MW00776916

THE ROUTLEDGE HANDBOOK OF PHILOSOPHY OF EMPATHY

Empathy plays a central role in the history and contemporary study of ethics, interpersonal understanding, and the emotions, yet until now has been relatively underexplored. *The Routledge Handbook of Philosophy of Empathy* is an outstanding reference source to the key topics, problems and debates in this exciting field and is the first collection of its kind. Comprising over thirty chapters by a team of international contributors, the *Handbook* is divided into six parts:

- Core issues
- History of empathy
- Empathy and understanding
- Empathy and morals
- Empathy in art and aesthetics
- Empathy and individual differences.

Within these sections central topics and problems are examined, including: empathy and imagination; neuroscience; David Hume and Adam Smith; understanding; evolution; altruism; moral responsibility; art, aesthetics, and literature; gender; empathy and related disciplines such as anthropology.

Essential reading for students and researchers in philosophy, particularly ethics and philosophy of mind and psychology, the *Handbook* will also be of interest to those in related fields, such as anthropology and social psychology.

Heidi L. Maibom is Professor of Philosophy at University of Cincinnati, USA. She works on empathy, psychopathology, responsibility, and theory of mind. She has edited *Empathy and Morality* (2014), co-edited *Neurofeminism* with R. Bluhm and A. J. Jacobsen (2012), and is currently writing a book on perspective taking.

Routledge Handbooks in Philosophy

Routledge Handbooks in Philosophy are state-of-the-art surveys of emerging, newly refreshed, and important fields in philosophy, providing accessible yet thorough assessments of key problems, themes, thinkers, and recent developments in research.

All chapters for each volume are specially commissioned, and written by leading scholars in the field. Carefully edited and organized, *Routledge Handbooks in Philosophy* provide indispensable reference tools for students and researchers seeking a comprehensive overview of new and exciting topics in philosophy. They are also valuable teaching resources as accompaniments to textbooks, anthologies, and research-orientated publications.

Also available:

THE ROUTLEDGE HANDBOOK OF PHILOSOPHY OF EMPATHY

Edited by Heidi L. Maibom

LONDON AND NEW YORK

First published 2017
By Routledge
2 Park Square, Milton Park, Abingdon, Oxon, OX14 4RN

and by Routledge
711 Third Avenue, New York, NY 10017

Routledge is an imprint of the Taylor & Francis Group, an informa business

British Library Cataloguing in Publication Data
A catalogue record for this book is available from the British Library

Library of Congress Cataloging in Publication Data
Names: Maibom, Heidi Lene, 1969- editor.
Title: The Routledge handbook of philosophy of empathy / edited by Heidi Maibom.
Description: New York : Routledge, 2017. |
Series: Routledge handbooks in philosophy |
Includes bibliographical references and index.
Identifiers: LCCN 2016031108 | ISBN 9781138855441 (hardback : alk. paper) |
ISBN 9781315282015 (e-book)
Subjects: LCSH: Empathy.
Classification: LCC BF575.E55 R695 2017 |
DDC 152.4/1-dc23
LC record available at https://lccn.loc.gov/2016031108

ISBN: 978-1-138-85544-1 (hbk)
ISBN: 978-1-315-28201-5 (ebk)

Typeset in Bembo
by Out of House Publishing

CONTENTS

Contents

NOTES ON CONTRIBUTORS

Robyn Bluhm is Associate Professor at Michigan State University, USA with a joint appointment in the Department of Philosophy and Lyman Briggs College. Her research examines philosophical issues in neuroscience and in medicine, with a particular focus on the relationship between ethical and epistemological questions in these areas. She is a co-editor of *Neurofeminism: Issues at the Intersection of Feminist Theory and Cognitive Science*.

Noël Carroll is Distinguished Professor of Philosophy at the Graduate Center of the City University of New York, USA. He has written over fifteen books, including most recently *Living in an Artworld*, *Art in Three Dimensions*, and *On Criticism and Humour: A Very Short Introduction*.

Mark H. Davis is Professor of Psychology at Eckerd College, St. Petersburg, FL, USA. His research areas include empathy, interpersonal conflict, and entrepreneurial mindset. He is the author of one of the most widely used measures of empathy, the Interpersonal Reactivity Index.

Remy Debes is Associate Professor of Philosophy at the University of Memphis, USA. He has published articles and book chapters on empathy, emotion, moral psychology, and moral sentimentalism, and human dignity. He also works in the history of ethics, with a special interest in the French and Scottish Enlightenment. He is co-editor of *Ethical Sentimentalism* (with Karsten Stueber) and *Dignity: A History*, both forthcoming.

Alison E. Denham works on topics in ethics, moral psychology, and aesthetics. She is the author of *Metaphor and Moral Experience* (2000) and, as editor, *Plato on Art and Beauty* (2011). She is jointly appointed to the Departments of Philosophy and Political Economy at Tulane University, New Orleans, USA. She is a Senior Research Fellow at St Anne's College, Oxford, and Visiting Professor at the University of Oxford.

Shaun Gallagher is the Lillian and Morrie Moss Professor of Excellence in Philosophy at the University of Memphis, USA, and Professorial Fellow at the Faculty of Law, Humanities and the Arts, University of Wollongong, Australia. He is currently a Humboldt Foundation Anneliese Maier Research Fellow (2012–18). Publications include *Phenomenology* (2012), *The*

Phenomenological Mind (with Dan Zahavi, 2012), *How the Body Shapes the Mind* (2005), and he is editor-in-chief of *Phenomenology and the Cognitive Sciences*.

Christine Cong Guo is Team Head of the Translational Neuroscience Group at QIMR Berghofer Medical Research Institute. She received a Ph.D. in Neuroscience from the Stanford University, followed by postdoctoral training at UCSF. She has broad research experience, from molecular biology and genetics to electrophysiology and systems neuroscience. Her work focuses on understanding functional brain networks in health and neurodegenerative diseases, using modern neuroimaging techniques.

Ishtiyaque Haji is Professor of Philosophy at the University of Calgary, Canada. He has research interests in ethical theory, philosophy of action, metaphysics, and philosophical psychology. He is the author of *Moral Appraisability* (1998), *Deontic Morality and Control* (2002), (with Stefaan Cuypers) *Moral Responsibility, Authenticity, and Education* (2008), *Freedom and Value* (2009), *Incompatibilism's Allure* (2009), *Reason's Debt to Freedom* (2012), and *Luck's Mischief* (2016).

Maurice Hamington is Executive Director of University Studies and Professor of Philosophy at Portland State University, USA. His research and writing focuses on care ethics. He is the author or editor of eleven books, including *Care Ethics and Political Theory* (with Daniel Engster), *Applying Care Ethics to Business* (with Maureen Sander-Staudt), *Socializing Care* (with Dorothy C. Miller), and *Embodied Care*. For more information on his other works please see https://pdx.academia.edu/MauriceHamington.

Douglas Hollan is Professor of Anthropology and Luckman Distinguished Teacher at UCLA, USA, an instructor at the New Center for Psychoanalysis in Los Angeles, and a practicing psycho-analyst. He has long been interested in cross-cultural and cross-disciplinary approaches to healing, mental health, and wellbeing. His recent research has focused on how sleeping and dreaming are implicated in health and wellbeing and on the role of empathy in human life and healing.

William Ickes is Distinguished Professor of Psychology at the University of Texas at Arlington, USA. He is a coeditor of the three-volume series New Directions in Attribution Research and the author of *Everyday Mind Reading* (2003) and *Strangers in a Strange Lab* (2009). His research on empathic accuracy has received three international research awards.

Imola Ilyes is a Ph.D. candidate in philosophy at York University, Toronto, Canada. Her dissertation reappraises contemporary work in moral psychology from a broadly Aristotelian point of view, with the aim of enlarging our notion of what it means to be an active, attentive moral agent, so as to overcome artificial divisions between the emotions and empathy on the one hand, and reason on the other.

James Jardine is a Ph.D. student in philosophy at the Center for Subjectivity Research, University of Copenhagen, Denmark. His dissertation explores the intimate connection between empathy and personhood, and seeks to engage Husserlian phenomenology in contemporary discussions of selfhood and recognition. He has published on these topics in *Deutsche Zeitschrift für Philosophie* and *Human Studies*.

Eileen John is Associate Professor of Philosophy at the University of Warwick, UK. Her research is in aesthetics and the philosophy of literature, with broad interests in how art and creative practices contribute to cognitive and ethical development. She has served as the Director of Warwick's Centre for Research in Philosophy, Literature and the Arts, and is the co-editor of the Blackwell anthology *The Philosophy of Literature*.

Antti Kauppinen is an Academy of Finland Research Fellow at the Department of Philosophy at the University of Tampere, Finland, and a Visiting Research Fellow at Trinity College Dublin, Ireland. He received his Ph.D. from the University of Helsinki in 2008, and has also held positions at the University of St Andrews and the University of Amsterdam. He works mostly in ethics and metaethics.

Jeanette Kennett is Professor of Philosophy at Macquarie University, Australia. She has published extensively on topics in moral psychology including autism, psychopathy, and moral and criminal responsibility and has held several research grants from the Australian Research Council. She is a Fellow of the Australian Academy of the Humanities.

Heidi L. Maibom is Professor of Philosophy at the University of Cincinnati, USA. She works on empathy, psychopathology, responsibility, and theory of mind. She has edited *Empathy and Morality* (2014), co-edited *Neurofeminism* with R. Bluhm and A. J. Jacobsen (2012), and is currently writing a book on perspective taking.

Derek Matravers is Professor of Philosophy at the Open University, UK and a Senior Member of Darwin College, Cambridge, UK. His recent work includes *Introducing Philosophy of Art: Eight Case Studies* (2013), *Fiction and Narrative* (2014), and *Empathy* (2016). He is the author of *Art and Emotion* (1998), as well as numerous articles in aesthetics, ethics, and the philosophy of mind.

Joshua May is Assistant Professor of Philosophy at the University of Alabama at Birmingham, USA. His articles have appeared in journals such as the *Australasian Journal of Philosophy*, *Canadian Journal of Philosophy*, *Journal of Medical Ethics*, *Philosophical Studies*, and *Synthese*. He is writing a book that argues for an empirically informed rationalism about moral psychology and defends ordinary moral thought and action against various scientific challenges.

Emily McRae is Assistant Professor of Philosophy at the University of New Mexico, USA. She specializes in Buddhist ethics, moral psychology, and feminism. She has published articles on a variety of topics, including anger, equanimity, open-mindedness, the role of philosophical therapy in moral life, and the ethics of interpersonal relationships. Her work has appeared in *American Philosophical Quarterly*, *Philosophy East and West*, *History of Philosophy Quarterly*, *Journal of Buddhist Ethics*, and *Sophia*.

Adam Morton has taught philosophy at Princeton, Ottawa, Bristol, Alberta, and UBC. He works on philosophy of language, philosophy of mind (folk psychology and philosophy of the emotions), and epistemology. His most recent books are *Bounded Thinking* and *Emotion and Imagination*. He is now thinking about the nature of scientific evidence, and has a quixotic intention to write something against human spaceflight.

Per Nortvedt is Professor of Medical Ethics at the University of Oslo, Center for Medical Ethics, Norway. He is trained as a nurse anesthetist and intensive care nurse and has a Ph.D. in medical ethics on the philosophical foundation of ethics of care and its relevance for health care.

His interests are in phenomenology, metaethics, and moral psychology, besides important issues in clinical medical ethics.

Matthew Ratcliffe is Professor for Theoretical Philosophy at the University of Vienna, Austria. Most of his recent work addresses issues in phenomenology, philosophy of psychology, and philosophy of psychiatry. He is author of *Rethinking Commonsense Psychology: A Critique of Folk Psychology, Theory of Mind and Simulation* (2007), *Feelings of Being: Phenomenology, Psychiatry and the Sense of Reality* (2008), and *Experiences of Depression: A Study in Phenomenology* (2015).

Ian Ravenscroft is Associate Professor of Philosophy at Flinders University, South Australia. His main research interests are empathy, emotions, and imagination. He is currently working (with Dan Hutto) on a radical enactivist approach to imagination and (with Lina Eriksson) on a critical assessment of theories linking disgust, purity, and conservatism. He occasionally dabbles in ethics.

Jenefer Robinson is Professor Emerita of Philosophy at the University of Cincinnati, USA and Honorary Visiting Fellow at the University of York, UK. She is the author of *Deeper than Reason: Emotion and its Role in Literature, Music and Art* (2005) and the editor of *Music and Meaning* (1997). She was President of the American Society for Aesthetics, 2009–11.

Thomas Schramme is Chair in Philosophy at the University of Liverpool, UK. His main research interests are in moral philosophy, political philosophy, and the philosophy of medicine. He has edited several collections of essays, for instance *Being Amoral: Psychopathy and Moral Incapacity* (2014). The anthology *Forms of Fellow Feeling: Empathy, Sympathy, Concern and Moral Agency* (co-editor: Neil Roughley) is forthcoming.

Armin W. Schulz is Associate Professor of Philosophy at the University of Kansas, USA. His research is primarily concerned with the substantive and methodological implications of attempts to combine evolutionary biology, psychology, and economics. He has published some nineteen pieces of peer-reviewed research, and co-edited a special section of the journal *Studies in the History and Philosophy of the Biological and Biomedical Sciences* on the evolution of psychological altruism.

David Shoemaker is a professor in the Department of Philosophy and Murphy Institute at Tulane University, USA. His research is in moral psychology, agency and responsibility, and personal identity and ethics. He is the general editor of *Oxford Studies in Agency and Responsibility*, and his book *Responsibility from the Margins* was published in 2015.

Shannon Spaulding is Assistant Professor of Philosophy at Oklahoma State University, USA. Her general philosophical interests are in philosophy of mind, philosophical psychology, and philosophy of science. The principal goal of her research is to construct a philosophically and empirically plausible account of social cognition.

Jane Stadler is Associate Professor in the School of Communication and Arts at the University of Queensland, Australia. She is author of *Pulling Focus: Intersubjective Experience, Narrative Film and Ethics* (2008) and co-author of *Imagined Landscapes* (2016), *Screen Media* (2009), and *Media and Society* (2012).

Kathleen Stock is Reader in Philosophy at the University of Sussex, UK. She mostly writes on fiction and imagination and the relations between them. Her monograph *Only Imagine: Fiction, Interpretation and Imagination* will appear in 2017.

Karsten R. Stueber is Professor of Philosophy at the College of the Holy Cross, USA. He specializes in philosophy of language, mind, and the social sciences. He is the author of *Rediscovering Empathy: Agency, Folk Psychology and the Human Sciences* and *Donald Davidsons Theorie Sprachlichen Verstehens*, and the co-author of *Philosophie der Skepsis, Empathy and Agency: The Problem of Understanding in the Human Sciences, Debating Dispositions*, and *Moral Sentimentalism*.

Thomas Szanto is a Marie-Curie Postdoctoral Research Fellow at the Center for Subjectivity Research, University of Copenhagen, Denmark, working on his project Shared Emotions, Group Membership, and Empathy. Previously, he has held postdoc positions in Copenhagen and at University College Dublin and lectured at four different Austrian universities. His recent publications include articles in the journals *Phenomenology and the Cognitive Sciences* and *Human Studies*, and the volume *Phenomenology of Sociality: Discovering the 'We'* (co-edited with Dermot Moran, 2016).

Vivian P. Ta is a doctoral student in the Department of Psychology at the University of Texas at Arlington, USA under Dr. William Ickes. Her research focuses on investigating latent semantic similarity in dyadic interactions. She is a NSF LSAMP-BD fellow, TEDx speaker, and has received recognition for her research from the Southwestern Psychological Association and the Society of Personality and Social Psychology.

Dan Zahavi is Professor of Philosophy and Director of the Center for Subjectivity Research at the University of Copenhagen, Denmark. In his systematic work, Zahavi has mainly been investigating the nature of selfhood, self-consciousness, intersubjectivity, and social cognition. He is author and editor of more than twenty-five volumes, including *Subjectivity and Selfhood* (2005), *The Phenomenological Mind* (with S. Gallagher, 2008), and most recently *Self and Other* (2014).

INTRODUCTION TO PHILOSOPHY OF EMPATHY

Heidi L. Maibom

What is empathy? Answers differ. To make things even more confounding, people disagree about how different the different definitions of empathy ultimately are! It is therefore a tricky topic to approach, but this handbook enters into this disputed territory fearlessly. It succeeds by giving voice to a range of different positions on empathy, from its Germanic origins in theories of art appreciation to its current appearance as an affective state that may play a significant role in morality. Philosophy, psychology, anthropology, and neuroscience are all represented, as are philosophy of mind, aesthetics, ethics, and phenomenology. The handbook therefore offers a little something to everybody, regardless of his or her taste or philosophical predilections. Because of its breadth of scope, there is plenty of opportunity for learning about different approaches and ideas, even for people well versed in empathy.

Although each chapter yields a wealth of information to the reader, it is nonetheless useful to have a brief overview of the study of empathy at the outset. I shall provide one such here. For a more comprehensive treatment, see Maibom (2014a) or Matravers (in press); for the psychology of empathy, see Davis (1994); for the history of the concept, see Stueber (2006); for neuroscience and empathy, see Iacoboni (2008) and Keysers (2011); and for empathy from a phenomenological perspective, see Zahavi (2014). For collections of essays on empathy, see Coplan & Goldie (2011), Decety (2012), and Maibom (2014b).

1. Varieties of empathy

People commonly distinguish between cognitive empathy and affective empathy. Cognitive empathy denotes the ability to ascribe mental states to others, such as beliefs, intentions, or emotions. This may be done by reflecting on how events, behavior, and psychological states co-vary, or by putting oneself in the position of the other to 'see' what one would think, feel, etc. The former kind is often called theory theory or theory of mind, whereas the latter is typically called perspective taking or simulation. Simulation, however, is technically speaking also a theory of mind (see Cognitive Empathy). Often, only perspective taking or simulation is thought to be cognitive empathy proper.

By contrast to cognitive empathy, affective empathy essentially involves affect on the part of the empathizer (see Chapter 2, 'Affective empathy'). There are at least four kinds of affect that are all called empathy: affective empathy (proper), emotional contagion, personal distress, and sympathy/empathic concern. I list them below with a reasonably representative characterization (Maibom 2012 2014a):

Affective empathy

Person S empathizes with person O's experience of emotion E in situation C if S feels E for O as a result of believing or perceiving that O feels E, or imagining being in C.

Sympathy/empathic concern

Person S sympathizes with person O when S feels sad for O as a result of believing or perceiving that something bad has happened to O, or S feels happy for O as a result of believing or perceiving that something good has happened to O.

Emotional contagion

Person S's feeling E is a case of emotional contagion if S feels E as a result of believing that person O feels E, perceiving that O's expressing E, or of imagining being in O's situation.

Personal distress

Person S is personally distressed by person O's experience of emotion E in situation C if S feels E – not for O, but for herself (S) – as a result of believing or perceiving that O feels E, imagining being in C, or as a result of believing that something bad has happened to O.

Whereas it is relatively clear that one can experience emotional contagion without much contribution from one's more cognitive faculties, personal distress and affective empathy depends on the subject having a certain attitude towards, or interpretation of, her emotional episode. Nonetheless, in order to *catch* another's emotions, one must at least possess the ability to discern *that* the other person experiences some affect and *what* affect he experiences. What such discernment comes down to is the topic of vigorous debate. Some are minimalists and believe that we can, as it were, *directly* perceive what others are feeling (see Chapter 14, 'Empathy and theories of direct perception'), perhaps due to the operation of mirror neurons (see Chapter 5, 'Empathy and mirror neurons' and Chapter 4, 'The neuroscience of empathy') or due to mimicry on the part of the 'receiver' (see Hatfield, Cacioppo, and Rapson 1994; Goldman 2006). When it comes to affective empathy proper, however, most researchers invoke more high-level cognitive abilities (but see Nichols 2001). First of all, one must be able to *ascribe* the emotional state in question to the other person. Second, one must be aware that one is feeling what one is feeling *because* the other person is feeling what he is feeling or because of the situation he is in. This involves some comprehension that one's own feeling is not a merited response to the situation one is in oneself, but is a response better suited to the other person's situation (or possibly state of mind). At the same time, one must understand that one's emotional response is not simply irrational or inappropriate. It is appropriate *as related to the other*. This is pretty complicated stuff, as I'm sure you can see, and so to maintain that affective empathy does not involve a heavy dose of cognitive activity would be foolish. And so it is better to say that cognitive empathy does not have to involve affect and that affective empathy typically involves a mix of cognitive and affective processes than to suppose that affective empathy somehow only involves affective processes.

Empathy with a person in need – someone who is in pain, sad, or in an upsetting situation – is the prototypical form of empathy, at least in the current literature. The term 'distress' is commonly taken to cover any of the individual emotions a person in need may feel. Empathic distress is the complementary term. It is experienced by someone in response to the distress of, or the bad situation of, the person in need (the 'target'). In typical cases of empathic distress, one is aware that one feels distressed *because* the target feels distressed or is in a bad situation, that one's distress is other-directed rather than self-directed, and that the object of one's distress overlaps with the object of the target's distress. One feels distress *with* and *for* the person in distress/need.

The flipside of empathic distress is personal distress. Personal distress is the *bête noire* of social psychology. It describes the tendency of a contagiously or empathically distressed individual to feel distressed as much for himself as for the target, or more distressed for himself than the target. This tendency is associated with less social adjustment, more aggression, and a tendency to distance oneself (often physically) from the distressing situation, e.g., the individual in need (Eisenberg 2000). It is worth noting, however, that people who are empathically distressed are *also* personally distressed, and that it is generally not the case that the individual is *confused* about the origin of the distress, that is, who is suffering. It is simply the case that the aversive affect becomes paramount, as does the need to escape the situation that causes it. Mounting evidence suggests that a decisive factor in determining a person's tendency to experience personal distress is their ability to regulate their emotions (Spinrad & Eisenberg 2014, López-Pérez & Ambrona 2015). However, personal distress can also be induced by making the situation of the person in need self-relevant. For instance, people who are asked to imagine how they themselves would feel in distressing situations, typically feel more personal distress than people who are asked to focus on the target's distress (Batson, Early, and Salvarani 1997). It is also likely that the more the other person suffers, the more the empathizer feels distress, including personal distress. Martin Hoffman (2000) and Nancy Eisenberg (2000) call this 'empathic overarousal.'

It turns out to be surprisingly hard to distinguish personal distress from empathic distress (see Chapter 2, 'Affective empathy'). This would be surprising if the two were quite different emotions. So perhaps they are not as distinct as all that. The two cannot be distinguished merely in terms of the affective quality of the distress. Indeed, distress forms the same qualitative grounding of both emotions, and what makes the difference is the *cognitive focus* of the distressed individual. When she focuses on the felt distress, she herself will be the locus of distress. *She* experiences distress, and to conceive of her distress this way is a way of experiencing personal distress. If, on the other hand, she focuses on the *origin* of the distress, the target becomes the most important locus of distress, and hence she comes to feel her distress *as empathic*. This duality of the empathic response makes sense once we consider that for our distress to be empathic, we must *feel* it. The idea also fits the data; people tend not to feel *only* personally distressed or empathically distressed. Most people feel distressed *both* for themselves and the target when another's bad situation makes them distressed. To complicate things even further, another's need evokes other emotions as well.

Sympathy is *also* typically felt when a person feels empathic and personal distress. But people differ in the degree to which they feel each of these three emotions. Psychologists agree that the optimal response to another in need is to feel more sympathy than distress, and more empathic distress than personal distress (Batson 2011, Eisenberg 2000, and Hoffman 2000). Sympathy is a less aversive feeling than distress (whether empathic or personal), and is more closely linked with prosocial behavior. Note, however, that the nomenclature here is quite mixed. What philosophers tend to call sympathy, psychologists generally call empathic concern. Empathic concern, however, is different from empathic *affect* because it need not match what the target is feeling, indeed typically it does not, and it is directed at the welfare of the person not their emotional situation. Its affective quality is as of being moved, and feeling softhearted and tender towards the target (Batson 2011).

How are all these emotional reactions to someone in need distinguished from one another, you ask. Partly by their affective quality – when it comes to distress and empathic concern – and

3

partly by their object – when it comes to determining whether the distress is personal or empathic (Batson, Early, and Salvarani 1997). Moreover, the behavioral effects are supposed to be distinct. Personal distress appears to lead to a concern about reducing the felt distress. If the easiest way of doing so is to help the person in need, the personally distressed person will help, but if it is easy to escape the situation that arouses distress, that tends to be the preferred option. By contrast, people experiencing more sympathy or concern for others help even when escape is easy. It should be noted, however, that as the costliness of helping goes up, helping tails off or largely disappears even for these individuals. Empathy-induced altruism, Batson says, is fragile (Batson 2011). Empathic distress is largely ignored as a separate category in social psychology, and so what its behavioral effects are is not clear.

This brings us to the real reason empathy and empathy-related phenomena have been studied so intensely: their connection with prosocial, altruistic, and moral behavior. Skepticism about altruism has a long history, and was unintentionally boosted by Darwin's theory of natural selection. Darwin himself appealed to group selection to explain what appeared to be human altruistic behavior (Darwin 1871/2004). Group selection, though, has mixed support (Wilson 2003, Richardson & Boyd 2006). Darwin also thought that sympathy was the more proximate mechanism of altruistic action. Since he was inspired by Hume, and Hume's sympathy is what we now call empathy, we can assume that he had empathy in mind (see Chapter 9, 'Empathy in Hume and Smith'). The idea has enjoyed a bit of a revival recently (see also Chapter 6, 'The evolution of empathy'). Others have focused on sympathy as the locus of altruistic motivation. For instance, David Sloan Wilson and Elliott Sober (Sober & Wilson 1998) have argued in favor of what they call psychological altruism by reference to parental care, something that looks much like sympathy/empathic concern. And Dan Batson has long argued that sympathy/empathic concern cause altruistic motivation (Batson 1991, 2011). For more on this, see Chapter 18, 'Empathy and altruism.'

The importance of empathy to morals generally has come under intense criticism by such people as Paul Bloom (2014) and Jesse Prinz (2011) (but see also Maibom 2009). According to them, not only does empathy not perform in the way it's made out to, it also often leads us in wrong direction, morally speaking (see Chapter 21, 'Empathy and moral responsibility' for details). We are told that empathy is biased, that it makes us more sensitive to the suffering of individuals than the suffering of groups of people, that it plays a questionable role in moral judgment, moral motivation, and moral development. What characterizes many of these critiques is a particular construal of what empathy is supposed to do to be morally relevant. By contrast, Hume and Smith thought of the role of empathy as foundational to our caring about others' welfare, and this basic point is not addressed in these critiques (see Chapter 9, 'Empathy in Hume and Smith'). Moreover, the Scottish sentimentalists pre-empted many of the current criticisms. For instance, they recognized that empathy is biased, but argued that this can be remedied by our taking the perspective of an impartial spectator.

Many contributors to this handbook are pretty stout defenders of the importance of empathy to morality, and so empathy may be making a comeback. Most of the chapters in Part IV 'Empathy and morals' argue that empathy is crucial for certain types of caring (Chapter 23, 'Empathy and care ethics,' Chapter 24, 'Empathy and medical therapy'), for moral judgment (Chapter 19, 'Empathy and moral judgment'), and for aspects of moral and legal motivation (Chapter 21, 'Empathy and moral responsibility,' Chapter 22, 'Empathy and legal responsibility'). It is, perhaps, unsurprising that contributors should be more optimistic about empathy, but it should not go unnoted that moral judgment is often thought to be more purely based in reason (Korsgaard 1996, Scanlon 1998), and that responsibility's connection to empathy is often questioned or not thought particularly relevant (Fischer & Ravizza 1998, Frankfurt 1969, Maibom 2008).

Before we move on to complicate matters more, I want to draw attention to the last section of the book, which concerns individual differences in empathy. There are rather large differences, culturally, when it comes to the role empathy plays and the importance it is accorded in interpersonal relationships. We see this, in part, in the Buddhist tradition (Chapter 11, 'Empathy, compassion, and "exchanging self and other" in Indo-Tibetan Buddhism'), but also in cross-cultural research (Chapter 30, 'Empathy across cultures'). In addition there are substantial individual differences (Chapter 31, 'Empathic accuracy'), although the male-female differences that are often taken for granted may be largely fictional (Chapter 33, 'Gender and empathy'). Differences are also apparent in mental disorders, and often examination of what lack of empathy correlates with has been taken to be significant for understanding the contribution of empathy to our lives (see Chapter 32, 'Empathy and psychopathology').

Empathy and mindedness

Our previous discussion of empathy, which keeps cognitive and affective empathy separate, more or less, applies poorly to other traditions in which the term 'empathy' plays a significant role. For instance, the very distinction between cognitive and affective empathy appears to break down in the phenomenological tradition, where 'empathy' designates our ability to directly apprehend the mindedness of another. English common-sense philosophy has long operated with the idea that there is a 'problem of other minds.' Probably inspired by Descartes, the question is how we know – even come to have beliefs about – the internal psychological states of others. Since they are not directly perceptible to us, we must *infer* the existence of such states and *a fortiori* the existence of other minds. Sadly, however, most inferential pathways are fraught with difficulties leading to such absurdities as the zombie problem (Chalmers 1996). The phenomenological tradition sidesteps such issues by insisting that we are directly confronted with the mindedness of other humans in a way that is perceptible and does not necessarily require a complex pattern of inference, particularly when they exhibit emotions (see Chapter 8, 'Empathy in the phenomenological tradition' and Chapter 3, and 'Phenomenology, empathy, and mindreading').

If I understand Zahavi's analysis of what we might call the phenomenological tradition correctly, there is no issue about you experiencing what the other person is experiencing in empathy. Emotional contagion therefore is not the intermediary process between third-personal and first-personal experience that it often appears as in social psychology and philosophy of mind. For whereas your empathic experience is experiential – rather than cognitive-inferential – it is not first-personal. The fact that you are empathizing means that you are presented *in experience* with the experience of another. This also means that the stress on empathy as sharing, which characterizes most other ways of thinking about this phenomenon, is resisted (cf. Zahavi & Rochat 2015). Moreover, others' experiences are not restricted to affective experiences, but include all mental phenomena, hence it makes little sense to distinguish between cognitive and affective empathy the way it is often done on this way of thinking about empathy. Note, however, that this view applies only to the types of empathy where we are directly presented with the body or bodily expressions of the other person.

The idea that we can directly apprehend what others feel through empathy has resurfaced in philosophy of mind partly due to the influence of embodied cognition approaches and recent neuroscience. With the discovery of mirror neurons, speculation that we *directly* apprehend not only what others feel, the nature of what they do, and so on, but also their *reasons* for action took off (see Chapter 5, 'Empathy and mirror neurons' and Chapter 4, 'The neuroscience of empathy'). Although some of these more expansive claims are no doubt exaggerated, the discovery has inspired new approaches to how we gain access to others' psychological states. Most of those reject the traditional view that we must *infer* what people think, feel, etc. from their behavior, and maintain that such states are in some sense *directly* given to us in perception (see Chapter 14, 'Empathy and theories of direct perception').

Empathy, imagination, and understanding

Even more direct approaches to social cognition must allow that much of our access to what others are going through is by inference from previous experience or through the *imagination* (see Chapter 16, 'Empathy and imagination'). Perspective taking is typically thought to involve the imagination. Psychologists tend to talk of two disparate forms of such activity: imagine-self and imagine-other perspective taking (see Chapter 10, 'Empathy in twentieth-century psychology'). In imagine-self perspective taking, the person imagines how she, herself, would feel, think, etc. in a certain situation. In imagine-other perspective taking, the subject is instructed to consider what the target would think, feel, etc. Usually, however, the focus is on emotions, which is why perspective taking is typically thought to induce empathy. It is therefore not terribly surprising that one is more likely to experience empathic affect when asked to imagine how one would *feel* or another person would *feel*. Having said that, Davis and colleagues have found that the self-focusing that results from imagine-self perspective taking with respect of empathic vs. personal distress also occurs in belief conditions (Davis et al. 2004).

It is worth noting that good perspective taking likely is neither imagine-self, nor imagine-other, but a blend of the two in which the self is inevitably involved through *imagining* being the other in her situation as best it can. Why psychologists have chosen to induce perspective taking in people that is bound to be different from what we would expect from ordinary perspective taking is an interesting question. Perhaps the idea was originally just to see whether it would make a difference to have the person focus either on himself or on the target (it does). Whatever the reason, it has now become a typical way of thinking of perspective taking. If, however, we turn to philosophical thinking about perspective taking, we see a very different tendency. Here there is real sensitivity to the partial projection that is involved – because we are using ourselves, in some sense, to understand the other – and to the partial self-transformation in the imagination that is required to actually get closer to understanding the other (e.g., Gordon 1986, Currie & Ravenscroft 2002, Goldie 2012). One imagines that people are well aware that simply imagining how they, themselves, would feel or act under certain circumstances is at best a guide to understanding others. A fuller understanding requires taking into consideration the individuality of the other.

Some philosophers argue that to understand reasons *as* reason-giving we must be able to simulate other people's reasons. Empathy thus becomes a way of unifying the somewhat schizophrenic existence of reasons-as-causes and reasons-as-justifications for actions (Stueber 2006, Chapter 12, 'Empathy and understanding reasons'). Moreover, taking another person's perspective helps us narrow down the range of possible psychological states that may be relevant to understanding others by means of our own experience-shaped ability to make decisions. It may be a way of getting around the so-called Frame Problem.

But empathy has also been thought to be connected with a more intimate way of relating to the other: in terms of her subjectivity (see Chapter 15, 'Empathy and intersubjectivity') or in terms of understanding *what it is like* for her (see Chapter 13, 'Empathy and knowing what it's like'). This approach may, in turn, be promising when it comes to the understanding and treatment of mental illness (see Chapter 17, 'Empathy and psychiatric illness').

Empathy and appreciating art

I come at last to the area that I'm probably least competent to talk about: the role of empathy in the aesthetic tradition of yore, and in current theories of how we appreciate art. Empathy was famously introduced as a term to denote a certain 'feeling into' that was supposed to accompany, or be part of, the aesthetic appreciation of the object of art. For instance, we might feel a certain straining of muscles as we behold the columns holding up a large pediment. This way of thinking about art appreciation, as a sort of projecting ourselves into the object, has not gained a lot of traction, in part because it is a difficult view to make sense of (see Chapter 7, 'Empathy in the aesthetic tradition'). Moreover, Noël Carroll shows why this is an untenable view of the role of empathy in appreciating pictures (Chapter 25, 'Empathy and painting').

The ways that an artwork can affect us ranges over the whole gamut of reactive emotions: emotional contagion, affective empathy, cognitive empathy (perspective taking), sympathy, and personal distress. In Chapter 26 ('Empathy in music'), Jenefer Robinson shows how both emotional contagion and affective empathy characterize music appreciation. And in art, there are many types of empathic experiences one might have: with the performer of the piece (in the case of music, for instance), with the creator of the piece (the artist), with the people or animate beings presented in the piece (as in literature or pictures), or, as some have argued, with the emotion expressed by the art work as a whole (e.g. Lopes 2011).

Whereas many people enjoy music because of the affect that it evokes, including empathic affect, art also contributes to our *understanding* of others' experiences, whether emotional or not. Literature is a case in point. In (good) literature, we are confronted with different points of views, are given vivid descriptions of experiences we might never have had or feelings we have never felt, and we often find ourselves being moved by people or situations that would not otherwise have moved us. Eileen John suggests that our lack of practical engagement with fictional characters helps us sidestep the limitations that typically characterize our empathic ability (Chapter 27, 'Empathy in literature'). Fiction may help us understand others better, broaden our understanding of the many possible viewpoints on the same event, and so on. Moving pictures have some of the same potential, even in the absence of irksome voice-overs.

Jane Stadler stresses the experiential nature of watching movies (Chapter 28, 'Empathy in film'), and relates this to Zahavi's idea that empathy provides a sort of knowledge by acquaintance of the mental lives of others. It gives us a sense of other people's experiences and it engages our affect, as when we feel with and for some of the cinematic characters. Arguably, engagement with fictional characters, either through literature or film, ultimately has moral and social implications by broadening our understanding of other experiences. But, of course, the capacity of art to make us imagine different experiences, thoughts, and feelings has its limitations. In the phenomenon known as 'imaginative resistance,' we fail or refuse to imagine a world in which what we take to be morally wrong in our world is morally right or at least morally acceptable. For instance, imagine a world in which not only is infanticide permissible, it is also (sometimes) the right thing to do. If you are like most, you cannot. This is a sort of failure of empathy. Why such failure exists is explored by Kathleen Stock (Chapter 29, 'Imaginative resistance and empathy').

Final words

The chapters here are meant to give the reader an overview of the particular area discussed, but they also often argue for a particular position on the matter. The chapters should therefore not taken to be entirely neutral as to the topic discussed. Most contributors are partial to empathy playing an important role in whatever area they discuss. However, there should be plenty of sources for people who are of a more skeptical bent also. It is my hope that this handbook will start many on a journey into the fascinating field of philosophy of empathy. Enjoy!

References

Batson, C. D. 1991. *The Altruism Question: Toward a Social-Psychological Answer*. Hove, UK: Lawrence Erlbaum Ass.

Batson, C. D. 2011. *Altruism in Humans*. New York: Oxford University Press.

Batson, C. D., Early, S., & Salvarani, G. 1997. Perspective taking: Imagining how another feels versus imagining how you would feel. *Personality and Social Psychology Bulletin*, 23, 751–8.

Bloom, P. 2014. Against empathy. *The Boston Review*, Sep. 10, 2014. https://bostonreview.net/forum/paul-bloom-against-empathy.

Chalmers, D. 1996. *The Conscious Mind*. Oxford: Oxford University Press.

Coplan, A., & Goldie, P. (eds.) 2011. *Empathy: Philosophical and Psychological Perspectives*. New York: Oxford University Press.

Currie, G., & Ravenscroft, I. 2002. *Recreative Minds*. Oxford: Oxford University Press.

Darwin, C. 1871/2004. *The Descent of Man*. New York: Barnes & Noble Books.

Davis, M. H. 1994. *Empathy: A Social Psychological Approach*. Boulder, CO: Westview Press.

Davis, M. H., Soderlund, T., Cole, J., Gadol, E., Kute, M., Myers, M., & Weihing, J. 2004. Cognitions associated with attempts to empathize: How do we imagine the perspective of another? *Personality and Social Psychology Bulletin*, 30, 1625–35.

Decety, J. (ed.) 2012. *Empathy: From Bench to Bedside*. Cambridge, MA: MIT Press.

Eisenberg, N. 2000. Empathy and sympathy. In: M. Lewis & J. Haviland-Jones (eds.) *Handbook of Emotions*, 2nd ed. New York: Guilford Press, 677–91.

Fischer, J. M., & Ravizza, M. 1998. *Responsibility and Control: A Theory of Moral Responsibility*. Cambridge: Cambridge University Press.

Frankfurt, H. G. 1969. Alternate possibilities and moral responsibility. *Journal of Philosophy*, 66, 829–39.

Goldie, P. 2012. *The Mess Inside: Narrative, Emotion, and the Mind*. Oxford: Oxford University Press.

Goldman, A. 2006. *Simulating Minds: The Philosophy, Psychology, and Neuroscience of Mindreading*. New York: Oxford University Press.

Gordon, R. 1986. Folk psychology as simulation. *Mind & Language*, 1, 158–72.

Hatfield, E., Cacioppo J. T., & Rapson R. L. 1994. *Emotional Contagion*. New York: Cambridge University Press.

Hoffman, M. 2000. *Empathy and Moral Development*. New York: Cambridge University Press.

Hume, D. 1777/1975. *Enquiries Concerning Human Understanding and Concerning the Principles of Morals*. L. A. Selby-Bigge & P. H. Nidditch (eds.). Oxford: Clarendon Press.

Iacoboni, M. 2008. *Mirroring People: The New Science of How We Connect With Others*. New York: Farrar, Straus, and Giroux.

Keysers, C. 2011. *The Empathic Brain*. Kindle E-Book.

Korsgaard, C. 1996. *The Sources of Normativity*. New York: Cambridge University Press.

Lopes, D. McIver. 2011. An empathic eye. In: A. Coplan & P. Goldie (eds.) *Empathy: Philosophical and Psychological Perspectives*. New York: Oxford University Press.

López-Perez, B., & Ambrona, T. 2015. The role of cognitive emotion regulation on the vicarious emotional response. *Motivation and Emotion*, 39, 299–308.

Maibom, H. L. 2008. The mad, the bad, and the psychopath. *Neuroethics*, 1, 167–84.

Maibom, H. L. 2009. Feeling for others: Empathy, sympathy, and morality. *Inquiry*, 52, 483–99.

Maibom, H. L. 2012. The many faces of empathy and their relation to prosocial action and aggression inhibition. *Wiley Interdisciplinary Reviews: Cognitive Science (WIRE)*, 3, 253–63.

Maibom, H. 2014a. Introduction: (Almost) everything you ever wanted to know about empathy. In: H. L. Maibom (ed.) *Empathy and Morality*. Oxford: Oxford University Press, 1–40.

Maibom, H. L. 2014b. (ed.) *Empathy and Morality*. Oxford: Oxford University Press.

Matravers, D. In press. *Empathy*. Cambridge: Polity Press.

Nichols, S. 2001. Mindreading and the cognitive architecture underlying altruistic motivation. *Mind & Language*, 16, 425–55.

Prinz, J. 2011. Against empathy. *Southern Journal of Philosophy*, 49, 214–33.

Richerson, P. J., & Boyd, R. 2006. *Not by Genes Alone*. Chicago, IL: Chicago University Press.

Scanlon, T. M. 1998. *What We Owe to Each Other*. Cambridge, MA: Harvard University Press.

Smith, A. 1759/1976. *The Theory of Moral Sentiments*. D. D. Raphael & E. L. Macfie (eds.). Indianapolis, IN: Liberty Fund.

Sober, E., & Wilson, D. S. 1998. *Unto Others: The Evolution and Psychology of Unselfish Behavior*. Cambridge, MA: Harvard University Press.

Spinrad, T., & Eisenberg, N. 2014. Empathy and morality: A developmental psychology perspective. In: H. L. Maibom (ed.) *Empathy and Morality*. New York: Oxford University Press, 59–70.

Stueber, K. 2006. *Rediscovering Empathy: Agency, Folk Psychology, and the Human Sciences*. Cambridge, MA: MIT Press.

Wilson, D. S. 2003. *Darwin's Cathedral: Evolution, Religion, and the Nature of Society*. Chicago, IL: Chicago University Press.

Zahavi, D. 2014. *Self and Other*. Oxford: Oxford University Press.

Zahavi, D., & Rochat, P. 2015. Empathy ≠ sharing: Perspectives from phenomenology and developmental psychology. *Consciousness and Cognition*, 36, 543–53.

PART I

Core issues

1

COGNITIVE EMPATHY

Shannon Spaulding

1. Introduction

Cognitive empathy is the capacity to understand another person's state of mind from her perspective. Consider the following real-life example, which I will return to throughout this chapter. Edward Snowden is a former subcontractor for the National Security Agency (NSA), the United States intelligence agency responsible for global monitoring of data for foreign intelligence and counterintelligence. Snowden began subcontracting for the NSA in March 2013. Two months later, Snowden flew to Hong Kong where he subsequently released many thousands of classified documents to journalists. These documents included information on global and domestic spying programs, military capabilities, operations, and tactics. In June of 2013, the US Department of Justice charged Snowden with violating the Espionage Act and stealing government property, and the US Department of State revoked his passport. Shortly thereafter, Snowden flew to Russia where he is now a resident.

Many people, including most in the US Government, have condemned Snowden's behavior as treasonous. His release of classified documents about military capabilities, operations, and tactics compromises military missions and endangers military personnel. Moreover, the journalists who received these classified documents often lack the capacity to protect the documents so that they do not end up in the hands of enemies of the US. For example, on January 27, 2014 the *New York Times* published one of these leaked documents but failed to properly redact classified information in the released PDF. As a result, the newspaper exposed the name of the NSA agent and the group that was the target of the operation (see http://nyti.ms/MluMBk). Though Snowden professes to have acted out of patriotism, many accuse Snowden of being a traitor.

Others, however, praise him as a courageous whistleblower. Snowden has said that his goal in releasing classified documents to journalists was to expose the NSA's spying programs so that Americans understand the extent to which their government monitors its own citizens and therefore can make an informed choice about whether they want their government doing these things. It is widely acknowledged that the American public would not have known that the NSA is collecting data on ordinary citizens' communications if not for Snowden's actions. Many regard Snowden as a hero for shedding light on these spying programs.

Understanding why Snowden judged that it was best for him to release thousands of classified documents to journalists is a difficult, real-world challenge of cognitive empathy. There are two main accounts of how we understand another person's perspective. One is based on theorizing and the other is based on mental simulation. In the next section, I will use the Snowden example to illustrate how these two accounts are meant to work. I shall argue in section 3 that we use both theorizing and mental simulation, but these strategies are not equally effective in all cases. I shall discuss a third underexplored pattern of reasoning in cognitive empathy. Self-serving goals, such as anxiety reduction, self-esteem, and confirmation of one's worldview, distort cognitive empathy. Finally, in section 4, I offer some concluding remarks on how to improve hybrid theories of cognitive empathy.

2. Theory Theory and Simulation Theory

The two main accounts of how we understand others' perspectives are the Theory Theory (TT) and the Simulation Theory (ST). Theory theorists argue that we understand others' perspectives by employing a folk psychological theory about other minds. For an overview of the TT, see the following collected volumes: Carruthers & Smith (1996); Davies & Stone (1995a). According to this view, we explain and predict behavior by theorizing about how mental states inform behavior. With our folk psychological theory, we infer from another person's behavior what his or her mental states probably are. And from these inferences, plus the psychological laws in the theory connecting mental states to behavior, we predict the next behavior of the other person.

When the TT was first proposed, proponents of the view argued that we understand others by employing a literal theory of mind, which involves folk psychological *laws* that connect mental states, unobservable theoretical entities, to behavior. Understanding others' perspectives, it was argued, consists in employing these folk psychological laws, along with auxiliary assumptions about the relevant circumstances, to *deduce* explanations and predictions of behavior. Theory theorists argued that we use our theory of mind just like, for example, physicists use the theory of gravity to explain and predict the behavior of physical objects. Jerry Fodor, for example, argues that theory of mind explanations "are frequently seen to exhibit the 'deductive structure' that is so characteristic of explanation in real science. There are two parts to this: the theory's underlying generalizations are defined over unobservables, and they lead to its predictions by iterating and interacting rather than by being directly instantiated" (Fodor, 1987, p. 7).

Contemporary theory theorists reject the idea that understanding others' perspectives literally involves applying folk psychological *laws* and *deriving* explanations and predictions from these laws. Instead, they characterize our capacity to understand others as underwritten by information-rich, interpretive processes (Nichols & Stich, 2003). More loosely conceived, theories may include models, heuristics, and a body of assumptions. A more general and modern way of characterizing the TT is in terms of an *information-rich* inference to the best explanation.

An example of a modern version of the TT is the Model Theory Theory, an account proposed by Heidi Maibom (2007, 2009) and Peter Godfrey-Smith (2005). Scientific theorizing, some argue, is best understood as a practice of constructing and applying scientific models (Giere, 1999). These models consist in a general structure or schematic pattern that can have many specific instantiations, and they can be elaborated in various ways to generate specific hypothetical systems to deal with particular empirical cases (Godfrey-Smith, 2005, pp. 2–4). According to Model TT, understanding another agent is analogous to this kind of scientific theorizing. There is a single, core folk psychological model, which consists in a distinction between beliefs and desires, the idea of sensory input and behavioral output, and characteristic dependence of action on perceptions, memories, goals, and temptations. This core folk psychological model can be elaborated in various ways with particular knowledge of social structures, institutions, and social roles, knowledge about a particular person's history and personality, etc. On this account, cognitive empathy is best described as facility with folk psychological models.

According to the TT, understanding Edward Snowden's perspective requires knowledge of the NSA, current laws relating to domestic spying, protections for whistleblowers, and the political environment. It also requires understanding the moral tension between liberty and safety. Crucially, understanding his perspective involves understanding the psychology of those who put their own safety (and to some extent others' safety) at risk for what they take to be a greater cause. On this view, understanding Snowden's perspective consists in sophisticated inference to the best explanation. Basically one must understand all the main factors that influenced his moral calculus.

In contrast to the TT, simulation theorists argue that we do not need to employ a *theory* about folk psychology to understand others. To understand a target's perspective, all we need to do is imagine what *we* would think, feel, and do in the target's situation, and on that basis we come to understand what the target thinks, feels, and will do. For an overview of this theory, see Davies and Stone's (1995b) collected volume on the ST. According to the ST, we use our own minds as a simulation of the other person's mind, putting ourselves in another's shoes, so to speak, and imagining what our mental states would be and how we would behave if we were that agent in that particular situation.

The basic idea of the ST is straightforward and intuitive, but the details of how this happen are quite nuanced (Spaulding, 2012, 2015). First, we retrodictively simulate to figure out what the target's mental states could have been to cause the observed behavior. Then we take the target's mental states in the form of pretend beliefs and pretend desires as input, run them through our own cognitive mechanisms, take the resulting conclusion and attribute it to the target in order to explain and predict the target's behavior.

In contrast to the TT, ST is sometimes characterized as an *information-poor* cognitive empathy process. It does not require access to large bodies of information about folk psychology. Simulation requires an ability to mentally put oneself in a target's position and figure out what one would feel, think, and do. One simply redeploys one's own cognitive mechanisms for the purpose of understanding the other person's perspective.

Despite the overall consensus that we understand others through mental simulation, there is considerable disagreement amongst simulation theorists about the nature of simulational mindreading. These disagreements concern whether we use high-level practical reasoning to figure out what it would be reasonable for us to think, feel, and do in the target's situation (Heal, 1996), whether the simulation heuristic requires introspective awareness (Gordon, 1995), and the extent to which simulation can be explained in simple reenactment or resonance terms (Goldman, 2006).

According to the ST, in order to understand Edward Snowden's perspective you need to imagine yourself in his position. Imagine that you have discovered at your new job that the government employs top secret programs that, unbeknownst to American citizens, allow the monitoring of ordinary Americans' phone calls, emails, texts, internet searches, etc. Imagine that you face the following dilemma: stay silent and let these secret programs continue illegally monitoring Americans' personal communications or give information to journalists that proves the extent of this monitoring and let them publicize these programs. Imagining facing this dilemma, you understand the difficult choice Snowden faced. According to ST, to understand Snowden's perspective you do not need to understand every significant factor that influenced his decision. Rather, you just need to mentally simulate being in his situation.

The TT and the ST offer different accounts of how we understand another's perspective. With respect to the Snowden example, the central difference is that the TT relies on consolidating a broad range of information about spying, whistleblowing, morality, and psychology whereas the ST relies on imagining oneself in Snowden's position facing the dilemma he faced. These are very different strategies for understanding another's perspective. I shall argue in the next section that we successfully use both the theorizing and simulational strategies, but we do so under different conditions.

3. A pluralist picture

The TT and the ST propose different strategies for cognitive empathy. As is well known in this field, both accounts are inadequate on their own. The TT – at least in its traditional formulation – faces a serious computational worry. Theoretical explanation requires categorizing observable behavior, applying general principles that link observable behavior to mental states, and mental states to other mental states, and mental states to behavior. One must figure out which of many principles could apply, whether appropriate background conditions hold, whether there are countervailing factors, and, for predictive purposes, the implications of the principle one chooses to apply. Combine this with the fact that many of our social interactions involve a range of people whose behaviors and mental states are interdependent, and you have an extremely computationally demanding and extended process of deriving a stable set of beliefs which will allow one to successfully take part in social interactions (Bermúdez, 2003, pp. 31–3).

A theoretical limitation of the ST is what is known as the "threat of collapse" (Davies & Stone, 2001; Heal, 1998). Theory theorists hold that we understand others via a *tacit* theory of other minds. Simulation theorists reject the idea that we understand others via a *theory* of other minds, tacit or not. They argue instead that we simply have to imagine ourselves in the other person's situation and figure out what we would think, feel, and do in that situation. This kind of simulation is successful to the extent the simulator's mental processes mirror the target's mental processes. The difficulty is that given a certain plausible account of tacit knowledge, the simulation process described above is indistinguishable from the employment of a tacit theory of other minds. But if that is right, then there would be no predictive differences between the ST and the TT, and the ST would simply collapse into the TT.

A related objection, which precedes the threat of collapse, is offered by Dennett (1987). To retrodictively simulate a person, I observe her behavior, imagine myself in her situation, generate hypothetical beliefs and desires that would explain why I would behave as she did if I were in that situation, and then attribute those mental states to her. A problem related to the threat of collapse is that there are indefinitely many mental state combinations that would explain the observed behavior. If we were to try to figure out, with simulation resources only, what our mental states could have been to cause us to behave like the target, our retrodictive simulation would have no way to decide between radically different belief-desire combinations that would explain the behavior. Moreover, there would be no stopping point for the retrodictive simulation. The simulation itself provides no way to determine when we have landed on a good-enough explanation of the observed behavior and can stop simulating. Retrodictive simulation reveals some of the possible mental states that a target may have, but it cannot, all by itself, provide knowledge of other minds. Theoretical information is required to move from identifying possible mental states to knowing a target's mental states. See Spaulding (2015) for more on this objection to ST.

Most contemporary theory theorists and simulation theorists recognize the inadequacy of *pure* TT and *pure* ST. Most theorists in this debate endorse a hybrid account that involves both theoretical and simulational elements (Davies & Stone, 1995b; Goldman, 2006; Heal, 1998; Nichols & Stich, 2003). The consensus is that sometimes we theorize to understand another person's perspective, while other times we mentally simulate. The current debate concerns under what conditions we use each of these strategies.

Consider first when the simulation strategy likely will be successful. You imagine yourself in another person's situation, figure out what you would think and feel in that situation, and attribute that perspective to the other person. This process will generate an accurate attribution only if you and the target are relatively similar. If the target evaluates information differently from you, if she has different values or ranks shared values differently from you, or if one of you has idiosyncratic beliefs and desires, your mental simulation will be inaccurate. In that case, you will fail to understand the target's perspective. For example, simulating Edward Snowden's perspective is likely to be successful only if the simulator shares Snowden's values (e.g., freedom from government intrusion), ranks those values the same way (e.g., privacy over safety), and evaluates risk and reward in the same way (e.g., the risk of being accused of treason vs. the reward of shedding light on domestic spying). If the simulator is different from Snowden in these ways, he will likely misrepresent Snowden's perspective and thus fail to understand his decisions.

Mental simulation is likely to be successful only when the simulator and the target are relatively similar. There is empirical evidence for this claim. Social psychologists have discovered that we automatically identify people as part of our in-group or as part of an out-group (Tajfel, 1974). This categorization appears to be a function of perceived similarity (Ames, 2004a, 2004b; Ames, Weber, & Zou, 2012). That is, those who we perceive to be like us are categorized as part of our in-group, and those who we perceive to be unlike us are categorized as part of an out-group. Age, race, and gender are salient features of people, thus one tends to identify people who share one's age, race, and gender as part of one's in-group. However, social categorization extends beyond these classifications. People have multiple, overlapping identities, and perceived similarity is relative to a context. For example, if hobbies are salient then only runners will count as part of my in-group. In that context, all non-runners are part of the out-group. However, if political ideology is salient, my in-group consists of liberal progressives, some of who are runners and some of who are not runners. Thus, I may consider someone as part of my in-group in one context but not in another.

As it turns out, the cognitive empathy strategies that we use depend on whether we perceive the target to be part of our in-group. When we perceive a target to be part of our relevant in-group, we use simulational heuristics to figure out the target's perspective (Ames, 2004a, 2004b). For example, we often project our own mental states onto those we perceive to be similar to us in some salient respect. That is, we figure out what we would think and feel in a particular situation and attribute that to the target. We also use our mental states as an anchor and adjust the interpretation based on how similar the individual is to us.

These simulational heuristics are likely to lead us to error when we *overestimate* the similarity between the target and ourselves and thus engage in more projection than is warranted. The resulting errors are called the Curse of Knowledge, a phenomenon where we falsely assume that others know what we know, and the False Consensus Effect, when we falsely assume that others share our opinion on some matter (Clement & Krueger, 2002; Epley & Waytz, 2010, p. 512). For both kinds of errors, we inappropriately project our own mental states onto others because we assume that we are more similar than we in fact are. The specific details on how this happens will differ from case to case, but in general inappropriate projection occurs when we attend to superficial similarities between others and ourselves and fail to notice or appreciate dissimilarities, e.g., in terms of situational context, personal background, knowledge, attitudes, values, and emotions.

The preceding paragraphs argue that simulation is an appropriate strategy for figuring out a target's perspective only when the simulator is relatively similar to the target. The other strategy for cognitive empathy is theorizing. Theorizing may be appropriate regardless of whether one is similar to the target. Theorizing involves considering a broad range of general, domain-specific, and folk psychological information, and this information will be relevant regardless of how similar the theorizer is to the target. Thus, when one is similar to a target, one may use either simulation or theorizing to figure out his perspective. However, simulation is more efficient when one is similar to the target. One need not consider all of the relevant evidence about the situation, target, and folk psychology in order to figure out the target's perspective because one can simply figure out what she would think and feel in that situation and project it to the target. Thus, though theorizing is an adequate strategy when the subject and target are similar, simulation has the advantage of being less cognitively demanding.

Theorizing is appropriate regardless of the target, however it is a distinctively superior strategy when one differs from the target in the relevant respects. In that case, it is better to infer the target's perspective on the basis of all of the relevant information rather than project one's own perspective onto the target. In addition, theorizing is a superior strategy when we want to ensure that we understand the target's perspective and that our own perspective does not skew our evaluation.

Empirical evidence supports this idea as well. In cases where something important depends on getting a target's perspective right, when we will be held responsible for our interpretation, or when the situation is unusual and unexpected, we tend to search for information about that person's perspective in a controlled and deliberative fashion (Fiske & Neuberg, 1990; Kelley, 1973; Tetlock, 1992). For example, when members of a job search committee make judgments about the candidates (e.g., whether a candidate will accept a job offer), the stakes are high. Thoughtful members of the committee will want to ensure that their judgments are accurate, consider all the relevant evidence, and make sure their decision is not based on mere superficial cues. This kind of reasoning is effortful, cognitively taxing, and difficult if one is under cognitive load or not well practiced in this kind of reflective reasoning (Gilbert, Krull, & Pelham, 1988).

To summarize, the consensus opinion in this literature is that we use both simulation and theorizing in order to understand others' perspectives. Theoretical and empirical considerations support the idea that we most effectively use simulation to understand a target's perspective when we are similar to the target. Simulation is ineffective and inappropriate when we are dissimilar to the target and therefore engage in more projection than is warranted. Theorizing about another's perspective is most effective when we are dissimilar to a target and when it is important that our attribution is correct. Theorizing is inefficient when we are similar enough to the target to project our own perspective onto the target and when getting the target's perspective *exactly* right is not the primary concern.

Sometimes accuracy is paramount in cognitive empathy. However, in other cases we just need a good-enough approximation of someone's perspective. In these cases, accuracy is only a secondary goal and efficiency is the primary goal. The interaction between accuracy and efficiency is familiar territory for the debate between the TT and the ST. However, accuracy and efficiency do not exhaust our goals in cognitive empathy. Before moving on to concluding remarks, I will discuss one final aspect of cognitive empathy that often is not considered by theory theorists or simulation theorists.

Another cluster of goals within social interaction includes anxiety reduction, self-esteem, and confirmation of one's worldview (Dunning, 1999; Kunda, 1990). The strategies we use when we have these self-serving goals may be effortful or efficient. Consider first the pattern of reasoning called Naïve Realism, which describes our tendency to regard others as more susceptible to bias and misperception than oneself (Pronin, Lin, & Ross, 2002). We think we simply see things as they are, but others suffer from bias. This tendency is prevalent in interactions in which people disagree. For example, one may regard those of a different political party as misguided and biased by their personal motivations, whereas one regards oneself (and to some extent other members of one's political party) simply as correct. This self-serving strategy influences the perspectives we attribute to others especially when the other person disagrees with us.

A second reasoning pattern that emerges when we have self-serving goals is called Confirmation Bias, which is a tendency to seek only information that confirms one's preconceived ideas and interpret ambiguous information in light of these preconceived ideas. Confirmation Bias is very common in all areas of cognition. With respect to cognitive empathy, we have preconceived ideas about other individuals and groups, and we tend to interpret events in terms of those preconceived ideas. For example, racists notice when individuals behave in ways that confirm their racist beliefs, but they often do not attend to the many cases where individuals act in ways that disconfirm their racist beliefs. As everyone with a racist relative can attest, pointing out this disconfirming evidence usually is ineffective. Confirmation bias affects both deliberative, controlled processes like theorizing and efficient processes like simulation. It occurs regardless of how the preconceived idea originated, how likely it is to be true, and whether accuracy is incentivized (Skov & Sherman, 1986; Slowiaczek, Klayman, Sherman, & Skov, 1992; Snyder, Campbell, & Preston, 1982).

We do not seek information in a systematic or unbiased way when we have self-serving goals. Instead, we seek information that validates our self-worth and confirms our pre-existing opinions. The processing of information is different in this context than the contexts in which accuracy or efficiency is the primary goal. The strategies employed for self-serving goals are compatible with deliberative, effortful cognitive empathy and efficient, simulation-based cognitive empathy. In either case, the cognitive empathy process is distorted by the subject's pre-existing opinions. Although both the TT and the ST are compatible with such distortions, neither view predicts the influence of self-serving goals on cognitive empathy. This is an important and neglected aspect of how we understand others' perspectives.

4. Conclusion

The goals we have in cognitive empathy determine the strategies we use to understand other people. Sometimes we have the motivation and ability to exhaustively review the available information and attribute mental states to others in that way. This is likely to be an effective strategy when it is important that we get the other person's perspective correct and when the other person is too dissimilar from us to simulate. For those who really want to understand Edward Snowden's perspective or for those who find his reasoning bafflingly different from their own reasoning, theorizing is the best strategy for understanding his point of view.

Sometimes, however, we lack the motivation or ability to do an exhaustive search for relevant information. In these cases, when efficiency is the primary goal we may use the simulation heuristic. This is likely to be an effective strategy when the target is similar to us in the relevant respect. For example, if, like Snowden, one values privacy over safety and one is wary of government overreach, then simulation may be an efficient and effective way to understand Snowden's perspective on releasing classified documents to journalists. There is little concern about egocentric bias in the simulation because one is sufficiently similar to the target.

Finally, our social interpretations sometimes are guided primarily not by accuracy or efficiency goals but by self-interest. In these cases, we search for information and interpret others' perspectives in light of what we antecedently believe. Both Naïve Realism and Confirmation Bias skew our understanding of others' perspectives. For example, if one disagrees with Snowden's decisions, one is likely to regard him as biased (e.g., by desire for fame or money) or misguided (e.g., in his belief that his actions will change the government's behavior or that the American public cares deeply about privacy). One will look for information that confirms these biases and misperceptions and ignore or downplay disconfirming evidence. The opposite pattern of reasoning applies if one regards Snowden's actions as, all things considered, good. In this case, Naïve Realism and Confirmation Bias skew our reasoning to confirm the belief that Snowden's behavior is virtuous. One is likely to seek information that Snowden is promoting the values we all hold dear and interpret those who disagree with his decisions as being biased and misguided. Whatever one's opinion, when we are motivated by self-serving goals such as anxiety reduction, self-esteem, and confirmation of one's worldview, these biases distort the cognitive empathy process.

Some of the results considered in this chapter support the TT, others support the ST, and others are not predicted by either view. Hybrid theories have the advantage of explaining more phenomena than either the TT or the ST alone, and they avoid the problems with pure TT and pure ST. For this reason, hybrids generally are the rule rather than the exception in this debate. I think hybrid theories are the most promising theories available. However, if a hybrid account is to offer a unified and informative explanation of how we understand others' perspectives, it has to do more than simply posit a conjunction of processes. Contemporary hybrid accounts gesture at the heterogeneity of cognitive empathy strategies. For a pluralistic account of social cognition that takes into account stereotypes, trait attribution, simulation, and theorizing, see Andrews (2008). But we need an explanation of how and when we shift between these strategies, which we use more often, and how accurate any of them are. For more on the conditions under which we use various strategies, see Spaulding (in progress). For more on the accuracy conditions of these strategies, see Spaulding (forthcoming). Though in some ways this chapter is critical of the current theories of how we understand others, I intend these arguments to be constructive. I hope they help improve hybrid theories so that they are more explanatorily adequate, predictively accurate, unified, and fruitful.

In this chapter I have sketched some of the components for an adequate hybrid theory of cognitive empathy. Specifically, I have described the various cognitive empathy strategies available to us, the conditions under which we are likely to use these strategies, when these strategies will be effective, and when they will lead us to error. There is more work to be done here in order to construct a unified and informative account of how we understand others' perspectives. However, I hope this chapter will serve as a roadmap for future development of hybrid theories of cognitive empathy.

References

Ames, D. R. (2004a). Inside the mind reader's tool kit: Projection and stereotyping in mental state inference. *Journal of Personality and Social Psychology*, 87(3), 340.

Ames, D. R. (2004b). Strategies for social inference: A similarity contingency model of projection and stereotyping in attribute prevalence estimates. *Journal of Personality and Social Psychology*, 87(5), 573.

Ames, D. R., Weber, E. U., & Zou, X. (2012). Mind-reading in strategic interaction: The impact of perceived similarity on projection and stereotyping. *Organizational Behavior and Human Decision Processes*, 117(1), 96–110.

Andrews, K. (2008). It's in your nature: A pluralistic folk psychology. *Synthese*, 165(1), 13–29.

Bermúdez, J. L. (2003). The domain of folk psychology. In A. O'Hear (ed.), *Minds and Persons* (pp. 25–48). Cambridge: Cambridge University Press.

Carruthers, P., & Smith, P. K. (1996). *Theories of Theories of Mind*. Cambridge: Cambridge University Press.

Clement, R. W., & Krueger, J. (2002). Social categorization moderates social projection. *Journal of Experimental Social Psychology*, 38(3), 219–31.

Davies, M., & Stone, T. (1995a). *Folk Psychology: The Theory of Mind Debate*. Oxford: Blackwell.

Davies, M., & Stone, T. (1995b). *Mental Simulation: Evaluations and Applications*. Oxford: Blackwell.

Davies, M., & Stone, T. (2001). Mental simulation, tacit theory, and the threat of collapse. *Philosophical Topics*, 29(1–2), 127–73.

Dennett, D. C. (1987). *The Intentional Stance*. Cambridge, MA: MIT Press.

Dunning, D. (1999). A newer look: Motivated social cognition and the schematic representation of social concepts. *Psychological Inquiry*, 10(1), 1–11.

Epley, N., & Waytz, A. (2010). Mind perception. In S. T. Fiske, D. T. Gilbert, & G. Lindzey (eds.), *Handbook of Social Psychology* (5th ed., Vol. 1, pp. 498–51). Hoboken, NJ: Wiley.

Fiske, S. T., & Neuberg, S. L. (1990). A continuum of impression formation, from category-based to individuating processes: Influences of information and motivation on attention and interpretation. *Advances in Experimental Social Psychology*, 23, 1–74.

Fodor, J. A. (1987). *Psychosemantics*. Cambridge, MA: MIT Press.

Giere, R. N. (1999). Using models to represent reality. In L. Magnani, N. Nersessian, & P. Thagard (eds.), *Model-Based Reasoning in Scientific Discovery* (pp. 41–58). New York: Kluwer Academic/Plenum Publishers.

Gilbert, D. T., Krull, D. S., & Pelham, B. W. (1988). Of thoughts unspoken: Social inference and the self-regulation of behavior. *Journal of Personality and Social Psychology*, 55(5), 685.

Godfrey-Smith, P. (2005). Folk psychology as a model. *Philosophers' Imprint*, 5(6), 1–16.

Goldman, A. I. (2006). *Simulating Minds: The Philosophy, Psychology, and Neuroscience of Mindreading*. New York: Oxford University Press.

Gordon, R. M. (1995). Simulation without introspection or inference from me to you. In M. Davies & T. Stone (eds.), *Mental Simulation: Evaluations and Applications* (pp. 53–67). Oxford: Blackwell.

Heal, J. (1996). Simulation, theory and content. In P. Carruthers & P. K. Smith (eds.), *Theories of Theories of Mind* (pp. 75–89). New York: Cambridge University Press.

Heal, J. (1998). Co-cognition and off-line simulation: Two ways of understanding the simulation approach. *Mind & Language*, 13(4), 477–98. Retrieved from <Go to ISI>://000078705900002.

Kelley, H. H. (1973). The processes of causal attribution. *American Psychologist*, 28(2), 107.

Kunda, Z. (1990). The case for motivated reasoning. *Psychological Bulletin*, 108(3), 480.

Maibom, H. (2007). Social systems. *Philosophical Psychology*, 20(5), 557.

Maibom, H. (2009). In defence of (Model) Theory Theory. *Journal of Consciousness Studies*, 16, 6(8), 360–78.

Nichols, S., & Stich, S. (2003). *Mindreading: An Integrated Account of Pretence, Self-Awareness, and Understanding Other Minds*. Oxford: Oxford University Press.

Pronin, E., Lin, D. Y., & Ross, L. (2002). The bias blind spot: Perceptions of bias in self versus others. *Personality and Social Psychology Bulletin*, 28(3), 369–81.

Skov, R. B., & Sherman, S. J. (1986). Information-gathering processes: Diagnosticity, hypothesis-confirmatory strategies, and perceived hypothesis confirmation. *Journal of Experimental Social Psychology*, 22(2), 93–121.

Slowiaczek, L., Klayman, J., Sherman, S., & Skov, R. (1992). Information selection and use in hypothesis testing: What is a good question, and what is a good answer? *Memory & Cognition*, 20(4), 392–405. Retrieved from http://dx.doi.org/10.3758/BF03210923.

Snyder, M., Campbell, B. H., & Preston, E. (1982). Testing hypotheses about human nature: Assessing the accuracy of social stereotypes. *Social Cognition*, 1(3), 256–72.

Spaulding, S. (2012). Mirror neurons are not evidence for the Simulation Theory. *Synthese*, 189(3), 515–34.

Spaulding, S. (2015). Simulation Theory. In A. Kind (ed.), *Handbook of Imagination* (pp. 262–73). Oxford: Routledge Press.

Spaulding, S. (forthcoming). Mind misreading. *Philosophical Issues*.

Spaulding, S. (in progress). Divergent Social Interpretations.

Tajfel, H. (1974). Social identity and intergroup behaviour. *Social Science Information*, 13(2), 65–93.

Tetlock, P. E. (1992). The impact of accountability on judgment and choice: Toward a social contingency model. *Advances in Experimental Social Psychology*, 25, 331–76.

2

AFFECTIVE EMPATHY

Heidi L. Maibom

'Affective empathy' denotes a range of emotional responses we can have to what others feel or the situation they are in, which include sympathy, empathic anger, and contagious joy. This stands in contrast to 'cognitive empathy,' which is typically taken to refer to our (more) cognitive ability to grasp what other people are thinking, feeling, or experiencing (see Chapter 1, 'Cognitive empathy'). The following emotional states may all be thought to be empathic (cf. Maibom 2012):

Affective empathy
Person S empathizes with person O's experience of emotion E in situation C if S feels E for O as a result of believing or perceiving that O feels E, or imagining being in C.

Sympathy (empathic concern)
Person S sympathizes with person O when S feels sad for O as a result of believing or perceiving that something bad has happened to O, or S feels happy for O as a result of believing or perceiving that something good has happened to O.

Emotional contagion
Person S's feeling E is a case of emotional contagion if S feels E as a result of believing that person O feels E, perceiving that O's expressing E, or imagining being in O's situation.

Personal distress
Person S is personally distressed by person O's experience of emotion E in situation C if S feels E – not for O, but for herself *(S)* – as a result of believing or perceiving that O feels E, imagining being in C, or as a result of believing that something bad has happened to O.

The consensus among philosophers tends to be that only what is described above under the title 'affective empathy' is affective empathy *proper*. Social psychologists, by contrast, mainly talk of what philosophers call sympathy, when they talk of empathy or, more precisely, empathic concern. This has led to some confusion in the literature. Most agree that emotional contagion is *not* empathy, although an influential account of empathy – the Perception-Action model of empathy – describes only such a process. The disagreement about nomenclature is not superficial. Indeed, the best way of understanding the problem is to consider that sympathy, personal distress, emotional contagion, and affective empathy are deeply interconnected structures, not as easy to pry apart as the above characterization suggests. To understand affective empathy, one needs to understand how it is connected to, yet different from, these other affective states.

1. What is affective empathy?

Martin Hoffman describes empathic emotion as an emotion that is more appropriate to the state or situation of someone else than to that of the person who experiences it (Hoffman 2000). If I am empathically sad that your cat was run over, my sadness is more appropriate to your situation – having lost a loved pet – than to my own, being a mere bystander to tragedy. So perhaps emotions can be experienced in one of two ways: 'directly,' in a way that is appropriate to our own situation, or 'empathically,' in a way that is more appropriate to another's situation (Batson 2011, Decety & Svetlova 2012, Haidt 2012, Maibom 2007, Prinz 2011a and 2011b). The way we ordinarily experience emotions is direct. I may be embarrassed that I forgot my colleague's name. However, I can also be embarrassed that my colleague said something insensitive about someone else within earshot of that person. In this case, even though I am embarrassed, I am not embarrassed *for myself*; I am embarrassed *for him*. Some philosophers prefer to say that we are embarrassed *with* someone if we empathize with her embarrassment because that highlights the fact that we are experiencing more or less the same emotion as the person we empathize with. By contrast, it seems possible to experience embarrassment *for* someone who is not embarrassed, herself. Is that empathy? If our view of empathy is that one only empathizes if one experiences much the same emotion the other person is experiencing – with respect to affective quality – then this case would not count. However, it seems natural to say that we are empathically embarrassed for, say, Basil Fawlty as he runs around his hotel making an arse of himself. We are embarrassed *for* him and our embarrassment is an emotion that would be appropriate for him to feel under the circumstances (or that *we* think is appropriate for him to feel). As Hoffman would say, our embarrassment is more appropriate to his situation than our own. Another way of putting the same point is that it would make sense for him to feel embarrassed under the circumstances, and that's why *we* feel embarrassed. If we feel embarrassed for someone in this way, our embarrassment is a good candidate for being empathic.

Conceiving of empathy as responsive also to the situation the other person is in brings it closer to its cousin, sympathy. Sympathy is generally thought to concern the *welfare* of the person. But whereas empathy is thought to match, more or less, the emotion the person would reasonably be expected to feel under the circumstances, or what she is actually experiencing, sympathy is typically expressed by a more narrow range of concerned emotions, such as soft-heartedness, concern, and tenderness (e.g. Batson 2011), which typically do not match the emotion the empathic target is actually experiencing or can reasonably be expected to experience. So sympathy seems to be a response to the welfare situation a person is in that is relatively uniform in its affective quality, and empathy varies as a function of the more particular situation the person is in. Another difference between empathy and sympathy is that when the person is immersed in his or her situation – i.e. experiences it from a first-person standpoint – she is unlikely to experience sympathy for herself. Sympathy seems to reflect a third-person standpoint. One can sympathize with oneself, to be sure, but when one does so it is typically from a more removed, less immersed, third-person perspective. We can therefore think of empathy as an emotional response to the situation of another that reflects a first-person stance towards that situation.

Theorists disagree about how much variance is deemed acceptable between the emotion experienced by the empathizer and the emotion felt by the subject. Because few people regard empathy as requiring success, sizeable differences can be accepted as long as the empathizer genuinely thinks that he or she is feeling what the other person feels or could reasonably be expected to feel. Nonetheless, the easiest way of conceptualizing key cases of empathy is simply to say that if *S* experiences an emotion *for O*, *S*'s affective state must be the same as, or very similar to, *O*'s. That is, if *O* is angry, *S* will be angry. On the other hand, we would be hard pressed to count *S*'s happiness on *O*'s behalf as empathic if *O* is upset about the very thing *S* is happy about on behalf of *O*.

An emotion is not simply an affective state. An emotion has what is variously called 'an object' or 'representational content.' It is *about* something. In the above example, my embarrassment is *about* forgetting my colleague's name. Because the above characterization of affective empathy demands that the empathizer and the target feel the *same* emotion, it is fair to suppose that *S*'s *E* must have the same object as *O*'s *E* for it to be empathic. After all, if I am embarrassed that I spilled a bit of red wine on myself and you are embarrassed that you're overdressed for the party, we are both embarrassed but evidently not about the same thing. But suppose I am simply sad that you are sad, without making any judgment about what made you sad in the first place. Am I empathically sad?

There is something odd about denying me empathic sadness in a case where my sadness has as its object just your sadness, but not the object of your sadness. For most people this would be an uncontroversial example of empathy. It might be better, then, simply to acknowledge that empathy comes in degrees. We empathize more fully with someone if our emotions also have the same object as his. Nonetheless, emotional resonance with the other *because* he experiences the affect he does is also a way of empathizing (though less fully). Clearly the object of our empathy is more complex than the object of the other person's emotion, because our empathy should encompass his affect as well. In other words, our empathic affect has as its object the other person's affect along with the object of that person's affect (in the fuller cases of empathy). In such cases, our emotions have the same affective quality and their objects overlap in part.

If we look at empathizing as being on a spectrum, we can also do away with another objection. Dan Zahavi and Philippe Rochat (2015) have argued that, contrary to what is typically thought to be a characteristic of affective empathy, the empathizer does not *share* the target's emotion *unless* the empathic act involves some form of mutual awareness. I think this may be taking the term 'sharing' too seriously, but we can concede that the fullest empathic affective experiences are those where there is sharing, as in mutual awareness. But many other experiences instantiate this ideal less fully, and are still well thought of as cases of affective empathy.

It might, however, be thought that experiencing the same emotion as someone else with the same object is *contrary* to empathy. Suppose that Harry is angry with his boss for treating him badly, and so am I. But if Harry is angry with his boss for treating him badly and *I* am angry with Harry's boss for treating him badly, what does the 'feeling *for*' amount to? Why aren't we just both (non-empathically) angry with Harry's boss? Why is my anger empathic? According to the story we have told so far, my anger must be related to Harry's anger or situation in the right way. We might say that my anger is empathic *because* I surmise that Harry is angry or that it would be appropriate for him to be angry. He might tell me that he is angry, I may be able to *see* that he is angry (his fists are clenched, he stomps around puffing, and so on), I imagine being him in his situation and see that I would be angry, etc. If my anger is in no way connected with Harry's state of mind – either as it is or as one might reasonably expect it to be – it would appear that I am just (non-empathically) angry with Harry's employer. Note, however, that in many cases it may be reasonable to expect that I would feel both: angry with Harry's boss because of the way he treats people, and angry *for* and *with* Harry because of what has happened to him.

If Harry's anger is only the source or origin of my own, my anger may simply be a case of emotional contagion. Emotional contagion is often thought to be the most basic affective reaction to the emotions of others that is still empathic in nature. It is said that we 'catch' others' emotions, e.g. their mirth, sadness, or anxiety (Hatfield, Cacioppo, & Rapson 1994). The term 'catch' is meant to reflect the fact that the process is often relatively automatic and involuntary. Reactive crying in infants is an early manifestation of emotional contagion (Simner 1971, Sagi & Hoffman 1976, Martin & Clark 1982). Reactive barking in dogs and contagious yawning in chimpanzees are likely animal equivalents (Campbell & de Waal 2011). As adults, too, we are susceptible to such contagion when in the company of others. Stepping into a room where people are talking and laughing, you may find the happy mood infectious, and therefore feel happy yourself. If, on the other hand, you spend an afternoon with your grieving friend, you might find yourself quite despondent at the end of it.

For my anger with Harry's boss to be more than a case of emotional contagion it is not enough that Harry's anger *caused* my anger, I must also *be aware* that I feel angry *because* Harry is angry. The anger must, in some sense, be ascribed to Harry even though I *also* feel angry. I feel *with* Harry, we might say. What I deem to be wrong about the world is not something that has happened *to me*, but something that has happened *to Harry*. In this way, awareness of the source of our anger is necessary for our emotion to be truly empathic.

Is it possible for me to experience the same affect, with a very similar object, *because* the other person experiences it, and be *aware* of it, without that emotion being empathic? Consider the following example. Sarah is quite upset because Keith failed to show up for an important family counseling meeting. When Keith realizes that she is upset, he becomes upset. He is upset that she is upset, he is upset *because* she is upset, and he *knows* that he is upset because she is upset. Nonetheless, he proceeds to berate her for making him upset (or worse). Instead of his upset making him more kindly disposed towards Sarah, he unleashes the distress he's caught from Sarah *on* Sarah.

Is Keith empathizing with Sarah's upset? To say 'yes' puts a strain on our ordinary conception of empathy as something beneficial and interpersonally useful. Indeed, most social psychologists would classify this type of upset along with 'personal distress' as an emotion that is self-centered and opposed to what they call empathy. In personal distress you are distressed *for* yourself even if you are made distressed by someone else's distress and you *know* that this is the case. Alternatively, we might think that Keith's distress is *reactive* distress. It is a reaction to Sarah's distress, and it happens to be similar to her emotion, but this seems more like an accident. It follows the same logic as reacting with fear to aggression, not the logic of catching or simulating the other person's emotion. Reactive emotionality is another important aspect of our emotional sensitivity to one another, but not typically one that is thought to rely on empathy.

This leaves us in a bit of a pickle. For if reactive or personal distress can look almost indistinguishable from empathic distress, how do we get a handle on empathic distress and, by extension, empathy at all? One might think that it is the choice of emotion – i.e. distress – that creates the problems. Perhaps the affective quality of distress is such that when one feels it, one tends to become more self-involved. And there is indeed evidence that empathic distress, itself, leads to increased self-focusing (López-Pérez et al. 2014). But one can easily see how empathic embarrassment, empathic joy, and empathic disgust can all lead to the same problem. This suggests that looking at empathic affect as a static phenomenon is a mistake. Emotions are dynamic processes that unfold over time in response to the person's thoughts and attitudes about the emotional experience, in response to the changing environment, and so on. And it is here that we must look to gain a better understanding of these phenomena.

2. Empathy as a process

One of the researchers whose work has been most sensitive to the idea of empathy as a process is Nancy Eisenberg. Her work has focused on how empathy is caused, its physiological measurement, what it later turns into, and how developmental factors influence this process (e.g. Eisenberg 2005). A rough outline of the empathic process – understood specifically as a response to another's distress – goes like this. At the initial stage of affective engagement with the situation of another, an emotion more appropriate to the other's situation is experienced, which the agent conceives of as empathic distress. This emotion later becomes transformed by the thoughts and attitudes of the empathizer into either personal distress or sympathy (cf. also Hoffman 2000). This affects what the initial empathic engagement motivates the agent to do. One way, then, to solve the problem that we faced above is to acknowledge that the empathic process may take different turns, and consequently lead to radically divergent outcomes. If, for instance, the empathic affect is strong and becomes the focus of the agent, he becomes self-focused and, as a result, he will be more motivated to get rid of the unpleasant affect *himself*. If, on the other hand, the agent focuses carefully on its *origin* in the affect or situation of the other, the emotion will be experienced mainly *for* the other, and will tend to turn into or co-occur with sympathy (empathic concern). The resulting motivation will be oriented towards bettering either the situation or the feelings of the target. Whether we decide to call these two processes by the same name, or by different ones, does nothing to change the fact they originate in the same way, share many of the same characteristics, and so on.

As the empathic process unfolds, closely related emotions morph into one another in a way that appears to be determined by the agent's attitudes, beliefs, and personality, and by the predicament of the target and how she reacts to it. Some people are more likely to experience personal distress when faced with a suffering other than others are, and the same holds true for sympathy (Eisenberg et al. 1988, Eisenberg et al. 1994, Batson 2011, Davis 1994). Nonetheless, personal distress and sympathy tend to co-occur as responses to an individual in distress (Batson 2011, Davis 1994, Carrera et al. 2013, López-Pérez et al. 2014). The critical question is usually taken to be *how much* of one versus the other the person feels. An important methodological confound is that personal distress is usually measured *purely* in terms of its affective qualities. That is, people who rate themselves as worried, distressed, disturbed, upset, troubled, and agitated (sometimes also alarmed, grieved, and perturbed) are typically simply assumed to experience *personal* distress (see, for instance, Batson 2011, Carrera et al. 2013). But these affective descriptors cannot capture whether the affect is felt *empathically* or *directly (personally)*. As Batson has previously found, people typically feel a mix of empathic and direct distress. In some studies, at least, people classified as high in personal distress actually report feeling as much distress for the target as for themselves. Personally distressed people are not confused about *why* they are distressed, they are just more distressed in general, and more personally distressed in particular, than people rated as being high in sympathy/empathic concern. Thus, at least three emotions tend to co-occur when a person is exposed to another in need or distress: empathic distress, personal distress, and sympathy. It should now be clear that the crucial question is not *which* of these emotions is experienced, but how much of one versus another is felt, and how they relate to one another and to the beliefs and attitudes of the person experiencing them.

To get an idea of the importance of such a nuanced view of the empathic process, let us consider a couple of ways an empathic process can unfold. Imagine that a colleague comes into your office in tears. Before even knowing about her situation, you feel sad yourself, presumably through emotional contagion. Your awareness that the person something bad has happened to is her, not you, makes you regard your own sadness in a certain way. It is sadness, not for yourself – though you are, of course, sad – but *for her*. It is, then, a mix of direct and personal sadness. Now sadness for her will tend to morph into a concern for her, best known as empathic concern or sympathy, assuming that you have no active dislike of her. On the psychologist's picture of sympathy, it involves feeling warm, softhearted, tender, compassionate, and moved (Batson, Early, & Salvarani 1997). As a result of such feelings for her, you will want to console her, make her feel better, or at least hear her out. This is a more positive empathic process. We can, however, imagine a less rosy one.

Suppose that one of your friends is in his characteristic pessimistic mood. He complains at length. The city that you both live in is mediocre, the politics is nuts, people are unfriendly or uninteresting, you've been to all the good restaurants many times, there's nowhere interesting to go, nothing to do, and life here is just dull, dull, dull. You start to feel despondent, depressed about living in this mediocre hole, and bitter about the low caliber of person populating the place (yourself excluded?). His mood has infected yours, you know it has, and you know you feel like he feels for very similar reasons to his. But you don't feel down *for* him; you just feel down. Before long you start getting irritated with him because you realize he is bringing you down. 'Why does he always do this?' you think, becoming surly in your attitude towards him, and plotting your escape.

Arguably both processes I have described are empathic, although they unfold in very different ways. They are both set off by emotional contagion. Your colleague's sadness and your friend's despondency directly affect your own mood. Suppose, further, that in both cases the contagion morphs into empathy before continuing on its way. You have a moment where you feel despondent on your friend's behalf, perhaps. But by contrast to your colleague's situation, that of your friend is very similar to your own, and if the reasons he enumerates to feel down about living where you live is enough for you to feel despondent or depressed on his behalf, they are reasons that *you* should feel despondent or distressed yourself. You are therefore led to reflect on your own situation stuck, as you are, in the middle of nowhere (let's imagine). You end up with what looks like the equivalent of personal distress, not sympathy for your 'downer' friend. And this, itself, may set off another process, one of irritation and resentment.

If I am right about why one process becomes more self-involved, it does rather seem that for the empathic process to unfold in a more positive way, a certain degree of personal disengagement is required. If the situation the target is in is relevant to your own and it makes you upset or distressed, the tendency will be to focus on your own predicament, not the target's. Paradoxically, this means that it is harder to empathize with someone who is in the same predicament as you are. Moreover, although empathizing with someone is ordinarily thought to be a way of being more involved with that person, it is clear that getting *too* involved carries the risk of tipping the empathic affect into direct affect, e.g. turning empathic distress into personal distress. That self-involvement makes a difference to the turn the empathic process takes is also clear in the experimental designs that induce personal distress. Here the subject is explicitly instructed to focus on how *she herself* would feel in the situation the other person is in, thus making the other person's situation self-relevant. When the situation he imagines he is in is distressing, the instruction has the predictable effect of inducing more distress generally, and more personal distress specifically.

One way to explain why direct/personal and empathic distress go hand in hand is to say that the person is experiencing the same affective quality in the two cases. When it comes to how the emotion *feels*, there is no need to separate the two. She is, however, aware of feeling distress *both* directly (since she is distressed) *and* empathically (since she is distressed *for* the target). Whether she ends up feeling more for herself or for the target depends on how she relates to her distress. Eisenberg has argued that some people are better at regulating their emotions than others, and low regulators are more likely to experience a preponderance of personal distress (Spinrad & Eisenberg 2014). Testing this hypothesis, Bélen López-Pérez and Tamara Ambrona (2015) exposed people to a person in distress (a picture of a child in a hospital bed with a pained expression) and then asked them to control their emotions by reappraising the situation. In one condition (the reappraisal condition) people were asked to think about the situation differently, and in the other (the rumination condition) they were asked to think 'repetitively' about their own thoughts and emotional reactions to the event. People in the reappraisal condition experienced a preponderance of empathic concern compared to personal distress; they were less aroused, experienced less negative affect, and focused less on their feelings. By contrast, people in the rumination condition experienced more arousal, more negative emotions and thoughts, as much personal distress as empathic concern, and focused more on their feelings. This provides further evidence that multiple factors influence the empathic process, including one's cognitive style.

It is therefore quite plausible that it is not the affective quality of the emotion itself that makes personal distress different from empathic distress. A large contributor is the belief that the other is the locus of suffering and that one's own distress is merely a result of hers. Having said that, there is some reason to expect that the more distressed one becomes, the more likely one is to become self-focused, as we have seen. Both Eisenberg and Hoffman have spoken about this phenomenon as 'empathic over-arousal' (Eisenberg 2005, Hoffman 2000). On the other hand, some evidence suggests that it is not a person's tendency to experience strong affect that determines their empathic affect, but how well regulated emotionally they are (Spinrad & Eisenberg 2014). Emotion regulation appears to be a matter of effortful control. That involves 'the ability to shift and focus attention as needed and to control behavior as needed' (Spinrad & Eisenberg 2014, 66). These are evidently skills that can be taught, perhaps through the caretaker's initial 'external' regulation of the child's emotions. Nonetheless, such skills tend to develop into dispositions to deal with affect, including contagious affect, in certain ways. It may be that everybody is subject to empathic over-arousal under certain circumstances, but that in less powerful situations those that are well regulated emotionally are less subject to it.

The story of the unfolding of the empathic process, in which sympathy springs from an emotion that is consonant with that of the other, has some limitations. When people are asked to report on the *timeline* of their particular affective response to another in need, they tend to report sympathy from the start. That is, on average, people report sympathy throughout the emotion process. Of course, since the results are averaged over individuals, we don't know whether *some* people feel empathic or personal distress initially, which then morphs into sympathy (Carrera et al. 2013). These studies also measure people's responses to a very limited number of scenarios, and are not necessarily representative of the empathic process generally. However, they do suggest that sympathy is often directly aroused by another in distress, and not by means of empathic or personal distress.

Carrera and colleagues (2013) also found that what affected helping a person in distress was *not* whether the agent felt more distress than sympathy throughout the episode. Rather, what mattered was whether the person felt a preponderance of distress *at the end* of the episode. People who experienced this were significantly less likely to help the target than were people who experienced a preponderance of distress during the beginning or middle of the episode, or who experienced less distress than empathic concern or an equal amount of both at the end of the episode. This result shows some fit with the dynamic process we posited above. We noted that the more positive empathic process ends with more sympathy for the other and less personal distress. The point of disagreement is whether or not sympathy *arises* from empathic distress or unfolds alongside it.

Lastly, there is more evidence that our empathic reactions to others is sensitive to whether the person experiences appropriate affect under the circumstances (cf. Fink, Heather, & de Rosnay 2015; Hepach, Vaish, & Tomasello 2013), the degree to which the empathizer is related or similar to the target, whether the target is seen as unsympathetic or blameworthy for their own predicament, and so on (Davis 1994, Batson 2011). I do not have space here to discuss all these nuances. As for interpersonal differences, we have already touched on the fact that some people are more empathic than others. However, people with psychopathy and people with autism are frequently mentioned in discussions of empathy because they are both thought to have deficiencies in this area (see Chapter 32, 'Empathy and psychopathology'). There is little doubt that psychopaths have attenuated responses to people who are upset, fearful, or sad (for a review, see Maibom 2016). Whether they also fail to empathize with more positive experiences is unclear. People with autism are widely thought to experience an intact affective response to distress in others, but have impaired ability to *recognize* such distress (Blair 1999a and 1999b, Nichols 2004). It is unclear, however, whether people with autism have a tendency to experience more *personal* than empathic distress in response to distressed others. People with autism tend to be highly anxious and have poorer emotional controls, and it may be that although they are responsive to others' distress, their empathic process tends to end with more personal distress than empathic distress or sympathy. This fits with Candida Peterson's (2014) finding that children with autism exhibit less empathy in their actions than neurotypicals. Peter and Jessica Hobson (2014) also suggest that a more basic difficulty with identifying with others lies at the root of autism.

3. Other empathic emotions

The literature on empathic affect and empathy-related emotions has been dominated by a focus on the feelings of those in need: pain, distress, sadness, and so on. It has been assumed that empathy with people suffering plays a crucial role in moral development and behavior, and in social adjustment. What role other empathic emotions play, if any, has remained underexplored. This is surprising given that the sentimentalist philosophers, who thought empathic affect was foundational to our making moral judgments, stressed the importance of both empathy with suffering and empathy with joy or happiness (Hume 1777/1975, Smith 1759/1976). Recent research on empathy with more positive emotions suggests that such empathy is *more* indicative of social adjustment and happiness than empathy with negative emotions (Blanke, Rauers, & Riediger 2016, Morelli 2013).

Famously, fMRI studies have found that empathic pain activates brain areas that overlap with the areas that are activated when the person feels pain or distress (for) herself (Singer et al. 2004, Cheng et al. 2007). It has also been found that disgust (Wicker et al. 2003, Jabbi, Bastiaansen, & Keysers 2008), fear (Gelder et al. 2004), anger (de Greck et al. 2012), anxiety (Prehn-Kristensen et al. 2009), pleasure (Jabbi, Swart, & Keysers 2007), embarrassment (Krach et al. 2011), and sadness (Harrison et al. 2006) activate overlapping brain areas when the person is feeling the emotion directly, or for themselves, and when they feel it for others (for a review, see Bernhardt & Singer 2012). In social psychology, there is now a handful of studies on empathic embarrassment (Miller 1987, Stocks et al. 2011). Whether what is found in these studies is evidence of empathy or emotional contagion is not always clear, and people are debating how to differentiate vicarious affective responses from empathic ones. Studies of so-called empathic fear (Gelder et al. 2004) may be better interpreted as finding fear *contagion* since it is associated with strong activation of action-oriented areas related to self-defense. Perhaps some emotions are primarily or exclusively felt vicariously – like fear – and others have a more complex standing. There are other findings of overlap in brain activation when something happens to the self and when something happens to another in other areas too, such as touch (Blakemore et al. 2005, Keyers et al. 2004), reward (Mobbs et al. 2009), and social exclusion (Masten, Morelli, & Eisenberger 2011). See also Chapter 5, 'Empathy and mirror neurons'.

4. Conclusion

Empathic affect rarely stands alone. It is part of a dynamic unfolding process in which the person empathized with, her reaction in her situation, and the personality, attitudes, and cognitive style of the empathizer all play a crucial role in determining its course. No one feels empathic distress without also feeling personal distress, and few people feel only empathy and not also sympathy (empathic concern) with a suffering other. Empathic affect comes in degrees. Sometimes we share others' emotions in the sense that we are mutually aware of experiencing the same type of affect with much the same object. At other times, the affective overlap and the object of the emotion vary more, and there may be no mutual awareness of the affective experience. Where we decide to draw the line is relatively arbitrary. The evidence suggests that empathic affect is continuous with more self-focused or direct affect. This is partly due to the fact that empathic distress *is* personal because the empathizer feels distressed, and partly due to the fact that a cognitive focus on the target of distress is required to keep the affect empathic. There are substantial interpersonal differences in the extent to which people empathize with others, some of which may be endogenous, some developmental, and others more situational. The upshot is that the empathic process need not be unequivocally positive. Empathy invoked can take a bad turn in people who are poor at regulating their emotions, or who are highly anxious, or to whom the other person's situation is personally relevant. Nonetheless, empathy has many positive effects, both personally and interpersonally. Arguably, it plays an important role in good social functioning. In the end, the most important factor in empathic affect may be how we deal with it.

References

Batson, C. D. 2011. *Altruism in Humans*. New York: Oxford University Press.
Batson, C. D., Early, S., & Salvarani, G. 1997. Perspective taking: Imagining how another feels versus imagining how you would feel. *Personality and Social Psychology Bulletin*, 23, 751–8.
Bernhardt, B., & Singer, T. 2012. The neural bases of empathy. *Annual Review of Neuroscience*, 35, 1–23.
Blair, R. J. R. 1999a. Psychophysiological responsiveness to the distress of others in children with autism. *Personality and Individual Differences*, 26, 477–85.
Blair, R. J. R. 1999b. Responsiveness to distress cues in the child with psychopathic tendencies. *Personality and Individual Differences*, 27, 135–45.
Blakemore, S. J., Bristow, D., Bird, G., Frith, C., & Ward, J. 2005. Somatosensory activation during the observation of touch and a case of vision-touch synaesthesia. *Brain*, 128, 1571–83.
Blanke, E. S., Rauers, A., & Riediger, M. 2016. Does being empathic pay off? Associations between performance-based measures of empathy and social adjustment in younger and older women. *Emotion*, February 24, 2016. Online first publication: http://dx.doi.org/10.1037/emo0000166.
Campbell, M., & de Waal, F. 2011. Ingroup-outgroup bias in contagious yawning by chimpanzees support link to empathy. *PLoS One*, 6, e18283.
Carrera, P., Oceja, L., Caballero, A., Muñoz, D., López-Pérez, B., & Ambrona, T. 2013. I feel so sorry! Tapping the joint influence of empathy and personal distress on helping behavior. *Motivation and Emotion*, 37, 335–45.
Cheng, Y., Lin, C., Liu, H. L., Hsu, Y., Lim, K., Hung, D., et al. 2007. Expertise modulates the perception of pain in others. *Current Biology*, 17, 1708–13.
Davis, M. H. 1994. *Empathy: A Social Psychological Approach*. Boulder, CO: Westview Press.

Decety, J., & Svetlova, M. 2012. Putting together phylogenetic and ontogenetic perspectives on empathy. *Developmental Cognitive Neuroscience*, 2, 1–24.

de Greck, M., Wang, G., Yang, X., Wang, X., Wang, X., Northoff, G., and Han, S. 2012. Neural substrates underlying intentional empathy. *Social Cognitive and Affective Neuroscience*, 7, 135–44.

Eisenberg, N. 2005. The development of empathy-related responding. In G. Carlo & C. P. Edwards (eds.), *Moral Development through the Lifespan: Theory, Research, and Application, The 51st Nebraska on Motivation.* Lincoln, NE: University of Nebraska Press, 73–117.

Eisenberg, N., Fabes, R. A., Murphy, B., Karbon, M., Maszk, P., Smith, M., O'Boyle, C., & Suh, K. 1994. The relations of emotionality and regulation to dispositional and situational empathy-related responding. *Journal of Personality and Social Psychology*, 66, 776–97.

Eisenberg, N., Schaller, M., Fabes, R., Bustamante, D., Mathy, R., Shell, R., & Rhodes, K. 1988. Differentiation of personal distress and sympathy in children and adults. *Developmental Psychology*, 24, 766–75.

Fink, E., Heathers, J. A., & de Rosnay, Marc. 2015. Young children's affective responses to another's distress: Dynamic and physiological features. *PLoS ONE*, 10, e0121735. doi:10.1371/journal.pone.0121735.

Gelder, B., Snyder, J., Greve, D., Gerard, G., & Hadjikhani, N. 2004. Fear fosters flight: A mechanism for fear contagion when perceiving emotion expressed by a whole body. *Proceedings of the National Academy of Science of the USA*, 101, 16701–6.

Haidt, J. 2012. *The Righteous Mind: Why Good People Are Divided by Politics and Religion.* New York: Pantheon.

Harrison, N. A., Singer, T., Rotshtein, P., Dolan, R. J., & Critchley, H. D. 2006. Pupillary contagion: Central mechanisms engaged in sadness processing. *Social Cognitive and Affective Neuroscience*, 1, 5–17.

Hatfield, E., Cacioppo, J. T., & Rapson, R. L. 1994. *Emotional Contagion.* Cambridge: Cambridge University Press.

Hepach, R., Vaisch, A., & Tomasello, M. 2013. Young children sympathize less in response to unjustified emotional distress. *Developmental Psychology*, 49, 1132–8.

Hobson, R. P., & Hobson, J. A. 2014. On empathy: A perspective from developmental psychopathology. In: H. L. Maibom (ed.), *Empathy and Morality.* New York: Oxford University Press, 172–92.

Hoffman, M. 2000. *Empathy and Moral Development.* New York: Cambridge University Press.

Hume, D. 1777/1975. *Enquiries Concerning Human Understanding and Concerning the Principles of Morals.* L. A. Selby-Bigge & P. H. Nidditch (eds.). Oxford: Oxford University Press.

Jabbi, M., Bastiaansen, J., & Keysers, C. 2008. A common anterior insula representation of disgust observation, experience, and imagination shows divergent functional connectivity pathways. *PLoS One*, 3, e2939.

Jabbi, M., Swart, M., & Keysers, C. 2007. Empathy for positive and negative emotions in the gustatory cortex. *Neuroimage*, 34, 1744–53.

Keysers, C., Wicker, B., Gazzola, V., Anton, J. L., Fogassi, L., & Gallese, V. 2004. A touching sight: SII/PV activation during the observation and experience of touch. *Neuron*, 42, 335–46.

Krach, S., Cohrs, J. C., de Echeverria Loebell, N. C., Kircher, T., Sommer, J., et al. 2011. Your flaws are my pain: Linking empathy to vicarious embarrassment. *PLoS One*, 6, e18675.

López-Pérez, B., & Ambrona, T. 2015. The role of cognitive emotion regulation on the vicarious emotional response. *Motivation and Emotion*, 39, 299–308.

López-Pérez, B., Carrera, P., Ambrona, T., & Oceja, L. 2014. Testing the qualitative differences between empathy and personal distress: Measuring core affect and self-orientation. *The Social Science Journal*, 51, 676–80.

Maibom, H. L. 2007. The presence of others. *Philosophical Studies*, 132, 161–90.

Maibom, H. L. 2012. The many faces of empathy and their relation to prosocial action and aggression inhibition. *Wiley Interdisciplinary Reviews: Cognitive Science (WIRE)*, 3, 253–63.

Maibom, H. L. 2016. Psychopathy: Morally incapacitated persons. In S. Edwards & T. Schramme (eds.), *Handbook of Concepts in the Philosophy of Medicine.* New York: Springer, 1109–29.

Martin, G. B., & Clark, R. D. 1982. Distress crying in neonates: Species and peer specificity. *Developmental Psychology*, 18, 3–9.

Masten, C. L., Morelli, S. A., & Eisenberger, N. I. 2011. An fMRI investigation for empathy for 'social pain' and subsequent social behavior. *Neuroimage*, 55, 381–8.

Miller, R. 1987. Empathic embarrassment: Situational and personal determinants of reactions to the embarrassment of another. *Journal of Personality and Social Psychology*, 53, 1061–9.

Mobbs, D., Yu, R., Meyer, M., Passamonti, L., Seymour, B., et al. 2009. A key role for similarity in vicarious reward. *Science*, 324, 900.

Morelli, S. A. 2013. *The Neural and Behavioral Basis of Empathy for Positive and Negative Emotions.* Dissertation Abstracts International: Section B: The Sciences and Engineering, vol. 73(10-B)(E).

Nichols, S. 2004. *Sentimental Rules: On the Natural Foundations of Moral Judgment.* New York: Oxford University Press.

Peterson, C. 2014. Theory of mind understanding and empathic behavior in children with autism spectrum disorders. *International Journal of Developmental Neuroscience*, 39, 16–21.

Prehn-Christensen, A., Wiesner, C., Bergman, T. O., Wolf, S., Jansen, O., et al. 2009. Induction of empathy by the smell of anxiety. *PLoS*, 4, e5987.

Prinz, J. 2011a. Is empathy necessary for morality? In A. Coplan & P. Goldie (eds.), *Empathy: Philosophical and Psychological Approaches.* New York: Oxford University Press, 211–29.

Prinz, J. 2011b. Against empathy. *Southern Journal of Philosophy*, 49, 214–33.

Sagi, A., & Hoffman, M. L. 1976. Empathic distress in the newborn. *Developmental Psychology*, 12, 175–6.

Simner, M. L. 1971. Newborn's response to the cry of another infant. *Developmental Psychology*, 5, 136–50.

Singer, T., Seymour, B., O'Doherty, J., Kaube, H., Dolan, R. J., & Frith, C. D. 2004. Empathy for pain involves the affective but not sensory components of pain. *Science*, 303, 1157–62.

Smith, A. 1759/1976. *The Theory of Moral Sentiments.* D. D. Raphael & A.L. Mackie (eds.). Indianapolis, IN: Liberty Fund.

Spinrad, T., & Eisenberg, N. 2014. Empathy and morality: A developmental psychology perspective. In H. L. Maibom (ed.), *Empathy and Morality.* New York: Oxford University Press, 59–70.

Stocks, E., Lishner, D., Waits, B., & Downum, E. 2011. I'm embarrassed for you: The effect of valuing and perspective taking on empathic embarrassment and empathic concern. *Journal of Applied Social Psychology*, 41, 1–26.

Wicker, B., Keysers, C., Plailly, J., Royet, J.-P., Gallese, V., & Rizzolatti, G. 2003. Both of us disgusted in my insula: The common neural basis of seeing and feeling disgust. *Neuron*, 40, 655–64.

Zahavi, D., & Rochat, P. 2015. Empathy ≠ sharing: Perspectives from phenomenology and developmental psychology. *Consciousness and Cognition*, 36, 543–53.

3

PHENOMENOLOGY, EMPATHY, AND MINDREADING

Dan Zahavi

Recent years have witnessed an upsurge of interest in and work on empathy in many different disciplines, including philosophy, cognitive science, developmental psychology, social neuroscience, anthropology, nursing, and primatology. Despite all the work being done, there is still no firm agreement about what precisely empathy is or how it might relate to or differ from motor mimicry, emotional contagion, imaginative projection, perspective taking, and sympathy. One attempt to map out some of the central options has been provided by Battaly (2011). According to her reconstruction, the three main positions are as follows:

1. Some conceive of empathy as a sharing of mental states, where sharing is taken to mean that the empathizer and the target must have roughly the same type of mental state. On this account, empathy does not involve knowledge about the other; it does not require knowing that the other has the mental state in question. Various forms of contagion and mimicry consequently count as prime examples of empathy.
2. Others argue that empathy requires both sharing and knowing. It is consequently not enough that there is a match between the mental state of the empathizer and the target, the empathizer must also cognitively assign or ascribe the mental state to the target. Insofar as empathy on this account requires some cognitive grasp and some self-other differentiation, low-level simulation like mimicry and contagion are insufficient for empathy.
3. Finally, there are those who emphasize the cognitive dimension and argue that empathy doesn't require sharing, but that it simply refers to any process by means of which one comes to know the other's mental state, regardless of how theoretical or inferential the process might be.

If empathy is supposed to be the label for a distinctive accomplishment, if it is supposed to constitute a distinct kind of interpersonal understanding rather than simply collapse into either emotional contagion or standard mindreading, it seems advisable to stay clear of both 1 and 3. But should we adopt 2, or might there be other options available, or should we perhaps abandon the attempt to reach a clear-cut definition, since it will inevitably amount to nothing but a terminological stipulation? Given how technical a term "empathy" is, and given how recently the term was coined and introduced into the scientific debate, it certainly doesn't seem particularly promising to appeal to ordinary usage when trying to reach a satisfactory definition.

One obvious move that is surprisingly rarely made, however, is to revisit the initial philosophical and psychological debate on empathy that took place during the first decades of the twentieth century. Were one to do so, it would quickly become clear that the term was used somewhat differently than is the case today. Lipps, who co-opted the term *Einfühlung* (which Titchener then proceeded to translate as empathy) from the field where it was originally introduced, namely aesthetics, insisted that empathy constituted a modality of knowledge *sui generis*. He argued that there are three distinct domains of knowledge: 1) knowledge of external objects, 2) self-knowledge, and 3) knowledge of others, and he took these domains to have three distinct cognitive sources, namely perception, introspection, and empathy (Lipps 1909, p. 222). The initial discussion of empathy was consequently quite epistemologically oriented, and motivated by a preoccupation with the problem of other minds and by a rejection of the argument from analogy. In the wake of Lipps's investigation, a number of phenomenologists, including Scheler, Stein, Husserl, Walther and Gurwitsch, engaged in further discussions regarding the nature and structure of empathy. Whereas they accepted the idea that empathy must be equated with a basic and quite fundamental form of other-understanding, they were more critical of Lipps's own positive proposal and rejected various attempts to explain empathy in terms of mirroring, mimicry, or imitation. As pointed out by the phenomenologists, whereas the latter processes might explain how and why I come to have a certain experience myself, they do not explain how I come to understand the other. For someone to have a feeling herself and for someone to empathically understand that another has a feeling are two quite different things (Gurwitsch 1979, pp. 24–5). Ultimately, the phenomenologists did not merely dismiss the proposal that imitation is sufficient for empathic understanding. They also questioned whether it was necessary. On a more positive note, the phenomenologists took empathy to be a perceptually based experience of foreign consciousness that more complex and indirect forms of social cognition presuppose as well as rely on.

1. What is empathy for?

Let me, in the following, try to further articulate and elaborate the phenomenological approach to empathy (by partially drawing on points that I have made in the past, cf. Zahavi 2010, 2011, 2014a, and 2014b). I will start elsewhere, however, namely by discussing a proposal by Joel Smith (2015). Smith's proposal is quite representative of a certain way of discussing empathy. It exemplifies the second option listed by Battaly and it can serve as a useful contrast to the position I am aiming to articulate and defend.

In his article "What is empathy for?" Smith defends the view that empathy, rather than being a psychological process or phenomenon, is an epistemic state or achievement that can be attained in various ways. Indeed, many different psychological processes might feed into and be recruited by empathy, which then "allows us to know how others feel" (Smith 2015, p. 1). More specifically, Smith argues that empathy involves sharing in another's affective state (Smith 2015, p. 4), and insists that two distinctive steps are needed in order for this sharing to occur. On the one hand, the empathizer must know *that* the target is in a certain affective state. But simply knowing *that* the target is in an affective state doesn't yet tell A *how* it feels for B to be in the state in question. In order for that to be possible, A must also know first-personally how it feels to be in the affective state in question. Smith consequently offers the following definition of empathy:

A empathises with B if and only if (1) A is consciously aware that B is ψ, (2) A is consciously aware of what being ψ feels like, (3) On the basis of (1) and (2), A is consciously aware of how B feels.

(Smith 2015, p. 5)

It is an important part of Smith's proposal that the first condition can be met in a number of different ways. One might know that B is ψ by being told so, by inferring it from other things that one believes about B, by simulating B and attributing to her the output, or simply by seeing that B is ψ. As for the second condition, Smith also allows for some variation. A might be acquainted with the feel of ψ, either by currently being in ψ, or by currently remembering a previous occasion where A was in ψ. In some cases, imagination might play the required role: one might be acquainted with the feel of ψ in virtue of the fact that one is imaginatively representing oneself as being in the state. It might even be possible to empathize with B's being ψ even if A has never been in ψ, namely insofar as A simply is, or has been, in some state that affectively matches ψ, for instance, a state of a similar kind. Furthermore, similarity of content is not a requirement. So if B is worried about the likelihood of a nuclear catastrophe, and A in the past has been worried about the fact that her parents will once die, a sufficient affective match might be in place. "Thus, even if A is not, and has never been, in exactly the same psychological state as B, she may nevertheless be, or have been, in a state that affectively matches it at some level of determinacy" (Smith 2015, p. 7). The greater the level of determinacy, the greater the match, the more A can be said to empathize with B, the more A will know how B feels (Smith 2015, p. 7) (see Chapter 13, "Empathy and knowing what it's like" in this volume).

To sum up, on Smith's proposal (as well as on many others', including, for instance, de Vignemont and Jacob (2012)), empathy involves sharing (and some amount of projection), it is restricted to affective states, and it has no foundational role to play in social cognition. As will become apparent in a moment, the phenomenological approach to empathy rejects all these claims.

2. Empathy and sharing

One significant problem with the widespread suggestion that empathy involves a sharing of affects (see also Decety and Lamm 2006, Preston 2007, Pfeifer and Dapretto 2009) is that people rarely define what they mean by sharing. Often all they mean is that empathy involves similar or isomorphic affective states in empathizer and target. But does that really amount to sharing? I think a moment's reflection ought to make it clear that the answer must be no. The fact that two individuals each have their own token of the same type of affective state does not make them share an affective state. The individuals in question might be completely unaware of each other and might simply have similar affective states out of pure coincidence. However, as defenders of the view might insist, in empathy surely the situation is different. Here the empathizer is precisely aware of the target and that is enough to convert similarity into sharing proper. But this reply is not convincing. Empathy can obviously be one-sided. A can empathize with B without B being aware of this. Sharing proper, however, arguably requires reciprocity. If you regularly borrow my car without my knowledge, we are not sharing the car. To claim that I am (aware of) sharing one of your emotions, while denying that you are (aware of) sharing one of mine, is equally problematic. Consider, by comparison, recent work on shared or joint attention. There is widespread consensus that joint attention is not simply a question of two unrelated people simultaneously looking at the same thing, nor is it simply a question of gaze following or gaze alternation. For joint attention to occur, the attentional focus of two persons (or more) shouldn't merely run in parallel, it must be joint in the sense of being shared, i.e., its occurrence must be mutually manifest to the co-attenders (cf. Sperber and Wilson 1986). This is precisely what makes joint attention quite unlike any kind of experience one might have on one's own. The emphasis here is clearly on the importance of bi-directionality and reciprocity for sharing (for a more extensive argument, cf. Zahavi & Rochat 2015).

What then about mere similarity? Is that a crucial requirement for empathy? As is also evident from Smith's account, the decisive difficulty concerns the question of how specific the match between empathizer and target must be in order to count as sufficiently similar. After all, everything resembles everything else in some respect. To claim that I can empathize with someone who is distressed because of the death of her two-year-old Spanish Timbrado or with someone who is suffering because of an attack of biliary colic, only if I have been distressed over the loss of the same kind of bird or undergone a gallbladder attack with the same kind of intensity in the past is hardly convincing. By contrast, to claim that I can only empathize with a minded creature if I have a mind myself seems eminently plausible, but also rather trivial. If the account is to say something plausible, yet nontrivial, it must position itself somewhere in between these two extremes. The question is where. Must the empathizer feel (or have felt or in principle be able to feel) the exact same kind of emotion or sensation, say, mortification or nausea? Is it enough if the empathizer is first-personally acquainted with a member of the same family of emotions, or might it be sufficient that the empathizer has simply had (or is in principle able to have) an emotion with the same kind of valence? The less specific the demand is, the more plausible the account might be (see also Chapter 2, "Affective empathy"). But obviously, this increase of plausibility goes hand in hand with a decrease in explanatory power. In any case, the belief that having experienced a life event oneself will give one more insight into another person's similar life experience is widespread, but might be unwarranted. Empirical research suggests that people with similar life experiences, such as childbirth and parental divorce, are not always more accurate at determining how another feels in the same situation compared to those without such experience. In some cases, having had the experience oneself might have a negative impact on one's ability to recognize that the other feels differently about x than oneself did (cf. Hodges 2005).

One implication of Smith's proposal is that empathy cannot provide us with knowledge of what it feels like to undergo new kinds of experiences, experiences we have not had ourselves. Indeed, contrary to Smith's claim, empathy cannot really give us new experiential knowledge; it does not allow me to recognize anything in the other that is new, anything with which I am not already familiar. It shares this limitation with other projective accounts of empathy. But is this a plausible outcome, or does it have, as Scheler once observed, as little merit as the claim that we can never come to understand something new, but only that which we have already experienced before? In some cases, this is undoubtedly true. The only way to know what it is like to taste elderberry syrup or smoked salmon is to try it oneself. But can one generalize from what holds true in the case of gustatory sensations to all phenomenal experiences or would such a generalization fail to do justice to the intuition that empathy can in fact expand our life and lead us beyond the confines of our own actual experiences (cf. Scheler 2008, pp. 46, 49)? Is it really true that one cannot empathize with, say, parents who have lost their only child, unless one had oneself in the past gone through such an ordeal or at least engaged in an explicit act of imagination to that effect?

As we saw, for Smith our understanding *that* the other is in a given state can be achieved in a number of ways. However different they might be (perceptual, inferential, testimonial, etc.), none of them can provide us with knowledge of *how* it feels like for the other to be in the state in question. How plausible is that claim? When seeing the other's anger, exhaustion, frustration, admiration, or joy, am I then really merely registering or detecting that the other is in some mental state while having no clue about what it is like for him or her to be in that state? Compare and contrast also the two following situations:

1) You enter your friend's home, discover that he has torn up all the letters from his ex-wife, and infer that he is anguished and distressed about his recent divorce.
2) You are together with your friend, when he suddenly breaks down and tells you about his divorce. You see his anguish and distress in his pained countenance.

How plausible is it to claim that both situations are alike in only providing you with knowledge *that* your friend is anguished and distressed? How plausible is it to claim that the face-to-face encounter in and of itself provides you with no information of how (or what) it is like for your friend to be in the affective state in question? How plausible is it to claim that that encounter provides you with no appreciation of the qualitative and hedonic character of the other's phenomenal state, and that your only access to that dimension is by somehow living through the state first-personally (be it online or offline)? Even if you have no children of your own, might spending time together with a couple who is bereaving the loss of their son not give you an understanding of what that is like; an understanding that is far more powerful than anything you might accomplish by means of certain feats of imagination?

3. Empathy and social cognition

One of the controversies in the empathy debate concerns the role that empathy plays in social cognition. Whereas some have argued that mindreading is an extended form of empathy (Goldman 2006, p. 4), and that empathy "is relevant when accounting for all aspects of behaviour enabling us to establish a meaningful link between others and ourselves" (Gallese 2001, p. 43), others have ascribed a far more modest role to empathy. On Smith's proposal, empathy is obviously not what establishes awareness of the other person's mental life in the first place. Rather, empathy requires a prior understanding of the other's mind in order to get off the ground, and is then supposed to allow for an enhanced understanding of the other's affective state. Over the years, empathy has been defined in various ways, just as many different types of empathy have been distinguished, including *mirror empathy*, *motor empathy*, *affective empathy*, *perceptually mediated empathy*, *reenactive empathy*, and *cognitive empathy*, to mention just a few of the options available. If Smith wants to use the term the way he does, he is, of course, free to do so, but it is striking how different his use is from the way the term was originally introduced and defined by early empathy theorists. Indeed, it might not be an exaggeration to say that we are dealing with a radical change in the meaning and use of the term.

One remaining commonality, however, is the idea that empathy somehow allows for a unique experiential understanding of others. But what is meant by "experiential understanding" differs dramatically. Consider, for example, Coplan, who has recently argued that empathy is a complex imaginative process through which the observer simulates another's situated psychological states, while maintaining clear self-other differentiation (Coplan 2011, p. 40). What, then, is the deliverance of empathy? Here is what Coplan writes:

> this process is the only one that can provide experiential understanding of another person, or understanding of another from the "inside." It is in virtue of its ability to provide this type of first-person access to another, however imperfect, that empathy is a unique and invaluable process – and one worth our attention.
>
> *(Coplan 2011, p. 58)*

But why should an act of imagination, even one that specifically accomplishes an other-oriented perspective taking (Coplan 2011, p. 54), provide for an *experiential understanding* of another person? Would we not normally insist on the difference between imagining a traffic accident and experiencing a traffic accident? In reply, it could be argued that although that difference does make good sense in our own case, it is far less obvious that it makes sense when it comes to our understanding of other people. Any convincing account of our understanding of others must respect the fact that we do not have the same kind of access to the minds of others that we have to our own, it must respect the asymmetry between self-ascription and other-ascription of mental states, it must respect that I do not have first-personal access to the minds of others. Since we cannot experience other people's mental states, the closest we can get to an experiential understanding of the other is by engaging in a particular kind of imaginative other-oriented perspective taking. But it is precisely this line of reasoning that the phenomenological account of empathy calls into question.

One useful way to pinpoint the difference in question is by briefly looking at the distinction between emotional contagion and empathy. One popular move in the more recent empathy literature has been to insist that one of the important distinctions between emotional contagion and empathy is that whereas the former is "self-centered," the latter is "other-centered" (cf. de Vignemont 2009). The other-centered character of empathy is then often cashed out with reference to the target of ascription. In emotional contagion as well as in empathy, the subject is living through the experience first-personally, the only difference being that in the former case, the experience is self-ascribed, whereas in the latter case, it is other-ascribed. The phenomenological approach views matters differently, and insists that we also have to factor in the other-centered givenness of the empathically grasped experience. Although the very experience of empathizing is given first-personally to the empathizer, the object or target of the act of empathy is not given first-personally to the empathizer, but is precisely given as an experience that is lived through first-personally by the other. It is, as Stein would say, located in the other and not in myself (Stein 1989, pp. 10–11). This is, of course, why phenomenologists have standardly rejected proposals according to which empathy should entail that the other's experience is literally transmitted to me, or at least require me to undergo the same kind of experience that I observe in the other (say, being sad that you are sad). Both proposals miss what is distinctive about empathy, and conflate empathy with emotional contagion and sympathy. To empathically experience, say, the emotion of another necessarily differs from the way you would experience the emotion if it were your own. In empathy, you are confronted with the presence of an experience that you are not living through yourself. If I empathize with your sadness, I have a sense of what it is like for you to be sad without being sad myself; I lack first-personal access to the sadness in question.

This might sound more mysterious than it really is. When insisting that empathy is what allows me to experience other experiencing subjects, and that we as a consequence do not exclusively have to rely on and employ internal simulations or imaginative projections, the idea is not to deny that second- (and third-) person access to psychological states differ from first-person access. The idea is rather to insist that it is a mistake to restrict and equate experiential access with first-person access. It is, to put it differently, possible to experience mental states in more than one way. Noticing a bottle of painkillers next to his bedside together with an empty glass of water and concluding that he is in pain is an example of knowing indirectly or by way of inference (Bennett & Hacker 2003, pp. 89, 93). By contrast, there is no more direct way of knowing that *another* is in pain than seeing him writhe in pain. Moreover, the fact that my experiential access to the minds of others differs from my experiential access to my own mind is not an imperfection or shortcoming. On the contrary, this difference is constitutional. It is precisely because of this difference, precisely because of this asymmetry, that we can claim that the minds we experience are *other* minds (cf. Husserl 1950, p. 139).

> Just as what is past can be originally given as past only through memory, and what is to come in the future can as such only be originally given through expectation, the foreign can only be originally given as foreign through empathy. Original givenness in this sense is the same as experience.
>
> *(Husserl 1959, p. 176)*

We might phrase this by saying that empathy provides a special kind of knowledge by *acquaintance*. It is not the standard first-person acquaintance, but rather a distinct other-acquaintance. Rather than blurring the distinction between self and other, rather than leading to some sense of merged personal identities (Cialdini et al. 1997), the asymmetry between self-experience and other-experience is quite crucial for empathy, at least according to the phenomenologists. When Coplan writes that the concept of empathy has not figured prominently in those discussions of intersubjectivity within Continental philosophy that have stressed the difference between self and others (Coplan 2011, p. 59), she is consequently mistaken.

When saying that empathy can provide a special kind of experiential understanding, this is not meant to suggest that empathy provides an especially profound or deep kind of understanding. In order to obtain that, theoretical inferences and imaginative simulations might very well be needed. No, the specificity of the access is due to the fact that it is basic and intuitive, i.e., the empathized experience is given directly as existing here and now. In short, there is a difference between empathically experiencing that another person is angry, and assuming or believing or inferring that another is angry. Just as we ought to consider the difference between thinking about a lion, imagining a lion, and seeing a lion, we also ought to acknowledge the difference between thinking about Anton's compassion or sadness, imagining in detail what it must be like for him to be compassionate or sad, and being empathically acquainted with his compassion or sadness in the direct face-to-face encounter. In the latter case, our acquaintance with Anton's experiential life has a directness and immediacy to it that is not possessed by whatever beliefs I might have about him in his absence.

This proposal is not committed to the view that everything is open to view or that others are totally transparent. The claim is not that *every* aspect of the mental life of others is directly accessible, but merely that we can be experientially acquainted with some aspects of the mental life of others. It has been argued that such a claim is hugely controversial in that it commits one to some form of behaviorism (Jacob 2011, p. 531). I have discussed the relation between experience and expressivity and rejected this criticism elsewhere (Zahavi 2014b), so let me here merely point out that the notion of social perception has gained popularity and been defended by philosophers coming from a variety of different traditions in recent years (cf. Rudd

2003, Green 2007, Cassam 2007, Newen & Schlicht 2009, Smith 2010, Stout 2010, Krueger & Overgaard 2012).

On the present proposal, there is no reason to delimit our empathic understanding to affective states. On the contrary, it is possible to empathize with the cognitive, affective, and conative experiences of the other, i.e., with his or her beliefs, perceptions, feelings, passions, volitions, desires, and intentions. After all, empathy concerns our general ability to access the life of the mind of others in their expressions, expressive behavior, and meaningful actions. Although Wittgenstein does not employ the term "empathy" in the following quote, what he is describing is precisely what the phenomenologists had in mind when they were discussing empathy:

> "I see that the child wants to touch the dog, but doesn't dare." How can I see that? Is this description of what is seen on the same level as a description of moving shapes and colours? Is an interpretation in question? Well, remember that you may also *mimic* a human being who would like to touch something, but doesn't dare.
>
> *(Wittgenstein 1980, Section 1066)*

We can see the other's elation or doubt, surprise or attentiveness in his or her face, we can hear the other's trepidation, impatience, or bewilderment in her voice, feel the other's enthusiasm in his handshake, grasp his mood in his posture, and see her determination and persistence in her actions. Thus, we certainly also express or manifest our mental states by acting on them. My fear or concern is not merely revealed to others in my facial expressions, but also in my running away from what terrifies me or in my attempts to console somebody who is grieving. When I experience the facial expressions or meaningful actions of another person, I am *experiencing* aspects of his or her psychological life, and not merely imagining it, simulating it, or theorizing about it. As Husserl writes, the mind of the other, his thinking, feeling, desiring, is intuitively present in the gestures, the intonation, and in the facial expressions. The expressivity of the other is imbued with psychological meaning from the start, and it is empathy that allows us to understand and grasp this psychological meaning (Husserl 1952, pp. 235, 244).

One implication (and limitation) of this account is that highlighting and emphasizing the intuitive character of empathy also restricts it to face-to-face based forms of interpersonal encounter. Importantly, this does not mean that empathy is necessarily restricted to dyadic relationships. It might very well be possible to empathize with a group, say, a mourning family. However, on many other accounts, and this is also reflected in colloquial speech, it makes good sense to say that we can also empathize with individuals or groups of people not present, and even with fictional characters. For the phenomenologists such uses of the term must at the very least be considered derivative. Moreover, any claim to the effect that, say, people in Copenhagen felt empathy with the Syrian refugees in Hungary might be problematic in that it blurs the distinction not only between empathy understood as a perception-based direct acquaintance with the minds of others and some kind of imaginative projection or theoretical inference, but also between empathy and sympathy. Thus, one should obviously also not overlook that the present proposal does not support or accord with the idea that empathy is per se morally significant and basically equivalent with compassion (see Chapter 21, "Empathy and moral responsibility").

In arguing for the difference between emotional contagion and empathy, Coplan has insisted that emotional contagion in contrast to empathy is a bottom-up or outside-in process. It is involuntary, it does not require any deliberate effort or higher-level processing such as imagination. It gets triggered by direct sensory engagement with another person expressing an emotion, and consequently requires a direct perception of the other (Coplan 2011, p. 46). On the phenomenological account, these features are very much features characterizing basic empathy, and this is what makes empathy different from other, more mediated forms of mindreading. So what would then on this account be the relation between empathy and mindreading? There are two different possibilities. The first would be to simply define empathy as faced-based mindreading. It is no coincidence that some of the recent work on phenomenology of empathy has been presented in the framework of the direct social perception debate (cf. Zahavi 2011). The other option would be to say that empathy is more basic and fundamental than mindreading proper. The coherency of this proposal obviously depends on what one understands by mindreading. On one popular proposal, mindreading involves the employment of a theory of mind and refers to our ability to attribute mental states to others, where these states are conceived of as unobservable, theoretical posits, invoked to explain and predict behavior in roughly the same way as physicists appeal to electrons and quarks in order to predict and explain observable phenomena. According to this usage, mindreading qua mental state attribution is a skill that has to be acquired just as we need to learn how to read texts (since there is no intrinsic or natural connection between the psychologically meaningful mental states and what is perceptually available). Given such a usage, empathy could be seen as immediate and direct form of social understanding (involving sensitivity to the animacy, agency, and emotional expressivity of others) any attempt to explain or predict the other's mental states and behaviors relies on and presuppose.

In the developmental literature, it is fairly uncontroversial that infants manifest an essentially innate sensitivity to social stimuli, that there is already an early form of intersubjectivity at play from around two months of age, where the infant has a sense of reciprocity with others, and that the "echoing of affects, feelings and emotions that takes place in reciprocal interaction between young infants and their caretakers" is a "necessary element to the development of more advanced social cognition, including theory of mind" (Rochat & Striano 1999, p. 8). Not surprisingly, however, a debate has sprung up regarding whether it might be possible to explain some of the findings in a more parsimonious way, i.e., in a way that doesn't ascribe any mindreading capacities to the infant. Perhaps the infant is merely very good at behavior-reading, i.e., sensitive to observable behavior and capable of reasoning about such behavior (for instance in a way that allows it to predict and anticipate certain outcomes) (Apperly 2011, p. 151). However, this dispute about whether infants are really mindreading or merely behavior-reading seems premised on the assumption that the former necessarily involves referring to purely interior and private states, i.e., states that are not visible in meaningful actions and expressive behavior. Given such a concept of mentality, there are good reasons to believe that children will only be able to master the capacity at a relatively late stage. But the obvious and crucial question is why one would want to opt for such a narrow, mentalistic understanding of the mind in the first place. Phenomenologists have in general taken an embodied approach to questions of intersubjectivity and interpersonal understanding. We begin from the recognition that the body of the other presents itself quite differently than any other physical entity, and accordingly that our perception of the other's bodily presence is unlike our perception of ordinary physical objects. I would consequently suggest that a more fortuitous route to explore is one that takes us beyond the dichotomy of behavior-reading and mindreading (cf. Sinigaglia 2008), and ultimately dispenses with the whole reading imagery. Moving beyond that dichotomy changes the nature of the challenge. The decisive question is no longer how to bridge the gap between visible but mindless behavior and invisible but disembodied mentality, but to understand the link between early forms of perceptually grounded empathy and more sophisticated forms of interpersonal understanding. To understand this link might itself pose many challenges, but to adopt a terminology from philosophy of mind, the challenges would belong to the easy problems, rather than the hard problem, of social cognition. As Merleau-Ponty puts it, the problem of knowing how

I can come to understand the other is infinitely less difficult to solve, if the other is understood primarily as an intentional comportment in the world, as a way of intending and grasping the world that surrounds us, than if she is understood as a radically alien psyche (Merleau-Ponty 1964, p. 117).

I hope it has by now become clear why the proposal I have outlined, a proposal that dates back to the earliest discussion of and debates on empathy, differs from the three main positions outlined by Battaly. On the phenomenological reading, empathy doesn't involve sharing, but nor is it merely just any kind of mindreading. Empathy is rather a form of "expressive understanding" that requires bodily proximity, and which allows for a distinct experiential grasp of and access to the other's psychological life.

Given the early and formative discussion of empathy, one might wonder whether one should not simply argue that the contemporary understanding and use of the notion is mistaken: it departs too radically from the original meaning of the term, which is the meaning to which we ought to return. This is, however, not a strategy I propose or endorse. To that extent, my main concern is not to argue that the classical phenomenological analysis of empathy is the right one. My point is rather that the phenomenological discussion of empathy – regardless of whether or not it *de facto* targets what we today would label empathy – contains various important insights regarding the foundations of social cognition that contemporary research on the topic ought to incorporate. For one, this analysis can offer a corrective to the widespread 'invisibility assumption' in the theory of mind literature, i.e., the assumption that other minds are concealed and hidden (cf. Johnson 2000, p. 22; Saxe, Carey, & Kanwisher 2004, p. 87).

References

Apperly, I. (2011). *Mindreaders: The Cognitive Basis of "Theory of Mind."* Hove and New York: Psychology Press.

Battaly, H. D. (2011). Is empathy a virtue? In A. Coplan & P. Goldie (eds.), *Empathy: Philosophical and Psychological Perspectives* (pp. 277–301). Oxford: Oxford University Press.

Bennett, M. R., & Hacker, P. M. S. (2003). *Philosophical Foundations of Neuroscience.* Oxford: Blackwell.

Cassam, Q. (2007). *The Possibility of Knowledge.* Oxford: Oxford University Press.

Cialdini, R. B., Brown, S. L., Lewis, B. P., Luce, C., & Neuberg, S. L. (1997). Reinterpreting the empathy-altruism relationship: When one into one equals oneness. *Journal of Personality and Social Psychology,* 73(3), 481–94.

Coplan, A. (2011). Will the real empathy please stand up? A case for a narrow conceptualization. *The Southern Journal of Philosophy,* 49, 40–65.

Decety, J., & Lamm, C. (2006). Human empathy through the lens of social neuroscience. *The Scientific World Journal,* 6, 1146–63.

de Vignemont, F. (2009). Affective mirroring: Emotional contagion or empathy? In S. Nolen-Hoeksema, B. Frederikson, G. R. Loftus, & W. A. Wagenaar (eds.), *Atkinson and Hilgard's Introduction to Psychology* (15th ed., p. 787). Florence, KY: Cengage Learning.

de Vignemont, F., & Jacob, P. (2012). What is it like to feel another's pain? *Philosophy of Science,* 79(2), 295–316.

Gallese, V. (2001). The 'shared manifold' hypothesis: From mirror neurons to empathy. *Journal of Consciousness Studies,* 8(5–6), 33–50.

Goldman, A. I. (2006). *Simulating Minds.* New York: Oxford University Press.

Green, M. S. (2007). *Self-Expression.* Oxford: Oxford University Press.

Gurwitsch, A. (1979). *Human Encounters in the Social World.* Pittsburgh, PA: Duquesne University Press.

Hodges, S. D. (2005). Is how much you understand me in your head or mine? In B. F. Malle & S. D. Hodges (eds.), *Other Minds: How Human Bridge the Divide Between Self and Others* (pp. 298–309). New York: The Guilford Press.

Husserl, E. (1950). *Cartesianische Meditationen und Pariser Vorträge.* Ed. S. Strasser. Husserliana, vol. 1. Den Haag: Martinus Nijhoff.

Husserl, E. (1952). *Ideen zu einer reinen Phänomenologie und phänomenologischen Philosophie. Zweites Buch. Phänomenologische Untersuchungen zur Konstitution.* Ed. E. M. Biemel. Husserliana, vol. 4. Den Haag: Martinus Nijhoff.

Husserl, E. (1959). *Erste Philosophie (1923/24). Zweiter Teil. Theorie der phänomenologischen Reduktion.* Ed. R. Boehm. Husserliana, vol. 8. Den Haag: Martinus Nijhoff.

Jacob, P. (2011). The direct-perception model of empathy: A critique. *Review of Philosophy and Psychology*, 2(3), 519–40.

Johnson, S. C. (2000). The recognition of mentalistic agents in infancy. *Trends in Cognitive Sciences*, 4(1), 22–8.

Krueger, J. & Overgaard, S. (2012). Seeing subjectivity: Defending a perceptual account of other minds. *ProtoSociology*, 47, 239–62.

Lipps, T. (1909). *Leitfaden der Psychologie.* Leipzig: Verlag von Wilhelm Engelmann.

Merleau-Ponty, M. (1964). *The Primacy of Perception.* Evanston, IL: Northwestern University Press.

Newen, A., & Schlicht, T. (2009). Understanding other minds: A criticism of Goldman's simulation theory and an outline of the person model theory. *Grazer Philosophische Studien*, 79(1), 209–42.

Pfeifer, J. H., & Dapretto, M. (2009). A mirror in my mind: Empathy and the mirror neuron system. In J. Decety & W. Ickes (eds.), *The Social Neuroscience of Empathy* (pp.183–98). Cambridge, MA: MIT Press.

Preston, S. D. (2007). A perception-action model for empathy. In T.F.D. Farrow & P. Woodruff (eds.), *Empathy in Mental Illness* (pp. 428–47). Cambridge, MA: Cambridge University Press.

Rochat, P., & Striano, T. (1999). Social cognitive development in the first year. In P. Rochat (ed.), *Early Social Cognition* (pp. 3–34). New Jersey: Lawrence Erlbaum Associates.

Rudd, A. (2003). *Expressing the World: Skepticism, Wittgenstein, and Heidegger.* Chicago, IL: Open Court.

Saxe, R., Carey, S., & Kanwisher, N. (2004). Understanding other minds: Linking developmental psychology and functional neuroimaging. *Annual Review of Psychology*, 55, 87–124.

Scheler, M. (2008). *The Nature of Sympathy.* London: Transaction Publishers.

Sinigaglia, C. (2008). Mirror neurons: This is the question. *Journal of Consciousness Studies*, 15(10–11), 70–92.

Smith, J. (2010). Seeing other people. *Philosophy and Phenomenological Research*, 81(3), 731–48.

Smith, J. (2015). What is empathy for? *Synthese*. DOI 10.1007/s11229-015-0771-8.

Sperber, D., & Wilson, D. 1986. *Relevance: Communication and Cognition.* Oxford: Blackwell.

Stein, E. (1989). *On the Problem of Empathy.* Washington: ICS Publishers.

Stout, R. (2010). Seeing the anger in someone's face. *Aristotelian Society Supplementary Volume*, 84(1), 29–43.

Wittgenstein, L. (1980). *Remarks on the Philosophy of Psychology*, vol. 1. Eds. G. H. von Wright & H. Nyman. Trans. C. G. Luckhardt & M. A. E. Aue. Oxford: Blackwell.

Zahavi, D. (2010). Empathy, embodiment and interpersonal understanding: From Lipps to Schutz. *Inquiry*, 53(3), 285–306.

Zahavi, D. (2011). Empathy and direct social perception: A phenomenological proposal. *Review of Philosophy and Psychology*, 2(3), 541–58.

Zahavi, D. (2014a). Empathy and other-directed intentionality. *Topoi*, 33(1), 129–42.

Zahavi, D. (2014b). *Self and Other: Exploring Subjectivity, Empathy, and Shame.* Oxford: Oxford University Press.

Zahavi, D., & Rochat, Ph. (2015). Empathy ≠ sharing: Perspectives from phenomenology and developmental psychology. *Consciousness and Cognition*, 36, 543–53.

4

THE NEUROSCIENCE OF EMPATHY

Christine Cong Guo

In recent decades, neuroscience, a discipline studying the nervous system, has evolved to a broad multidisciplinary field that attracts biologists, social scientists, computer scientists, and engineers alike. Modern neuroscience techniques are now commonly used to probe the neurophysiological basis underlying topics in social science and psychology; this chapter will discuss recent findings from neuroscience studies on empathy. While the scope of neuroscience encompasses many scales of the nervous system – from the molecular neuroscience at the microscopic level to systems and cognitive neuroscience at the macroscopic level – this chapter will primarily focus on the macroscopic perspective – the neural representations of empathy in the human brain. This field of study belongs to a relatively young but fast-growing domain of neuroscience, namely social neuroscience. Social neuroscientists often use a combination of neuroimaging and neuropsychological tests to identify the association between neural substrates and social behavior. The microscopic perspective on the neuroscience of empathy, though it won't be discussed here, is also a rapidly growing field – some prominent examples include the effect of oxytocin on empathetic behavior and its therapeutic potential (Bartz et al. 2011) and the role of von Economo neurons, a neuron type specific to higher mammals, in social behavior (Allman et al. 2011).

Empathy broadly refers to the capacity to experience the feelings and understand the thoughts of others. This capacity is pervasive in our daily life, and plays a central role in social interaction. Storytellers, filmmakers, musicians, and advertisers have known and capitalized on our innate capacity to resonate with the feelings of others for a long time. Thanks to the advance in non-invasive neuroimaging techniques, we are now able to examine brain activity during a wide range of empathetic behaviors. This progress hence enables neuroscientists to map the physiological correlates of the processes of empathy, describe its neuronal architecture, and specify empathy circuits in the brain (Rankin et al. 2006).

Broadly speaking, neuroscientists define empathy as a "complex form of psychological inference that enables us to understand the personal experiences of another person through cognitive, evaluative and affective processes" (Danziger, Prkachin, & Willer 2006). In this chapter, I will review two main streams of neuroscience research on empathy. Section I will discuss neuroimaging studies that examine brain activities during tasks designed to produce empathy in healthy participants. Section II will review lesion studies that examine the correlation between brain injuries and impairments in empathy in clinical populations.

I. Neuroimaging studies on empathy

The neuroimaging technique used by most social neuroscience studies is functional magnetic resonance imaging (fMRI). fMRI is a non-invasive imaging technique that uses MRI signals to measure brain activity. Compared to other neuroscience techniques, such as electroencephalogram (EEG), fMRI offers superb spatial resolution for inferring the neuroanatomical basis of empathy. fMRI experiments, however, are somewhat limited in their study paradigms – static and/or simple stimuli are almost always used, as participants need to lie still inside the scanner while images of their brain are taken. As the readers will discover later on, most studies discussed in this chapter examine relatively simple forms of empathy. This limitation is likely to be addressed as technological advances and innovations continue to expand the scope of what can be studied with fMRI, such as real-time interaction between two participants in two scanners (Koike et al. 2015).

Neuroimaging studies have unveiled two levels of neural processes contributing to empathy: a lower level/bottom-up process and a higher order/top-down process. The former represents a bottom-up process of automatic simulation of the observed by the observer. This process draws on somatic mimicry, i.e., the tendency to automatically mimic and synchronize facial expressions, postures, and movements with those of another person, and can lead to further convergence in emotion. It is viewed as the more primitive aspect of empathy, shared among non-human primates and lower mammals. I will use *emotional contagion* to refer to this lower level/bottom-up process. The higher order process, on the other hand, describes a top-down process that enables the observer cognitively to appreciate others' feelings. While this process is sometimes called perspective taking or Theory of Mind, I will use *affective perspective taking* here to refer specifically to the appraisal of others' feeling, as opposed to the appraisal of others' thoughts. This chapter is hence organized to discuss recent neuroimaging findings on neural mimicry/synchrony, emotional contagion, and finally affective perspective taking.

This section uses "emotional or affective empathy" and "cognitive empathy" only occasionally, as the meanings of these two terms tend to be ambiguous in neuroimaging literature. For example, both terms have been used to describe brain responses to observing or imaging others' experience of emotion. To avoid ambiguity, *emotional contagion* is used here when the research focus is the similarity of brain responses between the first-hand experience and the observation of others' experience of the same emotion; and *affective perspective taking* is used when the research focus is the brain responses contributing to cognitive appraisal.

Synchrony of neural activities across individuals

When searching for the neural basis of empathy, a fundamental criterion is the synchronization of neural activities between the observer and the observed. The earliest and perhaps the most prominent example of neural synchrony is provided by the "mirror neuron system" (see Chapter 5, "Empathy and mirror neurons"). "Mirror neuron system" takes its name from this class of neurons discovered in the premotor cortex of monkeys. Mirror neurons fire both when individuals perform a motor task and when they observe others performing that same task (Gallese et al. 1996). Follow-up electrophysiological studies also found mirror neurons in the inferior parietal lobule of monkeys. The fronto-parietal "mirror neuron system" is a neural mechanism that unifies action perception and action execution: when the monkey observes others' motor behaviors, the perceptual observation of action is matched with the monkey's own encoding of motor trajectories and the goal of motor act. Consequently, this matching is thought to underlie how the monkey understands the observed motor acts and predicts motor outcomes (Rizzolatti et al. 2001).

Building on these electrophysiological studies in monkeys, non-invasive neuroimaging experiments support the existence of a functionally analogous mirror neuron system in the human brain (Cattaneo 2009). The inferior frontal gyrus and the inferior and superior parietal cortices show increased activity both when human subjects observe and when they perform movements. The mirror neuron system is postulated to have evolved further in the human brain, so that it represents not only the process and goal of an action in the physical world, but also the intentions, thoughts, and feelings that motivated that action (Gallese 2001). Consequently, the human mirror neuron system appears to extend beyond the regions homologous to the monkey's fronto-parietal circuit to higher cognitive and affective domains. One prominent example is provided by the limbic system, which can be activated by both observation of others in pain and first-hand experience of physical pain (Singer et al. 2004; Morrison & Downing 2007; Morrison et al. 2004; Jackson et al. 2005). The next section will specifically deal with the neural substrates of emotional contagion, or affective experience sharing.

Emotional contagion

Emotional contagion describes an automatic mimicry and convergence of emotion when a person responds to the perceived emotion of others. Analogous to the synchronization of the neural codes between perceived and executed motor acts, emotional contagion is thought to rely on the synchronization of the neural codes between the perception and the first-hand experience of facial and visceral expressions of emotion. The neuroscience literature on emotional contagion primarily consists of studies on empathy with pain, owing to the robustness of pain in inducing empathy (Bernhardt & Singer 2012). I will first discuss the neural substrates underlying empathy for pain, and then summarize studies on empathic neural responses to other emotions.

The neural circuits involved in first-hand pain experience are relatively well understood. Painful stimuli activate thalamic and brainstem regions that receive direct nociceptive inputs, as well as premotor and prefrontal cortices, somatosensory cortices (S1 and S2), anterior cingulate cortex (ACC), and insula (Apkarian et al. 2005; Bushnell et al. 1999; Craig 2003; Peyron et al. 2000; Rainville & Rainville 2002). An interesting posterior-anterior axis has been suggested for the neural representation of pain, depending on whether it is a first-hand/physical or an observed/imaginary experience. In the insular cortex, the posterior insula is thought to be the primary interoceptive cortex (Craig 2009; Craig 2008), based on its reactivity to painful stimuli (Kong et al. 2006) and its connection to the thalamic pain center in non-human primate models (Craig 2014). The anterior insula (AI), on the other hand, is activated by conscious representations of painfulness, such as subjective appraisal and awareness of painfulness (Kong et al. 2006). A similar posterior to anterior division of pain reactivity has been reported in the ACC (Vogt 2005). Hence, the anterior portions of insular and cingulate cortices, namely the AI and dACC/pACC, are thought to encode the more affective-motivational dimensions of pain, as opposed to the primary encoding of painfulness in the posterior portions (Price 2000).

Empathy for pain describes a person's ability to undergo a painful experience without herself being directly exposed to a physically painful stimulus. Intriguingly, brain regions activated by empathy for pain are the same ones implicated in processing the affective and motivational aspects of pain, namely the AI and dACC (Craig 2009; Craig 2008; Bernhardt & Singer 2012). In their seminal study, Singer et al. examined the brain activity of healthy participants when they either received painful stimuli, or observed a signal indicating that their partner, who was present in the same room, would receive the same painful stimuli (Singer et al. 2004). Bilateral AI, rostral ACC, as well as regions in the cerebellum and brainstem, were activated during both the first-hand experience of pain and the observation of pain. In addition, the activations in the left AI and the ACC correlated significantly with individual differences in empathy: these limbic regions showed greater reactivity to pain in individuals who scored higher on two empathy scales – the Balanced Emotional Empathy Scale (Mehrabian 1997) and the Emotional Concern subscale of the Interpersonal Reactivity Index (IRI) (Davis 1983). The activations of AI and ACC by empathetic pain are further supported by fMRI paradigms which present facial expressions of others in pain, or of body parts receiving painful stimulation (Botvinick et al. 2005; Lamm et al. 2007; Saarela et al. 2007; Jackson et al. 2005; Gu et al. 2010). While both the AI and ACC were activated during the observations of pain, the AI appears to be more specific to the empathy for pain than the ACC (Gu et al. 2010). A recent meta-analysis across thirty-two fMRI studies further confirmed that the observation of others' pain activates the AI most robustly (Lamm et al. 2011). The inferior frontal gyrus (IFG) and dACC/aMCC are also consistently activated across fMRI studies on empathy for pain. Overall, the consistency of neural responses in the limbic pain regions to first-hand experience and the perception of others' experience of pain supports the notion that empathy involves shared neural representations between a person's experience of empathic pain and first-hand experience of physical pain (Bernhardt & Singer 2012).

Compared to the rich neuroimaging literature on the empathy for pain, reports on the empathy with other emotions are relatively limited. Nonetheless, evidence from a handful of studies has implicated a central role of the AI and ACC in vicarious responses to affective states other than pain, including social exclusion (Masten et al. 2011), disgust (Jabbi et al. 2008; Wicker et al. 2003), anxiety (Prehn-Kristensen et al. 2009), and taste (Jabbi et al. 2007). Using disgusting odorants, Wicker et al. implemented an fMRI paradigm to study empathy with disgust (Wicker et al. 2003). In this paradigm, participants both inhaled disgusting odorants and observed video clips showing facial expressions of disgust. Both feeling disgust and observing disgusted faces activated the same sites in the AI and to a lesser extent in the ACC. In a follow-up experiment, Jabbi and colleagues used bitter liquids to deliver first-hand experience of disgust in the scanner, and confirmed the co-activation of the AI by both observation and experience of disgust (Jabbi et al. 2008). Furthermore, observing facial expressions and bodily actions indicating various emotions was found to increase neural activity in the superior temporal sulcus, the AI, and other brain regions involved in the perception and the experience of emotion (Carr et al. 2003; Grosbras & Paus 2006; Jabbi et al. 2007).

So far, neuroscience research on empathy in dynamic social contexts remains scarce, partially due to the challenge of implementing dynamic social interactions in neuroscience experimental paradigms. Emerging findings suggest that the limbic regions could play a similar role in social empathy conditions as in pain and basic emotions discussed above. For example, AI could be activated by compassion and admiration, albeit with longer response time than in the observations of physical pain (Immordino-Yang et al. 2009). We expect to see growing interests in the higher forms of empathy in future neuroscience research.

Affective perspective taking (affective empathy)

When examining the neural substrate of empathy, Lamm and colleagues highlighted an important distinction between different pain induction experiments (Lamm et al. 2011): In one type of experimental design, participants directly observed visual displays depicting target persons in painful situations, whereas in the other, they were shown abstract visual symbols (cues) indicating whether the target person would be in painful situations. Compared to the picture-based design, the latter, referred to as the cue-based design, requires extensive top-down processing, as there are little explicit depictions of painful situations. Direct comparison between the two experimental designs revealed that cue-based studies preferentially activated ventral medial prefrontal cortex (vmPFC), superior temporal gyrus (STG), and posterior regions such as the inferior parietal cortex, precuneus, and posterior cingulate cortex (PCC) (Lamm et al. 2011). These brain regions have been associated with cognitive processes related to Theory of Mind or perspective taking (Frith & Frith 2003; Mitchell 2009). Clearly, empathy could be triggered by processes that are generated internally in the absence of explicit depiction of painfulness; this mechanism is likely to be served by neural underpinnings that are different from the ones that underwrite experience sharing or emotional resonance. This section is dedicated to discussing the neuroscience evidence regarding this cognitive, perspective-taking aspect of empathy.

In contrast to bottom-up emotional contagion, affective perspective taking is a top-down process whereby the subject strives to represent the state of the object. In the eighteenth century, Scottish philosopher and economist Adam Smith proposed that through imagination we place ourselves in the situation of another and become in some measure the same as that person. This act of imagination enables us to experience sensations as if we were the other person, although typically at a weaker intensity. Being a top-down process, affective and cognitive empathy emerge later than emotional contagion in development, as they heavily depend on the executive processing in the prefrontal cortex, which continues to mature from birth to adolescence.

As discussed above, affective perspective taking engages higher-order cognitive centers in the medial prefrontal and posterior parietal cortices (Lamm et al. 2011; Fan et al. 2011). Several functional neuroimaging studies were specifically designed to examine the neural substrates of affective perspective taking. These studies in general involved a 2 × 2 design, where the participants were presented with either emotional or neutral situations, and instructed to either imagine themselves (first-person perspective) or others (third-person perspective) in those situations (Schnell et al. 2011; Preston et al. 2007; Ruby & Decety 2004). The main effect of perspective taking (third-person > first-person conditions) reveals brain networks previously implicated for Theory of Mind, comprising medial prefrontal, medial-temporal, and medial and lateral parietal regions (Spreng et al. 2009; Frith & Frith 2006). The further step is to explore neural mechanisms specific to affective perspective taking. So far, the field is in general agreement that there are neural substrates specifically for affective perspective taking, beyond what is shared with perspective taking or Theory of Mind. The exact regions, however, remain debatable.

II. Human lesion studies on empathy

While functional imaging of healthy controls have identified the brain circuits involved in empathy (Lamm et al. 2011; de Vignemont & Singer 2006; Fan et al. 2011), only complementary data from human lesion studies can demonstrate which structures are required for normal empathy in real-life situations and which are not. Lesion studies have been conducted on several neuropsychiatric disorders associated with deficits in empathy, including schizophrenia, Asperger's syndrome, psychopathy, post-traumatic brain injury, and stroke. Here, I will focus on neurological conditions with measurable lesions in the brain, and review the insights they provide on the neural basis of empathy. Compared to the functional neuroimaging literature, lesion studies have placed a greater emphasis on the disassociation between affective and cognitive empathy: how they are differentially affected in patients and what their respective brain correlates are. Most of these studies used the IRI to assess empathy (Davis

1983). This test is a self-administered test, which includes four types of questions designed to evaluate cognitive empathy (perspective taking and fantasy scales) and affective empathy (empathetic concern and personal distress).

Frontotemporal dementia

The use of neurodegenerative diseases as lesion models has become increasingly common in clinical neuroscience. Compared to lesions created by strokes or the surgical removal of brain tumors, neurodegenerative diseases typically present specific but predictable patterns of brain damage, which are largely shared among patients with the same diagnosis. Typical examples include hippocampal atrophy in Alzheimer's disease, frontoinsular atrophy in behavioral variant frontotemporal dementia (bvFTD), and anterior temporal pole atrophy in semantic variant primary progressive aphasia (svPPA). These neurodegenerative diseases are increasingly used in lesion studies to elucidate structure-function relationships in the brain.

Patients with frontotemporal dementia (FTD) are a population uniquely suited to examine the neuroanatomical foundations of empathy. Progressive social impairment is a characteristic clinical feature of FTD, principally in the subgroup with predominantly frontal atrophy, the behavioral-variant FTD (bvFTD). Patients with bvFTD do not present with prominent speech, language, or general knowledge disorders, as in primary progressive aphasia, nor do they manifest short-term memory deficits, such as in Alzheimer's disease. Rather, subtle but progressively disabling social deficits are the characteristic symptoms for patients with bvFTD and can go unrecognized or misdiagnosed for years (Woolley et al. 2011).

Loss of empathy is an early symptom of bvFTD and constitutes one of its diagnostic criteria (Rascovsky et al. 2011). Patients with bvFTD display a diminished response to other's feelings, reduced social interest, or personal warmth (Mendez 2006; Rankin et al. 2006; Rankin et al. 2005). Eslinger et al. investigated aspects of interpersonal sensitivity and perspective taking in relation to empathy, social cognitions, and executive functioning in twenty-six patients with bvFTD (Eslinger et al. 2011). Patients with bvFTD were significantly impaired on caregiver assessments of empathy, but not on self-assessments, indicating impairments in both empathy and self-awareness. Combined with structural MRI images, the authors found that reduced perspective taking was related to bilateral frontal and left anterior temporal atrophy, whereas reduced empathic concern was related to right medial frontal atrophy. When expanding this brain-behavior analysis to broad neurodegenerative conditions, including FTD, Alzheimer's disease, corticobasal degeneration, and progressive supranuclear palsy, Rankin et al. found the integrity of brain tissue at the right temporal pole, the right fusiform gyrus, the right caudate, and right subcallosal gyrus correlated significantly with total empathy score (Rankin et al. 2006). These results from human lesion studies confirmed some of the findings from the functional neuroimaging literature on healthy participants, but interestingly unveiled a right predominance pattern. Critically, lesion studies in FTD demonstrated that cognitive and emotional empathy changes were associated with pathophysiology in different cortical and subcortical regions, supporting the idea that affective and cognitive empathy are embodied by distinct neural substrates (Rankin et al. 2006).

Focal lesion model

Focal brain lesions, typically resulting from stroke, tumors (meningiomas), and head injury, have been instrumental to the study of functional neuroanatomy. This type of lesion tends to be focal and circumscribed to a single brain region, hence offering superior anatomical specificity compared to the diffused and often bilateral damage in neurodegenerative disease. This anatomical specificity can be difficult to preserve in group studies. Nonetheless, because of the spatial localization and temporal acuity of such lesions, focal lesion studies provide the ultimate test of the casual relationships between brain and behavior, provided cases are selected carefully and the results undergo rigorous statistical analyses. Here, I will discuss clinical evidence from focal lesion studies on the neural basis of empathy, with a particular focus on group-level analyses. There have been many case reports on the impairments in empathy among patients with brain injuries and interested readers can refer to comprehensive reviews on this topic (Hillis 2014).

One of the early clinical observations on empathy and brain injury was made by Eslinger et al. (Eslinger 1998). The authors tested thirty-seven adults with diverse brain injuries on empathy, using a scale that evaluates perspective-taking ability. Although this early study provided no formal statistical analysis, it provided preliminary evidence that emotional and cognitive empathy could be disassociated. The author speculated that ventromedial prefrontal lesions were responsible for deficits in cognitive empathy, whereas orbitofrontal lesions might be responsible for deficits in emotional empathy. A recent study of thirty patients specifically tested the double disassociation of emotional and cognitive empathy in a cohort of thirty patients with focal lesions (Shamay-Tsoory et al. 2009). This study recruited eleven patients with ventromedial prefrontal lesions and eight patients with inferior frontal lesions, as well as additional clinical and healthy controls. Using the IRI self-ratings, they reported that patients with ventromedial prefrontal cortex lesions were significantly more impaired than other groups on perspective taking only, whereas patients with inferior frontal cortex lesions were more impaired on emotional contagion. There was some evidence that right more than left prefrontal lesions cause affective perspective-taking deficits, consistent with the right predominant patterns observed in FTD studies.

Several lesion studies have focused on understanding the neural underpinning of one of the two. The results are somewhat mixed, but most studies identified lesions involving right anterior insula and right anterior cingulate as critical to the function of empathy. Driscoll et al. examined emotional empathy in Vietnam veterans with traumatic brain injury and found that damages to ventrolateral prefrontal cortex, left and right posterior temporal lobes, and insula were associated with diminished affective empathy (Driscoll et al. 2012). Leigh et al. used a naturalistic task to assess affective empathy, where they asked patients about emotions of individuals in short videotaped scenarios or narrated stories (Leigh et al. 2013). They showed that acute impairment in affective empathy was associated with infarcts in the temporal pole and anterior insula. In a small cohort of patients, Gu et al. presented evidence that the anterior insular cortex lesions, but not anterior cingulate cortex lesions, result in deficits in explicit and implicit pain perception, supporting a critical role of anterior insular cortex in empathetic pain processing characterized by prominent deficits in higher-level social functioning (Gu et al. 2010).

Despite the fruitful findings from the lesion literature, some caveats should be considered when interpreting results from lesion studies. Lesions are highly variable across patients in regard to the location and the duration of the injuries, particularly focal lesion types such as stroke and brain tumor. Lesion studies therefore require careful selection of clinical cases with overlapping lesion locations. These studies assumed that the overlapping lesion regions among all cases are responsible for the functional impairments. This assumption, however, is not always valid, particularly when the sample size is small. A further concern relates to the natural recovery of brain injuries. The structure-function relationships in the brain are not static, and substantial reorganization could occur after brain injuries (Bütefisch 2004; Chen et al. 2002). If a patient is studied long after onset of the lesion, they may have partially recovered from the initial impairment caused by the lesion. Finally, deficits in empathy often interact with impairments in other cognitive and affective functions, such as working memory, emotion recognition, and mental flexibility. It is often challenging, sometimes impossible, to separate the effects contributing to empathy from confounds from these other functional domains.

III. Summary

With the advance of social neuroscience, we are beginning to uncover the neuroanatomical correlates of empathy, the neurotransmitters modulating empathy, and the alterations in empathy in neuropsychiatric disorders. Distinct neuroanatomical structures are likely to contribute to different components of empathy, including the bottom-up emotional contagion and top-down cognitive appraisal. The limbic regions in the brain, particularly the AI and ACC, are consistently engaged by observing others' pain in functional neuroimaging studies. Lesions to these regions, due to stroke or neurodegeneration, are often associated with functional impairments in emotion recognition and empathy, supporting the fundamental role of the AI and ACC in empathy. Furthermore, cognitive appraisal or cognitive empathy appears to engage high-order heteromodal brain regions including the dorsal medial prefrontal cortex. While the existing neuroscience literature is mostly developed on pain and basic emotions like disgust, further insights are likely to be gained with innovative paradigms using dynamic social contexts.

References

Allman, J. M., et al., 2011. The von Economo neurons in the frontoinsular and anterior cingulate cortex. *Annals of the New York Academy of Sciences*, 1225(1), pp. 59–71.

Apkarian, A. V., et al., 2005. Human brain mechanisms of pain perception and regulation in health and disease. *European Journal of Pain*, 9, pp. 463–84.

Bartz, J. A., et al., 2011. Social effects of oxytocin in humans: Context and person matter. *Trends in Cognitive Sciences*, 15(7), pp. 301–9.

Bernhardt, B. C., & Singer, T., 2012. The neural basis of empathy. *Annual Review of Neuroscience*, 35(1), pp. 1–23.

Botvinick, M., et al., 2005. Viewing facial expressions of pain engages cortical areas involved in the direct experience of pain. *NeuroImage*, 25(1), pp. 312–19.

Bushnell, M. C., et al., 1999. Pain perception: Is there a role for primary somatosensory cortex? *Proceedings of the National Academy of Sciences of the United States of America*, 96(14), pp. 7705–9.

Bütefisch, C. M., 2004. Plasticity in the human cerebral cortex: Lessons from the normal brain and from stroke. *The Neuroscientist: a review journal bringing neurobiology, neurology and psychiatry*, 10(2), pp. 163–73.

Carr, L., et al., 2003. Neural mechanisms of empathy in humans: A relay from neural systems for imitation to limbic areas. *Proceedings of the National Academy of Sciences of the United States of America*, 100(9), pp. 5497–502.

Cattaneo, L., 2009. The mirror neuron system. *Archives of Neurology*, 66(5), p. 557.

Chen, R., Cohen, L.G., & Hallett, M., 2002. Nervous system reorganization following injury. *Neuroscience*, 111(4), pp. 761–73.

Craig, A.D., 2003. A new view of pain as a homeostatic emotion. *Trends Neurosci.*, 26, pp. 303–7.

Craig, A. D., 2008. Interoception and emotion: A neuroanatomical perspective. In M. Lewis, J. Haviland Jones, and L. Fedlman Barrett (eds.), *Handbook of Emotion*, 3rd ed., New York: Guildford Press.

Craig, A. D., 2009. How do you feel – now? The anterior insula and human awareness. *Nature reviews. Neuroscience*, 10(1), pp. 59–70.

Craig, A.D., 2014. Topographically organized projection to posterior insular cortex from the posterior portion of the ventral medial nucleus in the long-tailed macaque monkey. *The Journal of Comparative Neurology*, 522(1), pp. 36–63.

Danziger, N., Prkachin, K. M., & Willer, J.-C. 2006. Is pain the price of empathy? The perception of others' pain in patients with congenital insensitivity to pain. *Brain*, 129, pp. 2492–507.

Davis, M. H., 1983. Measuring individual differences in empathy: Evidence for a multidimensional approach. *Journal of Personality and Social Psychology*, 44(1), pp. 113–26.

de Vignemont, F., & Singer, T., 2006. The empathic brain: How when and why? *Trends Cogn. Sci.*, 10, pp. 435–41.

Driscoll, D. M., et al., 2012. Empathic deficits in combat veterans with traumatic brain injury: A voxel-based lesion-symptom mapping study. *Cognitive and Behavioral Neurology: Official Journal of the Society for Behavioral and Cognitive Neurology*, 25(4), pp. 160–6.

Eslinger, P. J., 1998. Neurological and neuropsychological bases of empathy. *European Neurology*, 39(4), pp. 193–9.

Eslinger, P. J., et al., 2011. Social cognition, executive functioning, and neuroimaging correlates of empathic deficits in frontotemporal dementia. *The Journal of Neuropsychiatry and Clinical Neurosciences*, 23(1), pp. 74–82.

Fan, Y., et al., 2011. Is there a core neural network in empathy? An fMRI based quantitative meta-analysis. *Neuroscience and Biobehavioral Reviews*, 35(3), pp. 903–11.

Frith, C. D., & Frith, U., 2006. The neural basis of mentalizing. *Neuron*, 50(4), pp. 531–4.

Frith, U., & Frith, C. D., 2003. Development and neurophysiology of mentalizing. *Philosophical Transactions of the Royal Society of London. Series B, Biological Sciences*, 358(1431), pp. 459–73.

Gallese, V., et al., 1996. Action recognition in the premotor cortex. *Brain*, 119(2), pp. 593–609.

Gallese, V., 2001. The "shared manifold" hypothesis: From mirror neurons to empathy. *Journal of Consciousness Studies*, 8(5–7), pp. 33–50.

Grosbras, M. H., & Paus, T., 2006. Brain networks involved in viewing angry hands or faces. *Cerebral Cortex*, 16(8), pp. 1087–96.

Gu, X., et al., 2010. Functional dissociation of the frontoinsular and anterior cingulate cortices in empathy for pain. *The Journal of Neuroscience: the official journal of the Society for Neuroscience*, 30(10), pp. 3739–44.

Hillis, A. E., 2014. Inability to empathize: Brain lesions that disrupt sharing and understanding another's emotions. *Brain*, 137(4), pp. 981–97.

Immordino-Yang, M. H., et al., 2009. Neural correlates of admiration and compassion. *Proceedings of the National Academy of Sciences of the United States of America*, 106(19), pp. 8021–6.

Jabbi, M., Bastiaansen, J., & Keysers, C., 2008. A common anterior insula representation of disgust observation, experience and imagination shows divergent functional connectivity pathways. *PLoS ONE*, 3(8), p. e2939.

Jabbi, M., Swart, M., & Keysers, C., 2007. Empathy for positive and negative emotions in the gustatory cortex. *Neuroimage*, 34, pp. 1744–53.

Jackson, P. L., Meltzoff, A. N., & Decety, J., 2005. How do we perceive the pain of others? A window into the neural processes involved in empathy. *NeuroImage*, 24(3), pp. 771–9.

Koike, T., Tanabe, H. C., & Sadato, N., 2015. Hyperscanning neuroimaging technique to reveal the "two-in-one" system in social interactions. *Neuroscience Research*, 90, pp. 25–32.

Kong, J., et al., 2006. Using fMRI to dissociate sensory encoding from cognitive evaluation of heat pain intensity. *Human Brain Mapping*, 27(9), pp. 715–21.

Lamm, C., et al., 2007. What are you feeling? Using functional magnetic resonance imaging to assess the modulation of sensory and affective responses during empathy for pain. *PLoS ONE*, 2(12), p. e1292.

Lamm, C., Decety, J., & Singer, T., 2011. Meta-analytic evidence for common and distinct neural networks associated with directly experienced pain and empathy for pain. *NeuroImage*, 54(3), pp. 2492–502.

Leigh, R., et al., 2013. Acute lesions that impair affective empathy. *Brain: A Journal of Neurology*, 136(Pt 8), pp. 2539–49.

Masten, C. L., Morelli, S. A., & Eisenberger, N. I., 2011. An fMRI investigation of empathy for "social pain" and subsequent prosocial behavior. *NeuroImage*, 55(1), pp. 381–8.

Mehrabian, A., 1997. Relations among personality scales of aggression, violence, and empathy: Validational evidence bearing on the risk of eruptive violence scale. *Aggressive Behavior*, 23(6), pp. 433–45.

Mendez, M. F., 2006. The accurate diagnosis of early-onset dementia. *The International Journal of Psychiatry in Medicine*, 36(4), pp. 401–12.

Mitchell, J. P., 2009. Inferences about mental states. *Philosophical Transactions of the Royal Society of London. Series B, Biological sciences*, 364(1521), pp. 1309–16.

Morrison, I., et al., 2004. Vicarious responses to pain in anterior cingulate cortex: Is empathy a multisensory issue? *Cognitive, Affective & Behavioral Neuroscience*, 4(2), pp. 270–8.

Morrison, I., & Downing, P. E., 2007. Organization of felt and seen pain responses in anterior cingulate cortex. *NeuroImage*, 37(2), pp. 642–51.

Peyron, R., Laurent, B., & Garcia-Larrea, L., 2000. Functional imaging of brain responses to pain: A review and meta-analysis. *Neuropsychological Clinics*, 30, pp. 263–388.

Prehn-Kristensen, A., et al., 2009. Induction of empathy by the smell of anxiety. *PLoS ONE*, 4(6), p. e5987.

Preston, S. D., et al., 2007. The neural substrates of cognitive empathy. *Social neuroscience*, 2(3–4), pp. 254–75.

Price, D. D., 2000. Psychological and neural mechanisms of the affective dimension of pain. *Science (New York, N.Y.)*, 288(5472), pp. 1769–72.

Rainville, P., & Rainville, P., 2002. Brain mechanisms of pain affect and pain modulation. *Current Opinion in Neurobiology*, 12(2), pp. 195–204.

Rankin, K. P., Kramer, J. H., & Miller, B. L., 2005. Patterns of cognitive and emotional empathy in fronto-temporal lobar degeneration. *Cognitive and Behavioral Neurology: Official Journal of the Society for Behavioral and Cognitive Neurology*, 18(1), pp. 28–36.

Rankin, K. P., et al., 2006. Structural anatomy of empathy in neurodegenerative disease. *Brain: A Journal of Neurology*, 129(Pt 11), pp. 2945–56.

Rascovsky, K., et al., 2011. Sensitivity of revised diagnostic criteria for the behavioural variant of fronto-temporal dementia. *Brain: A Jurnal of Neurology*, 134(Pt 9), pp. 2456–77.

Rizzolatti, G., Fogassi, L., & Gallese, V., 2001. Neurophysiological mechanisms underlying the understanding and imitation of action. *Nature Reviews. Neuroscience*, 2(9), pp. 661–70.

Ruby, P., & Decety, J., 2004. How would you feel versus how do you think she would feel? A neuro-imaging study of perspective-taking with social emotions. *Journal of Cognitive Neuroscience*, 16(6), pp. 988–99.

Saarela, M. V., et al., 2007. The compassionate brain: Humans detect intensity of pain from another's face. *Cerebral Cortex*, 17(1), pp. 230–7.

Schnell, K., et al., 2011. Functional relations of empathy and mentalizing: An fMRI study on the neural basis of cognitive empathy. *NeuroImage*, 54(2), pp. 1743–54.

Shamay-Tsoory, S. G., Aharon-Peretz, J., & Perry, D., 2009. Two systems for empathy: A double dissociation between emotional and cognitive empathy in inferior frontal gyrus versus ventromedial prefrontal lesions. *Brain*, 132(3), pp. 617–27.

Singer, T., et al., 2004. Empathy for pain involves the affective but not sensory components of pain. *Science (New York, N.Y.)*, 303(5661), pp. 1157–62.

Spreng, R. N., Mar, R. A., & Kim, A. S. N., 2009. The common neural basis of autobiographical memory, prospection, navigation, theory of mind, and the default mode: A quantitative meta-analysis. *Journal of Cognitive Neuroscience*, 21(3), pp. 489–510.

Vogt, B. a, 2005. Pain and emotion interactions in subregions of the cingulate gyrus. *Nature Reviews. Neuroscience*, 6(7), pp. 533–44.

Wicker, B., et al., 2003. Both of us disgusted in My insula: The common neural basis of seeing and feeling disgust. *Neuron*, 40(3), pp. 655–64.

Woolley, J., et al., 2011. The diagnostic challenge of psychiatric symptoms in neurodegenerative disease: Rates of and risk factors for prior psychiatric diagnosis in patients with early neurodegenerative disease. *Journal of Clinical Psychiatry*, 72(2), pp. 126–33.

5

EMPATHY AND MIRROR NEURONS

Remy Debes

The most influential empirical discovery regarding empathy in the last few decades is undoubtedly the discovery of so-called mirror neurons. Mirror neurons are single-cell neurons that activate during both the execution of certain actions and the observation of those actions. For example, when you simply observe someone grasping a mug of coffee, the neurons (or groups of neurons) stimulated in your brain are the same, or very nearly the same, as the neurons that would be stimulated were it really *you* grasping a mug of coffee. And, apparently, our brains do this in response to a staggering array of human behavior. In particular, there is evidence suggesting that our brains "mirror" emotions: The neural pathways stimulated by merely seeing someone smiling or frowning or gagging, for example, are the same, or very nearly the same, as the pathways stimulated were we ourselves *actually* feeling joy or sadness or disgust. In light of these findings, some neuroscientists and philosophers have claimed that mirror neurons explain the human capacity for empathy.

In what follows, I offer a very brief overview of the empirical research on mirror neurons. I then review the standard claims researchers have made on the basis of this evidence. I focus first on claims about action mirroring, which have garnered the most attention in the literature. I then turn to claims about emotion mirroring and the uptake for the subject of empathy more generally, with the goal of trying to clarify what "empathy" might mean in the context of these claims. I end with some critical notes about these claims.

1. Monkeys, mirror neurons, and human "mirroring"

Mirror neurons were discovered serendipitously by a group of researchers in Parma, Italy, who first reported their finding in a short 1992 Research Note (di Pellegrino, Fadiga, Fogassi, Gallese, & Rizzolatti 1992). The group was studying neurons in the F5 region of the ventral premotor cortex (vPM) of macaque monkeys. These neurons were already well known for becoming active during specific sorts of goal-directed hand movements, such as pinching and holding. The surprise was that the same F5 neurons activated when the monkeys were merely *observing* certain actions, such as when a human attendant placed food in a box when the monkey was watching. These findings were backed up by two extensive reports by the same group a few years after (Gallese, Fadiga, Fogassi, & Rizzolatti 1996; and Rizzolatti, Fadiga, Gallese, & Fogassi 1996), at which point the name "mirror neurons" was dubbed and it was speculated for the first time that mirror neurons might exist in humans. It was a watershed moment in neuroscience. Since 1996 there have been more than a thousand articles published directly or indirectly on the subject of mirror neurons, prompting the noted neurobiologist Antonino Casile to proclaim that mirror neurons, "are one of the most, if not the most, influential discoveries in systems neuroscience of the last two decades" (Casile 2012, p. 3).

Looking back at the explosion of research that followed, four major points stand out. First, obviously the neural "copy" produced by mirroring is usually somehow inhibited or at sub-threshold levels for stimulating body movement. Otherwise mirroring would cause compulsory imitation. And while explaining imitation is one of the speculated applications of mirroring, of course we don't always imitate what we merely see others do or emote. We don't typically reach out when we merely see someone reaching or cry when we see someone crying, and so on. Notably, however, the mechanism of inhibition or control of mirroring remains one of the most open research questions at present. (Baldissera et al. (2001) suggest that the spinal cord may play a role in inhibition. More recent clues to an explanation can be found in Mukamel et al. (2010) and Grigaityte & Iacoboni (2015).)

Second, mirroring properties are not isolated to the F5 region of vPM where they were first discovered in macaques (see Casile 2012; but also Rizzolatti, Fogassi, & Gallese 2001; Fadiga, Craighero, & Olivier 2005; Buccino, Binkofski, & Riggio 2004; and Ferrari & Rizzolatti 2015). The F5 region remains the principal focus of research, but other brain regions have now been implicated. In the case of action, this includes the inferior parietal lobe (IPL), the supplementary motor area (SMA), Brodmann area 44 (pars opercularis of the Inferior Frontal Gyrus), the posterior sector of the Superior Temporal Sulcus (STS), and cingulate cortex. In the case of emotion, there is evidence implicating the somatosensory cortex and particular subcortical "limbic" structures (e.g. the insula or amygdala).

Third, although it is easy for non-specialists to walk away with the impression that mirror neurons are hyper-specialized in the sense of activating in the observation and performance of particular actions, in fact mirror neurons do not always operate with a strict one-to-one congruence. Instead, many of these neurons show what Collin Allen (2010) calls "broad" congruence: their activation during perception doesn't require the exact same stimulus as in their "motoric role." For example, while some of the neurons excited during actual reaching will only fire during the observation of reaching, others fire while observing other kinds of action. Indeed, only about one third of the neurons in the F5 region of the macaque brain show strict congruence, with the rest showing broad congruence, activating during the observation of a range of actions (Rizzolatti & Craighero 2004). Relatedly, as Allen also notes, the level and pattern of neural activation is not usually identical between the motoric and perceptual cases. These two facts about (1) broad congruence and (2) similar but not same activation levels and patterns – though sometimes occluded in the research – speak in favor of distinguishing between literal "mirror neurons" and more general "mirroring properties" of some brain systems.

Finally, there is strong evidence that human brains do have both mirroring properties and mirror neurons. To be clear, many claims about human mirror neurons have been misnomers. This is because hitherto most research on humans has not been based on direct electrophysiological evidence (i.e. single-neuron studies), which requires placing electrodes directly into the brain. Rightly or wrongly, this kind of direct testing is what was used in many monkey studies. But virtually all human research has used indirect methods to monitor brain activity. Most often, researchers have used functional magnetic resonance imaging (fMRI), a non-invasive technique that measures brain activity by tracking changes in blood flow, based on the fact that blood flow is coupled with neural activity (see Grigaityte & Iacoboni 2015). And while these tests have produced evidence that *fits* the mirror neuron hypothesis, technically what researchers recorded were neural *patterns* in the respective brain *regions* that were congruent between observation and performance conditions. In other words, strictly speaking most research supports only a conclusion about the mirroring *properties* of human brains.

Having said this, it is important to add that there is *some* direct evidence of the existence of literal mirror neurons in humans. Most notably, in 2010 Roy Mukamel and a team of supporting researchers reported findings from patients with pharmacologically intractable epilepsy, who agreed to the experimental mirror neuron testing while undergoing brain surgery to help relieve the epilepsy. Mukamel et al. (2010) presented twenty-one patients with movies of frowning and smiles, as well as of two hand actions (precision grips and whole-hand prehensions). The patients were also asked to perform these same expressions and hand motions. And to their great excitement, Mukamel and his team reported eleven single-cell neurons that discharged under both observation and execution, in the same way that has been observed in monkeys. And while this doesn't change my general recommendation for more circumspect language in the human case, it certainly stands as important evidence in the greater research project.

2. Understanding and empathy: the implications of mirroring

Researchers have suggested broad implications for mirroring systems, especially in areas of social cognition. In particular, it has been speculated that mirroring forms the basis of everything from imitation, language acquisition, action understanding, and empathy. It has also been suggested that deficits in mirroring capabilities might explain various cognitive-social disabilities, most notably autism (Rizzolatti & Craighero 2004; Keysers & Gazzola 2006; Iacoboni 2009; Rizzolatti & Craighero 2005; Williams et al. 2001; Ramachandran & Oberman 2006; for a counterpoint to the widespread optimism of this research, see Jacob & Jeannerod 2005 and Jacob 2008).

These suggestions and the attending research had an immediate uptake in philosophy. Perhaps most notably, research into mirror neurons has been brought to bear on the longstanding "theory of mind" debate over how to explain our folk psychological abilities of "mind reading" – that is, our ability to *understand* or *explain* what is going on in the minds of other persons and to make *predictions* about their behavior on the basis of this knowledge. This debate has so far been divided between so-called theory theorists (such as Paul Churchland or Peter Carruthers) and simulation theorists (such as Alvin Goldman or Robert Gordon). The theory theorists argue that we develop "naïve" psychological theories, which we use – typically tacitly – to *infer* the mental states of other persons, whether their beliefs, desires, or emotions. By contrast, simulation theorists argue, again roughly, that we reach such understanding by using our own psychological systems to *simulate* the mental states of other people. That is, based on what we observe about the person (e.g. her facial displays or other bodily behavior) or her situation (e.g. the task she is trying to perform), we activate in our own mind analogous cognitive systems *as if* we were that person or perhaps that person in that situation, and then somehow attribute or project the resulting mental states onto them.

This is not the place to dissect the many refinements theorists in these two camps make to the rough and ready sketches just offered, or to review the dispute between them (see Chapter 3, "Phenomenology, empathy, and mindreading"). Nor is my short review meant to suggest that that philosophy has a special purview over this debate. Theory Theory, in particular, has a long, steady backing in psychology by such eminent scholars as Alison Gopnik, Andrew Meltzoff, and Henry Wellman, just to name a few. My point is only to highlight the fact that simulation theorists pounced on the discovery of mirroring, which many of them took as manifest evidence of a cognitively "low level" kind of simulation, and the basis of cognitively more sophisticated forms of simulation. In particular, Vittorio Gallese (one of the original discoverers of mirror neurons in macaque monkeys) teamed up with Alvin Goldman (a principal defender of Simulation Theory) to defend the application of mirroring to simulation theories of mindreading.

Theory theorists have offered deflationary explanations to counter this annexing of the mirroring evidence (see e.g. Wellman 2014 or Spaulding 2012). But to reiterate, I am not here particularly interested in the Theory Theory vs. Simulation Theory debate. Instead, I want to review the basis of the supposed alliance between mirroring and Simulation Theory – what I call the "mirrored-understanding" claim – because this claim has also served as the bridge between mirroring and claims about empathy. And I am interested in claims about empathy.

So consider again: The empirical research suggests that observing an action or emotion triggers a neural pattern in brain regions corresponding to actual action or emotion. According to many, this neural "copy" is a plausible basis for a distinctive representation of the observed action or emotion. Mirroring, it can be said, provides the basis for representing the action or emotion "directly," by replicating the neural activity of actual action or emotion. This is sometimes called the "direct-matching hypothesis": We "understand" action or emotion when we combine or "map" – hence "directly match" – a visual representation of the action or emotion (from observation) *onto* the neural replication-representation of that action or emotion (from neural mirroring). For example, when we see someone reaching toward us, we understand what she is doing in virtue of combining our observation of her reaching with a neural replication-representation (in this case, a motor replication) of actual reaching. Moreover, much of the literature suggests that this understanding is robust. In particular, direct-matching is often claimed to yield understanding of the "meaning" of the action or emotion, in virtue of representing what the action or emotion is in some sense "about."

The direct matching hypothesis was implied as early as Gallese, Fadiga, Fogassi, & Rizzolatti (1996), and made explicit as early as 1999 (see e.g. M. Iacoboni et al. 1999. It is now common in the literature, albeit sometimes under different terminology. But before elaborating it further, I duly note that the connection between understanding and mirroring was initially drawn more cautiously. Gallese and Goldman, for example, originally argued that mirrored understanding does not represent "full grasp of mental states such as beliefs and desires" (Gallese & Goldman 1998, p. 500). Similarly, in one of their two seminal articles, the original mirror-neuron research team (Fadiga, Fogassi, Gallese, and Rizzolatti) wrote: "By this term ['understanding'] we mean the capacity to recognize that an individual is performing an action, to differentiate this action from others analogous to it, and to use this information in order to act appropriately. Self-consciousness is not necessarily implied in these functions" (Gallese, Fadiga, Fogassi, & Rizzolatti 1996, p. 606).

However, as I have argued elsewhere, even this seeming moderation should not be overestimated (Debes 2010). Whether the representation in question is "self-conscious" – as the preceding definitional claim states – bears little on its purported robustness. This is because *any* suggestion of "understanding" is already a relatively *thick* epistemic description. It is manifestly more suggestive, for example, than the kind of mere "recognition" or "differentiation" mentioned in the first two clauses. This thickness is further implied by the embedded claim that mirrored understanding facilitates an "appropriate" response by the observer. Otherwise the term "appropriate" becomes hard to interpret. After all, how would the mere recognition *that* someone is acting – say, the recognition *that* someone is moving her arm – absent any idea of what that movement is "about," provide the kind of information that could make a response "appropriate"? Even a thick notion of recognition, one that builds in action differentiation, won't do. Thus, suppose I recognize that you are *reaching*, as opposed simply to *moving* your arm. By itself this can't determine an "appropriate" response. Now, if I understand that you are reaching *for me* or *for the knife* – well, we can easily imagine how this sort of content about the object of action could be useful in determining an "appropriate" response. But this is also manifestly thick content.

In any event, more recent claims forthrightly assert the rich nature of "mirrored" understanding, both for action mirroring and emotion mirroring. This includes, more or less directly, Umiltà et al. (2001), Kohler et al. (2002), Wicker et al. (2003), Carr et al. (2003), Rizzolatti & Crighero (2004), Oberman et al. (2005), Iacoboni et al. (2005), Ramachandran & Oberman (2006), Keysers & Gazzola (2006), Kaplan & Iacoboni (2006), Niedenthal (2007), and Pfeifer et al. (2008). In Rizzolatti, Fogassi, and Gallese's 2006 feature article in *Scientific American*, for example, the subtitle advertises a "new avenue for human understanding." The article then begins by suggesting that mirroring can provide "true comprehension" of what others are doing, and goes on to describe mirroring as how we "discern," "grasp," or "understand" action *intentionally* – that is, that mirroring allows us to understand the literal intentions of an actor. They summarize: "A strict link thus appears to exist between the motor organization of intentional actions and the capacity to understand the intentions of others" (Rizzolatti, Fogassi, & Gallese (2006), p. 59). This comment is actually made in reference to monkeys, but the context of the overall argument clearly aims to establish a corresponding conclusion for humans, as betrayed already in that comment's anthropomorphizing use of "others."

A second mirrored understanding claim is then made in the same article, albeit more briefly, for emotion. The claim is initially made in terms of mere "recognition," that is, as a claim to explain our ability to know that, say, your angry facial gestures are *angry* gestures, as opposed to joyful, amused, or sad ones. However, it is quickly clear that Rizzolatti, Fogassi, and Gallese intend something more substantive than recognition. First, their claim about emotion understanding immediately follows the strong formulations of intentional action understanding, thus tacitly capitalizing on the thick connotation of understanding already in play. This is then reinforced by an explicit speculation that mirroring explains "empathy," and even the complementary use of the term "comprehension" to elucidate the nature of this supposed empathy. Rizzolatti, Fogassi, and Gallese write:

> [W]hen people use the expression 'I feel your pain' to indicate *both* comprehension and empathy, they may not realize just how literally true their statement could be.
>
> *(Rizzolatti, Fogassi, & Gallese (2006), p. 60,*
> *emphasis added)*

This talk of comprehension and empathy – which, to reiterate, is used by most of the prominent empirical investigators in the context of emotion – suggests a cognitive achievement much richer than mere recognition (see also Wicker et al. 2003, Carr et al. 2003, Iacoboni et al. 2005, Keysers & Gazzola 2006, and Pfeifer et al. 2008). The question now is, what achievement exactly? Can we, perhaps, translate claims about mirrored action understanding, which is usually cashed out in terms of intentions, to claims about mirrored empathy? And if not, then what does "empathy" mean in the context of mirroring research? I will conclude by trying to answer these new questions.

3. Can mirroring explain empathy?

For the sake of argument, grant that mirroring produces some kind of representation by direct matching. What is the content of this representation? It seems we can further grant that it must be richer than visual representation. After all, the thesis is not that mirroring simply compounds one visual representation – e.g. *that* some action is occurring, or *that* some emotion is being felt – with another visual representation. Instead, mirroring supposedly combines visual representation with something like a non-observational *experience* of the action or emotion. Consider: When we act or feel an emotion, we have somatic, experiential representations of our actions and feelings, even if we are not always attending to them. And the neural stimulation that corresponds to these somatic representations is precisely what is getting mirrored. At any rate, this is the plausible import of the neural stimulation being of a *motor, somatosensory,* or *limbic* kind, and why the literature often describes this non-observational component of the representation as "embodied" or "visceral" (see e.g. Gallese 2004). In short, it is in virtue of this "visceral" component that mirroring adds distinctive content to the compounded representation.

The foregoing might seem to imply a phenomenological point, namely, that mirroring combined a mere visual representation with a grasp of "what it's like" to do or feel the observed action or feeling (see Chapter 13, "Empathy and knowing what it's like"). Perhaps surprisingly, however, this is not the direction the literature has taken. Instead, as noted earlier, the tendency has been to explain what is "added" in terms of grasping what the action or emotion is "about." In particular, the implication is that mirroring allows us to grasp some aspect of the mental states of the *actor* or *emoter*, and it is this that allows us to understand what the action or emotion is about. So, how exactly is this connection supposed to go? Abstracting from the mirroring context, there are some obvious possibilities to flesh out a claim of understanding.

One might represent some mental state of the actor or emoter that:

(a) accounts for the object(s) of the action or emotion; e.g. *what* she was reaching for, or *who* she was angry at;
(b) accounts for the intention; e.g. not only that she was kicking the *ball* (the object of the kicking), but kicking the ball *to score*;
(c) explains how the actor guided the action toward its goal or object(s): e.g. that she used such-and-so body technique to kick the ball in *that way*;
(d) explains why the actor opted for the action in question or why the actor came to feel as he did, i.e. her *reasons* for intending the action or feeling the emotion.

All of these substantiate a prima facie claim to understanding. The challenge facing mirroring proponents, then, is to explain how layering representational states (direct matching) yields any of these cognitive achievements (a)–(d). In other words, what is it about the nature of the representations that mirroring provides, or their combination with visual representations, that would justify any of the claims above?

Unfortunately, as I have argued elsewhere, mirroring researchers have not clearly answered this question (Debes 2010). Indeed, because they have laid claim to more than one of the possibilities articulated in (a)–(d), it seems one must conclude is that there is no consensus on this critical questions, when it comes to cases of action. Of course, if empathy is what we want to explain, then it is ultimately cases of emotion mirroring that we want to know about. So what is the connection between these kinds of claims to understanding and cases of emotion mirroring?

As I said at the outset, most mirroring research explicitly refers to mirrored emotion as "empathy." Now, even if we read such claims charitably as claiming mirroring emotion constitutes *one* kind of empathy, given all I've said about claims about action mirroring, the implication of the mirroring research when it comes to emotion is still for a relatively *thick* notion of empathy. Consider: If, in cases of action mirroring, direct matching produces a kind of understanding, presumably the same is true in cases of emotion mirroring. In other words, presumably the kind of "empathy" in question involves "understanding" the emotion that one observes in others. So, what kind of understanding is this? Should we translate a version of the action understanding claims – namely, one of (a)–(d) above – to claims about emotion? Or, if no translation from action to emotion can be worked out – i.e. if no version of understanding (a)–(d) can sensibly be applied to cases of emotion mirroring – then is there really a meaningful sense of *understanding* in play for emotion? But if this is true, then does it really make sense to speak of *empathy* in the first place, in the context of mirroring, as the literature does?

Before attempting any answer to these questions, it is important to acknowledge that "empathy" is an eclectic concept. Indeed, it is so eclectic that it tolerates no dogmatic claim about what it "really" is. Nor has it ever been otherwise. The very inception of the English term in 1909 was an act of misinterpretation by the American psychologist Edward Titchener, who was trying to translate the German aesthetician Theodor Lipps's concept of *Einfühlung* (Debes 2015). And ever since Titchener introduced it, the term has been used in increasingly diverse ways to capture a range of phenomena in psychology, psychoanalysis, ethics, aesthetics, sociology, legal theory, and neuroscience (to name only the most prominent). In short, the worry is not that mirroring doesn't capture what empathy "really" is, but instead that mirroring proponents either (1) have been unclear about what they take "empathy" to be, using the term flippantly and without definition, or (2) they have claimed or implied that mirroring can substantiate a thicker notion of empathy than the evidence presently supports. Let me elaborate the second complaint.

It is easy to grant that mirroring emotion amounts to one obvious kind of empathy. After all, as we saw, the distinctive contribution of mirroring is supposedly visceral (in some sense). And whatever else emotions are, their embodied manifestation is obviously a salient aspect of our conception of them. In fact, unlike action, the mirrored representation of an emotion arguably just *is* an emotion, if only a rarefied and not always easily introspectible one. In short, in the case of emotion, there is good reason to say that the observation of another's emotion often results in a literal *felt* correspondence of feeling. That is, as a result of mirroring what the emoter feels, the observer in some sense also *feels* the relevant emotion. Hence, there is empathy, in one sense.

And yet, putting matters this way also highlights the central challenge in cases of emotion. The kind of empathy just described plausibly substantiates only a claim about *recognition*. That is, this kind of empathy plausibly explains my ability to recognize a given emotional expression or display for the kind of emotion it is; for example, my ability to recognize your furrowed brow and gritted teeth *as* anger. What is not clear, however, is whether this kind of empathy – which is something like a literal reflection in my brain of what others are feeling – lives up to, or substantiates, a claim of understanding.

To make this last point clearer, consider a contrasting way we often talk about empathy that lends itself to a clear connection to a claim about understanding (as opposed to mere recognition). Sometimes, perhaps often, we speak of empathy that turns on taking account of a person's *reasons to feel*, in sense (d) of "aboutness" elaborated above. Consider: Everyday conversation is replete with narratives about the various events of our lives, many of which hinge on the particular ways we are feeling or felt in some situation or other. For example, I tell you a story about my getting angry with a colleague. You tell me a story about your sorrow about the loss of your pet. And so on. Now notice that such stories often aim at laying out the reasons or considerations – the facts, impressions, and events – that we think *explain* our emotions. This is often our main objective in telling these stories to each other – a point buttressed by the fact that we often have the special explanatory goal of *defending* or *vindicating* the way we felt. Similarly, this seems to be the kind of empathy we have with characters in literature. Reading novels often involves firsthand appreciation of the relevant considerations – the events and qualities of a dramatic situation – that make up a character's reasons to feel. We virtually witness the features that *would* become the details of an emotion-focused narrative *were* the character to offer one. The point is that, on the one hand, it is the "route" through reasons that helps make empathy in these cases a plausible basis for claiming to "understand" another's emotion. And, on the other hand, it seems wildly implausible to think the kind of direct matching suggested by mirroring could ever produce this kind of empathy.

But perhaps the mirroring proponent only intends to substantiate understanding for emotion in senses (a)–(c). That is, perhaps the goal is to connect mirroring to the kind of representation that involves representing objects, goals, or intentions – but not reasons. After all, it is objects, goals, and intentions, rather than talk of reasons, which has been the usual emphasis in action cases.

But what would it mean to represent an emotion's "intention"? Do emotions have intentions? And how would mirroring an emotion allow us to grasp such a thing, even granting its existence? Similarly, what would it mean to represent an emotion as having a "goal" and how would mirroring allow us to grasp this? Granted, emotions typically have attentional objects – which is emphasized in sense (d) above. Thus, we don't simply get mad, or happy, or jealous. We get mad *at*, or feel happy *about*, or jealous *of*, *something* or *someone*. So perhaps focusing on intentional objections provides traction for a mirrored understanding claim in the case of emotion. How might this go?

It might be argued that observing emotion, in addition to mirroring, leads to gaze following, and, in turn, a closely associated representation of the attentional object of emotion. For example, gaze-reach association is strong for all primates and humans. Another person's reaching thus plausibly triggers in the observer not only an internal motor representation of the reaching (via the basic direct matching of mirroring) but also the kind of gaze following that will lead to visual representation of the object reached for. Thus, if you reach for your cup, I don't only often follow your gaze to the cup, I plausibly represent "the cup" in such close succession with any mirrored representation I form of your reaching, that my representation of the cup gets "bound up" with the mirrored representation of the reaching. So, why not think that something like this occurs when we mirror emotions?

First, emotions accept a more diverse array of objects than action. When you are reaching, for example, there are usually only so many kinds of objects for which you could be reaching, with each possible object tending to have a well-defined location. This is why gaze following has obvious explanatory potential in the case of action. By contrast, when you are angry, simply following your gaze will be less informative. You might be angry with a person, an action the person is performing, a physical object they are holding (such as a political sign), the facial expression or bodily gesture of the person, and so on. You might also be angry about a speech act, which would make gaze following irrelevant.

Second, even if we grant that gaze following in the observation of emotions is not chance, the connection to any representation mirroring provides is still objectionably contingent. This is because the representation at work in the gaze following (of the object of the emotion) is *external* to the mirroring process. That is, in the gaze-following explanation the "visceral" representation of the emotion, which purportedly distinguishes the mirroring phenomenon, especially in claims about empathy, is not itself contributing to the representational content. The explanatory move to understanding in this case of empathy would thus ironically make no essential reference to the visceral representation provided by mirroring, which is precisely what made a claim to mirrored "empathy" plausible in the first place. Or, to put all this another way, if *mirroring* really does provide understanding of another person's emotion, then it is the *mirroring* that should somehow "capture" the object of this person's emotion, not the merely associated process of gaze following. It is thus difficult to see how this strategy could justify the claim that mirroring emotion substantiates understanding.

Faced with these challenges, I think the mirroring proponent should give up the claim that mirroring yields understanding of another person's emotion. It provides only recognition. In other words, the concept of "understanding" ought to be reserved for the senses of understanding articulated under the distinctions (a)–(d) laid out above, all of which it is now far from clear that mirroring can explain.

To be clear, I am not suggesting that the foregoing worries entail that we give up any claim that mirroring yields "empathy" (see Chapter 3, "Phenomenology, empathy, and mindreading"). But the worries I've outlined are at least good reason for those who wish to explain empathy by reference to mirroring to specify far more precisely what they mean by "empathy" than they hitherto typically have. Indeed, the only safe conclusion at present is that it is unsettled what kind of "empathy" emotion mirroring really explains.

References

Adolphs, R. 2001. "The Neurobiology of Social Cognition." *Current Opinion in Neurobiology* 11: 231–9.
Allen, C. 2010. "Mirror, Mirror in the Brain, What's the Monkey Stand to Gain?" *Nous* 44(2): 372–91.
Baldissera, F., P. Cavallari, L. Craighero, & L. Fadiga. 2001. "Modulation of Spinal Excitability during Observation of Hand Actions In Humans." *European Journal of Neuroscience* 13: 190–4.
Buccino, G., F. Binkofski, & L. Riggio. 2004. "The Mirror Neuron System and Action Recognition." *Brain and Language* 89: 370–6.
Carr, L., M. Iacoboni, M. C. Dubeau, J. C. Mazziotta, & G. L. Lenzi. 2003. "Neural Mechanisms of Empathy in Humans: A Relay from Neural Systems for Imitation to Limbic Areas." *Proc. Natl. Acad. Sci. U.S.A.* 100: 5497–502.
Casile, Antonino. 2012. "Mirro Neurons (and beyond) in the Macaque Brain: An Overview of 20 Years of Research." *Neuroscience Letters* 540: 3–14.
Csibra, G. 2007. "Action Mirroring and Action Understanding: An Alternative Account." In P. Haggard, Y. Rosetti, & M. Kawato (eds.). *Sensorimotor Foundations of Higher Cognition. Attention and Performance*, vol. 22. Oxford: Oxford University Press, 435–59.
De Sousa, R. 1987. *The Rationality of Emotions*. Cambridge: MIT Press.
Debes, R. 2010. "Which Empathy? Limitations in the Mirrored 'Understanding' of Emotion." *Synthese* 175(2): 219–39.
Debes, R. 2015. "From Einfühlung to Empathy: Sympathy in Early Phenomenology and Psychology." In Eric Schliesser (ed.). *Sympathy: A History*. Oxford: Oxford University Press.
Di Pellegrino, G., L. Fadiga, L. Fogassi, V. Gallese, & G. Rizzolatti. 1992. "Understanding Motor Events: A Neurophysiological Study." *Explaining Brain Research* 91: 176–80.
Fadiga, L., L. Craighero, & E. Olivier. 2005. "Human Motor Cortex Excitability during the Perception of Others' Action." *Current Opinion in Neurobiology* 15: 213–18.
Ferrari, P. & G. Rizzolatti (eds.). 2015. *New Frontiers in Mirror Neuron Research*. New York: Oxford University Press.
Gallese, V. 2004. "Intentional Attunement: The Mirror Neuron System and its Role in Interpersonal Relations." Interdisciplines.org.
Gallese, V., L. Fadiga, L. Fogassi, & G. Rizzolatti. 1996. "Action Recognition in the Premotor Cortex." *Brain* 119: 593–609.
Gallese, V. & A. Goldman. 1998. "Mirror Neurons and the Simulation Theory of Mind-Reading." *Trends in Cognitive Sciences* 2: 493–501.
Gallese, V., C. Keysers, & G. Rizzolatti. 2004. "A Unifying View of the Basis of Social Cognition." *Trends in Cognitive Sciences* 8: 396–403.
Goldie, R. 2003. "Narrative and Perspective: Values and Appropriate Emotions." In A. Hatzimoysis (ed.). *Philosophy and the Emotions*. Cambridge: Cambridge University Press, 201–20.
Goldman, A. 2006. *Simulating Minds*. New York: Oxford University Press.
Goldman, A. Forthcoming. "Mirroring, Simulating and Mindreading." *Mind & Language*.

Grigaityte, K. & M. Iacoboni. 2015. "How to Study the Mirror Neuron System with Functional MRI: Challenges and Solutions." In P. Ferrari and G. Rizzolatti (eds.), 72–87.

Iacoboni, M. 2009. "Imitation, Empathy, and Mirror Neurons." *Annual Review of Psychology* 60: 1–19.

Iacoboni, M. et al. 1999. "Cortical Mechanisms of Human Imitation." *Science* 286: 2526–8.

Iacoboni, M. et al. 2005. "Grasping the Intentions of Others with One's Own Mirror Neuron System." *Public Library of Science Biology* 3(e79): 529–35.

Jacob, P. 2008. "What do Mirror Neurons Contribute to Human Social Cognition." *Mind & Language* 23: 190–223.

Jacob, P. & M. Jeannerod. 2005. "The Motor Theory of Social Cognition: A Critique." *Trends in Cognitive Sciences* 9: 21–5.

Kaplan, J. & M. Iacoboni. 2006. "Getting a Grip on Other Minds." *Social Neuroscience* 1: 175–83.

Keysers, C. & V. Gazzola. 2006. "Towards a Unifying Neural Theory of Social Cognition." *Progress in Brain Research* 156: 379–401.

Keysers, C. & V. Gazzola. 2010. "Social Neuroscience: Mirror Neurons Recorded in Humans." *Current Biology* 20: 353–4.

Kohler, E. et al. 2002. "Hearing Sounds, Understanding Actions: Action Representation in Mirror Neurons." *Science* 286: 846–8.

Mukamel, R., E. Ekstrom, J. T. Kaplan, M. Iacoboni, & I. Fried. 2007. "Mirror Properties of Single Cells in Human Medial Frontal Cortex." Program No. 127.4. San Diego, CA: Society for Neuroscience. Online.

Mukamel, R., E. Ekstrom, J. T. Kaplan, M. Iacoboni, & I. Fried. 2010. "Single-Neuron Responses in Humans during Execution and Observation of Actions." *Current Biology* 20: 750–6.

Niedenthal, P. 2007. "Embodying Emotion." *Science* 316: 1002–5.

Nussbaum, M. 1988. "Narrative Emotions: Beckett's Genealogy of Love." *Ethics* 98: 225–54.

Oberman, L. et al. 2005. "EEG Evidence for Mirror Neuron Dysfunction in Autism Spectrum Disorders." *Cognitive Brain Research* 24: 190–8.

Pfeifer, J. H., M. Iacoboni, J. Mazziotta, & M. Dapretto. 2008. "Mirroring Others' Emotions Relates to Empathy and Interpersonal Competence in Children." *NeuroImage* 39: 2076–85.

Ramachandran, V. & L. Oberman. 2006. "Broken Mirrors: A Theory of Autism." *Scientific American* 295: 63–9.

Rizzolatti, G. & L. Craighero. 2004. "The Mirror-Neuron System." *Annual Review of Neuroscience* 27: 169–92.

Rizzolatti, G. & L. Craighero. 2005. "Mirror Neuron: A Neurological Approach to Empathy." In J. P. Changeux, A. Damasio, W. Singer, & Y. Christen (eds.). *Neurobiology of Human Values*. Berlin: Springer Press, 107–23.

Rizzolatti, G., L. Fadiga, V. Gallese, & L. Fogassi. 1996. "Premotor Cortex and the Recognition of Motor Actions." *Cognitive Brain Research* 3: 131–41.

Rizzolatti, G., L. Fogassi, & V. Gallese. 2001. "Neurophysiological Mechanisms Underlying the Understanding and Imitation of Action." *Nature Neuroscience Reviews* 2: 661–70.

Rizzolatti, G., L. Fogassi, & V. Gallese. 2002. "Motor and Cognitive Functions of the Ventral Premotor Cortex." *Current Opinion in Neurobiology* 12: 149–54.

Rizzolatti, G., L. Fogassi, & V. Gallese. 2006. "Mirrors in the Mind." *Scientific American* 295: 54–61.

Smith, A. 1984. *The Theory of Moral Sentiments*. Indianapolis: Liberty Fund Inc.

Spaulding, S. 2012. "Mirror Neurons Are Not Evidence for the Simulation Theory." *Synthese* 189(3): 515–34.

Stueber, K. 2006. *Rediscovering Empathy*. Cambridge: MIT Press.

Turella, L., A. C. Pierno, F. Tubaldi, & U. Castiello. 2009. "Mirror Neurons in Humans: Consisting or Confounding Evidence?" *Brain and Language* 108: 10–21.

Umiltà, M. A. et al. 2001. "I Know What You Are Doing: A Neurophysiological study." *Neuron* 32: 91–101.

Velleman, D. 2003. "Narrative Explanation." *Philosophical Review* 112: 1–25.

Wellman, Henry. 2014 *Making Minds: How Theory of Mind Develops*. New York: Oxford University Press.

Wicker, B. et al. 2003. "Both of Us Disgusted in My Insula: The Common Neural Basis of Seeing and Feeling Disgust." *Neuron* 40: 655–64.

Williams, J. H. G. et al. 2001. "Imitation, Mirror Neurons, and Autism." *Neuroscience and Behavioral Reviews* 25: 287–95.

6

THE EVOLUTION OF EMPATHY

Armin W. Schulz

There is no doubt that humans frequently empathize (though exactly how often they do so is a matter of some controversy – see e.g. Hatfield & Rapson, 1994; Hoffman, 2000; Prinz, 2011). There is also increasingly little doubt that other species do so, too: in particular, chimpanzees have been shown to display empathetic reactions (see e.g. de Waal, 2008), and something similar seems to hold for dogs (Custance & Mayer, 2012), dolphins (Frohoff, 2013), and elephants (Hakeem et al., 2009; Plotnik et al., 2006). These facts raise the question of why the ability to empathize evolved: what evolutionary pressures brought it about that the ability to empathize spread through a number of different populations of organism? In what follows, I provide a partial answer to this question.

In particular, the goal in what follows is twofold. First, I outline some of the major factors that are likely to have influenced the evolution of empathy. Second, I show why knowing something about the reasons for which the ability to empathize has evolved is useful for answering various further questions concerning this ability.

This entry is structured as follows. In section I, I make clearer what I understand by empathy, and consider some methodological issues surrounding the evolutionary biological investigation of this trait. In section II, I then lay out the major driving force that is commonly thought to underlie the evolution of empathy: namely, the facilitation of cooperation. After that, in section III, I present another, less commonly discussed, factor that likely influenced the evolution of empathy: namely, the facilitation of the generation of non-cooperatively adaptive behavioral responses to the environment. In section IV, I consider some implications of these evolutionary biological points for the discussion surrounding the nature and moral importance of empathy. I conclude in section V.

I. What is empathy and how can it be evolutionary biologically studied?

In what follows, I take empathy to be a kind of "emotional mirroring": more specifically, organism A can be said to empathize with organism B to the extent that, upon obtaining evidence that B is feeling some emotion E, A is disposed to feel that same emotion E (Hatfield & Rapson, 1994; Hoffman, 2000; Prinz, 2011). Three points are important to note about this way of understanding empathy.

First, the view of empathy at stake here presupposes that organism B outwardly displays cues as to its emotional state. This is necessary, as only if B displays these cues is it possible for another organism A to react to B's emotional state by mirroring it. In the background here is the idea that cases of empathy should not be confused with situations in which two organisms just happen to share an emotion; rather, genuine empathizing is the *effect* of the fact that some other organism is in a relevant emotional state. Note further that this assumption of the presence of outward signs of an emotion that can be detected by other organisms is not guaranteed to be met in all populations of organisms. However, empirically, it does frequently seem to hold (Sauter et al., 2010; Ekman & Rosenberg, 1997; Prinz, 2007). For this reason, I will simply accept it here – i.e. the rest of the discussion should be seen to be restricted to populations in which this prerequisite to the evolution of empathy has already evolved. (It is possible that outward displays of cues pertaining to the emotional state of an organism coevolved with the ability to empathize. While raising some interesting issues, nothing in this chapter hangs on this, so I will not discuss it further here.)

Second, empathy as understood here involves more than just representing that another organism is in some emotional state: it involves actually being in that same state. Put differently: empathy goes beyond having a theory of another's mental states by requiring that the empathizer undergoes these mental states itself (for more on this, see e.g. Goldman, 2006; Schulz, 2011a). Relatedly, note that this view of empathy contrasts with *sympathy* – cases where an organism represents another organism as feeling some sort of (typically negative) emotion, and reacting accordingly (Prinz, 2011; Darwall, 1998). Unlike sympathy, empathy concerns cases where the same emotion – fear, disgust, joy, etc. – is *mirrored* in different organisms.

Third and finally, I here assume that a key adaptive function of many emotional reactions is to guide and initiate appropriate behavioral responses to the world. Put differently, I here assume that a key reason for why some emotions (like pain, fear, anger, or joy) have evolved is that they are highly adaptive as triggers for important behaviors – such as repair of damage, fleeing, fighting, grooming, etc. Note that I do not assume that this is true for all emotions, or that this is the only reason for why certain emotions have evolved; the claim is just that a key reason for why some emotions have evolved is that they enable the organism to better engage in adaptively appropriate behaviors. In this weak form, this is an assumption that is widely shared (Stich et al., 2010; Prinz, 2007).

Given all of this, then, the question to be answered here can be more precisely formulated as follows: why would an ability to feel what another organism feels – because this other organism feels it – spread and be maintained in a population of organisms? Before considering two different ways in which this evolutionary psychological question can be answered, it is useful to make two methodological remarks.

First, it needs to be acknowledged that evolutionary psychology, in general, is hard to do well (Richardson, 2007; Buller, 2005). In particular, for a full account of the evolution of any trait, we would need to know – at least – the ancestral state of this trait, the extent to which it is heritable, the size and origin of the relevant selection pressures on it, the extent to which it was variable (i.e. which alternatives existed in the population), and the size and structure of the population in question (Richardson, 2007; Brandon, 1990). Needless to say, this knowledge is hard to obtain even in the best of cases – and likely to be even harder for psychological traits like the ability to empathize, whose exact distribution on the phylogenetic tree is unclear, which do not fossilize, and whose genetic basis is not well understood.

However, this should not be taken to mean that asking about the evolutionary pressures on a trait like empathy is completely valueless (as has been suggested by Lewontin, 1998; Richardson, 2007). Rather, such an analysis can be seen to provide a partial account of what drove the evolution of the trait in question (Schulz, 2011a, 2011b, 2013). Put differently, if built on sufficiently well-grounded foundations, such an analysis can provide evidence – a reason – to think that a given trait evolved for a given set of reasons: while more work might be needed to fully confirm this account, this does not mean that, until this is the case, the account is completely epistemically worthless. Rather, such an account can provide a description of *some* of the major pressures on the evolution of the trait in question. As I try to make clearer in what follows, I think this is true when it comes to empathy: that is, I think that it is possible to provide reasonably well-grounded partial accounts of some of the major evolutionary pressures that have shaped this trait.

Second, in what follows, I focus in particular on *selective* accounts of the evolution of empathy. There are two reasons for why this is plausible. On the one hand – and as will also be made clearer momentarily – it is plausible that the selective pressures on empathizing are, in some contexts, very large. This suggests that natural selection is less likely to be easily swamped by other evolutionary factors in these contexts (Gillespie, 1998). On the other hand, empathizing is a relatively complex trait: it requires a sophisticated coordination between an organism's sensory systems – which need to detect which emotions another organism is feeling – and its emotional systems – which need to be disposed to mirror the detected emotions. This is important, as it is reasonable to think that, for complex traits like this, a selective explanation has a particularly high initial plausibility (Dawkins, 1986; Godfrey-Smith, 2001; Sterelny, 2003). With this is mind, consider the major account of the evolution of empathy in the literature: the idea that empathizing can facilitate cooperation.

II. Cooperative selective pressures on the evolution of empathy

One of the major and most widely accepted accounts of the evolution of empathy is based on the thought that empathy evolved to facilitate cooperation (de Waal, 2008; Churchland, 2011; Acebo & Thoman, 1995; Bowlby, 1958; MacLean, 1985). More specifically, the core idea behind this account can be set out as follows.

Assume that it is adaptive for organism A to cooperate with organism B: for example, assume that B is A's offspring, or that cooperating with B enables A to reclaim that help in the future when it (i.e. A) is in need of help. (I return to the adaptiveness of this and other kinds of cooperation momentarily.) Given this, emotional mirroring between A and B can make it easier for this cooperation to come about. In particular, the fact that the helping organism and the one in need of help share the same emotional state can make the need for help more salient to the helping organism.

More specifically, empathizing can make it more likely that a given organism provides (by assumption adaptive) help to another organism, as the helping organism does not just represent the other organism as in need of help – it *feels* the need for help. Given the fact (noted earlier) that many emotional states are known to be closely connected to certain behavioral outcomes, this thus makes it more likely that the helping organism will in fact cooperate with the organism in need (Damasio, 1994; Prinz, 2007). Put differently, the fact that organism A literally *feels* B's need for help plausibly functions as a reliable trigger for A to in fact help B.

In short: on this account, we should see empathy as a tool that has evolved so as to aid in the reliable establishment of cooperative interactions. Two further points about this account of the evolution of empathy need to be noted.

First, as should be quite obvious, this account of the evolution of empathy is tied to the evolution of cooperation: on this picture, empathizing is only adaptive when cooperating is, too. Fortunately, there are a number of cases where the latter is true – in fact, cooperation can be *highly* adaptive in some contexts. One of the most straightforward examples of this sort of situation concerns parent-offspring interactions: for many organisms, it is true that their own fitness is inextricably linked to that of their offspring (Sober, 2001; but see also Trivers, 1974). Indeed, parent-offspring can make for the major adaptive pressures for both members of the interaction (see e.g. Thometz et al., 2014). However, while this is one of the major cases in which cooperation – and thus, empathy – can be highly adaptive, it is not the only case: other examples include interactions among kin more generally (Griffin et al., 2004; Gardner & West, 2010; Griffin & West, 2002), reciprocal helping interactions (see e.g. Sachs et al., 2004; Carter & Wilkinson, 2013; Skyrms, 1996, 2004), and membership in cooperative groups (Sober & Wilson, 1998) – all of which can also provide major adaptive advantages to an organism (Sachs et al., 2004; Skyrms, 1996, 2004).

That said, it also needs to be acknowledged that, in many situations, the benefits from cooperation are small or cooperation is unlikely to evolve for other reasons (such as the fact that it has very demanding psychological or other prerequisites – see e.g. Hammerstein, 2003). For this reason, the evolution of empathy needs to be seen to be inherently limited on this account: in particular, the tether to the evolution of cooperation implies that, on this account, empathy will not be adaptive in all populations all of the time. This is important to note for what follows below.

The second point worth noting concerning this account of the evolution of empathy is that the latter is compatible with a number of different theories concerning the psychological role of empathy in the generation of helping behavior. To see this, note that, in general, organisms that are committed to cooperating with other organisms can be either altruists or egoists. (It is also possible that organisms cooperate for reasons that are neither altruistic nor egoistic; however, this is not so relevant here. See also Schulz, 2016.) Altruistic cooperators are organisms whose help is directly driven by concerns for the other organism (Sober & Wilson, 1998; Stich et al., 2010): psychologically, they cooperate because they aim to help the organism in need – while this help may also favor themselves biologically, this is not the psychological reason for their helping. By contrast, egoistic cooperators are organisms that help precisely because they think that helping is in their own best interest. This is important to note, as empathetic organisms, too, can be either psychological altruists or egoists.

To see this, note that an organism A will be altruistically empathetic if the mirrored emotion that drives its helping behavior makes a standing desire to help B be more salient or directive – without though altering the content of that desire (see also de Waal, 2008). In turn, this implies that, for altruistic helpers, empathizing is adaptive for making the commitment to help *clearer or more vivid*. Organisms are bound to have many commitments (including to themselves) and thus need to be able to decide which of these commitments to act on in a given situation. Here, an empathetic emphasis on the commitment to help can be highly useful in ensuring that the organism acts on this – by assumption – adaptive commitment. Put differently, empathizing can be useful for psychological altruists, as, by *emphasizing* their existing disposition to help B, it makes them more reliable in their helping behavior.

However, an organism A can also be egoistically empathetic. This will be so if it is the tokening of the mirrored emotion in A itself that drives the helping behavior: here, an organism helps another organism only to alleviate its own emotional state. So, if A helps B because (a) the perception of sadness on B's face makes A feel sad as well, (b) A is driven to reduce its own feelings of sadness, and (c) A thinks that the best way to reduce its own feeling of sadness is to make B happy, then A is an egoistic helper. In turn, this implies that, for psychological egoists, empathizing is adaptive, not for emphasizing an existing disposition to help, but for ensuring that they *in fact engage in* the – by assumption – adaptive helping behavior. Put differently: empathizing can be useful for egoistic helpers as, by *generating* a disposition to help B, it makes them more reliable in their helping behavior. (Note that while here is some controversy over whether we should expect the egoistic solution to be less reliable at motivating cooperative behavior than the altruistic one – see Sober & Wilson, 1998; Stich et al., 2010; Schulz, 2011b, 2016 – for present purposes, it is not necessary to discuss this further: what matters here is not the question of whether altruism is more reliable at causing cooperative behavior than egoism, but rather whether empathetic egoism is more reliable than non-empathetic egoism.)

Summing up, therefore: the key idea of the cooperative account of the evolution of empathy is that empathy is a tool to altruistically or egoistically facilitate the generation and maintenance of cooperative behavior. However, there is also another quite different – non-cooperative – perspective on the evolution of empathy. Bringing this out is the aim of the next section.

III. Non-cooperative selective pressures on the evolution of empathy

The non-cooperative perspective on the evolution of empathy focuses on the fact that emotional mirroring can be beneficial even in non-cooperative settings, provided that there is a correlation between the biological advantageousness of one organism feeling a particular emotion and another organism doing so. In a bit more detail, the core idea behind this account can be laid out as follows.

Assume that two organisms A and B live in close spatial proximity – perhaps because they are members of a large herd of zebras, or because they are members of a small family of chimpanzees. Further, assume that the organisms are often subject to a kind of collective attack: a predator charges both A and B (and perhaps the rest of the herd or family group as well), and tries to grab whoever it can reach. Finally, assume that flight responses in these organisms are at least sometimes mediated by emotional states – for example, assume that the organisms flee when becoming afraid, nervous, panicked, or anxious.

If these emotional reactions come with distinctive outer signs (as is assumed here), it can then be adaptive for A to react with fear to the sight of B's fear: for if B is afraid, there is good reason that a predator is near – which also is a good reason for A to be afraid (even if A has not yet spotted this predator). In turn, this is due to the fact that reacting with fear to B's fear gives A valuable time to initiate its own fleeing behavior: it does not have to wait until it has spotted the predator, but can engage in flight nearly simultaneously with those organisms that have spotted the predator. Here, then, empathy evolves not as a tool to enable cooperation, but as a way to exploit correlations in the adaptive behaviors of different organisms: if it is adaptive for A to feel X, then it is often also adaptive for B to feel X, simply because A and B are subject to the same sorts of environmental contingencies. (In fact, one could see this case of empathy as a special case of the evolution of signaling more generally: see e.g. Skyrms, 2010.) Three further remarks about this account of the evolution of empathy are useful to make here.

First, it is important to realize that, also in this context, the ability to empathize can allow for major adaptive advantages. As suggested in the above example of the predator attack, given that even a fraction of second's delay in responding to an attack can make the difference between escaping unharmed and being majorly injured or even killed, the time savings brought about by empathizing can be adaptively highly important. Moreover, this fleeing-focused case is not the only sort of case that makes non-cooperative empathizing adaptive. For example, it can be adaptive for a bird to react with excitement upon observing the excitement of another bird, as this can lead to faster generation of "mobbing" behavior – which can be highly adaptive (Hurd, 1996). Similarly, it can be adaptive to react with anger to the detection of anger in another organism: this can ready an organism for fighting behavior, which again can prevent major injury or death and can even lead to significant gains (e.g. in interspecific fights to gain access to mates: Plavcan & van Schaik, 1992; Fessler, 2010; Campbell, 2004). In short: since, for many animals, time is often of the essence, mirroring others' emotional states can be highly advantageous.

Second, note that it is plausible to think that this route towards the evolution of empathy is instantiated in quite different circumstances than the one based on cooperation. As noted earlier, the adaptiveness of cooperation – and thus, of cooperation-focused empathy – depends on the fact that a narrow set of particular conditions obtains. Here, by contrast, empathy is adaptive even if these conditions do not obtain (i.e. even if the organisms in question are not cooperative). However, this does not mean that there are no restrictions on the adaptiveness of empathy in non-cooperative settings whatsoever. In particular, as also noted earlier, for empathy to be adaptive on this account, a strong correlation in adaptive responses across individuals is needed. This, though, will not be the case in all contexts either. For example, if organisms are differentially robust, so that the dangers posed to them by predatory attacks are differentially great, then it is less adaptive for some of these organisms to be empathetic: there is little reason for A to be afraid when B is afraid if the sources of B's fear generally pose little threat to A. This is important, as it might be true across generations: for many organisms, it is true that much of what infants are adaptively afraid of (say) is not something that adults need to be afraid of (e.g. as the two groups are very differently physically robust). If so, though, then on the present account, we would not expect there to be much empathy across generations (though we might do so on the cooperative account).

Third and finally, on the present account of empathy, the direct adaptiveness of empathy is restricted to emotions signaling environmental conditions to which a speedy reaction is adaptive – emotions such as fear, anger, panic, anxiety, or excitement. This implies that, at least on the face of it, this account does not predict empathizing when it comes to emotions like joy or sadness: there is little to be gained for organism A to react to organism B's joy with joy (other than perhaps a few extra seconds of joy), and, similarly, there is little to be gained for organism A to react to organism B's sadness with sadness. Put differently: since empathy, on the present account, is adaptive because it mediates faster adaptive behavioral responses, it follows that in situations where fast adaptive responses are not required, empathy is not required either. Of course, it is possible that, for neurological or other reasons, organisms need to either be empathetic for all emotions or for none, so that an emotional specificity in empathizing cannot evolve. Still, it remains true that the situation here contrasts with the one at the heart of the cooperative account: there, the speed with which a behavioral response needs to be decided on is not greatly important to the adaptiveness of empathy, thus widening the range of emotions for which empathizing is directly adaptive. For non-cooperatively driven empathizing, by contrast, there are such decision-making speed constraints, so that empathizing is more narrowly adaptive only.

All in all, therefore: on the non-cooperative account of the evolution of empathy, empathy is adaptive for allowing organisms to react more quickly to time-sensitive environmental conditions. Instead of just reacting to the detection of the threat itself with the appropriate emotional state, empathetic organisms can react to the effects of this detection in other organisms – i.e. the outward display of their emotional states.

IV. Implications

There is no doubt that an understanding of the evolution of empathy is interesting in its own right: as noted above, the ability to empathize is a complex and relatively widespread trait about which we want to know more – and the reasons for its evolution are part of this. However, considering the above accounts of the evolution of empathy is important beyond this. This is due to the fact that these accounts have several implications that should be taken into account when developing a general theory of empathy.

First, considering the two accounts of the evolution of empathy – the cooperative and the non-cooperative one – together suggests that many organisms might find some form of empathy adaptive. This comes out clearly from noting that these two accounts are complementary to each other: a number of the cases in which the cooperative account does not apply (e.g. because they do not feature the adaptiveness of cooperation) are cases where empathy is adaptive for non-cooperative reasons – and the reverse. For example, while direct cooperation might not be adaptive in a herd of zebras, non-cooperative forms of empathy might be quite adaptive there, and while non-cooperative forms of empathy might not be adaptive across generations, cooperative ones might be. Of course, this does not mean that empathizing is always adaptive: even together, the two accounts do not cover all cases, as there are situations that feature neither adaptive cooperative interactions nor the needed correlations in time-sensitive responses to the environment. However, it does mean that empathizing is relatively frequently adaptive. This is important to note, as it provides a part of the explanation of why empathizing is widespread in the biological world: in fact, given the frequent adaptiveness of empathy, the two accounts of the evolution of empathy laid out above predict that future investigations will find evidence for empathetic abilities in even more species than what has been true thus far.

Second, both of these accounts suggest that empathy can reach across species boundaries – as long as the different organisms share similar enough emotional states so that some kind of emotional mirroring is possible. For example, since interspecies cooperation – e.g. in cases of mutualism – can be adaptive, it can also be adaptive for an organism of one species to empathize with an organism of another. Similarly, since different types of organisms often live in close spatial proximity, their adaptive responses can be correlated – again making empathizing adaptive. So, for example, it can be adaptive for a zebra to react with a given emotion – fear, say – if it sees a nearby wildebeest feel a closely related emotion – the wildebeest equivalent of zebra fear, say.

That said, it is also true that, third, both of the above accounts of the evolution of empathy support the idea that empathy is likely to be biased toward certain organisms. Specifically, organisms are more likely to empathize with others (a) that they are in cooperative relationships with, or (b) whose behavioral responses to the environment are sensitive to the same sort of factors that their own behavioral responses are sensitive to. In turn, this suggests that organisms (humans included) are unlikely to empathize well with organisms that live in distant places or times – which both makes cooperation harder and implies that the correlation in behavioral responses to the environment is likely to be weak – or which are removed from them in other ways – e.g. socially. This turns out to be empirically very plausible (de Vignemont & Singer, 2006; Langford et al., 2006; Singer et al., 2006; Lanzetta & Englis, 1989; Preston & de Waal, 2002).

Fourth, the above accounts of the evolution of empathy also bring out that, in many cases, empathy need not lead to or be based on psychological altruism, but can be inherently selfish (this thus contradicts the conclusion in de Waal, 2008). That is, empathizing organisms should not necessarily be thought to be altruists, since the reasons for why empathizing might have evolved need not have been to support existing altruistic desires. Instead, they might have evolved to support existing egoistic dispositions of one kind or another. Put differently: short of knowing more about the details of the conditions in which the ability to empathize has evolved – whether it concerned cooperative or non-cooperative situations, and if the former, what the particular nature of the disposition to cooperate was like – knowing that an organism has the ability to empathize does not tell one anything about whether it is also an altruist.

These last two points – viz. the biased nature of empathy and its lack of an essential connection to altruism – are worthwhile to note also because they bring out a fifth implication of the above discussion. In particular, these two points make clear that the moral value of empathy is not straightforward to assess. More specifically, to the extent that morality is seen as something that is inherently unbiased and other-directed – a relatively common view of morality (see e.g. Gill, 2007) – the fact that empathy is likely to be biased in its target and not necessarily altruistically oriented implies that empathy is unlikely to make, at least by itself, a universally good foundation for morality. This matters, as this supports a conclusion that others have reached as well. For example, Prinz (2011) argues on the basis of a number of social psychological and philosophical results that empathy should not be seen as the cornerstone of morality. The present evolutionary biological perspective can thus be seen to give some further partial support for Prinz's conclusion: while it is possible that empathy is altruistically based, it is also possible – and indeed plausible – that it frequently is not.

V. Conclusion

Empathy – i.e. the ability to mirror an emotional state upon detecting evidence of that emotional state in others – is a complex psychological trait whose evolution is likely to have been shaped by a number of different, though complementary, selective pressures. In particular, empathizing can facilitate the generation and maintenance of altruistic or egoistic cooperative interactions, and it can aid organisms in streamlining their behavioral responses to the environment by seeing the outward signs of others' emotional states as signals of the appropriate behaviors to engage in for themselves. While these points cannot be considered as having provided a complete and fully corroborated account of the evolution of empathy, they do provide a partial account of this evolution that is evidentially reasonably well grounded.

Apart from its inherent interest, this picture of the evolution of empathy is also worthwhile for its implications for a number of other issues. In particular, this picture suggests that (i) empathy is a trait that is likely to be relatively widespread among many different kinds of animals, (ii) it can be inter-specific, but (iii) it is biased in terms of the kinds of individuals it targets, (iv) it need not be altruistic in origin, and (v) it therefore is unlikely to make for a plausible basis for a universalist morality all by itself.

References

Acebo, C., & Thoman, E. B. (1995). Role of infant crying in the early mother-infant dialogue. *Physiol. Behav.*, 57, 541–7.

Bowlby, J. (1958). The nature of the child's tie to his mother. *International Journal of Psychoanalysis*, 39, 350–73.

Brandon, R. (1990). *Adaptation and Environment*. Princeton: Princeton University Press.

Buller, D. (2005). *Adapting Minds*. Cambridge, MA: MIT Press.

Campbell, A. (2004). Female competition: Causes, constraints, content, and contexts. *The Journal of Sex Research*, 41(1), 16–26.

Carter, G., & Wilkinson, G. (2013). Food sharing in vampire bats: Reciprocal help predicts donations more than relatedness or harassment. *Proceedings of the Royal Society* B, 280, 20122573.

Churchland, P. (2011). *Braintrust: What Neuroscience Tells Us About Morality*. Princeton: Princeton University Press.

Custance, D., & Mayer, J. (2012). Empathic-like responding by domestic dogs (Canis familiaris) to distress in humans: An exploratory study. *Animal Cognition*, 15(5), 851–9.

Damasio, A. (1994). *Descartes' Error: Emotion, Reason, and the Human Brain*. New York: Avon Books.

Darwall, S. (1998). Empathy, sympathy, care. *Philosophical Studies*, 89, 261–82.

Dawkins, R. (1986). *The Blind Watchmaker*. New York: Norton.

de Vignemont, F., & Singer, T. (2006). The empathic brain: How, when and why? *Trends Cogn. Sci.*, 10, 435–41.

de Waal, F. B. (2008). Putting the altruism back into altruism: The evolution of empathy. *Annual Rev. Psychol.*, 59, 279–300.

Ekman, P., & Rosenberg, E. (eds.). (1997). *What the Face Reveals: Basic and Applied Studies of Spontaneous Expression Using the Facial Action Coding System (FACS)*. Oxford: Oxford University Press.

Fessler, D. T. (2010). Madmen: An evolutionary perspective on anger and men's violent responses to transgression. In M. Potegal, G. Stemmler, & C. Spielberger (eds.), *International Handbook of Anger* (pp. 361–81). New York: Springer.

Frohoff, T. (2013). Lessons from dolphins. In P. Brakes & M. P. Simmonds (eds.), *Whales and Dolphins: Cognition, Culture, Conservation and Human Perceptions* (pp. 135–9). London: Routledge.

Gardner, A., & West, S. A. (2010). Greenbeards. *Evolution*, 64(1), 25–38.

Gill, M. B. (2007). Moral rationalism vs. moral sentimentalism: Is morality more like math or beauty? *Philosophy Compass*, 2(1), 16–30.

Gillespie, J. (1998). *Population Genetics: A Concise Guide* (2nd ed.). Baltimore: Johns Hopkins University Press.

Godfrey-Smith, P. (2001). Three kinds of adaptationism. In S. H. Orzack & E. Sober (eds.), *Adaptationism and Optimality* (pp. 335–57). Cambridge: Cambridge University Press.

Goldman, A. (2006). *Simulating Minds*. Oxford: Oxford University Press.

Griffin, A. S., & West, S. A. (2002). Kin selection: Fact and fiction. *Trends in Ecology and Evolution*, 17, 15–21.

Griffin, A. S., West, S. A., & Buckling, A. (2004). Cooperation and competition in pathogenic bacteria. *Nature*, 430, 1024–7.

Hakeem, A. Y., Sherwood, C. C., Bonar, C. J., Butti, C., Hof, P. R., & Allman, J. M. (2009). Von Economo neurons in the elephant brain. *Anat. Rec. (Hoboken)*, 292(2), 242–8.

Hammerstein, P. (2003). Why is reciprocity so rare in social animals? A Protestant appeal. In P. Hammerstein (ed.), *Genetic and Cultural Evolution of Cooperation* (pp. 83–94). Cambridge, MA: MIT Press.

Hatfield, E. C. J., & Rapson, R. L. (1994). *Emotional Contagion*. Cambridge: Cambridge University Press.

Hoffman, M. (2000). *Empathy and Moral Development: The Implications for Caring and Justice*. Cambridge: Cambridge University Press.

Hurd, C. R. (1996). Interspecific attraction to the mobbing calls of black-capped chickadees (Parus atricapillus). *Behavioral Ecology and Sociobiology*, 38(4), 287–92.

Langford, D. J., Crager, S. E., Shehzad, Z., Smith, S. B., & Sotocinal, S. G. (2006). Social modulation of pain as evidence for empathy in mice. *Science*, 312, 1967–70.

Lanzetta, J. T., & Englis, B. G. (1989). Expectations of cooperation and competition and their effects on observers' vicarious emotional responses. *J. Personal. Soc. Psychol.*, 56, 543–54.

Lewontin, R. (1998). The evolution of cognition: Questions we will never answer. In D. Scarborough & S. Sternberg (eds.), *Methods, Models, and Conceptual Issues: An Invitation to Cognitive Science* (vol. 4, pp. 107–32). Cambridge, MA: MIT Press.

MacLean, P. D. (1985). Brain evolution relating to family, play, and the separation call. *Arch. Gen. Psychiatry*, 42, 405–17.

Plavcan, J. M., & van Schaik, C. P. (1992). Intrasexual competition and canine dimorphism in anthropoid primates. *American Journal of Physical Anthropology*, 87(4), 461–77.

Plotnik, J. M., de Waal, F. B. M., & Reiss, D. (2006). Self-recognition in an Asian elephant. *Proceedings of the National Academy of Sciences*, 103(45), 17053–7.

Preston, S. D., & de Waal, F. B. (2002). Empathy: Its ultimate and proximate bases. *Behav. Brain Sci.*, 25, 1–72.

Prinz, J. (2007). *Emotional Construction of Morals*. Oxford: Oxford University Press.

Prinz, J. (2011). Is empathy necessary for morality? In A. Coplan & P. Goldie (eds.), *Empathy: Philosophical and Psychological Perspectives* (pp. 211–29). Oxford: Oxford University Press.

Richardson, R. (2007). *Evolutionary Psychology as Maladapted Psychology*. Cambridge, MA: MIT Press.

Sachs, J., Mueller, U., Wilcox, Thomas, & Bull, J. (2004). The evolution of cooperation. *The Quarterly Review of Biology*, 79(2), 135–60.

Sauter, D. A., Eisner, F., Ekman, P., & Scott, S. K. (2010). Cross-cultural recognition of basic emotions through nonverbal emotional vocalizations. *Proceedings of the National Academy of Sciences*, 107(6), 2408–12.

Schulz, A. (2011a). Simulation, simplicity, and selection: An evolutionary perspective on high-level mindreading. *Philosophical Studies*, 152(2), 271–85.

Schulz, A. (2011b). Sober & Wilson's evolutionary arguments for psychological altruism: A reassessment. *Biology and Philosophy*, 26, 251–60.

Schulz, A. (2013). The benefits of rule following: A new account of the evolution of desires. *Studies in History and Philosophy of Science Part C: Studies in History and Philosophy of Biological and Biomedical Sciences*, 44(4, Part A), 595–603.

Schulz, A. (2016). Altruism, egoism, or neither: A cognitive-efficiency-based evolutionary biological perspective on helping behavior. *Studies in History and Philosophy of Biological and Biomedical Sciences*, 56, 15–23.

Singer, T., Seymour, B., O'Doherty, J. P., Stephan, K. E., Dolan, R. J., & Frith, C. D. (2006). Empathic neural responses are modulated by the perceived fairness of others. *Nature*, 439, 466–9.

Skyrms, B. (1996). *Evolution and the Social Contract*. Cambridge: Cambridge University Press.

Skyrms, B. (2004). *The Stag Hunt and the Evolution of Social Structure*. Cambridge: Cambridge University Press.

Skyrms, B. (2010). *Signals: Evolution, Learning, and Information*. Oxford: Oxford University Press.

Sober, E. (2001). The two faces of fitness. In R. Singh, D. Paul, C. Krimbas & J. Beatty (eds.), *Thinking about Evolution: Historical, Philosophical, and Political Perspectives* (pp. 309–21). Cambridge: Cambridge University Press.

Sober, E., & Wilson, D. S. (1998). *Unto Others: The Evolution and Psychology of Unselfish Behavior*. Cambridge, MA: Harvard University Press.

Sterelny, K. (2003). *Thought in a Hostile World: The Evolution of Human Cognition*. Oxford: Wiley-Blackwell.

Stich, S., Doris, J., & Roedder, E. (2010). Altruism. In J. M. Doris & the Moral Psychology Research Group (eds.), *The Moral Psychology Handbook* (pp. 147–205). Oxford: Oxford University Press.

Thometz, N. M., Tinker, M. T., Staedler, M. M., Mayer, K. A., & Williams, T. M. (2014). Energetic demands of immature sea otters from birth to weaning: Implications for maternal costs, reproductive behavior and population-level trends. *J. Exp. Biol.*, 217(Pt 12), 2053–61.

Trivers, R. (1974). Parent-offspring conflict. *American Zoologist*, 14, 247–62.

PART II

History of empathy

7

EMPATHY IN THE AESTHETIC TRADITION

Derek Matravers

The aesthetic history of empathy, leading up to the coining of the term in 1909 by the psychologist Edward Titchener, is a confused affair. Fortunately, this history has been the subject of much recent expert research, to which I am greatly indebted. In particular, I would pick out work by Lauren Wispé, Harry Francis Mallgrave and Eleftherios Ikonomou, and Gustave Jahoda (Wispé 1987, Mallgrave and Ikonomou 1994, Jahoda 2005). As well as benefitting from their scholarship I have also, in the case of Jahoda, benefitted from translations of key passages. The relevant developments in aesthetics are also covered in Paul Guyer's *A History of Modern Aesthetics* (Guyer 2014: ch. 10). Titchener coined the term as a translation of the German 'Einfühlung'. The term 'empathy', even now, is used to refer to a wide variety of phenomena and (unsurprisingly) there is an 'aesthetic history' of at least some of such phenomena. There is also a history of the use of the word 'empathy' and its German predecessor, only some of which is properly aesthetic. The contribution from aesthetics to our understanding of empathy is, however, of mainly historical interest. Our contemporary understanding rests solidly within the philosophy of mind and cognate disciplines.

A good deal of stage-setting took place before the emergence of 'Einfühlung' as a technical term in aesthetic theory. In as much as Einfühlung broadly concerned the relation between active mental life and the inanimate world, at least part of that stage-setting is the concern with the relation between subject and object prevalent in German thought since Kant and Hegel. A further landmark in the history of the phenomena, which surely had an influence on the more concrete developments at the end of the nineteenth century, was Romanticism, in particular, German Romanticism. The Romantic movement of the late eighteenth and early nineteenth centuries was of such a disparate nature (geographically, politically, and in almost every way) that general claims about it will hardly rise above the banal. However, one characteristic was a yearning for unity against the distinctions characteristic of the time, whether subject and object, mind and body, man and world, or reason and the imagination. Finding a way in which our minds can enter into the world promises one way of approaching such a unity.

One manifestation of this, which took Romanticism closer to the modern use of the term 'empathy', was the work of Johann Gottfried von Herder. Herder uses the term 'Einfühlung' in his 'This Too a Philosophy of History for the Formation of Humanity' (Herder 1774). Herder's most notable contemporary commentator, Michael Forster, has argued that Herder was not talking about psychological projection (which would take his use close to one important aspect

77

of the modern use) but was using the term metaphorically; for 'an arduous process of historical-philological enquiry'. The cash value of the metaphor has five components, none of which are particularly part of aesthetics. Two of them, however, do take us close to at least some elements of the modern meaning of the term: 'in order to interpret a subject's language one must achieve an imaginative reproduction of his perceptual and affective sensations' and 'the interpreter should strive to develop his grasp of linguistic usage, contextual facts, and relevant sensations to the point where this achieves something of the same immediate, automatic character that it has for a text's original audience when they understood the text in light of such things (so that it acquires for him, as it had for them, the phenomenology more of a feeling than a cognition)' (Forster 2002: xvii–xviii). In short, when we read historical texts we should, in the first instance, imagine ourselves occupying the perspective of the producer of the text including imaginatively reproducing his or her mental states, and, in the second instance, we should do the same for the presumed readership of the text. Furthermore, in the second instance, doing so establishes a link to the feelings.

In 'On the Cognition and Sensation of the Soul', Herder describes the process that becomes central for the later writers we will be considering: 'The more a limb signifies what it is supposed to signify, the more beautiful it is; and only inner sympathy, i.e., feeling and transposition of our whole human self into the form that has been explored by touch, is teacher and indicator of beauty' (Herder 1778, quoted in Jahoda 2005: 154). Herder does not use the term 'Einfühlung' here, but rather 'inner sympathy'. This is symptomatic of things to come; although 'Einfühlung' emerges as the favoured term, plenty of other terms flourish in the same hedgerow to indicate either the same or some very similar concept.

The first signs of aesthetics taking up the term in a significant way is in the writings of Friedrich Theodor Vischer, Karl Köstlin, and Hermann Lotze (Mallgrave and Ikonomou 1994: 20). However, it was in the doctoral dissertation of Vischer's son, Robert, that 'Einfühlung' was first defined as a technical term. From the welter of Vischer's theorizing, we can identify three claims that, even if they did not originate with Vischer, were brought together under the concept 'Einfühlung'. First, he distinguishes between passive processes – bodily reactions to the world that involve no conscious involvement – and more active processes. He characterizes this distinction in several ways, including sensation versus feeling, sensory empathy versus kinesthetic empathy, and seeing versus scanning. Here is one characterization of the former: 'By sensation I mean the sensory process only and, more particularly, the sensory response to an observed object' (Vischer 1873: 95). In their discussion of Vischer's work, Harry Francis Mallgrave and Eleftherios Ikonomou list, along with 'Einfühlung', various other terms on the latter half of the divide: 'Anfühlung, Ineinsfühlung, Nachfühlung, Zufühlung, and Zusammenfühlung' (Mallgrave and Ikonomou 1994: 22). Whatever the details, all these feature the active involvement of the mind and imagination. Secondly, Vischer claims that a large part of the passive process lies in a similarity between the outward forms and the inner processes: 'This is not so much a harmony within an object as a harmony between the object and the subject, which arises because the object has a harmonious form and the formal effect corresponding to subjective harmony' (Vischer 1873: 95). Finally, Vischer introduces the notion of projection. In this, he was influenced by a book by Karl Albert Scherner, *Das Leben des Traums* (*The Life of the Dream*) that had been published in 1861 (Scherner 1861). The passage in which Vischer describes this influence, culminating in his definition of 'Einfühlung', is worth quoting in full.

> The longer I concerned myself with this concept of a pure symbolism of form, the
> more it seemed to me possible to distinguish between ideal associations and a direct

merger of the imagination with objective form. This latter possibility became clear to me with the help of Karl Albert Scherner's book *Das Leben des Traums* (*The life of the dream*). This profound work, feverishly probing hidden depths, contains a veritable wealth of highly instructive examples that make it possible for any reader who find himself unsympathetic with the mystical form of the generally abstract passages to arrive at an independent conclusion. Particularly valuable in an aesthetic sense is the section on 'Die symbolische Grundformation für die Leibreize' (Symbolic basic formation for bodily stimuli). Here it was shown how the body, in responding to certain stimuli in dreams, objectifies itself in spatial forms. Thus it unconsciously projects its own bodily form – and with this also the soul – into the form of the object. From this I derived the notion that I call 'empathy' [Einfühlung].

(Vischer 1873: 92)

There is at least one puzzle here: what Vischer means by 'objectifies itself in spatial forms'. He approaches, but never clearly says, that we identify ourselves with the object. The simile he uses to make his point – 'we have the wonderful ability to project our own physical form into an objective form in much the same way as wild fowlers gain access to their quarry by concealing themselves in a blind' – is hardly perspicuous (Vischer 1873: 100).

In short, in Vischer's work, we see the outline of the contemporary concept of empathy coming together. The three claims distinguished above foreshadow three elements of the contemporary concept. First, his distinction between passive and active processes is in some ways akin to the distinction between (as we would put it) the sub-personal and the personal. Secondly, he has the notion of a process whereby the inner mental states mirror outer forms. Finally, he has the notion of our projecting selves into an object and in that way imbuing the form of that object with content. However, quite what 'imbuing' covers here is unclear.

If Vischer deserves to be relegated to being a footnote in this history, the same should not be said of the man who picked up and developed his ideas: Theodor Lipps. Lipps was, in his time, a major intellectual figure in the English-speaking world. Had T. E. Hulme (an underrated thinker who was blown to bits by a German shell in 1917) lived to complete his planned work on 'Modern Theories of Art', two and a half of the projected nine chapters would have been devoted to Lipps (Hulme 1924: 261–4). This would also, no doubt, have led to more of Lipps's work being translated into English, which would perhaps have shored up his reputation in Anglophone countries.

At any particular time Lipps seems to have meant various things by 'Einfühlung', and he also shifted his view so that he meant different things at different times. His principal statement of his view was in his 1903 article, '"Empathy", Inward Imitation, and Sense Feelings' (Lipps 1903, translated by Johoda as 'Einfühlung, Inner Imitation, and Organic Feelings' (Jahoda 2005: 154)). A contemporary review of his work puts it in a recognizably Vischerean context:

Of late the question, or rather group of questions, which has excited most debate among German aestheticians has to do with the distinction between the object immediately presented to sense-perception – say a rose with its characteristic form and colouring – and the meaning which this has for our imagination, say full vitality and pride of life.

(Anonymous 1908: 459)

Lipps distinguishes 'aesthetic' imitation from what he calls 'voluntary' imitation (Lipps 1903: 254). His account of the first is radical. Faced with an aesthetic object, I feel various powerful and active emotions: 'I feel myself strong, light, sure, resilient, perhaps proud and the like.' Furthermore, 'It is myself' that I feel as having these emotions. So far, so good. The radical element is how he gets those felt emotions 'into' the object; he does so by identification: 'I do not so feel myself in relation to the thing or over against it, but in it …This is what I mean by Empathy: that the distinction between the self and the object disappears or rather does not yet exist' (Lipps 1903: 253). Lipps gives various other formulations of the same idea ('I am even spatially in its position, so far, as the self has a spatial position; I am transported into it' (Lipps 1903: 254)), although the idea does not become less obscure.There is some degree of back-tracking, which at least makes clear that Lipps is not claiming any straightforward identity between the observer and the object.

> In unimitative movement the activity belongs to my real self, my whole personality endowed as it actually is, with all its sensations, ideas, thoughts, feelings, and especially with the motive or inner occasion from which the movement springs. In aesthetic imitation, on the other hand, the self is an ideal self. But this must not be misunderstood.The ideal self too is real, but it is not the practical self. It is the contemplative self which only exists in the lingering contemplation of the object.
>
> *(Lipps 1903: 255)*

In common with other commentators, both those contemporary with Lipps and those writing more recently, I find his account of 'aesthetic empathy' obscure. However, it was the non-aesthetic use Lipps made of the concept that arguably has had the greater effect on contemporary thought.This is a significant step in the history of the concept; the move from empathy with objects to empathy with people.

Lipps moves seamlessly from talking of an object of beauty to talking of broader properties of – specifically – human beings. His example of something 'strong, proud, and free' is in fact 'a human figure'.

> I see a man making powerful, free, light, perhaps courageous motions of some kind, which are objects of my full attention. I feel a sense of effort. I may carry this out in real imitative movements. If so, I feel myself active. I do not merely imagine but feel the endeavour, the resistance of obstacles, the overcoming, the achievement.
>
> *(Lipps 1903: 253–4)*

We know from work produced by Lipps in 1907 that he put his concept of Einfühlung to work in thinking about the problem of other minds. Unconvinced by the argument from analogy, Lipps sought to replace it with an 'instinct' which gives us knowledge of other minds without involving an inference. (My discussion here is drawn directly from Jahoda's paper (Jahoda 2005).)

> In the perception and comprehension of certain sensory objects, namely, those that we afterward represent as the body of another individual (or generally as the sensory appearance of such), is immediately grasped by us.This applies particularly to the perception and comprehension of occurrences or changes in this sensory appearance, which we name, for example, friendliness or sadness.This grasp happens immediately and simultaneously with the perception, and that does not mean that we see it or apprehend it by means of the senses.We cannot do that, since anger, friendliness, or

sadness cannot be perceived through the senses. We can only experience this kind of thing in ourselves.

(Lipps 1907: 713; quoted in Jahoda 2005: 156; translated by Jahoda)

Lipps proposed that our grasp of other minds is a result of two processes. In the words of Jahoda, 'the object of sensory perception comes from the external world, while the inner excitation comes from within ourselves' (Jahoda 2005: 156). I witness another person's gesture of, for example, anger, and this raises a feeling within my consciousness. It is unclear how this could be a solution to the problem of whether other people have minds – we would simply be acquainted with more of our own mental states. However, if we put the 'whether' problem to one side (or assume it is solved) we do look to have a solution to the problem of how we know what is in the minds of others. We manage to 'read' the minds of others by re-experiencing their mental states for ourselves.

This leads naturally to the term's original introduction into English (at least as 'empathy' – in 1908 the term had been translated as 'infeeling' (Anonymous 1908: 466)). Here is the passage in which Edward Titchener coined the term:

Not only do I see gravity and modesty and pride and courtesy and stateliness, but I feel or act them in the mind's muscles. This is, I suppose, a simple case of empathy, if we may coin that term as a rendering of *Einfühlung*; there is nothing curious or idiosyncratic about it; but it is a fact that must be mentioned.

(Tichener 1909: 21–2; quoted in Jahoda 2005: 161)

'The mind's muscles' is an inspired description. In the same way as a frustrated football manager finds himself exercising his leg muscles by mimicking on the sidelines his players' kicks in the field, so our mind's muscles mimic in our minds what is going on in the minds of others. It is the non-aesthetic developments of Lipps's thoughts, the empathy with people and the subsequent broadening into the notion of other minds, that take us closer to the modern conceptions of empathy.

The non-aesthetic developments, however, are not my concern here. Lipps's influence continued to be felt in German aesthetics principally through the lens of Wilhelm Worringer, who co-opted the term (with acknowledgement to Lipps) in his immensely influential 1908 book, *Abstraction and Empathy*. The contrast between abstraction and empathy might seem surprising, given the focus on empathizing with forms in general, rather than figurative forms. However, Worringer is not concerned with the contrast between the abstract and the figurative, but rather with metaphysical attitudes to the world: the empathetic attitude is one of familiarity; of projecting oneself into the outside world and enjoying oneself. The attitude underlying abstraction is quite different:

Now what are the psychic presuppositions for the urge to abstraction? We must seek them in these people's feeling about the world, in their psychic attitude towards the cosmos. Whereas the precondition for the urge to empathy is a happy pantheistic relationship of confidence between man and the phenomena of the external world, the urge to abstraction is the outcome of a great inner unrest inspired in man by the phenomena of the outside world; in a religious respect it corresponds to a strongly transcendental tinge to all notions. We might describe this state as an immense spiritual dread of space.

(Worringer 1908: 70)

81

Lipps certainly did not restrict empathy to positive emotions; at least not in any simple sense (Lipps 1905). However, the difference between Worringer and Lipps is not a matter of detail. Worringer's comparisons between different 'world feelings' is some way from Lipps's concerns with empathy and hence part of a different debate.

I shall finish this chapter with a look at the brief history of the aesthetic use of the term in Anglo-American philosophy in the early twentieth century. This divides into two strands. The first was fundamentally experimental rather than theoretical, and concerned with the projection of movement rather than the projection of feeling. The second seems principally to have been pursued in Oxford, and was fundamentally theoretical, concerned with 'solving' the problem of beauty.

The first was principally pursued by the English writer Violet Paget, who wrote psychology under the name Vernon Lee. In 1897 Lee and her collaborator, Clementine Anstruther-Thomson, published 'Beauty and Ugliness', as essay largely devoted to the physiological relations of Anstruther-Thomson in front of works of art (Lee and Anstruther-Thomson 1897). At this time Lee had not read Lipps's work, and she was largely influenced by what she calls the 'Lange-James' account of the emotions, which identified emotions with bodily movements. The view put forward in 'Beauty and Ugliness' was that aesthetic appreciation was bound up with introspected perceptions of inner activity, some aspects of these changes subsequently being attributed to the object. The genesis and nature of Lee's theory has been brilliantly explored by Carolyn Burdett (Burdett 2011). In 1912, Lee republished the essay, together with a number of other essays (Lee and Anstruther-Thomson 1912). By this time she had read Lipps and (despite an unflattering review he had published of the earlier essay) moved away from a focus on introspecting activity to a more complicated view which married some of her earlier views with what she took from Lipps. Having said that, her book does contain some telling criticisms of Lipps. She rightly criticizes Lipps for theory-building in isolation from the results of empirical psychology, and for the obscurity of his idea that the whole ego is projected into the object as opposed to attributions of states of the ego (Lee and Anstruther-Thomson 1912: 66, 103).

It is not clear how seriously Lee was taken by the academic establishment. She describes herself as 'a novice in psychology' (Lee and Anstruther-Thomson 1912: 64) and is disarmingly modest about her work.

> My aesthetics will always be those of the gallery and the studio, not of the laboratory. They will never achieve scientific certainty. They will be based on observation rather than experiment; and they will remain, for that reason, conjectural and suggestive.
>
> *(Lee and Anstruther-Thomson 1912: viii)*

Either for these reasons, or for her pacifist stand in the First World War, Lee's influence declined. There has, however, recently been a revival of interest in her work. In addition to the paper by Burdett mentioned above, Susan Lanzoni has recently argued for the importance of her contribution to the development of the concept of empathy in turn-of-the-century psychology (Lanzoni 2009: 351).

The key figure in the reception of Lipps's work in Oxford seems to have been E. F. Carritt; a Fellow of University College who was unusual in his interest in aesthetics (another Fellow of University College, Bernard Bosanquet, had published the first history of aesthetics in English two decades earlier). Carritt published a collection of writing in the history of aesthetics, which included what is still the most extensive translation of Lipps in English (Carritt 1931). This includes a passage from Lipps in which he states what has been, since Kant, the central problem of aesthetics, that is, articulating the grounds of the aesthetic judgement in such a way as to account for the nature of that judgement. He puts the problem in a way reminiscent of Kant's 'antinomy of taste': 'The sensible appearance of the beautiful object is the object of aesthetic satisfaction; but, just as surely, it is not the ground of that satisfaction' (Lipps 1903: 252). This can be understood against a background of finding a middle way between two unsatisfactory accounts of beauty: that which takes it to be an objective property of objects, and that which take the judgement of taste to be an expression of a subjective state.

Lipps's positive proposal is characteristically obscure.

> Aesthetic satisfaction consists in this; that it is satisfaction in an object, which yet, just so far as it is aesthetically enjoyed, is not myself but something objective. This is what is meant by Empathy: that the distinction between the self and the object disappears or rather does not yet exist.
>
> *(Lipps 1903: 253)*

An echo of these words is found in the writing of Carritt's far more significant pupil, R. G. Collingwood. Collingwood is famous in aesthetics for his 1938 book, *The Principles of Art*. Less well known is an earlier book (1924), *Outlines of a Philosophy of Art*. In this, Collingwood echoes Lipps's view.

> The question has sometimes been raised, whether beauty is 'objective' or 'subjective', but which is meant, whether it belongs to the object and is by it imposed on the mind by brute force, or whether it belongs to the mind and is by it imposed on the object irrespective of the object's own nature … real beauty is neither 'objective' nor 'subjective' in any sense that excludes the other. It is an experience in which the mind finds itself in the object, the mind rising to the level of the object and the object being, as it were preadapted to evoke the fullest expression of the mind's powers. The experience of beauty is an experience of utter union with the object; every barrier is broken down, and the beholder feels that his own soul is living in the object, and that the object is unfolding its life in his own heart.
>
> *(Collingwood 1925: 43)*

It would be too quick to conclude that, at this stage, Collingwood had simply adopted Lipps's view. Evidence for is that, as editor of the collection from which the Lipps quotation is taken, Carritt gives a footnote directing the reader's attention to this passage from Collingwood (Collingwood is thanked by Carritt in the Introduction, so would presumably have approved). However, Collingwood's talk of 'the fullest expression of the mind's powers' is also reminiscent of Croce, a known influence on Collingwood and Carritt. Not only are the theoretical positions obscure, but Collingwood's and Carritt's writing at the time does little to clarify matters. Hence, unfortunately, I am unable to settle the issue.

Immediately after this, Lipps largely disappears from Anglo-American discussions (as does empathy). Even as early as 1908, Lipps's view was being condemned for its obscurity (Anonymous 1908). Carritt himself considers and rejects the view for the same reason in 1914: 'We have here nothing but an attempt to explain in figurative language an unconscious process by which some beautiful objects may have become so' (Carritt 1949: 278–9). If he had been attracted by Lipps's views, Collingwood had abandoned them in favour of an expression theory of beauty by the time he wrote *Principles of Art* (in the Preface to which he writes, with respect to the earlier book, that he had 'changed my mind on some things' (Collingwood 1945: v)). The aesthetic

83

doctrine of empathy, in which observers gave objects life by a process of total identification of the ego, was replaced by less obscure and psychologically more plausible doctrines.

Aesthetics, as with other branches of philosophy, saw a renewed interest in empathy following the 'simulation versus theory-theory' debate from the late 1980s. Within the visual arts, there has been a revival of interest in the stimulation of our 'inner feelings' by depictive representations, and the role such feelings play in our perceptions (see in particular Currie 2011 and Lopes 2011, as well as other essays in Coplan and Goldie 2011). However, the topic has been most discussed in the understanding of narratives, in particular fictional narratives. As with the earlier debates, the claims that are made generally concern reactions happening beneath the level of conscious awareness. Zanna Clay and Marco Iacoboni have argued that textual representations engage our primitive 'mirror neurons' (Clay and Iacoboni 2011), and Amy Coplan has argued that readers unconsciously adopt the perspective of certain of the characters (Coplan 2004).

As part of his general thesis that understanding a fictional narrative is a matter of imagining (or 'make-believing') the propositions that make up its content, Greg Currie has argued that we sometimes engage our capacity for empathy – something he refers to as 'secondary imagining': '*Secondary* imagining occurs when we imagine various things so as to imagine what is true in the story' (Currie 1995: 152).

> It is when we are able, in imagination, to feel as the character feels that fictions of character take hold of us. This process of empathetic re-enactment of the character's situation is what I call secondary imagining. As a result of putting myself, in imagination, in the character's position, I come to have imaginary versions of the thoughts, feelings and attitudes I would have were I in that situation. Having identified those thoughts, feelings and attitudes ostensively, I am then able to imagine that the character felt *that* way. That is how secondary imagining is a guide to primary imagining.
>
> *(Currie 1995: 153–4)*

Against this, philosophers such as Noël Carroll have argued that we generally do not access the fictional world via the perspective of its inhabitants: 'We do not typically emote with respect to fictions by simulating a character's mental state; rather … we respond emotionally to fiction from the outside. Our point of view is that of an observer of a situation and not … that of a participant in the situation' (Carroll 2001: 311; see also Kieran 2003). Whatever the truth of this, the tables have been turned. In the nineteenth century work done in aesthetics was delivering results that illuminated the philosophy of mind; in the late twentieth century and beyond, the debt is being repaid: it is work done in the philosophy of mind that is illuminating aesthetics.[1]

Note

1 In addition to thanking the editor for her comments, I would like to thank the members of the International Network for Sympathy/Empathy and Imagination (INSEI), in particular Maarten Steenhagen (who clarified the reception of empathy by Collingwood for me) and Anik Waldrow. INSEI meetings this year were made possible by a grant from the British Academy.

References

Anonymous (1908). Beauty and Expression. *The Edinburgh Review* 208(426): 458–86.
Burdett, C. (2011). The Subjective inside Us Can Turn into the Objective Outside: Vernon Lee's Psychological Aesthetics. *Interdisciplinary Studies in the Long Nineteenth Century* 12: 1–31.

Carritt, E. F., Ed. (1931). *Philosophies of Beauty: From Socrates to Robert Bridges Being the Sources of Aesthetic Theory*. Oxford, Clarendon Press.

Carritt, E. F. (1949). *The Theory of Beauty*. London, Methuen.

Carroll, N. (2001). *Beyond Aesthetics: Philosophical Essays*. Cambridge, Cambridge University Press.

Clay, Z. and M. Iacoboni (2011). Mirroring Fictional Others. In *Empathy: Philosophical and Psychological Perspectives*, ed. A. Coplan and P. Goldie. Oxford, Oxford University Press: 313–29.

Collingwood, R. G. (1925). *Outlines of a Philosophy of Art*. London, Oxford University Press.

Collingwood, R. G. (1938). *The Principles of Art*. Oxford, Clarendon Press.

Coplan, A. (2004). Empathic Engagement with Narrative Fictions. *The Journal of Aesthetics and Art Criticism* 62(2): 141–52.

Coplan, A. and P. Goldie, Eds. (2011). *Empathy: Philosophical and Psychological Perspectives*. Oxford, Oxford University Press.

Currie, G. (1995). *Image and Mind: Film, Philosophy and Cognitive Science*. Cambridge, Cambridge University Press.

Currie, G. (2011). Empathy for Objects. In *Empathy: Philosophical and Psychological Perspectives*, ed. A. Coplan and P. Goldie. Oxford, Oxford University Press: 82–95.

Forster, M. (2002). Introduction. In *Herder: Philosophical Papers*, ed. M. Forster. Cambridge, Cambridge University Press: vi–xxxv.

Guyer, P. (2014). *A History of Modern Aesthetics*, vol. 2. Cambridge, Cambridge University Press.

Herder, J. G. v. (1774). This Too a Philosophy of History for the Formation of Humanity. In *Philosophical Writings*, ed. M. Forster. Cambridge, Cambridge University Press: 272–358.

Herder, J. G. v. (1778). Plastik. *Herder's Werke*, vol. 3. Berlin, Aufbau: 70–154.

Hulme, T. E. (1924). *Speculations: Essays on Humanism and the Philosophy of Art*. London, Kegan Paul, Trench, Trubner, and Co. Ltd.

Jahoda, G. (2005). Theodore Lipps and the Shift From 'Sympathy' to 'Empathy'. *Journal of the History of Behavioral Sciences* 41(2): 151–63.

Kieran, M. (2003). In Search of a Narrative. In *Imagination, Philosophy, and the Arts*, ed. M. Kieran and D. M. Lopes. London, Routledge: 69–87.

Lanzoni, S. (2009). Practicing Psychology in the Art Gallery: Vernon Lee's Aesthetics of Empathy. *Journal of the History of Behavioral Sciences* 45(4): 330–54.

Lee, V. and C. Anstruther-Thomson (1897). Beauty and Ugliness. In *Beauty and Ugliness and Other Studies in Psychological Aesthetics*. London, John Lane, The Bodley Head: 153–239.

Lee, V. and C. Anstruther-Thomson (1912). *Beauty and Ugliness and Other Studies in Psychological Aesthetics*. London, John Lane, The Bodley Head.

Lipps, T. (1903). 'Empathy', Inward Imitation, and Sense Feelings. In *Philosophies of Beauty: From Socrates to Robert Bridges being the Sources of Aesthetic Theory*, ed. E. F. Carritt. Oxford, Clarendon Press: 252–6.

Lipps, T. (1905). A Further Consideration of 'Empathy'. In *Philosophies of Beauty: From Socrates to Robert Bridges, Being the Sources of Aesthetic Theory*, ed. E. F. Carritt. Oxford, Oxford University Press: 256–8.

Lipps, T. (1907). Das Wissen from fremden Ich. In *Psychologische Untersuchungen*, vol. 1. Leipzig, Engelmann: 694–722.

Lopes, D. M. (2011). An Empathic Eye. In *Empathy: Physiological and Psychological Perspectives*, ed. A. Coplan and P. Goldie. Oxford, Oxford University Press: 118–33.

Mallgrave, H. F. and E. Ikonomou (1994). Introduction. In *Empathy, Form, and Space: Problems in German Aesthetics, 1873–1893*, ed. H. F. Mallgrave and E. Ikonomou. Santa Monica, Getty Centre for Arts and Humanities: 1–85.

Scherner, K. A. (1861). *Das Leben des Traums*. Berlin, Verlag von Heinrich Schindler.

Titchener, E. (1909). *Lectures on the Experimental Psychology of the Thought Processes*. New York, Macmillan.

Vischer, R. (1873). On the Optical Sense of Form. In *Empathy, Form, and Space: Problems in German Aesthetics, 1873–1893*, ed. H. F. Mallgrave and E. Ikonomou. Santa Monica, Getty Center Publication Programs: 89–123.

Wispé, L. (1987). History of the Concept of Empathy. In *Empathy and Its Development*, ed. N. Eisenberg and N. Strayer. Cambridge, Cambridge University Press: 17–37.

Worringer, W. (1908). Abstraction and Empathy. In *Art in Theory: 1900–1990*, ed. C. Harrison and P. Wood. Oxford, Blackwell: 68–72.

8

EMPATHY IN THE PHENOMENOLOGICAL TRADITION

James Jardine and Thomas Szanto

Introduction

In the past few years, there has been a lively debate on whether and how phenomenology can contribute to social cognition research. Notably, some have doubted whether first-personal, phenomenological descriptions of intersubjective experience and interaction can support or disconfirm certain theories about social cognition (e.g., Spaulding 2015). In contrast to such an assessment, the aim of the present contribution will be to present an overview of the rich and detailed discussion of empathy found in the phenomenological tradition, focussing particularly on those aspects of this discussion that we believe to contain important and subtle insights of contemporary relevance.

Our approach in the following will be as follows. First, we will examine the account of empathy offered by the two phenomenologists whose writings on the topic we take to be the richest and clearest, Husserl and Stein, explicating their arguments for the claims that (i) empathy is a *sui generis* mode of intentional experience, (ii) the basic form of empathy can nevertheless be characterised as perception-like, and (iii) that a higher-order form of empathy is a more imagination-like way of understanding other persons from their own personal perspective. Moving beyond Husserl and Stein, we will then consider different types of empathic accomplishment that are more richly socially or collectively mediated, namely mutual, interactive, shared, and collective empathy, as well as the import of social roles and typification.

1. Empathy as a distinctive form of intentional experience

The English term "empathy" only dates back to the beginning of the twentieth century, when it was first coined by Titcherner (1909) to translate the concept of *Einfühlung* as employed by the German philosopher and psychologist Lipps. While the term first originated in nineteenth-century German aesthetics to designate an ability to "feel oneself into" (*Ein-fühlen*) works of art (Vischer 1873), the now ubiquitous association of empathy with interpersonal relations can be largely traced back to Lipps's work. Importantly for our purposes, Lipps was both a source of inspiration and a target of opposition for the phenomenologists, and outlining the basic features of his account can thus be of aid in clarifying their own position.

Lipps argued that there are three distinct regions of knowledge, namely, knowledge of things, self-knowledge, and knowledge of other selves. While the first region has as its source sensuous perception and the second inner perception, our knowledge of other selves is rooted in empathy, which should accordingly be understood as a basic concept for both psychology and sociology (1909: 222; 1907: 713). Consequently, for Lipps, empathy is "the name for an original and irreducible, yet simultaneously wondrous, state of affairs," namely the ability to "co-grasp" foreign mental states "in and with" the perceptual apprehension of foreign bodies. Lipps's claim that empathy is an irreducible source of knowledge of other minds partially stems from his belief that, rather than being rooted in analogical inference, our basic grasp of other minds is a more "immediate" accomplishment. As he hastens to add, however, this should not lead us to believe that we can "see" or "know immediately" the other's anger itself, since the latter is something non-perceivable which can only be directly known by the person who feels it. Rather, our awareness of another person's affective state "in" her bodily expressions must be attributed, not to a direct experience of that state, but to what he calls the "instinct of empathy," which itself has two components, the "tendency of expression," and the "instinct of imitation" (1907: 713–14). Lipps's proposal, briefly, is that when perceptually faced with another's body as physically contorted in a certain way, the empathiser feels an instinctive tendency to *imitate* the other's bodily contortion. If this bodily contortion coincides with one she has previously performed in instinctively expressing an emotion, then her tendency to imitate it in its turn reproduces an experience she has had earlier of this emotion. This recollected affect is then "represented" or "thought into" (*vorgestellt, hineingedacht*) the other's gesture as something which belongs to and is intimated in it (1907: 718–19; cf. 1909: 228). Furthermore, Lipps claims that empathy is not limited to the rather weak and preliminary ability to project one's own (past) emotional states into other people's bodily gestures; rather, in a second step, the empathising subject is instinctively moved to express and feel the otherwise merely recollected emotion in the present. Consequently, unless the natural course of empathising is interrupted by internal or external circumstances, empathy instinctively develops into a state of sympathy or emotional sharing (*Sympathie, Mitfühlen*), in which the empathising subject not only represents a mental state as belonging to the other's gesture, but actually feels and lives through the relevant emotion "with" the other (1907: 719–20).

Now, Lipps's core claim that empathy is a unique, irreducible, and immediate (i.e., non-inferential) experiential accomplishment and a basic source of knowledge of other minds was taken over and arguably radicalised by the phenomenologists. Thus, in her 1917 doctoral dissertation *Zum Problem der Einfühlung*, which Husserl supervised, Stein affirms that empathy is "a kind of experiential act *sui generis*," defining it as "the experience of foreign consciousness in general," or "the experience of foreign subjects and their lived experience" (1917: 11, 1, translation modified [20, 5]). However, not only did Husserl and Stein criticise almost every detail of Lipps's account of empathy (e.g., Husserl 1905–20: 38–41, 70–6; Stein 1917: 11–18, 22–4), they also offered a starkly different construal of this basic experiential and epistemic directedness towards others. One of the most important features of this controversy was the phenomenologists' insistence that the immediacy and distinctiveness of empathy was not only a matter of its non-inferential character, but also of its irreducibility to a Lippsian process which combines elements of body-perception, self-experience, and ultimately projection. This latter claim has two key components, which we will now explain.

(A) As Stein points out, the explanatory value of Lipps's account is questionable, in that somebody who perceived a physical entity whose movements evoked a recollection of her own prior expressive gestures would not thereby "arrive at the phenomenon of foreign lived experience, but at a lived experience of her own awoken by the seen foreign gestures" (1917: 23, translation modified [36]). That is, one must first have some understanding of what the other is going through in order to recognise a similarity between one's own experiences and those of the other, and it is therefore logically muddled to suggest that any understanding of other minds could be fundamentally based upon the reproduction of a past experience of our own that putatively approximates the other's current mental state. Indeed, such an explanation seems better equipped to account for emotional contagion or motor mimicry than for an epistemic grasp of other minds (1917: 23–4). An arguably more fundamental worry Stein expresses regarding Lipps's view is that in modelling our basic empathetic grasp of other minds on the (projection of) self-experience, one overlooks the phenomenological fact that the givenness of others' mental lives is entirely different from the givenness of one's own mental life, having its own distinctive structure which phenomenological reflection can tease apart (1917: 14, 17). To come face to face with another person's sadness is, after all, quite different from feeling sad oneself or remembering a sadness one felt earlier (1917: 11). And if, upon encountering another's sadness, one finds oneself sharing the other's sadness or sympathising with it, then this shared or sympathetic sadness is not the basic empathic access one has to the other's sadness but something more complex built upon and presupposing it (1917: 14, 17–18). In short, empathy and self-awareness (in its various forms) do not only target a different object; as intentional experiences they also differ fundamentally in type and composition.

(B) Furthermore, both Husserl and Stein attack Lipps's underlying presupposition that all that can be directly experienced of another person are the merely physical features of her body, arguing that such a postulated gap between foreign mindedness and the directly given is completely at odds with our lived acquaintance with others. As Husserl puts it, a basic form of empathy is rather "an immediate experience of others," in that our direct perception of another person is not merely instinctively accompanied by, but rather *includes* a certain "experience [of] the other's lived experiences," this being "accomplished as one with the originary experience of the [other's] body" (1912–16: 385, 208). As will become clear in the next section, rather than beginning with the presupposition that other minds are (invisible) entities accessible only through the projection of one's own mental states into otherwise inanimate bodies (Lipps), the phenomenological account of empathy begins by attempting to systematically articulate the sense and manner in which others are directly visible as minded persons.

For phenomenologists, then, empathy is both our basic mode of access to other minded beings, and an irreducible form of intentional experience with a unique structure. As we shall see in the next two sections, this unique mode of intentionality is nevertheless multi-layered, incorporating different modes of accomplishment. Moreover, while the claim that empathy has *sui generis* intentional structure stipulates that empathic acts are not composed of or identical to other intentional acts, this does not prevent it from exhibiting some of the characteristic features of other modes of intentionality. While the most primitive form of empathy can be described as a perception-like experience, a more active form of empathy is more akin to imagination.

2. Perception-like empathy

One of the more intriguing traits of phenomenological accounts of empathy is the frequent claim that a basic form of empathy shares important characteristics with the perceptual experience of non-minded entities, without nevertheless being strictly identical to the latter. Consider a perceptual episode which might be expressed by the following description:

(1) "On turning the street corner, I saw a blue car heading straight towards me."

(1) expresses a certain kind of perceptual episode, and by reflecting upon it one may identify certain general features of perceptual experience, of which we will emphasise just three. (i) In perceiving an object, such as "a blue car," or state of affairs, such as "a blue car moving towards me," what we are directly and immediately acquainted with is just the perceived object or state of affairs itself. In such cases, we take the object which *appears* to us to be the spatiotemporal object that *is* really there before us. This differs markedly from the way we experience an object in, say, imagination: in imagining "a blue car moving towards me," we do not typically take the imaginary object to be identical with an actual clunky entity heading in our direction. We can call this feature of perception its *directness*. (ii) A further general feature of perceptual experience is its epistemic role, namely that it can provide a *prima facie* justificatory basis for our (perceptual) judgements. Compare a person who thinks she was almost run over this morning, and does so *because* she earlier had a perceptual experience as of a car speeding towards her, with a person who holds the same belief but without having had any such experience. The former person surely has a justification for her belief that the latter lacks, even if her belief may ultimately be false. Call this the *justificatory import* of perception. (iii) A final feature of perception is what we will call its *perspectival* character. The perceptual experience expressed in (1) is an experience of a spatiotemporal object in motion, but it is one in which the moving object appears under a certain aspect or perspective, or more accurately, an aspectual series that unfolds as the blue car moves closer to the perceiver. Throughout this series, the perceiver does not experience each new aspect as a new object, but rather precisely sees *the car* as appearing *under* ever new aspects, in that with each aspectual shift certain visible features of an identical object come (more clearly) into view, while others cease to be visible. In short, even in a momentary perceptual appearance one can distinguish phenomenologically between the presence of the object and that of its visible aspect, where the former is irreducible to, and only partially revealed by, the latter (Husserl 1907; Merleau-Ponty 1945).

We can now consider to what extent empathic experience might embody these general features. Consider an experience expressed by the following description:

(2) "On turning the street corner, I saw someone glare at me angrily."

There is something inadequate in the suggestion that, were one to turn a corner and face such a person, what one would be experientially acquainted with is simply an inanimate entity. One might conclude from this that an empathetic grasp of the other's angry glare must then be rooted in an additional capacity which projects mental states into the directly given. However, it would also be phenomenologically inaccurate to claim that what appears *directly* in (2) is essentially the same as in (1), and that the subject turning the corner only thinks that someone is glaring at her angrily because the (wholly physical) entity she perceives is of such a kind as to set in motion a process of inference or simulation. Rather, a more accurate description of this experience would simply claim that what directly appears is just a *person staring angrily*, and that this is so irrespective of any process of imagining or thinking the subject may perform. In experiential episodes like this, what is immediately there before us experientially is surely not merely a material body, but a person, one whose facial expression displays an emotion (cf. Husserl 1912–16: 252). It therefore seems that a compelling description accords to this experience perceptual feature (i), in that here the intentional object of our experience (namely the person glaring at us angrily) directly appears to us, is visibly there. This claim gains further weight when we note that such cases also exhibit feature (ii). The person undergoing experience (2) would surely gain a *prima facie* justification to believe that "a person is glaring at me angrily," not that "an 'angry-looking' lump of flesh stands before me" – indeed, were she to believe the latter and claim to be perceptually justified in so doing, we might suspect her of suffering a pathology (or perhaps of being a particularly obstinate philosopher). It seems plausible, then, to claim that it is not only beliefs about the other's body, but also at least some that concern the other person as a whole (notably, a belief that she is currently angry), that gain a perceptual-like warrant in such cases. Finally, an encounter with another's angry glare exhibits feature (iii), in that we can distinguish between the object directly given and the aspect through which it perspectivally appears. While *what* we see is a person glaring at us angrily, the angrily glaring person is always given under a certain aspect; after all, in any moment of the perceptual episode only certain features of the other's body are directly visible.

One might think, however, that this last point actually counts against the claim that a basic form of empathy shares the directness characteristic of perception. If it is conceded that only certain features of the other's body can ever be directly visible, then it may seem to follow that a grasp of the other as a minded being could never be accomplished by any direct experience of her alone. The phenomenological account of empathy avoids this objection by insisting that, at least when it comes to the way others directly appear to us, the relationship between body and mind is not taken as a causal link between two separate entities, but as an *expressive* relation (cf. Jardine 2015a, 2016). We do not merely perceive the other person's directly visible countenances and gestures as meaningless physical events. Rather, to have such expressive movements directly in view just is to grasp their sense, that is, to *see* something of the other's emotive and practical condition:

> *Empathy into persons* is nothing else than precisely that apprehension which *understands the sense*, i.e., which grasps the body in its sense and in the unity of the sense it has to bear. To perform an act of empathy means to grasp *mind as an object*, to see a human being, to see a crowd of people, etc. Here we do not have an apprehension of the body as bearer of something psychic in the sense that the body is posited (experienced) as a physical object and then something else is added on to it, as if it was apprehended just as something in relation to, or in conjunction with, something else […] the body appears, but what we perform are the acts of comprehension, and what we grasp are the persons and the personal conditions "expressed" in the appearing content of the body.
>
> *(Husserl 1912–16: 256, translation modified [244])*

For the most part, we experience the other's bodily gestures and movements as intrinsically embodying mindedness, as movements lived through by someone; we see them as movements which the other purposively achieves or involuntarily suffers, which bring her perceptual world into ever new orientations, or as the manifestations of her affects (Stein 1917: 61–2, 67–8, 75–84; Scheler 1926b: 260). Similarly, we see the other's limbs and skin as loci for fields of sensation, such that when an object comes into contact with the other's body we immediately grasp this contact as tactually lived, and sometimes as painful or pleasurable (Stein 1917: 57–8). To quote again Husserl, the "body is not only in general a thing but it is indeed expression of the mind and *is at once organ of the mind*" (1912–16: 102, translation modified [96]). The conclusion that other people's mental states are inherently invisible only follows from the (valid) observation that their bodily features alone are directly visible if we picture the body as a meaningless physical entity. But once we appreciate that foreign bodies are directly visible as fields of expression, such reasoning loses much of its force.

It was emphasised earlier that both perceptual experience of non-expressive objects and perception-like empathy have a perspectival character. Another way of putting this point is that in the very act of seeing a thing or a person, we grasp the seen object as having more to it than what immediately meets the eye. To return to our earlier example, when facing a car heading towards us we do not merely see a free-floating bonnet; rather, we *perceptually* take the object to be *a car*, and as such we "co-perceive" or "co-intend" it as having other, currently non-visible features (a rear, an underside, a roof, etc.), these features being "co-present" in our perception in that they contribute to the overall sense the seen object has for us (Husserl 1918–26: 39–43). When it comes to perception-like empathy, on the other hand, the other's body is not only seen as having *materially* more to it than what meets the eye, it is also seen as an expressive body that displays elements of the other's experiential life. Consequently, in seeing the other person we are not *only* acquainted with her body in its materiality through the structures of direct visibility and co-perception; in understanding the expressivity of her body, Husserl claims, we also achieve a certain "envisaging" (*Vergegenwärtigung*) of the other's experiential life, which is "made present" to us in a certain way. It is crucial not to misunderstand this claim. On the one hand, Husserl is not suddenly conceding that our basic empathic contact with others is dependent upon imaginative capacities; rather, he consistently emphasises that the envisaging he has in mind is simply a moment in our perception of the other as an expressive, embodied whole, a moment that has essentially the same role as that played by co-perception in the seeing of non-expressive objects (1912–16: 208, 170–5 [198, 162–6]). The envisaging in question is, therefore, more of an ambiguous sense that the other is undergoing an experience of a certain type, namely the one which is seen as alive before me "in" her facial expressions and bodily movements. On the other hand, Husserl should not be understood as claiming that, while the other's physical features are directly presented, her mental features are only co-presented or envisaged. Such a claim cannot be correct, because as Husserl points out, much of what we directly encounter in other persons doesn't fall onto only one side of the mind-body distinction, being rather immediately embodied and experiential. Indeed, there is a sense in which every movement of the other's body is directly visible as, as it were, "full of soul"; consider how we see a person's "standing and sitting," or her "way of walking, dancing, and speaking" (1912–16: 252; cf. Overgaard 2012). The phenomenological claim that a moment of envisaging functions in perception-like empathy, then, simply affirms that our direct experience of persons as expressive unities necessarily involves a certain inarticulate awareness that the other's embodied enactments are not only directly evident to the empathising subject, but also lived through consciously by the other.

3. Imagination-like empathy and interpersonal understanding

We emphasised at the beginning of this chapter that, by empathy, the phenomenologists mean our experience of other subjects and their lived experience, and they claim that such experience encompasses a *sui generis* class of intentional acts. As should now be clear, this bold claim is partially motivated by the observation that our encounters with others involve a certain kind of perception-like experience, possessing the directness, justificatory import, and perspectival character of our perceptual experience of inanimate objects, but differing from the latter in it that involves a direct encounter with another person who is recognised as having an experiential life of their own. It would, however, obviously be a mistake to think that our (empathetic) experience and understanding of the personal lives of others is limited to our immediate quasi-perceptual contact with them. As Stein notes, when the other's sadness faces us as directly given in her facial expressions, we frequently "feel ourselves led by it" (1917: 19), in that the theme of our empathic interest becomes not only *that* the other is sad, but *what* she is sad about and *why* this state of affairs elicits sadness in her. In such cases, the other's experiential life "is no longer an object in the proper sense. Rather, it has pulled me into it, and I am no longer turned to the experience but to its object, I am in the position of its subject." Here, we are not merely directed towards the other in her embodied presence, but we enact a more active envisaging of the other's world-directed experiential life, bringing it to mind "as if" we were its subject, in a manner more similar to memory, expectation, or imagination than to perception. Importantly, Stein emphasises that this modality of empathy, which she characterises as a form of self-displacement or re-accomplishment (*Hineinversetzen, Mitvollzug, Nachvollzug*), is derivative to and explicates the more basic modality discussed above (e.g., 1917: 10–12, 20 [18–20, 32–3]). Moreover, just as the latter is not strictly identical to our perceptual experience of inanimate objects, this active envisaging or re-accomplishment should be distinguished from imagination, in that it targets a different domain of experiences (namely, those of the other, not an imaginary modification of oneself), and has a different type of epistemic import and motivation (1917: 10–1; cf. Jardine 2015b). Here too, then, empathy retains its irreducible and unique character.

In a similar vein, Husserl notes that the extent to which we take ourselves to have a sufficient understanding of the actions or emotions of another person is largely a matter of our practical interests. In our daily encounters with others, we often remain satisfied with "an intuitive presentation of a concrete minded being and mental life," that is, a direct and quasi-perceptual experience in which the other person is empathetically grasped merely in accordance with "the general types of human existence" (1915–17: 580, 578; cf. Taipale 2016). Namely, in the bustle of everyday life, we often lack the interest to go beyond our initial grasp of the other as a token of the universal type, "someone," or as someone exhibiting a type of comportment (as someone walking briskly, smiling happily, or lost in thought) or embodying a certain socio-cultural type or role (an issue we shall return to below). However, if we are so interested, it is also possible for us to aim at a deeper empathetic understanding of the others' comportment, to seek to uncover the person's operative motives, values, and goals (1915–17: 732–3). Husserl claims that this ability is closely connected to our knowledge of the person's individual character. On the one hand, a deep understanding of another person's actions, emotions, and beliefs benefits from our having some knowledge of their personal character, and on the other hand, such an understanding is exactly a way of acquiring and increasing such knowledge (1915–17: 734–5). Consequently, our ability to gain a richer understanding of the motivational context of another's actions is best seen as embedded within ongoing personal relationships, in which our epistemic familiarity with the other person's character has gradually developed through repeated empathic perception and, perhaps, communicative engagement (1912–16: 286–7, 170). However, when we know a person's character well, we are sometimes able to reach a fuller understanding of both the "what" and the "why" of their actions by actively envisaging and "re-living" the other's own agential perspective. This involves quasi-imaginatively representing the situation "as if" I were the other, taking into account the other's enduring values, habits, beliefs, and goals, and thereby understanding how the other's situation would lead *the other* to act. As Husserl emphasises, this is quite different from simply imagining how *I* would act in the other's situation, in that I may be able to accomplish such an understanding even if I would respond to the other's situation in a wholly different way, and it is for this reason that such an active envisaging of the *other's personal situation* is a form of empathy, and not merely a form of imagination (1915–17: 759, 755–6; cf. Goldie 2000: 178–205; Coplan 2011).

4. From social typification to "collective empathy"

In order to gain a multi-dimensional account of empathetic understanding, phenomenologists have typically emphasised that we have to move beyond the sole focus on bodily expressivity, and understand the role played by the broader social contexts in which self and other are embedded (cf. Chelstrom 2013; León & Zahavi 2016; Szanto & Moran 2015 and 2016). Generally, one may distinguish a number of related but distinct issues regarding empathy in broader social and collective contexts. First, there is the issue regarding the *direction* of empathic acts and, correspondingly, the respective (subject and object) *relata* of the empathic relation. For instance, in terms of the empathiser-target relation, we may want to know whether we have an individual-to-individual, an individual-to-pairs-of-individuals, an individual-to-group, or a group-to-group relation. Another issue concerns the role of *reciprocity* and *interaction* between empathiser and target, may these be individuals or, potentially, groups. Finally, the classical phenomenologists offer detailed discussions of the relationship between empathy and collective intentionality. Indeed, it is safe to say that phenomenology was the first intellectual tradition that has not only thoroughly investigated *both* these issues but, moreover, their complex interrelation (see Stein 1922; Walther 1923; Gurwitsch 1931; Schütz 1932; Husserl 1905–20, 1921–8; Scheler 1926a, 1926b; cf. Szanto 2015, 2016). Our purpose in the following is to outline how empathy can be mediated by different social and interactive contexts and accordingly assume different social forms. We will begin by considering the role of social typification in empathy, before considering certain additional forms of interpersonal understanding discussed by phenomenologists, namely *mutual* and *interactive empathy* and finally *shared* and *collective* empathy.

An important issue that has arguably not been sufficiently recognised in contemporary discussions concerns the central role played by *social typification* in empathy, an issue explored at length in the phenomenological sociology of Schütz. Schütz has convincingly argued that in all actual cases of interpersonal encounter, you will have a more or less explicit and more or less specific or fine-grained typification of the other(s) at play. Moreover, this process has no clear-cut boundaries, such that there will usually be an intermeshing or gradual transition from a more or less concrete, personal other in direct face-to-face encounters to a more or less "anonymous" representative or proxy of a social type. Such typification for Schütz involves the recognition and grasping of an "objective web of meanings" (*objektiver Sinnzusammenhang*), practices, or social facts in which subjects are always and already embedded. For instance, when greeting the postman who just handed you a letter, you become empathetically acquainted with both the nice, smiling young man, as well as the anonymous one whom you were eagerly awaiting this morning, and maybe even the surprisingly friendly representative of the state-owned service that has recently been criticised for their bad-tempered, poorly paid employees (Schütz 1932: 227–90; Schutz & Luckmann 1974: 98–139; cf. Zahavi 2010).

In a similar vein, Gurwitsch maintains that others are always given in specific and at the same time typical, more or less familiar horizons of sense, as "bearers of roles," and in more or less specific social "situations" (Gurwitsch 1931: 111). As he puts it:

> [others] do not surface "suddenly," "accidentally," or "by chance." [...] They immediately appear, instead, as existing concretely in the "co-included" situation. Not just any "human thing" emerges unexpectedly and sporadically [...]; it is rather the case that situations become visible in the horizons in which sellers, anonymous buyers, purveyers, employers, listeners, readers, masters, servants, etc., act out their roles.
>
> *(Gurwitsch 1931: 97)*

Moreover, Gurwitsch maintains, even basic facial expressions and gestures, such as shaking the head and wrinkling the brow, "are not in themselves unambiguous," but rather the comprehension of such "expressive phenomena smoothly arises from knowledge about the situation in which I am with others, and fits into this knowledge as one of its moments" (Gurwitsch 1931: 113). Here, Gurwitsch explicitly departs from Scheler's idea of "a universal grammar" regulating the "elementary" relations between experience and its expression (Scheler 1926b: 11; cf. Husserl 1912–16: 174–5).

Another important form of empathy arises where empathiser and target are, in multiple ways, *directly interacting* in empathising, and may even engage in joint agency.

First, consider what we might call *mutual* empathy and what, for example, Stein, following Lipps, labels *iterative empathy* or *reflexive sympathy* (1917: 18, 88–9). Here, the intentional content of a subject S_1's empathic act E_1 encompasses another subject S_2's empathic act, E_2, where E_2 might be directed at third-party subjects (viz. *iterative*) or at S_1 herself (viz. *reflexive empathy*). This may happen without necessarily presupposing that S_2 has an empathic understanding of, or in any way takes into account, S_1's empathising. Typically, however, in such situations both subjects will reciprocally understand that they are empathising with one another (and their empathic stances), and this understanding may or may not be made verbally explicit.

A related but distinct case is what Gurwitsch has explored in terms of "being together in a common situation" (*Zusammensein in einer gemeinsamen Situation*) and, in particular, in a situation of "partnership" of coordinated action, or generally, a so-called "consociate being together" (*gebundene Zusammensein*). According to Gurwitsch, by simply being assigned and grasping the *role* you play, or being an active participant in a situation, and perhaps even coordinating your actions with others, or *cooperating* in achieving a *joint goal*, you gain an intimate understanding of others' roles. This in its turn permits a richer understanding of others' desires, motivations, and intentions, since it familiarises you with the context of "relevance" (Schütz 1932; Schutz & Luckmann 1974), which is specific to the situation and which guides the intentions and motives of the agents. You thus gain, as it were, a "view from within," i.e., from within a situation of being together.

> While one confers with his partner, he faces the wishes, aims, and interests of the partner, which, even when not explicitly expressed, are provided by the setting of the things. In virtue of the partner's comportment during the negotiations, his aims, motivations, etc., can be discovered. One orients his comportment with respect to the position disclosed by his partner [...] As a result, one's own comportment in the situation (*Situationsverhalten*) is tuned in on the other and takes account of him.
>
> (*Gurwitsch 1931: 105*)

The point here is not only that such "interactive empathy," as one might call it, will facilitate the coordination of joint agency of the partners – though this may well happen – but, also, and conversely, that the very fact of being together in a shared situation with roles assigned to each person, or even in a situation of shared goals and coordinated action, provides clues for mutually empathising that might otherwise not be readily available or not be available at all.

Lastly – and probably most contentiously – there is the possibility of shared or collective empathy. *Shared* empathy applies in those cases where the object of empathy is either a *pair* of individuals or even a directly present *group*, whose members express, in their attuned bodily movements, a *shared* intentional state or experiential episode (cf. Salice & Taipale 2015). An illustrative example of shared empathy is Scheler's famous scenario of two parents, A and B, grieving over the loss of their deceased child, where a friend C sees them standing at the child's bedside, empathetically comprehends *their shared* feeling, and eventually commiserates upon *their* sorrow (Scheler 1926b: 12–13).

Moreover, there may be cases in which the empathising subjects jointly engage in *collective* empathetic understanding and thereby constitute a pair or group of empathisers. In this regard, it can be asked whether or not collectives, corporations, or other groups can be proper subjects (and not only objects) of empathising (cf. Szanto 2015). Were this possible, the empathic act would then not only be distributed across individual members but, rather, have a plural subject as its bearer. But even if one denies the possibility of such non-summative forms of empathy, one may still opt for genuinely collective forms of empathy in cases when two or more individuals cooperatively or jointly empathise with a third party and coordinate their respective empathic acts accordingly. Consider, as a kind of inverse case to Scheler's example, two empathisers A and B *jointly attending* to a third person C's expression of fear and distress. In doing so, A and B will not only share the focus of the empathic attention towards C, but may also reflexively empathise with one another, and signal this to each other and/or to C. When C bursts into tears, A and B, witnessing this together, may exchange worried glances, and may even signal to each other a desire not to let this be seen by C so as not increase her distress even more. In such a case, we are arguably dealing with a shared empathic experience, such that A and B can be said to constitute, as it were, an "empathiser of their own."

5. Concluding remarks

Our aim in this chapter has been to show that the phenomenological tradition harbours an elaborate conceptual framework for thematising empathy, one which remains relevant for contemporary discussions. For the phenomenologists, empathy is a *sui generis* kind of intentional act, whose most basic form consists in the direct and perception-like experience of other embodied minds as such. Moreover, they argue that a more cognitively demanding mode of empathetic understanding, which resembles imagination without being reducible to it, involves envisaging the emotions and actions of another person from their own personal perspective. Finally, they accompany this more abstract account with a nuanced consideration of the manner in which empathy is mediated by various social and collective contexts, and can accordingly assume different social forms. It is perhaps worth emphasising that such social modalities of empathy do not radically alter its basic structure as a *sui generis* intentional act that can be akin to either perception or imagination. Not only is it the case that, at least for mature human beings, empathetic understanding normally employs some degree of social typification. The phenomenologists would also maintain that we can distinguish between those cases of mutual, interactive, shared, and collective empathy that remain at the quasi-perceptual level, and those that progress to a quasi-imaginative level of accomplishment. On their view, then, empathy is a multi-layered and yet unitary mode of intentionality, encompassing a rich array of modes and possibilities for interpersonal understanding.

References

Chelstrom, E. (2013) *Social Phenomenology: Husserl, Intersubjectivity, and Collective Intentionality*, Lanham et al.: Lexington.

Coplan, A. (2011) "Will the Real Empathy Please Stand up? A Case for a Narrow Conceptualization," *The Southern Journal of Philosophy* 49(s1), 40–65.

Goldie, P. (2000) *The Emotions: A Philosophical Exploration*, Oxford: Oxford University Press.

Gurwitsch, A. (1931 [1979]) *Human Encounters in the Social World*, transl. F. Kersten, Pittsburgh: Duquesne University Press.

Husserl, E. (1905–20 [1973]) *Zur Phänomenologie der Intersubjektivität. Texte aus dem Nachlaß. Erster Teil: 1905–1920*, ed. I. Kern, The Hague: Martinus Nijhoff.

Husserl, E. (1907 [2010]) *Thing and Space: Lectures of 1907*, transl. R. Rojcewicz, Dordrecht: Kluwer.

Husserl, E. (1912–16 [1989]) *Ideas Pertaining to a Pure Phenomenology and to a Phenomenological Philosophy. Second Book: Studies in the Phenomenology of Constitution*, transl. R. Rojcewicz & A. Schuwer, Dordrecht: Kluwer. [(1952) *Ideen zu einer reinen Phänomenologie und phänomenologischen Philosophie. Zweites Buch: Phänomenologische Untersuchungen zur Konstitution*, ed. M. Biemel, The Hague: Martinus Nijhoff.]

Husserl, E. (1915–17 [2016]) *Ideen zu einer reinen Phänomenologie und phänomenologischen Philosophie. Zweites Buch: Phänomenologische Untersuchungen zur Konstitution und Wissenschaftstheorie*, ed. D. Fonfara, Dordrecht: Springer.

Husserl, E. (1918–26 [2001]) *Analyses Concerning Passive and Active Synthesis: Lectures on Transcendental Logic*, transl. A. Steinbock, Dordrecht: Kluwer.

Husserl, E. (1921–8 [1973]) *Zur Phänomenologie der Intersubjektivität. Texte aus dem Nachlaß. Zweiter Teil: 1921–1928*, ed. I. Kern, The Hague: Martinus Nijhoff.

Jardine, J. (2015a) "Husserl and Stein on the Phenomenology of Empathy: Perception and Explication," *Synthesis Philosophica* 29(2), 273–88.

Jardine, J. (2015b) "Stein and Honneth on Empathy and Emotional Recognition," *Human Studies* 38(4), 567–89.

Jardine, J. (2016) "Wahrnehmung und Explikation: Husserl und Stein über die Phänomenologie der Einfühlung," *Deutsche Zeitschrift für Philosophie* 64(2), 352–74.

León, F., & Zahavi, D. (2016) "Phenomenology of Experiential Sharing: The Contribution of Schutz and Walther," in A. Salice & H. B. Schmid (eds.), *Social Reality: The Phenomenological Approach*, Dordrecht: Springer.

Lipps, T. (1907) "Das Wissen von fremden Ichen," in T. Lipps (ed.), *Psychologische Untersuchungen I*, Leipzig: Engelmann.

Lipps, T. (1909) *Leitfaden der Psychologie*, Leipzig: Verlag von Wilhelm Engelmann.

Overgaard, S. (2012) "Other People," in D. Zahavi (ed.), *The Oxford Handbook of Contemporary Phenomenology*, Oxford: Oxford University Press.

Merleau-Ponty, M. (1945 [2012]) *Phenomenology of Perception*, transl. D. A. Landes, London, New York: Routledge.

Salice, A., & Taipale, J. (2015) "Group-Directed Empathy: A Phenomenological Account," *Journal of Phenomenological Psychology* 46(2), 163–84.

Scheler, M. (1926a [1973]) *Formalism in Ethics and Non-Formal Ethics of Values: A New Attempt Toward the Foundation of an Ethical Personalism*, transl. M. S. Frings & R. L. Funk, Evanston: Northwestern University Press.

Scheler, M. (1926b [1954]) *The Nature of Sympathy*, transl. P. Heath. London: Routledge & Kegan Paul.

Schütz, A. (1932 [1967]) *The Phenomenology of the Social World*, transl. G. Walsh & F. Lehnert, Evanston: Northwestern University Press.

Schutz, A., & Luckmann, T. (1974) *The Structures of the Life-World*, transl. R. M. Zaner & H. Tristram Engelhardt, London: Heinemann.

Spaulding, S. (2015) "Phenomenology of Social Cognition," *Erkenntnis* 80(5), 1069–89.

Stein, E. (1917 [1989]) *On the Problem of Empathy*, transl. W. Stein, Washington, D.C.: ICS Publication [(2008) *Zum Problem der Einfühlung*, Freiburg: Herder].

Stein, E. (1922 [2000]) *Philosophy of Psychology and the Humanities*, transl. M. C. Baseheart & M. Sawicki, Washington, D.C.: ICS Publication.

Szanto, T. (2015) "Collective Emotions, Normativity, and Empathy: A Steinian Proposal," *Human Studies* 38(4), 503–27.

Szanto, T. (2016) "Husserl on Collective Intentionality," in A. Salice & H. B. Schmid (eds.), *Social Reality: The Phenomenological Approach*, Dordrecht: Springer.

Szanto, T., & Moran, D. (eds.) (2015) Empathy and Collective Intentionality: The Social Philosophy of Edith Stein, *Special Issue: Human Studies* 38(4).

Szanto, T., & Moran, D. (eds.) (2016) *The Phenomenology of Sociality: Discovering the 'We'*, London, New York: Routledge.

Taipale, J. (2016) "From Types to Tokens: Empathy and Typification," in T. Szanto & D. Moran (eds.), *The Phenomenology of Sociality: Discovering the 'We'*. London, New York: Routledge.

Titchner, E. B. (1909) *Lectures on the Experimental Psychology of Thought-Processes*, New York: Macmillan.

Vischer, R. (1873) *Über das optische Formgefühl. Ein Beitrag zur Ästhetik*. Leipzig: Hermann Credner.

Walther, G. (1923) "Zur Ontologie der sozialen Gemeinschaften," *Jahrbuch für Philosophie und phänomenologische Forschung* 6, 1–158.

Zahavi, D. (2010) "Empathy, Embodiment and Interpersonal Understanding: From Lipps to Schutz," *Inquiry* 53(3), 285–306.

9

EMPATHY IN HUME AND SMITH

Imola Ilyes

For both Hume and Smith, the capacity to enter into or share the emotions of others is at the core of human emotional and social life. By entering into other points of view (a capacity they both call sympathy), we come to be concerned about the weal or woe of other people, becoming both motivated to help them and led to moral approval and disapproval of those actions that affect them. In this chapter, I will situate Hume's and Smith's theories of empathy in their broader views on cognition and imagination, clarifying the different foci of empathy, the role of the imagination, and the unique evaluative dimension in Smithian empathy. Then, I will explore how empathy lies at the foundation of moral motivation, clarifying how the differences between Humean and Smithian empathy explain differences in their conclusions about the nature and limitations of moral motivation. Lastly, I will show how both Hume and Smith construct privileged points of view to reconcile the impartial demands of moral judgment with the potential partialities of empathy. I aim to clarify how the role of empathy in moral judgment differs from its role in moral motivation, with resources being available in the former case that are explicitly rejected in the latter.

1. The basic nature and mechanics of empathy

1.1 Hume

For Hume, the workings of empathy make people's minds "mirrors to one another" (*Treatise* 2.2.6.21). He devotes much effort to explaining how it is that we empathize with each other. In the *Treatise* (Hume, 1739–40/2007), mental contents are broken down into ideas and impressions, and the sole difference between the two lies in the degree of "force and liveliness" (1.1.1.1) that they each possess. Impressions, which include "our sensations, passions, and emotions" (1.1.1.1), are the most lively or vivid, and ideas are the "faint images" or copies of those impressions in imagination and memory. The sight of an apple, for example, produces an impression of that apple; when I later recall that experience, I have an idea of that apple. Impressions such as love, anger, and joy, can also be "stored" in our minds as the ideas of those feelings.

The difference between impressions and ideas appears to be a matter of degree rather than of kind. As we can hold the same ideas in memory or in imagination, the difference between believing that something is the case and merely imagining that it is the case also lies in the "force and vivacity" that those ideas have (1.3.5.3). For example, the difference between believing that my office is painted orange and merely imagining that it is painted orange lies in the vivacity with which I experience the "idea-of-my-office-as-orange" in my mind. If my office actually is painted orange, "custom or habit" (1.3.5.6) will make the idea of it being orange more lively in my mind. This means that the memory of my office being orange is technically "somewhat intermediate betwixt an impression and an idea" (1.1.3.1), because it keeps some of the vividness of my original impressions. Interestingly, it follows – given that impressions include feelings like love and hate – that the difference between what we would call thoughts and emotions is also one of degree: degree of vivacity. And in the right circumstances, the thought of an emotion can be *converted* into the feeling of that emotion. This is what Hume thinks happens when we empathize with the emotions of another.

When we empathize with others, we "receive by communication their inclinations and sentiments" (2.1.11.2). In a nutshell, the process of empathy consists in seeing the signs of an emotion in another person (via her speech or body language), which gives us an idea of that emotion. If this idea is vivid enough, it can be converted into an impression of that emotion, thus allowing us to feel an emotion *with* the other person, *because* the other person is feeling it. Hume thinks that we effect this transformation from having the idea of another's emotion to feeling that emotion via our ever-present sense of ourselves, together with the way that our minds make regular kinds of associations between various sorts of ideas and impressions.

Whereas impressions and ideas constitute the *contents* or ingredients of thought, the principles of association explain the *process* of thought. Hume holds that there are three qualities by which our minds naturally associate one idea with another: resemblance, contiguity in time or place, and cause and effect (1.1.4.1). Thus, thinking of my orange office might make me think of an orange pumpkin (resemblance), or of the room next to my office (contiguity), or the painters who painted it orange (cause and effect). What is key is that "when any impression becomes present to us, it not only transports the mind to such ideas as are related to it, but likewise communicates to them a share of its force and vivacity" (1.3.8.1). If I witness someone weeping, such bodily changes naturally lead me to think about what caused them, which I know from experience to be sadness. Since my mind is transported to the idea of sadness, a degree of the vivacity of my impression of the weeping is transferred over to my idea of sadness. This is the foundation for the empathetic experience of sadness.

The explanation for the conversion of an idea of sadness into the *feeling* of sadness is our perennially lively idea of ourselves. Hume holds that "the idea, or rather impression of ourselves is always intimately present to us," and (given the principles of association) whatever is related to us or resembles us "must be conceiv'd with a like vivacity of conception" (2.1.11.4). Others do resemble us, and there is no emotion that they have experienced which we have not in some form felt ourselves (2.1.11.5). Hence I come to associate my idea of another person's emotion with my own experience of that emotion, and via my lively impression of myself, my idea of her sadness is converted into the feeling of sadness in me. Hence empathy typically consists in coming to share the emotions of another because of the movement from an impression of the signs of her emotion, to the idea of that emotion, to the very feeling of that emotion in oneself.

1.2 Smith

Rather than focusing solely on an apparent emotion, Smith thinks that we imagine the entire situation that another person is in, and then use this to imagine how we would feel in that situation. In *The Theory of Moral Sentiments*, Smith also uses the term sympathy to refer to "our fellow feeling with any passion whatsoever" (Smith, 1790/1982, I.i.1.5). Echoing Hume, he notes that the liveliness of our shared emotion will vary "in proportion to the vivacity or dullness of [our] conception" (I.i.1.2), though what is typically important is the vividness of our conception of the other's *situation*. We imagine the entire situation that another person is in, and use this to imagine how we would feel in that situation. Smith acknowledges that sometimes emotions may be shared "instantaneously, and antecedent to any knowledge of what excited them," chiefly if the expressed emotion is particularly violent (I.i.1.6). However, such cases are the exception rather than the rule, and even here our empathy is "extremely imperfect … [and] not very considerable," existing only insofar as such expressions of emotion "suggest to us the general idea of some good or bad fortune" (I.i.1.8–9). Smith is clearly responding to Hume's conception of empathy when he writes that, essentially, empathy "does not arise so much from the view of the passion, as from that of the situation which excites it" (I.i.1.10).

To underscore this point, Smith details a number of cases in which we empathize even when the object of our empathy is incapable of feeling certain emotions himself, "because, when we put ourselves in his case, that passion arises in our own breast from the imagination, though it does not in his from the reality" (I.i.1.10). For example, we feel anguish at the loss of sanity in others, even when that very loss of sanity renders another "insensible of his own misery." In such a case, we imagine what we would feel if in the same situation, while "at the same time able to regard it with [our] present reason and judgment," impossible as this would actually be (I.i.1.11). Likewise, the empathetic suffering of a parent with a sick child is amplified by a consciousness of its vulnerability and an anxiety about the future which the child cannot share. Indeed, we "sympathize even with the dead" (I.i.1.12), though they cannot feel anything at all.

There are two ways that I can engage in the point of view of another. I can imagine how *I* would feel in her situation, retaining my character and preferences in the process, or I can imagine how *she* feels in her situation, taking on her personality and desires. Amy Coplan (2011) refers to these alternatives as self- and other-oriented perspective taking (respectively). Generally, Smith holds that empathy involves self-oriented perspective taking, though at times he does suggest that we engage in a fuller "imaginary change of situations" with the person we empathize with. For example, "[w]hen I condole with you for the loss of your only son, in order to enter into your grief I do not consider what I, a person of such a character and profession, should suffer, if I had a son, and if that son was unfortunately to die: but I consider what I should suffer if I was really you, and I not only change circumstances with you, but I change persons and characters" (VII.iii.1.4). However, Smith generally understands empathy to involve self-oriented perspective taking, and as we shall see, it is important for him that empathy be so.

2. Imagination, cognition, and evaluation in empathy

2.1 Hume

The comparatively greater imaginative demands of Smithian perspective taking have led some to characterize Humean empathy (but not Smithian empathy) as emotional contagion (e.g., Darwall, 1998). However, if we go by the contemporary usage of emotional contagion, this characterization is misleading. Typically, emotional contagion is understood as automatic and unmediated by thought. I simply "catch" other people's emotional states as a result of being in their presence, as when I find myself happy in a cheerful crowd. It is often "below the threshold of awareness" and definitely does not "rel[y] on nor involves the imagination or any other higher-level processing" (Coplan, 2011, 45–6). This also means that when I experience an emotion as a result of emotional contagion, I may not know that the other is the cause of my emotion.

Both Hume and Smith leave room for catching the emotions of others in this way. Hume does, at one point, speak of emotions as "contagious" (3.3.3.5), and his remark that a "cheerful countenance infuses a sensible complacency and serenity into my mind; as an angry or sorrowful one throws a sudden damp upon me" (2.1.11.2) does suggest emotional contagion, given the spontaneity of the emotional transference here. Smith observes that "[w]hen we see a stroke aimed and ready to fall upon the leg or arm of another person, we naturally shrink and draw back our own leg" (I.i.1.3), an effortless bodily mirroring which is likewise suggestive of emotional contagion. However, for both Smith *and* Hume, the typical cases of empathy are conscious and at least minimally effortful, involving thought and imagination. When I am led, via the signs of an emotion, to an awareness of what the emotion of another person is, this is a conscious process that might even involve interpretation (as when I must rely on general causal knowledge to discern whether tears are tears of joy or sadness). When I come to feel the emotion myself, I know that I am feeling it in response to the emotion of another.

The role of cognition is evident given cases of empathy that Hume discusses in which we don't even form an impression of the emotions of another person at all, or in which the emotions we do see don't match those we come to feel. We might (given the principles of association) move from an impression of the cause of some emotions to imagining those emotions themselves, as when seeing surgical instruments laid out and doctors and nurses preparing for an operation leads us to feel "pity and terror" for the patient (3.3.1.7). Likewise, when we see that someone sleeping in a field is in danger of being trod on by my horses, we can come to feel fear by imagining his possible fate (2.2.9.13). In such cases, "[n]o passion of another discovers itself immediately to the mind. We are only sensible of its causes or effects. From *these* we infer the passion ... *these* give rise to our sympathy" (3.3.1.7). So Humean empathy cannot always be the mere triggering of emotions in us at the sight of others' emotions given that "we often feel by communication the pains and pleasures of others, which are not in being, and which we only anticipate by the force of imagination" (2.2.9.13). In other cases we come to feel different emotions from those we witness, as when we blush in shame at the behavior of those who don't feel any shame at all (2.2.7.5). We might even feel an empathetic emotion in inverse proportion to how another person appears to feel that emotion, as when our is sadness greater when a friend is bearing his misfortune with more reserve (2.2.7.5). Hume holds that custom or habit is generally important to explaining how people think and feel, and so in these cases "the imagination is affected by the *general rule*" (2.2.7.5), that is, by how people generally feel in response to good or bad fortune, or doing something shameful. The role of general rules shows that empathy is regulated by higher cognition.

2.2 Smith

While both Humean and Smithian empathy engage higher cognition, Smithian empathy has a distinctive evaluative element. We come to share the emotions of another if, upon entering imaginatively into her situation, we find that we would have the same feelings that she is actually experiencing: empathy consists in the *concurrence* of our emotions with another's emotions. This means that empathy always involves a comparison of the actual emotional response of another person with the emotional response I anticipate having in the same situation. For Hume, such a comparison is not essential to empathy: the imagination's task is to reconstruct what the other person is feeling, not what I would feel in her situation. It is this comparison that introduces an evaluative element in Smithian sympathy, for when I compare the other's emotion to my own, I inevitably either "second the other's feeling or dissent from it" (Darwall, 1998, 268). When there is "concord" between emotions, this is accompanied by the judgment that the emotions of the other are "just and proper, and suitable to their objects" (I.i.3.1): to empathize with another's emotion is to approve of it and find it appropriate. This is why Smithian empathy must, by its nature, involve self-oriented perspective taking. In order to find the emotions of another appropriate, there must be a "perspectival gap between spectator and agent" (Rick, 2007, 149). From another's point of view, her emotions will of course appear warranted, as our unregulated emotions tend to do. It is the gap between spectator and agent that leaves room for evaluation.

The fact that our own emotions naturally appear warranted to us explains why they are the benchmark for evaluating the emotions of others: "Every faculty in one man is the measure by which he judges of the like faculty in another. I judge of your sight by my sight ... of your resentment by my resentment" (I.i.3.10). This leaves Smith open to problems, for clearly there are cases in which we find another's emotion appropriate even though we don't share it. In order to explain this, Smith also appeals to general rules. We can still find laughter appropriate even though we're not in a jovial mood, because we know that we would usually laugh at the joke in question. Likewise, we can learn from experience which situations would lead us to feel sad, were we to take the time to consider them, even though we are too preoccupied to do so at the moment. Hence we rely on "general rules derived from preceding experience of what our sentiments would commonly correspond with" (I.i.3.4) to make judgments about the appropriateness of emotions.

Smithian empathy thus also has this regulative aspect, but the difference is that it is already built on an evaluative foundation that is not present in Humean empathy. While we can find emotions appropriate without at the moment sharing them, we cannot share emotions without finding them appropriate. Grief is an illuminating point of comparison discussed by both Hume and Smith in this context. For Hume, reliance on general rules means relying on our past experience of how much sadness we have observed to *commonly* be associated with a particular kind of situation in other people. It is because we are used to this association that even when a person bears grief with forbearance, we conceive an idea of, and so come to feel, the usual amount and tenor of sadness given the kind of loss he has suffered. For Smith, reliance on the general rule means relying on past experience of when *we* would enter into and find *appropriate* another's sadness. On this account, what makes a display of grief *excessive* is that spectators cannot enter into it. For Hume, the general rule tracks the amount of grief that we habitually witness; for Smith, it tracks the amount of grief we would usually come to feel, and so what we think is appropriate.

3. Malice, contempt, compassion, and sacrifice: empathy's breadth and phenomenology

For Hume and Smith, empathy has two roles in moral life. It explains compassionate or self-sacrificing moral motivation, and lies at the foundation of moral judgment, explaining how we come to approve of some actions and censure others. However, both thinkers observe that is it is naturally easier to empathize and so care about the suffering of some people rather than others, such as those we are emotionally attached to. Moreover, empathy-motivated compassion has natural rivals: feeling empathy does not always lead to helping behavior.

3.1 Hume

For Hume, whatever is connected to us becomes an object of concern for us. Hence, "[w]hoever is united to us by any connexion is always sure of a share of our love," including family, "countrymen, our neighbours, [and] those of the same trade" (2.2.4.2). As the "idea of ourselves is always intimately present to us, [it] ... conveys a sensible degree of vivacity to the idea of any other object, to which we are related" (2.2.4.7), and so the welfare of those connected to us is a matter of lively interest to us in the same way that our own welfare matters to us. Moreover, given that "[a]ll human creatures are related to us by resemblance," we can associate their emotions with our own and empathize with them and be concerned about their happiness.

It is possible for us to empathize with any person, but the very fact that empathy is predicated on resemblance means that it is naturally easier to empathize with some rather than others. Notwithstanding the role of the imagination in empathy and its power to carry us beyond the immediate signs (or lack thereof) of emotions, it is precisely because empathy involves *effort* that it is easier to empathize with those who are close to us in some way. For "[t]he stronger the relation betwixt ourselves and any object, the more easily does the imagination make the transition, and convey to the related idea the vivacity of conception, with which we always form the idea of our own person" (2.1.11.5). Hence it is both easier to empathize with those who are similar (sharing interests, ethnicity, etc.), and with those who are near us in space and time, for contiguity also serves to associate our idea of ourselves with that of the emotions of another person (2.1.11.6). As pity and care for others is grounded in empathy, it follows that it depends on such associations (2.2.7.4).

This means that however "contagious" emotions might sometimes be, observation of the emotions of another person is not always enough to produce empathy and so pity. For we are always at the center of our emotional universe, and so "our sentiments and passions … must strike upon us with greater vivacity than the ideas of the sentiments and passions of any other person" (2.2.2.15), and it is, as a general rule, difficult for our imaginative attention to shift from the consideration of something lively, like our idea of ourselves, to something faint, like our idea of the emotions or situation of another person (2.2.2.15). Hence when our impression of the emotion of another person is not vivid enough, thinking of the other's emotion is liable to simply carry our imagination back to thinking about ourselves. For example, if we get a faint impression of the sadness of another person, the imagination will focus not on the other's feelings, but rather on comparing her emotions to our relatively better state of mind. Whether comparison or empathy prevails depends upon the vividness of our impression of another's emotion. For as empathy involves the conversion of an idea of another's emotion into that emotion, it "demands greater force and vivacity in the idea than is requisite to comparison" (3.3.2.5). Given a faint impression, our sense of our own emotional state predominates, and the "misery of another gives us as more lively idea of our happiness … [and] therefore, produces delight" (2.2.8.8), an emotion Hume identifies as malice. And as Hume notes that we "always judge more of objects by comparison than from their intrinsic worth" (2.2.8.2), the pain of another can *increase* our sense of our own happiness.

Even when we do empathize with another, this is no guarantee of caring behavior. Hume holds that tonally similar emotions, such as anger and sadness, tend to be felt together (2.1.4.3). In contrast to malice, pity is an uneasy emotion, and so it seems that feeling pity might lead to scorn for those who suffer, rather than to care or tenderness for them, which are pleasurable. Tenderness for those who bring us pain appears to be a bit of a mystery. Hume's solution is that we can only feel positively towards those who suffer if we assume their own sufferings as our own: if, in other words, we *broaden* our self-interest so as to identify it with the good of others. This can happen when our impression of the suffering of another is so vivid that the imagination, rather than turning back to ourselves, instead considers the entire situation that the other person is in, beyond her immediate emotions. A vivid impression of the suffering of another "is not confined merely to its immediate object, but diffuses its influence over all the related ideas, and gives me a lively notion of all the circumstances of that person" (2.2.9.14). When we imagine the entire situation of another so vividly, it naturally becomes "our own concern" (2.2.9.13): we come to care about her as we care about ourselves. It is in such cases that we will rush to help the sleeping person in danger of being trod on by horses, as we vividly imagine his future suffering.

Feeling empathy directed at the entire situation of another, rather than merely her immediate pleasure or pain, is what Hume calls *extensive sympathy*, and this is what is necessary for love and tenderness. Extensive sympathy must, however, *begin* with a vivid impression of the immediate emotional state of another person. Here Hume uses a mechanical analogy: "as pipes can convey no more water than what arises at the foundation" (2.2.9.14), if there isn't a vivid initial impression to get the process going, the imagination will not get enough of a push to transcend what is immediately available to the senses and extend our empathy. Absent this push, we are liable to focus on the unpleasantness of the unease we feel in response to another's pain, which brings about hatred or contempt for the sufferer.

So, while it would not be fair to call Humean empathy automatic, it is nevertheless mechanistic in character: we need the right external content put into the gears of the imagination to produce the kind of empathy associated with care. Furthermore, however other-oriented we tend to intuitively think empathy-based moral motivation is, Humean empathy does not involve dethroning the self from our emotional concerns. Rather, it involves extending our sense of self-interest to include other people. This is neither automatic nor even easy, and malice and contempt are live options. As malice is a pleasant emotion and pity an unpleasant one, inter-emotional discordance (feeling pleasure at another's pain, or vice versa) has a prima facie advantage over concord in some cases.

It would seem that the notion of extensive sympathy brings Humean and Smithian empathy closer together, for recall that Smith holds that we share the emotions of another when we enter into her situation. But for Hume, extensive sympathy happens only with a vivid enough initial impression of a person's emotions, while for Smith, empathy is *normally* a response to another person's entire situation and awareness of another's emotion and situation, however vivid it is, will not occasion empathy if we think that her emotions are inappropriate.

3.2 Smith

Smith also acknowledges that our self-interest matters far more to us than the sufferings and joys of other people, however great they may be. The prospect of losing a finger tomorrow would cause a person far more mental anguish than the thought of thousands of deaths in a distant earthquake (III.3.4). However, Smith has other resources at his disposal to explain how we come to act generously towards others. He observes that "nothing pleases us more than to observe in other men a fellow-feeling with all the emotions of our own breast" (I.i.2.1), and on the other hand, "it is always disagreeable to feel that we cannot sympathize" (I.i.2.6) with the emotions of others. Even if the emotions empathized with are painful, arriving at emotional harmony with another person is pleasurable and so desirable. We not only feel ourselves disburdened when we share our sorrows with friends, but feel a kind of pleasure when we are able to share theirs.

This was a major point of disagreement between Hume and Smith, for Hume could not understand how the experience of suffering, whether our own or someone else's, could be pleasurable: suffering is, by its nature, a kind of unease. If Smith was right, it would mean (as Hume put it in a letter to Smith) that a "Hospital would be a more entertaining Place than a Ball" (Hume quoted in Smith, 1982, 46), which seems implausible. Smith responds by clarifying that the experience of empathy is accompanied by its own emotion, over and above the emotion empathized with. It is this second emotion (the sentiment of approbation) which is "always agreeable and delightful," whether or not the emotion empathized with is agreeable (I.iii.1.9). Given this, arriving at emotional concord with the emotions of others is a goal unto itself. For Hume, the affective quality of our empathizing depends wholly on the pleasantness of the emotions we are empathizing with, and so emotional concord is not itself a goal. One consequence of this is that for Smith malice will generally not be pleasant. There will be nothing pleasurable in comparing our discordant emotional states, even if we are happier in comparison, for the awareness of the discord between our sentiments will itself occasion a kind of unease.

Given our desire for emotional concord, the window to understanding Smithian moral motivation is our desire for others to share our motivating emotions and so approve of our actions. When it comes to our judgments of others, to approve of an action as suitable, just, or proper is to find that, upon entering into her situation, we share the emotions that motivated the agent's action (I.i.3.1). In addition to judging an action by the motive that caused it, we can also evaluate it by its effect on other people, that is, by whether it produces benefit or harm (I.i.3.7). If an action affects other people, we find it meritorious if we share, via empathy, the gratitude of the recipient of the action. Conversely, to find it demeritorious or deserving of punishment is to approve of the grief and resentment of the person hurt by the action (II.i.1.3).

We in turn want others to find our actions appropriate and meritorious. So while it may be true that we have a natural interest in our own life above that of others, "and to hear, perhaps of the death of another person, with whom we have no particular connexion, will give us less concern ... than a very insignificant disaster which has befallen ourselves" (II.ii.2.2), we know that for others, our interests are likewise not so important. Our concern for the approval of others leads us to "view ourselves not so much according to the light in which we may naturally appear to ourselves, as according to that in which we naturally appear to others" (II.ii.2.1). When we do so, we see that we cannot make simple self-love the principle upon which we act, because it is not a principle others could share. Instead, we must act in accordance with principles of fairness and respect for the rights of others, and pursue our good only in these parameters. In other words, "though the ruin of our neighbour may affect us much less than a very small misfortune of our own, we must not ruin him to prevent that small misfortune" (II.ii.2.1). Our desire for mutual emotional concord also gives us a motive to be humane and self-sacrificing, for the "amiable" virtues of kindness and tenderness stem from our effort to enter into the emotions of others, whilst the "respectable virtues of self-denial [and] of self-government" (I.i.4.10) stem from our effort to make both our motives and the pitch of our emotions such that others can enter into them.

Awareness of how others view us makes our own self-approval important to us. Remember, however, that for Smith approving of the emotions of another involves the recognition of a concord between the agent's actual emotions and the spectator's imagined response to the same situation, and so requires a perspectival gap between the spectator and the agent for such concord to make sense. When we turn our eye back to our own behavior, we create this gap by "plac[ing] ourselves in the situation of another man, and view[ing our actions] with his eyes and from his station" (III.1.2). However, the point of view of any particular observer is liable to have its own distortions and omissions, and we naturally desire "not only praise, but praiseworthiness; or to be that thing which, though it should be praised by nobody, is, however, the natural and proper object of praise" (III.2.1). If we only cared about the actual admiration of others, we might feign virtue and so would not really be "fit for society." To avoid this, we are by the natural order of things "anxious to be really fit" (III.2.7): to act admirably, rather than merely being admired. This desire also follows from the nature of our admiration for others. Admiration of a positive quality in another person involves the belief that they genuinely are acting on good motivations: our admiration would end if we found out they were merely feigning moral concern. Hence our desire to likewise be the objects of admiration cannot be satisfied unless we truly merit the evaluative content built into that emotion.

In order to be assured that our behavior is admirable, we view it from the point of view of an *impartial spectator*: an unbiased and fully informed observer of our behavior. We divide ourselves "into two persons" (III.1.6), spectator and agent, in order to determine whether our motives match up to what would be approved of by this spectator. Given such a standard, we don't even need to get the actual approval of others in order to be satisfied with our conduct. All we need is the ability to approve of our own actions, if we view them from the point of view of the impartial spectator (III.2.5).

For Smith, a desire for this self-approbation is the "love of virtue" (III.2.8), and it is the love of virtue that above all else motivates moral behavior. Our own "passive feelings" are often selfish, such that we would agonize more over losing our finger than thousands of deaths in an earthquake. Yet Smith doubts whether the most depraved villain would *agree* to the deaths of thousands in order to prevent such a loss. The difference between our passive feelings and the "active principles" that we are willing to act upon "is not the soft power of humanity, it is not the feeble spark of benevolence." Rather, "[i]t is reason, principle, conscience, the inhabitant of the breast, the man within, the great judge and arbiter of our conduct" (III.3.4). In other words, it is the noble love of virtue, the "sentiment of self-approbation" (III.6.13), that motivates action to help others. So while for Hume extensive empathy and acting on pity involve enlarging the boundaries of self-concern, for Smith moral behavior genuinely requires us to refrain from acting on our self-concern and be self-sacrificing. Fundamentally, the desire for emotional concord with others gives us a reason to set aside our self-interest that Hume's system does not have.

4. Partial empathy, impartial moral judgment: untying the knot

For Hume and Smith, empathy explains moral approval or disapproval. We know that empathy can be partial, and given that moral judgment presupposes a degree of impartiality, both acknowledge that it is useful and important to us to overcome these natural tendencies. Both propose the construction of a privileged perspective that will set the standard for moral right and wrong (Sayre-McCord, 2015).

4.1 Hume

For Hume, those qualities that are useful and agreeable (such as honesty or friendliness) give us a sense of pleasure because of our empathetic identification with other people. Moral judgment consists in the particular kind pleasure or pain that we feel in response to the character traits and comcomitant actions of another, when we think about how beneficial, harmful, agreeable, or disagreeable those traits and actions are to others. Whatever brings us this pleasure is what is virtuous, and whatever brings us this kind of pain is what is vicious (3.3.1.2–3). As we have seen, it is far easier to empathize with those who resemble us, who are close to us, or who we care about. It is thus impossible to "feel the same lively pleasure from the virtues of a person, who liv'd in Greece two thousand years ago, that I feel from the virtues of a familiar friend" (3.3.1.15). Yet in spite of this, "we give the same approbation to the same moral qualities in China as in England" (3.3.1.14). Hume explains that we abstract from our partial point of view and "fix on some steady and general points of view" (3.3.1.15) from which to assess character and action. Moral approval thus consists of the particular kind of pleasure that we feel if we assess people's characters and actions from this general point of view. There is hence a difference between calling a person our enemy, and judging this person to be vicious: in the latter case, we imply that we are assessing his character from a point of view that we expect our audience will be able to enter into as well (*Enquiry*, hereafter EPM, 9.1.6).

In the same way that we correct for our position in space when assessing the size of physical objects, in our judgments of character, we correct for the faintness of the emotions we feel towards those who are far away or unrelated to us (3.3.3.2). Within the structure of Hume's theory of empathy, this approach to correcting for partiality makes sense, for vivacity is the key to feeling empathy and to having that empathy translate into care for others. Thus we arrive at a common point of view for moral judgment by putting ourselves into an imaginative position where we think of experiencing the emotions of others with equal vivacity. The emotions of others are *brought near* to us in order for us to "see" – that is, imagine feeling – them clearly, "very much like removing obstructions from one's field of vision or of changing the angle and distance of one's gaze" (Rick, 2007, 146).

Hume sometimes holds that from the general point of view we consider how a person's character traits affect those in that person's "narrow circle," i.e., their family and friends (3.3.3.2). Given that people's benevolence is limited, we must when assessing anyone's character consider not how it affects us, but how it affects those within the natural sphere of concern of the person we are evaluating, which is itself a mechanism for vivifying our emotional response to the character of another. One concern with such a mechanism is that we are merely replacing one kind of partiality, that of our particular point of view, with another, that of the narrow circle of the agent. It is not clear why we should prefer the latter to the former, given that a person's narrow circle is likely to have their own partial points of view on the moral landscape. It is clear, however, that Hume thinks that all human beings have enough in common that consideration of how a person appears to her narrow circle would not involve us in evaluative conflict. For in the *Enquiry* he writes that the "notion of morals, implies some sentiment common to all mankind, which recommends the same object to general approbation, and makes every man, or most men, agree in the same opinion or decision concerning it" (EPM 9.1.5). There is "some universal principle of the human frame" (EPM 9.1.6) which leads people to share in moral judgments via the exercise of empathy. The purpose of imagining the points of view of the narrow circle is simply to make vivid to us those characters that we respond to more faintly.

However, Jon Rick (2007) raises worries about the narrow circle as a standard of character, observing that in some cases our moral judgments seem to clash with those of the narrow circle. In his discussion of tyrannicide, Hume himself notes that though Brutus may be "treated with indulgence on account of the prejudices of [his] time[]," subsequent experience has shown us that the practice of tyrannicide has bad consequences and so is wrong (EPM 2.2.19). We might explain this by saying that while perhaps the feelings of Brutus's narrow circle might be a reason to be indulgent to Brutus himself, we must extend our consideration beyond this circle when considering the merits of tyrannicide *in general*. In other words, when making judgments about the merits of action *types* (dishonesty, theft, etc.), the "narrow circle" might be the entire human community. Hume is hopeful that if we extend our vision widely enough we will come to find the same moral qualities to be useful and agreeable.

Hume holds that we have a pragmatic interest in fixing the content of our moral language so we can share assessments of characters and actions with other people. As each personal point of view is always changing, and is on its own terms irreconcilable with others, we "seek some other standard of merit and demerit, which may not admit of so great variation" (3.3.1.18). This is of vital practical interest for us to navigate our social landscape. In furtherance of this interest, correcting for partiality involves not only making vivid those characters that are faint, but also counteracting the prejudicial strongness of our emotional responses to the characters of friends and enemies. While from a personal point of view my enemy in war is hurtful to me, if I am "a man of temper and judgment" I can assess him to be brave and worthy of respect (3.1.2.4), in the same way as I can judge that my friend, though beloved, is not more virtuous than distant figures in history.

For Hume, there is thus a difference between the way empathy functions in moral motivation and in moral judgment. In moral judgment, "we over-look our own interest" (3.3.1.17) and aim to be impartial, something which he acknowledges is not possible when it comes to moral motivation. Our benevolence is limited, generally to our family and friends, which is indeed why we must consider how a person's character affects those in her narrow circle when we assess it (3.3.3.2). While our natural empathy is enough for us to prefer that other people do well rather than suffer, and so enough to lead us to approve of those things that help others do well, it is not enough to motivate us to sacrifice in order to help them (3.3.1.23). It might be that our generous sentiments are too weak "to move even a hand or finger of our body," even though they "still direct the determinations of our mind" (EPM 9.1.4). Indeed, the way to become morally motivated is not to be impartial, but to expand the scope of our partial concern by having such a vivid impression of the suffering of another person that we come to care about her as we care about ourselves. While this approach is in some ways admirable, it is not something that we can generalize beyond a fairly limited group of people or number of instances.

In the *Enquiry*, Hume does acknowledge that the fact that virtues are "cherished by society and conversation" means that the public approbation of virtue can act to gradually counteract people's natural selfishness and encourage the limited concern for others that they do have (EPM 9.1.9). Likewise, "our continual and earnest pursuit of a character, a name, a reputation" can give us the habit of surveying our behavior the way that other people are likely to, keeping "alive the sentiments of right and wrong" (EPN 9.1.10). However, it is not clear whether such a concern for a reputation is the same as a concern for admirability. Secondly, Hume is not clear as to whether the public praise of virtue encourages greater benevolence within our narrow circle, or actively encourages us to broaden that circle. Lastly, not enough is said to explain how the popular approval of benevolence is enough to help us overcome the risks of malice and contempt which are not a problem in Smith's system in the first place.

4.2 Smith

On the other hand, for Smith, the point of view of the impartial spectator is instrumental both in moral judgment and moral motivation. When I act morally, my concern is to be admirable or to merit the approbation of an impartial spectator. If the stakes are high enough (e.g., the loss of my finger versus the loss of thousands of lives), this concern *would* motivate me to sacrifice my own self-interest to help others. Indeed, Smith thinks that any reasonable person would be thus motivated, whilst for Hume, talk of reason only has a place when discussing the "calm determination of the passions" (3.3.1.18) that are involved in arriving at a general point of view in moral *judgment*. Whilst Smith focuses his attention on moral motivation, it is clear that the impartial spectator has a role to play in moral evaluation as well. In order, for example, to determine the right degree of resentment to feel at an offense, I must step back from the partial points of view of both the victim and offender, and indeed from my own point of view as an interested party, and consider the degree of resentment an impartial spectator would feel (I.i.5.4, I.ii.3.8). There is thus, for Smith, a greater unity between our roles as moral agents and moral judges. In both cases, we make use of the point of view of an impartial spectator to determine which emotional responses are proper and so which actions meritorious.

References

Coplan, A. (2011). Will the Real Empathy Please Stand Up? A Case for a Narrow Conceptualization. *The Southern Journal of Philosophy*, 49, 53–60.

Darwall, S. (1998). Empathy, Sympathy, Care. *Philosophical Studies*, 89, 261–82.

Hume, David (2006). *An Enquiry Concerning the Principles of Morals*. T. L. Beauchamp (ed.). Oxford: Oxford University Press. (Original work published in 1751.)

Hume, David (2007). *A Treatise of Human Nature*. D. F. Norton and M. J. Norton (eds.). New York: Oxford University Press. (Original work published in 1739 and 1740.)

Rick, Jon (2007). Hume's and Smith's Partial Sympathies and Impartial Stances. *The Journal of Scottish Philosophy*, 5, 135–58.

Sayre-McCord, Geoffrey (2015). Hume and Smith on Sympathy, Approbation, and Moral Judgment. In E. Schliesser (ed.), *Sympathy: A History* (pp. 208–46). New York: Oxford Univeristy Press.

Smith, Adam (1982). *The Theory of Moral Sentiments*. D.D. Raphael and A.L. Macfie (eds.). Indianapolis: Liberty Fund. (Original work published in 1790.)

10

EMPATHY IN TWENTIETH-CENTURY PSYCHOLOGY

Mark H. Davis

The story of empathy in twentieth-century psychology is of a gradual movement from general theoretical treatments to more specific empirical investigations of particular research questions. Its roots in philosophy, particularly the work of Scottish moral philosophers like Smith and Hume, are especially clear in the early years. Although the rising tide of empiricism later tended to obscure these origins, even the most recent empirical approaches still show their philosophical roots, especially with regard to the basic questions: What is empathy? What are its antecedents? What are its consequences?

History, definitions, and terminology

In the broadest sense, empathy refers to the reactions that one person has to the observed experiences of another. However, because responsiveness to others can take many forms, there has been a long history of definitional disagreement among those who have studied the phenomenon. Perhaps the earliest formal consideration of empathy was offered by the economist and moral philosopher Adam Smith (1759), who felt that we are imbued by nature with a nearly irresistible tendency to experience a "fellow-feeling" when we observe someone experiencing a powerful emotional state (see Chapter 9, "Empathy in Hume and Smith"). This feeling can take many forms: pity for the sorrowful, anguish for the miserable, joy for the successful, and so on. The source of these fellow feelings, Smith argues, is the power of imagination – we imaginatively transpose ourselves into the other person's situation, and in this way come to experience sensations that are generally similar to, although typically weaker than, those of the other person. This focus on the shared emotional states of observer and target became a recurring theme in later treatments of empathy. The name Smith gave to these imagined reactions was *sympathy*.

The term empathy came along later, and from a very different source. The word *Einfühlung*, initially used in German aesthetics, referred to the tendency of observers to project themselves "into" that which they observe, typically some physical object of beauty; the term was later broadened to encompass the process by which we come to know other people (see Chapter 7, "Empathy in the Aesthetic Tradition"). The English word empathy was actually invented by Edward Titchener

(1909) as a "translation" of the German term. Unlike Smith, Titchener believed that the mechanism through which empathy occurred was an inner imitation of the observed person or object – a process referred to today as motor mimicry. Importantly, Titchener additionally felt that the sharing of emotions created in this way also fostered a better understanding of the target.

Later approaches built upon this notion that empathy at its heart was about understanding other people. For example, the sociologist George Herbert Mead (1934) placed a heavy emphasis on the individual's capacity to take on the role of other persons, and understand how they view the world. The ability to do this was seen as a critical component in the developmental process of learning to live effectively in a highly social world. Jean Piaget (1932) placed a similar emphasis on a crucial cognitive skill – the ability to decenter, and to recognize that the experiences of others are separate from our own. The similarity between these two constructs – role-taking and decentering – is clear. Both describe a primarily cognitive process in which the individual suppresses his or her usual egocentric outlook and instead imagines how the world appears to others.

Later approaches to empathy have continued to reflect the two major threads apparent in this brief historical overview. Some emphasize emotion, and consider empathy to be the experiencing of some affective reaction in response to the observed experience of another person. (The often unspoken but critically important assumption underlying this approach is that the observer only "observes" the target's experiences, and does not participate in them. For example, it is empathy if I become angry when I witness someone being mistreated; it is not empathy if I become angry with someone who is clearly angry with *me*.) Other approaches conceive of empathy as an essentially cognitive phenomenon in which observers come to have knowledge or understanding of another person; emotional responses are not an essential part of this approach. In addition, a more inclusive approach has gained ascendance in recent years – one that begins with the assumption that empathy is a complex and multi-faceted phenomenon that of necessity includes both affective and cognitive components.

The cognitive tradition

As noted earlier, Piaget (1932) was among the first psychologists to argue for a primarily cognitive definition of empathy. His theory of cognitive development placed great emphasis on a crucial cognitive skill – the ability to *decenter*. In Piaget's view, the child begins as a creature incapable of differentiating between the experiences of self and those of others. Only as children progress through the stages of cognitive development do they become capable of making this distinction, and of recognizing that the experiences of others are separate from their own. The ability to suppress our usual egocentric outlooks, and instead imagine how the world appears to others, is thus an integral part of social development.

Given Piaget's tremendous stature, it is perhaps not surprising that the cognitive definition of empathy became quite widespread. One evidence of this can be seen in subsequent investigations of children's role-taking. Treatments of this topic (e.g., Eisenberg 1986) have typically distinguished between *perceptual* role-taking (the ability to imagine the literal visual perspective of another), *cognitive* role-taking (imagining others' thoughts and motives), and *affective* role-taking (the ability to infer another's emotional states). It should be noted that affective role-taking in this context refers only to an *awareness* of others' emotional states and does not necessarily include any affective reaction in the observer. Eventually an impressive array of techniques were developed to assess individuals' levels of role-taking capacity in both the cognitive (e.g., Chandler 1973; Flavell et al. 1968) and affective (e.g., Chandler & Greenspan 1972; Feshbach & Roe 1968) realms. Consistent with Piaget's views, the evidence suggests that role-taking skill generally increases throughout childhood (Eisenberg & Mussen 1989).

Outside of developmental psychology the cognitive tradition primarily took the form of an emphasis on empathy's role in enhancing accuracy in person perception, what is sometimes termed *social acuity*. In the 1940s and 1950s much of the research was predicated on the idea that empathy consists of an ability to accurately imagine others' viewpoints (e.g., Chapin 1942; Kerr & Speroff 1954). In fact, some of these approaches essentially equated empathy with the accurate perceptions of others (e.g., Dymond 1949; 1950). Although methodological difficulties plagued this early work, later investigations examined the same kind of questions with greater success. However, the methodological problems with early accuracy research contributed to a shift toward the emotional side of the empathy coin.

The affective tradition

Ezra Stotland and colleagues (Stotland 1969; Stotland, Sherman, & Shaver 1971) were perhaps the first of the more modern empathy theorists to again conceive of empathy in solely affective terms. Stotland (1969) defined empathy as "an observer's reacting emotionally because he perceives that another is experiencing or is about to experience an emotion" (p. 272). Thus, Stotland specifically distinguished affective empathy from cognitive processes related to accuracy, although he also discussed ways in which the two separate constructs might be related. Stotland's view of empathy therefore bears a strong resemblance to Smith's definition of sympathy discussed earlier; both definitions focus exclusively on the affective responses experienced by one person in reaction to the experiences of another. However, while the earlier views explicitly or implicitly assumed that the nature of the observer's emotion would parallel that of the target, no such assumption is made in Stotland's definition. For example, an observer's gleeful reaction to the pain of another would still qualify as empathy – what Stotland et al. (1971) refer to as *contrast empathy*.

Other theorists also tended to define empathy solely in terms of affective responses, but unlike Stotland, they also generally restricted the term empathy to emotional reactions which are at least broadly congruent with those of the target (e.g. Eisenberg & Strayer 1987; Hoffman 1984). In fact, one influential contemporary approach, that of Dan Batson (Batson 1991; Batson, Fultz, & Schoenrade 1987), is even more limited. Empathy, for Batson, consists specifically of other-oriented feelings of concern and compassion that result from witnessing another person suffer. Thus, in Batson's view even an exact *match* of emotions is not empathy; that term is reserved for compassionate feelings alone.

The multidimensional tradition

Eventually, and in retrospect inevitably, there was a growing realization that a more comprehensive approach to empathy, one that recognized its multifaceted nature, would be of considerable value (e.g., Davis 1980; Davis 1983; Deutsch & Madle 1975). The most ambitious of the modern empathy theorists to adopt this perspective is probably developmental psychologist Martin Hoffman (1984; 1987). He defined empathy in a fashion similar to most other contemporary theorists: as "an affective response more appropriate to someone else's situation than to one's own" (Hoffman 1987). However, within his larger theoretical framework, Hoffman also addressed a number of other important constructs related to empathy. In brief, children are said to move developmentally from a stage in which they have no sense of a self-other distinction – and therefore react to the distress of others with a personal distress of their own – to a more advanced state in which the growing cognitive sense of self allows the child to experience both a self-oriented distress and a more advanced distress experienced *for* other people. As role-taking

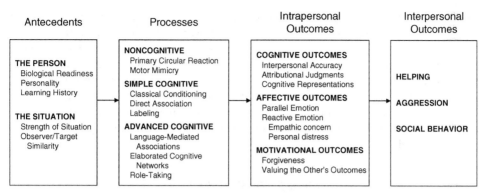

Figure 10.1. Organizational model of empathy antecedents, processes, and outcomes.

skills develop, this other-oriented distress increasingly becomes a form of true compassion for others. Thus, Hoffman's theoretical framework encompasses both cognitive role-taking and multiple types of affective responses to others' distress.

Eisenberg and colleagues (Eisenberg et al. 1991) also offered an analysis with a clear multidimensional flavor. A key part of this analysis focuses on the relations among various forms of affective responding; the single most crucial assumption they make is that observing a distressed target typically leads first to a parallel reaction – affective matching – which is then followed by a response of empathic concern or personal distress. As a rule, the immediate parallel response is transformed through some form of cognitive activity; cognitions that focus on the other's feelings and needs produce empathic concern, while those that focus on one's own arousal produce personal distress. Eisenberg's approach also places great emphasis on another type of cognitive process – the ability to deliberately regulate one's emotional state. Empathic over-arousal is aversive and leads to self-focus and self-concern. Thus, those who can effectively regulate their emotions tend to experience sympathy (an other-oriented response to another's emotion or condition) rather than personal distress (a self-focused, aversive response to another's emotional state or condition).

Based in part on the work of Hoffman and Eisenberg (as well as other theorists and researchers), Davis (1994) proposed a model of empathy (see Figure 10.1) based on a highly inclusive definition; empathy was broadly defined as a set of constructs having to do with the responses of one individual to the experiences of another. These constructs specifically include the processes taking place within the observer and the affective and non-affective outcomes that result from those processes. Based on this definition, the model conceives of the typical empathy episode as consisting of an observer being exposed in some fashion to a target, after which some response on the part of the observer – cognitive, affective, and/or behavioral – occurs. Four related constructs can be identified within this prototypical episode: antecedents, which refer to characteristics of the observer, target, or situation; processes, which refer to the particular mechanisms by which empathic outcomes are produced; intrapersonal outcomes, which refer to cognitive and affective responses produced in the observer which are not manifested in overt behavior toward the target; and interpersonal outcomes, which refer to behavioral responses directed toward the target.

Research questions

Given the heterogeneity of approaches to empathy, it is not surprising that this topic has been examined within a wide variety of contexts. Some of these are outside the scope of this chapter.

For example, empathy has figured prominently in clinical psychology, both in terms of its role in particular disorders such as antisocial personality disorder (e.g., Dolan & Fullam 2004) and autism spectrum disorders (e.g., Jones et al. 2010), as well as its role in the therapist-patient relationships (Rogers 1975). Late in the twentieth century, neuropsychology began to make rapid advances in identifying some of the neural underpinnings of both cognitive and affective forms of empathy (e.g., Decety & Ickes 2009). (See Chapter 4, "The neuroscience of empathy" and Chapter 5, "Empathy and mirror neurons.") For the remainder of this chapter I will briefly and selectively review four of the other major research questions in which empathy has figured most prominently.

Interpersonal accuracy

As mentioned previously, one of the first research questions to attract attention was empathy's potential role in producing accurate perceptions of other people. In the middle of the twentieth century one particular method for measuring such accuracy took center stage. Dymond's (1949; 1950) rating scale method assessed accuracy by having subjects rate targets on a series of traits, and then comparing these ratings with the targets' self-ratings on the same traits. The smaller the discrepancy between the observer's ratings and the target's own ratings, the more accurate (and empathic) the observer. This simple and intuitively appealing measure of accuracy was employed in numerous investigations (see Taft 1955). However, with the publication of several critiques of this method, especially that of Cronbach (1955), things came to a rather abrupt halt. The problem was that accuracy scores in the rating scale method are actually made up of several different constructs, some of which seem to be the result of response sets rather than any kind of empathic process.

To take just one example, consider a target and observer who both happen to have the same response tendency: they usually check the midpoint of a scale and seldom use the endpoints. This similar response style will make the observer appear more accurate because her rating will never be very different from the target's. This phenomenon ("Elevation" in Cronbach's terms) does not depend upon any ability to transpose oneself into the thinking or feeling of another individual, but it nevertheless contributes to an accuracy score which ostensibly reflects exactly this ability. As a result, such accuracy scores contain an unknown amount of statistical confounding. So thoroughly did these critiques discredit the rating scale method that almost all accuracy research was halted for twenty years.

However, eventually new and methodologically superior methods were found that did not rely on problematic discrepancy scores. The "gold standard" of accuracy measurement today is the naturalistic technique developed by William Ickes (see Chapter 31, "Empathic accuracy"). Ickes et al. (1990) introduced a procedure in which dyads made up of unacquainted undergraduates were secretly audio- and videotaped during a six-minute period as they sat waiting for an experiment to "begin." Later each participant separately viewed the tape and indicated the specific thoughts and feelings that s/he recalled having at specific points throughout the six-minute period. Finally, the participants individually viewed the tapes a second time, with the experimenter stopping the tape at every point where their dyad partners had reported having a specific thought or feeling; the subjects then estimated their partners' thoughts/feelings at each point. Accuracy was indexed by the frequency with which subjects were able to successfully estimate the dyad-partner's thoughts and feelings, and such accuracy was related to several characteristics of the dyadic interaction. For example, the degree to which the participants made attributions about each other was associated with greater accuracy, as was the degree to which they asked questions of one another.

Since then, this empathic accuracy (EA) technique has been used in dozens of studies in the U.S. and abroad (Ickes 2009). In addition to the original version described above (the "unstructured dyadic interaction" paradigm), another version has all observers view the same video of an interaction in which they have not participated (the "standard stimulus" paradigm). The former is especially useful for studying EA in existing relationships, and the latter for studying individual differences in EA and its correlates. These EA techniques have been used to examine clinical phenomena such as autism (Roeyers et al. 2001) and borderline personality disorder (Flury et al. 2008), and developmental issues such as the role of EA in adolescent peer relations (Gleason et al. 2009). Within social psychology it has been used most frequently in examinations of close relationships (e.g., Ickes & Simpson 1997; Ickes & Simpson 2001). One particularly fruitful line of inquiry has been the phenomenon of motivated inaccuracy, in which factors such as relationship instability and potentially threatening topics can lead romantic partners to actually *avoid* perceiving their partners accurately.

Cognitive structures

In the latter half of the twentieth century, one defining feature of psychology in general, and social psychology in particular, was an increasing emphasis on cognitive processes – the so-called "cognitive revolution" (Thagard 1992). During this time the subfield of social cognition made huge strides in explaining how social phenomena (and in particular, prejudice and stereotyping) result in large part from the way in which people perceive and mentally represent the elements in their social worlds (Kunda 2000). Reflecting this general trend, some forms of empathy research began to take on some of this flavor.

One such approach focused on the degree to which the cognitive representations of self and other can be said to overlap, or "merge" with one another. This view explains empathy's effect on emotion and behavior in terms of the degree to which empathizing makes the cognitive structures corresponding to self and other closer, more similar, and more intertwined. Evidence from at least two lines of research would suggest such a possibility. For example, Aron and colleagues (Aron & Aron 1986; Aron et al. 1991) found evidence that people in close relationships (e.g., best friends, spouses) appear to make fewer distinctions between the self and other when making cognitive judgments. In addition, cross-cultural research on "interdependent self-construal" (e.g., Markus & Kitayama 1991) suggests that in many collectivist cultures the self is defined largely in terms of its connections to outside entities: family, significant others, and important groups. This stands in contrast to the kind of self-definition more common in individualist cultures, which views the self as essentially separate from other social entities. Thus, an interdependent self-construal also appears to make fewer distinctions between "self" and "other."

Does empathy in fact contribute to a merging of self and other? Davis et al. (1996) conducted two experiments in which perspective-taking or control instructions were given to participants prior to viewing another student on videotape. Those who received the perspective-taking set were more likely to use traits they had earlier identified as characteristic of the *self* (especially positive traits) to describe the other student; thus, the cognitive representations of self and other shared more common content. Galinsky and Moskowitz (2000) extended this line of inquiry by examining the effect of perspective taking on the use of stereotypes to characterize outgroups. For example, college students who were instructed to take the perspective of an outgroup (the elderly) were less likely to later use stereotypes to characterize elderly people; moreover, this effect was mediated by the degree of overlap between self-traits and those seen as descriptive of the elderly. Taken together, these studies support the view that perspective taking affects the cognitive representation of others in a particular way – by making them more similar to our own self-constructs.

More recently, Wang et al. (2014) examined whether the effect of perspective taking on stereotyping depends on the nature of the target. If one effect of perspective taking is indeed to extend (largely positive) self-representations to the representations of others, then the overall effect on attitudes toward the target may depend on the target. Specifically, perspective taking should lead to *more* favorable views of negatively stereotyped targets, as the positive self-information is applied to the negative stereotype. However, perspective taking may lead to *less* favorable views of positively stereotyped targets, as the self-information is now applied to an already positive stereotype. Consistent with this view, Wang et al. found that taking the perspective of a negatively viewed target (e.g., laborer) led to seeing him as more intelligent and thoughtful; in contrast, taking the perspective of a positively viewed target (e.g., doctor) led to seeing the target as somewhat *less* intelligent and thoughtful.

Helping/altruism

Without question, the twentieth-century theoretical argument in which empathy figured the most strongly is the question of whether humans can act in truly altruistic ways (see Chapter 18, "Empathy and altruism"). For years this issue was the subject of a spirited empirical argument between two able protagonists, Dan Batson and Robert Cialdini. At the heart of this debate was a central question: whether emotional responses experienced by observers motivate helping for egoistic reasons (e.g., to reduce one's own discomfort), or altruistic reasons (e.g., to reduce the target's discomfort). Without denying that empathically induced affect can lead to helping behavior through the essentially egoistic means, Batson (1987; 1991) argued that at least some helping is not egoistic at all, but is in fact intended solely to benefit the needy target. Such helping would therefore qualify as "true" altruism. More specifically, the source of such true altruism is said to be the emotional response of empathic concern. In Batson's view these feelings of compassion and tenderness for the target are the source of a truly altruistic motivation; the stronger the feelings of compassion for the target, the greater is the motivation to reduce the target's need.

In a series of investigations (Batson et al. 1981; Batson et al. 1983; Toi & Batson 1982), Batson offered consistent support for the prediction that high levels of empathic concern produce helping, even when it is easy for the helper to avoid doing so. In these studies, participants were led to experience empathic concern or personal distress while exposed to a needy target, and were then given a chance to help; sometimes it was easy to physically escape the situations without helping and sometimes it was not. In every instance the subjects who were experiencing empathic concern provided relatively high levels of help, regardless of ease or difficulty of escape. Subjects who were primarily experiencing personal distress displayed the predicted sensitivity to the ease of escape manipulation; when escape was difficult they helped at the same level as those experiencing empathic concern, but when escape was easy the level of helping dropped dramatically. Importantly, this pattern held up over a variety of different need situations (e.g., target receiving electric shocks; target was in an auto accident).

The basic response to Batson's prima facie case for altruistic helping was the argument, made in a variety of ways, that what appears to be other-oriented helping might nevertheless be motivated by more selfish concerns. For example, it is possible that through socialization we learn that there are specific rewards (and punishments) associated with helping (or failing to help) people toward whom we are experiencing empathic concern. That is, we may learn that when we feel compassion toward another and then act on that compassion we may expect special rewards such as pride and praise, or that when we fail to help in such circumstances there are special punishments such as guilt and loss of social status. In a similar vein, situations that produce empathic concern may also cause increased sadness in the observer, and this increased sadness leads to greater helping; thus, the ultimate purpose of the helping may be to improve the mood of the observer/helper.

Research designed to evaluate such possibilities has produced somewhat equivocal results. Cialdini et al. (1987) used perspective-taking instructions to induce an empathic set (and presumably empathic concern) in some observers. For some of these empathizing observers, moreover, they provided a mood-enhancing experience (receiving praise or money) before the observers had the opportunity to help the target. If the motivation of the empathizing observers is primarily to enhance their own mood, then the introduction of a mood-enhancing experience should reduce the need for further mood management and thus reduce the likelihood of help. The results of the study generally supported this prediction. However, other similar investigations (Schroeder et al. 1988; Batson et al. 1989) found patterns more supportive of the altruism position.

Somewhat more recently, another challenge to the empathy hypothesis has been offered, one based upon the previously noted effect of perspective taking on the cognitive representations of other people. Cialdini et al. (1997) argued that if taking the perspective of a target produces a merging of the self and other at the level of cognitive representations, then help that is offered to the target is at least to some degree help "offered" to oneself. As such, it could not be considered truly altruistic. In support of this argument, Cialdini et al. had participants imagine a variety of targets (e.g., family member, acquaintance) facing a variety of problems. They were then asked how willing they would be to help, and the degree to which they were experiencing empathic concern, personal distress, and sadness; in addition, the degree to which they felt a sense of "oneness" with each target was assessed. The association between empathic concern and willingness to help was significant before the "oneness" variable was included in the analysis; however, once "oneness" was entered, the relationship between empathic concern and help was reduced to nonsignificance. As with the earlier challenges, subsequent research was somewhat mixed; some studies supported this challenge (e.g., Maner et al. 2002), but others continued to find support for the altruism position (e.g., Batson et al. 1997).

Social behavior

Finally, empathy's possible role in personal relationships has also attracted research attention. Both the affective and cognitive traditions argue that empathy in some form is necessary to help us deal with the fundamental obstacle in social life: namely, other people. Because others commonly have needs, desires, and goals that differ from our own, and because the attainment of their goals is frequently incompatible with ours, a powerful tendency toward conflict is inherent in all social life, resulting in potentially high levels of discord and disagreement. Empathy, in one form or another, can help to interrupt this sequence. Moreover, empathy can play a beneficial role in two ways: by aiding in the relatively minor, day-by-day process of keeping the relationship running smoothly (*routine maintenance*), and by contributing to the occasional, more serious efforts to repair substantial damage (*major repairs*).

With regard to routine relationship maintenance, considerable evidence indicates that the perspective-taking facet of empathy is especially important. To begin with, research examining the association between dispositional perspective taking and global relationship satisfaction routinely finds such associations. This pattern is especially strong when the perspective-taking measure specifically assesses the tendency to take the particular perspective of one's relationship partner. Measures of global perspective taking, on the other hand, tended to display similar but weaker associations (Davis in press).

One mechanism through which perspective taking (PT) might improve relationship satisfaction is by reducing the number and intensity of interpersonal conflicts. Higher levels of dispositional PT are associated with lower dispositional hostility (Davis 1994), fewer arguments with friends (Davis & Kraus 1991), and lower levels of hostile behavior toward intimate partners (e.g., Péloquin et al. 2011). Taken as a whole, the pattern that emerges from research in this area is that dispositional PT is the most consistent and reliable influence on social discord. Other facets of empathy may also play a role, but their effects are often moderated by other variables – most notably gender – and often not in consistent ways.

Another way in which empathy may help maintain relationships is through its influence on social support, broadly defined as everyday assistance that we provide to one another (Pasch & Bradbury 1998). Using a variety of assessment methods, recent research has documented the ways in which empathy is related to marital support. Some studies have focused on self-reports of spousal support and their relationship with dispositional empathy. Devoldre et al. (2010) carried out two studies to examine this question. In the first, they asked female college students to complete a measure assessing the degree to which they provided three types of support to their romantic partners: emotional (reassurance, encouragement), instrumental (suggestions, advice), and negative support (criticizing, minimizing the problem); in the second study they asked the same questions of both members of a sample of married couples. Overall, each of the three forms of dispositional empathy displayed significant associations with support provision. The most consistent effects may be summarized as follows: 1) dispositional PT was associated with providing more instrumental support; 2) dispositional PT was associated with providing less negative support; and 3) dispositional personal distress (PD) was associated with providing more negative support. Using a somewhat different method for assessing support, Devoldre et al. (2013) found that dispositional PT was associated with more instrumental support responses, and dispositional empathic concern (EC) was associated with more emotional support responses.

Another set of studies has focused not on dispositional empathy, but on a form of state empathy: accuracy at inferring the thoughts and feelings of one's romantic partner. The argument at the heart of this approach is that an accurate perception of the partner, including the partner's particular support needs at a given moment, will allow the support provider to offer more useful forms of support. Verhofstadt et al. (2008) employed a version of Ickes's empathic accuracy task in which married couples discussed a current personal problem of one of the partners. The interaction was videotaped, and subsequently that partner was asked at randomly chosen points to report what he or she had been thinking and feeling, and what he or she thought the partner had been thinking and feeling. This information was later coded to produce measures of empathic accuracy. Consistent with much of the research using trait empathy measures, empathic accuracy of the support provider was significantly associated with offering more instrumental support and less negative support. Empathic accuracy was unrelated to emotional support. Similar findings were also reported by Verhofstadt et al. (2011) using a sample of married couples.

In addition to everyday relationship maintenance, empathy also plays an important role when the relationship is threatened more profoundly as a result of serious misbehavior by one partner. In such cases, the key response from the wronged party is not the simple forbearance needed when partners are merely annoying, but a more fundamental willingness to forgive the guilty party. The end of the twentieth century saw an increasing amount of attention paid to this important interpersonal phenomenon (e.g., Enright et al. 1992; McCullough et al.

2000). Although a variety of definitions have been advanced, one influential approach is that of McCullough et al. (1997), who define forgiveness as a set of motivational changes characterized by lowered desires to retaliate against and maintain estrangement from an offending relationship partner, and a heightened desire for conciliation. Thus, forgiveness at its heart is a set of changes in the motivations of the offended party. The form of empathy most important by far in such circumstances turns out to be feelings of compassion and concern.

This can be seen quite clearly in a meta-analysis, carried out by Fehr et al. (2010), which analyzed the results from 175 studies and over 25,000 participants to evaluate the evidence for the situational and dispositional correlates of forgiveness. As part of this effort they considered three facets of empathy: trait PT, trait EC, and state EC. The trait variables exhibited relatively modest but reliable associations with forgiveness (dispositional PT, mean $r = .17$; dispositional EC, mean $r = .11$). In contrast, state levels of EC were strongly related to forgiveness (mean $r = .53$). In fact, state EC displayed the strongest association with forgiveness of any of the variables included in the meta-analyses. Thus, in sharp contrast to routine maintenance, for which perspective taking seems especially valuable, it is the affective response of empathic concern that matters most when forgiveness is required.

This intriguing pattern may result from the particular nature of forgiveness, which can be thought of as a kind of relationship "alchemy" – when we are faced with betrayal, it transforms the powerful immediate retaliatory response into a more benign and benevolent one. Understanding the partner's point of view may contribute to this transformation, but it seems to require more than mere understanding. What is required for this kind of change is the emotionally fueled power of a positive affective orientation toward the transgressor. What is required, in short, is a compassionate response of sufficient strength to turn relationship lead into gold.

References

Aron, A., & Aron, E. N. 1986, *Love as the expansion of self: understanding attraction and satisfaction*, Hemisphere, New York.

Aron, A., Aron, E. N., Tudor, M., & Nelson, G. 1991, 'Close relationships as including other in the self', *Journal of Personality and Social Psychology*, vol. 60, pp. 241–53.

Batson, C. D. 1987, 'Prosocial motivation: is it ever truly altruistic?' in *Advances in experimental social psychology*, vol. 20, ed. L. Berkowitz, Academic Press, New York, pp. 65–122.

Batson, C. D. 1991, *The altruism question: toward a social-psychological answer*, Lawrence Erlbaum Associates, Hillsdale.

Batson, C. D., Batson, J. G., Griffitt, C. A., Barrientos, S., Brandt, J. R., Sprengelmeyer, P., & Bayly, M. J. 1989, 'Negative-state relief and the empathy-altruism hypothesis', *Journal of Personality and Social Psychology*, vol. 56, pp. 922–33.

Batson, C. D., Duncan, B. D., Ackerman, P., Buckley, T., & Birch, K. 1981, 'Is empathic emotion a source of altruistic motivation?', *Journal of Personality and Social Psychology*, vol. 40, pp. 290–302.

Batson, C. D., Fultz, J., & Schoenrade, P. A. 1987, 'Distress and empathy: two qualitatively distinct vicarious emotions with different motivational consequences', *Journal of Personality*, vol. 55, pp. 19–39.

Batson, C. D., O'Quin, K., Fultz, J., Vanderplas, M., & Isen, A. M. 1983, 'Influence of self-reported distress and empathy on egoistic versus altruistic motivation to help', *Journal of Personality and Social Psychology*, vol. 45, pp. 706–18.

Batson, C. D., Sager, K., Garst, E., Kang, M., Rubchinsky, K., & Dawson, K. 1997, 'Is empathy induced helping due to self-other merging?', *Journal of Personality and Social Psychology*, vol. 73, pp. 495–509.

Berg, D. R., Lonsway, K. A., & Fitzgerald, L. F. 1999, 'Rape prevention education for men: the effectiveness of empathy-induction techniques', *Journal of College Student Development*, vol. 40, pp. 219–34.

Chandler, M. J. 1973, 'Egocentrism and antisocial behavior: the assessment and training of social perspective-taking skills', *Developmental Psychology*, vol. 9, pp. 326–32.

Chandler, M. J., & Greenspan, S. 1972, 'Ersatz egocentrism: a reply to H. Borke', *Developmental Psychology*, vol. 7, pp. 104–6.

Chapin, F. S. 1942, 'Preliminary standardization of a social insight scale', *American Sociological Review*, vol. 7, pp. 214–25.

Cialdini, R. B., Brown, S. L., Lewis, B. P., Luce, C., & Neuberg, S. L. 1997, 'Reinterpreting the empathy-altruism relationship: when one into one equals oneness', *Journal of Personality and Social Psychology*, vol. 73, pp. 481–94.

Cialdini, R. B., Schaller, M., Houlihan, D., Arps, K., Fultz, J., & Beaman, A. L. 1987, 'Empathy-based helping: is it selflessly or selfishly motivated?', *Journal of Personality and Social Psychology*, vol. 52, pp. 749–58.

Cronbach, L. J. 1955, 'Processes affecting scores on understanding of others and assuming "similarity"', *Psychological Bulletin*, vol. 52, pp. 177–93.

Davis, M. H. 1980, 'A multidimensional approach to individual differences in empathy', *JSAS Catalog of Selected Documents in Psychology*, vol. 10, p. 85.

Davis, M. H. 1983, 'Measuring individual differences in empathy: evidence for a multidimensional approach', *Journal of Personality and Social Psychology*, vol. 44, pp. 113–26.

Davis, M. H. 1994, *Empathy: a social psychological approach*, Westview Press, Boulder, CO.

Davis, M. H. in press, 'Empathy, compassion, and social relationships', in *Oxford Handbook of Compassion Science*, ed. E. Seppälä.

Davis, M. H., & Begovic, E. 2014, 'Empathy interventions', in *The handbook of positive psychological interventions*, ed. A. Parks, Wiley-Blackwell, New York, pp. 111–34.

Davis, M. H., Conklin, L., Smith, A., & Luce, C. 1996, 'Effect of perspective taking on the cognitive representation of persons: a merging of self and other', *Journal of Personality and Social Psychology*, vol. 70, pp. 713–26.

Davis, M. H., & Kraus, L. A. 1991, 'Dispositional empathy and social relationships', in *Advances in personal relationships*, vol. 3, eds. H. Jones & D. Perlman, Jessica Kingsley Publishers, London, pp. 75–115.

Deutsch, F. M., & Madle, R. A. 1975, 'Empathy: historic and current conceptualizations, measurement, and a cognitive theoretical perspective', *Human Development*, vol. 18, pp. 267–87.

Devoldre, I., Davis, M. H., Verhofstadt, L. L., & Buysse, A. 2010, 'Empathy and social support provision in couples: social support and the need to study the underlying processes', *The Journal of Psychology: Interdisciplinary and Applied*, vol. 144, no. 3, pp. 259–84.

Devoldre, I., Verhofstadt, L. L., Davis, M. H., & Buysse, A. 2013, *Are empathic people more supportive to their spouses? A scenario-based study.* Unpublished manuscript.

Dolan, M., & Fullam, R. 2004, 'Theory of mind and mentalizing ability in antisocial personality disorders with and without psychopathy', *Psychological Medicine*, vol. 34, pp. 1093–102.

Dymond, R. F. 1949, 'A scale for the measurement of empathic ability', *Journal of Consulting Psychology*, vol. 13, pp. 127–33.

Dymond, R. F. 1950, 'Personality and empathy', *Journal of Consulting Psychology*, vol. 14, pp. 343–50.

Eisenberg, N. 1986, *Altruistic emotion, cognition, and behavior*, Lawrence Erlbaum Associates, Hillsdale, NJ.

Eisenberg, N., & Mussen, P. H. 1989, *The roots of prosocial behavior in children*, Cambridge University Press, Cambridge.

Eisenberg, N., Shea, C. L., Carlo, G., & Knight, G. P. 1991, 'Empathy-related responding and cognition: a "chicken and the egg" dilemma', in *Handbook of moral behavior and development*, vol. 2: *Research*, eds. W. Kurtines & J. Gewirtz, Lawrence Erlbaum Associates, Hillsdale, pp. 63–88.

Eisenberg, N., & Strayer, J. 1987, 'Critical issues in the study of empathy', in *Empathy and its development*, eds, N. Eisenberg & J. Strayer, Cambridge University Press, Cambridge, pp. 3–13.

Enright, R. D., Gassin, E. A., & Wu, C. 1992, 'Forgiveness: a developmental view', *Journal of Moral Development*, vol. 21, pp. 99–114.

Fehr, R., Gelfand, M. J., & Nag, M. 2010, 'The road to forgiveness: a meta-analytic synthesis of its situational and dispositional correlates', *Psychological Bulletin*, vol. 136, pp. 894–914.

Feshbach, N. D., & Roe, K. 1968, 'Empathy in six- and seven-year-olds', *Child Development*, vol. 39, pp. 133–45.

Flavell, J. H., Botkin, P. T., Fry, C. L., Wright, J., & Jarvis, P. 1968, *The development of role taking and communication skills in children*, Wiley, New York.

Flury, J. M., Ickes, W., & Schweinle, W. 2008, 'The borderline empathy effect: do high BPD individuals have greater empathic ability? Or are they just more difficult to "read"?', *Journal of Research in Personality*, vol. 42, pp. 312–22.

Galinsky, A. D., & Moskowitz, G. B. 2000, 'Perspective-taking: decreasing stereotype expression, stereotype accessibility, and in-group favoritism', *Journal of Personality and Social Psychology*, vol. 78, pp. 708–24.

Gleason, K. A., Jensen-Campbell, L., & Ickes, W. 2009, 'The role of empathic accuracy in adolescents' peer relations and adjustment', *Personality and Social Psychology Bulletin*, vol. 35, pp. 997–1011.

Hoffman, M. L. 1984, 'Interaction of affect and cognition in empathy', in *Emotions, cognition, and behavior*, eds. C. E. Izard, J. Kagan, & R. B. Zajonc, Cambridge University Press, Cambridge, pp. 103–31.

Hoffman, M. L. 1987, 'The contribution of empathy to justice and moral judgment', in *Empathy and its development*, eds. N. Eisenberg & J. Strayer, Cambridge University Press, Cambridge, pp. 47–80.

Ickes, W. 2009, 'Empathic accuracy: its links to clinical, cognitive, developmental, social, and physiological psychology', in *The social neuroscience of empathy*, eds. J. Decety & W. Ickes, MIT Press, Cambridge, pp. 57–70.

Ickes, W., & Simpson, J. A. 1997, 'Managing empathic accuracy in close relationships', in *Empathic accuracy*, ed. W. Ickes, Guilford Press, New York, pp. 218–50.

Ickes, W., & Simpson, J. A. 2001, 'Motivational aspects of empathic accuracy', in *Interpersonal processes: Blackwell handbook in social psychology*, eds. G. J. O. Fletcher & M. S. Clark, Blackwell, Oxford, pp. 229–49.

Ickes, W., Stinson, L., Bissonnette, V., & Garcia, S. 1990, 'Naturalistic social cognition: empathic accuracy in mixed-sex dyads', *Journal of Personality and Social Psychology*, vol. 49, pp. 730–42.

Jones, A. P., Happé, F. G. E., Gilbert, F., Burnett, S., & Viding, E. 2010, 'Feeling, caring, knowing: different types of empathy deficit in boys with psychopathic tendencies and autism spectrum disorder', *Journal of Child Psychology and Psychiatry*, vol. 51, pp. 1188–97.

Kerr, W. A., & Speroff, B. G. 1954, 'Validation and evaluation of the empathy test', *Journal of General Psychology*, vol. 50, pp. 369–76.

Kunda, Z. 2000, *Social cognition: making sense of people*, MIT Press, Cambridge.

Maner, J. K., Luce, C. L., Neuberg, S. L., Cialdini, R. B., Brown, S., & Sagarin, B. J. 2002, 'The effects of perspective taking on motivations for helping: still no evidence for altruism', *Personality and Social Psychology Bulletin*, vol. 28, pp. 1601–10.

Markus, H., & Kitayama, S. 1991, 'Culture and the self: implications for cognition, emotion, and motivation', *Psychological Review*, vol. 98, pp. 224–52.

McCullough, M. E., Pargament, K. I., & Thoresen, C. E. 2000, 'The psychology of forgiveness: history, conceptual issues, and overview', in *Forgiveness: theory, research, and practice*, eds. M. E. McCullough, K. I. Pargament, & C. E. Thoresen, Guilford, New York, pp. 1–14.

McCullough, M. E., Worthington, L. L., Jr., & Rachal, K. C. 1997, 'Interpersonal forgiving in close relationships', *Journal of Personality and Social Psychology*, vol. 73, pp. 321–36.

Mead, G. H. 1934, *Mind, self, and society*, University of Chicago Press, Chicago.

Pacala, J. T., Boult, C., Bland, C., & O'Brien, J. 1995, 'Aging game improves medical students caring for elderly', *Gerontology and Geriatrics Education*, vol. 15, pp. 45–57.

Pasch, L. A., & Bradbury, T. N. 1998, 'Social support, conflict, and the development of marital dysfunction', *Journal of Consulting and Clinical Psychology*, vol. 66, no. 2, pp. 219–30.

Péloquin, K., Lafontaine, M., & Brassard, A. 2011, 'A dyadic approach to the study of romantic attachment, dyadic empathy, and psychological partner aggression', *Journal of Social and Personal Relationships*, vol. 28, pp. 915–42.

Piaget, J. 1932, *The moral judgment of the child*, trans. Kegan Paul, Trench, Trubner, London.

Roeyers, H., Buysse, A., Ponnet, K., & Pichal, B. 2001, 'Advancing advanced mind-reading tests: empathic accuracy in adults with a pervasive developmental disorder', *Journal of Child Psychology and Psychiatry*, vol. 42, pp. 271–8.

Rogers, C. R. 1975, 'Empathic: an unappreciated way of being', *The Counseling Psychologist*, vol. 5, pp. 2–10.

Schroeder, D. A., Dovidio, J. F., Sibicky, M. E., Matthews, L. L., & Allen, J. L. 1988, 'Empathic concern and helping behavior: egoism or altruism?', *Journal of Experimental Social Psychology*, vol. 24, pp. 333–53.

Smith, A. 1759/1976, *The theory of moral sentiments*, Clarendon Press, Oxford.

Stotland, E. 1969, 'Exploratory investigations of empathy', in *Advances in experimental social psychology*, vol. 4, ed. L. Berkowitz, Academic Press, New York, pp. 271–314.

Stotland, E., Sherman, S., & Shaver, K. 1971, *Empathy and birth order: some experimental explorations*, University of Nebraska Press, Lincoln, NB.

Taft, R. 1955, 'The ability to judge people', *Psychological Bulletin*, vol. 52, pp. 1–23.

Thagard, P. 1992, *Conceptual revolutions*, Princeton University Press, Princeton.

Titchener, E. 1909, *Elementary psychology of the thought processes*, Macmillan, New York.

Toi, M., & Batson, C. D. 1982, 'More evidence that empathy is a source of altruistic motivation', *Journal of Personality and Social Psychology*, vol. 43, pp. 281–92.

Verhofstadt, L. L., Buysse, A., Ickes, W., Davis, M., & Devoldre, I. 2008, 'Social support in couples: the role of emotional similarity and empathic accuracy', *Emotion*, vol. 8, no. 6, pp. 792–802.

Verhofstadt, L. L., Davis, M., & Ickes, W. 2011, 'Motivation, empathic accuracy, and spousal support: it's complicated', in *Managing interpersonal sensitivity: knowing when – and when not – to understand others*, eds. J. Smith, W. Ickes, J. Hall, and S. Hodges, Nova Science, Hauppauge, pp. 169–92.

Wang, C. S., Ku, G., Tai, K., & Galinsky, A. D. 2014, 'Stupid doctors and smart construction workers: perspective-taking reduces stereotyping of both negative and positive targets', *Social Psychological and Personality Science*, vol. 5, pp. 430–6.

11

EMPATHY, COMPASSION, AND "EXCHANGING SELF AND OTHER" IN INDO-TIBETAN BUDDHISM

Emily McRae

"Imagine yourself as an old yak," the nineteenth-century Tibetan master Patrul Rinpoche advises, "your back weighed down with a load far too heavy, a rope pulling you by the nostrils, your flanks whipped, your ribs bruised by the stirrups" (Patrul 1994: 204–5). This exercise in imaginative projection serves two related purposes for Patrul Rinpoche: it stimulates "intense and unbearable compassion" and causes us to relate to animals with more kindness and sensitivity. In Western moral psychological terms, we would say that Patrul Rinpoche is encouraging us to empathize with the yak. Empathy, basically, is the experience of vicarious feeling, feeling with another. This experience is different from taking on another's feeling as the object of our own feeling, which we do when we sympathize or feel compassion. In compassion we not only vicariously feel another's suffering, we feel distressed or concerned about it (Darwall 1998). Imagining oneself as the abused yak – and vicariously feeling that pain – is a form of empathy, which is phenomenologically distinct from the compassion or sympathy that it stimulates, even if they are experienced nearly simultaneously.

Yet in the traditional languages of Indo-Tibetan Buddhist philosophy there is no word that translates straightforwardly as "empathy" in this contemporary Western sense, although there are related concepts such as compassion (*karuna, snying rje*) and sympathetic joy (*mudita, dga' ba*). Even in English, "empathy," unlike "sympathy" or "compassion," is of relatively recent coinage, appearing in the Western psychological literature in the early twentieth century (Titchner 1909). In Nancy Sherman's discussion of the history of empathy, she notes that it was the English translation of the German *Einfühlung* – originally a term in aesthetics – which translates literally as "feeling one's way into another." According to Sherman's analysis, the main idea in these early usages of empathy in Western psychological contexts "is that of 'resonating' with another, where this often involves role taking, inner imitation, and a projection of the self into the objects of perception" (Sherman 1998, 83).

There is a deep recognition in Indo-Tibetan ethics of the moral significance of one's ability to "resonate" or "feel one's way into another" and no shortage of ethical practices of role taking, "inner imitation," and projecting of the self into objects of perception, such as imagining oneself as the old yak. In these practices, empathetic imaginative projection is cultivated as a central moral and spiritual skill that provides a foundation for two pillars of Mahayana Buddhist ethics: cultivating the positive emotionality of compassion, love, and joy (Section 1), and dismantling narratives of self-clinging (Section 2). These two pillars help form the main moral ideal of Mahayana Buddhism: *bodhicitta*.

Although the empathic imaginative projection employed in Indo-Tibetan Buddhist ethical practices shares some features with Western psychological accounts of empathy – for example, the recognition of the moral and epistemic value of empathic experience, and the role imagination can play in empathy – it differs from these accounts in at least two significant ways. First, empathy in Buddhist ethics is understood in the context of the larger ethical ideal of *bodhicitta* (Section 3). Second, empathy in this tradition is assumed to be highly trainable and our capacity for empathy is assumed to be vast, and vastly under-utilized; it is possible, with proper training, to empathize with any member of the moral community (Section 4).

In what follows, I draw on three Buddhist ethicists in the Indo-Tibetan tradition – the Indian philosopher Śāntideva (eighth century) and the Tibetan philosophers Tsongkhapa (fifteenth century) and Patrul Rinpoche (nineteenth century). In doing so, I do not mean to imply that these three are somehow representative of all Indo-Tibetan Mahayana Buddhist ethics; rather, I chose them for the depth and philosophical import of their discussions of the ways we come to feel with others.

1. Empathy as imaginative projection and cultivating compassion

First, a note on what I will not count as empathy in Buddhist ethical texts. I will diverge from Buddhologist Lambert Schmithausen and others who refer to Buddhist calls for impartiality between self and other as "empathy" (Schmithausen 2000; Taber 2013). Śāntideva, for example, makes such a case for impartiality: "I should dispel the suffering of others because it is suffering like my own suffering. I should help others too because of their nature as beings, which is like my own being" (Bodhicaryavatara (BCA) VIII.94). But this is essentially an argument, appealing to reason. Because it does not appeal to vicarious feeling – or feeling at all – I will not call this kind of reflection empathy, although it may be a precursor to empathy. (Śāntideva's argument directly precedes his discussion of "exchanging self and other," which is an empathy practice, as I argue in Section 2.)

I also do not consider the full range of ways we can vicariously feel with another, for example by mirroring or unconsciously imitating another's movements – as in Adam Smith's example of writhing and twisting when watching a tightrope walker (I.1.3) – or the subtle reading of micro-expressions. These cases of spontaneous and often unconscious simulation are not discussed at length in Indo-Tibetan Buddhist ethical texts (although they are taken up by contemporary psychologists interested in Buddhist meditation (Flanagan 2011, 45–9; Mascaro et al. 2013). Rather, these ethicists tend to employ empathic imaginative projection, projecting oneself, through one's imagination, into another's experience. This is perhaps because imaginative projection can be more obviously taught and cultivated, and explicit, intentional, moral self-cultivation is a core element of Indo-Tibetan Buddhist ethics.

Empathy as imaginative projection plays a significant role in two foundational Buddhist ethical practices: cultivating the Four Immeasurable Qualities (*tshad med bzhi*) and exchanging self and other (*bdag gzhan brje ba*). The Four Immeasurable Qualities are the main moral affective states in Buddhist ethics: love, compassion, sympathetic joy, and equanimity. They are called "immeasurable" (Tibetan: *tshad med*) because, with the proper training, one can increase one's capacity to feel them towards more and more sentient beings, whose numbers are immeasurable. I will focus here on compassion.

In Mahayana Buddhist ethics compassion (*karuna, snying rje*) is a complex moral virtue that includes being sensitive to and feeling with the suffering of others combined with the desire to alleviate that suffering and acting in accordance with that desire when possible. According to this tradition, it is not, as the moral sentimentalist theorist David Hume thought, a "calm" emotion; it is active and intensely felt. Patrul Rinpoche describes genuine compassion as "unbearable," making your heart "burst with the desire to do something right away," and filling your eyes with tears (202). Most Tibetan Buddhist compassion practices try to achieve this level of intensity by using empathic imaginative projection. Consider the following meditation by Patrul Rinpoche:

> Imagine a prisoner condemned to death by the ruler and being led to the place of execution, or a sheep being caught and tied up by the butcher. When you think of a condemned prisoner, instead of thinking of that suffering person as someone else, imagine that it is you. Ask yourself what you would do in that situation. What now? There is nowhere to run. Nowhere to hide. No refuge and no one to protect you. You have no means of escape. You cannot fly away. Now, at this very moment, all the perceptions of this life are about to cease. You will even have to leave behind your own dear body that you have sustained with so much care, and set out for the next life. What anguish! Train your mind by taking the suffering of that condemned prisoner upon yourself.
>
> *(201–2)*

Here we can see some explicit articulations of empathy as imaginative projection: "Imagine it is you," "Ask yourself what you would do in that situation," "Take the suffering of that condemned prisoner upon yourself." The assumption here is that this kind of empathic imaginative projection will stimulate compassion.

For Patrul Rinpoche, empathic imaginative projection need not be purely mental or abstract, despite relying on mental role-playing and inner imitation.

> Think carefully about these animals [who are about to be slaughtered]. Imagine that you yourself are undergoing that suffering and see what it is like. Cover your mouth with your hands and stop yourself breathing. Stay like that for a while. Experience the pain and the panic. When you have really seen what it is like, think again and again how sad it is that all those beings are afflicted by such terrible sufferings without a moment's respite.
>
> *(204)*

Here, more abstract imaginative projection is supplemented by a physical manipulation, covering one's own mouth to prevent breathing, in order to increase the intensity of the empathic resonance. The "experience the pain and the panic" is a direct command to empathize as a way into feeling compassion for "all those beings afflicted by such terrible sufferings."

Compassion in Buddhist ethics, then, employs empathy but does not reduce to empathy. Empathy is the moral skill, roughly understood as "feeling with another"; compassion is the emotional and conative response to the suffering. As such, it includes a certain kind of moral perception, moral reasoning, as well as certain habits of desire and action. But empathy plays a major role in compassion practices; it is what helps transition the moral agent from afflictive, self-centered emotionality (for example, of indifference or hatred) to a more virtuous emotionality. It can move us out of our habit of self-centeredness. If we are tempted to see another's suffering as not relevant to ourselves, Patrul Rinpoche simply suggests, "imagine it is you." This transition from the egocentric to an orientation sensitive to the needs of others is a major part of the Mahayana Buddhist conception of moral development, as is apparent in the ideal of *bodhicitta* (see Section 3).

2. "Exchanging self and other": empathy and dismantling narratives of self-clinging

"Exchanging self and other" (Tibetan: *bdag gzhan brje ba*) is a core moral concept in Buddhist ethics that utilizes empathetic imaginative projection in order to dismantle clinging to the self. It is a transformative practice that is designed to radically destabilize one's sense of self, and thus, it is claimed, liberate one from one's afflictive physical, mental, and emotional habits. One early and famous discussion of this practice is from Śāntideva's influential treatise *Bodhicaryāvatāra*, often translated as *A Guide to the Bodhisattva's Way of Life*, or *How to Live an Awakened Life*. Śāntideva advises identifying with an "inferior" (someone who has less than you, on some scale, for example power, privilege, virtue, health, or material wealth), identifying with an "equal" (someone who is comparable to you on some scale), and identifying with a "superior" (someone who has more than you on some scale). With regard to identifying with an inferior, Śāntideva writes:

> Creating a sense of self in respect of inferiors and others, and sense of other in oneself, imagine envy and pride with a mind free from false notions!
>
> *(VIII.140)*

The idea here is that one imagines oneself from the point of view of an "inferior," how one must seem to that person. One empathizes with the point of view of the "inferior" so thoroughly that one begins to see oneself as other, to the point where one actually feels envy towards *oneself* (who has now been othered). This is not an easy state to work oneself into (and one of the few times in Buddhist ethical literature that we are encouraged to cultivate envy and pride), but Śāntideva helpfully provides a script: "He is honored, not I. I do not receive such alms as he. He is praised. I am criticized. I suffer. He is happy. I do chores while he remains at ease. He, it seems, is great in the world. I, it seems, am an inferior, without virtues" (VIII.141–2). The "he" in this script is one's own self, now othered through empathy. This empathy practice allows one to gain distance from oneself and gives one the space to radically question one's own self-narratives. On Śāntideva's account, by seeing ourselves from the perspective of others, we will grow tired of, and even be repulsed by, our own self-clinging.

In later Tibetan commentaries, the practice of exchanging self and other is broadened to include so-called "taking on another's suffering," which is the practice of imaginatively exchanging one's own happiness and health and taking another's suffering and disease. Patrul Rinpoche describes this practice:

> ... look at a person actually suffering from sickness, hunger, thirst or some other affliction. Or, if that is not possible, imagine that such a person is in front of you. As you breathe out, imagine that you are giving that person all your happiness and the best of everything you have, your body, your wealth and your sources of merit, *just as if you were taking off your own clothes and dressing the other person in them*. Then, as you breathe in, imagine that you are taking into yourself all the other person's sufferings and that, as a result, he or she becomes happy and free from every affliction.
>
> *(223, my italics)*

In his commentary on this text, the twentieth-century Tibetan Buddhist scholar Khenpo (Abbot) Ngawang Pelzang makes the meditation even more vivid. He encourages us to first imagine one's own mother suffering:

> Imagine that this old mother of yours breathes out her suffering and its causes in the form of a stream of black vapor, and at the same time you inhale and it enters through your nostrils, so that now you have her suffering and its causes and she is freed of it all, just like the sun emerging from an eclipse.
>
> *(170)*

After exchanging self and mother, one gradually expands one's practice to include more and more members of the moral community.

These practices show that the exchanging self and other is not simply a heuristic for determining the limiting condition on action ("how would you like it if someone did that to you?") or a mental exercise in perspective taking. It is a transformative practice that uses empathic imaginative projection to chip away at self-clinging by softening the boundaries of self and other. The metaphors used encourage a dissolution of self/other boundaries: dressing another in one's own clothes and sharing breath with another (as in the Khenpo's meditation in which we inhale the very breath that the (m)other has exhaled) symbolize an intimacy that blurs the boundaries of identity. It does not seem coincidental, either, that one would start such a meditation with one's own mother, the person who, arguably, most shares in our identity (if only because her body literally created one's own body, a point that the Khenpo does not fail to make use of).

But if exchanging self and other is fundamentally about dissolving the (on the Buddhist view mistaken) categorical distinction between self and other, is it a practice of empathy at all? Empathy cannot entail a complete loss of sense of self, since, presumably, there needs to be an "other" for the "self" to empathize with. John Deigh has argued that what is "distinctive of empathy [is] that it requires imaginative participation in the other's life without forgetting oneself" (1995, 759). Perhaps exchanging self and other is a practice in what Max Scheler has called "emotional identification," in which "not only the separate process of feeling in another … is consciously taken as one's own, but his self (in all its basic attitudes) … is identified with one's own self" (2009, 18). Such identification – occurring during hypnosis, mystical experiences (to use Scheler's examples), or even Stockholm Syndrome – seems to put the one doing the identifying at some moral risk by making her vulnerable to manipulation through loss of moral agency. We may even worry that a complete identification with the other negates the moral import of empathy – if the other essentially becomes the self, are we really moving beyond the egocentric?

The fifteenth-century Tibetan philosopher Tsongkhapa pointed out that exchanging self and other is not a literal exchange – we are not thinking "I am others; Others are me." Through imaginative empathic projection we are reorienting ourselves emotionally, psychologically, and, importantly, morally. Tsongkhapa writes that the phrase "exchanging self and other" (*bdag gzhan rje ba*) "indicate[s] a change in the orientation of the two states of mind of cherishing yourself and neglecting others, wherein you develop the attitude of cherishing others as you presently do yourself and neglecting yourself as you presently do others" (2000, 53). So one intentionally disrupts one's habitual ways of identifying precisely to reorient one's patterns of desire, namely clinging to the self and indifference (or worse) towards others. There is no merger of self and other: I neither enlarge my sense of sense to include the other nor disown my self by identifying so completely with the other. Rather, exchanging self and other promotes a facility with identifying with others; after identifying with the "inferior," we swiftly move on to identifying with the "equal," and the "superior," and then back to our own, hopefully now morally reoriented, sense of self. Such fluidity allows one to see more clearly the afflictive mental states that arise from being so firmly anchored in one's narrow sense of who one is.

In Indo-Tibetan ethics, "afflictive mental states" (Sanskrit: *kleshas*, Tibetan: *nyon mongs*) is a technical term. It refers to a category of mental states that confuse us, feel out of our control (they "afflict"), and, if left untamed, cause harm to self and others. These include what in Western moral psychology would be called negative emotions, such as hatred, anger, obsessive craving, and states we would not typically categorize as affective, including ignorance, paralyzing doubt, and willfully holding on to a mistaken view. These afflictive states disturb one's own peace of mind, destroy mental health, motivate one to harm others, and make one oblivious to the real moral needs of self and others.

In Buddhist ethics, empathy practices – such as compassion and exchanging self and other – are some of the main ways by which we can reduce afflictive mental states. Compassion helps overcome cruelty and indifference, exchanging self and other corrects a morally problematic preoccupation with the self. Consider Patrul Rinpoche's commentary on Śāntideva's practice of exchanging self and other in BCA (V.140–56):

> We identify with the "inferior" and feel what such a person feels about us in order to give up envy. We identify with equal status person and feel what such a person would feel for us in order to give up competitiveness and rivalry. We identify with a "superior" and feel what that person feels toward us in order to give up pride.
>
> *(The Brightly Shining Sun, 5.ii.b)*

Empathizing with an "inferior" exposes the passive aggression and needless suffering of envy, which motivates giving up our own envy of others. Empathizing with a "superior" exposes the moral obliviousness of pride, making one's own pride seem embarrassing. With practice, these thinkers claim, we begin to see our own afflictive mental states as toxic and lose our attachment to them.

3. Empathy, *bodhicitta*, and altruism

Compassion and exchanging self and other are essential for cultivating the overarching moral ideal in Mahayana Buddhist ethics, *bodhicitta* (Tibetan: *byang chub*). Patrul Rinpoche, for example, calls the practice of exchanging self and others "the ultimate and unfailing quintessential meditation for all those who have set out on the path of the Mahayana teachings" (224). Compassion practices, he writes, "never fail to make us develop the extraordinary *bodhicitta*" (212). *Bodhicitta* is a radically altruistic moral orientation that centrally involves cultivating oneself in order to be the kind of person who can reliably, effectively, and wisely benefit others (Garfield 2011). The cultivation involved in becoming a person with *bodhicitta* – a *bodhisattva* (*byang chub sems dpa'*) – includes developing virtues such as patience, generosity, and wisdom, and moral skills such as mindfulness, moral reasoning, responsiveness, and, arguably, empathy (Garfield 2011; Garfield 2012). The empathy practices discussed above are traditionally presented in the context of cultivating *bodhicitta*, since empathy triggers both virtuous emotionality (through the Four Immeasurable Qualities practices) and the realization of no-self (through exchanging self and other practices), both of which are necessary for *bodhicitta*.

In Western and Buddhist moral psychology, empathy is widely regarded to be a foundational moral skill, and is often linked to altruism in both traditions (Deigh 1995; Sherman 1998; Sherman 2004). Given the role empathy plays in cultivating *bodhicitta* – a fundamentally altruistic ideal – it may seem that Buddhist ethics is committed to a strong empathy-altruism hypothesis, which seeks to explain the causal link between empathy and helping behavior (shown in the experiments of psychologist Dan Batson and others) by appeal to altruistic desire (Batson 1981; Batson 1998). But in Buddhist ethics the connection between empathy and altruism is complex. First, empathy is not directly linked to altruistic desires on this view; rather it helps develop compassion (and other positive emotionality) and reduces clinging to the self, which together help motivate one to help others. This may be true on Batson's model as well, since what he calls "empathy" includes a concern for the welfare of the other and is closer to Buddhist conceptions of compassion. Second, empathy does not act alone in strengthening positive emotionality and decreasing self-clinging; it works in conjunction with other skills and virtues such as wisdom, mindfulness, perceptiveness, and responsiveness.

It is also important to note that empathic imaginative projection in Buddhist ethics is not primarily linked to helping behaviors, but to the cultivation of the self as a moral agent. The cultivation of the self is a major part of becoming a *bodhisattva*, and one that can be easily overlooked if we think of *bodhicitta* simply in terms of altruism. Buddhist ethicists may agree with Peter Singer-type utilitarian arguments for radical generosity – in fact, the generosity encouraged by Śāntideva, for instance, makes Singer's position look somewhat self-indulgent – but the difference is that *bodhicitta* ethics is focused on becoming the kind of person who could actually alleviate suffering. Most of us understand that there is great and unbearable suffering in the world and that it would be better to alleviate that suffering than ignore or increase it. The moral problem, according to Buddhist ethics, is not that we do not understand what we should do, but we may not have the emotional and psychological resources to actually do it. The ideal of *bodhicitta* is becoming the kind of person (a *bodhisattva*) who has the psychological and emotional resources to adequately respond to suffering.

One of the basic assumptions – and, I would argue, insights – of Buddhist ethics is that most of us, most of the time, fail to adequately respond to suffering. This failure is not because we are especially bad people, or that human beings are inherently evil or selfish, but it is simply the result of the sheer amount of suffering that is part of the sentient condition (*samsara*) combined with the habits of thought, feeling, and action that make it difficult for most of us to respond to or sometimes even notice suffering. An appreciation of the myriad ways in which beings suffer and having an adequate response to that suffering is not a basic set of moral skills in Buddhist ethics; it is a rare moral accomplishment that requires a major transformation of our habitual ways of thinking, feeling, and acting. Empathy is one of the main ways by which this transformation can occur.

Buddhist ethicists, then, appear to be committed to an empathy-compassion hypothesis, the idea that empathic experience directly causes compassion, which is partly constitutive of *bodhicitta*. But empathic imaginative projection can come apart from compassionate response. As Max Scheler has argued, "This happens, for instance, where there is specific pleasure in cruelty … The cruel man owes his awareness of the pain or sorrow he causes entirely to a capacity for visualizing feeling! … As he feels, vicariously, the increasing pain or suffering of his victim, so his own primary pleasure and enjoyment at the other's pain also increases" (2009, 14). We need not even posit sadism to see how empathic projection may not lead to compassion, for instance in cases of "interrogators" who are masters of torturing others, not necessarily out of cruelty, but because they hope to obtain potentially helpful information (Biss 2014). To maximize their chance of extracting such information, these interrogators must understand the nuances of the victim's psychology, especially with regard to pain and distress, knowledge that vicarious feeling can provide.

The Buddhist ethical texts I discuss here do not specifically address the sadist's or the steely interrogator's unusual and morally problematic use of empathic experience. Nor do they consider the problem that someone may not be able to empathize at all, in any situation. This could be because such pathologies were not recognized or not thought important enough to mention. Or it could be because these ethical practices are designed for what Buddhist ethicists take to be the paradigmatic audience member for their work: the average human being (probably monastic, and, in many cases, male) who is interested in the moral and spiritual self-cultivation Buddhism offers. This is someone who suffers, probably more than he realizes, and is afflicted, but, simply because he is human, has great moral and spiritual potential; someone who cares about others – not impartially or as much as he cares about himself – but at least sometimes and in some ways; someone who can reason and feel. For such a person, empathic imaginative projection, it is reasonably assumed, will stimulate compassion. The real moral work on this view is to extend the sphere of those with whom we can empathize and, thus, feel compassion for.

But what about empathizing with people who do and feel terrible things? Is there any moral obligation to vicariously feel what a pedophile or rapist feels? Recall Patrul Rinpoche's discussion of empathizing with a death-row inmate. What is interestingly absent from his discussion is whether that prisoner deserves his sentence. This may seem like a glaring, and inexcusable, omission. But, I think, for Patrul Rinpoche, the question of whether the prisoner is guilty is not relevant to whether we should feel compassion for him (or empathize with him in order to stimulate that compassion). Presumably, it is relevant to how we should act toward him (by imprisoning him). In Indo-Tibetan Buddhist ethics, all suffering beings are proper objects of compassion, regardless of their criminal or moral history, which is not to say that they are therefore all treated the same. But, rather, the fact of suffering is always a morally relevant fact, even if it is not acted on because of more compelling or pressing moral considerations.

Because empathy (usually) aids in developing compassion, empathizing with the suffering of harm-doers (as they are called in some Buddhist texts) is appropriate, although clearly some care and caution is needed. We can empathize with the prisoner as a suffering being facing his imminent death without empathizing with the joy he may have taken in committing his crime. This is why empathy, as a moral skill, must be guided by *bodhicitta* and supported by other moral skills and virtues. For our empathy to help develop a wisely compassionate response or disposition, we must also be able to properly understand our situation (wisdom), perceive the salient features of situation (perception), and remember them (mindfulness), and effectively respond (responsiveness). It is the fact that empathy is guided by *bodhicitta* – constrained in some ways, expanded in others – that Buddhist ethicists explain the moral appropriateness of empathizing with, and eventually feeling compassion for, the suffering of harm-doers.

4. Conclusion: is empathy a trainable moral skill?

From the perspective of Western moral psychology, one of the striking features of Indo-Tibetan ethical practices is the assumption that we can, with training, improve our capacity for empathy and compassion. Psychologists Richard Davidson and Paul Ekman have noted that

> … an important difference between Buddhist and psychological approaches is that Buddhists provide a method for modifying affective states and cultivating *sukha* (happiness), whereas in psychology the only methods for changing enduring affective states are those that have been developed specifically to treat psychopathology … no effort has been invested in cultivating positive attributes of mind in individuals without mental disorders.
>
> *(Ekman et al. 2005, 61)*

In Buddhist ethics, as we have seen, serious effort has been invested in developing many practices designed to cultivate empathic skill, compassion, and other positive affective states. Recent psychological research supports the Buddhist assumption of the trainability of our emotions. It is now apparent that the neural networks in our brains can change in response to changes in our lives (a phenomenon known as neuroplasticity), and so we can modify our enduring affective traits through practice (Davidson & Begley 2012).

But Buddhist ethicists not only assume that we can cultivate empathic skill and positive emotionality, they also claim that there is no necessary limit to the degree or scope of our empathic experience or positive affective states; they can be felt boundlessly. Practices that require empathy, such as compassion and exchanging self and other, are designed so that, eventually, one is asked to empathize with and then feel compassion for any member of the moral community. "Start the meditation on giving happiness and taking suffering with one individual," Patrul Rinpoche advises, "and then gradually extend it to include all living creatures" (223).

But is it even possible for human beings to empathize impartially or universally? A moral ideal that does not take seriously the psychological limitations of human beings by making psychologically impossible demands is, presumably, not a good moral ideal. Is *bodhicitta* one such an impossible ideal? Is the expansive, empathic, imaginative projection that Buddhist ethicists assume is necessary for *bodhicitta* another one?

That Buddhist ethicists are sensitive to this worry is apparent in the ways that they take seriously the various psychological obstacles to empathizing. Recall Patrul Rinpoche's advice to increase one's empathy with animals about to be slaughtered by holding one's breath until one experiences pain and panic. Or Khenpo Ngawang Pelzang's suggestion that one visualize another's suffering as exhaled black vapor. These suggestions help one overcome the indifference, boredom, and distraction that may prevent empathic experience.

We also see a respect for psychological realism in the way that empathy practices are designed. One always begins by empathizing with someone for whom empathy comes easily, such as a family member. One slowly and gradually builds up one's capacity for empathy, empathizing with friends, strangers, animals, and, finally, enemies. Patrul Rinpoche warns against skipping the hard emotional work of empathizing in this gradual way and attempting to move right to empathizing with all sentient beings.

> When you start meditating on compassion, it is important to focus first on suffering beings individually, one at a time, and only then to train yourself step by step until you can meditate on all beings as a whole. Otherwise your compassion will be vague and intellectual. It will not be the real thing.
>
> *(202–3)*

But, gradually, over time (and lifetimes, in this tradition), with intentional practice, we can greatly increase our ability to empathize and feel "real" compassion.

Tsongkhapa claims that the current parochial limit to our ability to empathize with, feel compassion for, and benefit others is entirely due to "the influence of previous conditioning." This previous conditioning is a formidable obstacle, but, he claims, just as we can be conditioned for parochial empathy and partial compassion, we can, eventually, be conditioned for expansive empathy and impartial compassion. He uses the analogy of an enemy becoming a friend to explain this process:

… at first, when you heard even the name of your enemy, fear arose. Later you were reconciled and became such close friends that when this new friend was absent you were very unhappy. So, likewise, if you become habituated to viewing yourself as you presently view others and to viewing others as you presently view yourself, you will exchange self and other.

(2000, 52)

Tsongkhapa's everyday example – enemies becoming friends – highlights the fact that our ability to expand our sphere of concern is in many ways non-controversial: it is not uncommon to have an experience of coming to empathize with someone with whom we did not previously empathize. Even radical leaps of empathic ability, such as Tibetan prisoners who learn to empathize with and eventually feel compassion for their Chinese prison guards and, in some case, torturers, are not unheard of (Gyatso 1997).

But several empirical questions remain: Is it possible to expand one's empathy boundlessly, as is assumed by these practices (i.e. to include all sentient beings)? If that kind of expansion of empathy is possible, is it accomplished through training or are some rare individuals simply genetically predisposed to expansive empathy? If empathy can be expanded through practice, can it be expanded through these particular practices of the Four Immeasurable Qualities and exchanging self and other? At least some studies suggest that Buddhist compassion practices can increase one's ability to feel compassion and empathize with others, although, presumably, not boundlessly (Klimecki et al. 2013; Kristeller et al. 2005; Trautwein et al. 2013). One study found that long-term meditators on compassion are more sensitive to distressing stimuli than novice meditators, who are more sensitive still than meditation-naïve subjects (Mascaro et al. 2013; Lutz et al. 2008). Other studies suggest that long-term meditators on compassion have increased empathic skill, as measured by face-reading skills, which indicates that empathy and compassion form a sort of positive feedback loop (Mascaro et al. 2013; Flanagan 2011, 43–9). These studies, while fascinating, only provide evidence for Buddhist moral psychology's more modest claims, such as the claim that it is possible to change our affective habits with directed, long-term practice. But such studies have little to say about the more lofty claims of Buddhist moral psychology – the boundless nature of positive emotionality or the possibility of imaginatively exchanging oneself with another so thoroughly that one's sense of self is radically transformed. Clearly, more psychological research is needed to adequately assess the psychological plausibility of Buddhist accounts of empathic experience, compassion, and exchanging self and other.

In conclusion, empathy in Indo-Tibetan Buddhism is not a traditional category of psychological experience – at least not in a way that neatly lines up with contemporary Western accounts of empathy – but is clearly employed for the purposes of moral and spiritual cultivation, that is, for the cultivation of *bodhicitta*. *Bodhicitta* is a demanding moral ideal – as it includes wisdom, virtue, and boundless love, joy, and compassion – and empathy practices such as compassion and exchanging self and other provide the emotional and cognitive hook required to move us from an afflicted, self-centered perspective to one that recognizes and responds to the needs of others. The moral psychology underlying *bodhicitta* ethics requires that (i) our capacity for empathy can increase through intentional and disciplined training, (ii) there are no necessary limits on our capacity to empathize (and feel compassion), only the ever-changing limitations of previous conditioning, which can be undone, although not always easily, (iii) our capacity for empathy is currently vastly underutilized, and (iv) that, for most people, empathy helps cultivate compassion, which itself can be made boundless through training, and helps dismantle self-clinging.

References

Batson, C. D. 1998. "Altruism and prosocial behavior." In *Handbook of Social Psychology*, vol. 2, edited by D. T. Gilbert and S. T. Fiske, 282–316. Boston: McGraw-Hill.

Batson, C. D., et al. 1981. "Is empathic emotion a source of altruistic motivation?" *Journal of Personality and Social Psychology*, vol. 40: 290–302.

Biss, Mavis. 2014. "Empathy and interrogation." *International Journal of Applied Philosophy*, vol. 28, no. 2.

Darwall, Stephen. 1998. "Empathy, sympathy, and care." *Philosophical Studies: An International Journal of Philosophy in the Analytic Tradition*, 89: 261–82.

Davidson, Richard, and Sharon Begley. 2012. *The Emotional Life of Your Brain*. New York: Hudson Street Press.

Davidson, Richard, and Anne Harrington. 2002. *Visions of Compassion: Western Scientists and Tibetan Buddhists Examine Human Nature*. New York: Oxford University Press.

Deigh, John. 1995. "Empathy and universalizability." *Ethics*, vol. 105, no. 4: 743–63.

Ekman, Paul, et al. 2005. "Buddhist and psychological perspectives on emotion and well-being." *Current Perspectives in Psychological Science*, vol. 14, no. 2: 59–63.

Flanagan, Owen. 2011. *The Bodhisattva's Brain: Buddhism Naturalized*. Cambridge: MIT Press.

Garfield, Jay. 2011. "What is it like to be a bodhisattva? Moral phenomenology in Śāntideva's Bodhicaryāvatāra." *Smith Philosophy Department*. February 8. www.smith.edu/philosophy/docs/garfield_bodhisattva.pdf (accessed October 20, 2014).

Garfield, Jay. 2012. "Mindfulness and ethics: attention, virtue and perfection." *Thai International Journal of Buddhist Studies*, vol. 3: 1–24.

Gyatso, Palden. 1997. *The Autobiography of a Tibetan Monk*. New York: Grove Press.

Heim, Maria. 2008. "Buddhism on the emotions." In *Oxford Handbook of Religion and Emotion*, 190–210. New York: Oxford University Press.

Klimecki, O. M., et al. 2013. "Functional neural plasticity and associated changes in positive affect after compassion training." *Cerebral Cortex*, vol. 23, no. 7: 1552–61.

Kristeller, J. L., et al. 2005. "Cultivating loving-kindness: a two stage model of the effects of meditation on empathy, compassion, and altruism." *Zygon*, vol. 40, no. 2: 381–408.

Lutz, A., et al. 2008. "Regulation of the neural circuitry of emotion by compassion training: effects of meditative expertise." *PLoSOne*, vol. 3, no. 3: e1897.

Mascaro J. S., et al. 2013. "Compassion meditation enhances empathic accuracy and related neural activity." *Social Cognitive Affective Neuroscience*, vol. 8, no. 1: 48–55.

Motluk, A. 2001. "Read my mind." *New Scientist*, January: 22–8.

Patrul, Rinpoche. 1994. *The Words of My Perfect Teacher*. Translated by Padmakara Translation Group. San Francisco, CA: Harper Collins.

Pelzang, Khenpo Ngawang. 2004. *A Guide to the Words of My Teacher*. Translated by Padmakara Translation Group. Boston: Shambala.

Prinz, Jesse. 2011. "Against empathy." *The Southern Journal of Philosophy*, vol. 49, no. 1: 214–33.

Rifkin, Jeremy. 2009. *The Empathic Civilization*. New York: Penguin.

Rinpoche, Patrul. "The Brightly Shining Sun." www.lotsawahouse.org/tibetan-masters/patrul-rinpoche/bodhicharyavatara-brightly-shining-sun

Śāntideva. 1995. *The Bodhicaryāvatāra*. Translated by Kate Crosby and Andrew Skilton. Oxford: Oxford University Press.

Scheler, Max. 2009. *The Nature of Sympathy*. London: Routledge & Kegan Paul.

Schmithausen, Lambert. 2000. *A Note on the Origin of Ahimsa*. Reinbek: Verlag für Orientalistische Fachpublikationen.

Sherman, Nancy. 1998. "Empathy and imagination." *Midwest Studies in Philosophy*, vol. 22: 83–119.

Sherman, Nancy. 2004. "Empathy and the family." *Acta Philosophica*, vol. 13, no. 1: 23–44.

Taber, John. 2013. "Engaging philosophically with Indian philosophical texts." *Asiatische Studien Etudes Asiatiques*, vol. 67, no. 1: 125–64.

Thomson, Helen. 2010. "Empathic mirror neurons found in humans at last." *New Scientist*, April, www.newscientist.com/article/mg20627565-600-empathetic-mirror-neurons-found-in-humans-at-last/.

Titchner, E. 1909. *Experimental Psychology of the Thought Process*. New York: Macmillan.

Trautwein, F. M., et al. 2013. "Meditation effects in the social domain: self-other connectedness as a general mechanism." In *Meditation: Neuroscientific Approaches and Philosophical Implications*, edited by Stephan Schmidt and Harold Walsh, 175–98. Dordrecht: Springer.

Tsongkhapa. 2000. *The Great Treatise of the Stages of the Path to Enlightenment*. Ithaca, NY: Snow Lion.

PART III

Empathy and understanding

12

EMPATHY AND UNDERSTANDING REASONS

Karsten R. Stueber

There is widespread agreement among philosophers that behavior of rational agents qualifies as an intentional action if it can be explained in terms of an agent's reasons for acting. As Anscombe has famously remarked, intentional actions "are the actions to which a certain sense of the question 'Why?' is given application; the sense is of course that in which the answer, if positive, gives a reason for acting." And yet that definition is not fully transparent since, as she points out, "the question 'What is the relevant sense of the question "Why"' and 'What is meant by "reason for acting"?' are one and the same" (Anscombe 1957, 9). What is particularly perplexing about the nature of reasons is their bewildering duality. Reasons do not merely explain the occurrence of an action. They also constitute considerations that speak for an action and justify its occurrence within a variety of normative dimensions. Already Plato had trouble trying to account for the nature of such reasons, but ever since the scientific revolution the task has become especially difficult. From a scientific perspective it is almost impossible to identify ontologically acceptable features of the physical world and human beings within that world, which can play both the explanatory and evaluative role required for agents to be guided by their reasons in acting. All that we seem to find are causes and their effects but no reasons needed in order to normatively justify the actions of rational agency (see Turner 2010).

It is exactly within this context, and partly in reaction to the predominance of the scientific perspective, that philosophers have appealed to empathy in order to explicate further what it means for agents to act for reasons and to evaluate each other in terms of such reasons. Paradigmatic examples in this respect are the moral sentimentalists in the eighteenth century, particularly David Hume (1978 [1739]) and Adam Smith (1982 [1759]), the philosophers of history of the nineteenth and twentieth century (Droysen 1977, Dilthey 1961, and Collingwood 1946), and their successors within the contemporary metaethical and social cognition debate. The following discussion of the role of empathy in accounting for rational agency, and in allowing us to understand the nature of reasons, does not claim to be a comprehensive account of the twists and turns of the rather complex discussion of these controversial claims about empathy within the history of philosophy (see Stueber 2008/ 2014 in this respect). Rather, we will explore more systematically the claim that we can make sense of the notions of reasons for acting only in light of our empathic capacities. For that purpose, we will first identify the appropriate manner of understanding the concept of empathy within this context. In the second section, we will explain why empathy has been regarded as playing an epistemically central role in folk psychological reason explanations. We will conclude the chapter by indicating how empathy could also be thought of as playing a central role in conceiving of normative reasons.

1. Explicating the concept of empathy

As has often been noticed, the concept of empathy covers a rather wide range of related, but relatively distinct, psychological phenomena. Depending on their specific interests, researchers define empathy idiosyncratically in terms of the phenomenon they happen to focus on. Yet one should not forget that there is some system to this conceptual quagmire. Empathy-related phenomena have been the topic of a sustained philosophical discussion ever since the Enlightenment period (particularly within the Scottish Enlightenment), when philosophers and psychologists became interested in understanding the psychological mechanisms underlying human sociality and started to investigate how it is possible for individual human beings to care for one another, to know what the other person is thinking and feeling, and to evaluate each other from a normative and moral perspective. (For a detailed history of the empathy concept see Stueber 2008 and Coplan 2011. For a comprehensive history of the precursor concept of sympathy see Schliesser 2015.)

Even if there is no agreement about how to define empathy, the contemporary empathy literature distinguishes empathy proper from emotional contagion, sympathy, and personal distress, and regards them as distinct psychological phenomena (see Chapter 2, "Affective Empathy"). All of these phenomena are caused by observing or thinking about the situation, mental states, and feelings of another person. They can, however, be distinguished in terms of how aware the observer is of that causal history and the intentional object of his mental states so caused (see also the introduction in Maibom 2014). Sympathy and personal distress are seen as emotional reactions that, in contrast to empathy and emotional contagion, do not recreate the sentiments of the other person. In sympathizing with the hardship of another person I have to know about his hardship, but I do not necessarily have to feel or think the way he does. I am primarily concerned with the welfare of the other person. Similarly, in being personally distressed about other people's misfortune I do not share their emotions. In contrast to sympathy, I think, however, about their misfortune as something that constitutes a distressing state of affairs for my own wellbeing, since it constitutes a nuisance I have to deal with.

On the other hand, emotional contagion and empathy are understood as resonance phenomena in that the mind of the observer is resonating with or recreating another person's state of mind in his or her own mind. In emotional contagion we merely catch the emotion of another person, such as when we become happy in a room full of happy people or feel sad when surrounded by sadness, but without being aware of the fact that it is the other person's state of mind that makes us feel a certain way. Proper empathy, and in this respect all researchers on that topic concur, presupposes an awareness of the difference between self and other. I am in some sense aware that I experience or think in a certain manner because of my paying attention to another person's state of mind. Yet scholars differ in how exactly they fine-tune this general understanding of empathy. Coplan (2011) and Jacob (2011), for example, require that the empathizer recreate affective states that are isomorphic or sufficiently similar to the mental states of the person empathized with. Martin Hoffman (2000) suggests that we can also speak of empathy when we have feelings that are "more congruent with another person's situation" than our own, even if that person does not feel that way. Thus, we can talk about empathizing with another person when we feel an emotion that this person might feel if he were not ignorant about a specific aspect of his situation. (Think, for example, about a person who is seriously ill but has not been told about his condition.)

Prima facie, defining the concept of empathy mainly in terms of affective mental states seems to conform to our conception of empathy within ordinary language. This conception has been influenced by decade-long research in social psychology investigating the link between empathy or empathy-related phenomena and prosocial behavior, since in this context one focused on mental states that involve a motivational component. Nevertheless, in thinking about empathy as the fundamental method for understanding other minds, as proposed by Lipps (1907), or as the method uniquely suited for the historical and human sciences (Collingwood 1946, Dray 1957), scholars tended to have a much broader conception of empathy. They thought of it as the ability to recreate and resonate with any mental state of another person, regardless of whether or not that state included an affective component. Within the context of the contemporary discussion about the underlying mechanisms of social cognition, Goldman (2006) and Stueber (2006) continue to conceive of empathy in this more liberal sense. They also understand empathy as a resonance phenomenon involving different levels of cognitive complexity. More specifically, they distinguish between a developmentally early form of empathy referred to as *mirroring or basic empathy* – whose neurobiological basis is often understood as being provided by so-called mirror neurons – and a cognitively and developmentally more advanced form of *reconstructive, reenactive, or complex* empathy asking us to imaginatively take the perspective of another person (Goldman 2011, Stueber 2006, and Hollan 2014).

Accordingly, one should not expect to find the one correct definition of the concept of empathy that articulates all of its necessary and sufficient conditions. Rather, in adopting a conception of empathy one should make sure that it is clearly articulated, is a reasonable one in light of its discussion in the history of philosophy and psychology, and most importantly, is an illuminating one in regard to the chosen subject matter one wants to study (see also Batson 2009). Given these constraints, the type of empathy most naturally suited for the exploration of its role in understanding reasons and understanding agents acting for reasons is the cognitively more advanced form of reenactive empathy. Regardless of the controversy over how exactly mirror neurons contribute to social cognition – philosophers from the phenomenological tradition, for example, completely reject that idea (Overgaard and Zahavi 2012) – it is generally agreed that more basic forms of empathy allow us at most to grasp the type of emotion that is revealed in one's facial expressions or the goal-directedness of a bodily movement; that the hand is reaching for the glass, for example (see Stueber 2012, and Chapter 5 in this volume, "Empathy and Mirror Neurons"). However, it does not allow us to understand the reasons why an agent behaves a certain way, why a person has those emotions, and in what sense those emotions are indicative of his reasons for acting. Accordingly, if empathy is central for understanding those reasons, it is has to be a form of empathy that does not merely arise, as Adam Smith expresses it, "from the view of the passions, as from the situation which excites it" (Smith 1759/1982, 12). It is this form of reenactive empathy, which asks us to imaginatively put ourselves in the situation of the other person, that we will be dealing with in the next two sections, where we explore empathy's contribution to understanding reasons.

2. Empathy and folk-psychological reason explanations

In ordinary discourse we can identify the reasons for which a person acted in two ways. We refer to various mental states of the agent or we mention a specific state of affairs or an agent's goals. We point out, for example, that a student enrolled in a particular course because he wanted to fulfill a requirement and because he believed he could get an easy A. We might, however, just say that he enrolled in the course because it fulfills a certain requirement or in order to get an easy A. Within the recent philosophical literature there has been an intense discussion about which of the above idioms should be regarded as being primary in indicating the reasons for which somebody acts. According to the Davidsonian orthodoxy, one should think of mental states (particularly a specific belief/desire pair) as primary reasons for acting because only then can one also understand reasons as motivating causes of a person's action. On the other hand, it is a bit odd to identify mental states with reasons for acting since, most often, they do not normatively justify my action. If I falsely believe that the class satisfies a requirement or would allow me to get an easy A, I ultimately do not have any reason for taking this class. But then it is not my belief that p that provides me with a reason, but rather the reason is constituted by what makes my belief true, namely the fact that p. Similarly, if what I desire does not also possess some value, it seems my desire on its own does not really provide me with a reason for acting. Accordingly, some authors have argued that mental states should never be understood as reasons for actions. Rather reality itself provides us with reasons, which are grounded in "how things are and what is of value and not by (relations to) our beliefs and desires" (Dancy 2003, 423. See also Darwall 1983, Dancy 2000, Bittner 2001, and Alvarez 2010).

A detailed discussion of the above arguments and conceptions of reasons is certainly beyond the scope of this chapter (for a survey see Wiland 2012). It needs to be pointed out however that bifurcating the notion of a reason – as is quite common in the literature (Smith 1994) – and distinguishing between the psychological states of agents as their motivating reasons (dealt with in the philosophy of action) on the one hand, and facts or values as the normative reasons (to be addressed by meta-ethicists) on the other, is equally misleading. It suggests that motivating and normative reasons belong to different ontological categories. If that is so, it is no longer clear why normative reasons can be regarded as standards that provide appropriate criteria for the evaluation of rational agents, standards in light of which we directly address the agent. After all, we expect rational agents to be able to say something for their actions and to justify them on some level. Obviously, agents might be mistaken about the normative status of their subjective considerations and their behavior can be criticized for it. In order for objective normative reasons to constitute grounds for such criticism, they have to be considerations that could have been reasons for which agents actually acted. Accordingly, it might be best to conceive of a person's reasons for acting as a special ontological category such as dicta or things that can be said for an action (Darwall 1983), as potential states of affairs, or as propositions constituting the content of a person's psychological states.

Following Setiya (2007), one can then agree that it is literally incorrect to identify reasons for acting directly with what is in an agent's head or mind, that is, with his or her psychological states. At the same time, folk-psychological explanations purport to identify mental states in light of which an agent is subjectively attuned to considerations that speak for his actions and that play a causal role in bringing about his actions. It is exactly in this manner that folk-psychological explanations provide reason explanations and show the agent, as Davidson suggests, in "his role as rational animal," since it is in light of those beliefs and desires that we understand that there is "something to be said for the action, at least from the agent's point of view" (Davidson 1963, 8–9). In the remaining part of this section we will focus on the central involvement of empathy in understanding an agent's subjective reasons for acting before addressing the relation between empathy and normative reasons in the next section.

The claim that reenactive empathy plays an epistemically central role in understanding an agent's reason for acting has been defended most systematically by simulation theorists within the context of the so-called theory of mind debate; a debate concerned with delineating the underlying psychological mechanisms of making sense of other people with the help of the conceptual repertoire of folk psychology (see Chapter 1, "Cognitive Empathy"). Simulation theorists, in contrast to theory theorists, maintain that we do not utilize theoretical knowledge or rely on folk-psychological generalizations for these purposes. Rather, we use ourselves as a model with the help of our imaginative capacities and recreate another person's thought processes in our own mind (see Gordon 1995, Goldman 2006, Heal 2003, and Stueber 2006). In order for such simulation or reenactment to provide us with a reliable means for knowing other minds, it has to be sensitive to the relevant differences between the person empathized with and the empathizer. At a minimum we have to recreate another person's psychological perspective in our mind by imaginatively adopting some of his mental attitudes that we do not share with him and by quarantining some of the mental attitudes that he does not share with us, so that they do not interfere with our simulation.

In this context, psychologists also speak of two different forms of perspective taking and distinguish between self-oriented – imagining how oneself would feel or act in another person's situation – and other-oriented perspective taking – imagining how the other person would feel or act in his situation. For simulation theorists, the requirement of being sensitive to relevant differences between persons cuts across this distinction. In cases of overwhelming similarity, for example, self-oriented perspective taking is normally sufficient to satisfy this requirement. If both you and I are parents (come from the same cultural background and so on), imagining how I would feel and what I would do if my child were in a serious car accident is in all likelihood a reliable way of figuring out how you would feel and act. Yet, in other cases where such similarity does not exist, a more careful other-oriented approach is required.

In support of their position, simulation theorists have relied on both empirical and more a priori armchair arguments. They have suggested that it is very unlikely that humans could from a very young age onwards have acquired all of the very detailed theoretical knowledge required for understanding other people in all kinds of possible situations as theory theorists suppose. It is much more economical to assume that they use themselves as models in order to make sense of the other. Some simulation theorists have even appealed to neurobiological evidence in order to buttress their case (Currie & Ravenscroft 2002, Goldman 2006). More importantly, however, a number of authors have argued for the epistemic centrality of reenactive empathy in a more a priori manner. They emphasize that understanding a thought as a reason for acting requires situating that thought appropriately within a larger context of an agent's other mental states and the relevant aspects of the situation that the agent is aware of (Heal 2003, Stueber 2006). Consider and contrast in this respect our explanation of Peter going to the store in terms of his wanting to eat ice cream with an explanation that attempts to explain his behavior of going into the yard by referring to his desire to count every single blade of grass. In the latter case, we have difficulties understanding the explanatory force of the purported explanation because we have difficulties grasping how such a desire could indicate a consideration that speaks in favor of the action. In order to grasp it as a reason, we would have to hear a bit more about his other attitudes and beliefs (maybe he has been offered a huge sum of money for counting the blades of grass or somebody threatened his life).

It should be noticed that once additional information is provided, we grasp almost effortlessly how a thought fits in with other thoughts and can be understood as a reason for acting. In light of this information, we now know how to think more specifically about the mental framework of the other person, and how to integrate the mental attitude included in the attempted explanation of his behavior. In the first example of explaining the action in terms of a desire for ice cream, we do not need additional information because we assume that the other person shares most of our beliefs and attitudes. We also know how such a desire fits in with our other attitudes and is indicative of a consideration that speaks in favor of going to the store.

Nevertheless, one should be aware of the potential magnitude of this task of knowing how to appropriately integrate a mental state with all of our other mental attitudes in the appropriate manner. If we would have to consider all of them in their totality for that very purpose, it seems we would never be able to accomplish this task, or at least not very quickly, given our limited cognitive capacities. We therefore have to somehow grasp which smaller subset among the vast set of our mental states is relevant to consider in a particular context. Prima facie, we grasp that thoughts about China or Chinese philosophy do not seem to be relevant for considering and reflecting on whether to eat ice cream or to count all the blades of grass, unless we are organizing our lives according to Chinese philosophy. To solve the problem of relevance means to solve what, within research in artificial intelligence, is commonly referred to as the frame problem. To use Fodor's terminology, to identify the relevant aspects of our belief set means to be able to put a frame around them. Yet where to put the frame seems to be an irreducibly open-ended and contextual affair, not an activity that can be conceived of as the application of a theory or a theoretical algorithm, and certainly not a theory articulated in folk-psychological terminology (see Fodor 1983 and 2000, Henderson & Horgan 2000).

Aristotelian and Wittgensteinian rule-following considerations point in the same direction. Even following a simple rule like the rule of politeness telling us to hold the door open requires practical know-how of how to apply the general rule to specific circumstances. We must judge how far away the person is, take into account his or her physical abilities, age, handicaps, and conflicting normative commitments such as not wasting energy by holding the door open for too long. Certainly we can always formulate a rule more precisely, but ultimately such reformulations will still make use of general terms that need to be applied in concrete situations. The point of a rule is to guide behavior in a variety of yet unforeseen contexts, requiring agents to make the proper kinds of judgment. It is only in light of such practical capacities that we can also understand how an agent's commitment to rules provides him with reasons for acting in a particular situation (Stueber 2005).

Accordingly, understanding another person's reasons for acting – integrating his thoughts in the relevant way in a larger set of mental states – is possible only by activating our own practical capacities for making such judgments in light of the relevant and salient features of the situation that we and the other agent are aware of. We understand another person's reason only if we understand them as reasons that we could potentially have in the agent's situation, that is if we could imagine and reenact his reasons as our reasons. Ordinarily within the same cultural context such understanding proceeds effortlessly because we can just assume that agents are very similar to us and we grasp automatically that we would have acted in the same manner just by looking at the situation that the agent faces (in terms of a self-oriented form of perspective taking). At other times, when the other person comes from a very different background, for instance, such reenactment requires more effort. It also requires additional information about the relevant differences between us and the person we try to empathize with in order to be able to know how exactly to recreate his psychological perspective in our minds.

It is indeed true that within the original theory of mind debate, simulation theorists did not sufficiently emphasize this fact (see however Stueber 2006, chap. 6). To stress that further information about relevant differences between individuals is necessary might have muddied the water. In this respect, so-called narrativists (Gallagher & Hutto 2008) who criticize both simulation and theory theorists of distorting our capacity for social cognition have a point. Without such information, reenactive empathy on its own might not get off the ground, at least in a manner that would provide us with reliable means of knowing the other person's thought processes and reasons for action. Yet, admitting that we need further information for such purposes is not equivalent to admitting that such information makes the need for our empathic and reenactive capacities superfluous (Stueber 2008). Rather, the required narrative information about relevant differences is better understood as guiding us to appropriately take up the perspective of the other person. Moreover, one can admit that understanding the development of an individual person, his narrative so to speak, provides us with a deeper understanding of the larger significance of his decisions and actions without admitting that understanding such narratives proceeds independent of empathy. Narrativists, at least within the context of the discussion of social cognition, seem to take such narrative understanding as a form of understanding that cannot be further analyzed. Yet understanding a narrative implies grasping how the various events within that narrative hang together and are causally related. If the above argument is correct, this is possible only in light of the activation of our reenactive capacities, which allow us to understand the reasons for which an individual acted at specific times and circumstances (see Bittner 2001, Hutto 2008, and Stueber 2015).

To conclude this section, it is worth stressing three points. First, the above argument for the epistemic centrality of reenactive empathy in our understanding of subjective reasons and folk-psychological reason explanations is best understood as an argument for empathy being necessary for our grasping an agent's considerations as reasons for acting. Further information might be necessary to know how exactly to use our imaginative capacities to recreate another person's perspective. Moreover, empathic perspective taking is not sufficient for distinguishing between two prima facie equally plausible hypotheses about the reasons for which a person might have acted. Did a person, for instance, go to the store because he wanted to buy ice cream or because he wanted to challenge the amount charged for items that he bought before? We are certainly able to imagine both considerations as reasons in the appropriate circumstances. In order to decide the above interpretive question we need to appeal to further evidence about how plausible it is that an agent has certain psychological states in light of information about his biographical, cultural, or social context. Even information about his state of health might be helpful here. Yet again, appealing to such information does not make reenactive empathy superfluous because we are deciding between two interpretive hypotheses, whose prima facie plausibility can be established only in light of our empathic capacities.

Second, arguing that reenactive empathy is epistemically central and necessary for understanding reasons for acting should not be conceived as requiring that the empathizer become the other person, as Goldie (2011) seems to think. As indicated in the last section, empathy always requires an awareness of the distinction between self and other, and it is in light of this awareness that understanding other persons and their reasons for acting takes place. To think or wish otherwise is like wishing for a square circle for Christmas.

Finally, the above considerations should not be taken to imply that folk-psychological explanations constitute the whole realm of social cognition, or that every facet of human behavior can be explained by indicating an agent's subjective reasons for acting. Indeed, such a claim is rather counterintuitive as we often explain why somebody used his left hand to sign the contract by pointing out that he is left-handed. Normally we do not have reasons to use either our right or left hands. Accordingly, the above considerations are best understood as showing that the domain of folk-psychological explanations is circumscribed by our capacity for reenactive empathy and that whenever we do use such folk-psychological explanations, we use our empathic capacities.

3. Empathy and normative reasons

Our discussion so far has concentrated on an agent's subjective reasons for acting. Yet such subjective reasons might not be sufficient to fully justify an agent's actions, such as when he violates a moral norm for purely egoistic reasons. In that case one could say that a person's subjective reasons for acting fall short of being objectively normative reasons. Normative reasons are thus reasons that an agent has regardless of whether or not he also acts for these reasons. One might say that the fact that a person is in need always constitutes a normative reason for helping that person, even if one does not recognize that the person is in need. In talking about normative reasons, philosophers do not merely refer to moral reasons. Rather, normative reasons are any considerations that speak objectively for a certain kind of behavior independent of whether the agent herself recognizes it. In this respect the thinness of the ice and the fact that smoking causes cancer also constitute normative reasons not to walk on the ice and not to smoke.

Philosophers differ in regard to whether they view normative reasons as part of the ultimate furniture of the universe, as realists assert, or whether they regard them as constituted by our responses towards our environment, as anti-realist are inclined to think. Moreover, so-called reason internalists like Bernard Williams (1979) assert that the notion of a normative reason is essentially linked to an agent's set of psychological states, which motivate him to act, whereas reason externalists deny that claim and regard the relation between normative reasons and an agent's motivational states to be a contingent one (see the articles in Setiya and Paakunainen 2012). Here is certainly not the place to fully address the above issues, since they are part of a rather complex, far-reaching, and ongoing philosophical debate. But the question of whether or not empathy is also involved in understanding the nature of normative reasons is highly influenced by the philosophical choices one makes regarding realism and internalism in regard to the nature of reasons. From a historical perspective the claim that empathy is also relevant for understanding normative reasons (and not merely subjective reasons for acting) has its home in philosophical positions committed to moral anti-realism and internalism. More specifically, it can be traced back to the moral sentimentalism of the eighteenth century, particularly to David Hume and Adam Smith. Both of them have argued that it is in light of our empathic and sympathetic abilities to recreate the pleasure and pain of others (Hume) or their sentiments/reasons for feeling and acting a certain way (Smith) that we evaluate the moral appropriateness of particular types of actions and are provided with normative reasons. It is in this manner, they argued, that other people and their fate can be grasped as something that is of motivating concern for us. Given that we tend to empathize more with people whom we perceive to be similar to us, Hume and Smith introduced the idea of a general point of view or the impartial spectator perspective to account for the universality of moral reasons and judgments. The need of another person is thus a normative reason to help because we empathize with such a person from the impartial spectator perspective, a perspective where we abstract away from the fact that the involved person is our friend or our enemy, belongs to the same nationality, class, race, and so on.

Even if moral sentimentalism is an appealing option for some philosophers within contemporary meta-ethics, moral sentimentalism and the claim that empathy is constitutively involved in moral judgment and moral reasons is certainly a controversial thesis. It has been long challenged by philosophers committed to a more Kantian conception of morality and by a variety of philosophers committed to moral realism or realism about normative reasons. Moral realists have tended to regard the existence of moral reasons to be independent of the stances that humans take towards each other and have most often appealed to intuition or the method of reflective equilibrium as the main epistemic means for recognizing such reasons (Audi 2004, Scanlon 2014, Shafer-Landau 2003). Nevertheless, it needs to be pointed out that realism is logically compatible with claiming that our empathic capacity can play an epistemic role in recognizing normative reasons that are independently constituted (see also Oxley 2011). According to that line of thinking, one might conceive of another person's pain as a reason for helping to alleviate that pain, but at the same time maintain that only our empathic capacities allow us to recognize such a reason. Even people who lack our empathic abilities – like psychopaths – would therefore have a normative reason to alleviate the pain of another person. They would, however, be unable to recognize it, and one might therefore question whether they should be held morally responsible for their actions (see Chapter 21, "Empathy and Moral Responsibility").

On the other hand, realists and externalists about normative reasons tend not say very much about what it is that makes a fact an appropriate standard for the evaluation of a person's behavior. To use a slightly different terminology, they do not explicate the conditions under which a state of affairs is a reason that a person owns (Broom 2007) and in light of which it constitutes a normative obligation for the agent. Scanlon, for instance, seems to explicitly reject such concerns by suggesting that it is "nonsensical to ask what reason do we have to do what we have reasons to do" (2014, 98). Yet in taking such a stance Scanlon ultimately seems to fall short of philosophically elucidating a central assumption about our discourse about normative reasons, that is, that it is a discourse with broad intersubjective applicability. That very assumption (and thus the assumption of the reality of normative reasons) is something that needs to be explicated, since a central difficulty in evaluating an agent's behavior consists in deciding which reasons he or she owns. Without a philosophical response to this problem it seems we would have no way of distinguishing between a critical evaluation of an agent's behavior that is merely imposed from the external perspective of the interpreter, and an evaluation of it in terms of normative reasons to which, in some sense, the agents themselves subscribe.

As an example, one only needs to think of the rationality debate in the philosophy of social science and anthropology in the 1970s. This debate can be easily reframed as being about the nature of normative reasons that more "primitive" cultures can be appropriately understood to be obliged to respond to (see Wilson 1970). Are the facts, for example, that reveal themselves as reasons from the scientific perspectives also reasons that the Azande, with their commitment to systems of magic and witchcraft, can be reasonably said to own? Looked at it from this perspective, it seems as if the main argument for the involvement of reenactive empathy outlined in the last section carries over to the realm of normative reasons. Even normative reasons are ultimately reasons that an agent owns in the specific context in which he acts. Normative reasons have to be considerations that are normatively relevant in the specific context within which the agents act. Which reasons we normatively own is thus a question that can only be decided and negotiated from a perspective that takes into account the practical and deliberative perspectives of the agent and the interpreter. At the same time it has to be a perspective that is aware of the potential limitations and biases in the agent's and interpreter's points of view. It is a stance that requires not only the use of reenactive empathy, but also a commitment to impartiality, as the moral sentimentalist have suggested. It is in this manner that one might argue that empathy plays a central role in maintaining our discourse about objective normative reasons (see Stueber 2016, and the contributions by Debes, Kauppinnen, and Stueber in Debes & Stueber forthcoming).

Accordingly, empathy is not only centrally involved in our grasp of an agent's subjective reasons in terms of which we explain his or her actions, as I have argued in section 2. Such explanatory reasons have certainly been the main focus of the debate about the epistemic relevance of empathy in the nineteenth and twentieth century. Yet if we accept the suggestions in this section, empathy has also to be granted an important role in the elucidation of the domain of normative reasons. For it is only in light of our empathic capacities that we can comprehend to what specific objective reasons a rational agent is obliged to respond.

References

Alvarez, M. (2010) *Kinds of Reasons: An Essay in the Philosophy of Action*. Oxford: Oxford University Press.

Anscombe, G. E. M. (1957/2000) *Intention*. Cambridge, Mass.: Harvard University Press.

Audi, R. (2004) *The Good and the Right: A Theory of Intuition and Intrinsic Value*. Princeton: Princeton University Press.

Batson, D. (2009) "These Things Called Empathy: Eight Related but Distinct Phenomena," in J. Decety and W. Ickes (eds.), *The Social Neuroscience of Empathy*, 3–15. Cambridge, Mass.: MIT Press.

Bittner, R. (2001) *Doing Things for Reasons*. Oxford: Oxford University Press.

Broome, J. (2007) "Does Rationality Consist in Responding Correctly to Reasons?," *Journal of Moral Philosophy* 4, 349–74.

Coplan, A. (2011) "Understanding Empathy: Its Features and Effects," in A. Coplan and P. Goldie (eds.), *Empathy: Philosophical and Psychological Perspectives*, 3–18. Oxford: Oxford University Press.

Collingwood, R. G. (1946) *The Idea of History*. Oxford: Clarendon Press.

Currie, G., & I. Ravenscroft (2002) *Recreative Minds*. Oxford: Clarendon Press.

Dancy, J. (2000) *Practical Reality*. Oxford: Oxford University Press.

Dancy, J. (2003) "Précis of Practical Reality," *Philosophy and Phenomenological Research* 67, 423–8.

Darwall, S. (1983) *Impartial Reason*. Ithaca, NY: Cornell University Press.

Davidson, D. (1963/1980) "Actions, Reasons, and Causes," in *Essays on Actions and Events*, 3–19. Oxford: Oxford University Press.

Debes, R. & K. Stueber (eds.) (forthcoming). *Moral Sentimentalism*. Cambridge: Cambridge University Press.

Dilthey, W. (1961) *Gesammelte Schriften*, 15 vols. Leipzig: Teubner Verlagsgesellschaft.

D'Oro, G. & C. Sandis (eds.) (2013) *Reasons and Causes: Causalism and Anti-Causalism in the Philosophy of Action*. Basingstoke: Palgrave/Macmillan.

Dray, W. (1957) *Laws and Explanation in History*. Oxford: Clarendon Press.

Droysen, J. G. (1977) *Historik*. Stuttgart: Frommann-Holzboog.

Fodor, J. (1983) *The Modularity of the Mind: An Essay on Faculty Psychology*. Cambridge, Mass.: MIT Press.

Fodor, J. (2000) *The Mind Doesn't Work that Way: The Scope and Limit of Computational Psychology*. Cambridge, Mass.: MIT Press.

Gallagher, S. & D. Hutto (2008) "Understanding Others through Primary Interaction and Narrative Practice," in J. Zlatev. T. Racine, C. Sinha, & E. Itkonen (eds.), *The Shared Mind: Perspectives on Intersubjectivity*, 17–38. Amsterdam and Philadelphia: John Benjamins Publishing Company.

Goldie, P. (2011) "Anti-Empathy," in A. Coplan and P. Goldie (eds.), *Empathy: Philosophical and Psychological Perspectives*, 302–17. Oxford: Oxford University Press.

Goldman, A. (2006) *Simulating Minds: The Philosophy, Psychology, and Neuroscience of Mindreading*. Oxford: Oxford University Press.

Goldman, A. (2011) "Two Routes to Empathy," in Amy Coplan & Peter Goldie (eds.), *Empathy: Philosophical and Psychological Perspectives*, 31–44. Oxford: Oxford University Press.

Gordon, Robert M. (1995) "Folk Psychology as Simulation," in M. Davies and T. Stone (eds.), *Folk Psychology*, 60–73. Oxford: Blackwell Publishers.

Heal, J. (2003) *Mind, Reason and Imagination*. Cambridge: Cambridge University Press.

Henderson, D. & T. Horgan (2000) "Simulation and Epistemic Competence," in H.H. Kögler and K. Stueber (eds.), *Empathy and Agency: The Problem of Understanding in the Human Sciences*, 119–43. Boulder: Westview Press.

Hoffman, M. (2000) *Empathy and Moral Development*. Cambridge: Cambridge University Press.

Hollan, D. (2014) "Empathy and Morality in Ethnographic Perspective," in H. Maibom (ed.), *Empathy and Morality*, 230–50. Oxford: Oxford University Press.

Hume, D. (1978 [1739]) *A Treatise of Human Nature*. Oxford: Clarendon Press.

Hutto, D. (2008) *Folk-Psychological Narratives: The Sociocultural Basis of Understanding Reasons*. Cambridge, Mass.: MIT Press.

Jacob, P. (2011) "The Direct-Perception Model of Empathy: A Critique," *The Review of Philosophy and Psychology* 2, 519–40.

Lipps, Th. (1907) "Das Wissen von Fremden Ichen," *Psychologische Untersuchungen* 1, 694–722.

Maibom, H. (ed.) (2014) *Empathy and Morality*. Oxford: Oxford University Press.

Maibom, H. (forthcoming). "Knowing Me, Knowing You: Failure to Forecast and the Empathic Imagination," in A. Kind & P. Kung (eds.), *Knowledge through Imagination*. New York: Oxford University Press.

Overgaard, S. & Zahavi, D. (2012) "Empathy without Isomorphism: A Phenomenological Account," in J. Decety (ed.), *Empathy: From Bench to Bedside*, 3–20. Cambridge, Mass.: MIT Press.

Oxley, J. C. (2011) *The Moral Dimensions of Empathy: Limits and Applications in Ethical Theory and Practice*. Basingstoke: Palgrave Macmillan.

Scanlon, T. M. (2014) *Being Realistic about Reasons*. Oxford. Oxford University Press.

Schliesser, E. (2015) *Sympathy: A History*. Oxford: Oxford University Press.

Setiya, K. (2007) *Reasons without Rationalism*. Princeton: Princeton University Press.

Setiya, K. & H. Paakunainen (eds.) (2012) *Internal Reasons: Contemporary Readings*. Cambridge, Mass.: MIT Press.

Shafer-Landau, R. (2003) *Moral Realism: A Defense*. Oxford: Oxford University Press.

Smith, A. (1982 [1759]) *The Theory of Moral Sentiments*. Indianapolis: Liberty Fund.

Smith, M. (1994) *The Moral Problem*. Oxford: Blackwell Publishing.

Stueber, K. (2005) "How to Think about Rules and Rule-Following," *Philosophy of the Social Sciences* 35, 307–23.

Stueber, K. (2006) *Rediscovering Empathy: Agency, Folk Psychology, and the Human Sciences*. Cambridge, Mass.: MIT Press.

Stueber, K. (2008) "Reasons, Generalizations, Empathy, and Narratives: The Epistemic Structure of Action Explanation," *History and Theory* 47, 31–43.

Stueber, K. (2008/2014) "Empathy," *The Stanford Encyclopedia of Philosophy* (Winter 2014 edition), Edward N. Zalta (ed.), <http://plato.stanford.edu/archives/win2014/entries/empathy/>.

Stueber, K. (2012) "Varieties of Empathy, Neuroscience and the Narrativist Challenge to the Contemporary Theory of Mind Debate," *Emotion Review* 4, 55–63.

Stueber, K. (2015) "The Cognitive Function of Narratives," *Journal of the Philosophy of History* 9, 393–409.

Stueber, K. (2016) "Agents, Reasons, and the Nature of Normativity," in M. Risjord (ed.), *Normativity and Naturalism in the Social Sciences*, 96–112. New York/London: Routledge.

Turner, S. (2010) *Explaining the Normative*. Oxford: Polity Press.

Wiland, E. (2012) *Reasons*. London/New York: Bloomsbury Press.

Williams, B. (1979) "Internal and External Reasons," reprinted in *Moral Luck*, 101–13. Cambridge: Cambridge University Press (1981).

Wilson, B. (ed.) (1970) *Rationality*. New York: Harper and Row.

13

EMPATHY AND KNOWING WHAT IT'S LIKE

Ian Ravenscroft

1. Introduction

This chapter focuses on a common phenomenon: sometimes we experience the emotions of other people. Observing Arthur's sadness, Martha may feel sad; and when she observes his happiness, she may feel happy. Emotions have what are often called *phenomenological properties*. One way to grasp what phenomenological properties are is to talk about *what it is like* to experience this mental state or that one (Nagel 1974). There is something it is like to feel sad, and what it is like to feel sad is different from what it is like to feel happy. That difference is a difference in the phenomenological properties of sadness and happiness. Emotions are not the only mental states with phenomenological properties – there is something that it is like to see red, and what it is like to see red is different from what it is like to see green – but this chapter focuses on emotions. When Martha feels sad in response to Arthur's sadness, she has an experience with the same phenomenological properties as Arthur. In some respects, what it is like to be Martha is the same as what it is like to be Arthur.

A number of preliminary remarks are in order.

(i) Restricting our attention to experiencing other people's emotions is in some ways artificial. We could ask what it is like when another person sees red or experiences hunger.
However, for reasons of space I will restrict attention to the case of emotions.

(ii) The issue I will focus on is not emotional attribution, which is a variety of propositional knowledge: it is not about Martha's knowing that Arthur is angry in the way
that she knows he is a butcher. Rather it is about Martha re-enacting or recreating
Arthur's anger.

(iii) My use of the phrase "knowing what it is like to be someone else" raises the question of
what knowledge is in these circumstances. There is a vast literature on the correct analysis
of the concept of knowledge, but here I am using the term is a folksy way. We often say
things like "Arthur knows that Martha is tired" or "Martha knew Arthur was in pain,"
and these examples are adequate pointers for present purposes. I will not address skeptical arguments or subtle thought experiments intended to yield fine-grained analyses of
knowledge.

2. Knowing what it's like to be someone else

I will say that Martha knows what it is like to be Arthur when –

1. She is an emotional state phenomenologically similar to the one Arthur is in.
2. She knows that she is in a state phenomenologically similar to the state Arthur is in.
3. She knows that the state she is in was brought about by observing or imagining Arthur, where observing is taken to include actions like reading or hearing about Arthur.

The first condition guarantees that Martha's emotional state re-enacts or recreates Arthur's, but that it is not enough for knowing what it is like. She must in addition know that her emotional state matches Arthur's and that Arthur is the cause of her own emotional state. Without the second and third conditions she would not know that the experience she is having matches Arthur's – she would not know what it is like to be *Arthur*. Notice that the second and third conditions on knowing what it is like rule out emotional contagion as a variety of knowing what it is like (see Chapter 2, "Affective Empathy"). Wispé (1987: 76–7) defines emotional contagion as "an involuntary spread of feelings without any conscious awareness of where the feelings began in the first place." In cases of emotional contagion, people "catch" an emotion from someone else without realizing that their emotion originates in or matches the other person's. Thus emotional contagion involves the first condition of knowing what it is like but neither the second nor third.

2. Empathy and knowing what it's like

Knowing what it is like to be someone else might be described as a form of empathy, but the term "empathy" has been used in many ways, providing ample room for ambiguity and confusion (Coplan 2011, Goldman 2011 and Prinz 2011). As I have defined it, knowing what it's like shares some features of Vignemont and Singer's (2006) characterization of empathy:

> There is empathy if: (i) one is in an affective state; (ii) this state is isomorphic to another person's affective state; (iii) this state is elicited by the observation or imagination of … [that] person's affective state; (iv) one knows that the other person is the source of one's own affective state.

Notice, though, that on Vignemont and Singer's account of empathy the empathizer does not have to know that she is in the same affective state as the empathee; that is, empathy as defined by Vignemont and Singer does not meet the second condition on knowing what it's like to be someone else.

Sometimes "empathy" is used in ways that necessarily involve concern for the empathee. However, what it is like is neutral on the issue of the other's welfare: Martha may or may not be concerned about Arthur's welfare. Phrases like "sympathy" and "empathetic concern" are sometimes used to mark off those cases in which concern for the empathee is involved. Using this terminology we can say that whilst some instances of knowing what it is like may count as sympathy or empathetic concern, not all cases do.

Alvin Goldman (2011) argues that there are two distinct neurological pathways responsible for episodes of empathy. One route centrally involves mirror neurons and yields what I will call "mirror empathizing." This kind of empathizing is automatic in the sense that it is not consciously initiated and is effortless: we do not have to struggle to engage in mirror empathy.

Among several examples, Goldman discusses Wicker et al.'s (2003) research on empathetic disgust. The brain areas active when participants are exposed to a disgusting smell and of those who observed others responding to a disgust smell overlapped considerably. In both cases the anterior insula and the anterior cingulate cortex – areas populated by mirror neurons – exhibited increased activity. In contrast, participants who had smelled either pleasant or neutral odorants, or who had observed others smelling pleasant or neutral odorants, did not exhibit increased activity in these areas. The pattern of activation was due to smelling a disgusting odor, not merely smelling something.

Mirror empathy is not a form of knowing what it's like. Whilst mirroring involves the generation in the empathizer of a state phenomenologically similar to that of the empathee, it does not meet the second or third condition on knowing what it is like: the mirroring empathizer need not know that her state is phenomenologically similar to that of the empathizer nor that her state is caused by the empathee's state. Mirror empathy is a form of emotional contagion, not of knowing what it is like (see Chapter 5, "Empathy and Mirror Neurons").

Goldman distinguishes mirror empathy from reconstructive empathy, which requires a conscious effort to take on another's perspective. Knowing what it is like rarely involves making a conscious effort to reconstruct another's perspective. We are aware the outcome of knowing what it is like, but rarely consciously seek to know what it is like.

According to Goldman, reconstructive empathy involves theory of mind – the capacity to understand others' behavior in terms of their mental states (Goldman 2006). On the simulationist approach to theory of mind endorsed by Goldman (see Chapter 1, "Cognitive Empathy"), when Martha endeavors to understand Arthur's behavior she introduces "pretend" versions of Arthur's mental states into her own mental system (Goldman 1989, Stich and Nichols 1992, and Currie & Ravenscroft 2002). The pretend-belief that p shares some, but not all, of the characteristics of the belief that p. For example, say that Martha believes that Caffe Latte is the best place to get coffee and that she wants a coffee. Other things being equal, she will decide to go to Caffe Latte. In contrast, if Martha only pretend-believes that Caffe Latte is the best place to get coffee, she won't actually go to the cafe; rather, she will form the pretend-decision to go to the cafe. Her pretend-decision is "off-line"; that is, it is disconnected from her motor system so that she does not actually head for Caffe Latte. Beliefs typically originate in perception, or by reflecting on existing beliefs. How do pretend-beliefs that p originate? Simulationists sometimes say that pretend-beliefs originate in the "pretend-belief generator," but they have been rather coy about how it works.

Pretend mental states will be significant in the next section, but for the present let us return to Goldman's idea of reconstructive empathy. According to Goldman, Martha reconstructively empathizes with Arthur by introducing pretend versions of Arthur's mental states into her mental systems, which bring her into an emotional state congruent to Arthur's. Reconstructive empathy is not knowing what it is like because it fails to meet the second and third conditions on what it is like. However, Goldman argues that processes of mental simulation can also lead to the attribution of emotions to the object of the simulation (Goldman 2011). If Goldman is right, reconstructive empathy could form the basis of knowing what it is like.

3. What it is like and theories of emotion

Some theories of emotions have consequences for our understanding of what it is like to be someone else, and vice versa. For example, some theories of emotions make knowing what it is like implausibly difficult, and the existence of knowing what it is like raises important issues for other theories of emotions. A complete survey of the relationships between theories of emotions and what it is like is not possible in this chapter, so I restrict my discussion to simple cognitive theories and the James-Lange version of emotivist or "feeling" theories (Prinz 2004).

There are a variety of cognitive theories of the emotions, but they share a commitment to the idea that emotions are beliefs (or "judgments"), or complexes of beliefs and desires (Solomon 1980 and Nussbaum 2001). For example, to be afraid is to believe that danger is present and to desire to avoid danger. Notice that cognitivism entails that we will often be unable to know what it is like to be someone else. Say that cognitivism is true and that Arthur is afraid. According to cognitivism, if Martha is to know what it is like to be Arthur she too must believe that danger is present and desire to avoid it. But that can't be right. If Arthur believes that moths are dangerous but Martha does not, it would follow that Martha cannot empathize with Arthur's fear reaction in the presence of a moth – she cannot know what it is like to be Arthur. But it is plausible Martha *can* know what it is like to be Arthur in that situation, so something has gone wrong.

One way to avoid this problem is to appeal to pretend-beliefs introduced in the previous section. The idea of pretend-beliefs yields a modified cognitive theory of empathetic emotions: both beliefs and pretend-beliefs can be constituent parts of emotions. When Martha empathizes with Arthur's fear in the presence of a moth she pretend-believes that moths are dangerous. I remarked above that pretend-beliefs are typically off-line. Notice, though, that pretend-beliefs which are constituent parts of emotions are not entirely off-line. When she knows what it is like for Arthur to be afraid of moths, Martha will exhibit at least some of the bodily responses of fear. She may, for example, sweat or have an elevated heart rate.

Much more needs to be said about pretend-beliefs. Somehow Martha's pretend-belief that p must be prevented from interacting with her belief that not-p. For if Martha simultaneously entertained both of these beliefs, she would arrive at a contradiction. Some kind of process for temporarily quarantining Martha's belief that not-p must be postulated. In the empathy case, if Martha both believes that moths aren't dangerous and pretend-believes that they are, then, on the cognitive theory of empathy, Martha should both fear and not fear moths. Once again her belief that not-p must be temporarily quarantined. It would be very helpful if a theory of quarantining were available.

Cognitive theories contrast with emotivist theories. The simplest emotivist theories identify emotions with phenomenological properties: to be sad is to feel a certain way. The James-Lange theory says that emotions are the feeling of bodily changes, including cardiovascular, respiratory, muscular-skeletal, and endocrine changes (James 1884, Lange 1885/1922). On the James-Lange theory, the bodily changes associated with an emotion *precede* the emotion itself. Notice that if the James-Lange theory is correct, in order for Martha to know what it is like to be Arthur when he is afraid, she must first recreate in herself the bodily changes Arthur is experiencing, but she cannot do so by first empathetically experiencing Arthur's fear because, as we have noted, according to the James-Lange theory the bodily changes precede the emotion. It follows that, in cases of knowing what it is like to be someone else, the James-Lange theory requires that somehow Martha perceives the bodily changes Arthur is undergoing, reproduces them, experiences their feeling, and thereby empathizes with him. Clearly this is implausible for some bodily changes because they are not readily detectable by simple observation. For example, amongst other physiological responses, fear causes reduced levels of gastric activity, and yet it is unlikely that Martha can observe this (Thompson 1988: 146).

One important class of bodily changes associated with emotions are facial expressions. It has been widely noted that deliberately producing a smile tends to engender feelings of happiness. When Strack et al. (1988) got participants to hold a pencil in their mouths in a way that forced them to smile, they typically reported feeling happy. We know that there are systems of mirror neurons that fire both when Martha sees Arthur smile and when she smiles herself. The feel of the bodily changes constituent of smiling would then be a constituent of Martha's knowing what it is like to be Arthur (Goldman and Sripada 2005).

Damasio (1994) endorses a version of the James-Lange theory according to which some emotions are the feelings of bodily changes, but others are due to what he calls "as-if loops" which endogenously generate the feelings associated with bodily change. He locates the as-if loops in the ventromedial prefrontal cortex, whereas emotions with exogenous sources are primarily processed in the amygdala. Perhaps the as-if loop is activated when Martha empathetically feels Arthur's fear: to empathize with Arthur's fear, Martha must activate the as-if loop for fear. However, an account is still required of the processes by which Arthur's fear responses trigger Martha's as-if loops.

4. The limits of knowing what it is like

In this section I discuss some issues relating to the limits of knowing what it is like.

Cross-cultural limitations. A major source of information about the emotional states of others is the characteristic facial expressions of emotions. Ekman and Friesen (1971) presented evidence that facial expressions of basic emotions (anger, fear, surprise, disgust, happiness, and sadness) are essentially pan-cultural. In a typical experiment, Ekman and Friesen presented participants from the Fore group in New Guinea with a story in pictures in which a man's child has died. The participants were then presented with photos of faces that the Western experimenters took to be expressing one of the basic emotions. Overwhelmingly the participants selected the face that the Western investigators took to be expressing sadness. It is important to stress that Ekman's thesis is that emotional *expressions* are universal, not that the *triggers* of emotional responses are universal. The latter is clearly false. The professional snake-catcher and I do not experience the same emotion in the presence of a snake.

The universality of the facial expressions characteristic of emotions suggests that facial expressions might allow us to know what it is like to be someone from a different culture. However, Ekman himself provided evidence that facial expressions of emotions are not straightforwardly pan-cultural. Ekman and his collaborators demonstrated that facial expressions of emotions can be modulated by cultural norms (Griffiths 1997: 53–5). Ekman showed both Japanese and American college students a horror film and observed that they had very similar facial expressions when watching *except when an authority figure was present*. In the presence of an authority figure the American students continued to express fear whilst the Japanese students very briefly expressed fear but quickly masked it. Importantly, the expression of the fear response by the Japanese participants was so quick as to be undetectable under normal viewing conditions – Ekman and colleagues had to slow down a video recording of the students' faces considerably to detect the initial fear response. Ekman used the phrase "display rules" for the cultural masking of emotional expressions. The existence of culturally influenced display rules presents a serious challenge to knowing what it is like across cultural divides. Because the masking of facial expressions of emotion happens very quickly, non-Japanese observers unfamiliar with Japanese display rules will have difficulty knowing what it is like to be one those students.

There is also evidence that American and Japanese participants attribute different levels of emotional intensity to the same facial image (Matsumoto & Ekman 1989). The mean emotional intensity ratings of the American participants exceeded those of the Japanese on all basic emotions except disgust, and this result was independent of both the gender and ethnicity of the person in the photo. This outcome suggests – although certainly doesn't prove – that Americans may have more intense empathetic responses to most basic emotions than do Japanese. If this is the case, we would have further evidence that it is difficult to know what it is like across cultures.

It is often suggested that the Japanese experience an emotion – *amae* – not experienced by Westerners (Griffiths 1997: 101). *Amae* has been described as a pleasurable feeling of indulgent dependence. If *amae* really is a culturally dependent emotion, then non-Japanese people will have trouble knowing what it is like to be a person experiencing *amae*. There is reason to doubt, however, that *amae* is a culturally dependent emotion. As noted above, the triggers of emotions vary from person to person and culture to culture. *Amae* can be thought of as a form of pleasure with culturally dependent triggers – it is triggered by a certain kind of social dependence. But even if this is true, it may be difficult for a Westerner to know what it is like to be a person experiencing *amae* because emotional triggers are an important clue to the emotional states of others.

What it is like and gender. Are there gender differences in the capacity to know what it's like? It is often suggested that women are better at emphasizing than men and, if that is right, men maybe less capable than women at knowing what it's like. In an early review Hoffman (1977) concluded that women are more empathetic than men, but in a later review Eisenberg and Lennon (1983) concluded that reported gender difference in empathy varied with the experimental approach. Women exhibited greater empathetic responses than men when measured by self-report, but the gender difference was not observed when the empathetic response was measured by unobtrusive observation of non-verbal behavior or physiological responses. More recent research found that under some circumstances, women were better at empathizing than men (Klein and Hodges 2001, see Chapter 33 in this volume, "Gender and Empathy").

As is so often the case, there are definitional issues concerning the meaning of "empathy." Hoffman defined empathy as "the observer's vicarious affective response to another person" (1977: 713). In contrast, Eisenberg and Lennon defined empathy as "emotional matching and/or sympathetic responding" (1983: 101). Klein and Hodges (2001) focused on what Ickes (1993) calls empathetic accuracy, that is, the capacity to accurately attribute emotions to others. None of these conceptions of empathy match the definition of knowing what it is like given in Section 1 and so we cannot assume that these results carry over to knowing what it is like. The existence of gender differences in the capacity to know what it is like is therefore an open question.

Simulation theory. On Goldman's (2011) reconstructive model of empathy, when Martha empathizes with Arthur she provides her emotional system with pretend-inputs that correspond to the "real" inputs to Arthur's emotion system. As we have seen, what Goldman calls "reconstructive empathy" is one of the constituents of knowing what it is like and, consequently, limitations on the capacity for reconstructive empathy will be reflected in the capacity for knowing what it is like. Goldman distinguishes between two kinds of errors that might impact on reconstructive empathy: errors of omission and errors of commission. Errors of omission occur when the empathizer does not have adequate information about the empathee to generate the appropriate pretend-inputs. Errors of commission occur when the empathizer generates pretend-inputs that do not correspond to the "real" inputs experienced by the empathee. Goldman points out that failure by the empathizer to quarantine her own mental states from engaging in the empathetic process can lead to errors of commission. If the simulationist model of reconstructive empathy is right, both of these kinds of errors are likely to impact on knowing what it is like. For example, if Martha does not quarantine her own relaxed attitude to moths when she observes Arthur's fear of moths, she is unlikely to know what it is like to be Arthur.

5. What is it like to be a fictional character?

So far it has been assumed that causal relations between empathee and empathizer play a central role in knowing what it is like. Arthur's facial expressions, bodily movements, and situation, his words and tone of voice: these causally interact with Martha in ways that lead her to know what it is like to be Arthur. However, it seems that we can sometimes empathize with fictional characters – Martha experiences Oliver Twist's fear of Sikes – and yet there are no causal connections between Martha and Sikes because Sikes does not exist.

In Section 3, I discussed a cognitive theory of empathetic emotions and noted its reliance on pretend-beliefs. Applied to the case of Martha's knowing what it is like to be Oliver, Martha would have to pretend-believe that Sikes is dangerous. But as noted, the idea of pretend-belief generation has not been well articulated. On the other hand, applied to knowing what it is like to be a fictional character, the James-Lange theory requires that Martha re-enacts the bodily changes Oliver would undergo if he were confronted by Sikes. In Section 3, I noted that mirror neurons may play a part in re-enacting bodily changes, but mirror neurons require causal relations with the target – relations that don't exist in the fictional case. Again as noted earlier, Damasio has appealed to as-if loops to explain the rise of endogenous emotional responses, but if the as-if loop model is to be applied to what it is like to be a fictional character, an account needs to be developed of how fiction engages the as-if loop in appropriate ways. It must be concluded that at present we lack a satisfactory account of knowing what it's like to be a fictional character.

The concerns I have expressed about knowing what it is like to be a fictional character carry over to the temporal case: what is it like to be your future self? Say that Martha mentally time travels forward to a predicted situation in which she loses her job. Intuitively, it seems that she can know what it will be like to be her future self even though there are no causal links back from her future state to her present one, just as there are no causal links from Oliver Twist to Martha. So again we have need of an account of endogenously generated knowledge of what it is like. Moreover, there is considerable evidence that we *cannot* accurately predict our future mental states, including our emotional states. There is a very large literature on our incapacity to know how we would react in certain situations (see for example Ross & Nisbett 1991). For example, few people correctly predict how they would behave were they a subject in Milgram's (1963) notorious obedience experiment. Drawing on this literature, Maibom (2016) argues that our predictions of our future mental states are normative in this sense: our predictions are often erroneously based on how we think we *should* behave rather than how we *would* behave. This strongly suggests that our capacity to know what it is like to be our future selves is limited.

Notice that in both the fictional and mental time travel cases it is not enough to appeal to the imagination; it is not enough to say that Martha imagines what it is like to be Oliver in the presence of Sikes. We can use this locution if we wish, but the problem remains the same. How does Martha imagine what it is like to be Oliver? Simulationist theories of imagination propose that imagining involves introducing pretend-inputs into the relevant processor that has been taken off-line. Visual imagination, for example, is said to involve introducing pretend-states into the visual processor when it is off-line (Currie 1995, Currie & Ravenscroft 1997). However, once again we need a detailed account of pretend-input generation.

6. Ethics and what it is like

The capacity for empathy has often been connected with ethics, most prominently by Adam Smith (1759/1976) and David Hume (1739/1978). Hume and Smith used the term "sympathy" in a variety of ways, raising questions about the extent to which it maps onto the more recent term "empathy" (Coplan & Goldie 2011). I will assume that Hume's and Smith's preferred term maps onto the more recent term "empathy." In the *Treatise* we find this remark:

> We partake of [the victim of injustice's] uneasiness by sympathy; and as every thing, which gives unease in human actions, upon the general survey, is called Vice, and whatever produces satisfaction, in the same manner, is denominated Virtue ... [S]ympathy with public interest is the source of the moral approbation, which attends that virtue.
>
> *(Hume 1939/1788: II.ii)*

Hume is offering an emotivist theory of moral judgment (Ayer 1936, Prinz 2007). Roughly, A's action towards B is morally wrong if our empathetic reaction to B involves an unpleasant emotion, and morally right if our empathetic reaction involves a pleasant emotion. What might an emotivist say about cases in which A does not know what it is like to be B? One response is to embrace subjectivism: accurate or not, A's action is wrong if it produces a negative empathetic response in the observer (Prinz 2007). Alternatively, the emotivist could follow Smith (1759/1976) and appeal to the empathetic response of a well-informed and impartial spectator – an ideal empathizer whose empathetic responses are always accurate. On this view, A's action towards B is right if the ideal empathizer's reaction to B involves a pleasant emotion and wrong if the ideal empathizer's reaction to B involves an unpleasant emotion (see Chapter 19, "Empathy and Moral Judgment" and Chapter 9, "Empathy in Hume and Smith").

Both Hume and Smith thought of empathetic responses as, at least in part, necessary for moral judgments, but there are also contingent relations between ethics and empathy. Some emotional responses are of significance to how we morally regard the person experiencing them. A person who is delighted by the suffering of others is rightly described as immoral. We can know what it is like for that person to witness torture, and that knowledge can drive our moral response to them. Knowing what it is like provides evidence of their moral culpability. If this is right, the limits of our capacity to know what it is like places limits on our ethical capacities. If I misjudge what it is like to be the person witnessing torture, I may morally misjudge them.

7. Conclusion

Knowing what it is like is both important and puzzling. It is important in that it is such a striking feature of human experience, because of its links to ethics, and because of the role it has played under the label "sympathy" in the history of philosophy. It is puzzling because we have yet to develop a well-worked out theory of knowing what it is like. We need a deeper understanding of its limits and of its implementation in the brain, of its relation to current theories of emotion, and of our seeming ability to know what it is like to be a fictional character. Knowing what it is like will remain an important focus of research for sometime.

Acknowledgements I would like to thank Heidi Maibom and Dan Hutto for their feedback and encouragement.

References

Ayer, A. 1936. *Language, truth and logic* (London: Victor Gollancz).
Batson, C., Batson, J., Todd, R., Brummett, B., Shaw, L., & Aldeguer, C. 1995. Empathy and the collective good: Caring for one of the others in a social dilemma. *Journal of personality and social psychology* 68: 619–31.

Coplan, A. 2011.Understanding empathy: Its features and effects. In A. Coplan and P. Goldie, *Empathy: Philosophical and psychological perspectives* (Oxford: Oxford University Press).

Coplan, A., & Goldie, P. 2011. Introduction. In A. Coplan and P. Goldie, *Empathy: Philosophical and psychological perspectives* (Oxford: Oxford University Press).

Currie, G. 1995.Visual imagery as the simulation of vision. *Mind and language* 10: 25044.

Currie, G., & Ravenscroft, I. 1997. Mental simulation and motor imagery. *Philosophy of science* 64: 161–80.

Currie, G. & Ravenscroft, I. 2002. *Recreative minds: Imagination in philosophy and psychology* (Oxford: Oxford University Press).

Damasio, A. 1994. *Descartes' error: Emotion, reason and the human brain* (New York: Putnam).

Eisenberg, N., & Lennon, R. 1983. Sex differences in empathy and related capacities. *Psychological bulletin* 94: 100–31.

Ekman, P., & Friesen 1971. Constants across cultures in the face and emotion. *Journal of personality and social psychology* 17: 124–9.

Goldman, A. 1989. Interpretation psychologized. *Mind and language* 4: 161–85.

Goldman, A. 2006. *Simulating minds: The philosophy, psychology and neuroscience of mindreading* (Oxford: Oxford University Press).

Goldman, A. 2011.Two routes to empathy. In A. Coplan and P. Goldie, *Empathy: Philosophical and psychological perspectives* (Oxford: Oxford University Press).

Goldman, A., & Sripada, C. 2005. Simulationist models of face-based emotion recognition. *Cognition* 94: 193–213.

Griffiths, P. 1997. *What emotions really are: The problem of psychological categories* (Chicago: University of Chicago Press).

Hoffman, M. 1977. Sex differences in empathy and related behaviors. *Psychological bulletin* 84: 712–22.

Hume, D. 1739/1978. *A treatise of human nature.* P. Nidditch (ed.) (Oxford: Oxford University Press).

Ickes, W. 1993. Empathetic accuracy. *Journal of personality* 61: 587–610.

James, W. 1884.What is an emotion? *Mind* 9: 188–205.

Klein, K., & Hodges, S. 2001. Gender differences, motivation, and empathetic accuracy: When it pays to understand. *Personal and social psychology bulletin* 27: 720–30.

Lange, C. 1885/1922. *The emotions: A psychophysiological study* (trans. I. Haupt). In K. Dunlap (ed.) *The emotions* (Baltimore: Williams and Wilkins).

Maibom, H. 2016. Knowing me; knowing you: Failure to forecast and the empathic imagination. In A. Kind and P. Kung (eds.) *Knowledge through imagination* (Oxford: Oxford University Press).

Matsumoto, D., & Ekman, P. 1989. American-Japanese cultural differences in intensity ratings of facial expressions of emotion. *Motivation and emotion* 13: 143–57.

Milgram, S. 1963. Behavioral study of obedience. *Journal of abnormal and social psychology* 67: 71–8.

Nagel, T. 1974.What is it like to be a bat? *The philosophical review* 83 (4): 435–50.

Nussbaum, M. 2001. *Upheavals of thought: The intelligence of emotions* (Cambridge: Cambridge University Press).

Prinz, J. 2004. *Gut reactions: A perceptual theory of emotions* (Oxford: Oxford University Press).

Prinz, J. 2007. *The emotional construction of morals* (Oxford: Oxford University Press).

Prinz, J. 2011. Is empathy necessary for morality? In A. Coplan and P. Goldie, *Empathy: Philosophical and psychological perspectives* (Oxford: Oxford University Press).

Ravenscroft, I. 1998.What is it like to be someone else? Simulation and empathy. *Ratio* 11: 170–85.

Ravenscroft, I. 2012. Fiction, imagination, and ethics. In R. Langdon and Catriona Mackenzie (eds.) *Emotions, imagination and moral reasoning* (New York: Psychology Press).

Ross, L., & Nisbett, R. 1991. *The person and the situation.* New York: McGraw-Hill.

Smith, A. 1759/1976. *The theory of moral sentiments.* D. Raphael and A. Macfie (eds.) (Oxford: Clarendon).

Solomon, R. 1980. Emotions and choices. In A. Rorty (ed.) *Explaining emotions* (Los Angeles: University of California Press).

Stich, S., & Nichols, S. 1992. Folk psychology: Simulation or tacit theory. *Mind and Language* 7: 35–71.

Strack, F., Martin, L., & Stepper, S. 1988. Inhibiting and facilitating conditions of the human smile: A nonobtrusive test of the facial feedback hypothesis. *Journal of personality and social psychology* 54: 768–77.

Thompson, J. 1988. *The psychobiology of emotions* (Amsterdam: Elsevier).

Vignemont, F. de, & Singer, T. 2006. The empathetic brain: How when and why? *Trends in cognitive science* 10: 435–41.

Wicker, B., Keysers, C., Plailly, J., Royet, J.-P., Gallese, V., & Rizzolatti, G. 2003. Both of us disgusted in *my* insula: The common neural basis of seeing and feeling disgust. *Neuron* 40: 655–64.

Wispé, L. 1987. History of the concept of empathy. In N. Eisenberg and J. Strayer (eds.) *Empathy and its development* (Cambridge: Cambridge University Press).

14

EMPATHY AND THEORIES OF DIRECT PERCEPTION

Shaun Gallagher

Numerous authors agree that one should distinguish between low-level empathy and high-level empathy. High-level empathy may involve higher-order cognitive processes such as imagination, simulation, or narrative understanding. Among theories of high-level empathy one can distinguish between those theories that differentiate between ordinary everyday social cognition (sometimes called "mindreading") and empathy, and those that do not. Thus, for example, although Karsten Stueber (2006) distinguishes between basic empathy and a higher-order re-enactive empathy, he conceives of the latter as a sophisticated mindreading ability, namely, a higher-order simulation of mental states taken as reasons for action. Likewise, Alvin Goldman (2006) distinguishes low-level from high-level empathy but explains the latter as a specific kind of simulative mindreading imagination (called enactive or E-imagination). Other theorists, in contrast, focus on the same kind of simulative forms of imagination but provide detailed criteria meant, in part, to distinguish empathy from ordinary mindreading (Vignemont and Singer 2006; Vignemont and Jacob 2012; Jacob 2011). Narrative theories also distinguish between ordinary social cognition and empathy, maintaining that higher-order understanding and subtle attunement to context matter for empathy (Gallagher 2012a).

In part, the issue of whether empathy is equivalent to ordinary everyday social cognition is even more complicated in discussions of low-level forms of empathy. In some respects this complication goes back to the original conception of *Einfühlung*, the German term translated by the novel English term "empathy" (Titchener 1909). Theodor Lipps (1906), for example, considered *Einfühlung* to be a low-level imitative process automatically activated whenever we encounter the expressions or actions of another person. Its purpose is to help us understand what the other person is experiencing. Contemporary theories of low-level, mirror neuron (MN) based simulation seem to make the same claim. Both Stueber and Goldman, for example, are happy to associate low-level empathy with MN activation and to understand that activation as a mode of simulation. In this respect, when they speak of low-level empathy, they come close to the position of Gallese (2001)

According to Gallese, one's empathic response to the other person's action is instantiated in an MN mechanism that matches (simulates) observed action. The three levels of his "shared manifold model" – the neurological level of MN activation; the functional level of simulation; and the experiential or phenomenal level of empathy – however, are meant to be an explanation of a basic form of social cognition. "It is just because of this shared manifold that intersubjective communication and mind-reading become possible … Empathy is deeply grounded in the experience of our lived-body, and it is this experience that enables us to directly recognize others not as bodies endowed with a mind but as *persons* like us" (Gallese 2001, 43). Although Gallese is usually careful to distinguish empathy from mindreading understood as mental state attribution (e.g., Gallese 2008), the significant point is that for Gallese MN activation, and therefore empathy, are automatic and involved with action understanding. MNs activate automatically whenever I see another person engage in intentional action. Thus, our everyday simulation-based, automatic social cognition processes are, by definition and by default, empathic encounters. On this conception of empathy, we empathize with almost everyone we encounter throughout the day. On a different reading, however, MN activation may be a necessary, but not sufficient condition for empathy. Rizzolatti and Sinigaglia (2006), for example, maintain this view. They distinguish between MN activation and empathy. They suggest that "sharing someone's emotive state at [a] visceromotor level and feeling empathy for that person are two very different things" (191), because empathy depends on factors other than motor or emotional resonance. They point to more contextual factors, including high-level imagining of myself in the other's place.

Although I think that the term "empathy," in contrast to its original sense of *Einfühlung*, has evolved in meaning to signify something closer to high-level processes that are not automatic and default, in this chapter I explore its more original meaning as a low-level response, and how we should understand it. I'll focus on the question of whether it is a form of direct perception, or rather requires other cognitive processes such as imagination, simulation, or inference. I've referred to the low-level form of empathy as "elementary empathy" in a previous publication (Gallagher 2012b), and I'll continue to use that term here.

Some old debates about empathy

A good historical starting point for further exploration is Moritz Geiger's essay (Geiger 1910/2015), which provides an overview of the field at that time. Geiger finds the origins of the concept of *Einfühlung* in Romanticism, specifically tied to an emotional contemplation of nature. In this context it was not considered a perception, but a cultivated aesthetic feeling. He suggests that Rudolf Hermann Lotze (1858) and Robert Vischer (1893) carried the concept over into psychology, adding an explicit notion of mental content to aesthetic feeling. Theodor Lipps (1906), thereafter, employed the term to refer to our sense of other minds. For Lipps, *Einfühlung* is neither external perception, which allows us to know objects or things in the environment, nor internal perception (introspection), which allows us to know ourselves. It's rather a different mental process that allows us to know other minds.

Geiger identifies three questions to be addressed in regard to the phenomenon of *Einfühlung* or elementary empathy: the question of phenomenology (what we experience when we experience empathy), the question of psychological mechanism (how empathy is caused in us), and the developmental question (how we come to have this ability). The notion that elementary empathy involves a "transposing" process was frequently mentioned (Dilthey [1926], for example, used the term *Hineinversetzen*), but for Geiger it was not clear whether this was an answer to the phenomenological or the psychological question.

Geiger focuses on the phenomenology of elementary empathy and distinguishes between theories that equate it with a form of imagination, and those that think of it as a real instantiation of the other's emotion. According to the first view, although I perceive outward expressions (gestures, facial expressions, etc.) of emotions, in order to grasp the other person's experience I have to use my imagination to gain a sense of the emotion itself, although gaining such a sense does not require that I actually experience that emotion. A contemporary version of this view is expressed by Baron-Cohen (2005, 179):

> Empathy involves a leap of imagination into someone else's headspace. While you can try to figure out other persons' thoughts and feelings by reading their faces, their voices, and their postures, ultimately their internal worlds are not transparent, and to climb inside their heads requires imagining what it must be like to be them.
>
> *(Baron-Cohen 2005, 170)*

In contrast, on the real instantiation view, embraced by Lipps, sometimes through the act of imagining we come to experience (not just imagine) the same thing that the other person experiences. If we experience the anger of the other person, "this anger is not something that is simply objectively there facing us, but we are in it. We live in this anger, it fully gives itself [*Selbstgegebenheit*], although for other reasons it does not have the same effectiveness [*Wirkungsfähigkeit*] as anger in daily life" (Geiger 1910/2015, 22, trans. revised). Here's a more contemporary expression of this view provided by Ravenscroft (1998, 172): "When we empathise with the distressed climber we do not merely hold a series of propositions about his mental life. We personally experience states very much like his. ... We experience what it is like to be the distressed climber." (See also Chapter 13, "Empathy and Knowing What It's Like.")

On this view, elementary empathy involves instantiating a kind of identity with the other. A common objection to this latter view is that it doesn't ring true phenomenologically: when we grasp that another person is angry, we do not necessarily feel anger ourselves; if we notice that someone else is fearful, we do not experience fear ourselves. We find this objection in Husserl (1973, 188), and more recently and succinctly expressed by Zahavi: "How plausible is it to claim that I have to be scared myself in order to understand that my child is scared, or that I need to become furious myself if I am to recognize the fury in the face of my assailant?" (Zahavi 2014, 113).

In Geiger's analysis it's clear that imagining someone's anger is different from feeling anger, which is different from simply knowing the fact that someone is angry, and these are all different from perceiving the other's anger. On the theories reviewed by Geiger, one doesn't perceive the other's anger; one only perceives the external gestures or expressions of anger, which then triggers or activates the imagination or feeling to attain an empathic experience. Lipps, for example, refers to the symbolic relation of empathy [*symbolische Einfühlungsrelation*] (1906, 23ff.). That is, the physical gesture or expression operates as a symbol of the other's mental state or emotion.

In terms of the psychological mechanism that explains how elementary empathy is possible, Geiger notes that all of the theories agree on one basic idea, namely, that it involves a projection of one's own experience into the other. Again, one can point to a more contemporary expression of this position: "In all cases, observing what other people do or feel is transformed into an inner representation of what we would do or feel in a similar, endogenously produced, situation" (Keysers & Gazzola 2006, 394). Although we know of the other's experience only through external signs, "we add something mental from our own inwardness – here we have a special act of the spontaneity of a mental nature, and not a simple intake of the data transmitted to us from the outside" (Geiger 1910/2015, 24, trans. revised; see, e.g., Lipps 1905, 17; 1909, 225). This involves a kind of filling in (*Einfüllung*); that is, we use our own experience to fill in what we cannot access of the other's experience. The mechanism for this projection or filling in may be a matter of psychological association (Stern 1897), where I produce the feeling that is associated with the physical gesture or expression, which may lead to a kind of empathic fusion (*Verschmelzung*) (Volkelt 1905). Alternatively, the projection of my feeling into the other may be the result of an inferential process based on analogy. Just as my own feelings generate a set of gestures or expressions, when I see the same set of gestures or expressions made by a different body I infer that there must be similar feelings behind them. Lipps objects to this solution since it seems to already assume that there is another experiencing ego behind the expressions of experience (1907, 697–8). What we might gain by such an inferential process is something more like a projection of my own ego into the other's body, which Geiger calls "empathy by self-objectification" (1910/2015, 25; see Lipps 1909, 222).

Developmentally, if one rejects the nativist view, or the idea of empathy as an "inherited disposition" (Geiger 1910/2015, 26; Darwin 1873; Fechner 1907), then empathy depends on learning how gestures and expressions correlate with inner feelings by either association or imitation. By learned association I link a feeling (e.g., anger) that I have experienced with a proprioceptive-kinesthetic image of my expressive movement. There is then a cross-modal connection between proprioception and vision, so that I learn to associate the visible kinematic movements of others with my own kinesthetic experience, and thence to the feeling of anger that I have previously experienced. Alternatively, on the imitation view, one posits an imitative instinct or tendency in which the visible movements of others motivate a similar movement in me. If the movement is an expression of anger, my imitation will generate the feeling of anger in me (Prandtl 1910). This would be a case of contagion. Then, on this basis, i.e., by means of the bodily feeling that is generated, elementary empathy would emerge as the projection or attribution of anger to the other's psyche (Volkelt 1905; Wundt 1874). The processual order is as follows: the other's feeling – the other's expressive movement – my movement – my similar feeling, and then projection. Lipps, however, suggests a different ordering to the imitation: one sees the other's expression, imitates the mental experience, which then generates the bodily feeling, i.e., one's own gesture, which may be inhibited to some degree. For Lipps, however, the bodily feeling is a by-product of empathy and not an essential part of it.

Empathy as a perceptual experience

Such explanations of projective mechanisms are consistent with the idea of elementary empathy as either the result of imaginative processes or the instantiation of emotion. It's only in the classic phenomenologists – Husserl, Stein, Scheler – that we begin to find a *perceptual* account of elementary empathy. Phenomenological views were developed in part through a critique of Lipps. As indicated, according to Lipps, we project our own experience (an inner imitation) onto the other. This suggests that we have to have experienced X to understand X in the other. But this does not explain why we should (or why we are warranted to) project our own experience onto the other. At best, according to Stein (2010), we get an explanation of automatic mimicry/contagion, but not empathy, since contagion falls short of empathy. For empathy, we need to make the other's affective state the intentional object of our own awareness (Stein 2010).

For both Husserl and Stein empathy is a unique form of intentionality directed at the experience of others. It is not a case of attributing, imagining, inferring, or cognizing the experiences of others; it is rather a complex case of perceiving the other's experiences "in" her gestures and bodily expressions (Stein 2010, 4). The perception is complex because it involves the apprehension of the physical gestures and expressions, plus a co-apprehension (an apperception) of the experience expressed in those bodily movements. Stein contrasts the situation in which I learn about someone's experiences by means of a letter that describes a sad event in their life (this would involve a more imaginative or inferential understanding) and the situation of being with that person as they live through the experience. The latter is more directly a case of perception than imagination or inference. Husserl also considers that in cases where we encounter the other in person, her intentions and feelings are perceptually present in her gestures and expressions (Husserl 1952, 235).

It's not clear that for Husserl or Stein empathic perception is a form of direct perception, although this depends on how one defines perception (Gallagher 2008). Indeed, Husserl suggests that it is not a case of direct perception (Husserl 1966, 240) and that rather it involves a form of appresentation or apperception (Husserl 1973, 27; 2002, 107). Such apperception, however, is involved in all perception. Thus, Joel Smith (2010) suggests, just as in the perception of physical objects we do not have a direct vision of all sides of the object but, as Husserl explains, we apperceive the sides of the object that are not visible so that in effect we perceive the object as a whole, so we may also visually perceive the bodily gestures and expressions of the other person and likewise apperceive the non-appearing aspects of emotion. As defined by Husserl, apperception is part of the structure of perception itself. Whereas in the case of physical objects, however, we can walk around to see the previously occluded sides and thereby make visible what was previously non-visible, and whereas this implicit anticipatory or "protentional" aspect of perception is what allows us to perceive/apperceive the object as a whole, we cannot do this in the case of emotions. As Smith notes, however, the apperception of the other's emotion is part of an ongoing perception of her ongoing behavior, and as the behavior develops over its time course, it fulfills or confirms the continuing perception. It's only if one thinks of perception as delivering a momentary snapshot that it seems that by perception alone we cannot get to the non-visible aspects of the other's experience. Still, the claim is not that we have direct perceptual access to all aspects of the other's experience. The claim is that what we call empathy is perceptual in nature.

> Actually, no [imaginative transposition] occurs … Nor does any kind of analogizing occur, no analogical inference, no transference by analogy … Rather the apperception of the other's psychic life takes place without further ado.
>
> *(Husserl 1973, 338–9; trans. Zahavi)*

For Husserl, the fact that we do not have complete access to the other's full experiential life shows us that our experience of the other is different from our own self-experience. It is also the basis for claiming that we experience the otherness of the other, and not simply a self-replication or what Geiger had called a self-objectification.

Likewise, for Scheler (2008), elementary empathy involves the perception of the other (*Fremdwahrnehmung*) (on Scheler's use of the term "empathy," see Zahavi (2014)). In contrast to Lipps, and perhaps in a stronger claim for *direct* perception than we find in Stein or Husserl, he defends the idea that we can directly perceive emotion in the expression of the other. In doing so, he rejects the idea that we have to introduce our own experience into a constructive mix of empathy, or that empathy for another's emotion requires that we have past experience with that emotion.

> For we certainly believe ourselves to be directly acquainted with another person's joy in his laughter, with his sorrow and pain in his tears, with his shame in his blushing, with his entreaty in his outstretched hands … And with the tenor of this thoughts in the sound of his words. If anyone tells me that this is not "perception"… I would beg him to turn aside from such questionable theories and address himself to the phenomenological facts.
>
> *(Scheler 2008, 260–1)*

His perceptual theory of empathy rejects the identification of empathy with emotional contagion or motor mimicry. In effect, Scheler rejects everything about the terms of the empathy debate as summarized by Geiger.

Scheler's notion of direct perception doesn't mean that prior experience cannot inform one's perception, or contribute to one's understanding of the other. Also, the claim is not that all aspects of the other's experience are available perceptually. If I can perceive bodily expressions, I am not able to perceive the precise bodily sensations that might be part of the emotion (Scheler 2008, 66). We note, however, that Scheler makes no attempt to explain the psychological or subpersonal mechanisms that could account for our ability to perceive emotions in others, although he does provide a number of arguments against the theory of inference from analogy. For example, he notes that young infants seem to be able to understand another's emotion even before they are able to make inferences. Indeed, recent research suggests that we find non-conscious contagion, and a consonance of facial gestures and vocal intonations, between infant and caregiver as early as the second month (Stern 1995; Rizzolatti & Sinigaglia 2006), although infants can perceptually distinguish and respond to different emotions even earlier (happy *versus* sad faces at 2–3 days (Field et al. 1982)). Scheler points out that the logic of the argument from inference is also wrongheaded since rather than getting us to the experience of the other it gets us no further than our own experience (as projected) in self-objectification.

Merleau-Ponty helps to clarify the phenomenological claim about direct perception. "For Husserl the experience of others is first of all 'esthesiological' ... The whole riddle of *Einfühlung* lies in its initial, 'esthesiological' phase; and it is solved there because it is a perception" (Merleau-Ponty 1964, 170). Perception already involves an inner activation that comes close to a motor resonance. Indeed, Husserl had pointed to the activation of the kinaesthetic system, a motor reverberation in correlation with visual perception, as early as 1907 (Husserl 1997). Merleau-Ponty emphasizes the idea that empathy is not equivalent to a narrow attribution of mental states (or a form of mindreading). As Husserl had indicated, our empathic response targets the entire person, not just a mind as distinguished from a body.

> By the effect of a singular eloquence of the visible body, *Einfühlung* goes from body to mind. When a different behavior or exploring body appears to me through a first "intentional encroachment," it is the man as a whole who is given to me with all the possibilities (whatever they may be) that I have in my presence to myself in my incarnate being, the unimpeachable attestation. I shall never in all strictness be able to think the other person's thought ... On the other hand, I know unquestionably that that man over there sees, that my sensible world is also his, because *I am present at his seeing*, it is *visible* in his eyes' grasp of the scene.
>
> *(Merleau-Ponty 1964, 169)*

I see the other as a full person, not in the same way that I have a detached observation of an object, but in a relational accomplishment that is underscored by a *vinculum* formed neither by "comparison, nor analogy, nor projection or 'introjection'" – nor theoretical inference, nor simulation – but by an embodied perception as a starting point for interaction or potential interaction (see 1964, 168–70). Through this analysis of social perception, Merleau-Ponty carries the phenomenological conception of a perceptual form of elementary empathy forward and into the contemporary debates.

Contemporary debates about empathy and direct perception

Contemporary debates about empathy have become quite complex, in part because they have become even more interdisciplinary. Geiger, a philosopher, had presented his 1910 review of the philosophy and psychology of empathy at the 4th Congress of Experimental Psychology, but as subsequent questioning at that conference revealed, there hadn't been much experimental science conducted in this area. Today, as the present collection of papers in this volume attests, we still have philosophers and psychologists involved in the debate, but also neuroscientists and social scientists. Here I'll continue the focus on direct perception models of empathy and simply acknowledge that there are many other models and a large amount of continuing debate about the nature of empathy. I focus on two questions. First, how is it possible to talk about the direct perception of another person's mental states? In this respect I'll limit the focus to emotions and intentions. Second, in what sense is such direct perception a form of empathy?

In response to the first question, the answer depends, not only on how we conceive of perception and what makes it direct, but also on the nature of the mental states that are being perceived. In the older debate, for example, the assumption was that the bodily expressions associated with an emotion were mere outward signs or symbols of the inner experience, but were not part of the emotion itself. A more contemporary view argues that an emotion consists of (is constituted by) a pattern of various elements that include autonomic processes, "action tendencies" (i.e., bodily changes preparatory for actions, see Frijda 1986); overt expressions (including expressive posture and movement, facial expression, gesture, and vocal expressions, e.g., intonations); phenomenal feelings; cognitive aspects (such as attitudes, shifts of attention, and changes to perception); intentional objects (that is, the perceived, remembered, or imagined object the emotion is about, see Goldie 2000), and perhaps even situational aspects. This pattern theory of emotion (see Newen et al. 2015; Gallagher 2013) maintains that such elements are variables that can take different values and weights in the dynamic constitution of an emotion where we can distinguish typical patterns of aspects and values and define an emotion as involving some variation of that pattern. On the pattern theory of emotion one can have a token of the same type of emotion lacking a particular characteristic feature, although there may be some minimal number of characteristic features and their values that are sufficient to constitute a particular pattern that counts as that emotion. On this account of emotion, it is very easy to say that we can perceive emotions in others. If emotions are constituted by features that may include bodily expressions, behaviors, action expressions, relations to intentional objects, etc., then emotion perception can be considered a form of pattern recognition (Newen et al., 2015; Gallagher & Varga, 2014). When I see the gestures and bodily expressions, situated in relation to an intentional object or event that, in part, constitute the emotion, I see the emotion. There are elements, of course, that I cannot perceive, e.g., the phenomenal feelings, cognitive aspects, etc. But this does not prevent me from having a direct perception of a sufficient amount of the pattern that constitutes the specific emotion.

A similar argument can be made for the notion of intention. Traditional accounts of intentions usually view them as unobservable internal states or representations. Intentions, however, can be distinguished into three types: prior or distal intentions (D-intentions); intentions-in-action or present intentions (P-intentions); and motor intentions (M-intentions). One can argue, however, that M-intentions (embodied in the precise motoric processes of carrying out an action) are in fact visible in the kinematic aspects of the bodily movements that make up an action, and indeed, there is empirical evidence to this effect (Ansuini et al. 2013; Becchio et al. 2012). We can literally distinguish, perceptually in the kinematics, what a person intends to do in very basic actions, such as picking up an apple in order to eat it, or to throw it, or to offer it to someone. Even critics of direct social perception admit that M–intentions are perceptible (see e.g., Spaulding 2015). Although the same critics tend to deny that P–intentions are perceptible, one can argue that, to the extent that P–intentions are in–the–action and are contextualized by the particular arrangements of the environment in which the action is carried out, they are also perceptible. I can see your intention to cross the street in your action of crossing the street. The formation of D–intentions may be a private matter conducted out of sight within another person's reflective cognition, but in some collective cases even D–intention formation may involve a public process of deliberation and communication that can be perceived, not only by participants, but by other observers. A D–intention may be written down or expressed orally, and if such expressions are normatively (or even legally) binding agreements (or contracts), one may be able to claim that such D–intentions can be perceived (see also Chapter 5, "Empathy and Mirror Neurons").

Whether one can directly perceive other mental states may depend to what extent one holds to the notion that the mind is embodied and situated, and to what extent one understands mental states generally as consisting of patterns, some elements of which may be perceived. If emotions and intentions and possibly other mental states are such that they can be perceived, what does it mean to say that they can be *directly* perceived? Although this is also an issue that is currently under debate, for present purposes we can say simply that I *directly* perceive something if I do not have to add an inference or other non–perceptual cognitive process to perception in order to access it (Gallagher 2008). Helmholtzian and predictive processing models of perception hold that at a sub–personal level perception itself is inferential (e.g., Hohwy 2013). Some theorists (Carruthers 2015; Lavelle 2012) argue that even if perception is not itself inferential, to actually perceive emotions or intentions involves top–down, extra–perceptual inferential processes at the sub–personal level. Moreover, some simulationists argue that at neuronal levels, perceptual processes must be combined with MN activation in order to simulate (rather than directly perceive) another person's emotions and intentions (Gallese 2001). Whether this is the best way to conceive of perception is open to debate (see Gallagher & Varga 2014; Orlandi 2013). In contrast, enactivist interpretations consider MN activation to be part of the sensory–motor processes involved in direct perception, rather than a form of simulation or inference (Gallagher 2012c). One can also develop a more enactivist account of predictive processing that does not rely on the Helmholtzian notion of inference (e.g., Bruineberg & Rietveld 2014). Furthermore, if we take emotions and intentions to consist of patterns, some elements of which are perceptible, we can at least exclude the need for *conscious* inference as we perceive the emotions and intentions of others.

Empathic perception in context

To what extent, however, is the direct perception of emotion or intention a form of empathy? Here again, current debates about the nature of empathy, mentioned in the opening paragraphs, are relevant. Unless one thinks that every perception of another person's actions or bodily expressions, or every automatic activation of the MN system, is a case of elementary empathy (which is consistent with the early understanding of *Einfühlung*), then one might consider that the direct perception of embodied mental states can be either empathic or non–empathic. However, rather than think that there are some necessary or sufficient criteria that would allow us to define whether the perception of another's mental state is intrinsically empathic or non–empathic (cf., e.g., Vignemont & Jacob 2012), I suggest that we need to appeal to context. In fact, at least in everyday life, there is no non–situated perception that is purely synchronic, snapshot, or *simpliciter*; no perception that is outside of diachronic, dynamic, contextualized situations. Social perception is always embedded in social, and often interactive, contexts. In other words, outside of experimental situations, I never perceive bodily expressions or actions that are not already richly contextualized in pragmatic or social situations. The relevant notion of perception is an enactive, action-oriented perception that operates in interactive situations and that is attuned to one's own social affordances (Gallagher 2012c), and to the affordances of others (Kiverstein 2015; also De Bruin, Strijbos, & Slors 2011). In this case, we are already beyond the idea of a perception that pieces things together from partial profiles. As Merleau-Ponty suggests, that's not something we do; perception is already the accomplishment of the body in its relation to the material environment – a relationship that he consistently characterizes as a form, structure, or Gestalt.

The idea that perception is always contextualized means that the distinction between low-level and high-level empathy is ambiguous, and is better conceived as a matter of degree along a spectrum rather than an absolute distinction. In terms of embodied, enactivist conceptions of perception, I directly perceive the other in terms of how I may be able to interact with her in the specifics of the pragmatic or social context, that is, in terms of the possibilities afforded by the social context – which include the possibilities afforded to her (Kiverstein 2015), the possibilities afforded to me in response to her (Gallagher 2012c), as well as any affordances that are co-constituted in joint actions (Abramova & Slors 2015). Direct perception of the other, accordingly, is interaction oriented and context dependent.

The possibility of empathic perception is, in the words of Merleau-Ponty, "the effect of a singular eloquence of the visible body" situated in the world. Empathy, as an embodied direct perception, is the perception of a situated embodied mind, i.e., the perception of meaningful bodily movements, gestures, and expressions in context. I perceive the other person in her circumstances, and it is only *with*-her-in-her-circumstances that my perception is empathic or not. The meaning of "situation" or "circumstance" includes the idea that it is not only the perceived other who is in the situation, but also the perceiving agent. Indeed, it is often the case that I am part of what the other takes as her intentional object, and that itself may modulate my perception of her. The context includes a perceiver-perceived structure, which is related to Merleau-Ponty's notion of form (this is an important hermeneutical point that I can't develop here, but see Gallagher 2009). Direct perception, *intrinsically*, is neither empathic nor non-empathic, since even lower-level empathy depends on the particulars of circumstance. In the case of empathic perception, the particulars of the situation will typically elicit the kind of other-related affective interest that defines it as empathic.

Acknowledgements The author acknowledges support received from the Humboldt Foundation's Anneliese Maier Research Award.

References

Abramova, E., & Slors, M. (2015). Social cognition in simple action coordination: A case for direct perception. *Consciousness and Cognition* 36: 519–31.

Ansuini, C., Cavallo, A., Bertone, C., & Becchio, C. (2013). The visible face of intention: Why kinematics matters. *Frontiers in Psychology* 5: 815. doi: 10.3389/fpsyg.2014.00815.

Baron-Cohen, S. (2005). Autism-'autos': Literally a total focus on the self? In: T. E. Feinberg & J. P. Keenan (eds.) *The Lost Self: Pathologies of the Brain and Identity* (166–80). Oxford: Oxford University Press.

Becchio C., Manera V., Sartori L., Cavallo A., & Castiello U. (2012). Grasping intentions: From thought experiments to empirical evidence. *Frontiers of Human Neuroscience* 6: 117.

Bruineberg, J., & Rietveld, E. (2014). Self-organization, free energy minimization, and optimal grip on a field of affordances. *Frontiers in Human Neuroscience* 8. doi:10.3389/fnhum.2014.00599.

Carruthers, P. (2015). Perceiving mental states. *Consciousness and Cognition* 36: 498–507.

Darwin C. (1873). *The Expression of the Emotions in Man and Animals*. New York: Appleton.

De Bruin, L. C., Strijbos, D., & Slors, M. (2011). Early social cognition: Alternatives to implicit mindreading. *Review of Philosophy and Psychology* 2: 499–517.

Dilthey, W. (1926). *Gesammelte Schriften*, vol. 7. Göttingen-Stuttgart: Vandenhoeck & Ruprecht. Partially translated in K. Mueller-Vollmer (ed.), *The Hermeneutics Reader* (152–64). New York: Continuum, 1988.

Fechner, G.T. (1907). *Über die Seelenfrage*. Hamburg and Leipzig: L. Voss.

Field, T. M., Woodson, R., Greenburg, R., & Cohen, D. (1982). Discrimination and imitation of facial expression by neonates. *Science* 218: 179–81.

Frijda, N. H. (1986). *The Emotions: Studies in Emotion and Social Interaction*. Paris: Maison de Sciences de l'Homme.

Gallagher, S. (2008). Direct perception in the intersubjective context. *Consciousness and Cognition* 17: 535–43.

Gallagher, S. (2009). Philosophical antecedents to situated cognition. In: P. Robbins & M. Aydede (eds.) *Cambridge Handbook of Situated Cognition* (35–51). Cambridge: Cambridge University Press.

Gallagher, S. (2012a). Empathy, simulation and narrative. *Science in Context* 25(3): 301–27.

Gallagher, S. (2012b). Neurons, neonates and narrative: From embodied resonance to empathic understanding. In: A. Foolen, U. Lüdtke, J. Zlatev, & T. Racine (eds.) *Moving Ourselves, Moving Others* (167–96). Amsterdam: John Benjamins.

Gallagher, S. (2012c). In defense of phenomenological approaches to social cognition: Interacting with the critics. *Review of Philosophy and Psychology* 3(2): 187–212.

Gallagher, S. (2013). A pattern theory of self. *Frontiers in Human Neuroscience* 7(443): 1–7. doi: 10.3389/fnhum.2013.00443.

Gallagher, S., & Newen, A. (in preparation). *A Pattern Concept of Mind*.

Gallagher, S., & Varga, S. (2014). Social constraints on the direct perception of emotions and intentions. *Topoi* 33(1): 185–99.

Gallese, V. (2001). The 'shared manifold' hypothesis: From mirror neurons to empathy. *Journal of Consciousness Studies* 8: 33–50.

Gallese, V. (2008). Empathy, embodied simulation, and the brain: Commentary on Aragno and Zepf/Hartmann. *J. Am. Psychoanal. Assoc.* 56: 769–81.

Geiger M. (1910/2015). Über das Wesen und die Bedeutung der Einfühlung. In: F. Schumann (ed.) *IV. Kongress für experimentelle Psychologie* (29–73). Verlag J. A. Barth, Leipzig 2010/2011. Translated by F. Gödel and M. Aragonaas (2015). On the essence and meaning of empathy (Parts I & II). *Dialogues in Philosophy, Mental and Neurosciences* 8(1): 19–31 and 8(2): 75–86.

Goldie, P. (2000). Explaining expressions of emotion. *Mind* 109(433): 25–38.

Goldman, A. (2006). *Simulating Minds: The Philosophy, Psychology and Neuroscience of Mindreading*. Oxford: Oxford University Press.

Hohwy, J. (2013). *The Predictive Mind*. Oxford: Oxford University Press.

Husserl, E. (1952). *Ideen zu einer reinen Phänomenologie und phänomenologischen Philosophie. Zweites Buch. Phänomenologische Untersuchungen zur Konstitution*. Husserliana 4. Den Haag: Martinus Nijhoff.

Husserl, E. (1966). *Analysen zur passiven Synthesis. Aus Vorlesungsund Forschungsmanuskripten 1918–1926*. Husserliana 11. Den Haag: Martinus Nijhoff.

Husserl, E. (1973). *Zur Phänomenologie der Intersubjektivität I*. Husserliana 13. Den Haag: Martinus Nijhoff.

Husserl, E. (1997). *Thing and Space*. Trans. R. Rojcewicz. Dordrecht: Springer.

Husserl, E. (2002). *Einleitung in die Philosophie. Vorlesungen 1922/23*. Husserliana 35. Dordrecht: Kluwer.

Jacob, P. (2011). The direct perception model of empathy: A critique. *Review of Philosophy and Psychology* 2(3): 519–40.

Keysers, C., & Gazzola, V. (2006). Towards a unifying neural theory of social cognition. *Progress in Brain Research* 156: 379–401.

Kiverstein, J. (2015). Empathy and the responsiveness to social affordances. *Conscious Cogn.* 36: 532–42.

Lavelle, J. S. (2012). Theory-theory and the direct perception of mental states. *Review of Philosophy and Psychology* 3(2): 213–30.

Lipps, T. (1905). *Die ethischen Grundfragen*. Hamburg: Leopold Voss Verlag.

Lipps, T. (1906). *Ästhetik*. Leipzig: Verlag von L. Voss.

Lipps, T. (1907). Das Wissen von fremden Ichen. In: T. Lipps (ed.) *Psychologische Untersuchungen I* (694–722). Leipzig: Engelmann.

Lipps T (1909). *Leitfaden der Psychologie*. Leipzig: Verlag von Wilhelm Engelmann.

Lotze, R. H. (1858). *Mikrokosmus*, vol. 2. Leipzig: Hirzel.

Merleau-Ponty, M. (1964). *Signs*. Evanston: Northwestern University Press.

Newen, A., Welpinghus, A., & Juckel, G. (2015). Emotion recognition as pattern recognition: The relevance of perception. *Mind & Language* 30(2): 187–208.

Orlandi, N. (2013). Embedded seeing: Vision in the natural world. *Noûs* 47(4): 727–47.

Prandtl, A. (1910). *Die Einfühlung*. Leipzig: J. A. Barth.

Ravenscroft, I. (1998). What is it like to be someone else? Simulation and empathy. *Ratio* 11(2): 170–85.

Rizzolatti, G., & Sinigaglia, C. (2006). *Mirrors in the Brain: How our Minds Share Actions and Emotions*. Oxford: Oxford University Press.

Scheler, M. (2008). *The Nature of Sympathy*. London: Transaction Publishers. Original: *Wesen und Formen der Sympathie*. Bonn: Verlag Friedrich Cohen, 1923.

Smith, J. (2010). Seeing other people. *Philosophy and Phenomenological Research* 81(3): 731–48.

Spaulding, S. (2015). On direct social perception. *Consciousness and Cognition* 36: 472–82.

Stein, E. (2010). *Zum Problem der Einfühlung*. Freiburg: Herder.

Stern, D. N. (1995). Self/other differentiation in the domain of intimate socio-affective interaction: Some considerations. *Advances in Psychology* 112: 419–29.

Stern P. (1897). *Einfühlung und Assoziation in der neueren Ästhetik*. Hamburg: L. Voss.

Stueber, K. R. (2006). *Rediscovering Empathy: Agency, Folk-Psychology and the Human Sciences*. Cambridge, MA: MIT Press.

Titchener, E. B. (1909). *Lectures on the Experimental Psychology of Thought-Processes*. New York: Macmillan.

Vignemont, de F., & Jacob, P. (2012). What is it like to feel another's pain? *Philosophy of Science* 79(2): 295–316.

Vignemont, de F., & Singer, T. (2006). The empathic brain: How, when and why? *Trends in Cognitive Sciences* 10: 435–41.

Vischer, R. (1893). *Über ästhetische Naturbetrachtung*. Leipzig: Deutsche Rundschau.

Volkelt, J. (1905). *System der Ästhetik*. Munich: Beck.

Wundt, W. (1874). *Grundzüge der physiologischen Psychologie*. Leipzig: W. Engelmann.

Zahavi, D. (2014). Empathy and other-directed intentionality. *Topoi* 33(1): 129–42.

15

EMPATHY AND INTERSUBJECTIVITY

Joshua May

1. Introduction

Watching my daughter erupt in joy while celebrating an accomplishment, I empathize and am similarly filled with joy at her success. In this way, empathy involves sharing similar mental states of another, whether positive or negative. Contrast this with sympathy or concern, which are likewise other-oriented but seem to predominantly involve only negative feelings and ones that needn't match those of the person with whom one sympathizes. For example, I may sympathize with a woman giving birth, even though I don't take myself to be feeling similar pain or anguish. There are many characterizations of *empathy*, but let's work with a rough conception of it as the ability to take on the perspective of another and as a result have similar feelings (and perhaps thoughts).

Intersubjectivity concerns how one is mentally connected with and distinguished from others. Undoubtedly, various conceptions of empathy are intimately related to this. Empathizing may even conceptually blur or eliminate the normal distinction one has between oneself and another. Seeing a parent wallow upon learning her child has been kidnapped, I might vividly imagine what it's like and feel anguish myself, as though I had my own child taken from me.

The idea that empathy and intersubjectivity are connected is an old one. Consider, for example, how Adam Smith characterizes the process he calls "sympathy" in 1759:

> By the imagination we place ourselves in [another's] situation, we conceive ourselves enduring all the same torments, we enter as it were into his body, and become in some measure the same person with him, and thence form some idea of his sensations, and even feel something which, though weaker in degree, is not altogether unlike them.
>
> *(Smith 1759/2004: 12)*

How is this supposed fusion or merging best construed? Do we literally perceive ourselves as becoming one with the other? Or do we merely share in another's psychological states vicariously, experiencing a similar emotion or thought while representing the other as an entirely distinct person?

The answers have great philosophical import. Like technology, magical powers, and celebrity, empathy can be used for good or evil. We see the positive side when a stranger feels

169

compassion for another in need and is motivated to help. The dark side of empathy is on display when a sadist uses it to figure out other people's concerns in order to harm and manipulate them. By itself empathy is arguably a morally neutral aspect of the mind (compare Prinz 2011). The relation between empathy and intersubjectivity, however, is one area in which the rubber hits the road, connecting directly to core issues in moral philosophy. In fact, when empathy meets intersubjectivity, we encounter some of the most exciting questions about our social lives, such as altruism, compassion, self-interest, immortality, and the connection between morality and rationality.

2. Altruism and compassion

Taking self-other merging seriously can have different philosophical implications. Arguably the most common view about empathy and intersubjectivity is that empathizing with another has positive effects. Empathy is typically tied to compassion, for example, since it allows one to become vividly aware of another's situation, often another's plight (Nussbaum 2001: ch. 6.3). Our attention is not just focused on another's circumstances; empathy seems to at least typically come with an altruistic concern for others, at least when they are perceived to be suffering or in need.

This concern may arise because empathy leads to feeling another's pain or joy to some degree as if it were one's own. In other words, the kind of intersubjectivity so common in empathy involves a kind of self-other fusion that seems to motivate altruism. In a different context (defending a particular moral theory), Peter Railton alludes to this point vividly:

> When one studies relationships of deep commitment ... it becomes artificial to impose a dichotomy between what is done for the self and what is done for the other. We cannot decompose such relationships into a vector of self-concern and a vector of other-concern, even though concern for the self and the other are both present. The other has come to figure in the self in a fundamental way ... If it is part of one's identity to be the parent of Jill or the husband of Linda, then the self has reference points beyond the ego, and that which affects these reference points may affect the self in an unmediated way.
>
> *(Railton 1984: 166–7)*

Similar thoughts arise in Schopenhauer's work on ethics (Nussbaum 2001: 327 n.46). He writes that acting from compassion for another "requires that I am in some way *identified with him*" such that the "entire *difference* between me and everyone else, which is the very basis of my egoism, is eliminated, to a certain extent at least ... the difference between him and me is now no longer absolute" (Schopenhauer 1840/1999: 143–4). For these reasons, Schopenhauer believes compassion is the cement of the moral universe (see also Slote 2010).

Ample experimental evidence now confirms what common experience and reflection suggest. An *empathy-helping relationship* exists in humans whereby increased feelings of empathy for someone perceived to be in need makes one more likely to help that person. We might explain this relationship in terms of egoism or altruism, however. The *empathy-altruism hypothesis*, most prominently championed since the 1980s by social psychologist Dan Batson, states that empathy for those in need induces altruistic motivation to help (Batson 2011). That is, empathy generates a desire to help the other for her own sake – an ultimate, non-instrumental, or intrinsic motive. Of course, in such contexts, the relevant kind of empathy seems to involve or lead to compassion more specifically (Nussbaum 2001: 339). Batson's official term is "empathic concern," which is so inclusive that we might just be talking about sympathy here. But it's at least not implausible that empathy is doing the work.

Alternative egoistic explanations of the empathy-helping relationship have been proposed and tested experimentally. Several decades of evidence, however, have produced a powerful case for the empathy-altruism hypothesis (Batson 2011). For example, empathic concern continues to increase rates of helping even when empathizers can easily leave and avoid the other in need. So increased helping doesn't appear to be explained by an egoistic desire to reduce one's aversive reaction to the shared pain or anxiety. Similarly, helping rates remain higher among participants experiencing high empathy, even if they can receive a boost in mood prior to being presented with the opportunity to help or if they decline to help. These are just two of the various egoistic alternatives that have failed to match the consistent predictions of the empathy-altruism hypothesis.

3. From radical altruism to immortality

So it seems we have powerful evidence that empathy typically leads to altruistic concern for others who are perceived to be in need. But how far can this go? Ordinarily we don't, say, feel another's pain literally, at least not to the same degree. My best friend's severe depression might make me feel down too, but I don't feel exactly the same, despite empathizing with him.

People with *mirror-touch synesthesia*, however, commonly report a kind of "hyper-empathy," in which they seem to experience the very same bodily sensations they perceive in others, even in the same locations. Fiona Torrance (2011), for example, reports feeling "as if my body was being beaten" when watching an unexpected torture scene in a film. Mirror-touch synesthesia thus comes with the burden of vividly experiencing the plight of others. However, the condition does have some positive effects on how one relates to others. Torrance's experience is reminiscent of the commonly posited link between empathy and compassion: "I'm hugely considerate of other people – after all, I know exactly what it feels like to be them."

Some neuroscientific evidence suggests that the hyper-empathy characteristic of mirror-touch synesthesia is connected to, not just empathy, but intersubjectivity specifically. One study, for example, compared gray matter in people with mirror-touch synesthesia to controls. In synesthetes' brains, there was less gray matter in an area that includes the right temporal parietal junction, which is associated with empathy, understanding the minds of others, and distinguishing self from other. The researchers note the possibility that the hyper-empathy patients experience may be "a consequence of faulty self-other monitoring" (Holle et al. 2013: 1049).

Perhaps this represents something like the moral ideal. Some philosophers have argued that we ought to weaken the distinction between self and other. Derek Parfit (1984), for example, famously argues that we must develop impersonal principles of morality, reminiscent of utilitarianism, that do not rely so heavily on what he sees as a dubious separateness of persons (see also Schopenhauer 1840/1999). This picture of personhood and its moral implications is similar to the Buddhist notion of no-self (*anātman* or *anattā*), according to which our concept of an individual person – designated by "I" – is merely a useful fiction (Siderits 1997).

Drawing on these traditions, Mark Johnston perhaps takes such considerations to their limits. He urges us to embrace *agape* "or radical altruism" (2010: 49) based on a merging of self and other:

> The conception of goodness that I have in mind is one shared by the best forms of Judaism, Christianity, and Buddhism. The good person is one who has undergone a kind of *death of the self*; as a result he or she lives a transformed life driven by *entering*

imaginatively into the lives of others, anticipating their needs and true interests, and responding to these as far as is reasonable. The good person is thus a caretaker of humanity, in himself just as in others. By living this way, the good person encounters himself objectively, as just another, but one with respect to which he has a special trust.

(2010: 14, emphasis added)

Moreover, Johnston strikingly argues that by being "really good" one can "survive death," without appeal to a supernatural afterlife. If we were to follow "the command of agape," we "would survive wherever and whenever interests are to be found," living on "in the onward rush of humankind" (296).

These are no doubt lofty claims, connecting personal identity to morality. But there is increasing empirical evidence suggesting that this isn't far from how we conceive of ourselves across time (Strohminger & Nichols 2014). While continuity of memory accounts for much of how we identify individuals, changes to one's moral opinions and behavior are apparently the greatest perceived threat to loss of one's identity. Such research suggests there may be something to the way Johnston connects moral character to individuality.

However, while this research helps to support one aspect of Johnston's theory, it puts pressure on the claim that extreme empathic altruism amounts to *survival*. Very few of us are so altruistic. If I were to care about others the way I care about myself (extending beyond my close friends and family), then I might have already failed to survive as the same person. Suppose, say, that through meditation a previously callous and crass grandmother is able to undergo a "death of the self" and become one with everyone. She is suddenly kind and considerate, for she loves all just as much as she loves herself. If truly radical enough, this may make us think she is no longer really with us, similar to the effects of severe dementia.

4. Egoism and nonaltruism

Thus far we have seen that many theorists connect the intersubjectivity in empathy to positive ideals, such as altruism, beneficence, impartial concern, and even immortality. This has long been the dominant view among philosophers, who have rarely taken seriously the theory that we are all ultimately self-interested (*psychological egoism*). However, given that experimental research connects helping behavior with empathy, self-other merging raises a worry about whether such concern is ultimately egoistic.

The problem is that empathy blurs the distinction between self and other such that one may in some sense be concerned with oneself. Consider the great love we have for family and friends and the personal sacrifices we make for them. The thought that this may in fact be egoistic goes back to at least Francis Hutcheson, who considered (but ultimately rejected) the challenge: "Children are not only made of our bodies, but resemble us in body and mind; they are rational agents as we are, and we only love our own likeness in them" (1725: 162). Similar worries briefly arise in Nussbaum: "if it is to be for *another*, and not for oneself, that one feels compassion, one must be aware of both the bad lot of the sufferer and of the fact that it is, right now, not one's own" (2001: 327).

In fact, some psychologists have argued that it is not empathy that increases helping behavior but rather only self-other merging or "oneness," which sometimes co-occurs with empathic arousal. Robert Cialdini and colleagues, for example, write: "close attachments may elevate benevolence not because individuals feel more empathic concern for the close other but because they feel more at one with the other – that is, because they perceive more of themselves in the other" (Cialdini et al. 1997: 483). This at least provides a "nonaltruistic" alternative to the empathy-altruism hypothesis, although on common accounts of the egoism-altruism distinction, it counts as egoistic (May 2011a).

In a series of experiments, Cialdini and his collaborators apparently provide some evidence in favor of their oneness hypothesis. They had participants imagine various people in need and report their level of empathy, personal distress, and oneness. Crucially, oneness was measured using two items. One asked participants to indicate "the extent to which they would use the term *we* to describe their relationship" with the person imagined to be in need (Cialdini et al. 1997: 484). The other item involved pairs of increasingly overlapping circles that represent self versus other, and participants "selected the pair of circles that they believed best characterized their relationship" with the other (484). Across several experiments, high measures of oneness, not empathy, predicted increased helping.

There are several issues with these experiments. First, they did not, as Batson typically does, get participants to believe that someone is actually in need, providing what they perceive to be a genuine opportunity to help. Instead, participants were asked to *predict* what they would do in an imagined situation, which might not be a reliable means of measuring helping behavior. Second, the measure of oneness is rather metaphorical and ambiguous (Batson et al. 1997: 497; see also Badhwar 1993: §2). For example, use of the pronoun "we" is hardly indicative of mentally representing oneself as merging with another. It is interesting that oneness apparently predicted increased predictions of helping. But oneness and empathy cannot so easily be separated with such measures, as some participants may report increased oneness as a way of indicating greater compassion or closeness. Third, Batson and colleagues (1997) conducted a series of experiments attempting to avoid these problems and found no support for the oneness account. (To better measure only oneness, the researchers compared participants' ratings of themselves, and a person believed to be in need, on various personality traits.)

These issues raise serious problems for the experimental support of the oneness account. The problem, however, may be even more fundamental, for the account faces conceptual difficulties.

5. Dividing self from other

So far we have taken rather seriously the idea that empathy can involve a merging of self and other. A common view puts a *positive* spin on this: merging leads to altruism, impartial concern for others, and perhaps even immortality. Taken quite literally, however, the fusion of self and other seems to lead to a *negative* (or at least neutral) upshot: the intersubjectivity in empathy actually motivates egoism or makes the egoism-altruism divide inapt.

Some philosophers, however, are more skeptical and resist taking self-other merging literally (e.g. Deigh 1995; Nussbaum 2001; May 2011b). Many scientists likewise explicitly characterize empathy as involving separateness from others or "no confusion between self and other" (Decety & Jackson 2004: 75). On this view, as Nussbaum puts it, at least typically empathy is like "the mental preparation of a skilled (Method) actor: it involves a participatory enactment of the situation of the [e.g.] sufferer, but is always combined with the awareness that one is not oneself the sufferer" (2001: 327).

There are numerous skeptics about the extent of self-other fusion. But are there any powerful arguments in favor of a skeptical position? One is primarily conceptual and applies even if we had solid experimental evidence that oneness predicts increased helping behavior, not compassionate empathizing (developed in May 2011b). The precise problem, however, depends on how we interpret the idea of self-other merging.

The most straightforward and literal interpretation of merging is that one mentally represents oneself as strictly (quantitatively or numerically) identical with "another." Compare someone, say Kanye, who believes he is Jesus Christ – not just similar to this historical individual but literally him. This interpretation of self-other merging has the implausible implication that feeling empathy for someone in need tends to induce what would normally be classified as delusional beliefs (May 2011b; compare Nussbaum 2001: 328). Of course, we have seen that some prominent philosophers and traditions have denied there's a sharp distinction between self and other. But they recognize that this isn't typically part of ordinary people's thinking, even when empathizing (especially clear on this is Parfit 1984). Compare even the so-called "hyper-empathy" in mirror-touch synesthesia: patients don't appear to perceive themselves in the other's shoes. Rather, a feeling is generated in themselves, which is presumably represented as occurring in their own body. The other person's experience merely triggers a similar feeling in oneself.

Some proponents of merging, however, seem to explicitly reject this interpretation. Cialdini and his collaborators, for example, write: "We are not suggesting that individuals with overlapping identities confuse their physical beings or situations with those of the other" (1997: 482). They speak only of "blurring" the distinction between self and other, in which the self is "dynamic" and "malleable."

However, it is difficult to see how this can appropriately explain people's helping behavior, for this seems to require a sharp division between self and other. Suppose John looks across the room and sees a man with a spider in his hair. If he mentally represents that individual "de se" or *as himself* (say he believes he's looking in a mirror), then this will normally motivate vigorous patting of his own head. If, on the other hand, John represents the individual *as another* (as distinct from himself), then this will typically motivate rather different behavior, such as calling out to notify the other of the spider. In predicting and explaining behavior, then, it is normally crucial whether the actor conceives of an individual first-personally or third-personally. As John Perry (1979) famously points out, this is similar to indexical expressions – like "I," "here," and "now" – which have irreducible egocentric reference, e.g. to the speaker or to the speaker's location in space or time (for some dissent, see Cappelen & Dever 2013). Of course, such egocentricity is a mere reference point and is distinct from egoism.

Emotions are also often egocentric, possessing an essential connection to the self that impacts action. For example, there may be a sense in which I fear for a soldier as she charges into battle, but normally fear is for a predicament one conceives *as one's own* (compare Williams 1970; Nussbaum 2001: 30–1). Similarly, I would not feel guilt unless I distinguished what I did from what someone else has done. I might in a loose sense feel "guilty" for what my child has done, but arguably this is really a feeling of guilt for not teaching her better or taking some other action myself that relates to her mistake. Even if egocentricity isn't an essential component for the emotion, when this element conjoins with emotion its character and effects on action are again distinctive. I may empathize with my coworker's financial windfall and share in the excitement, but the feeling of excitement would be different if I were to win the lottery *myself* (and will certainly motivate different actions).

Return now to empathy-induced helping behavior. If we suppose that empathically aroused individuals mentally blur the distinction between themselves and the other, then we would expect rather different behavior. Perhaps they would be unsure how to act, who to help, which pronouns to use (not just "we" but "me" versus "her"), and so on. Mentally blurring the self-other distinction would normally have dramatic and distinctive effects on behavior. Yet participants in studies offer to help another individual without any confusion or evidence of self-other blurring. This makes it plausible to attribute to them a third-personal representation of the other as distinct from themselves (May 2011b).

There is certainly a sense in which empathy causes us to experience the world from another's perspective. People with mirror-touch synesthesia often describe their experience as if they are living another person's experience. Torrance (2011) writes: "When I watch a film, I feel as if I'm starring in it." Compare ordinary reactions of flinching when witnessing someone about to incur bodily damage. However, such descriptions are compatible with representing the threatening force and its subsequent effects as occurring in another's body. Presumably, when empathizing with someone in physical danger at a distance, one doesn't jump out of the way as if representing oneself as literally in the other's shoes. Instead, we cringe, flinch, or avert our eyes – actions that presume a representation of oneself as distinct from the other. Indeed, common descriptions patently represent another as distinct from oneself – e.g. "I was constantly crying – not because something had happened to me, but because I had seen someone else crying or felt someone else's pain" (Torrance 2011).

Finally, one might weaken the merging proposal to simply say that empathy tends to make us locate, not our identities, but shared properties or qualities in others. We do not represent ourselves as strictly identical but rather as similar to the other. The empirical evidence does suggest that we empathize more strongly with others who are similar to ourselves – e.g. in race or gender (Batson 2011). But the weakened account of course is entirely compatible with the skeptical view, which denies that empathy leads us to think of ourselves as another (May 2011b).

It is thus difficult to take literally the idea that empathizing with another in need tends to make us collapse or blur the self-other distinction. The intersubjectivity in empathy is most easily captured by positing a strong mental divide between oneself and another. So it doesn't seem that we can appeal to merging to ground an egoistic, or even "nonaltruistic," account.

The foregoing problems also threaten to make radical altruism (and the immortality it may promise) impossible for humans, because it may not be a psychological or conceptual possibility. Psychologically, it may require pathology to achieve (compare mirror-touch synesthesia), which comes with great burdens. Conceptually, radical altruism (or *agape*) may prevent anyone from appropriately interacting with the world. How, after all, could John get the spider out of his own hair (or another's) if he mentally blurs or abandon's the distinction between self and other? The Upanishads are certainly right: "Who sees all beings in his own self and his own self in all beings, loses all fear" (Isha Upanishad 6). But an egocentric element in fear is important for navigating one's own environment. Radical altruism may, paradoxically, yield a failure to effectively help anyone, including oneself.

At this point, one might ask how we can explain the effects of empathy without positing at least some substantial self-other blurring, especially given that one empathizes better with those similar to oneself. Otherwise, why should empathy make us more concerned for others if we don't somehow merge ourselves with them? The answer may lie in the simple idea that empathy for another's plight draws our attention to them, connecting them to ourselves (compare Hume 1739: 2.2.7). We needn't conceive of this in egoistic terms. Empathy may simply induce *relational desires*, which concern both self and other. I might, for example, desire to *be the one* to help Nathan or desire to have a *mutually* enjoyable game of tennis with Mr. Robinson. Arguably, such desires aren't egoistic, since they represent another person as an essential beneficiary, not an individual who is merely essential to one's own benefit (May 2011a). On this picture, empathy can increase altruism, not so much because we merge self and other, but rather because empathy involves focusing one's attention on the other and vividly representing their plight.

6. Intersubjectivity without merging

We have seen various reasons for being skeptical about empathy blurring the divide between self and other. A more modest level of intersubjectivity, however, is still important for various projects in ethics. Obviously, for theories that ground morality in sentiments, empathy can serve as a crucial element in moral knowledge and virtue (Hume 1739; Slote 2010). Perhaps more surprisingly, modest forms of intersubjectivity are even important for theorists who ground morality ultimately in reason.

Many ethical theories invoke the notion of impartiality, which is intimately related to the distinction between self and other. Appeals to impartiality are especially common among moral *rationalists*, who maintain that the truth and appropriateness of moral judgments are chiefly grounded in reason as opposed to sentiment. Consider just two varieties of rationalism: Kantian and utilitarian (or, more broadly, consequentialist).

Utilitarian rationalists tend to hold that moral facts are simply facts about what maximizes overall happiness. No individual's happiness matters more than anyone else's; each person's happiness counts equally in the calculation. Many utilitarians believe this basic moral truth can be known by reason alone. In fact, they are typically wary of appeals to emotion in ethics and have few, if any, commitments to common-sense morality (Greene 2013). However, utilitarians tend to recommend empathizing with others as a way of overcoming our partiality toward our friends and family (compare the views of Parfit and Johnston in section 3). For example, Peter Singer (1981/2011) famously refers to expanding one's circle of concern beyond the usual default, which is narrowly focused on those with whom we share personal relationships. Importantly, Singer treats this process as one of empathizing and being grounded in the rational insight that there is no intrinsic moral difference between oneself and others. Empathy may then be a source of great moral progress, as it vividly informs us of how various actions and policies affect others.

There are several issues with appealing to empathy to support utilitarian rationalism. One well-known limitation is in empathy itself: it's notoriously partial and myopic. We feel it more strongly toward those we happen to already care most about, like friends and family, but also those who happen to be similar to oneself, even just in ethnicity (for review, see Prinz 2011). Related to this, empathy appears to be easily manipulated by arbitrary factors, like how vividly another's plight is represented, as when we feel more compassion for fewer identifiable victims than for large groups of "statistical victims" (e.g. Jenni & Loewenstein 1997). As John Rawls points out, the utilitarian "conception of justice is threatened with instability unless sympathy and benevolence can be widely and intensely cultivated" (1971: 155). Empirical evidence seems to confirm that the requisite level of impartiality and inclusiveness may be impossible to achieve with empathy.

The situation might not be so dire. Some evidence does suggest that we can expand compassion toward large groups when we're not focused on the costs of empathizing (Cameron & Payne 2011). And some theorists conceive empathy more narrowly as an imaginative process in which one maintains such a sharp distinction between self and other that one does not illicitly import one's own perspective and biases (e.g. Coplan 2011; Batson 2011). This specific kind of empathizing, which is associated with distinct brain circuits, may make it more suitable for extreme impartiality and inclusivity. Nevertheless, such forms of empathizing remain rare and taxing for most of us.

Another issue concerns the ability to understand what others are thinking and feeling ("theory of mind"). This capacity, intimately related to empathy, seems to be intact in some individuals, such as psychopaths, who are nevertheless typically depraved. What seems to aid moral knowledge in an empathic response is the compassionate concern that typically comes with it, not the rational recognition that everyone's happiness matters equally. Moreover, autism seems to involve an impairment in social understanding, not sentiment, but a moral deficit doesn't apparently follow (Nichols 2004). Some Kantians have argued that psychopaths have cognitive deficits in their capacity to reason appropriately (e.g. Maibom 2005). But, if psychopaths can recognize what others think and feel, what other cognitive element could be missing that is part of the *utilitarian* appeal to empathy?

Kantian rationalists tend to hold that morality is chiefly grounded in reason, particularly in reasoning about what to do or the appreciation of others as free and rational beings, like oneself. Not all Kantians draw on empathy (e.g. Rawls 1971), but it can become relevant to the recognition of the interests and autonomy of others. Thomas Nagel (1970), for example, grounds morality in reason by a comparison to prudence. Why should I act for the benefit of my future self (e.g. save for retirement)? Nagel's answer is, roughly, that my current self is merely one among many across time and it would be irrational to arbitrarily privilege my *current* self over later incarnations. Similarly, Nagel argues that morality arises out of the recognition that one is merely one among many distinct people and that it would be irrational to arbitrarily privilege *me* over *them*.

Nagel explicitly denies that sympathy is the relevant mechanism here (1970: 80), but this is only because he conceives of sympathy as opposed to reason. Presumably, though, even if empathy has an affective component, it can serve as an epistemic aid by drawing one's attention to morally relevant facts. Empathizing with others (or one's future self) might, for example, generate an appreciation for their personhood and the irrationality of treating them unfairly. Moreover, it may be precisely empathy's intersubjectivity that allows it to play this role in the Kantian project, for one must recognize others' interests but also that they are distinct autonomous persons (Deigh 1995).

Empathy does seem to increase the tendency to impute agency. Sharing the pain or joy of others provides vivid reminders that they too are individuals with their own concerns, relationships, and values. This may explain why empathizing with fictional characters and animals amplifies anthropomorphism. Consider the negative reactions to videos in which engineers at Google kicked a dog-like robot to test its ability to remain upright while moving. Some viewers expressed concern for Spot, describing the treatment as cruel and rude, despite knowing full well that the machine is a mindless automaton.

Kantian theories also needn't rely on empathy to generate purely impartial concern for all. Such theories can more easily accept that empathy motivates greater concern for select individuals, such as family, friends, and members of one's in-group. Kantians simply prescribe impartiality in the form of treating all persons fairly, respecting their capacity for choosing their own path through life autonomously (Rawls 1971). Empathy needn't make people act in ways that eschew special obligations to kith and kin; it must only aid in the recognition of others as deserving of a minimal level of respect (compare Deigh 1995).

But don't psychopaths understand what others think and feel, but simply don't care? The missing element seems to be a sentiment or feeling, not a rational recognition. Perhaps; but the Kantian appeal to empathy may involve more cognitive elements than theory of mind. One might appeal in particular to a recognition of intersubjectivity – e.g. that others are distinct persons with concerns relevantly similar to one's own (compare Deigh 1995). For example, there is some evidence that psychopaths have shorter attention spans and do not respond well to certain kinds of learning by negative reinforcement (Maibom 2005). Such deficits impair reasoning about what to do, including universalizing one's reasons for action or appreciating that it is irrational to arbitrarily privilege one's own interests over the like interests of others.

It's no wonder that egocentricity (grandiose sense of self-worth) is a diagnostic element of the psychopathy checklist.

Autism is a different matter, but some Kantians contend that their deficits in social understanding do indeed lead to some impairment in moral reasoning, even if nowhere near as severe as the psychopath's (Kennett 2002). Those with severe autism do often struggle to navigate the social world, failing to fully appreciate common moral norms that are grounded in what other people think and feel. This is a more superficial deficit than in psychopathy, because autism only limits understanding of what others care about, not the recognition that their concerns, whatever they may be, are no less important just because they aren't one's *own*.

The Kantian project may ultimately do no better than the utilitarian one. The point for our purposes is simply that empathy has the potential to do important work for various ethical theories, even in the absence of a literal merging between self and other. As empathy tends to militate against egocentricity, it provides a level of intersubjectivity that can still do heavy lifting in ethics.

7. Conclusion

Empathy and intersubjectivity are certainly related, but the connection can seem to point in multiple directions. Optimists believe empathy puts us in touch with others in a way that generates a compassionate concern that forms the foundation of morality and even immortality. Pessimists argue that empathy merely blurs the distinction between oneself and others, yielding self-interested motivation or at least precluding genuine altruism. The truth may lie somewhere in between, for both of these camps may oversell the idea that empathy leads to self-other merging. Still, while maintaining a sharp distinction between self and other, empathy's intersubjectivity can inform debates about the very foundations of morality. Even if empathy makes one neither a self-interested snake nor a selfless saint on a path to immortality, it can perhaps ground altruistic concern for others and an appreciation of oneself as merely one among many moral beings in the universe.

Acknowledgements For helpful feedback, I thank George Graham, Heidi Maibom, and Colin Marshall.

References

Badhwar, N. (1993) "Altruism versus Self-Interest: Sometimes a False Dichotomy," *Social Philosophy and Policy* 10 (1): 90–117.

Batson, C. D. (2011) *Altruism in Humans*, New York: Oxford University Press.

Batson, C. D., K. Sager, E. Garst, M. Kang, K. Rubchinsky, & K. Dawson (1997) "Is Empathy-Induced Helping Due to Self-Other Merging?" *Journal of Personality and Social Psychology* 73 (3): 495–509.

Cameron, C. D., & B. K. Payne (2011) "Escaping Affect: How Motivated Emotion Regulation Creates Insensitivity to Mass Suffering," *Journal of Personality and Social Psychology* 100 (1): 1–15.

Cappelen, H., & J. Dever (2013) *The Inessential Indexical*, Oxford: Oxford University Press.

Cialdini, R. B., S. L. Brown, B. P. Lewis, C. Luce, & S. L. Neuberg (1997) "Reinterpreting the Empathy-Altruism Relationship: When One into One Equals Oneness," *Journal of Personality and Social Psychology* 73 (3): 481–94.

Coplan, A. (2011) "Will the Real Empathy Please Stand Up? A Case for a Narrow Conceptualization," *The Southern Journal of Philosophy* 49 (s1): 40–65, Spindel Supplement: Empathy and Ethics, Remy Debes (ed.).

Decety, J., & P. L. Jackson (2004) "The Functional Architecture of Human Empathy," *Behavioral and Cognitive Neuroscience Reviews* 3 (2): 71–100.

Deigh, J. (1995) "Empathy and Universalizability," *Ethics* 105 (4): 743–63.

Greene, J. (2013) *Moral Tribes*, New York: Penguin Press.

Holle, H., M. J. Banissy, & J. Ward (2013) "Functional and Structural Brain Differences Associated with Mirror-Touch Synaesthesia," *Neuroimage* 83: 1041–50.

Hume, D. (1739) *A Treatise of Human Nature*, D. F. Norton & M. J. Norton (eds.), Oxford: Oxford University Press, 2000.

Hutcheson, F. (1725) *Inquiry into the Original of Our Ideas of Beauty and Virtue*, Fifth ed., London.

Jenni, K., & G. Loewenstein (1997) "Explaining the Identifiable Victim Effect," *Journal of Risk and Uncertainty* 14 (3): 235–57.

Johnston, M. (2010) *Surviving Death*, Princeton, NJ: Princeton University Press.

Kennett, J. (2002) "Autism, Empathy and Moral Agency," *Philosophical Quarterly* 52 (208): 340–57.

Maibom, H. L. (2005) "Moral Unreason: The Case of Psychopathy," *Mind and Language* 20 (2): 237–57.

May, J. (2011a) "Relational Desires and Empirical Evidence against Psychological Egoism," *European Journal of Philosophy* 19 (1): 39–58.

May, J. (2011b) "Egoism, Empathy, and Self-Other Merging," *Southern Journal of Philosophy* 49 (s1): 25–39, Spindel Supplement: Empathy and Ethics, Remy Debes (ed.).

Monroe, K. R., M. C. Barton, & U. Klingemann (1990) "Altruism and the Theory of Rational Action: Rescuers of Jews in Nazi Europe," *Ethics* 101 (1): 103–22.

Nagel, T. (1970) *The Possibility of Altruism*, Oxford: Oxford University Press.

Nichols, S. (2004) *Sentimental Rules: On the Natural Foundations of Moral Judgment*, New York: Oxford University Press.

Nussbaum, M. (2001) *Upheavals of Thought*, New York: Cambridge University Press.

Parfit, D. (1984) *Reasons and Persons*, New York: Oxford University Press.

Perry, J. (1979) "The Problem of the Essential Indexical," *Noûs* 13 (1): 3–21.

Prinz, J. (2011) "Against Empathy," *The Southern Journal of Philosophy* 49 (s1): 214–33.

Railton, P. (1984) "Alienation, Consequentialism, and the Demands of Morality," *Philosophy & Public Affairs* 13 (2): 134–71.

Rawls, J. (1971) *A Theory of Justice*, Boston, MA: Harvard University Press.

Schopenhauer, A. (1840/1999) *On the Basis of Morality*, E. F. J. Payne (trans.), Indianapolis, IN: Hackett.

Siderits, M. (1997) "Buddhist Reductionism," *Philosophy East and West* 47 (4): 455–78.

Singer, P. (1981/2011) *The Expanding Circle: Ethics, Evolution, and Moral Progress*, New Afterward Edition, Princeton, NJ: Princeton University Press.

Slote, M. (2010) *Moral Sentimentalism*, New York: Oxford University Press.

Smith, A. (1759/2004) *The Theory of Moral Sentiments*, Knud Haakonssen (ed.), Cambridge: Cambridge University Press.

Strohminger, N., & S. Nichols (2014) "The Essential Moral Self," *Cognition* 131 (1): 159–71.

Torrance, F. (2011) "I Feel Other People's Pain," *The Guardian* (March 18), <www.theguardian.com/life-andstyle/2011/mar/19/i-feel-other-peoples-pain>.

Williams, B. (1970) "The Self and the Future," *The Philosophical Review* 79 (2): 161–80.

16

EMPATHY AND IMAGINATION

Adam Morton

1. Introduction

Human beings do a lot of imagining. We imagine what would happen if various things were to pass, how to get to various destinations, how to achieve various ends, and nearer to the target of this volume, what it is like for other people. Children and adults engage in imaginative play, and the use of the imagination is central to many forms of art. It is controversial how these different situations, which we describe with the verb "to imagine/in," are related, and how much unity there is to the psychological capacities that we bring to them. It is widely suspected that childhood development imaginative play, such as pretending that a banana is a telephone or that a teddy bear can understand what is said to him (Harris 2000), develops alongside the capacity for counterfactual thinking ("what would happen if I dropped this glass") (Williamson 2005), the capacity to reason from an assumption "for the sake of argument" (Johnson Laird 2006), and the capacity to imagine the feelings and reactions of others (Leslie 1987, Byrne 2005, Tomasello et al. 2005). And it is often argued that artistic traditions similarly scaffold such capacities in adults. The title of one of the most influential works on the imagination in art, *Mimesis as Make-Believe* (Walton 1990, for doubts see Moran 1994), reveals the suspicion that childhood play and adult art build on similar human traits. And it is also often argued that some failures of the imagination unite such different syndromes as autism and psychopathy (Happé 1994). But the evidence is ambiguous. (My own suspicion, no more than that, is that there are a number of human capacities, all of which are employed in these different areas, which do not have names in everyday language, and which in normal human life support one another in a way that makes them hard to separate.)

The aim of this chapter is to give a systematic description of imagining the plight of others, without begging questions that await more evidence and analysis. I connect most of the work I shall refer to by linking it to a puzzle about the role of imagining what someone is feeling, and to a proposed resolution of the puzzle (for imagination, see Gendler 2013).

2. The puzzle

The puzzle can be described by contrasting two rather different functions of empathy. The first function is that of grasping facts about how situations feel to others in a way that allows one to manage one's relations with them. (It is not our only resource for doing this.) And contrasting with this, there is the function of *showing* solidarity with people in their situations. There is a tension between these two functions. It can be described in everyday terms as an issue about honesty. The honesty in question is admitting that you do not know what another person is going through, and the context is that in which that person needs sympathy and support. The tension is between understanding and doing. For many purposes we need explanations, models, predictions, and the like, of other people's thoughts, motives, and feelings. These are things that can be true or false, accurate or inaccurate, known or unknown. Very often we simply do not have them: the other person is in some respect a mystery to us. For other purposes we need to show commiseration, sympathy, even understanding. Often human social life demands that we act in these "empathetic" ways, even when we do not have the cognitive grasp of the other that might seem to be presupposed. So perhaps we can and even should simply fake it, act according to a script without understanding what lies behind the other role in the script. That is what makes it an issue of honesty.

The possibility of fake empathy raises a central issue. People want to be treated empathetically, but they want it to be real, to arise from a real concern with their real predicaments. I take that as obvious, but also think of the Greek root in "em*pathy*" or the root of the German "Mit*gefühl*," signifying that one person shares the painful feelings of another. So the problem is that we want something that is often impossible. The resolution I shall propose amounts to saying that that the understanding of people we need in many situations does need to be accurate, but it does not need to be accurate in the ways one might naïvely expect. In particular, it does not need to represent their feelings and emotions accurately.

3. Empathy and imagination: definitions and contrasts

I shall take empathy as a broad family of states where one person's emotion causes another to have a closely related emotion. This in turn puts pressure on the concept of emotion. I shall require that emotions have affective and cognitive components – they are associated with characteristic feelings and they affect thought and motivation – which are non-accidentally correlated. (For an introduction to accounts of emotion in philosophy see Goldie 2003, for a survey of psychological data see Fox 2008, and for a comprehensive collection with a helpful introduction see Goldie 2010.) I will not define "closely related" for the pairs of the emotion of the empathizing person and that of the person with whom she empathizes, except to require that the subjective affect of the two should be similar, and in particular they should match in hedonic quality: an unpleasant state should be matched with another unpleasant one. Typically the empathizer's emotion causes her to act in a way that helps the person she is empathizing with. But on some accounts of empathy and especially sympathy, the motive to help is incidental. There are many ways of organizing the components of these emotions and attitudes, but we can distinguish between resonance – feeling what another person feels; appropriateness – having a suitable reaction to their situation; and identification – having an attitude that makes their aims and troubles into your concern (Coplan 2011, Maibom 2007, 2014). A person can have any of these alone, without the others. The possibility that is relevant to our puzzle is that of having appropriateness and identification without resonance. One can care about another and react well to them without feeling what they do, or even knowing what they feel.

In order to make the contrasts between empathy with and without imagination starker, I shall work with the very broad and basic definition of empathy above as the sharing of states, knowing that there are important distinctions that it ignores. (This is like the account in Stotland 1969.) I will refer to empathy that may not satisfy more than the bare bones of this definition as "basic empathy." A dog can show basic empathy when she picks up that you are upset and licks your face.

Imagination, as I shall use the term, always involves the representation of one thing by a state of mind whose cognitive properties reflect some of its own properties. (See Strawson 1970, Brann 1991, Casey 2000, Stevenson 2003, Currie & Ravenscroft 2002, and Nichols 2006. Few writers argue that there is a deep unity to the range of processes we label as imagination. For an exception see McGinn 2004.) For example, imagining spatial relations between things differs from simply having beliefs about their locations, because imagined spatial relations can be rotated, translated, and so on, in ways that parallel the spatial relations of the things themselves. Imagination here tends to be associated with visual and spatial images, though the connection is controversial. (See Block 1981, Kind 2001, Pylyshin 2003, Kosslyn, Thompson, & Gannis 2006.) Imagination of states of mind is in a general way similar: when you imagine a person's psychological states you represent them with states that respond to your cognitive processes in ways that imitate, though typically simplifying, the ways that the other person's states respond to their cognition. You make a mental model of mental states. Imagination is not our only way of grasping the states of mind of others; we also have explicit and implicit theories of their states and how they interact. Proponents of imagination-based or "simulation" accounts and proponents of theory-based or "theory theory" accounts opposed each other for decades, but the consensus now is that we have mind-grasping resources of both kinds. (For early simulation accounts see Gordon 1986 and Goldman 2006. The term "theory theory" comes from Morton 1980. For their eventual reconciliation see Nichols & Stich 2003, Morton 2009, and Maibom 2007.)

Imagination, even of emotion, and empathy are different. Imagination fits its target largely in terms of how accurate it is as a representation of the target, as I explain below, and empathy fits its target largely in terms of the extent to which it is caused by it. We can have imagination without empathy, trivially if it does not represent emotions, and less trivially if it does not motivate empathetic behaviour. More subtly, imagination that centres on a state to which it gives roughly the cognitive and motivational states that it actually has, but which has the wrong hedonic tone, will not be empathy. (A pathological but psychologically acute risk taker imagining an extremely cautious one.) Even more subtly, consider imagination that represents the state as having the psychological properties that it does in fact have, in terms of a state which in fact is similar, but which the imagining person takes mistakenly to have a different affective tone. Then the state is being imagined, but the status of the process as empathy is very problematic. (An old-fashioned, self-deceiving, closeted gay person imagining a charming encounter with someone they are not in fact attracted to: he thinks it is empathy because he thinks both he and the target feel delight, but in fact the target's emotion is delight and his is discomfort labelled as delight.)

Empathy without imagination is also possible. One example is given by cases of emotional contagion (Hatfield, Cacioppo, & Rapson 1994, Goldie 2003), in which one person's visible emotion causes someone else to have a similar emotion in much the way that yawns are catching, without any cognition directed at the other. In a more interesting class of cases the empathizing person associates another person with a group of people who they think of as having some emotion, which, as a result, they feel with reference to that person. Call this empathy by association. In yet other cases the empathizer situates the empathizee in a situation in which it is normal to feel a particular emotion, and experiences some variety of that emotion. (See Coplan 2011, Maibom 2007.) Call this situational resonance.

Imagination is always partial and very often inaccurate. This is evident and inescapable in non-psychological imagination. Even imagining the layout of some very familiar location, such as your own home, you will leave out many details and get many others, for example the relative proportions of different walls, wrong. Incompleteness and limited accuracy is a feature of all imagination. Another way of saying this is that we imagine representations of facts, and we humans can never imagine all of any fact and always misimagine something about it. Imagination is in this respect like belief or expectation or memory, even when its vehicle is image-like. (For relations between imagination and belief see Byrne 2005.)

Incompleteness and inaccuracy are also to be expected when one person is imagining the mind of another. This will take different forms on different accounts of psychological imagination, but as long as there is a claim that the imagination is accurate then inaccuracy is a possibility, and as long as some imagination is more extensive than others, incompleteness is inevitable given the vast range of potential states to imagine. Representation brings with it the possibility of misrepresentation, and no single state will represent all of any person's mental states, not even most of those that are causally connected. It is easy to give examples of mis-imagination. There is all the data on the variety of contradictory emotions that one can attribute on the basis of facial configuration (Hastoff et al. 1970). There is the great range of explanations of people's behaviour that is consistent with everything one knows about them. And people are not as consistent as we tend to suppose, often acting out of what we take to be their characters and influenced by tiny details of their situations in ways that we find intuitively hard to digest (Nibett & Ross 1991). So consider how easily one can suppose that someone is acting out of affection when they are in fact calculating their own interest, or the reverse, or how easily one can suppose that someone is crying from sorrow, at a break-up say, when in fact they are crying from relief. In all these cases, I shall say that one's reaction is not accurate imagination (Matravers 2011, Morton 2013, part I).

4. Why does accuracy matter?

There are times when basic empathy is all we want. A friendly lick from a pet who is sensitive to your distress or an echoing groan from a companion is enough to make us feel better. But these are fairly rare. Much of the time we want something more individual, predicated more on our particular distress. This is particularly so with the reactions of other humans, especially those in a position to appreciate our particular plight. We can resent empathy that is automatic and based on superficial aspects of our behaviour. Consider for example a person, Melanie, in an unusual and delicate trap. She has encouraged George to become attached to her because Eric has jilted her. Now George has suggested marriage and she might be favourably inclined since she has come to appreciate his straightforward affection and his undeviousness. But Eric has just contacted her and intimated that he has made a terrible mistake and would like to get together again. Her time with George has made her realize quite how devious Eric is, and she is far from sure that Eric is not just trying to mess with George or her, and will be off again once the damage is done. But she retains a deep longing for him. Does she love him? Not really, though she finds him exciting. She meets her friend Helen, who sees how upset she is and asks about it. Helen's reaction on being given the barest outline is, "Oh you poor thing; these hard decisions can really take it out of you." Melanie snaps at her and changes the topic. The reason for her annoyance is that she is not bothered by the difficulty of the decision at all, but by her knowledge that after a ritual indecision she will choose Eric, knowing that it is a mistake and that it will lead to heartbreak for her and hurt the devoted George. She doesn't bother even trying to explain this to Helen because she has seen enough of Helen to know that Helen will not understand, and that more evidence of her immunity to the morally and psychologically subtle situation will be even more annoying.

Enough melodrama. Life is full of situations in which you want someone to feel a congruent emotion, but want her to feel it for the appropriate reasons. We want accuracy. And inasmuch as empathy serves a central role in human life, we want it to be more or less accurate. Some of the reasons for this are clear. We don't bond with people who misunderstand us, because they are likely to misjudge our feelings and preferences on other occasions. And there are times when knowing the reasons for our emotions is needed for helpful action. Helen is unlikely to be able to help Melanie either with her decision or with her emotions. And, harder to express clearly, there is a kind of loneliness that comes when people cannot grasp why you feel what you do.

This presents us with a problem. It is both a philosophical problem and one that arises frequently in our lives. We can rarely imagine the affective tone of other people's emotions at all accurately. This may seem surprising, since most people exhibit a fair amount of empathy, and this kind of imagination seems to be required to do it right. But, as I shall argue, it is rarely more than a rough approximation to the affect that is the target of our imagining.

5. What we do and do not imagine

We experience a lot of what I have called simple empathy. One kind is emotional contagion, already mentioned. Another is situational resonance. We see someone in a situation and we have the emotion that we associate with the situation. (People tend to speak of empathy more when the emotion is unpleasant: pain, loss, or frustration. Then it motivates sympathetic action.) Someone hits her thumb with a hammer and we say "ouch" while feeling an echo of the agony. But if we were to judge these like real imagination, as representations of someone else's mind, we can ask how often they would be accurate.

The answer is surely that they would often not be very accurate. Even when it comes to pain, what the empathetic person feels and what the target person feels are rarely very similar. The hammer hits the thumb and the person curses and bounces around. How high is their pain threshold, and for that matter is the reaction really to the damage or to the thought "Oh shit, I've missed the nail and hit my thumb"? Questions such as these multiply for more complicated unpleasant situations. Someone has just learned that she is losing her job, and you really feel for her, as you say. This is partly a reaction to the disturbed look on her face, partly from summoning your own uncertainties about your job situation, and partly because you know that losing one's job is a notoriously stressful thing. But do you understand the balance between fear for her future and anger at her boss? Do you have any sense of whether some anticipation of this was lurking beneath everyday awareness? Do you know whether the fallback plans and opportunities that are now open are occurring to her, or whether they are buried in the tempest of bad feeling? (See Goldie 2011.)

Where there is little precedence in your own experience you are likely to feel a wide stereotypical reaction rather than something tuned to the person's state and situation. Consider the Helen and Melanie example again. Does Helen have any hope of reproducing the balance between fear, indecision, anger, despair, and self-loathing in Melanie's mind? Can she even identify these components of Melanie's upset, explicitly or implicitly, as part of imagining them, let alone imagine the balance between them? I have portrayed Helen as reacting mechanically and unsubtly, but accuracy would be a tall order even for a focused and intuitive person. Most of us would take ourselves to have empathy for what it is like to be a refugee forced to give up the life that was familiar and live somewhere without status or grasp of the language or social customs, and no way of earning anything other than the most menial living. But we are very unlikely to be able to capture the real combination of desperation, despair, and hope – the feeling of out of the fire and into an unknown frying pan – that a refugee may actually experience (Maibom 2016).

The difficulties pertaining to imagining feelings stand out, even if we grant that any imaginative grasp of another person is incomplete and of limited accuracy. Contrast imagining feeling with imagining spatial navigation and reasoning. Two people have a plan to meet around noon at a downtown restaurant. One is arriving by train at 11:30 and the other is coming from their apartment ten busy city blocks away. The second person would like to arrive at the restaurant at the same time as the first, and so she imagines the first person's route from the station to the restaurant. She begins by imagining the shortest series of roads and crossings that will get him there, and then she imagines him walking it, knowing him well enough that she can simulate his pace and progress. She concludes that the trip as imagined will take him between 25 and 30 minutes, though she could do it in less time, and she knows from her experience that she can get to the restaurant in 15 minutes. So she leaves at 11:55. Or consider imagining another person doing arithmetic. You want to know what he will say if asked what 13×14 is. So you do it yourself, see what you get, and report that as the answer he is likely to give. Similar things hold when the task is more difficult or the other person would do it in a way that is different to yours but which you can imagine (Heal 1986).

We can also imagine other people's decision-making and action-planning with a fair degree of accuracy. This is one of our resources for anticipating the actions and reactions of others, without which human social life would be impossible. Though we think of others as affective creatures, with feelings and experience, it is their cognitive side that we most easily imagine. This can be put in a paradoxical way: simulated experience grasps thought and simulated thought grasps experience.

Perhaps then imagination – or any capacity that can be judged for accuracy – is not a good tool for empathy. Perhaps we should stick to emotional contagion, situational feeling, and whatever else makes us upset when others are upset. But these are not attractive options. We have already seen why: people's need for empathy is a need to be understood, to be the object of fellow-feeling for the right reasons. Is this a deep desire for the impossible?

6. Empathetic behaviour

It is important to comfort people, support them, make them feel that they are not alone. This hardly needs defence. Clumsy comfort is often resented, though. People don't want others assimilating their situation to that of everyone else whose case has some generic similarity. But, also, people don't want to be probed, analysed, or generally have their state of mind be the object of someone else's speculation and curiosity. Or, very often they do not. Even when it seems that one person has miraculously resonated to the way that someone else's situation feels to that very person, the person who is being imagined will often resent it, thinking that the other person is exhibiting some intuitive impudence or presumption in being right about them. It seems that we cannot win.

These considerations are somewhat less important when it is not a matter of giving comfort to someone in their presence, but helping them, possibly without their knowledge. But this too requires an accurate understanding of what will be of use to the other. And with this, some element of the same danger returns. The person may either find that the supposed help is not what they want or need, or, less common but still a real possibility, find that an accurate assessment is presumptuous or demeaning. For an example of this, consider an offer to help with someone's education that takes into account their actual tendency to boredom and distraction, and therefore avoids the high-level fantasy education that the person might want to be offered.

So it is delicate. One might just pretend, with whatever level and kind of assumed understanding that will please the other person. But of course we usually want to do good, in a way that is deeper than simply acting in a pleasing way. And we don't want our efforts to be wasted, as they often will be if the manner of our efforts to help is constrained by the style in which it would please the person to be helped.

Simply asking the person may not solve the problem. In fact it is often does not. One reason is that they may not reply frankly, perhaps because they anticipate that you will react badly to an admission of their true feelings. Another reason is that in the situations in which people are most in need of empathy they are often not at their most introspective or expressive. In fact, there is another theme here, that of the tension between accurate capture of someone's emotional state and faithfulness to what they take their state to be, often mis-imagining themselves (Sherman 2015).

Sometimes expression of empathy does not enter the picture. One case is that in which one suddenly comes to understand what it was like for the recipient of one of one's past actions. This can result in unexpected remorse. Although this is fairly frequent in human life, at least in mine, I shall say no more about it.

7. A solution

I have organized my exposition around a problem, which is as much a problem of practical social life as it is one of theoretical understanding. The problem was that of producing the kind of empathetic behaviour that is likely to be emotionally useful to other people in the ignorance we usually have of their detailed mental states, and in particular of the way they will react to our well-meaning gestures. It looks as if we cannot win: either we act on inadequate evidence, and thus often get it wrong, or we hesitate because the evidence is inadequate, and are blamed for lack of empathy.

Well, nothing is going to make the problem go away. There is a divide between large-hearted, hasty, and often mistaken empathetic styles, on the one hand, and more careful styles in danger of seeming cold or aloof, on the other. The discussion of imagination in previous sections, though, gives us some suggestions about how to handle it. In a way, the solution is obvious.

We are rarely very accurate in imagining the detailed feel of others' emotions (but see Chapter 13, "Empathy and Knowing What It's Like"). That is an understatement, if what I have been saying is correct. But we are much better at imagining their thoughts, desires, intentions, and so on. There is a basic reason why we imagine beliefs, desires, and the like more accurately than we do affective states. They are propositional attitudes, taking the form "person p desires/wants/hopes/fears/etc. that s" where the s space is occupied by an English sentence. So to understand that someone hopes that, say, Sally is elected to the senate, one has only to understand the meaning of "to hope" and of "Sally is elected to the senate." And any normal ten-year-old can do this without drawing on great depths of psychological intuition. It is an analogue/digital distinction: imagination of feeling is analogue, with arbitrarily fine distinctions and gradations, while imagination and attribution of propositional attitudes is digital, based on fixed relations to discrete objects without intermediary cases. Moreover, on one now dominant account of propositional attitudes they are relations to individual things in the environment rather than to mental contents (Braun 1998). To give a standard example, "Hammurabi believes the evening star will soon rise" and "Hammurabi believes the morning star will soon rise" are both relations between Hammurabi and the planet Venus, which is both the evening star and the morning star. This leaves even less room for variety and subjectivity.

One might object to this that while ascription of propositional attitudes is in this way, digital imagination of them is a more varied and nuanced business. Now not all ascription draws on the imagination, unless pure simulation accounts are correct, but imagination-based ascription is still ascription. One person imagines that another wants to drink some water, so she grasps imaginatively his relation to the proposition "I want a drink of water": the grasp is imaginative, and may tell her something about him besides this particular desire, but it is a grasp of the relation to this proposition and no other. The implications for anticipating his reactions and other behaviour are the same whether the procedure used is imaginative or not, though the mechanisms of both ascription and prediction may be different. In the example, the ascription in both cases supports the prediction that the person is likely to walk over to the water cooler, and that he is likely to become angry if told to stay at his desk for an hour. So while imaginatively attributing propositional attitudes may give one less of a feel for what it is like to be a particular person, it opens a less delicate way to the anticipation of some of that person's future actions, on which much human cooperation and interaction depend.

As a result, we can consider different ways of interacting with the person who needs our attention, and we can assess which ones will be judged as callous, sympathetic, supportive, intrusive, presumptive, or whatever. We can focus on the other person's reactions to our rough take on their feelings rather than on the details of their feelings themselves. In fact, imagining the emotions of the other is often the least important aspect. Our imaginative efforts are best expended at grasping the other person's reactions to our expressions of empathy. If we get the reactions to our empathetic actions and gestures right, then accuracy about the person's feelings about their situation is much less crucial. If we are wrong about them and still do the right thing, our efforts will be appreciated, while if we are right about them and do the wrong thing, all is wasted.

Here are two examples, to illustrate this theme. First, consider refugees again. The situation of a refugee is so different from that of average middle-class academics in comfortable countries that our attempts to imagine the states of mind of a refugee are inherently suspect. You can know a lot about a refugee's objective situation without having any idea whether they are elated (to have escaped a grim situation), demoralized (because their present situation is grim), or incomprehending (because the new grimness is so puzzling). And trying to decide between these is presumptuous. All you need to know is that these people need help, and know how it will be best received. The second example is a real recent situation in my town, Vancouver. Disabled people in a welfare hotel have been stuck on the upper floors without food because the landlord refuses to repair the elevators. Are these people resigned, in the face of the latest assault on their dignity, or angry, in the face of offensive indifference, or desperate, in the face of imminent hunger? I have no idea, although my situation is just a little bit nearer to theirs than those of the average reader of this piece. (I too live on an upper floor, cannot get down by myself, and am trapped when the elevators are not functioning. But mine is a nice building and I have money.) But we don't need to know any of this: all that matters is that these people are stuck with no access to food, and that we find a way of alleviating the situation that does not offend or demean them. The solution to being bad at imagining some things is to imagine more things and to situate the areas of feeble imagination among them.

This may seem arrogant or impersonal, as it may seem to recommend pleasing the other without really understanding how it is for them. No: it is our best bet for helping, comforting, and aligning our interests with those of the other person. It may require sacrifices on our part. And that is the point of being empathetic. We can do well by putting a lot of effort into entering into an imaginative grasp of our relations with other people, even at the price of a very rudimentary grasp of what that particular person in that particular situation feels.

In fact, there is a way in which the strategy I am describing does engage with details of what people are feeling. First, it creates a line of communication between people, giving time and a suitable context to get more information. More profoundly, though more controversially, it allows and encourages a lot of mutual imagining. Each person can get a sense of the other person's reactions to their reactions to whatever it is that they are reacting to. Among these reactions are thoughts that each person has about their feelings. "This is a really painful topic for me but she seems insensitive to that," "If I say this more carefully he may understand that jealousy isn't a factor here," "I find it frustrating that she isn't comforted by my pointing this out." But if you know how somebody thinks they feel, and what they make of somebody else's reactions to what that person thinks they feel, you have at any rate a sense of what their subjective life is like. If we combine this with an assumption that our naïve emotions of fellow feeling are at any rate a starting point for grasping the affect of the other, then the gap between what we are good at imagining and what eludes us is beginning to close. (A picture somewhat like this is sometimes associated with Wittgenstein and called "expressivism." See Wittgenstein 1953: sections 285, 304, 580, Mulhall 1990, and Morton 2003: exploration II.)

References

Block, N. (ed.) (1981) *Imagery*, Cambridge, MA: MIT Press.

Brann, E. T. H. (1991) *The World of the Imagination*, Lanham, MD: Rowman & Littlefield.

Braun, David (1998) "Understanding Belief Reports," *Phil. Rev.* 107, 555–96.

Byrne, R. (2005) *The Rational Imagination*, Cambridge, MA: MIT Press.

Casey, E. (2000) *Imagining: A Phenomenological Study*, 2nd ed., Bloomington, IN: Indiana University Press.

Coplan, A. (2011) "Understanding Empathy: Its Features and Effects," in A. Coplan & P. Goldie (eds), *Empathy: Philosophical and Psychological Perspectives*, Oxford: Oxford University Press, 3–18.

Currie, G., & I. Ravenscroft (2002) *Recreative Minds: Imagination in Philosophy and Psychology*, Oxford: Oxford University Press.

Davies, M., & T. Stone (eds) (1995) *Mental Simulation*, Oxford: Blackwell.

Fox, E. (2008) *Emotion Science*, London: Palgrave Macmillan.

Gendler, T. (2013) "Imagination," *Stanford Encyclopedia of Philosophy*, http://plato.stanford.edu/entries/imagination/ accessed 25 May 2016.

Goldie, P. (2003) *The Emotions: A Philosophical Exploration*, Oxford: Oxford University Press.

Goldie, P. (2010) *The Oxford Handbook of Philosophy of Emotion*. Oxford: Oxford University Press.

Goldie, P. (2011) "Anti-Empathy," in A. Coplan & P. Goldie (eds) *Empathy: Philosophical and Psychological Perspectives*, Oxford: Oxford University Press, 302–17.

Goldman, A. (2006) *Simulating Minds*, Oxford: Oxford University Press.

Gordon, R. (1986) "Folk Psychology as Simulation," *Mind and Language* 1, 158–71; reprinted in M. Davies & T. Stone (eds) (1995) *Mental Simulation*, Oxford: Blackwell.

Happé, F. (1994) *Autism: An Introduction to Psychological Theory*, London: UCL Press.

Harris, P. L. (2000) *The Work of the Imagination*, Oxford: Blackwell.

Hastorf, D., D. J. Schneider, & J. Polefka (1970) *Person Perception*, Reading: Addison-Wesley.

Hatfield, E., J. T. Cacioppo, & R. L. Rapson (1994) *Emotional Contagion*, Cambridge: Cambridge University Press.

Heal, J. (1986) "Replication and Functionalism," in J. Butterfield (ed.), *Language, Mind, and Logic*, Cambridge: Cambridge University Press, 135–50; reprinted in M. Davies & T. Stone (eds) (1995) *Mental Simulation*, Oxford: Blackwell.

Johnson Laird, P. N. (2006) *How We Reason*, Oxford: Oxford University Press.

Kind, A. (2001) "Putting the Image Back in Imagination," *Philosophy and Phenomenological Research* 62, 85–109.

Kosslyn, S. M., W. L. Thompson, & G. Ganis (2006) *The Case for Mental Imagery*, Oxford: Oxford University Press.

Lacewing, M. (2015) "Emotions and the Virtues of Self-Understanding," in S. Roeser & C. Todd (eds), *Emotion and Value*, Oxford: Oxford University Press.

Leslie, A. (1987) "Pretense and Representation: The Origins of 'Theory of Mind'," *Psychological Review* 94(4), 412–26.

Maibom, H. (2007) "The Presence of Others," *Philosophical Studies* 132, 161–90.

Maibom, H. (2014) "Everything You Ever Wanted to Know about Empathy," in H. Maibom (ed.), *Empathy and Morality*, Oxford: Oxford University Press, 1–40.

Maibom, H. (2016) "Knowing Me, Knowing You: Failure to Forecast and the Empathic Imagination," in A. Kind & P. Kung (eds), *Knowledge through Imagination*, New York: Oxford University Press, 185–206.

Matravers, D. (2011) "Empathy as a Route to Knowledge," in A. Coplan & P. Goldie (eds), *Empathy: Philosophical and Psychological Perspectives*, Oxford: Oxford University Press, 19–30.

McGinn, C. (2004) *Mindsight: Image, Dream, Meaning*, Cambridge, MA: Harvard University Press.

Moran, R. (1994) "The Expression of Feeling in Imagination," *Philosophical Review* 103(1), 75–106.

Morton, A. (1980) *Frames of Mind*, Oxford: Oxford University Press.

Morton, A. (2003) *The Importance of Being Understood: Folk Psychology as Ethics*, London: Routledge.

Morton, A. (2009) "Folk Psychology," in Brian McLaughlin & Ansgar Beckermann (eds), *The Oxford Handbook of Philosophy of Mind*, Oxford: Oxford University Press, 713–26.

Morton, A. (2013) *Emotion and Imagination*, Cambridge: Polity.

Mulhall, S. (1990) *On Being in the World: Wittgenstein and Heidegger on Seeing Aspects*, London: Routledge.

Nichols, S. (ed.) (2006) *The Architecture of the Imagination: New Essays on Pretense, Possibility, and Fiction*, Oxford: Oxford University Press.

Nichols, S., & S. Stich (2003) *Mindreading: An Integrated Account of Pretense, Self-Awareness and Understanding Other Minds*, Oxford: Oxford University Press.

Nisbett, R., & L. Ross (1991) *The Person and the Situation*, New York: McGraw-Hill.

Pylyshyn, Z. W. (2003) *Seeing and Visualizing*, Cambridge, MA: MIT Press.

Shepard, R. (1982) *Mental Images and their Transformations*, Cambridge: Bradford Books.

Sherman, Nancy (2015) "Self-Empathy and Moral Repair," in S. Roesser & C. Todd (eds), *Emotion and Value*, Oxford: Oxford University Press, 183–99.

Stevenson, L. (2003) "Twelve Conceptions of Imagination," *British Journal of Aesthetics* 43(3), 238–59.

Stotland, E. (1969) "Exploratory Investigations of Empathy," in L. Berkowitz (ed.), *Advances in Experimental Social Psychology*, vol. 4, New York/London: Academic Press, 271–314.

Strawson, P. F. (1970) "Imagination and Perception," in L. Foster & J. W. Swanson (eds), *Experience and Theory*, Amherst, MA: University of Massachusetts Press, 31–54.

Tomasello, M., M. Carpenter, J. Call, T. Behne, & H. Moll (2005) "Understanding and Sharing Intentions: The Origins of Cultural Cognition," *Behavioral and Brain Sciences* 28(5), 675–91.

Tye, M. (1991) (repr. 2000) *The Imagery Debate*, Cambridge, MA: MIT Press.

Walton, K. (1990) *Mimesis as Make-Believe*, Cambridge, MA: Harvard University Press.

Williamson, T. (2005) "Armchair Philosophy, Metaphysical Modality, and Counterfactual Thinking," *Proceedings of the Aristotelian Society* 105, 1–23.

Wittgenstein, L. (1953) *Philosophical Investigations*, Oxford: Blackwell.

17

EMPATHY AND PSYCHIATRIC ILLNESS

Matthew Ratcliffe

Introduction

It has become something of a commonplace for philosophers to observe that the term "empathy" has been and continues to be used in a number of different ways (e.g. Coplan, 2011, p. 40; Zahavi, 2014, p. 152). I accept that this is the case, although I am less sure that it *should* be. Nevertheless, given the possibility that "empathy" legitimately refers to a range of different cognitive achievements, I will restrict my enquiry here to something that people often (but by no means always) refer to as empathy in the context of psychiatric illness. I will sketch an account of what it is to empathize with experiences of psychiatric illness by asking, "What, exactly, is lacking or judged to be lacking when the sufferer states that others do not or cannot empathize with her?" and, conversely, "When she does feel empathized with, what is it that she recognizes?" The answer to these questions, I will suggest, points to a conception of empathy that differs markedly from the kinds of cognitive achievement philosophers tend to associate with the term.

Most recent philosophical accounts of empathy appeal to one or another form of mental simulation. Empathy is said to consist, partly or wholly, of person A's generating a first-person experience that is similar to person B's experience, in order to understand the latter. Proponents of the view tend to distinguish two types of simulation: an explicit, effortful modelling of somebody else's experience, and an implicit replication process that facilitates a perceptual or at least perception-like appreciation of experience. For instance, Goldman (2011, pp. 33–6) describes both "reconstructive" empathy and automatic "mirroring" (see also Goldman, 2006; Stueber, 2006). A further distinction has been drawn between two types of explicit simulation. One might think of simulation in terms of putting oneself in another person's physical or psychological situation and then imagining what one would experience, think, or do. However, it has been argued that this is insufficient for empathy: one has to somehow occupy the other person's perspective, rather than attempt to model what he experiences while retaining one's own first-person perspective. Hence Gordon (1995, p. 734) appeals to an ability to "recenter" one's "egocentric map", while Darwall (1998, p. 268) maintains that "projective empathy" involves feeling "as though we were they", and Coplan (2011, p. 53) similarly insists that empathy involves "other-oriented" rather than "self-oriented" perspective-taking.

I will show how empathizing with experiences of psychiatric illness often involves something importantly different from both kinds of explicit simulation. It is not so much a matter of generating similarities, as recognizing the possibility of profound forms of phenomenological difference that people are more usually oblivious to. Indeed, when acknowledgement of difference by A is successfully conveyed to B, this sometimes suffices for B's recognition of empathy on the part of A. Furthermore, understanding someone else's experience by means of simulation is psychologically impossible in at least some cases. Insofar as empathy is still achievable in these cases, it must therefore be something else.

Empathy is generally taken to involve more than just *understanding*; one must also *experience* something of what another person experiences. And this, one might worry, is something that an emphasis on difference-recognition does not capture. So there may still be a role for implicit simulation mechanisms, which facilitate a perceptual or quasi-perceptual appreciation of at least some aspects of the other person's experience. However, I will distinguish three ways in which one might be said to "experience someone else's experience", at least two of which are not principally a matter of simulation. These two, I will suggest, play a more central role in the kind of empathy described here. In so doing, I will also distinguish my account of empathy from an approach that originates in the phenomenological tradition of philosophy and is often pitted against simulation theory. According to that approach, empathy is a distinctive kind of intentionality, which enables a perceptual or perception-like appreciation of another person's experience (e.g. Stein, 1917/1989; Zahavi, 2007, 2011, 2014, Thompson, 2007). Even though this kind of appreciation has some role to play, it is just one part of a larger picture.

Hence I will arrive at a distinctive conception of empathy, one that may also have wider applicability. It does not conform to any simulationist approach to empathy, and neither is it to be identified with the "phenomenological" alternative. It is, however, quite consistent with many descriptions of empathy that have been offered by clinicians, in psychiatric contexts and more widely, and could be pieced together from their various remarks (e.g. Halpern, 2001, 2003; Havens, 1986; Margulies, 1989).

Disturbances of empathy

The theme of feeling estranged from other people in general features in many first-person accounts of psychiatric illness, and is not specific to any particular diagnosis. J. H. van den Berg (1972, p. 105), in a phenomenological characterization of what he calls the "typical psychiatric patient", describes this as follows:

> The psychiatric patient is alone. He has few relationships or perhaps no relationships at all. He lives in isolation. He feels lonely. He may dread an interview with another person. At times, a conversation with him is impossible. He is somewhat strange; sometimes he is enigmatic and he may, on rare occasions, be even unfathomable. The variations are endless, but the essence is always the same. The psychiatric patient stands apart from the rest of the world.

Experiences of interpersonal and social isolation are no doubt heterogeneous, and I do not wish to make sweeping generalizations concerning the kinds of experience associated with a specific psychiatric diagnosis or with psychiatric diagnoses in general. Nevertheless, it is safe to say that feeling cut off from other people is a frequent and prominent aspect of psychiatric illness experience, even though the details of the experience may vary considerably. If we start by construing empathy in a fairly permissive way, as a matter of *understanding what others experience*, it is clear that actual and perceived failures of empathy are a central theme in the testimonies of many psychiatric patients. Other people either are, or at least appear to be, incapable of understanding what the person is going through – they seem unsympathetic, distant, and even hostile towards him. For instance, the claim that others do not or cannot understand what one is going through features consistently in first-person accounts of depression:

> "… they are all selfish and don't understand"; "they don't understand and so act like nothing is wrong"; "It feels like no one else has ever experienced anything like this before, like you're all on your own"; "I find other people irritating when depressed, especially those that have never suffered with depression, and find the 'advice' often given by these is unempathetic and ridiculous"; "nobody understands or loves me"; "However much they say they understand, I don't believe them"; "There is the realization that you have never connected with anybody, truly, in your life"; "everyone seems so annoyingly normal, happy, able to cope, unaware of the turmoil that is filling my room, my head, my life, my world"; "You feel alone and in a world that cannot be easily explained or described."

On the other hand, the patient may knowingly or unknowingly fail to engage with the perspectives of others. Many of those who reflect back on their experiences of depression remark on their own failure to appreciate and engage with the perspectives of others, as well as their tendency to misinterpret other people in general as indifferent, disapproving, or hostile:

> "… when I am depressed very small things annoy me. I get angry with my partner and children for any reason, yet really they are being themselves. I also find it hard to show kindness and emotion to them"; "when I start to get depressed, I only filter through the negative messages from friends and family, so even the most benign comment can be perceived as an insult"; "They seem distant, inaccessible, critical, hostile. I find it much harder to understand their points of view and they seem to struggle to understand mine."

Depression can involve a kind of self-absorption, a preoccupation with one's own predicament. Thoughts about other people are often principally concerned with one's own suffering. Others fail to understand, regard one as worthless, or harbour hostile intentions: "When I am depressed I interpret many of the things that my family and friends do and say as being negative and most of the time persecutory. It is like everything they do is about me." (These testimonies were obtained via a 2011 questionnaire study on depression experiences, which I conducted with colleagues as part of the AHRC- and DFG-funded project "Emotional Experience in Depression: a Philosophical Study." For further details, see Ratcliffe, 2015, ch. 1.) In some cases, others are described not as specific individuals with distinctive emotions and concerns but in terms of an undifferentiated "they", whose sole role in the depression narrative is to convey disapproval of the author (Ratcliffe, 2015, p. 227). An extreme privation of interpersonal experience, more often associated with schizophrenia diagnoses, involves others not only starting to lose their distinctiveness as individuals but ceasing to be recognized as subjects of experience at all. They become "phantoms", or generic judges and persecutors that are bereft of other psychological characteristics (Minkowski, 1933/1970, p. 329). Hence, despite the diversity of experience encompassed by the label "psychiatric illness", and also by more specific diagnostic categories such as "major depression" and "schizophrenia", the actual and/or perceived lack of empathy by one or both parties is a conspicuous and wide-ranging theme. But what exactly is it that is lacking or perceived to be lacking?

Recognition of difference

Perhaps, one might suggest, lack of empathy in the context of psychiatric illness is best accounted for in terms of one or another form of mental simulation: we ordinarily come to understand others' experience by replicating them in the first person, a process that is more likely to fail in challenging cases such as these. It is not entirely clear how the relationship between empathy and simulation (of whatever kind) is supposed to be understood. Assertions to the effect that simulation *is* empathy, simulation *is necessary for* empathy, empathy is *partly constituted by simulation*, or empathy somehow *depends upon* simulation processes could be construed as debatable – and perhaps empirically testable – claims concerning the relationship between two independently identifiable accomplishments, x and y. Then again, it sometimes appears that the two are being treated as synonyms, rendering the claim that "empathy" is "simulation" true by definition. For example, Stueber (2006, pp. 3–4) labels the view that simulation is our primary means of accessing other minds as the "empathy view". Whichever the case, one of the philosophical lessons we can learn by considering psychiatric illness is that empathy does *not* have to be construed as wholly or principally a matter of simulation, or even as necessarily involving simulation.

It could well be that, in severe depression for instance, a sufferer's ability to simulate the minds of those who are not depressed is limited, and vice versa. But this is not usually what is at stake when it is stated that others do not or cannot understand what the person is going through. In some such cases, it could be that others do in fact understand but are misinterpreted as incapable or indifferent. Nevertheless, I think there is some truth to remarks that feature frequently in first-person accounts of psychiatric illness, to the effect that others do not or cannot comprehend the experience, or at least central aspects of it. Experiences of severe psychiatric illness are often described in terms of inhabiting a radically different world, an isolated, alien realm that is set apart from the consensus reality taken for granted by others as an unwavering backdrop to their experiences, thoughts, and activities:

> When people suggested to me that I had no good reason for being so full of self-disgust, their words made no sense. I was torpid, a sham, and deserved no self-respect. Most of all I was terribly alone, lost, in a harsh and far-away place, a horrible terrain reserved for me alone. There was nowhere to go, nothing to see, no panorama. Though this landscape surrounded me, vast and amorphous, I couldn't escape the awful confines of my leaden body and downcast eye. I didn't want to live, but I couldn't bear to die.
>
> *(Shaw, 1997, p. 40)*

Sufferers describe a global change in the structure of their experience. As the author of a well-known autobiography of schizophrenia puts it, madness is a "country" that is "opposed to reality" (Sechehaye, ed., 1970, p. 44). What is altered or lost is a sense of being comfortably immersed in a shared world, something that is so deep-rooted for many of us that it does not become an object of explicit reflection or enquiry. However, one does come to explicitly contemplate this aspect of experience when it is diminished or distorted. And, in seeking to describe it, one faces the challenge of conveying a change in x to those who have not yet recognized the existence of x:

> You know that you have lost life itself. You've lost a habitable earth. You've lost the invitation to live that the universe extends to us at every moment. You've lost something that people don't even know is. That's why it's so hard to explain.
>
> *(Quoted by Hornstein, 2009, p. 213)*

To comprehend such experiences, it must first be recognized that something we more usually take for granted is susceptible to disturbance, that radical phenomenological difference is possible. This recognition of potential difference is quite different from the task of attempting to bridge already established differences by means of simulation. Of course, some phenomenological differences are effortlessly and routinely recognized, and so it might be objected that recognition alone is not much of an achievement at all. For example, suppose that I am sitting at a table with person B, looking at a glass of wine. I recognize that B's position in the room gives her a perspective on the glass that differs from my own. I also recognize that the glass does not look inviting to B in the way it does to me, as B has just told me she does not like the taste of wine. Whenever I interact with another person, I register any number of phenomenological differences, some or all of which could conceivably be bridged by means of simulation. However, at the same time, I continue to take it as given that *we* inhabit the same social space, where chairs are for sitting on, tables are for placing drinks on, bars are for ordering drinks from, it is appropriate to talk informally, it is not appropriate to throw glasses against the wall, and so forth. In other words, one does not have to project, wholesale, an appreciation of norms, roles, artefact functions, and so forth onto the other person. It is something that both parties presuppose in the guise of a shared situation: it is "ours", rather than "mine" and also "yours". Much of what we experience is like this; it is not differentiated into yours and mine, but accepted as *our world*. I think this is partly what Jaspers (1912/1968, p. 1315) seeks to convey with the following passage:

> We understand other people, not through considering and analysing their mental life, but by living with them in the context of events, actions and personal destinies. Even when we do on occasion give consideration to mental experience as such, we do this only in a context of causes and effects as understood by us, or else we make a practice of classifying personalities into categories, etc.

Where potential or actual differences between A and B are more radical, where the "world" is not shared to such an extent, the task of understanding requires us to suspend assumptions of commonality. And there is more to this suspension than just recognizing that person B may not share a common, habitual, unthinking appreciation of norms, roles, and functions, which more usually appear as integral to the experienced world. B may have lost the sense that things could ever be different in a meaningful way, the sense of being spatially and temporally situated in a shared world, the sense that reality is separate from her imaginings (Ratcliffe, 2012). The task of understanding may be further obfuscated by B's sense of irrevocable estrangement from others, which may involve indifference to A's attempts to communicate or hostility towards A.

Hence acknowledging the possibility of profound phenomenological difference is essential to empathy in this context. This theme is all but absent from simulationist accounts, and also from phenomenologically inspired alternatives that emphasize some form of perceptual or quasi-perceptual relation. However, the need for heightened "openness" is a consistent theme throughout the clinical literature on empathy. For example, Halpern (2001, pp. xi–xii) states that "genuine curiosity and openness to learning something new" is the "most important pathway to empathy" in clinical settings, and Margulies (1989, p. 12) remarks that empathy involves "the capacity to go against the grain of needing to know". Havens (1986, pp. 16–21) talks of "finding the other", something that involves entering "that person's world". One might think of "entering" in terms of duplicating the other person's experiential world, but what Havens actually emphasizes is the recognition and exploration of phenomenological difference: the "empathic visitor discovers what he has taken for granted in his own world: that it is a world of particular time and space". This kind of interpersonal openness is arguably not just an aspect of empathy but itself sufficient for a kind of empathy: when A is recognized by B as adopting such an attitude towards her, A is recognized as empathic. For instance, Pienkos and Sass (2012, p. 32) stress how empathy involves "recognizing what is *otherwise* in persons with psychosis", and observe how "patients can feel quite moved in being asked about these experiences". Havens (1986, p. 24) also describes how clients can "light up in recognition of your sudden presence in their lives", something that involves a sense of being "found".

This poses a further problem for accounts of empathy that emphasize A's replicating B's experience. B's all-enveloping sense of interpersonal isolation is to some extent *mitigated* by recognition of empathy on the part of A. So empathy, at least where there is a sense of mutual recognition, does not just involve understanding a pre-formed experience; the act of successfully empathizing with an experience can itself change the nature of that experience. This is especially so when the initial experience involves a sense of isolation from everybody, a pervasive lack of interpersonal connection. So the object of empathy is a moving target, not something episodic or constant that one holds in suspension and duplicates. As Havens (1986) further remarks, an initial experience of mutual recognition can serve as the starting point for a variably collaborative process, whereby the nature of interpersonal difference is progressively clarified and a more positive understanding of experience assembled. No doubt, this could involve various acts of imagination on the part of the empathizer, some of which will meet the criteria for one or another type of simulation. However, more central is an acknowledgement of the other person's predicament as something that falls outside what many of us take as given. This acknowledgement involves a kind of openness to the distinctive perspective of a particular person, which resists the temptation to typify her or impose one's own perspective upon her.

The limits of simulation

So far, I have suggested that empathic openness does not centrally involve simulation, but there are also grounds for believing that the kinds of experience I have described *could not* be understood in such a way. As well as replicating circumscribed experiences and thoughts, one would have to replicate a much wider-ranging sense of belonging to the world. And it is arguable that wholesale replication of a "phenomenological world" is psychologically impossible. Goldie (2011) maintains that *"empathetic perspective-shifting"*, where one comes to somehow adopt the subjective perspective of another person, is more generally unachievable. To do this, one would have to take on the person's various psychological dispositions. However, many character traits, moods, and the like play the phenomenological roles that they do in virtue of their *not* being explicit objects of attention. Goldie therefore argues that one could not feed them into an explicit simulation without distorting them in the process: "B's full-blooded agency, including his characterization, becomes merely another empirical fact for A to take into account in her imaginative project" (Goldie, 2011, p. 309). For similar reasons, Slaby (2014) maintains that simulation theories of empathy presuppose an overly atomistic conception of experience; one cannot replicate the more enveloping, background structure of experience. Margulies (1989, p. 34) also remarks that localized experiences presuppose the "totality of the person" and must be understood in relation to it.

Ev   en if such objections can be resisted, there is a more specific and compelling objection to be made in cases of severe psychiatric illness. Suppose one seeks to empathize with an experience that itself centrally involves a diminishment or absence of empathic ability (where empathic ability is understood in a maximally permissive way, as an ability to understand, to varying degrees, another person's experience). One could not replicate the experience without also replicating the absence of empathy: A would replicate B's lack of receptiveness to others' experience and would then be unable to attribute it to B, due to that same lack of receptiveness. A partial replication, which did not incorporate the lack of empathy, would be ineffective in all those instances where B's lack of empathy is inextricable from and central to wider-ranging changes in B's relationship with the social world. Neither is it plausible to maintain that A first replicates B's experience and later draws on the memory of doing so in order to empathize with A, where remembering one's lack of empathy does not involve a continuing inability to empathize. This would imply that A ultimately comes to grasp B's experience via something that is not a simulation of B's experience, thus raising the question of why a simulation is needed in the first place. If empathy depends proximally on *x*, which is not a simulation of experience, the simulationist needs an account of how *x* itself depends upon something that is a simulation.

I think it is more plausible to maintain that empathy, in the kinds of case I am concerned with, involves acknowledging an enduring phenomenological distance between two parties, rather than traversing that distance. One could of course draw upon memories and exercises of imagination in order to aid the task of understanding, but not in a way that closes this gap. I should add that the point applies not only to "empathic perspective-shifting" but also to the less ambitious goal of "putting oneself in her shoes". When one asks, "What would I do in her shoes?", the shoes in question are partly comprised of a profoundly different way of experiencing and relating to the world. Person A either recognizes that she cannot accomplish this, or she is mistaken when she thinks the desired result has been achieved. Of course, one could maintain that empathy is outright impossible in these cases. Hence, as we never manage to empathize with experiences that themselves involve a lack of empathy, there is no problem for the simulationist to address. In response, we need only note that when empathy *is* recognized as arising in these situations (and it frequently is), the term must be referring to something other than simulation, and it is this achievement that I seek to further clarify here.

Three kinds of second-person experience

It might be objected that I have so far offered an overly negative conception of empathy. It involves only the recognition of difference, whereas empathy is more usually construed in terms of experiencing something of what the other person experiences. It thus involves a more positive understanding of someone else's mental life, as well as something more specific than understanding (where the term "understanding" is used in a general, noncommittal way): *experiencing*. This, one might add, is surely still to be construed in terms of simulation. Even if explicit simulation can rightly be said to involve "experiencing something of what someone else experiences", I have already ruled that out. However, it is not the only sense in which one might be said to do so, and I will conclude by considering three other candidates.

In the phenomenological tradition of philosophy, empathy has been construed not as a matter of simulation but as a distinctive, *sui generis* type of intentional state, which has another person's experience as its object. Just as I might *perceive* an object or *believe* a proposition to be true, I *empathize* with the experiences of others. This involves a perception-like apprehension of a person's experience, which is manifest in her perceived expressions, gestures, movements, and tone (e.g. Stein, 1917/1989; Zahavi, 2007, 2011, 2014; Thompson, 2007). The claim that empathy involves a distinctive way of relating to another person is compatible with what I have so far said. One directs one's attention towards her, in a way that involves a distinctive degree and kind of openness to specifically *interpersonal* forms of difference. Empathy can thus be construed in terms of a certain *type* of second-person relation. However, the claim that this relation gives one some degree of access to another person's *experience* is more specific and contentious. The extent of this access is also unclear: can you experience that someone else is happy, that they are happy about *p*, or even that they are happy about *p* because of *x*? Moreover, given the emphasis on a perceptual or perception-like experience, it has been objected that this view is in fact compatible with an implicit simulationist account of empathy. In short, the perceptual or quasi-perceptual grasp of second-person experience that certain phenomenologists describe could be reliant upon the operation of implicit simulation mechanisms (e.g. Currie, 2011). However, others have disputed this, maintaining that the perception of second-person experience does not involve simulation (e.g. Gallagher, 2007).

I allow, for the sake of argument, that empathizing with psychiatric illness can involve a fairly superficial, perception-like appreciation of what another person experiences. I also allow that this may turn out to be somehow reliant on implicit simulation processes (which are to be distinguished from the kinds of explicit simulation that have been my main concern up to this point). However, it needs to be added that this operates in conjunction with an importantly different kind of "second-person experience". When interacting with someone who is profoundly socially isolated, a more usually harmonious interplay of word, expression, gesture, and action breaks down to varying degrees. Interactions become awkward and uncomfortable, and the other person's experiences no longer appear embodied in her expressions, gestures, and tones in an unambiguous, unproblematic way. Consider, for instance, the so-called "praecox feeling", which is said to characterize interactions with schizophrenia patients (no doubt only some people's interactions with some people who have that diagnosis). This involves a general feeling of unease and lack of interpersonal connection that can serve as a fairly reliable guide for diagnosis (see Varga, 2013, for a discussion). Peter Hobson (2002, p. 49) describes having a similar kind of experience when interacting with autistic people: "A person can feel that there is something missing when relating to someone who is autistic – it is as if one is in the presence of a changeling, someone from a different world – but this escapes the net of scientific methods."

Now, if empathy is construed as a quasi-perceptual appreciation of experience (something that operates most effectively in the context of harmonious interactions between people), we can simply construe these experiences in terms of a breakdown of empathy. On the other hand, such breakdowns can make a positive contribution to the kind of empathy that I am addressing. It would be an oversimplification to state that, even if explicit simulation is ineffective when we seek to understand radically different forms of experience, implicit simulation persists. In fact, it is the disruption of a quasi-perceptual process (a process that may or may not be legitimately construed in terms of implicit simulation) that should be emphasized. The experience of disruption is at the same time a way of experiencing the other person. Insofar as one's interaction with her is out of synch or otherwise lacking, she may appear strange, somehow different. Hence the distance between one's own world and hers is something that can, to some extent at least, be experienced. This is a prominent theme in the work of Minkowski (1933/1970, part II, ch. 1), who invites the clinician to reflect upon how she feels when interacting with a patient, upon "the feeling we have in the presence of certain patients when we attempt to grasp their living personality" (pp. 223–4). Such feelings, he suggests, are double-sided: how one feels is also a way of experiencing the other person. They can therefore feed into the empathic project, helping one to grasp the nature of the difference and, ultimately, to achieve a positive characterization. One can come to better understand the person by spending a prolonged period of time with him, interacting with him, and attending to one's feelings:

> It was like two melodies being played simultaneously, although these two melodies are as dissonant as can be, a certain balance becomes established between the notes of one and the other and lets us penetrate a little further into our patient's psyche.
>
> *(Minkowski, 1933/1970, p. 182)*

So the person is understood, not through the kind of experience allegedly enabled by implicit simulation routines, but through its disruption. However, it might still be objected that all of this provides us with an inadequate grasp of what the other person *does* experience. A sense of difference, regardless of whether or not it is experienced, does not add up to a positive empathic understanding. And perhaps, one might reiterate, it is only through one or another kind of simulation that this can be achieved. However, I think there is a third way in which one can rightly be said to "experience someone else's experience" in this context, something that can involve a positive phenomenological appreciation of profoundly different "worlds". In short, one can elaborate on the initial experience of difference by means of narrative. An obvious objection to this proposal is that narrative cannot contribute to one's *experience* of someone else's world; narrative supplies us instead with a supplementary, non-phenomenological appreciation. But there are reasons to resist that view. Consider gazing at a work of art while someone explains to you the circumstances in which it arose, the intentions of the artist, the artistic techniques employed, what makes it unique and important, how it is best viewed, and so forth. In cases like this, one's attention may remain directed at the piece, rather than distracted by the narrative. At the same time, experience of the piece is altered and enriched. One comes to see it differently and more discerningly; it *looks* different. It is debatable whether this kind of enriched experience is properly regarded as "perceptual". However, the only point I want to insist on is that, phenomenologically speaking, one's immediate experience of the piece is not wholly insulated from the narrative one acquires, but somehow shaped by it.

I think something analogous to this occurs in the case of second-person experience. One's attention remains directed at the other person and her experiences, rather than turned inwards towards one's own mental life. However, an increasingly elaborate and nuanced narrative is assembled, which continually shapes and reshapes what one experiences of the other person's world. This is especially so when there is some degree of cooperation between the two parties. As Gallagher (2012, p. 370) suggests more generally, empathy is not a matter of replicating other people's experiences so much as situating those experiences in a wider context of meanings, "getting to know their stories". Furthermore, it is arguable that narrative and experience, especially emotional experience, are inextricable, that some or all emotions are partly constituted by narrative structure and content (Goldie, 2012). Hence, insofar as a narrative is shared by two parties, it comprises a kind of bridge between them that aids interpretation. Recognition of difference is thus embellished with a positive phenomenological appreciation of experience, something that does not require "having the same experience as the other person" in a first-person way.

This is not to suggest that first- and second-person narratives will always be congruent or that interpretations will ever fully converge. Even if it is admitted that narrative and experience cannot be cleanly separated, there remains the possibility of outright misinterpretation (on the part of one or both parties) and self-deceit. It can be added that A's interpretation of B's experience may involve insights into its nature that B lacks, opening up the possibility of B's reinterpreting and reshaping her experience by engaging with A's narrative (e.g. Margulies, 1989). First-person narratives may also be fragmented or lacking in some respect, something that can itself be revealing and contribute to empathic interpretation. And the relationship goes both ways. A's interaction with B is also self-affecting, serving to reshape her own experience to varying degrees and in different ways. So the difference between first- and second-person perspectives on experience is preserved throughout. The end result is not a final, fixed narrative, given that the relationship between experience and self-interpretation is a dynamic and open-ended one. These points complement another prominent theme in the clinical literature: that empathy generally takes the form of a variably cooperative interpersonal *process* of whatever duration, rather than an episodic achievement by a single individual. As Coulehan et al. (2001, p. 222) suggest, empathy "allows the patient to feel understood, respected, and validated", thus facilitating a kind of "feedback loop" through which her experience is progressively clarified. This process not only enables one to appreciate another person's experience; it also shapes and reshapes the experiences of both parties as it progresses (Havens, 1986, p. 21; Margulies, 1989, p. 97).

We therefore arrive at an account of what it is to empathize with profound phenomenological changes that arise in psychiatric illness (and, no doubt, in various other circumstances as well). It minimally involves a distinctive kind of openness to another person's experience. In addition, it may involve the narration of experience, something that can be achieved through an interpersonal process, involving differing degrees of cooperation or lack thereof. I do not wish to deny that a narrative, empathic appreciation of very different forms of experience can be accomplished in other ways as well, such as interpreting texts and other sources. However, as Jaspers remarks, interpersonal interactions generally yield greater insight:

> The most vital part of the psychopathologist's knowledge is drawn from his contact with people. What he gains from this depends upon the particular way he gives himself and as therapist partakes in events, whether he illuminates himself as well as his patients. The process is not only one of simple observation, like reading off a measurement, but the exercise of a self-involving vision in which the psyche is glimpsed.
>
> *(1913/1963, p. 21)*

This "giving", I suggest, is to be construed in terms of a distinctive way of relating to another person, one that involves an unusual degree of sensitivity to the possibility of phenomenological difference, and the "self-involving vision" in terms of an interpersonal process that empathic openness facilitates. From here, we can go on to address the questions of how widely applicable this conception of empathy might be, whether there are there are also other, quite different kinds of empathy, and whether certain philosophical approaches to empathy sometimes *refer* to the kind of achievement I have described here, but inadvertently mischaracterize it.

Acknowledgements: Thanks to Heidi Maibom for reading and offering helpful comments on an earlier version of this chapter.

References

Berg, J. H. van den. 1972. *A Different Existence: Principles of Phenomenological Psychopathology*. Pittsburgh: Duquesne University Press.

Coplan, A. 2011. Will the Real Empathy Stand Up? A Case for a Narrow Conceptualization. *The Southern Journal of Philosophy* 49, Spindel Supplement: 40–65.

Coulehan, J. L., Platt, F. W., Egener, B., Frankel, R., Lin, C.-T., Lown, B., & Salazar, W. H. 2001. "Let Me See if I Have This Right ..." Words that Help Build Empathy. *Annals of Internal Medicine* 135: 221–7.

Currie, G. 2011. Empathy for Objects. In Coplan, A. & Goldie, P., eds. *Empathy: Philosophical and Psychological Perspectives*. Oxford: Oxford University Press: 82–95.

Darwall, S. 1998. Empathy, Sympathy, Care. *Philosophical Studies* 89: 261–82.

Gallagher, S. 2007. Simulation Trouble. *Social Neuroscience* 2: 353–65.

Gallagher, S. 2012. Empathy, Simulation and Narrative. *Science in Context* 25: 355–81.

Goldie, P. 2011. Anti-Empathy. In Coplan, A. & Goldie, P., eds. *Empathy: Philosophical and Psychological Perspectives*. Oxford: Oxford University Press: 302–17.

Goldie, P. 2012. *The Mess Inside: Narrative, Emotion, and the Mind*. Oxford: Oxford University Press.

Goldman, A. 2006. *Simulating Minds: The Philosophy, Psychology and Neuroscience of Mindreading.* Oxford: Oxford University Press.

Goldman, A. 2011. Two Routes to Empathy: Insights from Cognitive Neuroscience. In Coplan, A. & Goldie, P., eds. *Empathy: Philosophical and Psychological Perspectives.* Oxford: Oxford University Press: 31–44.

Gordon, R. 1995. Sympathy, Simulation, and the Impartial Spectator. *Ethics* 105: 727–42.

Halpern, J. 2001. *From Detached Concern to Empathy.* Oxford: Oxford University Press.

Halpern, J. 2003. What is Clinical Empathy? *Journal of General Internal Medicine* 18: 670–4.

Havens, L. 1986. *Making Contact: Uses of Language in Psychotherapy.* Cambridge, MA: Harvard University Press.

Hobson, P. 2002. *The Cradle of Thought.* London: Macmillan.

Hornstein, G. 2009. *Agnes's Jacket: A Psychologist's Search for the Meanings of Madness.* New York: Rodale.

Jaspers, K. 1912/1968. The Phenomenological Approach in Psychopathology. *British Journal of Psychiatry* 114: 1313–23.

Jaspers, K. 1913/1963. *General Psychopathology.* Trans. from the German. Seventh edition by Hoenig, J. & Hamilton, M. W. Manchester: Manchester University Press.

Margulies, A. 1989. *The Empathic Imagination.* New York: W.W. Norton & Company.

Minkowski, E. 1933/1970. *Lived Time: Phenomenological and Psychopathological Studies.* Trans. Metzel, N. Evanston: Northwestern University Press.

Pienkos, E., & Sass, L. A. 2012. Empathy and Otherness: Humanistic and Phenomenological Approaches to Psychotherapy of Severe Mental Illness. *Pragmatic Case Studies in Psychotherapy* 8: 25–35.

Ratcliffe, M. 2012. Phenomenology as a Form of Empathy. *Inquiry* 55: 473–95.

Ratcliffe, M. 2015. *Experiences of Depression: A Study in Phenomenology.* Oxford: Oxford University Press.

Sechehaye, M., ed. 1970. *Autobiography of a Schizophrenic Girl.* New York: Signet.

Shaw, F. 1997. *Out of Me: The Story of a Postnatal Breakdown.* London: Penguin.

Slaby, J. 2014. Empathy's Blind Spot. *Medicine, Healthcare and Philosophy* 17: 249–58.

Stein, E. 1917/1989. *On the Problem of Empathy.* Trans. Stein, W. Washington, D.C.: ICS Publications.

Stueber, K. R. 2006. *Rediscovering Empathy: Agency, Folk Psychology and the Human Sciences.* Cambridge, MA: MIT Press.

Thompson, E. 2007. *Mind in Life: Biology, Phenomenology, and the Sciences of Mind.* Cambridge, MA: Harvard University Press.

Varga, S. 2013. Vulnerability to Psychosis, I-Thou Intersubjectivity and the Praecox-Feeling. *Phenomenology & the Cognitive Sciences* 12: 131–43.

Zahavi, D. 2007. Expression and Empathy. In Hutto, D.D. & Ratcliffe, M., eds. *Folk Psychology Re-assessed.* Dordrecht: Springer: 25–40.

Zahavi, D. 2011. Empathy and Direct Social Perception: A Phenomenological Proposal. *Review of Philosophy and Psychology* 2: 541–58.

Zahavi, D. 2014. *Self and Other: Exploring Subjectivity, Empathy, and Shame.* Oxford: Oxford University Press.

PART IV

Empathy and morals

18

EMPATHY AND ALTRUISM

Thomas Schramme

Introduction

Altruism is the opposite of egoism. In a philosophical context altruism and egoism are regularly discussed as contrasting theories regarding the ultimate motivation of human behavior. Psychological egoism claims that any conduct, even if on the surface it promotes the welfare of others, can ultimately be traced back to the motive of promoting an agent's self-interest. Altruism is hence not a reality, according to psychological egoism. Once the debate is reduced to such a contrast, focusing on ultimate motives of human conduct, important theoretical decisions have been made, which then also affect the discussion around the impact of empathy on altruism. Even where psychological egoism is rejected, discussions are aligned along the problem whether a person's motive is to benefit or increase the welfare of another person.

But altruism need not be reduced to its opposition to egoism. In this chapter, altruism is discussed as a psychological basis for moral conduct more generally, not just in terms of motivations to benefit others. Here, *altruism* stands for the capacity to take the moral point of view and to be disposed to act accordingly. It is argued that empathy indeed might have an important role in the development and maintenance of such a disposition.

The chapter sets out to provide, first, a conceptual landscape regarding the notion of altruism. It seems obvious that only on the basis of conceptual precision is it possible to eventually query the significance of empathy for altruism. We will draw several important distinctions, most importantly between psychological, behavioral, and biological altruism. For the purposes of philosophical debate in moral theory the psychological perspective is the most relevant.

Second, I will introduce two kinds of explanations of the relation between empathy and altruism. Descriptive theories aim to explain empathy's causal contribution to altruism, either in individual instantiations of altruistic motivation or in developmental terms, regarding the maturation of an altruistic disposition as an aspect of the personality of a person. This is mainly the perspective of psychologists. Normative theories of altruism, which are discussed in philosophy, are usually laid out in terms of a theory of practical reason. Again, empathy might play a role in accounting for reasons for action. Several examples of these kinds of explanations are briefly introduced.

Finally, some objections to linking empathy and altruism are critically examined. We will see that many of these objections are based on particular conceptions of the relevant terms, which are only of limited interest to the psychological account of the capacity for altruism. Because these objections therefore miss the target set in this chapter, they do not undermine the claim that empathy has a significant role for altruism.

Throughout the chapter it will become obvious that an important problem of a straightforward discussion regarding the relation between empathy and altruism is due to a widespread confusion over the relevant terms. Before determining the role of empathy in altruism and morality, we must therefore get a clear grasp of the conceptual landscape.

Altruism as taking the moral point of view

Moral demands often oppose our own self-concerned desires. We are regularly required to do, or to refrain from doing, certain acts, which we would like to (not) do, as a matter of morality. Since self-concerned desires can be called egoistic, the demands of morality can be described in opposition to egoism. According to this picture, morality and egoism are opposing forces acting on the agent. Moral rules and demands are initially external to us; we need to internalize them before they gain psychological force. This process can be described as individual development of altruism, here using the term that was originally introduced as a contrasting term to egoism in the nineteenth century by Auguste Comte. Seen this way, altruism is a short word for the psychological phenomenon of the internalized pull of morality, or of taking the moral point of view. An altruistic person takes the normative force of moral demands into account. Altruism requires the acknowledging of moral demands in the form of being ultimately motivated by a concern for others (Nagel 1970: 16, 79; Joyce 2013). But the concept of altruism need not be restricted to the category of motives. It might also contain elements of recognizing another person as someone who counts morally, or of feeling with another being. So the notion of altruism describes a psychological stance, which might contain affective, cognitive, and motivational elements. Still, the main and often exclusive focus in the philosophical debate is on motives. As we will see, other disciplines have their own conceptualizations of altruism that are also linked to empathy, most notably biology and economics. These conceptions of altruism are not restricted to psychological features, but mainly concern overt behavior and its consequences.

To have an altruistic disposition does not always mean that a person acts altruistically in a given situation. After all, there might be other aspects of the situation that prevent a person from doing what is morally required, such as stress or ignorance. Also, since altruism is only one force that operates on the agent, it is not certain that it will win against any egoistic or otherwise undermining forces that may be present in an agent.

The way altruism has been presented so far needs some defense. Above it was identified with a moral stance quite generally. In contrast, many people would probably regard altruistic conduct as helping behavior more specifically. For example, a person sacrificing her life to save another person would be altruistic on this view. Other, less extreme examples of moral behavior – say when a person returns a borrowed item to another person – would usually not be deemed altruistic, because there seems to be no active promotion of the welfare of another person involved. The fact that we can understand altruism both as referring to moral behavior quite generally and as restricted to a more specific set of helping behaviors may lead to confusion. But note that we described altruism above as a psychological notion. So it is not the kind of conduct that makes it altruistic or not, but its psychological basis. Returning a borrowed item might be called altruistic if it is done because the agent deems it the kind of action that will protect the welfare – broadly conceived – of the person who lent the item. It can be called altruistic conduct because it is done for the sake of the other person and not for any other reasons, such as fear of punishment or loss of esteem. The latter kind of reasons would be deemed to be egoistic, and hence conduct based on such motives could not properly be called altruistic. As we will see, this description fits the discussion in moral psychology. In conclusion, altruism can be understood in contrast to egoism and is not restricted to helping behavior.

Possible links between empathy and altruism

Empathy comes into play as a kind of psychological mechanism that might account for moral motivation. Indeed, both common sense and moral psychology frequently assume that there is a strong link between empathy and altruism. We have to be wary, though, of conceptual confusion. Sometimes empathy is identified with a "feeling with" another person, or with "empathic concern." This then seems to straightforwardly account for altruism. But note that in such an account empathy is roughly the same as sympathy. The potential moral role of empathy might then be smuggled into the theory by a conceptual move, because sympathy by definition involves a concern for others. Such a conceptual shortcut ought therefore to be avoided, though admittedly the way we use concepts in theories is rarely completely neutral.

The relationship between empathy and altruism can, first, be described in factual terms. For instance, moral psychologists Daniel Batson and Martin Hoffman explain altruism and moral development, at least partially, in terms of the psychological mechanisms related to the general concept of empathy. This makes the connection between empathy and altruism mainly empirical and hence testable. More specifically, despite theoretical differences, Batson and Hoffman both think that empathy or empathy-related psychological mechanisms have a causal role in the development of altruistic motivation.

An alternative, second, model draws a connection between empathy and altruism in normative terms. A common way to account for a normative perspective on the force of morality is in terms of reasons for action. Why should I be moral? This is a basic question that is asked in moral philosophy. According to this framework the question is whether empathy can play a role in providing altruistic reasons for action. This makes the connection between empathy and altruism mainly a conceptual and theoretical matter, because it is based on an account of practical rationality, or acting for reasons.

The two ways of looking at a connection between empathy and altruism cannot always neatly be separated, of course. After all, they are merely two different perspectives on the same phenomenon, namely individual agency. Yet it will be seen in this chapter that some terminological confusion might stem from not properly distinguishing between the descriptive and the normative project.

In addition to a factual as opposed to a normative project of explaining the connection between empathy and altruism, there is another important distinction that has been alluded to before. It concerns the difference between an isolated motivation of an act and a psychological disposition to act. The latter can be described as a character trait of a person. It seems that the already mentioned terminology of "being moral," which is often used in moral philosophy, is helpful in this respect. It allows for two different readings, which are both important, though they need to be distinguished: First, being moral might mean to be motivated, in a certain situation, to act in accordance with what is morally required. We might then ask what role empathy might play in such instantiations of altruism. Being moral might also mean, second, to be a moral person who is disposed to act altruistically. Empathy might play a role in achieving such a disposition. The distinction between individual acts of altruism and individual instantiations of empathy in contrast to a disposition for altruism and for empathic reactions is important. Indeed, as we will see, several objections to seeing a strong connection between empathy and altruism only focus on the former interpretation in terms of individual acts and their psychological bases.

To make things even more complicated, there are of course various interpretations of the notion of empathy. This is a recurrent theme within this handbook. Depending on which interpretation of empathy is subscribed to, the specific role of empathy in morality might support a specific metaethical position. In moral philosophy, empathy is widely regarded to be a kind of feeling. Accordingly, it is often assumed that if empathy indeed somehow grounds altruism, moral sentimentalism is supported, as opposed to its rival, moral rationalism. Moral sentimentalism sees a significant role for emotions and affective elements in morality; moral rationalism denies such a role and accounts for morality in terms of rationality or the human capacity to reason. The kind of argument in favor of sentimentalism just mentioned, however, is of course based on a particular reading of empathy, namely on an interpretation of empathy as a kind of affective feature of the mind. But, as readers of this volume will be aware, an interpretation of empathy in terms of affective or emotional psychological mechanisms is not the only convincing option. If cognitive elements are emphasized, the link between empathy and morality might also be used in favor of moral rationalism.

Occasionally philosophers discuss specific psychopathologies in order to establish a link between empathy and altruism. Two mental disorders are of considerable interest in this regard, because they involve a lack, or a serious defect, in empathy and, arguably, impairments in moral capacity as well. These cases are psychopathy and autism. Some scholars have argued that the respective empirical findings can indeed be used to test ethical theories and to solve certain metaethical problems. In addition to the debate between moral sentimentalism and rationalism, psychopathological findings have been used as arguments in discussions about moral motivation. According to motivational internalism, a particular belief that it is morally right to do a certain thing involves a motivation to do it. In contrast, motivational externalism holds that moral judgment and moral motivation can come apart. Since psychopaths seem to know right from wrong but are not motivated to act accordingly, they seem to refute internalism. Yet, it might not be straightforward to determine whether psychopaths indeed make full-fledged moral judgments. This depends on an interpretation of the notion of moral judgment (Sinnott-Armstrong 2014). Hence, the philosophical debate between internalism and externalism cannot be decided on empirical grounds only. It requires conceptual commitments.

From what has been said so far it is clear that the way we conceive of the relationship between empathy and altruism has important repercussions on debates in moral philosophy. Yet it still has to be seen how we can best account for the link between empathy and altruism. There is some hope that empirical findings will contribute to debates in moral philosophy, but there are also considerable conceptual issues involved.

Three concepts of altruism

An important source of confusion is the fact that different disciplines use the term *altruism* in different ways. In the scholarly literature it has become common to distinguish three concepts of altruism: psychological, behavioral, and biological (or evolutionary) altruism (Clavien & Chaupisat 2012; Batson 2011: 23ff.; Kitcher 2011: 18ff.). Each of these kinds of altruism will be briefly introduced in this section, but the focus of this chapter is psychological altruism, as this version is usually used in philosophical approaches. Very briefly, psychological altruism refers to "a motivational state with the ultimate goal of increasing another's welfare" (Batson 2011: 20). This definition is useful as a starting point, though later some problems will be pinpointed. Psychological altruism is regarded as psychological because it refers to mental states of agents, such as intentions, motives, and the like.

Behavioral altruism is connected to approaches that look into outcomes of psychological states, namely particular acts. If some given behavior benefits other beings and is somehow costly (all things considered) for the agent, it is regarded as altruistic. For instance, Dominique de Quervain and his collaborators describe altruism in that way (de Quervain et al. 2004: 1254). There is no direct reference to the motives of agents. Other publications in similar research areas arguably acknowledge motives as being important (Fehr & Fischbacher 2005: 8), though it is contested whether this reference to motives bears any substance (Peacock et al. 2005). Psychological theories also discuss individually costly behavior, of course, but they would then usually avoid the term "altruism" and rather refer to prosocial behavior (Eisenberg & Miller 1987).

Biological altruism, which is also sometimes called evolutionary altruism, refers to behavior that is costly in a biological sense, for instance reducing reproductive success over the life span of an animal and conferring a benefit to another animal, usually a group or species member. This notion is obviously not congruent with accounts of altruism we find in philosophy, as it does not even require intentionality. It is closely related, though, to behavioral altruism. It mainly differs in its account of costs and benefits, which are purely biological in the case of biological altruism. Costs and benefits within this research paradigm are usually fleshed out in terms of reproductive success. One might argue against such an approach that the language of altruism is necessarily motivational and that evolutionary biologists "hijacked" the terminology (de Waal 2008: 280). Similarly, it is common for philosophers to object that biological altruism is in fact not about altruism at all, but rather concerned with complicated and convoluted stories of selfishness. After all, the motives for this kind of behavior seem self-regarding. Indeed, fairly often what biologists talk about would perhaps better be described as cooperation (Okasha 2008).

Biologists reply that if we reserve the term *altruism* for what philosophers see as "real altruism," we will not be able to explain how altruism could evolve at all. After all, it is a major task of evolutionary biology to give an account of non-selfish behavior (Sober & Wilson 1998: 6). It would therefore be detrimental to this task if we give up the notion of biological altruism. To be sure, a more pluralist view can highlight the difference between ultimate, i.e. evolutionary, and proximate, i.e. psychological, causes of behavior. There is no contradiction in using both perspectives on altruism, though it can obviously lead to misunderstandings. For instance, to call mutually beneficial, i.e. cooperative, behavior altruistic seems to stretch the notion too far. Such kind of behavior seems clearly based only on self-interest, if only in a complicated way, as it includes future beneficial events that have a certain probability. So "reciprocal altruism," as still used in biology, seems to be a misnomer. Even biologists themselves occasionally acknowledge this (West et al. 2007: 420). There are however some differences between biological and psychological accounts of altruism, which cannot be explained away by misuses of terminology. These are due to different research interests or different foci of explanation (Kitcher 2011: 86f.). Probably it would therefore help to sort out potential cross-purposes by distinguishing between altruism generally and human altruism more specifically, or to stick explicitly to the mentioned distinctions between psychological, behavioral, and biological altruism.

Some worries regarding common conceptions of altruism

As just explained, a recurrent theme within the literature is that altruism requires on balance some cost for the agent (e.g. West et al. 2007: 422). This is mainly a perspective we find in theories of biological and behavioral altruism, but it bears relevant similarity with psychological accounts. According to such a view, whenever there is a long-term or all-things-considered gain for the supposedly altruistic agent that would make the action overall beneficial for the agent, it should not count as altruistic. Interestingly, this seems to be the flip side of a traditional debate in philosophy regarding the actual possibility of altruism. Here it is a common move of so-called psychological egoists to highlight ever more hidden and indirect benefits to the agent, and use these as the basis for their assertion that there is no such thing as real altruism. The latter is a kind of recursive strategy, because it can be used over and over again in case someone comes up with stories of putative altruism (Stich et al. 2010). But this ends up in a linguistic quandary: "If psychological egoists … refuse to accept any … examples of unselfish behavior, then we have a right to be puzzled about what they are saying. Until we know what they would count as unselfish behavior, we can't very well know what they mean when they say that all voluntary behavior is selfish. And at this point we may suspect that they are holding their theory in a 'privileged position' – that of immunity of evidence" (Feinberg 2007: 192).

By virtue of the recursive strategy, psychological egoism achieves a kind of invulnerability, but this comes at a price. To lose such an important distinction as the one between altruism and egoism by insulating the latter from falsification seems clearly unhelpful and there has been accordingly a plethora of critics of this move in moral philosophy. To merely focus on benefits and costs therefore seems unhelpful. After all, it always seems possible to give an account of an overall benefit of actions to the agent, if only in terms of immaterial gains. Indeed, when drawing the distinction between egoism and altruism in terms of the aggregated costs and benefits involved, a terminological arms race about the welfare of the agent is started. The problem here is one of simply opposing altruism and egoism and to define the former as overall welfare cost and the latter as overall welfare gain for the agent. Consequently, on the basis of an interpretation of altruism in terms of costs to the agent, we cannot allow an altruistic act to be altogether beneficial for the person herself. But this result seems unwanted. Especially when people act benevolently because they want to be that kind of person, they seem to be both helping others and benefiting themselves. Hence it appears more sensible to focus instead on other significant aspects of altruism than merely overall costs to the agent.

The psychological account too considers benefit to others as a decisive element of altruism but it is less the actual result – a benefit – that counts, but the intent or motive of an agent to benefit someone else. Altruism here means to do something because of a concern for other persons' welfare. In addition theorists often claim that the aim of benefiting someone else needs to be pursued for its own sake (Frankena 1963: 21) or as the ultimate aim of an action in order to be altruism proper. This is required, because we can benefit other people by our actions without having a concern for their welfare. It might simply happen that to benefit others is the road to take when agents pursue their own wellbeing. To be sure, an agent may gain in terms of welfare as a kind of by-product when acting to the benefit of someone else, for instance in form of the proverbial "warm glow" of such an action. Such an indirect benefit is consistent with the psychological account of altruism. But the ultimate aim, according to the standard view, needs to be the welfare of someone else.

The reference to ultimate goals (Batson 2011: 20; Feinberg 2007: 190) or ultimate desires (Stich et al. 2010) might cause confusion. The idea of ultimate goals, both in psychology and philosophy, is based on the general idea of instrumental actions. Ultimate goals are seen as the final ends of actions, which are served by other goals of actions. Hence instrumental goals are opposed to ultimate goals in this perspective. For example, an agent might help a person in need, but her ultimate aim might not be to benefit the other person, but to earn esteem and gratitude.

It is often assumed that all human behavior follows such a pattern, where we can distinguish instrumental aspects, usually called means, from final ones, usually called ends. Since ends can be means to other ends we get a picture of action where we assume a final end, something that is, in philosophical parlance, done "for its own sake." Altruistic action, as we have seen, is usually regarded as something that is done for the sake of benefiting others. This aspect explains why theories of altruism regularly refer to motives instead of actual behavior. According to common theories of psychological altruism, we need to know what the agents aim at in order to find out whether they act altruistically. However, this is a highly stylized picture of human action. Fairly often people do something because they value it intrinsically and see an instrumental value in it as well. To define altruism as being based on an ultimate goal or desire therefore does not seem to help to distinguish real altruism from fake altruism. This is not only a problem of actually identifying the psychological states of agents but also a deeper problem of modeling altruism. The common model requires a kind of motivational purity, which simply does not exist in the real world.

There is another concern that has to do with the notion of aiming at the welfare of someone else. There seem to be two aspects involved here, or two ways of aiming at the welfare of others, which were mentioned earlier. We can interpret altruism as a positive concern for others, which leads people to increase the welfare of others. This is, for instance, in line with Batson's definition. Alternatively, it might be enough for altruism to respect others' welfare and to omit engaging in any harmful behavior (Schmidtz 1993: 53). Again, for some philosophers, most notably Philip Kitcher, the second motive – respect for others or "normative guidance," as he calls it – is a kind of fallback capacity in case of failures of genuine altruism (Kitcher 2011: 67ff.). Now, it is true that lack of respect calls for normative guidance, which is usually related to some kind of sanction. Fear of sanctions makes the motivation not to harm others a non-altruistic one. But in contrast to a restricted and demanding account of altruism, it seems that at least some cases of not harming others, especially in situations where one could easily get away with it, can plausibly be deemed examples of altruism. This then seems to allow for less demanding instances of behavior to be outcomes of genuine altruism. Altruism is then basically identical with taking the moral point of view, i.e. an individual appreciation of the normative force of morality. Admittedly, such a close connection of general moral motivation and altruistic motivation is sometimes explicitly rejected (Batson 2014: 46), but it can certainly be found in the philosophical debate.

Empathy and altruism: descriptive explanation

The descriptive perspective on the relationship between empathy and altruism focuses on possible explanations of the presence of altruistic motivation in agents and specifically the role that empathy has in this regard. Although it has just been called a descriptive approach it should also be clear that any such scientific explanation relies on conceptual commitments, which might contain normative elements. Most importantly, what altruism is – as opposed to egoism – is a philosophical problem, which apparently is at least partly determined by a particular account of moral agency. We have just learned about some of the intricacies of the conceptual landscape.

Descriptive explanations might focus on the proximate causes of altruistic conduct, which are usually psychological mechanisms in individual instantiations of such behavior, or they might aim at an account of the ultimate causes. The latter perspective is taken in developmental theories of altruism. Again, these might differ in that they can focus on evolutionary aspects in phylogeny or on the development of individual personality, especially during childhood and adolescence.

A well-known and hugely influential theory that explains altruism by reference to empathic concern is Dan Batson's empathy-altruism hypothesis, which he has developed with his team over a couple of decades of research. His theory is psychological, and it focuses on the proximate causes of behavior, i.e. individual motives. The hypothesis states that "empathic concern produces altruistic motivation" (Batson 2011: 11). Note that Batson refers to empathic concern, which seems a different idea than empathy. Indeed, the former seems to already have a normative stance – a focus on other's welfare – built into it. Batson interprets empathy, or rather empathic concern, mainly as an emotional phenomenon, as a kind of feeling. His theory is inconclusive regarding the cognitive elements of empathy, although he seems to partially account for them in terms of "antecedents of empathic concern" (Batson 2011: 37f., 43f.), since these include perceiving the other as in need and valuing the other's welfare. Finally, his research is mainly pursued in a negative fashion. It aims at undermining interpretations of certain conduct – studied in carefully devised laboratory experiments – in virtue of egoistic motivations. For instance, some experiments allow subjects to easily escape a morally demanding situation, which would be deemed the egoistic option. When they do not try to escape, but rather help, this seems to support an interpretation of the underlying motive as altruistic.

The aforementioned features of Batson's thesis – that it is expressed in terms of altruistic concern; that it understands empathy as affective phenomenon; and that it is pursued in opposition to egoism – make his theory somewhat hard to assess within the landscape of the philosophical debate on the role of empathy for altruism. Even when we disregard the quarrel over the empirical evidence for *ultimate* altruistic motivation (Stich et al. 2010; Sober & Wilson 1998: 232), the result regarding the link between empathy and altruism is in any case fairly modest, as has been acknowledged by Batson himself. After all, there is no evidence for empathy being necessary or sufficient for instantiations of altruistic behavior. There might always be circumstantial and other psychological aspects undermining the motivational impact of empathic concern, hence empathy might not be sufficient for genuine altruism. In addition, there might be other motivational routes to overtly altruistic behavior, if not to altruistic motivation, such as distress at the plight of others. In sum, it should be noted that Batson's theory is targeted at a descriptive explanation of the presence of altruistic motivation by empathic concern. He does not explain overtly altruistic, i.e. helping behavior, or moral behavior more generally (Batson 2014).

Other important psychological developmental theories regarding the link between empathy and altruism have been offered by Nancy Eisenberg and her collaborators, by Carolyn Zahn-Waxler and her team, as well as by Martin L. Hoffman (Eisenberg & Miller 1987; Zahn-Waxler et al. 1992; Hoffman 2000). In contrast to Batson, these researchers do not focus on the proximate causes of individual behavior but on the development of altruistic concern during the maturation of individual personality. It should also be noted that they do not explicitly distinguish between altruistic motivation in particular and moral or pro-social motivation in general. Accordingly, their research does not establish a descriptive explanation of the link between individual instantiations of empathy and altruism, but deems empathy to be a significant developmental contributor to an altruistic, or moral, disposition. Again, there is also no assumption of a necessary or sufficient role of empathy in developing such disposition in the relevant psychological literature. This is important, because for philosophers a mere contingent correlation is usually not of particular interest. They regularly direct their interest toward theses that explain a necessary role for empathy in altruism, either on an empirical or a conceptual basis. Hence there is again a potential occasion for misconceived dialogue between philosophers and psychologists.

There are also developmental approaches to the link of empathy and altruism that focus on ultimate causes of behavior, most notably in evolutionary terms. It has already been stressed that these descriptive explanations are not easily adaptable to the philosophical point of view. After all, they target different purposes and levels of explanation (Joyce 2013).

Empathy and altruism: normative explanation

It has been emphasized above that in the philosophical debate altruism often stands for moral motivation more generally, and not just for a specific motivation to increase others' welfare. This has to do with the fact that philosophers often contrast moral motivation and egoistic motivation. In a Kantian tradition, we find a similar contrast between genuinely morally motivated conduct and conduct that is only in conformity with moral requirements. The latter kind of conduct might well be based on self-interested concerns, most notably fear of sanctions. Philosophical theories that explain and justify the demands of morality in virtue of these mechanisms, i.e. sanctions, are usually aligned with psychological egoism. Hence the common dichotomy of egoism and altruism leads naturally to an identification of altruism with a general and genuine moral motive, not just a specific motive to benefit others.

In contrast to the empirical explanations, in moral philosophy altruism is usually explained by theories of practical rationality. Since human agency is here conceived under the guise of norms of rationality, the kind of explanation is normative. An explanation of altruism, as opposed to egoism, requires reference to motivating and justifying reasons that account for genuine moral conduct. But if there is no specific moral motive, then morality seems to be based only on a generic characteristic of human beings, that is, on practical rationality. This seems to naturally lead to an explanation in terms of what is good for the agent, hence apparently to an egoistic account.

We have already seen, though, that it does not seem right to insulate egoism from any counter-examples by conceptual moves. Accordingly, it is not right to simply define practical rationality in terms of self-interested agency. When we aim at a normative explanation, the main focus should be on providing the most convincing philosophical theory of practical rationality and reasons for action. Such a theoretical problem cannot be solved by defining the relevant concepts in a particular way.

Different theories of practical rationality may have recourse to the phenomenon of empathy. As has been alluded to before, when empathy is understood as a kind of feeling with the other, it can be used in terms of a sentimentalist account of explaining altruism. In the tradition of moral philosophy, such a perspective has been aligned with David Hume. Modern moral philosophers follow this lead; probably Michael Slote is most explicit here in his commitment to empathy (Slote 2011: 13ff.).

Other aspects of empathy, especially the element of perspective-taking, can be used in a rationalist theory. In his book *The Possibility of Altruism*, Thomas Nagel argued, for instance, that the "possibility of putting oneself in the place of another" (Nagel 1970: 83) leads to a judgment involving the recognition of others; a judgment that anyone who is practically rational would make. In other words, perspective-taking allows the universalization of moral demands. Hence cognitive empathy, though not explicitly mentioned by Nagel in these terms, can here be seen as a formal feature of practical rationality, which makes altruism possible. Altogether, both a reference to an emotional aspect of empathy and to a cognitive aspect of empathy may therefore account for a normative explanation of altruism.

In a similar vein, Stephen Darwall has developed a theory of care and respect in terms of reasons for action, which bases both mentioned normative attitudes, care and respect, on empathy and sympathy (Darwall 2002: 15f.). Morality's demands, according to Darwall, are due to the second-person standpoint, and hence rely on claims of particular persons against each other. Again, empathy plays a crucial role in accounting for the second-person standpoint (Darwall 2006: 43ff., 151ff.).

Objections to the link between empathy and altruism

Many objections have been leveled against empathy making any significant contribution to altruism and morality. As we will see shortly, almost all of these concerns are based on a particular understanding of both empathy and morality, which are not necessarily the ones that are, or need to be, put forward by defenders of such a role for empathy.

For the purposes of this chapter, we can disregard objections that aim to undermine the very possibility of empathy. For instance, Peter Goldie argued that we cannot really imagine being another person (Goldie 2011). This is a point about the insurmountability of the first-person perspective. Whether convincing or not, it is not a specific problem of empathy in its relation to altruism. It is true, of course, that if taking the perspective of someone else from their subjective point of view is impossible, and if we as agents erroneously assume that we do have such access to other persons' minds, we might end up with a faulty basis for certain decisions, including decisions about what to do in a moral situation (Slaby 2014). Still, the potential fault here is not specific to morality and it is not a problem with empathy per se, but with a particular assumption about empathy's functions and results.

More to the point it has been objected that empathy might lead us astray in certain situations (Prinz 2011a; 2011b; cf. Maibom 2014: 35ff.). Certain biases, say due to the urgency of a need perceived in one person, as opposed to an abstract entitlement of another person, might cause an unjust moral judgment. There are also demands of morality that cannot be based on empathy, because there is no particular person involved to emphasize with. Problems of distributive justice, which are usually concerned with groups of people, are examples to this point. These kinds of objections target specific situations where a moral agent comes to a wrong moral judgment because of empathic feeling. But we have seen before that many researchers who claim a significant role for empathy in morality discuss general moral dispositions, not specific judgments or actions. Surely they would agree that instantiations of empathy in particular situations cannot guarantee the morally right judgment, never mind the right actions, and might even occasionally undermine moral motivation. In addition, defenders of the moral significance of empathy point out that empathy needs to be discussed in its proper form (Song 2015). Like other skills empathy should be developed and honed. So it is not empathy as such, but a qualified version of empathy, which is supposed to strengthen empathy in humans. More specifically, it is said that empathy needs to be "regulated" (Kauppinen 2014), or "morally contoured" (Carse 2005).

So the main point of critical debate should be empathy's role in the development of the moral point of view in agents. Some authors claim that moral development can be explained without reference to empathy and indeed better explained in other terms (Prinz 2011a: 221f.; 2011b: 216ff.). But it seems that the jury is still out in this respect. Indeed, without a clear view on the conceptual landscape – on what exactly altruism is, and what exactly the different forms of empathy are – we will probably never identify the proper role of empathy in the development of morality.

Conclusion

Although empathy by itself is not a moral phenomenon (Maibom 2014: 33), it has been argued in this chapter that it does have an important role in the development of the moral point of view of agents. It seems that empathy is significant in both its cognitive and affective aspects. To be able to take the perspective of others – if not from their very own perspective – seems to be important to ground the judgment that other persons count normatively. Similarly, to be able to feel with another person, especially feeling their pain and needs, seems important to ground the moral motivation to alleviate their suffering. In terms of moral agency, empathy might therefore have epistemic and motivational roles. All of this, however, is highly speculative. In the future it needs to be seen, from the point of view of empirical and normative explanations of the role of empathy within altruism and morality, just how important empathy really is and what roles, exactly, it might have in accounting for human (and perhaps other animals') morality.

References

Batson, C. Daniel. 2011. *Altruism in Humans*. Oxford: Oxford University Press.

Batson, C. Daniel. 2014. Empathy-Induced Altruism and Morality: No Necessary Connection. In: *Empathy and Morality*, ed. Heidi Maibom. Oxford: Oxford University Press, 41–58.

Carse, Alisa L. 2005. The Moral Contours of Empathy. *Ethical Theory and Moral Practice* 8: 169–95.

Clavien, Christine; Chaupisat, Michel. 2012. Altruism: A Philosophical Analysis. In: eLS. John Wiley & Sons Ltd, Chichester. www.els.net [doi: 10.1002/9780470015902.a0003442.pub2].

Darwall, Stephen. 2002. *Welfare and Rational Care*. Princeton, NJ: Princeton University Press.

Darwall, Stephen. 2006. *The Second-Person Standpoint: Morality, Respect, and Accountability*. Cambridge, MA: Harvard University Press.

de Quervain, Dominique J.-F.; Fischbacher, Urs; Treyer, Valerie; Schellhammer, Melanie; Schnyder, Ulrich; Buck, Alfred; Fehr, Ernst. 2004. The Neural Basis of Altruistic Punishment. *Science* 305 (1254): 1254–8.

de Waal, Frans B. M. 2008. Putting the Altruism Back into Altruism: The Evolution of Empathy. *Annual Review of Psychology* 59: 279–300.

Eisenberg, Nancy; Miller, Paul A. 1987. The Relation of Empathy to Prosocial and Related Behaviors. *Psychological Bulletin* 101 (1): 91–119.

Fehr, Ernst; Fischbacher, Urs. 2005. Human Altruism: Proximate Patterns and Evolutionary Origins. *Analyse und Kritik* 27 (1): 6–47.

Feinberg, Joel. 2007. Psychological Egoism. In: *Ethical Theory: An Anthology*, ed. Russ Shafer-Landau. Oxford: Blackwell, 183–95.

Frankena, William K. 1963. *Ethics*. Second edition. Englewood Cliffs, NJ: Prentice-Hall.

Goldie, Peter. 2011. Anti-Empathy. In: *Empathy: Philosophical and Psychological Perspectives*, eds. Amy Coplan & Peter Goldie. Oxford: Oxford University Press, 302–17.

Hoffman, M. L. 2000. *Empathy and Moral Development: Implications for Caring and Justice*. Cambridge: Cambridge University Press.

Joyce, Richard. 2013. Altruism and Biology. In: *The International Encyclopedia of Ethics*, ed. Hugh LaFollette, 215–22.

Kauppinen, Antti. 2014. Empathy, Emotion Regulation, and Moral Judgment. In: *Empathy and Morality*, ed. Heidi Maibom. Oxford: Oxford University Press, 97–121.

Kitcher, Philip. 2011. *The Ethical Project*. Cambridge, MA: Harvard University Press.

Maibom, Heidi. 2014. Introduction: (Almost) Everything You Ever Wanted to Know about Empathy. In: *Empathy and Morality*, ed. Heidi Maibom. Oxford: Oxford University Press, 1–40.

Nagel, Thomas. 1970. *The Possibility of Altruism*. Princeton, NJ: Princeton University Press.

Okasha, Samir. 2008. Biological Altruism. *Stanford Encyclopedia of Philosophy*. (Fall 2013 Edition). In: Edward N. Zalta, ed. URL: https://plato.stanford.edu/archives/fall2013/entries/altruism-biological/.

Peacock, Mark S.; Schefczyk, Michael; Schaber, Peter. 2005. Altruism and the Indispensability of Motives. *Analyse und Kritik* 27 (1): 188–96.

Prinz, Jesse. 2011a. Against Empathy. *Southern Journal of Philosophy* 49. Spindel Suppl.: 214–33.

Prinz, Jesse. 2011b. Is Empathy Necessary for Morality? In: *Empathy: Philosophical and Psychological Perspectives*, eds. Amy Coplan & Peter Goldie. Oxford: Oxford University Press, 211–29.

Schmidtz, David. 1993. Reasons for Altruism. *Social Philosophy & Policy* 10 (1), 52–68.

Sinnott-Armstrong, Walter. 2014. Do Psychopaths Refute Internalism? In: *Being Amoral: Psychopathy and Moral Incapacity*, ed. Thomas Schramme. Cambridge, MA: MIT Press.

Slaby, Jan. 2014. Empathy's Blind Spot. *Medicine, Health Care, and Philosophy* 17 (2): 249–58.

Slote, Michael. 2011. *Moral Sentimentalism*. Oxford: Oxford University Press.

Sober, Elliott; Wilson, David Sloan. 1998. *Unto Others: The Evolution and Psychology of Unselfish Behavior*. Cambridge, MA: Harvard University Press.

Song, Yujia. 2015. How to Be a Proponent of Empathy. *Ethical Theory and Moral Practice* 18: 437–51.

Stich, Stephen; Doris, John M.; Roedder, Erica. 2010. Altruism. In: *The Moral Psychology Handbook*, eds. John Doris & The Moral Psychology Research Group. Oxford: Oxford University Press, 147–205.

West, S. A.; Griffin, A. S.; Gardner, A. 2007. Social Semantics: Altruism, Cooperation, Mutualism, Strong Reciprocity and Group Selection. *Journal of Evolutionary Biology* 20 (2): 415–32.

Zahn-Waxler, C.; Radke-Yarrow, M.; Wagner, E.; Chapman, M. 1992. Development of Concern for Others. *Developmental Psychology* 28 (1): 126–36.

Further reading

Bagnoli, Carla (ed.). 2011. *Morality and the Emotions*. Oxford: Oxford University Press.

Blum, Lawrence. 1980. *Friendship, Altruism, and Morality*. London: Routledge & Kegan Paul.

D'Arms, Justin; Jacobson, Daniel (eds.). *Moral Psychology and Human Agency: Philosophical Essays on the Science of Ethics*. Oxford: Oxford University Press.

Davis, Mark H. 1996. *Empathy: A Social Psychological Approach*. Boulder, CO: Westview Press.

Decety, Jean (ed.). 2012. *Empathy: From Bench to Bedside*. Cambridge, MA: MIT Press.

Deigh, John (ed.). 1992. *Ethics and Personality: Essays in Moral Psychology*. Chicago, IL and London: University of Chicago Press.

Miller, Christian. 2013. *Moral Character: An Empirical Theory*. Oxford: Oxford University Press.

Narvaez. Darcia; Lapsley, Daniel K. (eds.). 2009. *Personality, Identity, and Character: Explorations in Moral Psychology*. Cambridge: Cambridge University Press.

Rottschafer, William A. 1998. *The Biology and Psychology of Moral Agency*. Cambridge: Cambridge University Press.

Roughley, Neil; Schramme, Thomas (eds.). 2015. *On Moral Sentimentalism*. Newcastle upon Tyne: Cambridge Scholars Publishing.

Roughley, Neil; Schramme, Thomas (eds.). Forthcoming. *Forms of Fellow Feeling: Empathy, Sympathy, Concern and Moral Agency.* Cambridge: Cambridge University Press.

Schramme, Thomas (ed.). 2014. *Being Amoral: Psychopathy and Moral Incapacity*. Cambridge, MA: MIT Press.

19

EMPATHY AND MORAL JUDGMENT

Antti Kauppinen

At the beginning of September 2015, shocking images of a drowned Syrian refugee boy on a Turkish beach aroused widespread criticism of European policy. Although the crisis had started much earlier, many people apparently only then formed the belief that it is the moral obligation of rich Europe to take care of people in desperate need, and demanded that politicians act. Why? Speaking for myself, as a parent of a boy of similar age, I felt sadness and anger at those responsible for forcing parents to take such risks – I couldn't help thinking that this could have happened to my own son, had I not had the luck to live in a stable and peaceful country. The striking picture resonated emotionally with me, as it did with many others who had hitherto paid little attention to the refugee problem, in spite of knowing that large numbers of people were risking their lives to escape war. The best explanation for this reaction is likely to be the capacity and tendency of human beings to take on the feelings they attribute to other people, when they come to be vividly aware of the situation of individual others they can identify with. Evidently, such empathic feelings sometimes causally influence the moral judgments that people make.

This modest claim about causal influence is hardly controversial. But some philosophers have made stronger claims for empathy, maintaining that it is *necessary* for or even constitutive of moral judgment, or that it is part of the best explanation of why we endorse pro-social moral norms and distinguish them from conventional norms. Some have also argued that empathy is needed for making *good* moral judgments, while others claim it's often morally problematic, because it is biased and insensitive to numbers, among other things. This chapter examines arguments for and against such claims, focusing largely on the contemporary debate, though I will discuss the historical views that have directly influenced it.

1. Empathy causation

In keeping with established terminology, I will distinguish between cognitive and affective empathy, where the former is roughly a matter of imaginatively taking another's perspective, and the latter involves roughly coming to feel as the other does, because one takes the other to feel that way. (I will leave the details of these processes for other chapters.) Here's a simple form of the hypothesis that empathy is causally necessary for moral judgment:

Minimal Empathy Causation hypothesis

Any moral judgment made by any subject B regarding a situation that elicits emotion
or affect in another subject A is caused at least in part by affective empathy with A.

If Minimal Empathy Causation is true, we can't make moral judgments concerning others
without first empathizing with someone. (As Jesse Prinz (2011a) points out, it is silent on judgments concerning oneself.) Why would this be? One classical argument is provided by David
Hume (whose own view is nevertheless ultimately more complex, as we'll see). Hume argues,
first, that what makes us approve or disapprove of something is that surveying it gives rise to a
distinctive kind of pleasure or pain (*Treatise* (T) 78). In the case of moral judgment, he maintains
that "'Tis only when a character is consider'd in general, without reference to our particular
interest, that it causes such a feeling or sentiment, as denominates it morally good or evil" (T 79).
Second, something pleases or pains us without reference to our particular interest only when we
empathize with the pleasure or pain it gives rise to in others. Using "sympathy" for what is now
called empathy, he summarizes: "When any quality, or character, has a tendency to the good of
mankind, we are pleas'd with it, and approve of it; because it presents the lively idea of pleasure;
which idea affects us by sympathy, and is itself a kind of pleasure" (T 155). This suggests that
empathy is causally necessary for (other-directed) moral judgment, since it alone enables us to
have the distinctive kind of disinterested pleasure or pain on which moral approbation or disap-
probation is based. This is a parsimonious hypothesis, as it allows us to explain why people make
the moral judgments they do without appeal to some kind of innate moral capacity, intuition,
or practical reason. (Hume and other sentimentalists separately argue against these alternative
explanations, but this is not the place to discuss these arguments.)

Nevertheless, Minimal Empathy Causation faces such serious challenges that it has few if any
defenders. Leaving aside issues that arise for sentimentalist explanations in general, Hume himself observed that our empathy can vary without variation in our moral judgment. For example,
he noted that like sense perception, our natural empathy is influenced by the position of the
object relative to us: "We sympathize more with persons contiguous to us, than with persons
remote from us: With our acquaintance, than with strangers: With our countrymen, than with
foreigners" (T 156). Yet our approval doesn't (always) vary accordingly. Hume's explanation of
this was that we learn to *regulate* our empathy when making judgments. That is, we "correct
the momentary appearances" (T 157) by adopting a "common point of view" (T 163), since
otherwise our sentiments would constantly clash and uncertainty would reign. We do this "by
a sympathy with those, who have any commerce with the person we consider" (T 158). So it is
not enough that empathy helps us transcend our own perspective in *some* way. For Hume, our
moral verdicts depend on empathizing with the feelings of those affected by an action (or the
agent's character traits) regardless of their relationship to us. Call this kind of view the Regulated
Empathy Causation hypothesis.

Adam Smith's account builds on Hume's, but highlights the role of *cognitive* empathy. He
believes that what leads us to approve of someone's response to a situation is that we imaginatively
place ourselves in their shoes and find that we would respond the same way. His account of moral
judgment is complex, but roughly, he claims that we morally disapprove of someone if we imaginatively place ourselves in the shoes of both the agent and those affected, and find that we would
ourselves resent the agent for the ill will her action displays (see Gordon 1995 and Kauppinen
2010). Like Hume, Smith thinks we learn to regulate our response, in his case by reference to how
an impartial spectator would feel. An impartial spectator is just any normal person who doesn't
favor any particular person, so that her responses are not influenced by the identity of the agent or

the patient of the action, and who doesn't think of herself as more important than others. When I approach a situation as an impartial spectator, I feel just the same way about an insult to a stranger as I do about an insult to a friend, and I take it that any ordinary person who treats others as equals would feel the same way. It is the sense that *any* normal, decent person who doesn't take sides would feel in a certain way that lends a distinctively moral force and quality to our sentiment.

So, Hume and Smith agree that making moral judgments on the basis of empathy involves counteracting some of our natural tendencies. In contemporary terms, it demands a form of *emotion regulation*: we need to both *up-regulate* our empathic reaction on behalf of strangers and *down-regulate* our empathic reaction on behalf of those close to us (see Kauppinen 2014 for discussion with reference to empirical psychology). However, while this kind of view explains why natural empathy and our moral judgments diverge, it is hardly credible as a hypothesis about the causal history of *each and every* moral judgment. The problem is that it is cognitively quite demanding to place ourselves impartially in another's position before judging, and we certainly seem capable of making judgments without doing so.

Even if we leave the above issues aside, it is questionable whether empathizing could account for the content of all our moral judgments. As Jesse Prinz has emphasized, there are many situations in which we make moral judgments, but there is no possibility of empathic affective reaction. For example, there seem to be victimless crimes, which we disapprove of even though there is by definition no one to empathize with. Many people disapprove of masturbating with an already dead chicken, for example (Haidt, Koller, & Diaz 1993). In yet other cases, there are too many victims to empathize with (think of the Great Famine), or it is indeterminate who suffers from the bad action, such as tax evasion (Prinz 2011a, 220). These cases strongly suggest that empathy can't be causally necessary for moral judgment. Indeed, they support a simpler explanation, which Prinz puts as follows:

> My moral response is linked to action-types. If I classify your behavior as an instance of "stealing," then that is enough to instill moral ire. Disapprobation can follow directly from certain types of action without any need to contemplate the suffering of victims.
>
> *(2011a, 220)*

This simple alternative hypothesis appears to be superior to any Empathy Causation account. But it requires an answer to the question of how we come to disapprove of actions of certain types, and there empathy might yet have a role to play.

2. Empathy constitution

Could empathy be *constitutively* involved in each and every moral judgment? If it were, the following would be true. Here is the thesis:

Empathy Constitution

> Moral judgments are constituted by affective empathy either with the patient or the agent of the action.

In its patient-focused form, Empathy Constitution is vulnerable to many of the challenges faced by Empathy Causation, or their analogs. For example, if we consider ourselves to be wronged, but can't empathize with ourselves, clearly our judgment isn't constituted by our empathic emotion. How about the agent-focused variant? It has recently been defended by Michael Slote. Slote begins by observing that "empathic concern for others is itself a psychological state that may be the subject or object of empathy" (Slote 2010, 34). Suppose that someone goes out of their way to help the homeless, thus manifesting a high degree of empathic concern. In Slote's terminology, she displays warmth and tenderness towards the homeless. If I come to share her feelings, I feel warmth and tenderness towards her, and such "empathy with empathy" constitutes moral approval (ibid., 35). On the other hand, if someone acts towards others with cold indifference, taking on that person's feeling means that I have a cold feeling towards the agent, and that constitutes my disapproval, according to Slote. Such emotional approval and disapproval then "enters into making moral judgments" (ibid., 53), which helps explain why moral judgments coincide with motivation.

Many philosophers have criticized Slote's proposal (see e.g. Stueber 2011). One problem that I'll leave aside here is a more general metaethical issue of whether moral judgments could consist even in part of feelings of any kind, given their semantic and inferential properties. Apart from this issue, one obvious concern is that if I take on your warm feeling towards the homeless, I seem to end up with a warm feeling towards the homeless, not towards you. Slote's response to this is to claim that the intentionality of the empathic feeling is determined by its causal origin, which is the agent's feeling (2010, 39). But this view of the intentionality of empathic emotions has odd implications. Suppose you're angry with Eilis, and I empathize with you. Since the cause of my empathic anger is your feeling, Slote's view implies that I'm now angry with you! This is unacceptable. Second, feelings of warmth or chill towards someone seem to have very different characteristics than moral approval or disapproval (Prinz 2011a). For example, while feeling cold toward someone is no doubt a negative feeling, it only accidentally motivates us to impose sanctions on the agent. It contrasts with blaming attitudes like resentment or indignation, which are hardly phenomenally "cold" in any sense. Finally, agential empathy seems to be neither sufficient nor necessary for approval, nor its absence for disapproval. For example, we can disapprove of actions that are not done out of unempathic motives, such as an animal rights activist throwing a cake in the face of a politician out of empathy for the suffering of farm animals (cf. D'Arms 2011). In short, neither the patient- nor the agent-focused variant of Empathy Constitution is particularly plausible.

3. Empathy's role in explaining moral norms

Given the challenges to Empathy Causation and Empathy Constitution, one might think that empathy can't play a role in explaining moral judgment. But what has been said so far doesn't yet rule out a more indirect, yet still necessary role for empathy in the *development* of moral judgment. Consider Prinz's hypothesis that "moral response is linked to action-types" (2011a, 220). As I noted, it requires an explanation of how such a link is formed. That is, why do we embrace certain *specific* moral norms or rules, and why do we regard certain norms as specifically *moral*, as opposed to conventional? Here's one hypothesis:

Empathy Explanation hypothesis

Empathic feelings are a necessary part of the best explanation of a) why subjects endorse pro-social norms b) in a distinctively moral way.

By "pro-social norms" I mean norms that prohibit harming other people in certain contexts, require respecting people and their property, demand fair treatment, and so on. Not all norms that people have historically endorsed in a distinctively moral way are pro-social in this sense. Obviously, practices like slavery or marital rape have been considered morally permissible, and some people think chauvinistic patriotism is morally required. The best explanation for the existence of such norms will likely appeal to the self-interest of privileged populations rather than empathy. But empathy might play a role in explaining why people hold *some* central moral norms, even when it is against their self-interest or what they've been taught.

3.1 Empathy and rules

The first part of the Empathy Explanation hypothesis is that empathy is necessary for explaining why people form judgments regarding certain pro-social act-types. There are several ways in which this explanation might work. Hume and Smith appealed to what might be called our *induction disposition*: once we perceive a pattern across cases, we project it to future instances as a generalized expectation. As Smith puts it:

> The general maxims of morality are formed, like all other general maxims, from experience and induction. We observe in a great variety of particular cases what pleases or displeases our moral faculties, what these approve or disapprove of, and, by induction from this experience, we establish those general rules.
>
> *(The Theory of Moral Sentiments (TMS) 377)*

It is, as I said, relatively uncontroversial that we do sometimes form judgments as a result of empathizing with someone. Suppose that during our formative years we encounter several people who have been cheated by someone else, empathize with their anger or hurt, and consequently disapprove of the people who cheated them. (Insofar as we empathize impartially, we'll disapprove of cheating anyone, not just cheating people like us.) If we have the induction disposition, we'll come to disapprove all instances of cheating by default, without having to empathize in each and every case of cheating.

A different but potentially complementary kind of empathy-based explanation says that over time we (collectively) come to embrace pro-social moral norms out of a set of candidates, because those norms resonate with our empathic tendencies. Individuals might then pick up these norms through socialization without themselves empathizing. This would be an empathy-based variant of the view that Shaun Nichols (2004) has developed, according to which norms that match our affective reactions enjoy greater "cultural fitness" than those that don't, and thus get transmitted from generation to generation. Nichols's own account appeals to a "Concern Mechanism," which is triggered by attributions of negative hedonic or affective states to others, and generates concern for them, reactive distress, and contagious distress (2004, ch. 2). It is these emotional responses that explain why norms against causing harm to others are widely adopted, according to Nichols. However, our actual pro-social moral norms are much more complex than blanket prohibitions against harming people – it matters to us what the agent's motives are, whether the harm is a means to an end or a side effect, whether the harm is the result of an action or of an omission, whether the harm is intended, negligent, or merely accidental, and so on (for some empirical data, including data about cultural variation, see Young & Tsoi 2013 and Barrett et al. 2016). Arguably, a simple Concern Mechanism cannot account for the greater cultural fitness of such norms that are sensitive to the agent's quality of will. Instead, explaining them may require appealing to perspective-taking along the lines of the regulated empathy hypothesis (see Kauppinen forthcoming for some details).

How successful is this part of Empathy Explanation? Properly answering this question would require a detailed comparison with alternative explanations of why we embrace pro-social moral norms. While philosophers sometimes appeal to the ability to intuit moral principles or pure practical reason, psychologists tend to prefer evolutionary explanations that appeal to innate affective dispositions to disapprove of behavior that reduces fitness at the group level (Haidt 2012) or an innate moral 'grammar' that generates moral principles (Mikhail 2011). Jesse Prinz (2011a, 2011b) offers parental conditioning and imitation as an alternative. However, such a story is evidently incomplete, since it leaves unexplained why *parents* endorse and transmit some norms and not others. In any case, if any of these hypotheses is true, empathy is not necessary for explaining our adherence to our moral norms. What Empathy Explanation has going for it is parsimony, since it doesn't require assuming any kind of innate moral capacity (see Nichols 2005). It also predicts that empathic reactions to novel situations will result in specification or rejection of pre-existing principles (Masto 2015) – for example, we might come to rethink our convictions regarding slavery or treatment of refugees as a result of vivid descriptions that arouse empathic feelings.

3.2 Empathy and the moral/conventional distinction

The second part of Empathy Explanation is that empathy is necessary for explaining why we regard certain pro-social norms as distinctively *moral*. Clearly, not all norms belong in this category. We can, for example, think that something is against the law without thinking that it is morally wrong. What is distinctive of moral norms, then? Since the work of Elliot Turiel (1983), it has been common for psychologists to focus on different ways of responding to transgressions of norms. According to this tradition, some transgressions are regarded as wrong independently of whether they are permitted by social, political, or even religious authorities (authority-independence), as wrong everywhere (universality), as more seriously wrong (seriousness), and more severely punishable. These norm-violations include what are often considered paradigmatic moral wrongs, such as injustice or harming others. Other transgressions, such as dressing in a particular way, are regarded as wrong only when prohibited by some local authority, such as a teacher, legislator, or custom, wrong only locally, as less seriously wrong, and less severely punishable. These features are taken by many psychologists to mark what is called the moral/conventional distinction. Many studies have found that children distinguish between these two kinds of transgression from an early age, roughly two to three years old (Smetana 1981). Although this distinction has recently become controversial (see Kelly et al. 2007 and Shoemaker 2011), the critiques arguably misconstrue what authority-independence in the relevant sense entails, so I will assume in the following that it is nevertheless along the right lines. (Space constraints prevent a more detailed examination here.)

Supposing this is the right way to draw the moral/conventional distinction, what could be the role of empathy in explaining it? Start with the contrast between a paradigmatic moral transgression that involves one person deliberately harming another in order to further their own perceived interests, and a paradigmatic conventional violation, such as wearing different colored socks. In the first case, if we either affectively empathize with the person harmed, or imaginatively put ourselves in her position, we will predictably have a negative reactive attitude such as resentment towards the agent. Typically, at least as far as we ourselves see it, this attitude doesn't depend on our personal relationship to either the agent or the patient, or on taking ourselves to be more important than other people, so we take it that any normal, decent person would feel the same way. Consequently, we emotionally construe the action as being wrong, whether or not we've been told by someone that it is impermissible (see Kauppinen 2013). Further, we're in a position to appreciate *why* the action is wrong – say, that it manifests insufficient regard for the victim's will or interests. And when we have a negative reactive attitude towards the agent, we're already blaming them, and if we take it that any informed and impartial spectator would feel the same way, we already construe blame as fitting. In the second case, we won't have these emotional responses towards different colored socks. So even if both harming and dressing in a certain way go against rules that we've been taught, it's no surprise that we regard the first violation to have a different status, and consider it to be wrong regardless of whether someone in a position of authority permits it.

These considerations suggest that empathizing of a certain kind is *sufficient* to distinguish moral from conventional norms. It's a much more demanding task to make that empathy is *necessary* for recognizing the distinction. One challenge is that other emotional responses, such as disgust, seem sufficient to get some people to regard certain transgressions, such as masturbating with a dead animal or spitting into a glass from which one is going to drink, as authority-independently wrong (Nichols 2004). One line of response would be to emphasize that authority-independence isn't the sole mark of a moral norm. There's also the fittingness of blame and guilt. A defender of Empathy Explanation might insist that when we think that a disgusting behavior is morally wrong, there is an element of cognitive empathy involved in our disapproval – we imagine any normal person would blame the agent for such behavior. It would support this hypothesis if people who lack empathy couldn't genuinely distinguish between moral and conventional violations. I'll turn to this issue next.

3.3 *Empathy deficits and moral judgment*

Empathy Explanation predicts that people with empathy deficits should manifest deficient moral judgment. (I will restrict my attention to judgment, not moral agency in general.) In this context, two populations, psychopaths and autists, have received particular attention. In the following, it is worth bearing in mind that both conditions are spectrum disorders – any deficits associated with them can be expected to be a matter of degree.

Let's start with psychopaths. One characteristic of the disorder is that psychopaths care little or nothing about how other people feel. Nevertheless, psychopaths appear to be good at attributing feelings to others, possibly by way of perspective-taking. Thus, they seem to be deficient in affective empathy in particular, and seemingly a good test case for its necessity for moral judgment. Are psychopaths capable of moral judgment, then? This is controversial. They do well in some tests of moral reasoning, and generally classify as wrong the same actions as normal people do. But since they appear to be unmoved by the wrongness of certain actions, some philosophers deny that they genuinely consider them to be morally wrong – rather, they're only parroting what they've been taught. Whether this is the case hangs on whether moral judgment internalism is true or not (for the current state of the debate, see Björnsson et al. (eds.) 2015).

A metaethically more neutral test is whether psychopaths can distinguish between moral and conventional violations. Some evidence suggests that they can't – in particular, one study found that convicted criminal psychopaths say all transgressions are authority-independently wrong (Blair 1995). R. J. R. Blair's (1995) interpretation is that psychopaths can't tell the difference between moral and conventional norms since they lack an affective response to the suffering of others (so, unsurprisingly, they rarely appeal to harm as a justification for why a violation is wrong), but try to create a good impression in the eyes of authorities by erring on the side of caution and classifying all violations as authority-independent. However, more recent studies suggest that psychopaths may, after all, be able to make the distinction. For example, when Aharoni et al. (2012) gave a forced-choice test, in which subjects had to classify eight out of sixteen transgressions as authority-independent, they "found no evidence that high-psychopathy offenders – as measured by total psychopathy score – were any poorer at distinguishing moral from conventional transgressions than were low-psychopathy offenders." However, total psychopathy score includes a number of components, such as interpersonal and lifestyle facts, in addition to affect, and they found that the affective facet taken alone *did* influence performance. (For an alternative interpretation of the data, see Levy 2014.)

In brief, then, evidence from psychopaths must be regarded as inconclusive at the moment. Matters are further complicated by the fact that psychopaths suffer from other deficits as well. Prinz (2011a) argues that their generally low affect levels suffice to explain any deficiencies in moral judgment, while Jeanette Kennett (2002) argues that it is problems with reasoning and impulse control that are the cause – in particular, she claims psychopaths are unable to appreciate how considerations independent of one's present desires provide reasons that extend over time (2002, 355). In the latter vein, Heidi Maibom draws on various empirical studies to support the hypothesis that psychopaths have deficient practical rationality in the sense of willing means to their ends and ensuring that their aims are consistent, among other things, due to "impairments in attention width and span, impulsivity, deficient self-understanding, and difficulties adjusting their responses" (Maibom 2005, 253–4).

However, Aaltola (2014) observes that so-called secondary psychopaths are "hot-headed" and aggressive, though not empathic, so Prinz's hypothesis doesn't seem to work for them. In contrast, primary psychopaths are extremely controlled and intelligent, while being emotionally detached and fearless. These "snakes in suits," as they're sometimes called, don't seem to have the problems with reason that Kennett's and Maibom's hypotheses require (although such individuals have not yet been studied as carefully as incarcerated psychopaths). So it seems empirically plausible that it is the common problem with both kinds of psychopath, lack of empathy, which *best explains* the deficits in their moral judgment. But any definite conclusions would be premature.

Autistic people are another population of interest, since, roughly speaking, it is characteristic of them that they can't adopt the perspective of others, and thus rate low on cognitive empathy. At the same time, autists are often conscientious, and both autistic children (Leslie et al. 2006) and adults (Zalla et al. 2011) distinguish between moral and conventional norms. Kennett concludes from these facts that "the case of autism shows that both selves and moral agents can be created in the absence of empathy" (2002, 357). But this conclusion, too, may be premature. Many researchers believe that autists are capable of *affective* empathy, even if they are bad at mindreading (Dziobek et al. 2008), so a version of Empathy Explanation might still be true (Blair 2005). However, there is at least some reason to think that autism involves deficient affective empathy as well. Hobson & Hobson (2014) draw on various studies to argue that since the cognitive deficits of autists make it hard for them to experience others as persons with minds in the first place, the range, depth, and likelihood of their emotional response to the feelings or situations of others is severely limited.

Adding to the complexity of the issue, some recent research has called into question the assumption that autists are capable of making the moral/conventional distinction. In particular, Zalla et al. (2011) gave autistic subjects not only questions regarding standard moral and conventional violations, but also disgust violations drawn from Nichols (2004). What they found was that while normal subjects regarded moral and disgust violations as authority-independent, they nevertheless distinguished between them. But autists didn't. They also rarely appealed to the welfare of the victim to justify their judgment in moral cases. Other studies have shown that autists' violation judgments aren't as sensitive to agents' intentions as normal subjects' judgments – roughly, they judge unintended harms to be as bad as deliberate harms (Moran et al. 2011, Buon et al. 2013). These results are unsurprising – given the trouble autists have in putting themselves in other people's shoes, they can be expected to have difficulty appreciating the moral significance of the agent's and patient's perspective on an action. On the basis of such considerations, Tiziana Zalla and co-authors conclude:

> We argue that while the affective component of the empathy is sufficient to distinguish affect-backed from affect-neutral norms, an intact cognitive empathy, which is specifically involved in moral appraisal, is required to distinguish moral from disgust violations.
>
> *(Zalla et al. 2011, 123)*

This is good news for Empathy Explanation, since it suggests that cognitive empathy may after all be necessary for being able to properly make the moral/conventional distinction, possibly by way of making possible more cognitively demanding forms of affective empathy.

To sum up, although the empirical evidence regarding psychopathy and autism is controversial, it seems plausible that while members of both empathy deficient populations may be capable of distinguishing between moral and conventional violations in at least some cases, they have a poor grasp of the grounds for authority-independent rules for blaming people (cf. McGeer 2008 and Shoemaker 2015). This suggests that both cognitive empathy and affective response to putting oneself in the shoes of others may be necessary for *moral insight* and perhaps *moral intuition*. This more modest hypothesis predicts that empathy-deficient people, regardless of their reasoning capacity, will be poor at making moral judgments when moral insight is needed – in particular, when the rules that one has learned from others don't yield an answer, or yield answers that conflict with one another. While it has not, to my knowledge, been empirically tested yet, this hypothesis does fit well with observed behavior.

4. Is empathy good or bad for moral judgment?

Regardless of how empirical controversies regarding the causal or explanatory role of empathy turn out, we can ask whether empathizing with others before making moral judgments makes it more likely that those judgments are correct. In one kind of situation, this is the case rather trivially. The correctness of some moral judgments hangs on facts about the feelings and other psychological states of other people. For example, whether Emily is to blame for hurting Joe's feelings depends in part on what Emily's intentions were and whether Joe's feelings were indeed hurt. Assuming that cognitive empathy is one way of learning about other people's intentions and feelings, it will in such cases be conducive to making correct judgments. Further, we occasionally ask each other to "walk a mile in our shoes" before blaming us. In this kind of case, too, cognitively empathizing with someone is likely to change our moral responses for the better – typically, it leads us to better appreciate the presence of excusing factors. (The data from autists supports this hypothesis.) So, in brief, cognitive empathy with the agent or those affected by an action can be expected to improve moral judgment whenever the moral status of the action depends on empirical facts about mental states that are accessible via empathy.

But what if our moral judgments result from affective empathy with the actual feelings of other people? Is that a good thing? It is a commonsense notion that empathy serves as a check to bias and self-interest, so we should try to be more empathic if we can before we judge. But recently, some philosophers and psychologists have argued that empathy is inherently morally problematic. Paul Bloom (2013) maintains that it is "parochial, narrow-minded, and innumerate," so we shouldn't rely on it. He notes that psychological research has revealed what is called the identifiable victim effect: people seem to care more about the plight of one individual they can relate to than about the suffering of many people that show up in statistics (Jenni

& Loewenstein 1997). Indeed, we can't possibly empathize with everyone, and people who are strangers to us might be particularly difficult for us to empathize with, so we're better off relying instead on "more abstract principles of justice and fairness, along with a more diffuse compassion" (Bloom 2015). Sometimes this means going against empathy's verdict, as when punishment is warranted, or fair allocation of resources means that someone has to suffer. Jesse Prinz (2011a, 2011b) makes similar criticisms, adding that empathy is easily manipulated (for discussion and a response to Prinz, see Chapter 21, "Empathy and moral responsibility"). We might also note that since it can be difficult for the privileged and powerful to put themselves in the shoes of the underprivileged – the poor, the disabled, or ethnic minorities, for example – relying on empathy in a political context may lead to reinforcing the unjust status quo.

With the notable exception of Michael Slote (2010), who thinks moral demands are as partial as empathy is, most partisans of empathy find these observations troubling. Alas, these concerns are not new. As already discussed, none other than David Hume himself was keenly aware of the biases and limitations of our empathy. We've seen that he believed we can, to some extent, correct for the inbuilt biases. Nevertheless, he acknowledged that empathy ("humanity") can easily come into conflict with justice:

> When I relieve persons in distress, my natural humanity is my motive; and so far as my succour extends, so far have I promoted the happiness of my fellow-creatures. But if we examine all the questions, that come before any tribunal of justice, we shall find, that, considering each case apart, it wou'd as often be an instance of humanity to decide contrary to the laws of justice as conformable to them. Judges take from a poor man to give to a rich; they bestow on the dissolute the labour of the industrious; and put into the hands of the vicious the means of harming both themselves and others.
>
> *(T 155)*

So far, Hume is in agreement with critics like Bloom. But he digs deeper. Hume believes that justice is an "artificial virtue," a system of rules that has arisen, because it serves, on the whole, each individual's enlightened self-interest. But why should we think that serving not just our own interest but the interests of all (or at least most) others is good or just? Hume's answer is that it's because we empathize with those others, and thus disinterestedly approve of justice and other artificial virtues. Given his view of the nature of empathy, Hume thought this would result in endorsing a kind of rule-utilitarianism. Adam Smith, in contrast, held that since we might empathize with the resentment of one person sacrificed for the benefit of many even if we're impartial, empathy-based rules are non-consequentialist.

Either way, such indirect empathy is arguably a good thing, when it comes to settling on principles of justice – someone who lacked such empathy might end up endorsing rules that fail to serve the general good, or show insufficient regard for the dignity of each individual. Consider someone like Adolf Eichmann, who possibly quite sincerely thought that morality required him to do his duty as defined by his superiors (Arendt 1963). It is safe to assume that had he reflected on the rules he was told to obey by placing himself in the position any one of those negatively affected by them, he wouldn't have been equally enthusiastic about obedience to Nazi authorities. After all, empathy, in particular when it is regulated by reference to an ideal of impartiality, tends to result in embracing pro-social norms of the kind that most of us regard as correct (cf. Hoffman 2011).

So, philosophers who think empathy is a good thing for morality have always been aware that our natural tendency to take on other people's feelings is an unreliable guide in moral judgment. Instead, they have argued that empathy must be tempered by regulating our emotional responses to particular cases so that we won't miss the big picture. Nevertheless, they maintain that the alleged conflict between empathy and justice is illusory, since our regard for justice itself stems from empathy. They would thus agree that we shouldn't base decisions about immigration policy on how we feel when contemplating a dead boy, for example. Untutored empathy can blind us to the non-actual and the wider context. But it can spur us to reflect on what the alternatives to the actual situation are, and to consider their impact in the light of principles that may get their grip on us in virtue of resonating with impartially empathic responses.

5. Conclusion

It is likely an exaggeration to claim that empathy is the "cement of the moral universe," as Michael Slote (2010) does. It is not plausible that empathy is either causally or constitutively involved in each and every moral judgment, and it may not be necessary for having the capacity to distinguish moral from other norms. But people who lack the ability to put themselves in the place of others and feel for them do appear to have trouble with moral insight and appreciating the grounds of pro-social moral principles, even if their rational powers are largely intact. This suggests that empathy may have an irreplaceable role in the development of good moral judgment after all, although it wouldn't be wise to rely on it in each individual case.

References

Aaltola, Elisa 2014. Affective Empathy as Core Moral Agency: Psychopathy, Autism and Reason Revisited. *Philosophical Explorations* 17 (1), 76–92.
Aharoni, Eyal, Sinnott-Armstrong, Walter, & Kiehl, Kent A. 2012. Can Psychopathic Offenders Discern Moral Wrongs? A New Look at the Moral/Conventional Distinction. *Journal of Abnormal Psychology* 121 (2), 484–97.
Arendt, Hannah 1963. *Eichmann in Jerusalem: A Report on the Banality of Evil.* New York: Viking Press.
Barrett, H. et al. 2016. Small-Scale Societies Exhibit Fundamental Variation in the Role of Intentions in Moral Judgment. *PNAS* 113 (17), 4688–93.
Blair, R. J. R. 1995. A Cognitive Developmental Approach to Morality: Investigating the Psychopath. *Cognition* 57, 1–29.
Blair, R. J. R. 2005. Responding to the Emotions of Others: Dissociating Forms of Empathy through the Study of Typical and Psychiatric Populations. *Consciousness and Cognition* 14, 698–718.
Bloom, Paul 2013. The Baby in the Well: The Case Against Empathy. *New Yorker*, May 20.
Bloom, Paul 2015. Imagining the Lives of Others. *New York Times*, June 6, SR8.
Björnsson, Gunnar, Björklund, Fredrik, Strandberg, Caj, Eriksson, John, and Ragnar Francén Olinder 2015 (eds.). *Motivational Internalism.* Oxford: Oxford University Press.
Buon, Marine, Dupoux, Emmanuel, Jacob, Pierre, Chaste, Pauline, Leboyer, Marion, & Zalla, Tiziana 2013. The Role of Causal and Intentional Judgments in Moral Reasoning in Individuals with High Functioning Autism. *Journal of Autism and Developmental Disorders* 43, 458–70.
Coplan, Amy, & Goldie, Peter (eds.) 2011. *Empathy: Philosophical and Psychological Perspectives.* Oxford: Oxford University Press.
D'Arms, Justin 2011. Empathy, Approval, and Disapproval in Moral Sentimentalism. *Southern Journal of Philosophy* 49, Supplementary Volume, 134–41.
Dziobek, Isabel, Rogers, Kimberley, Fleck, Stefan, Bahnemann, Markus, Heekeren, Hauke R., Wolf, Oliver T., & Convit, Antonio 2008. Dissociation of Cognitive and Emotional Empathy in Adults with Asperger Syndrome Using the Multifaceted Empathy Test (MET). *Journal of Autism and Developmental Disorders* 38, 464–73.
Gordon, R. M. 1995. Sympathy, Simulation, and the Impartial Spectator. *Ethics* 105, 727–42.
Haidt, Jonathan 2012. *The Righteous Mind.* New York: Pantheon Books.
Haidt, Jonathan, Koller, Silvia H., & Dias, Maria G. 1993. Affect, Culture, and Morality, or Is It Wrong to Eat Your Dog? *Journal of Personality and Social Psychology* 65, 613–28.

Hobson, R. Peter, & Hobson, Jessica A. 2014. On Autism: A Perspective from Developmental Psychopathology. In Maibom (ed.) 2014, 172–92.

Hoffman, Martin 2011. Empathy, Justice, and the Law. In Coplan & Goldie (eds.) 2011, 230–54.

Hume, David 1739–40/1978. *A Treatise of Human Nature*. Ed. L. A. Selby-Bigge, 2nd rev. edn., P. H. Nidditch. Oxford: Clarendon Press.

Jenni, Karen, & Loewenstein, George 1997. Explaining the "Identifiable Victim Effect." *Journal of Risk and Uncertainty* 14, 235–57.

Kauppinen, Antti 2010. What Makes a Sentiment Moral? *Oxford Studies in Metaethics* 5, 225–56.

Kauppinen, Antti 2013. A Humean Theory of Moral Intuition. *Canadian Journal of Philosophy* 43 (3), 360–81.

Kauppinen, Antti 2014. Empathy, Emotion Regulation, and Moral Judgment. In Maibom (ed.) 2014, 97–121.

Kauppinen, Antti forthcoming. Sentimentalism, Blameworthiness, and Wrongdoing. In Remy Debes and Karsten Stueber (eds.), *Ethical Sentimentalism*. Cambridge: Cambridge University Press.

Kelly, Daniel, Stich, Stephen, Haley, Kevin J., Eng, Serena J., & Fessler, Daniel M.T. 2007. Harm, Affect, and the Moral/Conventional Distinction. *Mind and Language* 22 (2), 117–31.

Kennett, Jeanette 2002. Autism, Empathy, and Moral Agency. *Philosophical Quarterly* 52 (208), 340–57.

Leslie, Alan, Mallon, Ron, & DiCorcia, Jennifer 2006. Transgressors, Victims, and Cry Babies: Is Basic Moral Judgment Spared in Autism? *Social Neuroscience* 1 (3–4), 270–83.

Levy, Neil 2014. Psychopaths and Blame: The Argument from Content. *Philosophical Psychology* 27 (3), 351–67.

Maibom, Heidi 2005. Moral Unreason: The Case of Psychopathy. *Mind and Language* 20 (2), 237–57.

Maibom, Heidi (ed.) 2014. *Empathy and Morality*. New York: Oxford University Press.

Masto, Meghan 2015. Empathy and its Role in Morality. *Southern Journal of Philosophy* 53 (1), 74–96.

McGeer, Victoria 2008. Varieties of Moral Agency: Lessons from Autism (and Psychopathy). In Walter Sinnott-Armstrong (ed.), *Moral Psychology*, vol. 3: *The Neuroscience of Morality*. Cambridge, MA: MIT Press, 227–57.

Mikhail, John 2011. *Elements of Moral Cognition*. Cambridge: Cambridge University Press.

Moran, Joseph, Young, Liane, Saxe, Rebecca, Lee, Su Mei, O'Young, Daniel, Mavros, Penelope, & Gabrieli, John 2011. Impaired Theory of Mind for Moral Judgment in High-Functioning Autism. *PNAS* 108 (7), 2688–92.

Nichols, Shaun 2004. *Sentimental Rules*. New York: Oxford University Press.

Nichols, Shaun 2005. Innateness and Moral Psychology. In Peter Carruthers, Stephen Laurence, & Stephen Stich (eds.), *The Innate Mind: Structure and Contents*. New York: Oxford University Press, 353–69.

Prinz, Jesse 2011a. Against Empathy. *Southern Journal of Philosophy* 49, Supplementary Volume, 214–33.

Prinz, Jesse 2011b. Is Empathy Necessary for Morality? In Coplan and Goldie (eds.) 2011, 211–29.

Shoemaker, David 2011. Psychopathy, Responsibility, and the Moral/Conventional Distinction. *Southern Journal of Philosophy* 49, Supplementary Volume, 99–124.

Shoemaker, David 2015. *Responsibility from the Margins*. Oxford: Oxford University Press.

Slote, Michael 2010. *Moral Sentimentalism*. New York: Oxford University Press.

Smetana, Judith 1981. Preschool Children's Conceptions of Moral and Social Rules. *Child Development* 52 (4), 1333–6.

Smith, Adam 1759–1790/2002. *The Theory of Moral Sentiments*. Ed. Knut Haakonssen. Cambridge: Cambridge University Press.

Stueber, Karsten 2011. Moral Approval and the Dimensions of Empathy: Comments on Michael Slote's Moral Sentimentalism. *Analytic Philosophy* 52 (4), 328–36.

Turiel, Elliot 1983. *The Development of Social Knowledge: Morality and Convention*. Cambridge: Cambridge University Press.

Young, Liane, & Tsoi, Lily. 2013. When Mental States Matter, When They Don't, and What That Means for Morality. *Social and Personality Psychology Compass* 7 (8), 585–604.

Zalla, Tiziana, Barlassina, Luca, Buon, Marine, & Leboyer, Marion (2011). Moral Judgment in Adults with Autism Spectrum Disorders. *Cognition* 121(1), 115–26.

20

EMPATHY AND MORAL MOTIVATION

Alison E. Denham

Any justification ends finally with the rationally gratuitous presence of the emotion of sympathy; if that condition were not met, one would simply have no reason to be moral.

Thomas Nagel, The Possibility of Altruism (11)

1 The Empathic Motivation Hypothesis

The thought that empathy plays an important role in moral motivation is almost a platitude of contemporary folk psychology. Unlike many folk platitudes, however, it also has a long and distinguished history in philosophical theory. Early British sentimentalists accorded to it (or to "sympathy," as it was then labeled) a central role; Hume's premiss that "the minds of men are mirrors to one another's" lay at the heart of his etiology of the "moral distinctions" and their ability to move us to action (Hume, 1739/1978: 365). In the nineteenth century, Adam Smith followed him in locating the affective power of moral claims in our natural propensity to reflect one another's behaviors and inner lives (Smith, 1759/2002). Parallel themes were mooted in German moral philosophy and aesthetics in the 1700s, and versions of the empathy construct remained prominent in continental accounts of moral motivation through the nineteenth century and early twentieth centuries (Schiller, 1794/1967; Schopenhauer, 1840/1995; Lipps, 1903; Scheler, 1923/1954; Husserl, 1931/1988). In the second half of the last century, however, mainstream analytic philosophers largely abandoned empathy and its cognates, notwithstanding its close association with prominent notions such as universalizability, interpersonal cognition, and internal reasons. With a few notable exceptions, moral philosophy then regarded empathy with suspicion, as an ill-defined, psychological construct that had no place in reasoned moral justification and motivation.

The current resurgence of interest in whether and how empathy motivates moral conduct owes something to the experimental turn in moral theory, but it is even more indebted to developments in experimental psychology. One principal catalyst was Daniel Batson's landmark studies of moral motivation in the 1980s and 1990s (Batson, 2011; Batson, 2012). These studies put to the test what Batson called the "egoistic hypothesis" – the claim that the ultimate goal of all human action is to promote the agent's own welfare. The competing hypothesis was that, in certain facilitating conditions, agents' choices and actions can be altruistically

227

motivated – motivated directly by a non-instrumental or ultimate desire to benefit another, even when doing so incurs personal costs. Batson's particular focus was empathic concern, which he understood as involving "vicarious other-focused emotions, including feelings of sympathy, compassion, tenderness and the like" (Batson, 1991: 113). His studies explored the effect of empathic induction on subjects' preparedness to respond altruistically to others, both in attitude and in action choices, using experimental designs that controlled for egoistic motives of reward seeking, punishment avoidance, and relief from aversive arousal. While his findings have met with many challenges, they are widely regarded as lending support to the 'empathy-altruism' hypothesis – the claim that as "empathic feeling for a person in need increases, altruistic motivation to have that person's need relieved increases" (Batson, 1991: 72). Batson's claim that empathy evokes altruistic motivation harmonizes well with the common assumption that empathy moves us to do the right thing, and is a force for the (moral) good (see Chapter 19, "Empathy and altruism").

In everyday life, however, human empathy can be capricious and double-edged. As Primo Levi observed, its workings are often unreliable and "elude all logic." There is no proportion, for instance, "between the pity we feel and the extent of the pain by which the pity is aroused: a single Anne Frank excites more emotion than the myriads who suffered as she did but whose image has remained in the shadows" (Levi, 1988: 56). Levi's skepticism about the contributions of empathy to moral conduct is at least partly borne out by its role in countless everyday, moral failings; as Jesse Prinz has observed, empathy can move us to be "grotesquely partial to the near and dear" and lead us into "profound moral error" (2011b: 224). Even if one rejects the thought that partiality and morality are incompatible, it is clear that empathy can sometimes deform our moral judgments. The same may be said of empathy's contributions to moral motivation. There is compelling experimental evidence that its force is fickle (ebbing and waning whimsically), irrational (unmodulated by the seriousness or size of its targets), and wildly prejudicial (subject to in-group biases, to proximity, salience, and cuteness effects) (Konrath & Grynberg, 2013). Perhaps worst of all, the allure of its verdicts can persist even when they contradict our considered moral judgments (Navarete, 2012; Batson et al., 2004; Batson, Klein, Highberger, & Shaw, 1995). So does morality really want empathy on its side?

Perhaps it does, despite these perils. It is generally (and, I think, correctly) assumed that empathy can, in some circumstances, provide a powerful motive to right action that sometimes defeats, and often competes with, the two forces most hostile to morality: indifference and self-interest. Empathy competes with indifference in its epistemic role, by alerting us to circumstances that demand moral attention, and in its motivational role, it serves as a corrective to our default position of egocentrically pursuing our own ends, and only our own ends. The reasoning behind the assumption is straightforward. Other-regarding or altruistic moral requirements often enjoin actions that compete with our concern for our own welfare. If we are to be moved by them, indifference and self-interest must be counteracted by a motive force of equal or greater power. In our species, empathic concern is that motive. Hence empathy is, in such cases, necessary for moral motivation.

This reasoning is plausible so far as it goes. Nonetheless, any identification of empathy and moral motivation *tout court* would clearly be a mistake: countless moral requirements do not directly concern personal welfare at all, and enjoy no direct connection with empathy. Among these empathy-irrelevant norms are various sexual, dietary, and hygiene prohibitions, norms deriving from religious commandments, and norms based on conceptions of social honor and prestige. Empathic responsiveness to human weal and woe will not dissuade a man from acts of necrophilia, nor keep him Kosher, nor prompt him honorably to fall on his sword.

These exceptions acknowledged, considerations of other persons' interests still justify a central and ubiquitous core of moral prescriptions. Others-welfare or altruistic norms prescribe actions that are pro-social; they direct the agent to protect or promote the interests of another person or persons. Among these are certain harm norms (prohibitions against harming persons and their property) as well as norms reflecting Aristotelian and Humean natural virtues, such as friendship, kindness, generosity, compassion, and loyalty. There is good reason to suppose that a *sine qua non* of being moved by such norms is a propensity to be moved by other *people*, and that being moved by other people involves being moved empathically.

I will put a label to the basic hypothesis that empathy is necessary to motivate compliance with our others-welfare judgments: the Empathic Motivation Hypothesis (EMH). The EMH is ambiguous as between two claims. First, it may be taken as a claim about the motivational contributions of immediate and occurrent empathy to token others-welfare judgments. This is the synchronic claim that, necessarily, whenever an agent is motivated to act on a judgment of that kind, he is then empathically motivated. Second, it may be read as making a claim about the developmental contributions of empathy to moral motivation. This is the diachronic claim that empathy is necessary for the development of the capacity to be motivated by others-welfare judgments.

Is the EMH true, in either version? That question can be addressed from several different perspectives in both philosophy and psychology. I cannot investigate all of the options here, and will focus on elucidating the EMH and setting out some of the conceptual and empirical challenges it faces. §2 deals with preliminaries, distinguishing empathic concern from other dimensions of empathy (resonance, attunement, distress, and non-empathic concern). §3 presents the skeptical case against the synchronic version of EMH. §4 examines the merits of EMH as a developmental, diachronic claim, focusing in particular on the evidence from psychopathologies and attachment theory.

2 Dimensions of empathy: mindreading, resonance, attunement, distress, and concern

What is empathy, and how does it matter to moral motivation? In this section I will navigate some of the conceptual territory these questions inhabit.

Empathy is not an emotion, but a way of identifying and representing emotions and other affective states. I will use the terms "empathy" and "affective empathy" interchangeably; when we empathize, affective states are our objects of thought. Some use "empathy" more broadly, to include exercises in cognitive mindreading or perspective-taking. However, it is now generally recognized that mindreading and affective empathy are distinct capacities: a plethora of experimental evidence testifies to this at both the functional and neurophysiological levels (Decety et al., 2013; Blair, 2006). "Mindreading," as psychologists use the term, refers to a capacity reliably to identify others' action-explaining intentional states – typically their beliefs, desires, and intentions. It is an ability accurately to represent the propositional attitudes that render actions intelligible, and to exercise these representations in explaining and predicting others' behavior. Affective empathy can also represent propositional attitudes, but it does so by a different mechanism and in a different mode. Jean Decety refers to affective empathy as empathy "proper," and defines it as "a construct broadly reflecting a natural capacity to share and understand the affective states of others, comprising emotional, cognitive, and motivational facets" (Decety & Cowell, 2014). This requires that the empathizer not only represent, but also *share* in another's target states: affective empathy is an experiential as well as a representational capacity. When we empathize, we do not only identify and individuate another's affective/motivational states (emotions, sensations, aversions, etc.) but do so by instantiating some of their first-personal experiential character. The distinction between first-personal and other-personal representations of experiential states is key to empathy's motivating force: a solely conceptual or propositional representation of, e.g., another's pain or pleasure, however detailed and accurate, does constitute affective empathy, and indeed requires no affective or motivational engagement whatever. An empathic representation, by contrast, is what elsewhere I have called a "subjective conception" – a conception as from the first-personal perspective of the experiencing subject (Denham, 2000; Denham, 2012). If one represents another's pain by way of affective empathy, one's own experience must feature some of the target state's phenomenology – its qualitative and motivational characteristics. To some degree, it is itself painful.

So described, affective empathy is not yet a capacity for the solicitous concern that matters to moral motivation. To get there from here, we must trace four different dimensions of affective empathy: empathic resonance, empathic attunement, empathic distress, and empathic concern. I will briefly sketch each in turn.

Empathic resonance. Infants famously mimic the facial musculature of their caregiver's expressions, probably from only a few hours after birth (Hoffman, 2000). Such motor mimicry is a) reflexive and b) non-referential: the mimicking subject does not exercise voluntary control over his motor state, nor is he typically consciously aware of its occurrence. Nonetheless, motor empathy arguably plays an important role in the development of affective empathy and interpersonal emotion regulation in the first few months of life; at the neurological level, the causal pathways between motor and affective responses are bi-directional (Hoffman, 2008). Motor mimicry persists throughout our lives, and is an early and basic form of what is often called "empathic resonance" – an innate capacity to reflect some features of the behavior (especially facial expressions) and experiential states (especially the affective states) of others. Resonance is vividly illustrated by Hume's analogy between our responses to one another's sentiments and the sympathetic vibrating of strings on a violin: when one string is plucked or bowed, it directly causes a vibration in the others (Hume, 1739/1978). Empathic resonance is automatic and non-rational. As Hoffman observes, resonance (in his terms, "emotional contagion") is "passive, involuntary, and based on surface cues; it requires little cognitive processing or awareness that the source is [someone else]" (Hoffman, 2008: 441). It is not yet a representational state, save in the attenuated sense of representing the resonating subject's own condition. It serves no interpersonal, referential function.

Empathic attunement. Most developmental psychologists regard empathic resonance as a developmental precursor to a second, cognitively more complex dimension of affective empathy: I will call this (empathic) attunement. Attunement occurs when (a) a subject conceives of (represents in thought) another's experiential state, the conception being typically elicited by observing or remembering or imagining the other; (b) via resonance, the subject's occurrent state reflects (some constituents of) the content and phenomenological character of the target experience (or what he takes that experience to be), and (c) the subject regards his reflective states as referring to and informing him of the other's experience (Vignemont & Singer, 2006: 435).

This last feature (c) registers that attunement constitutes a first-person conception of the target affective/motivational states as belonging to another subject of experience; the agent regards his conception as representing the content and character of the other's inner life. Attunement is thus essentially referential. Where the referent states are aversive ones such as fear, sadness, or other kinds of distress, attunement presents the agent with a motive for two further responses: empathic distress or empathic concern.

Empathic distress names a familiar development of empathic attunement. (Batson terms it "personal distress") (Batson, 2011). When empathic attunement is persistent and intense, the empathizer can become "empathically over-aroused" (Hoffman, 2008): his focus of attention and his dominant motivation is then to relieve his own distress. In empathic distress, a subject (a) encounters another's aversive state, typically by directly perceiving or imaginatively engaging with him, (b) empathically attunes to that aversive state, recognizing the other as its source and referent, and (c) incurs a *self-focused* motivation to remove the aversive stimulus (the target subject's distress) from his perceptual and/or cognitive environment – for instance, to abandon the victim or to pursue attentional diversions (Hoffman, 2008). Empathic distress is thus an "egoistic" motivational state in Batson's sense of that term, which sometimes conflicts with our moral convictions – as when we guiltily bin the charity circular with its images of starving children, or change the television channel to avoid scenes of desperate refugees.

Empathic concern. When attunement is manifested as empathic distress, it is *negatively* correlated with moral motivation – the opposite of the pro-social influence with which empathy is typically associated. Attunement must develop via a different transformation, as empathic concern, if it is to be recruited into the service of morality. Empathic concern is closely allied with Hume's notion of benevolence – a non-instrumental desire to promote the welfare of another. A benevolent desire may, of course, arise by way of various causal trajectories, and not all are empathic; I will discuss one alternative shortly (Nichols, 2004). As I (stipulatively) use "empathic concern" here, it names a species of the genus of concern, viz., concern that is a development from and conceptual elaboration of (empathic, affective) attunement: the former occurs contiguously or concurrently with the latter, and its content is informed by it. Empathic concern is thus distinguished from other modes of concerned attention by having resonance and attunement as *constituents* as well as causal conditions. Resonance and attunement do not just precede empathic concern, but contribute to its content and felt character, in part determining its valence, intensity, attentional focus, and motivational force. If John responds to Sally's painful toothache with empathic concern, he then is *already* in an internal state that refers to Sally, is aversive and negatively valenced, relatively intense, and motivates a desire to help her.

Empathic and non-empathic concern. Benevolence or concern of some kind is analytically necessary to (psychological) altruistic motivation. But must that be specifically empathic concern? Shaun Nichols proposes a different account of altruistic motivation. On Nichols's view, helping behavior is best explained by a "Concern Mechanism" – a dedicated, independent mechanism motivating us to act in ways that will relieve or reduce others' distress. The role of this mechanism is both epistemic and motivational: it alerts the agents to the other's distress, identifying it *as* the other's distress, and it "triggers" an independent motivation to act altruistically (Nichols, 2001: 444). As Nichols describes the process, "altruistic motivation depends on a mechanism that takes as input representations that attribute distress, e.g., *John is experiencing painful shock*, and produces as output affect that *inter alia* motivates altruistic behaviour" (Nichols, 2001: 446).

Nichols's Concern Mechanism does not rely on sophisticated perspective-taking skills, such as the ability to imaginatively elaborate the detail of the other's experience, or to grasp its causes and consequences for someone in his position. His evidence for this derives from three sources. First, as a matter of chronology, very young children exhibit altruistic behavior (at between twelve to eighteen months) before they have developed sophisticated perspective-taking/mindreading abilities – for instance, the ability to pass False Belief tests and to make relatively fine-grained predictions of beliefs, desires, intentions, and actions. These do not emerge until thirty-two to forty-eight months (Nichols, 2001: 447). Secondly, autistics also have restricted mindreading abilities and yet

231

exhibit spontaneous altruistic behaviors (Nichols, 2001: 449). Finally, psychopaths provide some negative evidence: they are (bar some noteworthy lacunae) skilled mindreaders, but exhibit significant deficits in their abilities to feel empathic concern and to behave altruistically towards others (Nichols, 2001: 449).

This evidence is compatible with the relatively minimalist account I have given of empathic concern. However, while that construct inherits its motivational efficacy from the valence, intensity, and direction inherent in empathic attunement, Nichols's Concern Mechanism can operate directly, both in signaling to the agent that another is in distress and motivating his altruistic response (Nichols, 2001: 245). As Nichols puts it, it is possible "that the representation of the other's distress produces a distinctive emotion of sympathy or concern for the other person and this emotion is *not homologous to the emotion of the person* in need" (Nichols, 2001: 444, emphasis added). The idea is not a new one: Darwin, for instance, maintained that sympathy constituted a "separate and distinct emotion" (Darwin, 1871: 215). More recent evidence in its favor derives from studies associating altruistic behavior with a distinctive facial expression (Roberts & Strayer, 1996: 456; Miller et al., 1996: 213).

All of this matters to the prospects of the EMH. If it can be demonstrated that benevolent concern is regularly yielded by an empathy-independent mechanism and realized by a distinctive state at the neurophysiological level, this would largely put paid to the idea that affective empathy is necessary for altruistic motivation. At most, empathy might play a modest epistemic role, providing detail of the distress "inputs," with a functionally and neurophysiologically discrete concern mechanism producing the altruistic "outputs." How plausible is this proposal?

While the jury will be out for some time to come, I believe that we should regard Nichols's proposal with skepticism, for three reasons. First, evolution rarely replicates functions to no point, and empathic attunement is *already* inherently motivating, with the same attentional focus (the other subject) and part of the same motivational direction (aversion to his/her distress or attraction to his/her well-being). Why render attunement redundant with a functionally independent system? It would be more efficient for empathic concern to develop out of and exploit both the information and the motivation inherent in resonance and attunement, perhaps modulated by certain cognitive skills (Preston & de Waal, 2002). Second, the chronology of developmental histories of resonance, attunement, and concern tells against their independence. Ontogenetically, resonance is followed by attunement, which is in turn followed by concern (Preston & de Waal, 2002). Phylogenetically, too, the neurological states realizing resonance and attunement (such as the amygdala, anterior insula, and anterior cingulate cortex) antedate those associated with concern (the ventromedial prefrontal cortex and lateral orbitofrontal cortex) (Decety & Cowell, 2014).

Finally, the separate chronology of the ontogenetic development of cognitive skills required by concern recommends that resonance is modulated and recruited into higher-level thought as these make available the requisite conceptual repertoire – for instance, a self-other distinction, awareness of one's powers as a discrete agent, and recognition of others as independent loci of malleable affective experience (Hoffman, 2008; Decety & Svetlova, 2012). If we think that concern matters to morality, we do best to look to its *first* appearance in the dynamics of empathy.

3 The synchronic Empathic Motivation Hypothesis: is occurrent empathy necessary for moral motivation?

The synchronic version of the EMH claims that, necessarily, when an agent is moved to act on a token others-welfare judgment, occurrent empathy contributes to that motivation. Is the synchronic EMH true?

Let us consider the positive case first. Batson's initial experiments showed that subjects who are primed to empathize with victims are more strongly motivated to help them; "high empathy" subjects are altruistically motivated even when helping comes at a significant cost to personal interests (Batson, 2011). In later studies using the same basic design, Batson found further that empathy priming led subjects to act more altruistically even when (a) the help- ing was anonymous and offered no personal credit (thus challenging reward incentives), (b) there were good reasons to avoid helping, making helping demanding and not helping justi- fied (challenging anticipated guilt incentives), (c) subjects were advised that they would receive no feedback on their assistance (challenging incentives of praise/victim's gratitude), and (d) when refusing to help promises a positive experience on par with that of helping (challenging anticipated pleasure incentives) (Batson, 2011, Appendices B, C, D, F, G). These results are not conclusive, but they strongly suggest that empathy can promote attitudes and behavior that are *better explained* by altruistic rather than egoistic motivation, at least in a context of heightened, targeted empathy induction. This is encouraging news for the friend of the synchronic EMH.

Beyond Batson, numerous other studies have found strong correlations between empathy and other-regarding actions and attitudes. Konrath and Grynberg's extensive survey of the lit- erature identifies a number of results supporting the claim that empathy promotes pro-social motivation. To mention only a few:

- For both attunement and empathic concern, and regardless of how these were measured (i.e., observer-reports, self-reports, self-reported vicarious emotion, or targeted situational induc- tion), empathy is positively associated with pro-social behaviors towards strangers (sharing, assisting, giving) (Eisenberg & Miller, 1987).
- Empathy induction increases interpersonal cooperation, even in Prisoner's Dilemma games in which the subjects know that their game partner has defected. In one study, situational empathy induction increased cooperation rates from 5% (control) to 45% in a one-time play (Batson & Ahmed, 2001).
- Empathy induction has been shown to improve outcomes in negotiations between par- ties with competing goals, producing better outcomes on both sides relative to controls (Galinsky, Maddux, Gilin, & White, 2008).
- Parents who rank high in empathy (on both self-reports and observer reports) have more positive and effective interactions with their children. As Konrath and Grynberg note, this is unsurprising if, as the aforementioned studies suggest, "empathizing makes people kinder and more cooperative" (Konrath & Grynberg, 2013: 2).

These are just a few examples of a large body of evidence indicating that *some* dimension of empathy is causally efficacious in motivating our other-regarding judgments. Hoffman confi- dently asserts that there is "overwhelming evidence that people who feel empathically distressed at another's misfortune are more motivated to help, that empathic distress makes people help more quickly, and that people who are empathically responsive to another's distress feel better when they help than when they don't" (Hoffman, 2008: 441). What more could the friend of the EMH require?

The answer is "a great deal." First, many of the associations noted are merely correlational, and do not establish that empathy is the horse rather than the cart. This is not, in fact, a serious worry in every case: sometimes other considerations, such as the order in which stimuli are presented (as in Batson's studies), make the causal claims compelling. But there are other meth- odological worries as well, including inconsistencies in how "empathy" is conceptualized. Some conceptualizations, for instance, include personal distress as an indicator of empathy, whereas others exclude it; again, some take perspective-taking or cognitive mindreading as constituents of empathy and others do not. Measurement procedures are also inconsistent. Some studies rely solely on self-report, which is notoriously unreliable for subjects who are independently invested in an empathic self-conception. Others use observer reports, and still others assess autonomic, physiological correlates of affective arousal. Why should we suppose that all of these are measuring the same conditions? To further complicate matters, some studies target dispositional or trait empathy, while others assess empathy as aroused in a particular situation (situational empathy). Finally, and most problematic of all for the synchronic EMH, even very high positive correlations between empathy and pro-social attitudes and behaviors can only show, at best, that empathy facilitates moral motivation, not that it is an indispensable condition of it.

For these and other reasons, several philosophers, including Peter Goldie, Heidi Maibom, and Jesse Prinz, have argued that, the experimental evidence notwithstanding, the synchronic EMH is a non-starter (Goldie, 2011; Maibom, 2014; Prinz, 2011a, 2011b). Prinz has been perhaps its most vociferous critic. He holds that empathy makes no indispensable (or even desirable) contribution to moral experience, arguing that it is neither constitutively, causally, epistemically, developmentally, nor motivationally necessary. Let us consider some of his arguments against its role in moral motivation.

A first objection echoes §1's observation that many norms fail even to be candidates for empathic motivation. Sometimes empathic concern even directly recommends against them. Empathy – *pace* our usual norms and intuitions –would likely recommend, for instance, that we steal from the rich to give to the poor, and that we refuse to punish transgressors. Recognized moral norms suggest otherwise. The objection is well taken so far as it goes, but it does not go very far if the EMH is indexed only to *others-welfare* moral judgments directly justified by persons' interests, and manifesting natural virtues such as kindness, generosity, compassion, pity, fidelity, and forgivingness. Could we ever be moved by these judgments without some kind of empathic responsiveness to others' wants and needs?

Prinz insists that we could. His second argument is that empathic concern fails to provide the *best explanation* of moral motivation, even in this restricted class. The argument relies on his particular meta-ethical commitments, which are both internalist and sentimentalist. In brief, Prinz holds that moral judgments are intrinsically motivating because they have an emotional basis or "contain" emotions, as he sometimes puts it. The emotions they contain may be negatively valenced (disapprobative) responses such as anger, disgust, guilt, and shame, or positively valenced (approbative) ones such as gratitude, admiration, or pride. A token moral *judgment* is in part *constituted* by such emotions, and that is why it is intrinsically motivating (Prinz, 2011a: 219). This account of moral motivation, Prinz argues, already delivers everything we need to explain moral motivation; empathy is simply surplus to requirements. There is no explanatory gap in the motivational story for it to fill.

Might not empathy nonetheless be our most effective and reliable source of motivation, even if it is not a necessary one? Against this suggestion, Prinz's third argument is that the emotions constitutive of moral judgments are also more powerful motivators than empathy: anger, disgust, happiness, and shame all, he claims, yield stronger effects than empathy (Prinz, 2011a: 218–20). For example, he cites one study as showing "no correlation in children between empathy and pro-social behaviour" (Underwood & Moore, 1982), another indicating only a modest correlation in adults between pro-social behavior and shared sadness (Eisenberg et al., 1989), and he claims that in studies using economic games, "empathy does not motivate moral behavior when there are significant costs" (Fehr & Gächter, 2002). This is puzzling data for the punter immersed in the experimental evidence adduced at the beginning of this section. What of Hoffman's "overwhelming evidence" for the very correlations Prinz denies?

The puzzle arises because Prinz conceptualizes empathy solely in terms of "shared" or "vicarious" affect (effectively, just resonance and attunement), excluding empathic *concern*. The handful of studies on which he relies accordingly attribute empathy only to subjects who directly evidence affect-sharing *independently* of concern. The Eisenberg study, for instance, distinguished displays of "concerned attention" (e.g., a child wrinkling her brow) from displays of "shared emotion" (direct mimicry of the target's sadness); only the latter counts as manifesting empathy. This makes all the difference, for it assumes that subjects' responses of sympathy or concern are *not* empathically driven. But this is almost to assume what Prinz aims to prove. Indeed, as Prinz judiciously acknowledges in a footnote, Batson's "notion of empathic concern may be immune to many of the worries raised here" (Prinz, 2011a). Just so.

Even if Prinz's best-explanation objection fails, however, the coast is hardly clear for the synchronic EMH, for it stands to be defeated if agents' others-welfare/altruistic judgments are *ever* motivating in the absence of occurrent empathy. And in fact this often happens; there are many modes and manifestations of interpersonal concern apart from occurrent *empathic* concern. An overworked nurse suffering from compassion fatigue and long past empathic attunement can continue to be motivated by her commitment to caring for her patients; a dedicated humanist may serve the homeless, even when he ceases to be animated by empathy for them. In both cases, their (non-empathic) concern may even see them through occasional episodes of irritation or distaste or revulsion. That gives us no reason to deny that their ultimate goal is to relieve the plight of those in need.

Cases such as these and countless other everyday acts of benevolence testify that altruistic concern need not be underwritten by occurrent empathy. The motivational force of our token others-welfare judgments requires no here-and-now empathic input: while attention to and concern for others may be indispensable, these often motivate agents independently of any present empathic engagement. The synchronic EMH is false.

4 The diachronic Empathic Motivation Hypothesis: is empathy developmentally necessary for moral motivation?

Even if the synchronic EMH fails, empathy may yet connect with moral motivation in other ways. Indeed, it is difficult to believe that empathy plays *no* significant role in shaping the norms that govern our personal relationships, and moving us to act on them. As Maibom observes, "without the influence of empathy-related affect, morality might be unrecognizable to us" (Maibom, 2014: 38). This seems correct, and its correctness highlights how unilluminating is the conclusion that the synchronic EMH is false. Instead, empathy may be *diachronically* necessary for moral motivation, playing an indispensable role in the development of moral motivation, as a precondition for (a) concerned attention to others and (b) regulating (restraining or deferring) one's concern for oneself, balancing others' needs against our egocentric ends. Even if occurrent empathy has moved largely off-stage by the time mature moral judgment makes its entrance, it may have played a leading role earlier in the developmental drama. That is the possibility I will now consider.

One principal source of evidence for the diachronic EMH has been developmental psychopathology; another is attachment theory. These are not entirely independent sources, for dysfunctional attachment is strongly correlated with a range of moral disorders. For reasons of space, this section will focus on the arguments from psychopathology, mentioning in conclusion some prospects for further research within the framework of attachment theory.

Empathic concern and moral psychopathology

Over the last two decades, several psychologists and philosophers have argued that psychopathic personality disorder provides evidence favoring some version of the diachronic EMH (Deigh 1995; Blair 2005; Soderstrom, 2003; Denham, 2000, 2011). It is widely believed that psychopaths exhibit deficits in affective empathy; indeed, 'lack of empathy' is among the disorder's diagnostic criteria. This is supported by behavioral observations as well as autonomic measures such as skin-conductance and startle-blink responses. EEG and fMRI data have further indicated that psychopaths are hypo-responsive to others' distress, and especially to fear and sadness (Blair, 1995; Blair et al., 2001; Patrick, 1994; Decety & Cowell, 2014). That psychopaths lack moral motivation is also built into the diagnostic criteria: they appear to understand the moral rules holding sway in their communities, but they systematically fail to be guided by them in their practical judgments – they know what morality requires, but are unmoved by it. Moreover, some studies (albeit not all) indicate that psychopaths are less sensitive than controls to the special authority of moral as opposed to conventional rules (Blair, 1995; Blair, 2006). These anomalies are unlikely to be owed to deficits in cognitive mindreading, for most psychopaths typically perform as well as neurotypicals in that respect (Blair, 1995).

These observations have suggested to many that the psychopath's failures of moral motivation are caused developmentally by a deficit in affective empathy. In normal moral development, affective empathy generates negative emotions in response to actions yielding distress in others (e.g., physical abuse) and positive emotions in response to actions promoting their well-being (e.g., helping, comforting). On one standard developmental narrative, these action types come to be regularly associated with the elicited emotions; stable patterns of response thus are acquired throughout childhood and early adolescence, and develop into settled dispositions to respond with disapproval to negative elicitors and approval to positive ones. Once this habituation has taken place, empathic responses are no longer required to motivate token moral judgments; our settled dispositions do the job. While affective empathy may continue to be activated on occasion, its motivational contribution to *moral* development is largely completed by late adolescence. In the case of the psychopath (the hypothesis goes), this process goes awry: because of his empathic deficits, he fails to lay down the requisite associations in the first place, and this explains his failure later to respond to moral transgressions/observances with appropriately valenced motivations.

Unfortunately, the hypothesis is underdetermined by the evidence. In particular, it ignores the possibility of a third *explanans* – a third condition which might independently explain both the psychopath's empathy deficits *and* his lack of moral motivation, yielding a mere correlation (Prinz, 2011a, 2011b; Maibom, 2014). Maibom, for instance, observes that psychopaths' general hypo-responsiveness to fear and high pain thresholds might fill that role. Owing to these deficits, "their understanding of, and ability to feel with and for people who are afraid, would also be impaired … lack of fear may itself cause a number of the deficits associated with psychopathy, including the moral ones" (Maibom, 2014: 16). This is one candidate explanation. Is it the best one, or at least better than some version of diachronic EMH?

Perhaps not. The EMH finds further support from comparative data on autistics. Autistic subjects suffer significant mindreading deficits, as well as deficits in emotion recognition. However, their affective responsiveness – and particularly their responsiveness to others' distress – is largely intact: high-functioning autistics' affective empathy is often (if not always) on a par with that of neurotypicals, as assessed by a variety of measures including expression mimicry, autonomic arousal, and fMRI (Baron-Cohen, 1995; Blair, 1995; Vignemont, 2009). In view of this profile, the diachronic EMH would predict that autistics are not, on the whole, deficient in moral motivation. This prediction is largely fulfilled: while autistics struggle with subtler rules of social interaction, and show developmental delay on false belief and other mindreading tasks (especially in early years), they are not systematically transgressive of other-regarding norms. Taking the evidence from psychopathy and autism together, then, seems to recommend some version of the diachronic EMH over "third condition" hypotheses. For the joint evidence suggests that while mindreading is neither necessary (being impaired in morally compliant autistics) nor sufficient (being intact in morally unmotivated psychopaths), affective empathy is indispensable for moral competence.

Unfortunately, consideration of the wider evidence delivers a less straightforward picture. For one thing, recent research focusing on the psychopath's cognitive abilities has suggested that their deficits may not be specific to affective responsiveness as such, but to a failure to integrate affective and cognitive information (Decety, 2015). Several other cognitive deficits, too, have been identified, including impairments in semantic processing (Kiehl, 2004) and emotion recognition (Wilson, Juodis, & Porter, 2011). Secondly – and more fatally for the diachronic EMH – recent studies have challenged the pivotal claim that psychopaths have profound affective empathy deficits at all. An impressive body of recent experimental evidence has challenged this longstanding view, including one study indicating that psychopaths "resonate" with others' distress at a sensorimotor level on par with controls (Maibom, 2014: 14–16; Domes et al., 2013; Lishner et al., 2012). Skepticism seems also to be justified by Decety's important finding that the neural regions in which psychopaths differ from non-psychopaths are *not* those associated with affective resonance (amygdala and anterior insular cortex) but rather those associated with *concern* (ventromedial prefrontal cortex and lateral orbitofrontal cortex) (Decety, 2015). If Decety is correct, intact affective resonance can combine with an absence of other-regarding moral motivation, suggesting that the sort of concern altruism requires is not borne out of resonance/attunement-based empathic concern, but has some independent source. In that case, the psychopath's particular toolbox of capacities may even offer evidence *against* the diachronic EMH. All considered, the evidence from psychopathology is mixed and inconclusive. The idea that empathy is a developmental precondition of other-regarding motivation will not be so easily vindicated.

Nonetheless, the diachronic EMH is hardly falsified by these findings, and experimental evidence in other arenas suggests that it merits further investigation. One promising direction is the psychological construct of *attachment*, especially as this figures in theories of early child development. In its wider sense, "attachment" refers to an enduring, intimate emotional bond that develops between two or more persons, normally through sustained personal contact, yielding a felt need for personal proximity and conditioning the attached person's sense of security and safety. In the context of child development, "attachment" refers more particularly to this bond as it holds between an infant or toddler and his primary caregiver – a connection that is instrumental in the child's cognitive, affective, and social development (Bowlby, 1969/2008; Ainsworth & Bell, 1970; Fonagy & Target, 1997). Securely attached children manifest behaviors consistent with a trusting, affectionate intimacy with their caregiver. Theorists dispute the details of how best to characterize the complex dynamics of this bond, but all delineate it in part in terms of interpersonal affective "synchrony," or the harmonious and spontaneous sharing of affect, perceptual focus, and motivational direction – the hallmarks of joint empathic attunement. Longitudinal studies indicate that successful synchronization and secure attachment strongly predict mature empathic responsiveness (Kestenbaum, Farber, & Sroufe, 1989), with mother-infant synchrony measures in the first year of infancy being directly associated with empathy levels at ages six and sixteen (Feldman, 2007). Secure attachment is also a powerful predictor of optimal development in respect of a range of other morally relevant capacities, including cooperativeness, self-regulation (including gratification deferral), and "mindedness" – the ability to reliably identify, predict, and harmonize with others' cognitive and affective states (Fonagy & Target, 1997). These same capacities are, in turn, both causally and constitutively related to altruistic motivation, and pro-social motivation of other kinds as well. In one study directly examining the development of moral conscience it was found that the degree of mutually responsive orientation between an infant and caregiver, especially of positive affective states, was directly correlated *both* with higher empathic resonance at twenty-two months and greater guilt awareness at forty-five months (Zahn-Waxler et al., 1992; Knafo et al., 2008).

In sum, while research on attachment is still in its early stages, it is now generally acknowledged to be a robust predictor of several capacities closely associated with mature, pro-social dispositions. A better understanding of the developmental role of attachment and its contributions to moral motivation may yet allow us to construct a clearer narrative of how and why affective empathy interacts with our ability to be concerned for and moved by others. From a developmental perspective, it could turn out that our earliest empathic engagements underwrite the distinctive regard we have for our human fellows, and the special claims that they make on us as moral agents.

Endnote: empathy in theory and experience

Wittgenstein mocked the idea that we understand others by analogically reasoning from our own experience. "Do you look into *yourself*," he asked, "in order to recognize the fury in his face?" (Wittgenstein, 1980, §927). To see the fury, the pain, or the sorrow in another's face we of course typically look at that person directly. Indeed, recognizing and responding to others' inner lives is part of what it is to see them as persons at all, and this seems, prima facie, to require no special exercises of introspection. It does not follow, however, that our propensity to identify and respond to others as persons floats free of our affective attunement to them. My survey of the territory has assumed that it makes sense to speak of experiencing concern for and being moved by another, absent all empathic engagement. That assumption pervades most contemporary experimental and philosophical models of empathy, and it is unavoidable if one is to engage with those models on their own terms. It is not clear, however, that the assumption is fully intelligible. Perhaps to see another human being as a fellow subject of experience is *already* to interact with him as a locus of perception, emotion, and will – to regard him as a source of motivations in which we share, even when those motivations are contrary to our own. Although we may not need to "look within" ourselves to see someone animated by despair or delight, it does not follow that we could see him in these ways were we not already engaged with and imbued by the reality of his inner life. Perhaps it is our separateness and individuality that must be learned, not our common humanity. If so, human morality could not exist in its present shape or form without a natural foundation in empathy. It may yet turn out to best explain our recognition of the reality and value of others, and their ability to move us as they do.

References

Ainsworth, M. D. S., & Bell, S. (1970) "Attachment, exploration, and separation: illustrated by the behavior of one-year-olds in a strange situation," *Child Development*, 41(1), 49–67.
Baron-Cohen, S. (2009) "Autism: the empathizing-systemizing (E-S) theory," *Annals of the New York Academy of Sciences*, 1156(1), 68–80.
Baron-Cohen, S., Campbell, R., Karmiloff-Smith, A., Grant, J., & Walker, J. (1995) "Are children with autism blind to the mentalistic significance of the eyes?" *British Journal of Developmental Psychology*, 13(4), 379–98.

Batson, C. D. (1991) *The Altruism Question: Toward a Social-Psychological Answer*, Hove, UK: Lawrence Erlbaum Associates.

Batson, C. D. (2011) *Altruism in Humans*, Oxford: Oxford University Press.

Batson, C. D. (2012) "The empathy-altruism hypothesis: issues and implications," in: J. Decety (ed.) *Empathy: From Bench to Bedside*, Cambridge, MA: MIT Press.

Batson, C. D., & Ahmad, N. (2001). "Empathy-induced altruism in a prisoner's dilemma II: what if the target of empathy has defected?" *European Journal of Social Psychology*, 31(1), 25–36.

Batson, C. D., Ahmad, N., & Stocks, E. (2004) "Benefits and liabilities of empathy-induced altruism," in: A. G. Miller (ed.), *The Social Psychology of Good and Evil*, New York: Guilford Press.

Batson, C. D., Klein, T. R., Highberger, L., & Shaw, L. L. (1995). Immorality from empathy-induced altruism: When compassion and justice conflict. *Journal of personality and social psychology*, 68(6), 1042.

Blair, R. J. R. (1995) "A cognitive developmental approach to morality: investigating the psychopath," *Cognition*, 57(1), 1–29.

Blair, R. J. R. (2005) "Responding to the emotions of others: dissociating forms of empathy through the study of typical and psychiatric populations," *Consciousness and Cognition*, 14(4), 698–718.

Blair, R. J. R. (2006) "Fine cuts of empathy and the amygdala: dissociable deficits in psychopathy and autism," *Quarterly Journal of Experimental Psychology*, 61(1), 157–70.

Blair, R. James R., et al. (2001) "A selective impairment in the processing of sad and fearful expressions in children with psychopathic tendencies," *Journal of Abnormal Child Psychology*, 29(6), 491–8.

Blair, R. J. R., Peschardt, K. S., Budhani, S., Mitchell, D. G. V., & Pine, D. S. (2006) "The development of psychopathy," *Journal of Child Psychology and Psychiatry*, 47(3–4), 262–76.

Bowlby, J. (1969/2008) *Attachment and Loss*, New York: Basic Books.

Darwin, C. (1871/2004) *The Descent of Man*, New York: Barnes & Noble Books.

Decety, J. (2015) "The neural pathways, development and functions of empathy," *Current Opinion in Behavioral Sciences*, 3, 1–6.

Decety, J., & Cowell, J. (2014) "The complex relation between morality and empathy," *Trends in Cognitive Sciences*, 18(7), 337–9.

Decety, J., & Svetlova, M. (2012) "Putting together phylogenetic and ontogenetic perspectives on empathy," *Developmental Cognitive Neuroscience*, 2, 1–24.

Decety, J., Chen, C., Harenski, C. L., & Kiehl, K. A. (2013) "An fMRI study of affective perspective taking in individuals with psychopathy: imagining another in pain does not evoke empathy," *Frontiers in Human Neuroscience*, 7, 489.

Deigh, J. (1995) "Empathy and universalizability," *Ethics*, 105(4), 743–63.

Denham, A. E. (2000) *Metaphor and Moral Experience*, Oxford: Oxford University Press.

Denham, A. E. (2011) "Psychopathy, empathy and moral motivation," in: J. Broakes (ed.), *Iris Murdoch: Philosopher*, Oxford: Oxford University Press.

Domes, G., Hollerbach, P., Vohs, K., Mokros, A., & Habermeyer, E. (2013). "Emotional empathy and psychopathy in offenders: an experimental study," *Journal of Personality Disorders*, 27(1), 67.

Eisenberg, N., & Miller, P. A. (1987) "The relation of empathy to prosocial and related behaviors," *Psychological Bulletin*, 101(1), 91.

Eisenberg, N., et al. (1989) "Relation of sympathy and personal distress to prosocial behavior: a multi-method study," *Journal of Personality and Social Psychology*, 57, 55–66.

Feeney, B. C., et al. (2008) "The generalization of attachment representations to new social situations: predicting behavior during initial interactions with strangers," *Journal of Personality and Social Psychology*, 95(6), 1481.

Fehr, E., & Gächter, S. (2002) "Altruistic punishment in humans," *Nature*, 415, 137–40.

Feldman, J. B. (2007) "The effect of support expectations on prenatal attachment: an evidence-based approach for intervention in an adolescent population," *Child and Adolescent Social Work Journal*, 24(3), 209–34.

Fonagy, P., Steele, M., Steele, H., Moran, G. S., & Higgitt, A. C. (1991) "The capacity for understanding mental states: the reflective self in parent and child and its significance for security of attachment," *Infant Mental Health Journal*, 12(3), 201–18.

Fonagy, P., & Target, M. (1997) "Attachment and reflective function: their role in self-organization," *Development and Psychopathology*, 9(04), 679–700.

Galinsky, Adam D., et al. (2008) "Why it pays to get inside the head of your opponent: the differential effects of perspective taking and empathy in negotiations," *Psychological Science*, 19(4), 378–84.

Goldie, P. (2011) "Anti-empathy," in P. Goldie & A. Coplan (eds.), *Empathy: Philosophical and Psychological Perspectives*, Oxford: Oxford University Press.

Hoffman, M. (2000) *Empathy and Moral Development*, New York: Cambridge University Press.

Hoffman, M. (2008) "Empathy and prosocial behavior," in: M. Lewis, J. Haviland Jones, & L. Fedlman Barrett (eds.), *Handbook of Emotion*, 3rd ed., New York: Guildford Press.

Hume, D. (1739/1978) *A Treatise of Human Nature*, ed. L. A. Selby-Bigge, 2nd rev. ed., P.H. Nidditch, Oxford: Clarendon Press.

Husserl, E. (1931/1988) *Cartesian Meditations*, trans. D. Cairns, Dordrecht: Kluwer.

Kestenbaum, R., Farber, E.A., & Sroufe, L.A. (1989) "Individual differences in empathy among preschoolers: relation to attachment history," *New Directions for Child and Adolescent Development*, 1989(44), 51–64.

Kiehl, Kent A., et al. (2004) "Temporal lobe abnormalities in semantic processing by criminal psychopaths as revealed by functional magnetic resonance imaging," *Psychiatry Research: Neuroimaging*, 130(1), 27–42.

Knafo, A., Zahn-Waxler, C., Van Hulle, C., Robinson, J. L., & Rhee, S. H. (2008) "The developmental origins of a disposition toward empathy: genetic and environmental contributions," *Emotion*, 8(6), 737.

Konrath, S., & Grynberg, D. (2013) "The positive (and negative) psychology of empathy," in: D. Watt & J. Panksepp (eds.), *The Neurobiology and Psychology of Empathy*, New York: Nova Science Publishers, Inc.

Levi, P. (1988) *The Drowned and the Saved*, New York: Summit Books.

Lipps, T. (1903) *Asthetik*, vol. 1. Leipzig: Leopold Voss Verlag.

Lishner, D.A., Vitacco, M.J., Hong, P.Y., Mosley, J., Miska, K., & Stocks, E. L. (2012) "Evaluating the relation between psychopathy and affective empathy: two preliminary studies," *International Journal of Offender Therapy and Comparative Criminology*, 56(8), 1161–81.

Maibom, H. L. (2014) "Introduction: (almost) everything you ever wanted to know about empathy," in: H. Maibom (ed.), *Empathy and Morality*, Oxford: Oxford University Press.

Miller, Paul A., et al. (1996) "Relations of moral reasoning and vicarious emotion to young children's prosocial behavior toward peers and adults," *Developmental Psychology*, 32(2), 210.

Nagel, T. (1979) *The Possibility of Altruism*, Princeton: Princeton University Press.

Navarrete, C. D., McDonald, M. M., Mott, M. L., & Asher, B. (2012) "Virtual morality: emotion and action in a simulated three-dimensional 'trolley problem,'" *Emotion*, 12(2), 364.

Nichols, S. (2001) "Mindreading and the cognitive architecture underlying altruistic motivation," *Mind & Language*, 16, 425–55.

Nichols, S. (2004) *Sentimental Rules: On the Natural Foundations of Moral Judgment*, New York: Oxford University Press.

Patrick, C. J. (1994) "Emotion and psychopathy: startling new insights," *Psychophysiology*, 31(4), 319–30.

Prinz, J. (2009) *The Emotional Construction of Morals*, Oxford: Oxford University Press.

Prinz, J. (2011a) "Is empathy necessary for morality?" in: A. Coplan & P. Goldie (eds.), *Empathy: Philosophical and Psychological Approaches*, New York: Oxford University Press.

Prinz, J. (2011b) "Against empathy," *The Southern Journal of Philosophy*, 49(s1), 214–33.

Preston, S. D., & de Waal, F. (2002) "Empathy: its ultimate and proximate bases," *Behavioural and Brain Sciences*, 1, 515–26.

Roberts, W., & Strayer, J. (1996) "Empathy, emotional expressiveness, and prosocial behavior," *Child Development*, 67, 449–70.

Scheler, M. (1923/1954) *The Nature of Sympathy*, trans. P. Heath, London: Routledge.

Schiller, F. (1794/1967) *On the Aesthetic Education of Man: In a Series of Letters*, trans. and ed. E. M. Wilkinson and L.A. Willoughby, Oxford: Clarendon Press.

Schopenhauer, A. (1840/1995) *On the Basis of Morality*, trans. E. F. J. Payne; intro. D. E. Cartwright, Providence: Berghahn Books.

Smith, A. (1759/2002) *The Theory of Moral Sentiments*, K. Haakonssen (ed.), Cambridge: Cambridge University Press.

Soderstrom, H. (2003) "Psychopathy as a disorder of empathy," *European Child & Adolescent Psychiatry*, 12(5), 249–52.

Underwood, B., & Moore, B. (1982) "Perspective-taking and altruism," *Psychological Bulletin*, 91(1), 143–73.

Vignemont, F. (2009) "Drawing the boundary between low-level and high-level mindreading," *Philosophical Studies*, 144(3), 457–66.

Vignemont, F., & Singer, T. (2006) "The empathic brain: how, when, and why?," *Trends in Cognitive Sciences*, 10, 435–41.

Wilson, K., Juodis, M., & Porter, S. (2011) "Fear and loathing in psychopaths: a meta-analytic investigation of the facial affect recognition deficit," *Criminal Justice and Behavior*, 38(7), 659–68.

Wittgenstein, L. (1980) *Remarks on the Philosophy of Psychology*, vol. 1, eds. G.E.M. Anscombe & G. H. von Wright; trans. G. E. M. Anscombe, Oxford: Blackwell.

Zahn-Waxler, C., Robinson, J. L., & Emde, R. N. (1992) "The development of empathy in twins," *Developmental Psychology*, 28(6), 1038.

21

EMPATHY AND MORAL RESPONSIBILITY

David Shoemaker

Empathy has come in for a beating lately. From public exchanges in the *New York Times* and the *Boston Review* to a series of pointed scholarly articles by leading intellectual figures, empathy's oft-assumed status as an essential element in our moral lives has been systematically trashed. It is instead claimed to be useless, badly deployed, or even downright pernicious.

To the contrary, I think many of these recent indictments of empathy are, at best, overblown or misguided. I will not defend empathy in all its moral roles here, though; rather, I will restrict my focus to its purported role in moral responsibility. In what follows, I will tell a plausible story about how empathy seems necessary for moral responsibility, and then I will show how three recent objections to empathy's playing such a role fail to dent it, at least once we have enriched it in key ways.

1. A plausible story about empathy's role in moral responsibility

Empathy has long been thought necessary to our *holding* people responsible, helping us figure out the target's quality of character or the nature of his merits or demerits. More recently, however, writers have focused on empathy's role in enabling people to *be* morally responsible. This discussion has been generated almost entirely because of a flurry of attention on *psychopaths*.

There is widespread agreement about two essential components of being morally responsible for some action: knowledge and control (for resisters to including one or the other component, see Scanlon 1998; Arpaly 2003; Smith 2005; and Sher 2009). The former, *epistemic*, component says that in order to be morally responsible, one must have performed that action knowingly, i.e., for one to be blameworthy (i.e., responsible plus culpable) for some wrongful action, one must have known what one was doing and that what one was doing was wrong (not necessarily under that description, though; see Arpaly & Schroeder 2014: Ch. 7). The latter, *control* component, says that in order to be morally responsible for some action, one must have performed it freely. Of course, what counts as "freely" has been the subject of debate for nearly 2,000 years, but at the least it includes a lack of interference, from sources either external (e.g., manipulating or coercing agents) or internal (e.g., psychological compulsions and manias). The discussion about psychopaths and responsibility has thus tended to focus on whether their specific disabilities undermine one or the other of these components.

Many theorists come to the table intuiting that psychopaths are not morally responsible, and by way of explanation they point to psychopaths' empathic disabilities, which have been widely and well documented in the psychological literature. Now it's important to flag immediately that there is an important distinction between *cognitive* and *emotional* (or "affective") empathy. The former involves either an intellectual understanding of what someone else is going through or an ability to simulate someone else's cognitive states, whereas the latter involves actually feeling and caring about what other people feel and care about. Now while it has seemed to many that psychopaths are perfectly able to engage in cognitive empathy (see, e.g., Blair et al. 1996; I will question this notion below), it is nonetheless clear that psychopaths have significant impairments in their ability to engage in emotional empathy (Decety et al. 2013). They experience very little arousal to events in their lives (either physiologically or psychologically), so it is no surprise that what happens in the lives of other people has little to no emotional impact on them either.

So how precisely would an emotional empathic disability undermine their moral responsibility? Some have argued that psychopaths' empathic disabilities make them unable to recognize moral right and wrong, preventing them from meeting the epistemic component (e.g., Deigh 1995; Fine & Kennett 2004; Levy 2007; and Haji 2010). Others have argued that psychopaths' empathic disabilities make them unable to care about others in the way necessary to motivate them to adhere to moral norms, preventing them from meeting the *control* component (e.g., Fingarette 1967; Murphy 1972; Shoemaker 2007). Most plausible, though, is a third position, holding that psychopaths' empathic disabilities prevent them from meeting *both* the epistemic and control components by gutting their *moral sense* (see Pritchard 1974; Russell 2004; McKenna 2012: 80–2; Watson 2011: 308–9). Consider an analogy. To have a good sense of humor requires both that one fully appreciate the reasons why things are funny and also that one be disposed to respond to such things with amusement (and for those reasons). To have a good moral sense, by analogy, one must both fully appreciate the reasons why things are right and wrong and also be disposed to respond to those things with the right attitudes and motivations (and for those reasons). To the extent that empathic disabilities undermine both aspects, psychopaths lack a moral sense, and thus they are not morally responsible for what they do.

Call this the *Plausible Story* about how empathic deficits undermine moral responsibility, a story according to which *emotional empathy is necessary for moral responsibility*. This story is vulnerable to three objections. I turn now to explore these objections and to point the way toward defenses against them.

2. Are we bad at empathizing?

In a recent essay for *The New York Times*, Paul Bloom argued that empathy is a terrible ground for public policy, despite the claims of many politicians and public commentators, given that we just aren't very good at it (Bloom 2015). In making his case, he mentions several studies that purport to show either that we do about as well as chance in seeing things as others do or judging the thoughts of strangers, and several more studies that purport to show that we are *worse* than chance in judging others' thoughts and emotions (cf. Epley 2014; Chapter 31 in this volume, "Empathic accuracy"). And even if we are urged to try harder, or undergo empathy training, there are simply cognitive limits to what we can understand (from the inside) about others. For example, how could we *really* understand what it's like to fight in a war, become poor, undergo a religious conversion, or suffer in solitary confinement for years (if, in each case, we haven't already) (Paul 2014)? Consequently, those who advocate empathy for others as the only or best way to generate moral or political change are sadly mistaken.

How might we apply this criticism of empathy to its purported role in moral responsibility? It would be rather straightforward. If moral responsibility requires the (capacity for the) good exercise of empathy in order to gain epistemic access to the relevant moral reasons (grounded in the interests of others), but most of us are incapable of the good exercise of that mechanism, then most of us would lack a crucial condition for moral responsibility. Surely this is false, though: Most of us *are* morally responsible for what we do, even if we're no good at empathy. Consequently, moral responsibility can't require the (capacity for the) good exercise of empathy.

How effective would this objection be as wielded against the *Plausible Story*? As it stands, not very. Recall that the *Plausible Story* as originally told is really only about the necessity of *emotional* empathy for moral responsibility, as that is what psychopaths are said to lack. But Bloom's story is implicitly about *cognitive* empathy, about (merely) taking up and intellectually understanding the perspectives of others. Consequently, this Bloom-inspired objection to the *Plausible Story* is a non sequitur.

One might amend Bloom's objection by claiming that emotional empathy requires cognitive empathy: How could I feel what you're feeling if I don't understand what you're going through? This form of the objection is vulnerable to counterexamples, though, for it seems that many real-life agents (individuals at the high end of the autism spectrum or with mild intellectual disabilities) are capable of emotional empathy without (much in the way of) cognitive empathy. I will say more about this point in the final section. But Bloom's objection may still have force against what I think is a necessary expansion of the *Plausible Story*. That's because the recognition of (at least some) moral reasons (i.e., meeting the epistemic component) actually does require cognitive empathy and its good exercise. After all, simply feeling others' pain as they feel it (emotional empathy) may not reveal any *reasons for action* at all. Sure, such feelings may tend us toward altruism of a kind (Batson et al. 1987; Batson and Shaw 1991; Batson 2014), but such a process may work more or less automatically, effectively hijacking our more deliberative motivational system, and it would also be hostage to an objectionable contingency: I might happen to feel for a limping rat in the same way I feel for a limping Tiny Tim Cratchett in the same way I feel for a limping Hitler. What cognitive empathy can do, though, is enable us to determine the overall *worthiness* of certain pursuits by revealing to us facts about other agents that become actual reasons in our own deliberations. How so?

Suppose that I am considering starting jackhammer work on my driveway Sunday morning at 5 a.m., but I know my neighbor tends bar till 3 a.m. on Sunday mornings and values sleeping in late. Now perhaps the fact of his sleeping habits initially seems no different to me than the fact that his upstairs bathroom window is 26 inches wide. But then I take up his perspective as if I were him, imagining being jackhammered awake. I would hate this (were I him), as it would completely derail my day.

Such cognitive empathy on my part will tend, if my various psychological mechanisms are properly functioning, to enable a new and important recognition: When I see sleeping in peacefully as worthwhile from his perspective (roughly in the way that he would see it), then when I return to my own perspective, his assignment of *value* to sleeping in will come along as well. In other words, I will come to see that fact about him (that he assigns great worth to sleeping in on Sunday) in a newly "reasonish" way, i.e., as at least a putative reason for me to take seriously in my own deliberations about what to do (and so that fact about him now has a different status than the fact about his bathroom window size) (cf. Stueber 2006). This is one crucial way we come to have *regard* for one another. A failure to do so is what we call *inconsiderate*. And if coming to regard him in the right way requires cognitive empathy, as it seems to, then cognitive empathy is required for responsibility after all.

But does this now mean psychopaths, who are ostensibly capable of cognitive empathy, are responsible after all? No. For one thing, if emotional empathy is *also* required, and psychopaths are incapable of that, then they would still lack a crucial capacity for responsibility. But more importantly, I believe psychopaths actually lack a key component of the story I just told about the role of cognitive empathy in moral responsibility, namely, the ability to see facts about others' interests in a "reasonish" way, as providing putatively worthy constraints on their own pursuits. This claim is strongly suggested by their severe (and well-documented) prudential impairments: they often flit from project to project, making lots of money in one arena, say, only to give it up one day without explanation to pursue something else. Or they may insist that they don't want to go to prison while nevertheless continuing to do those things that are guaranteed to send them there. Their lives tend to have no direction, and they very often act against their own interests (see, e.g., Cleckley 1976; Hart & Dempster 1997; Watson 2013; Shoemaker 2015: 160–2). What I think this evidence reveals is that they lack the ability to see value *anywhere*. In other words, they have desires but not *ends*, things they deem worth pursuing. But if they cannot see worth in their own lives, how much less likely they are to see it in the lives of others! Consequently, even if they can imaginatively take up the perspectives of other people, this is not enough to get them what they need for moral responsibility, which is the further ability to see others' interests as worthy of pursuit from those others' – and then subsequently from their own – perspectives. They lack the capacity, in other words, for having regard for people. This would actually incapacitate them from moral responsibility even if their emotional disabilities didn't.

Now if we take the more developed version of the *Plausible Story* seriously, a story that includes cognitive empathy as necessary to moral responsibility, would the Bloom-inspired objection have bite? I doubt it. The objection to requiring cognitive empathy for moral responsibility would be grounded in the (alleged) fact that we are bad at it. But being bad at something doesn't disqualify one from responsibility for it. Indeed, sometimes that's the precise reason one *is* (and ought to be) blamed for something. Being a bad friend, for instance, is grounds for blame by one's friend, as is being bad at having regard for others generally. What typically gets one off the hook for responsibility is not just badness in exercising one's capacities but a genuine *incapacity* (or a serious capacity impairment relative to others). But merely being bad at the exercise of one's (unimpaired) cognitive empathic capacity would seem to be evidence that one simply *disregards* others, and that would be a ground for blame if anything is.

And what of Bloom's stronger claim, that the relevant sort of cognitive empathy (with soldiers, the poor, etc.) may be *impossible*? This does implicate incapacity. But notice that it's an incapacity, if it is, for *fully* understanding the very specific plight of certain other people. But the sort of cognitive empathy required for moral responsibility may require no such robust capacity. Rather, one may need only rough or partial understanding to recognize the relevant "reasonish" facts. And relatedly, while one may not be able to understand what it's like to be a soldier, say, one may nevertheless be able to understand what it's like to be in danger (even if it's not life-threatening danger), or what it's like to have comrades one has an extra-close relationship with, or what it's like to slog through horrible environmental conditions, given (relatively) analogous experiences in one's own life. One's understanding of these simulacra experiences may then be sufficient to enable one's recognition of the "reasonish" facts necessary to being morally responsible.

Finally, we should hesitate in swallowing whole the empirical science Bloom dishes out. Some very recent studies actually suggest that we may have more of a choice in exercising empathy than his studies would imply. For instance, when people were told about child refugees from Darfur, those who were not told they'd be asked for a donation had greater empathy for the children than those who were told they'd be asked for a donation. Such financial considerations should make no difference, however, if our capacity for exercising good empathy were limited (Cameron, Inzlicht, & Cunningham 2015). In another study, people told that empathy could be improved actually made a greater effort to understand different racial groups, and were more successful in doing so (Schumann, Zaki, & Dweck 2014). So while empathy might be hard, or we might see various costs attached to engaging in it, such facts give us no reason not to demand it from one another in our moral responsibility practices. After all, *virtue* is hard too, and surely involves costs, but we have no problem holding each other responsible for our failures in its pursuit.

3. Empathy as a bad moral guide

In a series of influential articles, Jesse Prinz has argued that empathy isn't the moral boon most people have thought it to be (Prinz 2011a, 2011b; cf. Bloom 2013, 2014). Prinz's primary target is the view that empathy is necessary for morality. Through a series of compelling examples, he not only challenges this necessity claim but also argues that empathy can actually interfere with the ends of morality. Prinz is talking here explicitly about *emotional* empathy, "a kind of emotional mimicry ... feeling what one takes another person to be feeling" (Prinz 2011b: 212). But why would this be a bad thing, both unnecessary to, and even undermining, morality?

Prinz surveys the purported role of empathy in moral *judgment*, *development*, and *motivation*. He takes these three to be exhaustive of the ways in which empathy might be seen as having a necessary role to play in morality, and he shows that it does so in none of them. It is often thought, first, that we need to empathize with the victim of wrongs to judge those things wrong, but it is obvious, by contrast, that we quite often make judgments about the moral status of actions – that they are or would be greedy, or callous, or kind – without having to make any sort of empathic leap, and there are also wrongs we judge as such that are victimless (e.g., necrophilia, consensual incest, desecrating a grave). Further, even if emotional responses are necessary to moral judgment, they don't have to be empathic emotions, as responses like (anticipated) guilt or anger could do the trick instead (Prinz 2011b: 213–16).

With regard to its purported role in moral development, Prinz claims that the psychological literature reveals no more than a *correlation* between empathy and the development of moral competence (facility with making moral judgments), and so nothing like a necessary connection.

The third domain Prinz explores is moral motivation, and he rejects empathy as necessary there too. Feeling others' pain isn't essential to motivate us to help them, he argues, as our moral judgments (about the value of helping them) likely have *other* motivating emotions like guilt, anger, or shame built into them, and if so, then additional motivational empathic oomph would be redundant (Prinz 2011b: 218–20).

Perhaps empathy isn't *necessary* for morality, then, but isn't it still valuable to have and develop? Prinz argues no, for empathy has a very dark side. In collectivist cultures, it generates an in-group-think mentality, and outsiders are bullied and killed. It motivates suicide bombers. Empathy has proximity effects – how much empathy you tend to feel depends on how close you are to the victim – and empathy can also be manipulated: in criminal trials, those showing emotion tend to get lower sentences than those who don't (Prinz 2011b: 225–7; see also Bloom 2013). Consequently, empathy "is not especially motivating and it is so vulnerable to bias and selectivity that it fails to provide a broad umbrella of moral concern" (Prinz 2011b: 227).

This is a barrage of criticisms. Should the *Plausible Story*teller be worried? The last complaint, that empathy might actually be bad for morality generally, is, I think, one we might easily respond to. All of the faults cited – in-group bias, preferential treatment, proximity effects, manipulability – are bad things that could be eliminated or mitigated simply by *more empathy*, by increasing the range of those with whom we empathize (cf. Shoemaker 2014: 513–14). It's not that empathy itself is bad or causes bad things; rather, it's the incomplete or improper deployment of empathy that does so. But then we should correct the deployment, not dismiss the empathy.

The more compelling worries have to do with whether empathy plays any necessary role in morality, as the *Plausible Story* insists that it does. Now it is odd right from the start that Prinz thinks that empathy's potential role in morality is exclusively limited to moral judgment, development, or motivation, given the role the *Plausible Story*tellers have also thought it plays in moral responsibility. Nevertheless, how might we most charitably apply Prinz's criticisms to this domain? Perhaps all we need ask is this: If empathy isn't necessary to moral judgment, development, or motivation, then how could it possibly be necessary to moral responsibility, which just implicates a failure (or success) with respect to one of those three elements?

Here is how. Prinz's criticisms are directed against emotional empathy, remember, which involves a vicarious feeling of what another person is feeling. But this, I will argue, is (as with cognitive empathy) a crucial form of moral regard, the capacity for which is indeed necessary for one type of moral responsibility, even if it's not necessary to moral judgment, development, or motivation in Prinz's terms. Let's begin with what ought to be a familiar case. Suppose you are in a close romantic relationship, and your partner comes home from work and is completely emotionally wrought in telling you of having been humiliated publicly by his or her boss that day. You respond by patting your partner on the back and saying, in an even voice, "There, there," but you feel no emotional disturbance whatsoever. It sure seems in such a case that it would be appropriate for your partner to morally blame you, to be angry with you. But why? It's because you should be feeling emotionally simpatico with him or her in circumstances like this. Failure to do so is what we call *insensitive*.

Insensitivity – a failure of emotional empathy – does not just play this role in close personal relationships. It may also play a role among strangers. Suppose my young daughter has just fallen on an icy sidewalk and broken her arm. Several people rush to our aid, but I notice some young men on the other side of the street laughing at what they saw. I will very likely tremble with anger, blaming them for their gross insensitivity. And importantly, it is not the laughing that enrages me; rather, it is the mere fact of their amusement. Were one of them trying desperately to squelch his laughter, I would still be just as angry at him, and, it seems, appropriately so (Shoemaker 2015: 99–103). Our anger in such cases seems distinctly moral, and the angry response is certainly among our designated "responsibility responses." To the extent that it explicitly targets a lack of emotional empathy, then, emotional empathy is necessary to moral responsibility of this sort, even if it implicates no lack of facility with moral judgment, development, or motivation, as Prinz thinks of them.

Of course, emotional empathy may not be necessary to moral responsibility for the other kind of regard discussed earlier, namely, responsibility for taking others' ends seriously through the recognition of "reasonish" facts typically enabled by *cognitive* empathy. But given how much it matters to us that our friends, lovers, and even some strangers are emotionally in tune with us, it is at least necessary to the domain of emotional interactions and responsibility that is rife in our interpersonal lives. And what's important here is that it is precisely the *empathy* that we expect of one another in such circumstances, and not the emotional responses as such. Suppose that, as it so happens, I have been magically constructed simply to mirror my wife's emotions, no matter where or when they occur (so I don't even have to be in her presence for this to occur). That I feel what she's feeling when she is emotionally wrought about her humiliation won't be sufficient to get me off the hook in such a scenario; rather, what will matter, I think, is that I have actually *imagined things from her emotional perspective*. It is thus feeling what others feel *via* that emotional perspective-taking that we expect from one another, and a failure in the perspective-taking is what tends to generate blame.

What this means is that the *Plausible Story*, suitably developed along the lines I have suggested, could still be correct about psychopaths, as well as about the empathic capacities necessary for moral responsibility. Even if, as Prinz argues, there can be alternative emotional sources of moral judgment and motivation, there is no alternative for the emotional empathy *itself* that we often expect of one another. So even if the source of psychopaths' failures of empathy is their general emotional impairment, it is the empathic failure that is most directly implicated in moral responsibility. And this is a story that will be relevant in the next section as well.

4. Alternative routes to moral responsibility

The previous two objections were not originally designed to target the *Plausible Story* about moral responsibility. The next one has been. Recall that the *Plausible Story* has two main features: (a) psychopaths lack empathy, *and so* (b) they are not morally responsible for what they do. Heidi Maibom, in a series of articles (Maibom 2005, 2008, 2009, 2010), questions both elements.

Regarding psychopaths' alleged lack of empathy, Maibom allows that while they are indeed less empathetic than non-psychopathic controls, they nevertheless do have *some* empathy. So while their palmar sweating is lower in response to pictures of people in distress than that of neurotypicals (Blair et al. 1996), they still have a greater response to such pictures than to neutral ones (Maibom 2008: 172). Similarly, their reflex response to startling events is, while abnormal, not utterly lacking (Levenston et al. 2000; Patrick 2007). And there are some self-reports of psychopaths, including Ted Bundy, which seem to reflect some degree of empathy for their victims (Maibom 2008: 172). Consequently, psychopaths as a group cannot be said to lack empathy.

I do not take this argument to strike very deeply at the heart of the *Plausible Story*, however. First, we should be extremely dubious of the self-reports of psychopaths, who lie all the time, just for the fun of it. But second, and more importantly, the *Plausible Story*, in order to be at all plausible, must recognize – and easily can – the *scalar* nature of psychopathy, i.e., that it comes in degrees, and so the more empathic impairment psychopaths have, the less moral responsibility they have. If we think of the *Plausible Story* as merely being about psychopaths' empathic *impairments* – which neither side disagrees they do have – and so consequently about psychopaths' *impaired* responsibility, we can sidestep Maibom's worries.

Even if we make such a move, though, or even if we grant that psychopaths lack empathy altogether, Maibom's much stronger argument is that it wouldn't matter for their responsibility. This is because the *Plausible Story* claims that only via empathy can one reach true moral understanding. But this is a mistake; rather, Maibom claims, moral understanding may be reached by many non-empathic routes.

Consider a paradigm moral norm: it is wrong to harm others (other things being equal). How might one achieve sufficient understanding of this moral norm to be responsible for violating it? The *Plausible Theorist* seems to say that it is only via one's empathy with someone that one can fully morally appreciate why harming that person would be wrong. But this is unrealistically restrictive, argues Maibom. Rather, one can come to this understanding in numerous ways, e.g., by recognizing "that it would be unjust, that one would infringe on someone's rights, or that harming others can lead to loss of one's soul, loss of sanity, or cause one to move over to the dark side" (Maibom 2008: 173). One may also come to recognize this moral norm by thinking about what God would want one to do, what a virtuous person would do, what maxims one can consistently will as universal laws of nature, or what principles no one could reasonably reject. Now perhaps some (or many) of these justifications for the norm in question are mistaken. But so what? Why should it matter *what* justification people have for the normatively binding status of the norm, just as long as they can – somehow, some way – come to have *a* moral justification for it? Indeed, how could a realistic demand for moral understanding ask for anything more than this? Imagine how absurd it would be for us to excuse someone who harmed you because he thought it was wrong to do so only in virtue of its corrupting his soul (Maibom 2008: 174–5). What Maibom ultimately argues, then, is that while psychopaths do have a disorder, it is a specifically *moral* disorder, that is, they lack regard for moral norms. They know what the moral norms are, but they just don't care, and this is precisely what makes them bad people. But badness is not madness, and so does not constitute sufficient grounds for excuse; indeed, it constitutes sufficient grounds for blame and punishment (Maibom 2008: 176–81).

My response begins by pointing out that it often does matter, at least in interpersonal morality, what justifications people have for their adherence to or transgressions of harm norms. Suppose, for example, that I don't cheat on my wife, but solely because I think God will punish me if I do, and suppose my wife finds out about this reason of mine. Or suppose that I am your best friend, and I go to visit you when you are laid up at the hospital, but I explain that I'm only doing so insofar as I couldn't consistently will my maxim to stay home watching *Judge Judy* as a universal law of nature. In both cases, I may be blameworthy, and precisely in virtue of my bad justifications for doing the right thing. And such responses would seem appropriate only if I had access to – but rejected or ignored – better justifications.

Let me explain and expand this point. What such cases suggest is a crucial difference between the justifications relevant to moral permissibility/impermissibility and those relevant to moral responsibility (of a kind). Some action might be wrong for a very specific reason, but when you intentionally avoid performing it you count as doing what's permissible, period, *regardless* of your reasons, and when you intentionally perform it you count as doing what's wrong, period, again regardless of your reasons. This means there is room for you to do something impermissible, but for *blameless* reasons, just as you may do something permissible, but for *blameworthy* reasons (cf. Scanlon 2008: 124–5; Shoemaker 2013). Our praising and blaming responses, then, seem often to target your reasons for doing what you do, i.e., your *motives*. And what tends to be targeted by blaming responses, e.g., anger, are motives expressing a failure to take someone and their interests sufficiently seriously, i.e., failures of *regard* (Shoemaker 2015: Ch. 3). So what makes my wife angry when I say I haven't been cheating on her because I'm worried about what God might do to me is that she has been left entirely out of my deliberative and motivational mix. It's as if she and her interests don't matter at all in my marital fidelity; instead, all that matters is God's opinion of me. But that won't be a reason getting me off the blame hook. So too when I visit you in the hospital solely because I failed to be able to universalize my maxim about watching *Judge Judy*, it seems clear that *you* don't really matter to me; rather, all that seems to matter is my avoiding rational inconsistency.

The suggestion being made here is that certain responsibility responses involve holding others *accountable*, but it's not their being accountable to moral norms that matters; rather, it's their being accountable *to us* that matters. And while any number of different justifications might suffice for the former, most won't do for the latter, which often requires a very specific motivating reason. But if one really lacks access to that specific reason, then it would seem inappropriate for one to be blamed for failing to grasp or act on it.

Psychopaths' empathic impairments strongly suggest they lack such access, though. Recall psychopaths' prudential flaws, which suggests that they can't see worth in their own desires and interests, let alone those of other people. They thus cannot see a range of facts about people's interests as putative reasons in their own deliberations about what to do, i.e., they lack access to reasons of regard for other people. Consequently, even if they have sufficient understanding to recognize and adhere to moral norms and so engage in the world of moral permissibility and impermissibility, they may yet lack sufficient moral understanding of the specific reasons relevant to being accountable to one another to be morally responsible in the end.

But isn't Maibom right that psychopaths are still *bad*? Indeed she is: psychopaths can be cruel, manipulative, and all-around jerks. So doesn't that mean they are morally responsible for being that way? I think they are, just as Gandhi and Martin Luther King, in being generous, kind, and courageous, are morally responsible for being that way. But this allowance isn't in tension with what I have been saying, for there may be *multiple* types of moral responsibility, and so one might be responsible on one type but not another (see, e.g., Watson 2004: 260–88). Being a cruel, manipulative, generous, or kind person generally, and so being the appropriate target of one range of responsibility responses (such as admiration, disdain, contempt, or esteem) implies nothing about whether one might, in any specific circumstance, fail or succeed in being accountable to others, and so be an appropriate target of a different range of responsibility responses (such as anger or gratitude). Kind people break their promises, and cruel people occasionally give friends a pass. Psychopaths might thus be responsible in one way but not another, being bad people and so being appropriate targets of contempt or disdain for their poor character, while having impaired (empathic) capacities for the kind of moral understanding necessary to be accountable to others and so being inappropriate targets of anger (Shoemaker 2015: Part I, Chs. 5–6).

Even so, considerations from a different sort of real-life agent may give defenders of the *Plausible Story* one last headache. Instead of claiming with Maibom that psychopaths are morally responsible, this objection allows that psychopaths are not responsible but denies that it's for empathy-related reasons. Here is the succinct argument: If we deny that psychopaths are accountable, yet we also recognize that many individuals with high-functioning autism (HFA) have the exact same empathic impairments as psychopaths but *are* accountable, then empathic capacities cannot be necessary for accountability (Kennett 2002). Now the empathic impairments of individuals with HFA are fairly well documented, as they have great difficulty taking up the internal psychological perspectives of others (see, e.g., Hobson et al. 2006, 2011), but they nevertheless seem to be able to identify alternative (non-empathic) methods for discovering others' reason-giving interests, and so adhering to moral norms (Kennett 2002: 350–5). If this is sufficient for their having the kind of moral understanding and concern necessary to responsibility, then empathic impairments cannot be what grounds psychopaths' responsibility impairments.

While I have doubts that the empirical science is sufficiently up to speed on the precise deficits of those with HFA to come to a determinate verdict here or that there is even a unified disorder to discuss, the defender of the *Plausible Story* could still have a few outs, even granting a coherent version of the objection. One is simply to bite the bullet by denying the accountability of individuals with HFA (in virtue of their empathic deficits), while allowing that such individuals may nevertheless be morally responsible in a different sense, being, for instance the appropriate target of admiration and esteem (i.e., they may have good characters). A supplemental move expresses skepticism that individuals with HFA actually have the moral understanding and concern they are thought to have by the objector. Instead, some empirical research suggests that those with HFA may care less about taking others' interests as reason-giving and more about their "need to abide by whatever rules they have been taught without sharing our understanding of the ends those rules are meant to serve" (McGeer 2008: 24; see also Zalla et al.

2011). They thus might again be examples of people capable of behaving morally permissibly/impermissibly but not accountably, i.e., they may lack access to the relevant moral motivational reasons to make anger, for example, appropriate, given their empathic impairments. Both moves would thus deny that individuals with HFA are actually accountable to others after all. But as I noted, the empirical science doesn't yield a univocal view of individuals with HFA yet, so we may have to remain agnostic. At any rate, this final version of the "alternative routes" objection may be staved off by the *Plausible Story*teller.

5. Conclusion

Despite multiple attacks on empathy's purported role in morality, there is no reason (yet) for the *Plausible Story*teller to worry. Emotional empathy, suitably understood, does seem necessary for moral responsibility. Indeed, the *Plausible Story* may be more than plausible; it could well be true.

References

Arpaly, Nomy. 2003. *Unprincipled Virtue*. Oxford: Oxford University Press.
Arpaly, Nomy, & Schroeder, Timothy. 2014. *In Praise of Desire*. Oxford: Oxford University Press.
Batson, C. Daniel. 2014. *The Altruism Question: Toward a Social-Psychological Answer*. New York: Psychology Press.
Batson, C. Daniel, Fultz, Jim, and Schoenrade, Patricia A. 1987. "Distress and Empathy: Two Qualitatively Distinct Vicarious Emotions with Different Motivational Consequences." *Journal of Personality* 55: 19–39.
Batson, C. Daniel, & Laura L. Shaw. 1991. "Evidence for Altruism: Toward a Pluralism of Prosocial Motives." *Psychological Inquiry* 2.2: 107–22.
Blair, James, et al. 1996. "Theory of Mind in the Psychopath." *Journal of Forensic Psychiatry* 7: 15–25.
Bloom, Paul. 2013. "The Baby in the Well: The Case Against Empathy." *New Yorker* 20.
Bloom, Paul. 2014. "Against Empathy." *The Boston Review*.
Bloom, Paul. 2015. "Imagining the Lives of Others." *The New York Times* (The Stone, June 6, 2015). URL: http://opinionator.blogs.nytimes.com/2015/06/06/imagining-the-lives-of-others/?_r=0.
Cameron, Daryl, Inzlicht, Michael, & Cunningham, William A. 2015. "Empathy Is Actually a Choice." *The New York Times* (Gray Matter, July 12, 2015). URL: www.nytimes.com/2015/07/12/opinion/sunday/empathy-is-actually-a-choice.html.
Cleckley, Hervey. 1976. *The Mask of Sanity*. Fifth Edition. St. Louis: C.V. Mosley.
Decety, Jean, et al. 2013. "An fMRI Study of Affective Perspective Taking in Individuals with Psychopathy: Imagining Another in Pain Does Not Evoke Empathy." *Frontiers in Human Neuroscience* 7: 489.
Deigh, John. 1995. "Empathy and Universalizability." *Ethics* 105: 743–63.
Epley, Nicholas. 2014. *Mindwise: Why We Misunderstand What Others Think, Believe, Feel, and Want*. New York: Vintage.
Fine, C., & Kennett, J. 2004. "Mental Impairment, Moral Understanding and Criminal Responsibility: Psychopathy and the Purposes of Punishment." *International Journal of Law and Psychiatry* 27: 425–43.
Fingarette, Herbert. 1967. *On Responsibility*. New York: Basic.
Haji, Ishtiyaque. 2010. "Psychopathy, Ethical Perception, and Moral Culpability." *Neuroethics* 3: 135–50.
Hart, Stephen D., & Demptster, Rebecca J. 1997. "Impulsivity and Psychopathy." In Christopher D. Webster & Margaret A. Jackson, eds, *Impulsivity: Theory, Assessment, and Treatment* (New York: The Guilford Press), pp. 212–32.
Hobson, Peter R., et al. 2006. "Foundations for Self-Awareness: An Exploration through Autism." *Monographs of the Society for Research in Child Development* 71: 1–166.
Hobson, Peter R., et al. 2011. "Autism and the Self." In Shaun Gallagher, ed., *The Oxford Handbook of the Self* (Oxford: Oxford University Press), pp. 571–91.
Kennett, Jeanette. 2002. "Autism, Empathy, and Moral Agency." *Philosophical Quarterly* 52: 340–57.
Levenston, G., Patrick, C., Bradley, M., & Lang, P. 2000. "The Psychopath as Observer: Emotion and Attention in Picture Processing." *Journal of Abnormal Psychology* 109: 373–85.

Levy, Neil. 2007. "The Responsibility of the Psychopath Revisited." *Philosophy, Psychiatry, & Psychology* 14: 129–38.

Litton, Paul. 2010. "Psychopathy and Responsibility Theory." *Philosophy Compass* 5.8: 676–88.

Maibom, Heidi. 2005. "Moral Unreason: The Case of Psychopathy." *Mind & Language* 20: 237–57.

Maibom, Heidi L. 2008. "The Mad, the Bad, and the Psychopath." *Neuroethics* 1: 167–84.

Maibom, Heidi L. 2009. "Feeling for Others: Empathy, Sympathy, and Morality." *Inquiry* 52: 483–99.

Maibom, Heidi L. 2010. "Imagining Others." *CRÉUM – Revue les ateliers de l'éthique* 5: 34–49.

McGeer, Victoria. 2008. "Varieties of Moral Agency: Lessons from Autism (and Psychopathy)." In Walter Sinnott-Armstrong, ed., *Moral Psychology, Volume 3: The Neuroscience of Morality: Emotion, Brain Disorders, and Development* (Cambridge, MA: The MIT Press), pp. 227–57.

McKenna, Michael. 2012. *Conversation and Responsibility*. New York: Oxford University Press.

Murphy, Jeffrie G. 1972. "Moral Death: A Kantian Essay on Psychopathy." *Ethics* 82.4: 284–98. Reprinted in *Retribution, Justice, and Therapy* (Netherlands: Springer, 1979), pp. 128–43.

Patrick, C. 2007. "Getting to the Heart of Psychopathy." In H. Hervé & J. Yuille, eds., *The Psychopath: Theory, Research, and Practice* (Mahwah, NJ: Lawrence Erlbaum Associates), pp. 207–52.

Paul, Laurie Ann. 2014. *Transformative Experience*. Oxford: Oxford University Press.

Prinz, Jesse. 2011a. "Against Empathy." *The Southern Journal of Philosophy* (Spindel Supplement) 49: 214–33.

Prinz, Jesse. 2011b. "Is Empathy Necessary for Morality?" In Peter Goldie & Amy Coplan, eds., *Empathy: Philosophical and Psychological Perspectives* (Oxford: Oxford University Press), pp. 211–29.

Pritchard, Michael S. 1974. "Responsibility, Understanding, and Psychopathology." *The Monist* 58: 630–45.

Russell, Paul. 2004. "Responsibility and the Condition of Moral Sense." *Philosophical Topics* 32: 287–305.

Scanlon, T. M. 1998. *What We Owe to Each Other*. Cambridge, MA: The Belknap Press of Harvard University Press.

Scanlon, T. M. 2008. *Moral Dimensions*. Cambridge, MA: The Belknap Press of Harvard University Press.

Schumann, Karina, Zaki, Jamil, & Dweck, Carol S. 2014. "Addressing the Empathy Deficit: Beliefs about the Malleability of Empathy Predict Effortful Responses when Empathy is Challenging." *Journal of Personality and Social Psychology* 107: 475–93.

Sher, George. 2009. *Who Knew? Responsibility without Awareness*. Oxford: Oxford University Press.

Shoemaker, David. 2007. "Moral Address, Moral Responsibility, and the Boundaries of the Moral Community." *Ethics* 118: 70–108.

Shoemaker, David. 2013. "Blame and Punishment." In D. Justin Coates & Neal Tognazzini, eds., *Blame: Its Nature and Norms* (Oxford: Oxford University Press), pp. 100–18.

Shoemaker, David. 2014. "Emotional Lobbying." *The Georgetown Journal of Law & Public Policy* 12 (Special Issue): 505–19.

Shoemaker, David. 2015. *Responsibility from the Margins*. Oxford: Oxford University Press.

Smith, Angela M. 2005. "Responsibility for Attitudes: Activity and Passivity in Mental Life." *Ethics*: 115: 236–71.

Stueber, Karsten R. 2006. *Rediscovering Empathy: Agency, Folk Psychology, and the Human Sciences*. Cambridge, MA: MIT Press.

Watson, Gary. 2004. *Agency and Answerability*. Oxford: Oxford University Press.

Watson, Gary. 2011. "The Trouble with Psychopaths." In R. Jay Wallace, Rahul Kumar, & Samuel Freeman, eds., *Reasons and Recognition* (Oxford: Oxford University Press), pp. 307–31.

Watson, Gary. 2013. "Psychopathy and Prudential Deficits." *Proceedings of the Aristotelian Society* 113: 269–92.

Zalla, Tiziana, et al. 2011. "Moral Judgment in Adults with Autism Spectrum Disorders." *Cognition* 121: 115–26.

22

EMPATHY AND LEGAL RESPONSIBILITY

Ishtiyaque Haji

1. Introduction

Empathy may be thought to be relevant to legal culpability for many reasons, including the following. First, empathy plays a key role in aspects of moral and legal reasoning; taking the perspective of another, for example, facilitates fair or impartial decision-making. Second, empathy is important to motivate apt reactions to injustice. Third, empathy is essential to being good persons; its lack is correlated with future bad behavior (whether criminal or immoral), aggressive behavior, and causing pain to others. Finally, each of these preceding characteristics of empathy seems conducive to framing good public policies about, for instance, gender discrimination in the workplace and affordable access to legal representation, especially for the indigent. Pertinent parties are divided on these (and other) putative virtues of empathy. Among those favorably inclined toward empathy, Glannon (1997) stresses the importance of empathy in legal responsibility. Nichols (2004) and Blair (e.g., 1996, and Blair et al. 2005) regard intact empathic affect as central to making moral judgments (see also Slote 2010). Shoemaker (2015; see also Chapter 21 in this volume, "Empathy and moral responsibility") argues that empathy plays an essential role in our practices of interpersonal moral responsibility. Among the dissenters, Bloom (2014; 2015) proposes that empathy can lead to detrimental outcomes such as empathic distress, depression, anxiety, and myopia in policymaking. Prinz (2011a; 2011b) says that empathy is not crucial to good decision-making, is not a great motivator, can be manipulated to give preferential treatment to those who do not deserve it (in criminal trials, for instance, those showing emotion tend to get lower sentences than those who do not (Prinz 2011b: 225–7)), and is biased, increasing when the people in need are in close proximity and similar to ourselves.

In this chapter, I will use psychopathy as a special case to explore connections between empathy and legal responsibility. The germane literature reveals mounting evidence for the postulate that lack of empathy and the overall emotional depravity of psychopaths impedes internalization of moral norms. I propose that this impediment, in turn, affects what the empathically or emotionally deprived individual sees, on occasions of choice, as salient alternatives from which to choose, and how this individual weighs or judges the importance of such alternatives. I explain how these two factors – salience and ranking of alternatives – bear on legal culpability. My overall thesis, then, is that there is reason to believe that empathic or emotional depravity may well have untoward implications for reasoning.

2. Emotional depravity and moral norm internalization

Eysenck (1977; 1998) and other researchers (e.g., Fowles 1980; Lykken 1995) have hypothesized that fearful anticipation of punishment is fundamental to socialization. In early development, parents, teachers, or peers (among others) punish or negatively reward children's transgressions. This punishment reinforces the lesson that the relevant behavior is impermissible and ought to be avoided. In addition, Dienstbier (1984) and fellow investigators (e.g., Kagan 1998; Kochanska 1993; 1994; Kochanska et al. 2002; Lykken 1995) report that children who are susceptible to high emotional reactivity are more prone to experience guilt. Their findings strongly suggest that fear is a prerequisite to develop guilt or induce discomfort pursuant to a transgression. Guilt, in turn, is thought to be an important harbinger to moral norm internalization (e.g., Blair 1995; Hoffman 2000; Kochanska et al. 2002).

Influential accounts of empathy (e.g., Blair 1995; Hoffman 2000) explain that mentally healthy children develop the capacity of anticipatory guilt by reflecting both on acts they perform that are deemed to be moral transgressions and on attendant reactions to committing them. Exercising this emerging facility inhibits future repetition of such acts. Endowed with embryonic powers of anticipatory guilt, fearful anticipation of punishment, and nascent empathy, children begin to shape their competence for identifying and appreciating normative concerns; they start to learn from past experiences to differentiate moral right from wrong. Even young children, it seems, distinguish between moral wrongdoing or breaching moral rules from conventional wrongdoing or contravening conventional rules (e.g., Blair 1996; Fine & Kennett 2004; Levy 2007a; 2007b; Smetana & Braeges 1990; Song, Smetana, & Kim 1987). As a result of acquiring emerging capacities of anticipatory guilt, fear, and empathy, mentally healthy children are already partly equipped to view the world through moral lenses.

Unlike such children, psychopathic infants suffer from deficits in fear, guilt, and empathic response. In a striking and provocative paper Viding et al. reaffirm that psychopathic tendencies in childhood and adulthood involve "both affective-interpersonal impairment (callous-unemotional traits [CU]; e.g., lack of empathy, lack of guilt, shallow emotions) and overt antisocial behaviour" (Viding et al. 2005: 592). They propose that antisocial individuals who "present with the affective core of callous-unemotional traits (individuals with psychopathy) start offending at a young age and continue across the lifespan with acts that are often predatory in nature," and that the predatory nature of their crimes "reflects the lack of empathy (CU personality core) of psychopaths" (2005: 592). What is perhaps most striking is one of the primary findings of their research:

> Our results indicate that exhibiting high levels of callous-unemotional traits (CU) at 7 years, as assessed by teachers at the end of the first year of school, is under strong genetic influence ... Moreover, antisocial behavior ... for children who are high on CU (i.e., children with psychopathic tendencies) is highly heritable.
>
> *(2005: 595–6)*

In their synopsis of the pertinent contemporary scholarship on moral development, Fine and Kennett conclude that "there are pre-existing suggestions in the literature that psychopathic individuals may have deficits that cause them to fail to internalise moral norms during the course of their development" (2004: 431).

In sum, there appear to be strong grounds to support the thesis that deficits in fear, guilt, and empathy in children with psychopathic tendencies prevent internalization of moral norms of conduct (see also, e.g., Anderson et al. 1999). Psychopaths will then not bring these norms to bear in interpreting their circumstances and, as I propose below, in their practical deliberations.

3. A digression: impermissibility and culpability

Culpability is associated not with wrongness *per se* but with belief in wrongness. In other words, the condition that culpability requires wrongness – one is culpable for an action only if it is impermissible for one to perform this action – is false. A preliminary rendering of the replacement thesis I propose is that one is culpable for an action only if one takes that action to be impermissible for one. ("Culpability" and "blameworthiness" are used interchangeably, as are "wrongness" and "impermissibility.") There are several reasons to renounce the former condition. In this section, I first summarize two of these reasons, one having to do with so called "Frankfurt examples" and the other with suberogation. I then comment on the replacement thesis. Its significance to whether relevantly emotionally impaired individuals are morally culpable for their offenses is discussed in the ensuing two sections on alternatives.

Among other things, Frankfurt examples attempt to establish that a person can be morally responsible for doing something despite not being able to do otherwise, as long as the conditions that render her unable to do otherwise play no role in bringing about her action. Think of such an example as unfolding in two stages. In Stage 1, Augustine is morally culpable for stealing some pears. Next, in a "rerun" of Stage 1, Stage 2, something precludes Augustine from doing anything incompatible with stealing but without in any way interfering in Augustine's actually stealing as it turns out. A mind reader, Ernie, who can tell what Augustine is about to do, will do nothing if he detects some reliable and involuntary sign Augustine displays that he, Augustine, is about to steal, but will force Augustine to steal if he discerns the reliable and involuntary sign that Augustine is about to refrain from stealing. But Augustine proceeds exactly as before, so Ernie has no need to intercede. As Augustine in the absence of Ernie in Stage 1 is culpable for stealing, and since in Stage 2 Augustine does not behave any differently, he is morally culpable for stealing here too, even though he could not have done otherwise (Frankfurt 1969; Fischer & Ravizza 1998; Pereboom 2001; Fischer 2006; Mele 2006; Kane 2013; Haji 2016).

Assume that in Stage 1 it is morally wrong for Augustine to steal the pears. In Stage 2, however, it is *not* wrong for him to steal them. For if it is wrong for him to steal, he ought not to steal. But if he ought not to steal, he can refrain from stealing, given that "ought not" implies "can refrain from." In Stage 2, Augustine cannot refrain from stealing the pears because of ever-vigilant Ernie. It is, then, false that it is wrong for Augustine to steal the pears in Stage 2. He is, however, *still* culpable for stealing them (Haji 1998; 2012; 2016).

Suberogatory acts also tell against the principle that blameworthiness requires wrongness. To elaborate briefly, start with a more familiar category of acts, the supererogatory. Supererogatory acts are permissible acts that have a special sort of value. Stock illustrations of supererogatory behavior include a mailperson's rescuing a child from a burning room at considerable risk to her own life (Feldman 1978: 48), or the soldier's sacrificing his life by throwing himself on the grenade to save his comrades (Urmson 1958). Many advocates of the supererogatory concede that the supererogatory is not confined to the saintly or heroic; mundane action, doing small favors, for example, can also qualify as going beyond duty (see, e.g., Heyd 1982: 142). Although there is controversy on just how the concept of the supererogatory is to be analyzed, there is a fair measure of agreement on these elements: An act is supererogatory for one if and only if it is optional for one to do it (i.e., it is neither obligatory to do it nor obligatory to refrain from doing it), one is praiseworthy for doing it, one would not be blameworthy for omitting to do it, and it "goes beyond duty." (See McNamara 2011 for an insightful account of what it is for an act to go beyond duty.)

Suberogatory acts, are, roughly, the symmetric flip sides of supererogatory ones; they are permissible acts with a special sort of disvalue. In one of Driver's putative examples of a suberogatory act, a man who takes a seat on a train, thereby intentionally preventing two other people from sitting together despite availability of another seat, does no wrong but falls short of decency (1992: 286–7). Chisholm & Sosa propose that minor discourtesy, such as taking too long in a restaurant when others are waiting, may also be suberogatory (1966: 326). Roughly, an act is suberogatory for one if and only if it is optional for one to do it, one is blameworthy for doing it, one would not be praiseworthy for omitting to do it, and it is offensive or bad in some way.

Frankfurt examples and the suberogatory, among other considerations, motivate reconceptualizing the connection between culpability, on the one hand, and wrongness, on the other (see, e.g., Haji 2012 for further considerations). The two may frequently go together, but they sometimes come apart, as they do, for instance, in Frankfurt cases. Elsewhere (e.g., Haji 2012; 2016), I have argued that vital to culpability is, roughly, belief in wrongness:

> *Blame-1*: An agent is morally culpable for performing an action only if she believes that it is morally wrong for her to perform it.

Blame-1 suffers from the problem that one might not believe that doing something is impermissible but nonetheless be (indirectly) blameworthy for doing it due to being blameworthy for the ignorance of wrongdoing from which one does it. Accepting this, I have been initially inclined toward *Blame-2*:

> *Blame-2*: An agent is blameworthy for performing an action only if she nonculpably believes that it is impermissible for her to do it.

But *Blame-2* still does not encapsulate what I want precisely because one might not believe that doing something is impermissible and yet still be blameworthy for doing it. Suppose you believe that it's permissible for you to do something on the advice of an acquaintance you do not trust. Assume, then, that you do not believe that doing this thing is impermissible, and do it. You may still be blameworthy for doing it because you are blameworthy for not believing that it is impermissible for you to do it. Something along the lines of the following is needed:

> *Blame-3*: An agent is morally blameworthy for performing an action only if either she believes that doing it is impermissible or she is blameworthy for failing to believe that doing it is impermissible (see, e.g., Haji 2016 for further discussion).

For our purposes, and in the interests of simplicity, the relevant principle may be abridged to this: If one is culpable for performing an act, then one takes this act to be impermissible for one. It should be noted that many who, in my view, mistakenly believe that culpability requires wrongness will not accept this principle (see, e.g., Widerker 1991; Copp 1997; Fischer 2003).

4. Lack of moral norm internalization and weighing alternatives

It is assumed that, typically, when we make choices about what to do or refrain from doing, there are several alternatives or options available to us. But (somehow) we are able to narrow down the alternatives to a manageable and salient few. We may say that these pared down alternatives are what we regard as *salient* options, they are members of our *salient* alternative sets, and it is these options that we reflect upon or are at the forefront of our attention when we make decisions. In addition, we may assume that, consciously or unconsciously, we rank or weigh these alternatives. Among other factors, our normative cares or investments dictate the sort of ranking. For example, when long-term self-interest is our primary concern, we rank alternatives in terms of what we judge to be their prudential value. Similarly, depending on the relevant circumstances in which we find ourselves and things such as our involvements that we take to be of significance in those circumstances, we weigh salient alternatives on the basis of what we regard to be, for instance, their moral, legal, etiquettical, or religious value. Sometimes we ponder the all-things-considered-from-our-point-of-view value of our salient alternatives. I want to theorize about the effects of empathy or emotional deprivation on what we take to be our salient alternatives and how we rank these alternatives.

To facilitate discussion, consider a possible moral ranking of alternatives assuming the following familiar utilitarian view about moral obligation. On every occasion of choice, we confront a set of possible acts. Each of these possible acts has a "total consequence" – all the results that would occur if the act were performed. Further, each of these acts has a "net goodness value" – the act's utility – which is determined by subtracting the total amount of intrinsic badness (or evil) that its total consequence contains from the total amount of intrinsic goodness it contains. Again, in the interests of simplicity, assume that, roughly, pleasure is the sole ultimate intrinsic good, and pain the sole ultimate intrinsic evil. The utility of an act, dictated by the outlined "hedonic calculus," is a measure of the net pleasure that would be contained in its total consequence if it were performed. Act utilitarianism is the view that an act is morally obligatory if and only if its utility exceeds that of all other alternatives.

It is one thing for an act to have a utility, quite another to determine its utility. Assume that as we make decisions we consciously or unconsciously attempt to rank salient alternatives, in the hope that these subjective rankings coincide with their actual values as determined by the hedonic calculus. Suppose, in ranking alternatives, one takes seriously what may be regarded as a moral norm – the *Impartiality Norm*. For our aims, the norm may be formulated in this way:

Impartiality Norm: No one's pleasure (or pain) is to count as more (or less) important than anyone else's.

When one feels pleasure at a time, there is an episode that then occurs that is one's feeling pleasure at that time. If Sally the baker were to feel a certain amount of net pleasure on biting into a chocolate bar, and Barack the president and Satan, too, were to feel that very same amount of net pleasure on biting into that bar, we would assign, or so suppose, the very same cardinal or ordinal ranking to each of the three episodes of pleasure if we were to rely on the *Impartiality Norm*.

Here is another moral norm:

Interest Norm: When deciding on the moral course of action, take the interests of others into account, including the pleasure or pain they may feel as a result of our actions. (Again, this is rough and ready, the imprecision compatible with our goals.)

I now float some hypotheses, which should help us to conceive of possible connections between lacking empathy and ranking alternatives. Each hypothesis can be sufficiently regimented or appropriately modified to be tested empirically. Let's say that an empathically depraved or impaired agent is an agent who either lacks the capacity for empathy or whose capacity for empathy is severely compromised.

> *Hypothesis-1*: Agents (such as psychopaths) who are empathically depraved and emotionally impaired do not internalize moral norms (see section 2), and, consequently, do not rank their salient alternatives on the basis of these norms (such as the *Impartiality Norm* and the *Interest Norm*).
>
> *Hypothesis-2*: Lack of empathy and the capacity to have pertinent emotions significantly impair an agent's ability to be concerned about others or to take their interests into account when, for example, reasoning about what one morally or legally ought to do.

Among these interests are the interests, generally, to feel or receive pleasure and to avoid or minimize pain. As a result of being empathically depraved, if others' interests of this sort are not among one's concerns, then (as I shortly explain) this may well have an effect on how one ranks alternatives. This leads naturally to a third hypothesis.

> *Hypothesis-3*: The disposition to identify empathically with others influences the very way in which one weighs reasons for action.

Some comments on these hypotheses are in order. Cognitive empathy, experiencing the world from the perspective of or what one believes to be the perspective of others, is to be distinguished from emotional empathy, feeling and caring about what one takes other people to feel and care about. Regarding Hypothesis-1, the distinction between these two types of empathy is of no great moment: Lack of empathy, whether cognitive or emotional or both, has an adverse effect on moral norm internalization. As for Hypothesis-2, some may worry that while agents, such as psychopaths, may be deprived of emotional empathy, their capacities for cognitive empathy could well be intact. Furthermore, it is this latter sort of empathy, it may be claimed, that is central to concern about others or being sensitive to the interests of others. However, Christov-Moore & Iacoboni (2014) propose that cognitive and emotional empathy cannot be easily separated: There is evidence that neural systems for emotional and cognitive empathy influence each other. Being deficient in one sort of empathy may well have an adverse effect on the other sort. Even if either one of these sorts of empathy has no interesting bearing on the other, there is a further problem. A prominent feature that distinguishes psychopaths from other mundane criminals is their lack of prudence. Their deficiency in prudential reasoning and their inability to carry out long-term plans appear, again, to be a function of their emotional impairment. Like many others (e.g., Cleckley 1976; Hart & Dempster 1997; Watson 2013; Shoemaker 2015: 160–2), Levy underscores the observation that psychopaths commit crimes in the face of awareness of the high risks of being caught, and will "gamble the proceeds of a large haul for a small gain" (Levy 2007a: 130). If such individuals cannot take their *own* interests into account, there is little reason to believe that they can take the interests of *others* into account. As Shoemaker remarks, it appears that psychopaths:

> lack the ability to see value *anywhere*. In other words, they have desires but not *ends*, things they deem worth pursuing. But if they cannot see worth in their own lives, how much less likely they are to see it in the lives of others!
>
> *(p. 245, this volume)*

Concerning Hypothesis-3, reflect on the following imaginary case. Suppose, in virtue of empathic or emotional deficiency or depravity (the germane effects of which were summarized in section 2), norms such as the *Impartiality Norm* and the *Interest Norm* do not influence Psyo's assessment of his salient alternatives. How might he rank these alternatives? In discordance with the *Impartiality Norm* and the *Interest Norm*, Psyo regards his pain or pleasure as far more important than the pain or pleasure of others when weighing alternatives to make decisions. In an example like the previous one involving the chocolate bar, Psyo assigns the episode that is *his* feeling pleasure at some time to some degree on biting into the bar an ordinal ranking higher than the one he assigns to the episode that is Barack's feeling pleasure at some time to some degree.

Consider two broad possibilities (not meant to be exclusive) regarding Psyo's assessing the alternatives in the skewed way in which he does. (a) The option he sees as morally right (or obligatory) differs from what *is* morally right (or obligatory), given his peculiar weighting. To be clear, on this option, Psyo recognizes moral categories of rightness and wrongness but ranks his salient alternatives in a nonconventional way. When he performs the alternative he deems to be morally obligatory for him, an alternative that typically favors *his* short-term interests, cares, or concerns, he fails to do it in light of the belief that it is morally impermissible for him to do it. He may, for instance, falsely believe that it is obligatory for him to gamble away his week's salary because of the proximal pleasure he will enjoy as a result of doing so, even though this imprudent act will in fact cause him, and others dependent on him, to feel net pain.

(b) Psyo simply does not regard his ranking as a moral one. He chooses to do what he takes to be in his *immediate* short-term self-interest. (He fails to rank his salient alternatives in the way in which he would if he were a mentally healthy moral or a prudential agent.) Here, again, it is false that Psyo takes the act he performs to be impermissible for him. He may believe that the option he performs is wrong in some conventional sense of being proscribed – perhaps the people with whom he hangs out frown upon such acts – but he does not see these options as *moral* options.

Some may propose that it is only via empathy that one can grasp what the relevant norms, such as the *Impartiality Norm* and the *Interest Norm*, are. Maibom (2008) has questioned this. She claims that one can appreciate what these norms are by means that require no empathy. (Shoemaker (Chapter 21, this volume) has an interesting discussion of this view of Maibom.) Arguably, Maibom is right about this, but it would not undermine what I have said about Psyo's unconventional ranking of alternatives. Despite not having internalized a norm (and, hence, in the pertinent circumstances not acting on the basis of this norm), one may comprehend it. We may grant that Psyo understands the *Impartiality Norm* and the *Interest Norm* but he simply doesn't care about them. Psyo's deficiency in prudential reasoning precludes him from taking the interests of others into account or giving sufficient weight to the interests of others in his deliberations about what to do.

In the American Law Institute's test for its Model Penal Code, "a person is not responsible for criminal conduct if at the time of such conduct as a result of mental disease or defect he lacks substantial capacity either to appreciate the criminality of his conduct or to conform his conduct to the requirements of the law." There is, thus, an epistemic dimension of criminal conduct having to do with recognizing the criminality of one's conduct, and a control dimension concerned with conforming one's conduct to what the law demands. Principle *Blame-3* is one element of the former dimension. Needless to say, there are differences between moral and legal culpability. For example, there are strict liability laws – something with no parallel when it is just moral culpability at issue – and the scope of moral culpability, that is, the things for which one can be morally culpable, far exceeds the scope of legal culpability. In addition, reaction to legal culpability is institutionalized whereas response to moral culpability is not. To facilitate discussion, I assume that, at least in the criminal law, ideally legal and moral culpability should coincide.

The details of our clinical test case involving Psyo imply that Psyo would not be culpable for his pertinent actions because he fails to satisfy a necessary condition of culpability: Roughly, doing what one believes it is morally impermissible for one to do (see *Blame-3*).

Now for a conjecture, psychopaths may rank alternatives and deliberate in the way in which Psyo does. To mention only one set of complications with real-life cases involving agents who are empathically or emotionally depraved in the manner in which psychopaths are, psychopathy, empathic impairment, and culpability come in degrees. (Maibom (2008: 172) cites evidence for the view that psychopaths do have some empathy, even for their victims.) It would be an interesting exercise to expose factors that bear on degree of culpability, and see whether these factors enhance or mitigate, whatever the case may be, the empathically depraved individual's degree of culpability.

5. Ranking, salience, and probability shaping

Empathic depravity may affect not only one's ranking of alternatives but also which alternatives one deems salient, and one's motivation to translate salient alternatives into action. I address salience first and then motivation.

Regarding salience, we have noted that mentally healthy adults have the ability to pare down their alternatives to those they believe to be fundamental or salient. Suppose Psyo ranks his morally obligatory alternative – the option not to harm Philly – so low that it is not in his salient alternative set. Then it is as if this alternative does not appear on Psyo's "radar screen" at all, and he does not even contemplate it in his deliberations about what to do. Furthermore, Psyo is not culpable for this option's not being in his salient alternative set because Psyo is not culpable for his skewed ranking. In turn, he is not culpable for his skewed ranking because this ranking is a function of, or significantly affected by, his failure to internalize moral norms. Moreover, he is not responsible for *this* additional failure because he is not responsible for his deficiencies in empathy or emotion.

In section 3, I ventured that an agent is not culpable for an action if it is false that (loosely) she takes it to be morally wrong for her. In section 4, I proposed that an empathically depraved agent, such as Psyo, may fail to meet this necessary condition of culpability because of his skewed *ranking* of alternatives. His assessment may be way out of line with the actual utilities of the alternatives. While the option is in fact morally wrong, given his ranking, in Psyo's estimation it is morally obligatory. In this section, what I have argued for so far is that an empathically depraved agent may not be culpable for failing to perform the action it is morally obligatory for him to perform because this action may not even appear in his salient alternative set. Once again, this excuse has more to do with the epistemic dimension of culpability than with the control dimension.

Turning, next, to motivation, through our capacities of normative reflection and learning from past experiences we can affect our propensities for future choice and conduct. To illustrate, as young Peg begins to appreciate the value of promise keeping, her desires not to be branded as untrustworthy, to avoid other possible detrimental consequences of breaking trust, to cultivate good character, or to be accepted as part of her peer group may all contribute to her raising the probability that she will decide to keep some promise she made. More generally, through their past behavior, agents shape present practical probabilities, and in their present behavior they shape future practical probabilities (e.g., Mele 2006: 122). In the vast majority of directly free actions – free actions that do not inherit their freedom from other free actions to which they are suitably related – mentally healthy individuals bear some responsibility for these probabilities. Assuming such antecedent probabilities affect motivational strength of, for instance, desires to perform pertinent actions (such as Peg's future desires to perform actions of promise-keeping), probability shaping influences motivation. If, through pertinent past actions, Peg has raised the probability of performing a certain act, say keeping a promise, then, barring unusual circumstances, her desire to keep this promise will have been correspondingly strengthened as well.

Suppose Psyo performs the alternative he takes either to be morally obligatory for him or best for him (the latter in the event of not discerning this option to have a primary *moral* status of being right, wrong, or obligatory). Suppose this option – his seriously harming Philly – is in fact morally wrong for him. With a mentally healthy individual, the resulting negative reaction from others would tend, over time, to *decrease* the antecedent probability that she perform this sort of action. Not so with Psyo. Owing to his empathic or emotional depravity, Psyo is largely insensitive to such external reaction. Moreover, since he takes the salient option he performs to be morally *obligatory* or *best* for him, his so regarding this option would tend to *augment* antecedent probabilities of performing similar sorts of action in the future. In addition, Psyo is largely not morally culpable for decreasing or increasing the antecedent practical probabilities (whatever the case may be). Again, he is not culpable for his empathic or emotional depravity, and it is in virtue of this depravity that his ability to shape practical probabilities is what it happens to be.

Assuming, again, that such antecedent probabilities can have a salutary effect on motivational strength, we would expect Psyo to perform what would in fact be the alternative it would be morally wrong for him to perform but which *he* deems to be morally obligatory or best for him to perform. In sum, empathic and emotional depravity, as a result of (indirectly) affecting the probabilities of performing (or failing to perform) what psychopaths deem to be their salient alternatives, should affect which of their salient alternatives they are motivated to perform.

Regarding possible exculpation, as we have seen, there is reason to believe that the psychopath is not morally responsible for shaping practical probabilities, or his responsibility for such shaping is diminished. But such shaping bears directly on moral motivation. We should, then, entertain seriously the proposal that relevantly empathically or emotionally depraved individuals are either unable to act on numerous mundane moral reasons – reasons such as the fact that an alternative is indeed morally wrong for one to perform – or they experience difficulty in translating moral reasons into action, even assuming that they recognize what is obligatory or impermissible. Here the exculpating or mitigating factor in question – lack of motivation to conform one's conduct to the requirements of law or morality – is more closely associated with the control rather than epistemic dimension of legal culpability.

In conclusion, I have proposed that emotional depravity may lead to legal nonculpability (or diminished culpability) in at least three ways. First, assuming the pertinent empirical evidence or research is cogent, empathically depraved or emotionally impaired individuals fail to internalize moral norms, such as the *Impartiality Norm*, and as a result fail to *rank* alternatives on the basis of the prescriptions of such norms. Their failure to so rank alternatives may well result in their not satisfying a necessary condition of culpability capsulized in principle *Blame-3*. Second, owing to not internalizing moral norms, the morally (or legally) obligatory option may not even be among the emotionally or empathically depraved individual's salient alternatives. This, again, may serve as grounds for exculpation or mitigation, and the grounds here are more closely associated with the epistemic and not the control dimension of culpability. Third, emotional or empathic depravity may contribute to the deprived individual's failing to influence the probabilities of performing future offenses in ways in which mentally healthy individuals shape these probabilities. As the deprived individuals are not culpable for their empathic depravity, and they are not culpable for the fact that if they are relevantly deprived, then they will not influence practical probabilities as normal others do, they are not culpable for failing to shape probabilities as normal others do. This, too, may provide grounds for exculpation or mitigation, and the grounds here have to do with the control dimension of culpability.

References

Anderson, S. W., Bechara, A., Damasio, H., Tranel, D., & Damasio, A. R. (1999) "Impairment of Social and Moral Behavior Related to Early Damage in Human Prefrontal Cortex," *Nature Neuroscience* 2: 1032–7.

Blair, R. J. R. (1995) "A Cognitive Development Approach to Morality: Investigating the Psychopath," *Cognition* 57: 1–29.

——— (1996) "Brief Report: Morality in the Autistic Child," *Journal of Autism and Developmental Disorders* 26: 571–9.

Blair, R. J. R., Mitchell, D., & Blair, K. (2005) *The Psychopath*, Oxford: Blackwell Publishing.

Bloom, P. (2014) "Against Empathy," *Boston Review*, September.

——— (2015) "Imagining the Lives of Others," *The New York Times* (The Stone, June 6, 2015). URL: http://opinionator.blogs.nytimes.com/2015/06/06/imagining-the-lives-of-others/?_r=0.

Chisholm, R. M., & Sosa, E. (1966) "Intrinsic Preferability and the Problem of Supererogation," *Synthese* 16: 321–31.

Christov-Moore, L., & Iacoboni, M. (2014) *Boston Review*, September.

Cleckley, H. (1976) *The Mask of Sanity*, Fifth Edition, St. Louis: C.V. Mosley.

Copp, David (1997) "Defending the Principle of Alternate Possibilities: Blameworthiness and Moral Responsibility," *Nous* 31: 441–56.

Dienstbier, R. (1984) "The Role of Emotion in Moral Socialization," in C. Izard, J. Kagan, & R. Zajonc (eds.) *Emotions, Cognitions, and Behavior*, New York: Cambridge University Press, pp. 485–514.

Driver, J. (1992) "The Suberogatory," *Australasian Journal of Philosophy* 70: 286–95.

Eysenck, H. J. (1977) *Crime and Personality*, London: Routledge and Kegan Paul.

——— (1998) "Personality and Crime," in T. Millon, E. Simonsen, M. Birket-Smith, & R. D. Davis (eds.) *Psychopathy: Antisocial, Criminal, and Violent Behavior*, New York: The Guilford Press, pp. 40–9.

Feldman, F. (1978) *Introductory Ethics*, Englewood Cliffs, NJ: Prentice Hall.

Fine, C., & Kennett, J. (2004) "Mental Impairment, Moral Understanding and Criminal Responsibility: Psychopathy and the Purposes of Punishment," *International Journal of Law and Psychiatry* 27: 425–43.

Fischer, J. M. (2003) "'Ought-Implies-Can', Causal Determinism, and Moral Responsibility," *Analysis* 63: 244–50.

Fischer, J. M. (2006) *My Way: Essays on Moral Responsibility*, New York: Oxford University Press.

Fischer, J. M., & Ravizza, M. (1998) *Responsibility and Control: A Theory of Moral Responsibility*, Cambridge: Cambridge University Press.

Fowles, D. C. (1980) "The Three Arousal Model: Implications of Gray's Two-Factor Learning Theory for Heart Rate, Electrodermal Activity, and Psychopathy," *Psychophysiology* 17(2): 87–104.

Frankfurt, H. (1969) "Alternate Possibilities and Moral Responsibility," *The Journal of Philosophy* 66: 829–39.

Glannon, W. (1997) "Psychopathy and Responsibility," *Journal of Applied Philosophy* 14: 263–75.

Haji, I. (1998) *Moral Appraisability*, New York: Oxford University Press.

——— (2012) *Reason's Debt to Freedom*, New York: Oxford University Press.

——— (2016). *Luck's Mischief: Obligation and Blameworthiness on a Thread*, New York: Oxford University Press.

Hart, S. D., & Dempster, R. J. (1997) "Impulsivity and Psychopathy," in C. D. Webster & M. A. Jackson (eds.) *Impulsivity: Theory, Assessment, and Treatment*, New York: The Guilford Press, pp. 212–32.

Heyd, D. (1982) *Supererogation*, Cambridge: Cambridge University Press.

Hoffman, M. L. (2000) *Empathy and Moral Development: Implications for Caring and Justice*, Cambridge: Cambridge University Press.

Kagan, J. (1998) "Biology and the Child," in N. Eisenberg & W. Damon (eds.) *Wiley Handbook of Child Psychology. Social, Emotional, and Personality Development*, Vol. 3, New York: Wiley, pp. 177–235.

Kane, R. (2013) "Frankfurt-Style Examples and Self-Forming Actions," in I. Haji & J. Caouette (eds.) *Free Will and Moral Responsibility*, Newcastle upon Tyne: Cambridge Scholars Publishing, pp. 58–73.

Kochanska, G. (1993) "Toward a Synthesis of Parental Socialization and Child Temperament in Early Development of Conscience," *Child Development* 64: 325–47.

—— (1994) "Beyond Cognition: Expanding the Search for the Early Roots of Internalization and Conscience," *Developmental Psychology* 30: 20–2.

Kochanska, G., Gross, J. N., Lin, M., & Nichols, K. E. (2002) "Guilt in Young Children: Development, Determinants, and Relations with a Broader System of Standards," *Child Development* 73(2): 461–82.

Levy, N. (2007a) "The Responsibility of the Psychopath Revisited," *Philosophy, Psychiatry, and Psychology* 14(2): 129–38.

—— (2007b) "Norms, Conventions, and Psychopaths," *Philosophy, Psychiatry, and Psychology* 14(2): 163–70.

Lykken, D. T. (1995) *The Antisocial Personalities*, Hillsdale, NJ: Lawrence Erlbaum Associates.

McNamara, P. (2011) "Supererogation, Inside and Out: Toward an Adequate Scheme for Common-Sense Morality," in M. Timmons (ed.) *Oxford Studies in Normative Ethics*, Volume 1, New York: Oxford University Press, pp. 202–35.

Mele, A. (2006) *Free Will and Luck*, New York: Oxford University Press.

Nichols, S. (2004) *Sentimental Rules*, New York: Oxford University Press.

Maibom, H. (2008) "The Mad, the Bad, and the Psychopath," *Neuroethics* 1: 167–84.

Pereboom, D. (2001) *Living Without Free Will*, Cambridge: Cambridge University Press.

Prinz, J. (2011a) "Against Empathy," *Southern Journal of Philosophy* 49: 214–33.

Prinz, J. (2011b) "Is Empathy Necessary for Morality?" in Amy Coplan & Peter Goldie (eds.) *Empathy: Philosophical and Psychological Perspectives*, Oxford: Oxford University Press, pp. 211–29.

Shoemaker, D. (2015) *Responsibility from the Margins*, Oxford: Oxford University Press.

Slote, M. (2010) *Moral Sentimentalism*, Oxford: Oxford University Press.

Smetana, J. G., & Braeges, J. L. (1990) "The Development of Toddlers' Moral and Conventional Judgments," *Merrill-Palmer Quarterly* 36: 329–46.

Song, M., Smetana, J. G., & Kim, S.Y. (1987) "Korean Children's Conceptions of Moral and Conventional Transgressions," *Developmental Psychology* 23: 577–82.

Urmson, J. O. (1958) "Saints and Heroes," in A. I. Meldin (ed.) *Essays in Moral Philosophy*, Seattle: University of Washington Press, pp. 198–216.

Viding, E., Blair, J., Moffitt, T.E., & Plomin, R. (2005) "Evidence for Substantial Genetic Risk for Psychopathy in 7-Year-Olds," *Journal of Child Psychology and Psychiatry* 46: 592–97.

Watson, G. (2013) "Psychopathy and Prudential Deficits," *Proceedings of the Aristotelian Society* 113: 269–92.

Widerker, D. (1991) "Frankfurt on 'Ought Implies Can' and Alternative Possibilities," *Analysis* 51: 222–4.

23

EMPATHY AND CARE ETHICS

Maurice Hamington

Introduction: what is care ethics?

Led by feminist scholars, care ethics grew out of a groundswell of dissatisfaction with traditional ethical theorizing. Early theorists include Carol Gilligan, who first used the term "care" to describe an alternative form of relational moral deliberation that did not fit existing ethical categories (1983); Nel Noddings, who provided the philosophical and phenomenological basis for care, including the central role for attentiveness in the caring relationship (1984); and Joan Tronto, who framed care in terms of its political implications (1993). Each of these theorists has evolved and refined their thinking through many publications beyond their original work on the subject. Subsequently, care ethics has grown into a burgeoning interdisciplinary field of study, with applications in health care (e.g. Benner & Gordon 1996), education (e.g. Monchinski 2010), business (e.g. Hamington & Sander-Staudt 2011), environmental studies (e.g. Goralnik et al. 2014), and social policy (e.g. Mahon & Robinson 2012). Although care ethics retains strong ties to feminism, scholars who are not explicitly connected to feminist theory have begun addressing care in earnest (e.g. Engster 2007, Slote 2007).

The impetus for care ethics came from feminist theorists who observed the absence of women's experience in moral philosophy. This critique was not only about a lack of examples from women's lives but also about how traditional approaches, namely deontological and teleological ethics, evolved and flourished without taking the situatedness of individuals into consideration. In other words, care ethics was a reproach to the presumed disconnected objectivity found in ethical theory that implicitly favored the biases of the dominant male identity that formulated it. Moral philosophers, almost exclusively the domain of socially privileged males, framed ostensibly objective ethical theory in a manner consistent with upper-class, able-bodied, masculine experience of independent agents capable of making isolated transactions in the world. Women and other marginalized identities did not usually have this experience and their lives were not commonly reflected in the development of Western theory (Tuana 1992). In particular, care ethicists claim that relationships matter and should be at the heart of moral consideration. Concern for relationship has historically been disregarded and devalued as a "feminine" concern, so much so that caring labor continues to be among the least compensated work in society.

In a similar departure from the mainstream, care ethics has also uniquely honored emotion's role in moral deliberation (e.g. Noddings 2010a, 157–79; Petterson 2008, 51–64). As Noddings describes, "Caring depends on a form of attention that requires continuous interaction between the cognition that assesses needs and the emotion that moves a carer to respond to them" (Noddings 2010a, 163). Care is more than just emotion, however, the affective dimension of care foments attentiveness and motivates action. In other words, emotions can focus caring. This phenomenon can be witnessed in the transition of an abstract problem experienced by an unfamiliar other into one that we care about. For example, there is no issue more important to care ethicists than how to expand the circle of caring inclusion. Caring for family and friends is a pervasive experience given the established emotional bonds, but caring for unfamiliar and distant others is a greater challenge. Moral sentimentalism, through works of thinkers such as David Hume and Adam Smith, achieved some traction in the eighteenth century. For mainstream philosophers, emotion and compassion have largely been devalued as producing bias and thus detracting from objective moral truth. Immanuel Kant's concern for categorical imperatives – absolute, unconditional requirements that must be obeyed in all circumstances and are justified as ends in themselves – has come to dominate modern Western ethical theorizing. Care posits a relational ontology or the notion that humans exist in a dynamic web of relationships that define who they are and participate in every decision. Therefore, care ethics is primarily described as a relational approach to morality and thus it has provided a theoretical space for considering emotions. Empathy, and the emotions it can engender, is an important part of the motivation for caring action.

Given its relational basis, another significant attribute of care is its responsiveness. Kantian and utilitarian ethics endeavor to answer the question "what is the right thing to do?" regardless of the individuals and context (Held 2006, 83). As a result of the concern for decision making, these approaches create rubrics of moral assessment such as "one should never lie" or "act to create the greatest amount of happiness for the greatest number of people" that can be applied *a priori* to a given experience. Care does not take a preemptive formulaic approach to right action (Noddings 1984, 24) and thus the normative response is one that emerges from the situation. The care giver must be attentive and responsive to the other. For example, an ethics driven by categorical principle can simply adjudicate a lie as morally wrong and unacceptable. A care approach focuses on the relationship and individuals involved rather than applying a rigid assessment of ethics to behavior. This knowledge is generated out of an attentiveness and openness to the other that can help shape the moral response. The moral concern is for the other, not for any particular action abstracted from the relational context. The moral approach opened up by the central concern for relationship also opens a role for empathy as a skill of understanding. However, before turning to empathy, in addition to relationality, one more aspect of care theory bears addressing because of its central role in care and its implications for empathy: particularism.

Care is a particularist ethic, which means that context – the particulars – matters in care theory because care is responsive to an individual other in relationship. To be responsive, one must know the circumstances of the other's situation. Generalized responses to others are not experienced as caring with any depth. For example, handing a dollar to every panhandler may assuage personal guilt or offer a modicum of generosity but it is hardly a significant performance of care. Care requires an attention to the other (Noddings 2010a, 28), which shapes the caring response. In the example above, handing a dollar to a panhandler may demonstrate a low level of care on a continuum that extends to much deeper forms. Stopping to talk to the panhandler and learning about their circumstances and responding in accord with those circumstances constitutes a deeper form of care. Responsiveness and particularity go hand in hand. It should be noted that this particularism does not imply relativism (Hekman 1995, 45–6). There is a caring attitude that guides the care giver toward effective response that helps the one cared for to grow and flourish. Counterexamples of abusive behavior within ostensibly caring relationships (e.g. corporal punishment in the name of love) are sometimes offered to expose the dark side of care but such actions hardly meet the criteria of authentic responsiveness in the service of growth and flourishing suggested by care theorists. In other words, the personal claim that one is caring is insufficient evidence that one is caring. In this manner, care ethics is postmodern in resisting the polar categories of objectivity, characterized as a universal interchangeable moral rubric, and relativism, defined by subjectivity.

In summary, care is a relational and responsive approach to morality that takes into account the particulars of a situation and acknowledges both the emotive and the cognitive elements of ethical action. Before moving to the particulars of the relationship between care ethics and empathy, it is important to address the definition of empathy used by care ethics and in the rest of this chapter. One common method for categorizing empathy amongst scholars who study it is as either cognitive empathy, which is the mental understanding of other people's feelings, or emotional empathy, which describes vicarious feeling with the emotions of others (Smith 2006). Care ethicists do not consistently or explicitly delineate between cognitive and emotional empathy. Rather than the product of sloppy thinking, the alternating and intermingling of the two ideas is consistent with the notion of care as combining cognitive and emotive elements, as described above. On the one hand, emotional empathy is disruptive and compels the caregiver to engage with the individual in need. Care ethics has always valued emotion as part of the moral process (Held 2006, 10). On the other hand, cognitive empathy provides knowledge that can be articulated and generalized, forming the basis for policy and institutional decisions in political care. Although care theorists do not clearly prioritize one category of empathy over the other, the discussions below between Michael Slote and Nel Noddings favor a definition of empathy more consistent with cognitive empathy.

Nel Noddings and Michael Slote

The most prolific care ethicist of the late twentieth and early twenty-first century is Nel Noddings. In her early work, Noddings was reluctant to use the term empathy and favored sympathy as crucial to care ethics. One reason for Noddings's original distrust of the term empathy is her concern that it involves a projection by the care giver onto the one cared for. Accordingly, she was critical that empathy meant imagining oneself in the other (Noddings 2002, 13). For Noddings, such an approach made the caring relationship overly one-sided. Noddings emphasizes the caring relationship as central whereby the care giver and one cared for interact in a responsive ongoing exchange. A second reason that Noddings was wary of employing the term empathy had to do with her feminist sensibilities. Noddings was concerned that "empathy" had replaced "sympathy" because the latter had become associated with the feminine and was not worthy of moral theorizing in a field dominated by men. Beginning in 2010 with *The Maternal Factor*, Noddings warms up to the term "empathy" by using it as a shorthand for "a constellation of processes" that includes "attention; cognitive apprehension, or reading (the results of which may or may not be reevaluated); a strong possibility of sympathy; and connection to one's own sympathetic structures" (2010a, 56).

In the mid-2000s, virtue ethicist Michael Slote embraced care ethics and promoted a form of care that explicitly placed empathy at the center. Slote claimed that care ethics is a comprehensive normative ethical theory suitable for both individual and political adjudication (2007, xiii). For Slote, "caring motivation is based in and sustained by our human capacity for empathy with others" (2007, 4). Slote claims that moral distinctions correspond to empathetic tendencies. For example, Slote points to the linkage between empathy and depth of knowledge: "we understand/judge an unwillingness to relieve pain we perceive to be morally worse than an unwillingness to relieve pain that is merely known about" (2007, 128). Slote constructs care ethics in such a way that it can make normative claims in a manner consistent with the processes of traditional ethical approaches and thus can be the basis for rights, justice, and respect for autonomy. By framing care ethics as an approach that can support tenants of moral and political philosophy, Slote engages care ethics through an approach that some have resisted: framing care ethics as an alternative ethical approach rather than a radical paradigm shift. Nevertheless, Slote offers unique insights into the relationship of empathy and care ethics. Perhaps counter-intuitively, Slote claims that empathy allows the caring individual to be more objective (2010a, 143–58). He claims that the individual who brings a caring attitude to an encounter with someone they ostensibly disagree with can employ empathy to set aside their bias and genuinely understand the other. For Slote, "Objectivity requires one to be able, and in various situations actually, to empathize with another person's intellectual point of view, and … seeing another person's position or argument from that person's point of view means empathically (i.e. through empathy) seeing it in something like the favorable light in which the other person sees it" (Slote 2010a, 149–50). Slote draws the provocative conclusion, "empathy is sufficient, not just required for objectivity." (See also Chapter 12 in this volume, "Empathy and understanding reasons.")

Noddings, rather grudgingly, and Slote, somewhat enthusiastically, are two care ethicists who have maintained something of a running dialogue about the prominence of empathy in caring (e.g. Noddings 2010c and Slote 2010b).

The role of empathy in care ethics

In what follows, I summarize some of the roles for empathy in a care ethical relationship. These are not explicit conclusions found in the literature but rather my own extrapolations.

1. *Looking beyond stereotype.* Empathy can help us care for others as individuals rather than categories or stereotypes. To empathize is to imaginatively engage in psychological displacement – to endeavor to understand what another person is feeling based on available evidence. Empathy not only acknowledges another sentient being, it makes the abstract into the particular and allows for a more nuanced grasp of the other (e.g. Todd et al. 2012; Galinsky & Moskowitz 2000). A caveat here is that one must ensure that their basis for empathetic perspective taking is not based on a stereotype (Skorinko & Sinclair 2013). Noddings refers to this concern as "empathetic accuracy" (Noddings 2010a, 175). Feelings of empathy can be misplaced or falsely constructed. Nevertheless, accurate empathy is crucial for the epistemic processing of care. For example, the abstract concept of homelessness elicits a limited depth of moral motivation but, when coupled with the particularity of an individual's story of homelessness, can bring rich connection and understanding that animates moral motivation and caring action (Benhabib 1987, 164).

2. *Reinforces an alternative moral ontology.* Care ethics posits a different ontology than other mainstream moral philosophies. Humans are viewed as relational beings rather than autonomous agents making discrete ethical transactions. Empathy reinforces a relational ontology by valorizing efforts to think and feel with other moral agents rather than simply respond to external phenomenon. For example, within the context of a caring relationship, one might be concerned with what motivated someone to steal rather than judging their actions to be morally wrong. The context and relationship share significance with individual acts. A relational ontology situates care as a liminal notion that exists between the polar concepts of human sameness and human difference. To empathize means to

have some basis or evidence to understand and feel with the other but it also reinforces difference in that were humans not different there would be no need to empathize, as we would just know what the other person is feeling (Noddings 2010a, 53). Accordingly, empathy and care give us the means to create common cause across intersectional identity differences (Hamington 2015b).

3. *Foundation for moral action.* Ultimately, care ethics is concerned with actions taken that help the one cared for to flourish and grow. There is no evidence of care without action (Collins 2015, 65–73). Care ethicists make it clear that care is more than simply a sentiment or good will. Caring action is motivated by empathy because the empathetic feelings help create a visceral connection between people. Although empathy may not be the only reason that people take caring action, it is a substantial one.

4. *Spurs moral progress.* Traditional approaches to ethics including utilitarian and Kantian moral philosophy endeavor to establish means for value judgment in anticipation of experience. Accordingly, moral rules or rubrics guide ethical action. Such approaches can have a degree of inertia, as witnessed in efforts to use sacred texts written thousands of years ago for contemporary moral answers. Because empathizing with the other is central to care, one begins with an epistemic process, namely understanding the other, before determining which caring action to undertake. This responsiveness through empathetic attentiveness allows for an emergent normativity that is nimble enough to be open to change. A striking recent instance of the power of empathetic concretization is the recent revolution in public opinion on same-sex marriage. In less than two decades, the United States went from passing constitutional amendments defining marriage as heterosexual to acknowledging the rights of gays and lesbians to marry. This change was largely accomplished through the public and private coming out of many gay people, making them visible and normalizing their lives in the eyes of the American public. As a result more people began empathizing with the anguish of not being allowed to enter into publicly recognized life commitments. Gay marriage transformed from an abstract concept in a heteronormative society to a seemingly undeniable expression of human flourishing.

5. *Basis for expanding the circle of cared for.* A potential pitfall of empathy is its parochial nature. It is much easier to empathize with those who are most familiar and like ourselves. However, the knowledge gained from thoughtful empathizing can be the basis for making imaginative leaps to care for less familiar others. Some leaps are easy and others require more inquiry. If I witness someone who is unfamiliar to me fall and hit their head, I do not have to wonder if my empathetic feelings are misplaced. I know it hurts because we share embodiment despite any cultural, linguistic, political, or social differences. This knowledge is based in my common understanding of what it means to have a body (Hamington 2004). Embodied existence becomes the basis for a degree of empathy. Everyone gets hungry, fears violence, and is vulnerable to disease because they have a body. The body is the starting point for my empathetic imagination to expand the circle of those I might care for. In addition to our fundamental embodied commonality, we can gain empathetic understanding through the knowledge that comes from inquiry into the lives of others.

The roles for empathy in caring listed above are not unrelated to one another. The ability of empathy to concretize the particularities of human experience (#1) creates the potential for treating unfamiliar others in a more than superficial manner thus expanding the circle of care (#5). Seyla Benhabib describes the ability of care to move between a specific "concrete" understanding of an individual and a general conclusion about others.

> My purpose is to develop a universalistic moral theory that defines the "moral point of view" in light of the reversibility of perspectives and an "enlarged mentality." Such a moral theory allows us to recognize the dignity of the generalized other through an acknowledgement of the moral identity of the concrete other.
>
> *(Benhabib 1987, 164)*

Accordingly, if I get to know some particular prison inmates and see the richness of their humanity and make an empathetic connection with them, it may change my perspective on prison inmates more generally despite the fact that most of them remain unknown to me.

In summary, empathy plays a variety of interrelated roles in the process of caring.

Empathy as necessary but insufficient condition of care

Although care ethicists view empathy as vital for care, they do not equate empathy with care. In other words, even if empathy may be a necessary condition of care, it is not a sufficient condition of care, particularly if care is defined as an action taken that promotes the growth and flourishing of another. Empathy can be experienced without being motivated to act. One might choose not to act because it is better not to, given the circumstances. For example, because of personal experience, I may empathize with someone who is having a seizure but I may choose not to act because trained medical personnel are on the scene and any action on my part would not be beneficial. Similarly, I may empathize with someone I see on the news who lives in a part of the world that is a great distance from me so I may not have the ability to effectively act on their behalf. In such cases, I might imagine possible courses of action yet I do not imagine that I could act in such a way that makes a significant difference (Hamington 2010, 683). Furthermore, without sufficient inquiry, empathy can lead to inadequate or misguided caring action. In such cases, my empathy does not run deep and my understanding is superficial and it would have been better had I not acted at all. For example, if I see a colleague crying and I offer them a tissue and tell them they should go home and take care of themselves, the gesture is superficial and minimal and possibly aimed at assuaging my discomfort with the display of emotion. It could be that something that happened at home has led to their distress and my quick action just became the source of further anguish. Had I engaged in greater inquiry, thus taken the time, effort, and risk to listen, I might have learned something that would have led to an action experienced as deeper caring by the person crying.

Empathy clearly plays a critical part in care, but it does not always lead to a caring act. The causal chain is complicated by the nonlinear relationship between inquiry, empathy, and action. Skilled care can create more opportunities for empathy and understanding. In the example above, I described the effort to learn why the colleague was crying as a risk. In many situations, we know that further inquiry may lead to an empathetic connection, which may make a difference to our decision to listen and ask questions. It's not just that it takes time and effort but there is the possibility that my heart will be pulled in and I will feel compelled to act. As Noddings describes, "the caring person, one who in this way is prepared to care, dreads the proximate stranger, for she cannot easily reject the claim he has on her" (Noddings 1984, 47). Accordingly, there are times when we are otherwise engaged that we do not wish to endeavor to know more because we realize that such inquiry will pull us in to care. In such cases knowledge can be said to activate empathy, which in turn can lead to caring action. One can avoid the causal chain by retreating from knowledge. As novelist Leslie Jamison describes, "Empathy isn't just listening, it's asking the questions whose answers need to be listened to. Empathy requires inquiry as much as imagination" (2014, 5).

In recent years, feminist theorists have developed the seemingly contradictory notion of "epistemologies of ignorance" (Tuana & Sullivan 2006, vii). These scholars are asking whether there is intentionality behind gaps of knowledge. Such gaps may be socially or politically motivated to maintain inertia around existing structures of privilege. For example, if I don't know much about the plight of incarcerated individuals, I will not necessarily feel compelled to tackle injustice in our criminal justice system. Empathizing with others can lead to a causal trajectory resulting in my compulsion, so I may avoid the whole thing by not learning about them – by avoiding empathy. The idiom "burying my head in the sand" is apropos of the relationship between knowledge and care. Empathy is an important linkage but it is fed by knowledge.

Conclusion: teaching empathetic care

How do we define moral education if we take the ideal of care driven by empathy seriously? In traditional approaches that treat ethics as a purely cognitive endeavor, teaching rules or rubrics of consequences and how to apply them in complex situations is the bulk of moral education. Although such education can be very enlightening and thought provoking, it avoids the hard work of exercising the empathy and inquiry skills needed for care. What care ethics suggests is that moral education should be more holistic and inclusive, and thus take inquiry and empathy skills into account. Once again, the work of Slote and Noddings is particularly useful because of their ongoing dialogue.

Slote draws upon the work of psychologist Martin Hoffman, who emphasizes the use of empathy induction as an important tool in a child's moral development. If a child hurts another child, the parent will encourage her to explore, by means of the imagination, how the actions affects the other child. "Induction in its earliest stages involves getting a child to recognize the harm he has caused *people he knows* (like a younger sibling or schoolmate) and teaching him to both put himself in their place and to be concerned about the harm his actions might cause them" (Slote 2007, 29). Here Slote ties empathy to imagination, indicating that the teaching moment is one that prompts the child to pause and make an effort at imaginative displacement. Moving from the personal to the societal, Slote then extends this kind of inductive experience to structured educational opportunities for students to make a foray into understanding unfamiliar others, as in, for example, exchange programs.

Noddings indicates that when it comes to moral education, she is somewhat persuaded by Slote, but she also maintains that there is more to caring than empathy. Noddings offers a four-part approach to moral education where empathy features only implicitly (2010b). For Noddings, moral education should consist of *modeling*, where the instructor demonstrates caring behavior, and presumably empathy; *dialogue*, where authentic speaking and listening takes place, which creates the foundation for empathy; *practice*, when the student is given the opportunity to inhabit caring behavior, a version of Slote's notion of induction; and *confirmation*, which Noddings describes as a positive version of induction where the student's motives are credited even if the actions are not morally praiseworthy (Noddings 2010b, 147–8). Noddings also notes that care and empathy are in a circular relationship whereby it is unclear which comes first: "An agent's act may invite our entry; results of which we approve may induce empathy for an agent we believe is responsible; or we may enter the empathic circle before the event as it were – our empathy has already been aroused" (2010b, 149). In summary, Slote suggests that induction in moral development and its extension to structured experiences are a means of developing the empathy needed for a care ethical approach. Noddings offers a comprehensive approach to fostering care in the classroom, which includes modeling, dialogue, practice, and confirmation, with empathy being developed through each element.

Philosopher Susan Verducci provides a novel approach to educating for empathy in the service of care ethics through drama. Verducci, a former student of Noddings, claims that it is possible to develop the kind of empathy needed for caring through learning the skills necessary for method acting. Recognizing the shortcomings of dramatic empathy versus authentic empathy, Verducci still finds sufficient skill development in theater exercises for efficacious ethical benefit: "With practice and guidance, one hopes that students will cultivate not only their capacity to empathise, but the habit of doing so. Ideally, students would develop a way of being in the world that centres on the connections between their own lived lives and those of others" (2000, 97). Specifically, Verducci claims that method acting can contribute to the development of empathy in at least four ways. First, actors engage in cognitive understanding through textual and contextual analysis (2000, 90–2). In other words, method actors do their homework and develop a deep understanding of the character through the dialogue and actions in the script, and by understanding the writer and time period. Context matters as much in the theater as it does in the development of empathy. A second contribution of acting is its emphasis on attention and attunement to the behavior of others (2000, 92–3). Actors use all of their faculties to communicate and as such must master nuances of human behavior. An effective care giver is able to capture information from the subtleties of human expression – an epistemic skill that supports empathy. A third benefit of acting skill is the emphasis on motivational shifts and substitutions (2000, 93–4). One of the major premises of method acting is that if the actor cannot find an authentic personal motivation for their portrayal, the audience will know and the acting will be ineffective. Empathy involves imaginatively understanding the other, which is a significant undertaking given that I can never be the other. Empathizing usually requires a foundation of commonality to realize at least a partial visceral understanding. Finally, Verducci describes method acting as engaging duality in a manner needed for empathetic care (2000, 94–5). Here, she is describing the experience of being both oneself and the one being portrayed at the same time. This is as true for acting as it is in empathy. I never cease being myself but if I try to empathize, I am endeavoring to feel with the other.

Verducci offers what some might consider a radical pedagogy for fostering empathy in service of care. However, care can be characterized as a radical departure from traditional ethical approaches. Care values emotions and context in a moral approach that resists formulaic moral responses. Relationships are central and thus empathy is indispensable. As such, a care ethical approach to moral education may indeed require new methods for promoting empathy in the context of ethical development (Hamington, 2015a).

References

Benhabib, Seyla. (1987) "The Generalized and the Concrete Other: The Kohlberg-Gilligan Controversy and Moral Theory" in Eva Feder Kittay & Diana T. Meyers, eds., *Women and Moral Theory*. Lanham, MD: Rowman and Littlefield.

Benner, Patricia, & Suzanne Gordon. (1996) "Caring Practice" in Suzanne Gordon, Patricia Benner, & Nel Noddings, eds., *Caregiving: Readings in Knowledge, Practice, Ethics, and Politics*. Philadelphia, PA: University of Pennsylvania Press.

Collins, Stephanie. (2015) *The Core of Care Ethics*. London: Palgrave Macmillan.

Engster, Daniel. (2007) *The Heart of Justice: Care Ethics and Political Theory*. New York: Oxford University Press.

Galinsky, Adam D., & Gordon B. Moskowitz. (2000) "Perspective-Taking: Decreasing Stereotype Expression, Stereotype Accessibility, and In-Group Favoritism." *Journal of Personality and Social Psychology* 78: 708–24.

Gilligan, Carol. (1983) *In A Different Voice: Psychological Theory And Women's Development*. Boston, MA: Harvard University Press.

Goralnik, Lissy, Matt Ferkany, Laurie Thorp, & Kyle Powys Whyte. (2014) "Philosophy in the Field: Care Ethics, Participatory Virtues, and Sustainability." *Resilience: A Journal of the Environmental Humanities* 1: 3.

Hamington, Maurice. (2004) *Embodied Care: Jane Addams, Maurice Merleau-Ponty and Feminist Ethics.* Champaign, IL: University of Illinois Press.

———— (2010) "The Will to Care: Performance, Expectation, and Imagination." *Hypatia* 25(3): 675–95.

———— (2015a) "Performing Care Ethics: Empathy, Acting, and Embodied Learning" in Julinna C. Oxley, ed., *Experiential Learning in Philosophy.* New York: Routledge.

———— (2015b) "Care Ethics and Confronting Intersectional Difference through the Body." *Critical Philosophy of Race* 3(1).

Hamington, Maurice, & Maureen Sander-Staudt, eds. (2011) *Applying Care Ethics to Business.* New York: Springer.

Hekman, Susan J. (1995) *Moral Voices, Moral Selves: Carol Gilligan and Feminist Moral Theory.* University Park, PA: Pennsylvania State University Press.

Held, Virginia. (2006) *The Ethics of Care: Personal, Political, and Global.* New York: Oxford University Press.

Jamison, Leslie. (2014) *The Empathy Exams.* Minneapolis, MN: Graywolf Press.

Mahon, Rianne, & Fiona Robinson, eds. (2012) *Feminist Ethics and Social Policy: Towards a New Global Political Economy of Care.* Vancouver: University of British Columbia Press.

Monchinski, Tony. (2010) *Education in Hope: Critical Pedagogies and the Ethic of Care.* New York: Peter Lang.

Noddings, Nel. (1984) *Caring: A Feminine Approach to Ethics and Moral Education.* Berkeley, CA: University of California Press.

———— (2002) *Starting At Home: Caring and Social Policy.* Berkeley, CA: University of California Press.

———— (2010a) *The Maternal Factor: Two Paths to Morality.* Berkeley, CA: University of California Press.

———— (2010b) "Moral Education and Caring." *Theory and Research in Education* 8(2): 145–51.

———— (2010c) "Complexity in Caring and Empathy." *Abstracta* 5: 6–12.

Petterson, Tove. (2008) *Comprehending Care: Problems and Possibilities in the Ethics of Care.* Lanham, MD: Lexington Books.

Skorinko, Jeanine L., & Stacey A. Sinclair (2013) "Perspective Taking Can Increase Stereotyping: The Role of Apparent Stereotype Confirmation." *Journal of Experimental Social Psychology* 49: 10–18.

Slote, Michael. (2007) *The Ethics of Care and Empathy.* New York: Routledge.

———— (2010a) *Moral Sentimentalism.* New York: Oxford University Press.

———— (2010b) "Reply to Noddings, Cottingham, Driver, and Baier." *Abstracta* 5: 42–61.

Smith, Adam. (2006) "Cognitive Empathy and Emotional Empathy in Human Behavior and Evolution." *The Psychological Record* 56: 3–21.

Todd, Andrew R., Adam D. Galinsky, & Galen V. Bodenhausen. (2012) "Perspective Taking Undermines Stereotype Maintenance Processes: Evidence from Social Memory, Behavior Explanation, and Information Solicitation." *Social Cognition* 30: 94–108.

Tronto, Joan. (1993) *Moral Boundaries: A Political Argument for an Ethic of Care.* New York: Routledge.

Tuana, Nancy. (1992) *Woman and the History of Philosophy.* New York: Paragon House.

Tuana, Nancy, & Shannon Sullivan. (2006) "Introduction: Feminist Epistemologies of Ignorance." *Hypatia* 21(3): vii–ix.

Verducci, Susan. (2000) "A Moral Method? Thoughts on Cultivating Empathy through Method Acting." *Journal of Moral Education* 29(1): 87–99.

24

EMPATHY AND
MEDICAL THERAPY

Per Nortvedt

Introduction

Human empathy makes it possible to understand another person's states of mind, and in particular (with relevance for medicine) patients' subjective experiences of illness and health. As pointed out elsewhere in this handbook, empathy represents a particular form of interpersonal understanding and embodies a basic sensitivity to the mindedness of other persons (Zahavi 2014, and Chapter 3 in this volume, "Phenomenology, empathy, and mindreading"). Empathy gives access to the experiences, thoughts, and emotions of other persons indirectly as well as directly: indirectly, as a form of social cognition in which one tries to understand the situation from the perspective of the other person by means of the imagination. This kind of cognitive empathy has many forms, from the imagining how it might be to be a starving and freezing child in a camp for Syrian refugees in Turkey, how it is for a patient to live with constant lumbar pain or to feel the relief of recovery from serious illness. Indirect or cognitive empathy epitomizes a deliberate and imaginative shift from self-knowledge to taking the perspective of the other person. Cognitive empathy might be enforced by shared vulnerabilities, by one's own experiences of loss, of being in pain or being hospitalized. Even though we cannot fully understand the minds of other persons, and the other is always *an other*, as humans we have shared vulnerabilities. Even when not having lived with chronic pain, all of us know and have experienced some kind of pain. We are all susceptible to loss, to disease and the same existential conditions of finitude and interpersonal dependency. This universal human condition of existential vulnerabilities is a genuine basis for empathy, and is a source of understanding the other person. And cognitive empathy, even though it is inferential and imaginative by nature, may evoke emotions of pain, anger, pity and compassion and make us affected by the weal and woe of others (Vetlesen 1994).

Secondly, as argued both by psychologists (Hoffman 2000) and phenomenologists (Zahavi 2014; and Chapter 14 in this volume, "Empathy and theories of direct perception"), empathy can also be primary affective, non-inferential, pre-reflective and based on experience. Hoffman argues that affective empathy is the "vicarious affective response to another person" and further that: "The key requirement of an empathic response according to my definition is *the involvement of psychological processes that make a person have feelings that are more congruent with another's situation than with his own situation*" (Hoffman 2000, 29–30). As illustrated by

Scheler (1913/2008), it is important to understand empathy as a form of shared intentional state; a direct grasp, emotionally and cognitively, of a particular situation and its significance for a person. When you perceive the worry on a person's face, you immediately perceive this as something of importance and in most circumstances empathy causes a concern for worrying about the other person. "The pained awareness" of another person's vulnerability and pain is inseparable from a certain grasp of the significance of this empathic experience. Scheler argues: "We certainly believe ourselves to be directly acquainted with another person's joy in his laughter, with his sorrow and pain in his tears, with his shame in his blushing, with his entreaty in his outstretched hands, with his love in his look and affection" (Scheler 2008, 260).

Theories of direct empathy argue that when you see a person in pain, you also immediately recognize this pain as some kind of suffering. You do not conclude that he is suffering from some kind of deductive inferential process of comparing his diagnosis with his mental status, the expression on his face etc. You can see his suffering as an immediate and spontaneous process of joint empathic, emotional-cognitive perception. Zahavi claims: "The state is experienced as actually present to me, thereby making the experience in question very different from, say, reasoning that the other is upset, because the letter she received has been torn up, or inferring that the other is drunk because he is surrounded by a dozen empty beer bottles, or concluding that the other must be furious if I had been subject to the same treatment as he has. I take all of the latter cases to be more indirect forms of social cognition, and to insist that my recognition of, say, the other's joy or fear in her facial expression is also indirect simply blurs important distinctions" (Zahavi 2011, 548).

As I will show in this chapter, all forms of empathy are significant for medical therapy, be they direct or indirect, cognitive or affective. Moreover, there is a prosocial and altruistic aspect of empathy that is not so much recognized by phenomenologists. Mostly, empathy is reduced to a morally neutral form of other-oriented understanding (Zahavi 2014). But as argued by Vetlesen (1994) and Hoffman (2000), empathy is not morally neutral. In particular, empathy represents a basic form of affectedness, or as Hoffman stresses, a distress evoked by the pain and suffering of others, which has strong moral connotations. To be empathically affected by the human vulnerability of others is fundamental for moral concern and hence a precondition for what many call sympathy. This chapter cannot give a full philosophical argument for the relationship between empathy and morality, but by means of clinical examples I will show how this is a view that has much merit with regard to medical practice. But first some remarks about empirical research on empathy in medicine.

Research on empathy in medicine

Empathy in medicine can be broadly defined as having a proper understanding of the patient's experiences and empathy encompassing cognitive, affective, behavioral, interpretive, and moral aspects (Pedersen 2010). An extensive survey on research on empathy in medicine showed that empathy was categorized as a joint affective and sensory response, as well as a cognitive way of understanding the experiences and minds of other persons (Pedersen 2010; Halpern 2001). In this research, a variety of paradigms are used, with some emphasizing empathic cognition, and others sensory/affective empathy. Most research on empathy in medicine has been quantitative in nature and has investigated the role of empathy in the clinical encounter, as well as in the education of medical students. With regard to medical education, many studies have focused on empathy decline and how empathy tends to decline during medical schooling and medical training (Eikeland et al. 2014). The studies show that medical students may develop some degree of cynicism in clinical practice, in the sense that they distance themselves from patients' emotions in situations where the patients present the doctor with their personal stories, worries, hopes and suffering. Here is what one student says:

> "There are some of the elderly patients [...] that ask if someone can cut their nails [...]. My idea of empathy is that that is something I could have done, [...] I changed the bedding for a patient who had vomited [...] then I was told, 'Then you should call the nurse because she's supposed to do that,' because we were seven people, we were supposed to interview [...] and I thought, 'Well, there's only two people talking. I can do this in the meantime'."
>
> *(Eikeland et al. 2014, 4)*

Instead of seeing their empathic emotions as sources of clinical knowledge and responding with sympathy, the students are corrected by their clinical supervisors and told to exhibit a higher degree of personal control and to hide their emotional reactions. The students generally struggle with finding a proper balance between their own emotions of personal care and keeping a proper emotional and personal distance from the patients' suffering and pain. Instead of seeing their empathy as sources of clinical knowledge and a part of their clinical responsibilities, they are concerned about being too affected. In their view, affective empathy in particular can reduce their professionalism. They favour detachment in the sense of not being too concerned with the vulnerability of their patients and not showing emotional concerns, but rather focusing strictly on the relevant biomedical information:

> "I also think that as a student you can become a bit cynical [...] when you have bed-side teaching [...] and you listen and you auscultate back No. 8, it is no longer humans [...] with names, but it's more back No. 8. So I think you can quickly become cynical if you are not aware. When you are sitting in the Emergency Department and hoping for an acute myocardial infarction and trauma [...], I think you can quickly become cynical."
>
> *(Eikeland et al. 2014, 5)*

Extensive reviews on empathy research in medicine and medical education also reveal that there has been a systematic neglect of seeing empathic emotion as intrinsically related features of empathic interpretation and understanding (Pedersen 2010). Literature reviews state that: "Cognitive and emotional aspects are involved in most or all understanding, however, to various degrees, and it is generally very difficult to know when or if only cognitive aspects are involved" (2010, 98). As a basis for a comprehensive systematic investigation of literature and research on empathy in medicine, Pedersen argues that affective empathy will always involve some kind of interpretation, for instance that the pain of the patient represents some instances of suffering (2010).

Empathy and medical care

The rest of this chapter will show how empathy in important ways is essential for good medical care and therapy. Empathy is clinically important in several ways. First, empathy is important for displaying the authentic attitudes of care and concern that are crucial in the relational encounter with patients and relatives. Hence, there is a virtue-theoretical part of medical care in which empathy plays a formative role in clinical competence.

Secondly, empathy plays a significant epistemological role in clinical therapy and observation. Jodie Halpern discusses the role of gut feelings as part of empathy and quotes the psychoanalyst Michael Basch, arguing that "gut feelings are a necessary basis for social recognition of others' emotional states, including the kind of recognition needed for empathy" (Halpern 2001, 48). The empathic physician may additionally profit from increased diagnostic accuracy, more meaningful work, an increased sense of wellbeing, and reduced symptoms of burnout. I will argue that empathic gut feelings are cues of great clinical significance, because they alert the clinician to alterations in the patient's clinical condition, and these are alterations that are both biomedically and morally important (Nortvedt 2008; Oernes 2016).

Finally, empathy is a precondition for making medical therapy morally significant. Empathy is constitutive for the interpersonal and relational morality that is so essential to medical therapy. Medicine is not about treating persons solely as objects, as if their bodies were just biological material, devoid of subjectivity. Medicine is crucially about treating disease and illness for the human good and for the health of the human being. In doing so, attending to and understanding the subjective experiences of patients are crucial. And in low-level empathy (see Chapter 14, "Empathy and theories of direct perception"), affective empathy represents a fundamental emotional affectedness that alerts attention to the weal and woe of other persons. It is therefore morally significant.

Empathic perception moral attitudes in medicine

In the *Nichomachean Ethics*, Aristotle famously argues that the virtue of *phronesis* is not only doing the right thing towards the right person at the right time, but also acting with the right attitude, i.e. acting in the right manner (Aristotle, NE 1106 b, 15–25). And Nancy Sherman in a chapter on emotions in Kantian morality argues that

> [e]ven if action is to have a predominant role in moral theory, the emotional tone of one's action may make a moral difference. Action that is unfeeling may simply not be received in the same way as action conveyed through more gentle care.
>
> *(Sherman 1990, 150)*

It is apparent that empathy is crucial for acting towards the patient *in the right way, at the right time and with the right attitude*. The main reason for this is that empathy is crucial for understanding what is at stake for the patient, and for seeing what is morally relevant (Vetlesen 1994). Empathy makes us aware of how to act in ways that take into consideration a given patient's particular vulnerability. Just imagine a patient with cancer, who is in great psychological distress and very anxious before surgery. A good doctor must be attentive, and he or she must decide about the right time to inform the patient fully of the prognosis, and must do so with the appropriate emotional tone and compassion. To employ Sherman's phrasing, both cognitive and affective empathy contribute to behaving in the right way and with the proper attitude.

Acting with proper attitude and empathy is particularly important in order to counter the objectification of medical therapy. One important precondition for medical therapy is that persons are objectified. Doctors are trained in diagnostic labeling, in focusing on the disease rather than the subjectivity of the sick person. Grodin argues: "For example, though a surgery to amputate a gangrenous limb is a healing act, it involves cutting and maiming of the human body, which under nonmedical circumstances would be an act of harm and criminality" (Grodin 2010, 59). Detached concern is crucial in many cases of medical therapy, but emotional detachment can also blur medical vision and make the doctor incapable of seeing what is personally at stake for the patient. Therefore, empathy is so crucial for medical therapy.

Here is one example:

> A young medical student in the mid-term of her medical training is accompanying twelve students and their teacher on a round in the ward. They visit a young man, a refugee from the war in Bosnia in the 1990s. He is seriously ill with cancer and the doctor teaches the students about CT scans and how to examine the abdomen, which is full of ascites – the patient has all signs of serious liver failure. After the students have examined the patients they all leave the room, while one student hesitates in the door and returns to the patient. He seemed so lonely and afraid, alone in a foreign country waiting to die. She felt pity for him, she saw his misery, she empathized with him and she went to talk with him.
>
> *(Martinsen 2003)*

In this case, empathy alerts the student, and makes her a responsible and caring physician. Empathy focuses attention upon the personal and subjective experiences of the sick person. In this case it is exemplified by the person from Bosnia enduring his illness as a refugee in a far-off country.

Empathy shapes *how one cares*, in expressing friendliness, behaving carefully, and minimizing pain and suffering as part of medical treatment and therapy (see also Chapter 23, "Empathy and care ethics"). This is very important because many of the procedures and therapies of medical care, as well as prognostic medical information, are potentially technical, impersonal, and painful. It is easy to imagine how medical injections and manipulations of limbs that are broken can hurt. Also manipulations and mobilizations of the body stricken with cancer can be extremely painful.

Empathy creates awareness about how it is for a person to endure painful therapies and procedures. But this attentiveness to the subjectivity of the other person must also in general be manifested by authentic attitudes of concern for the patient as a person. A person displaying empathic understanding and emotion usually and naturally displays attitudes of friendliness and compassion as part of his or her attention to a patient and/or his family, for instance. In clinical practice there is usually a neat connection, I think, between understanding the impact of the illness on the patient, his feeling, his behavior and his relationships, feeling concern for him, and the reality of this felt concern and empathy being displayed in the attitudes with which we meet the patient. For the most part, empathy is expressed in the phenomenology of the body, in the gestures, in the look and in the handshake of the medical clinician. Empathy humanizes therapy and creates atmospheres of consolation and trust. Empathic understanding is a concerned understanding, expressed in the attitudes of the clinical doctor towards the patient.

In professional care it is also important to balance personal feelings of empathic concern with an emotional distance that must fit professional and competent therapy. As has been explicitly recognized in literature on empathy, there can be too much empathy (Hoffman 2000). The emotional strain of empathic distress and identification can be overwhelming in situations of great trauma, in accidents and in situations involving the death of children. Clinical and professional empathy, even if it involves spontaneous perception and care, must always incorporate a proper emotional distance. In situations that can create great empathic distress, and when giving prognostic information that can be devastating such as when tragic accidents happen, a certain control over one's emotions is necessary. Empathy has to be balanced to express authentic attitudes of care as well as adjusting the personal expressions of the clinician to the situational constraints of clinical therapy.

Empathy and clinical therapy

From what has been outlined so far, there are several ways in which empathy is central to clinical therapy in medicine. For good clinical therapy, it is essential to understand the experiences of the patient suffering from illness. Empathy is a capacity of understanding and identifying with the subjectivity of other persons. Empathy gives the medical clinician important access to the subjectivity of the patient, that is to see and understand personal experiences of illness, of anxiousness, pleasure, relief and mourning (Nortvedt 2008).

Clinical care is continuously animated by signals and cues of bodies in pain, faces in strain, muscles in tension or bleeding vessels. These facts of pathology have a bearing on empathic perception. Clinical empathy is epistemologically significant. It reveals information that is important for successful therapy. Jodie Halpern has done much to illuminate this epistemological role of empathy with regard to psychiatric care (Halpern 2001).

My background in intensive care medicine and anaesthesiology shows many similar examples of empathy contributing to more fully fledged clinical knowledge. For instance, an unconscious patient, for example a child, may show different signs of stress, which can be manifested in bodily cues. It can be a slight change in the respiratory pattern, redness in the upper part of the thorax or on the patient's neck. These clinical signs are easier to see for the empathic clinician; they alert him or her and are of great clinical concern. In clinical medicine, empathy does not only make us understand and be aware of the moods of persons, but also of gestures, bodily changes and visceral signs. Cognitive empathy will be important in understanding clinical cues in the larger medical context of diagnosing, labeling and prognosticating, while affective empathy initiates the first awareness of clinical alterations. Empathy with the patient in a particular situation has two important bearings upon medical therapy. It alerts and fine tunes clinical observation by raising awareness of alterations in the clinical condition. Secondly, a clinician who is empathically concerned is also motivated to conduct further clinical examinations. In somatic health care, we see that affective empathy is the motivational force behind spontaneous manifestations of care, and in seeing that the patient needs comfort care and kindness. In clinical therapy, empathy enforces clinical observation, sensitizes the clinicians to signs of stress, discomfort, etc. The focus in the phenomenological tradition on direct empathic and social perception also encapsulates central features of clinical and medical perception. For instance, when a physician examines a painful abdomen, he or she directly sees, feels and understands significant aspects of the patient's condition, such as the severity of the clinical situation, as well as the suffering and anxiousness of the patient. This kind of empathic perception is important in order to supplement a clinical reflection and deliberation that paradigmatically is very biomedically oriented.

Clinical empathy is both epistemologically and morally significant. It is epistemologically important because it reveals and saturates clinical knowledge and observation. It is morally important because it shapes the authentic attitudes of being personal in professional settings, of showing personal concern within a context of medical care. Finally, empathy structures and informs moral perception, i.e. perception of the morally relevant features that are pertinent in clinical situations of medical care. Here is another example where an empathic attitude helps us see what one would not see otherwise. Parents of a seriously ill child have now stayed at their child's bed for several days. When you meet them this morning you immediately recognize their strained and worried faces. You tell them that they have to go and sleep for a while and that their child is in safe hands under professional care. You also ask if they want to see the doctor for more information. I think empathy makes one see and be alert to the agony of the parents and the moral significance of their experience.

The morality of empathy

Particularly in clinical empathy, there is a neat connection between empathy and care, between empathic perception and concern for another person's wellbeing. This empathic concern is often called sympathy, while empathy is taken to be a morally neutral way of understanding the minds and experiences of other persons (Zahavi 2014). However, I will argue that this narrowing of empathy to merely a way of understanding and reacting upon the distress and suffering of a person ignores the normative dimension of empathy. Empathy is not merely a neutral way of identifying with and understanding another person's pain and suffering. Empathy must also be understood in a normative context of the kind that American philosopher Thomas Nagel calls altruistic reasons. Nagel does not discuss empathy but importantly he argues that "[s]ympathy is not, in general, just a feeling of discomfort produced by the recognition of distress in others, which in turn motivates one to relieve their distress. Rather it is the pained awareness of their distress as *something to be relieved*" (Nagel 1978, 80).

In my view, this paraphrase by Nagel touches on a central nerve in the understanding of empathy in medicine and in medical therapy. Principally, empathy is an awareness of another person's condition as a condition in which to partake and to care about. Empathy is about interpersonal identification and the sharing of human experiences. Empathy is an emotional faculty that gives us as humans and clinicians an access to the moral domain understood as the weal and woe of other persons (Vetlesen 1994). This is also the principal hermeneutical insight that Jodie Halpern emphasizes in her book on empathy in medicine (Halpern 2001). Empathy in medicine is central because it humanizes the clinical encounter, it informs clinical observation and invites the clinician to notice more than the pure manifestations of pathology and disease (Nortvedt 2008). It situates clinical observation within a normative context. Just imagine the spontaneous and concerned worry in a physician confronted with the anxiousness of his patient before a difficult surgery. Or the concern evoked in a nurse perceiving an evolving infection and pain in a serious injury.

These assertions can be grounded. Affective empathy is morally significant because there is a spontaneous feeling of discomfort when perceiving the pain and suffering of another person. The primary affectedness caused by affective empathy may be a source of concern and compassion, and in many cases motivates and results in caring for the person's wellbeing. Hoffman describes affective empathy as a rudimentary distress caused by seeing the distress of another person, and that empathic distress is an important source of prosocial action and moral responsible behavior. But cognitive empathy can also invoke human sympathy and emotions of pity and concern. Thus we can say that both affective and cognitive empathy may serve as a precondition for moral concern. The question is how to explain the sources of normativity in empathy altogether.

Cognitive empathy can be a morally neutral way of understanding the mindedness of another person. The most prominent example is that even a torturer must have access to the minds of the victim, of understanding his or her responses, of accessing the consequences of the pain inflicted, so as to reach the aim of the torture, for instance getting the relevant information. Affective empathy, on the other hand, as a distress evoked by the pain of another, is a situational, sensory, and direct response that makes a person vulnerable to the vulnerability of another person. There is an immediate disturbance, like the kind that Martha Nussbaum describes as a "tug in the stomach" when she hears about the death of her mother (Nussbaum 2001). In clinical situations it could be a concerned worry caused by seeing the anxiousness in the patients' eyes before surgery. But how can this disturbance caused by another person's worry be understood as a normative incident? Why is it not just a sheer disturbance? Why does the perception of a person being anxious evoke a concerned worry for the person's wellbeing? It is a fact that the discomfort caused by seeing the agony and pain of another person could just as well cause aversion, making one run away instead of helping (Korsgaard 1996). Empathic overarousal (Hoffman 2000) may cause severe personal distress that may cause actions contrary to helping behavior. And it is a similar fact that simply understanding the vulnerable situation of a person may cause no moral concern. So, what is it in the empathic arousal that motivates a person morally, that motivates caring for the other person? What is "the pained awareness of another's situation" as a reason to help him or her (Nagel 1978)? How may empathy be envisioned as giving humans an access to morality understood as care and concern for another person?

To argue that empathy has a direct moral connotation means to address the question about the origin of moral reasons itself. Nagel explains altruistic motivation as a reason for helping endorsed by rational justification and role taking. And rationality can explain and justify the empathic reasons that we can all share as universal reasons for acting within a community of rational equals. But I find it hard to see that rational and cognitive endorsement of shared values can fully explain the fact of moral motivation, i.e. why the pained awareness of another person's situation works as a spontaneous reason to help, and not just to run away. Rational endorsement of reasons can explain the justification of moral reasons, but not the origin of these reasons as moral reasons. Even Kant at the end of the *Groundwork* acknowledged the incomprehensibility of the moral law, that the origin of the Good Will is a mystery, when he states: "And this, while we do not comprehend the practical unconditioned necessity of the moral imperative, we do comprehend *its incomprehensibility*" (Kant 2012 131).

However, there are other ways of establishing arguments for the normativity of empathic perception than the ones given by Kantian constructivism. It can be argued that empathic perception is a perception of moral realities, a perception of moral properties, properties that have moral value in their own right. Empathy would thus be an important faculty in revealing the moral realities of a particular situation. Moral realists argue that values, and in particular moral values, are part of the fabric and furniture of reality in the same way as a thing, a chair, or a tree is (McNaughton 1988). Moral realism would hold that moral values exist as properties independent of subjective perception, that they are not a function of subjective projection, but that they are properties of real things in the world. For instance, a moral realist would argue that to see pain is to see it as irreducibly normative, as it were, as something bad. This means that the normativity of pain is not merely a function of rational endorsement, as some Kantians seem to argue (Korsgaard 1996). "The painfulness of pain" is not merely a perception of a reason, e.g. a reason to remove that pain, as Korsgaard argues. According to moral realism, the painfulness and hence the moral magnitude of pain as suffering is a property of the pain independent of how the individual person evaluates the significance of the pain *for him or her*. Pain is not merely a moral problem in so far as it is a problem for the patient. Pain is crucially something that is communicated to the world as expressions of painfulness, and this moral reality of the painfulness of pain is perceptually available for persons caring for the one who is in pain and for those seeing that a person whom they know is in pain (Nortvedt 2012). The normative significance of pain is expressed to the world as a moral call, and the normativity of this call is not exhausted by a person's evaluation of the meaning of the pain for him or her. It is still a moral reality and a moral reality which is accessible for perceptual empathy.

So, certain intuitions in clinical medicine, such as the imperative to care for a person suffering, are due to the fact that they represent not merely clinical realities, but also moral realities, evincing a certain moral pull. Such clinical moral realities show up in the experience of the clinician, and they are manifested in the phenomenology of the sick body, in signs of pathology and in pain and suffering. This assessment of the moral dimensions of empathy needs further philosophical grounding than that given by me here. It is, however, important to note that without empathy, one will be numbed; one will not see another person's suffering as something to care about (see also Chapter 19, "Empathy and moral judgment"). In this sense, empathy is the basic condition for sympathy and care (Vetlesen 1994). But the moral metaphysics of empathy, why empathy is a genuine source of normativity, is a larger philosophical question which might have several possible answers: Kantian ones, realist and subjectivist ones, as well as phenomenological and metaphysical ones. Maybe a theory of reasons can give an answer to these questions about the sources of normativity, as Nagel tries to flesh out in his recent book *Mind and Cosmos* (Nagel 2012), but I am not sure. There he argues that "[t]he most conspicuous consequence of realism would be that human beings are able not to detect but to be motivated by value. In the case of basic experiential values such as the goodness of pleasure and the badness of pain, an instinctive motivation is built into the experience itself: The desire that it continue is part of the pleasure and the desire that it stop is part of the pain" (Nagel 2012, 112). It is a further challenge for empathy- and care-based moral theories to give a more extensive account of normativity that can reconcile the intuitions of emotion and experience with the reason-generating force of critical moral reflection.

Conclusion

Empathy is crucial for medical treatment in several ways. First, empathy is essential for identifying with and understanding the experiences of illness and disease. Hence, it is central to holding on to the subjective and personal dimension of biomedical science and practice, as distinct from the impersonal and objective view of the mechanisms of disease and human functioning. This is important, since disease and loss of health is always also deeply personal, experiential, and normative in nature (see also Chapter 17, "Empathy and psychiatric illness"). Second, empathy is crucial in moral perception and clinical observation, as it makes it possible to reveal the normative significance of clinical cues and alterations in bodily and human functioning. Finally, empathy in medical therapy shapes the attitudes of human concern that is necessary to perform medical therapy in a way that is good and compassionate.

References

Aristotle (1985) *Nicomachean Ethics*, Indiana: Hackett Publishing Company.
Eikeland, H., Oernes, K., Finseth, A. and Pedersen P. (2014) The physician's role and empathy: a qualitative study of third year medical students, *BMC Medical Education*, 14: 165.
Grodin, M. (2010) Mad, bad, or evil: how physician healers turn to torture and murder, in *Medicine after Holocaust*, S. Rubenfeldt (ed.), New York: Palgrave Macmillan, pp. 49–67.
Halpern, J. (2001) *From Detached Concern to Empathy: Humanizing Medical Practice*, Oxford: Oxford University Press.
Hoffman, M. L. (2000) *Empathy and Moral Development: Implications for Caring and Justice*, Cambridge: Cambridge University Press.
Kant, I. (2012) *Groundwork for the Metaphysics of Morals*, Cambridge: Cambridge University Press.
Korsgaard, C. (1996) *The Sources of Normativity*, Harvard: Harvard University Press.
MacNaughton (1988) *Moral Vision: An Introduction to Ethics*, Malden, MA: Blackwell.
Martinsen, E. H. (2000) Å la seg følelsesmessige berøre i medisinstudiet (To be emotionally affected during the study of medicine), *The Journal of the Norwegian Medical Association*, 120(3): 374–6.
Nagel, T. (1978) *The Possibility of Altruism*, Oxford: Oxford University Press.
Nagel, T. (2012) *Mind and Cosmos: Why the Materialist Neo-Darwinian Conception of Nature Is Almost Certainly False*, Oxford: Oxford University Press.
Nortvedt P. (2008) Sensibility and clinical understanding, *Medicine, Health Care and Philosophy*, 11: 209–19.

Nortvedt, P. (2012) The normativity of clinical health care: perspectives on moral realism, *Journal of Medicine and Philosophy*, 37(3): 295–310.

Nussbaum, M. (2001) *Upheavals of Thought: The Intelligence of Emotions*, Cambridge: Cambridge University Press.

Pedersen, R. (2010) *Empathy in Medicine: A Philosophical Hermeneutic Reflection*, Oslo: University of Oslo.

Scheler, M. (1913/2008) *On the Nature of Sympathy*, London: Transaction Publishers.

Sherman, N. (1990) The place of emotions in Kantian morality, in *Identity, Character and Morality*, Flanagan, O. and Rorty, A.O. (eds.), Cambridge, MA: MIT Press, pp. 149–73.

Vetlesen, A. J. (1994) *Perception Empathy and Judgment: An Inquiry into the Preconditions of Moral Performance*, University Park, PA: Penn State University Press.

Zahavi, D. (2011) Empathy and direct social perception: a phenomenological proposal, *Review of Philosophy and Psychology*, 2: 541–58.

Zahavi, D. (2014) *Self and Other: Exploring Subjectivity, Empathy and Shame*, Oxford: Oxford University Press.

Further reading

Doris J. M. (2010) *The Moral Psychology Handbook*, Oxford: Oxford University Press.

PART V

Empathy in art and aesthetics

25

EMPATHY AND PAINTING

Noël Carroll

Introduction

Discussing the relationship of empathy to painting is complicated because of the ambiguity of one of its central terms, namely "empathy" (Carroll, 2012; Wispé, 1987). For some philosophers, empathy and sympathy are distinct. "Empathy" means "feeling as the other feels because he/she feels that way." Sympathy, on the other hand, does not necessarily require emotionally feeling anything at all, but does involve a pro-attitude toward the object of one's concern, a disposition to help or, at least, to wish that the plight of the other be alleviated.

But ordinary language is not so tidy. The cliché "I feel your pain" (when used non-ironically) sounds like the very epitome of empathy, yet, when used sincerely, it typically connotes the speaker's desire that the pain be palliated. In other words, it is an expression of sympathy.

Moreover, the imprecision of the laity is often echoed by the experts, including psychologists who frequently run empathy and sympathy together. Of course, empathy and sympathy may occur in tandem. Indeed, it is frequently thought, especially by aestheticians arguing in defense of the value of art, that empathy is a prelude to sympathy. Walk in another's shoes and one will be disposed to feel *for* him/her, not merely only *with* him/her. Empathy, it is thought, will engender at least tolerance. Nevertheless, even if that occurs sometimes or even regularly, empathy and sympathy can be distinguished conceptually, as illustrated by the possibility of the sadistic empath who uses his/her ability to discern what the other fears and to feel his/her pain in order to torture the victim ever so more effectively.

So far I have discussed empathy solely in terms of feeling. But there is no consensus even here among commentators. From some perspectives, empathy only requires mutual understanding. That is, empathy could be a cognitive affair, transpiring affectlessly.

Nor need empathy be construed as only a relationship between persons or even sentient creatures. The term was originally coined to describe a phenomenon putatively experienced through inanimate objects, like art works (Wispé 1987; Currie, 2011). "Empathy," in this usage, was a matter of "feeling *into*," as one was said to feel the pressure of gravity in the tension in one's own muscles while gazing upon the bulge in the columns supporting the roof of a temple. In such cases, empathy could not involve sharing feelings, since the columns felt nothing. Rather, the phenomenon might be more accurately described as projection.

Given the lack of agreement about the scope of empathy, we must tread gingerly, gradually assembling a concept of empathy that seems helpful in characterizing at least some of our relationships with painting.

In order to approach this problem, I will begin with what I think is clearly a false conception of empathy – namely, *empathy-as-identification* – in the hope that by noting its shortcomings critically, we will be on our way to a more applicable notion of empathy in regard to the case of painting.

(Unless indicated otherwise, it will be presupposed that *empathy* is a relation involving *emotional* feelings between human beings or, at least, animals and aliens that have been anthropomorphized.)

Empathy-as-identification

Perhaps the most common idea of empathy rests on the notion of *identification*, as evidenced by my students with numbing, albeit unreflective, regularity. On this view, to empathize with another person or anthropomorph, whether actual or fictional, is to feel like that person. Here "like," I take it, means "just like" or "exactly like." That is why the process is called "identification" – because it involves identity, namely, identity in feeling states.

But even this is not strong enough to capture the phenomenon of empathy. Consider, for instance, *The Deposition* by Gerard David (1515). It is a picture of Jesus Christ being lowered from the cross. A woman off to the right wipes away a tear. The faces of all the members of the assembled group are somber. They are sad. Suppose that we are sad, even sad in the same way, if we are fervent Christians. Is this a case of empathy conceived in terms of identification?

No. And the reason is that we are not sad *because* the disciples of Christ are sad. That is not the source of our sadness. Rather we are sad, if we are sad, for the same reasons that his disciples are sad – because this good man has suffered and died a horrible death. Likewise when we view Correggio's *Assumption of the Virgin* (1530), we are not joyous because the onlooking angels are beaming with exultation. We are joyous, as they are joyous, by witnessing the Blessed Virgin Mary speeding upwards toward heaven, swathed in a golden light that raises our spirits.

What both these examples show, then, is that empathy-as-identification requires not only shared feelings, but that the feelings in the viewer be caused by the objects of his/her attention – in the preceding examples, the onlookers to Christ's Deposition and Mary's Assumption respectively – having exactly those self-same feelings. This is not the case in the two works just canvassed. Rather, they are cases of what we might call coincident feeling states. We feel as the characters feel because we are responding comparably to the same stimulus to which the characters in the pictures are reacting. They gaze upon the dead body of Christ and are sad; we do likewise and feel sorrow. But our sorrow is *for* Christ, just as our joy has Mary's apotheosis as its source, not the feelings of the ebullient seraphim.

In both cases, the situation is analogous to the members of a sporting team who are cheering their side onward as it heads toward victory. Each member of the crowd is cheering for the success of their guys. They are not thrilled because their athletic heroes are feeling thrilled nor because other members of the crowd are thrilled. They all are coincidently thrilled in response to the same state of affairs, the prospect of their team's victory.

Of course, there are undoubtedly cases where we viewers are moved in the way in which we are moved because of the feeling states of the figures in paintings. In response to Titian's *The Flaying of Marsyas* (1570–8), the viewer is undoubtedly moved by the satyr's unhappy predicament. And yet this case reveals another inadequacy with the notion of *empathy* at hand. For empathy-as-identification requires not only that the empath's feeling be caused by its subject but that his/her feeling be *identical* to the object of his/her attention. Yet it is improbable that the viewer of Titian's masterpiece can be feeling what Marsyas is feeling.

This is clearly obvious with respect to pain. No normal human could be literally feeling the pain of being flayed by gazing upon Titian's Marsyas. Even in everyday life, it is unlikely that we undergo exactly the *same* pain when, for example, we see someone cut her finger or scrape his knee when falling (see Chapter 2, "Affective empathy"). We may experience a twinge in the same vicinity of the wounded subject's body, but it will be no way as intense, nor will it even duplicate the exact sensations of those whose agony we witness. As we scrutinize the plight of Marsyas, we may feel something, perhaps a slight tremor or chill. But it will be nothing (exactly) like the pain that Marsyas is suffering. Could we even imagine what the sensation of being flayed alive feels like precisely? (See Chapter 16, "Empathy and imagination.")

Of course, in discussions of empathy, the reference to *feelings* most often refers to *emotions* rather than to bare sensations. Presumably, Marsyas' situation calls up an emotional response in us, one caused in part by Marsyas' own affective reactions to his situation. His countenance, with its downturned mouth, signals, as one might expect of anyone in his condition, an extremely high degree of unhappiness. But we do not experience the same emotions that Marsyas does. He probably feels remorse over having incurred Apollo's ire. However, we have no cause to be remorseful.

Marsyas' distress may cause us to feel sorrow for him, but we are not sorrowful for having incited the wrath of Apollo. We are not feeling remorse. We are sorry for Marsyas' imprudence in angering the god. Perhaps we even feel some indignation. The punishment seems too excessive for the "crime."

Marsyas is feeling regret. We are feeling sorrow. The object of Marsyas' regret is his recklessness in entering a contest with the god. The object of our sorrow is the torture that Marsyas is suffering. Marsyas' feelings of remorse may contribute to our sorrow for him, since his remorse adds psychological misery to his physical ordeal; but our sorrow is a qualitatively different emotional state. Indeed, contributing to our sorrow for Marsyas may be some quotient of disgust in response to the gruesome manner in which he is being punished. But Marsyas is not feeling disgust. Thus, we are not empathizing with Marsyas in the strong sense of empathy-as-exact-identification.

Empathy-as-vectorially-converging-emotions (Carroll 2012)

Typically our emotional states in relation to depicted persons in paintings cannot be a matter of identification because the viewers' emotional states take different objects and/or targets than do the states of the depicted characters. In Goya's *The Third of May, 1808* (1814–15), a representation of a firing squad executing a group of rebels, the prisoner in the white shirt and those next to him evince fear, while the onlookers, probably the friends and family of the prisoners, weep. But we viewers are neither afraid – the soldiers cannot pose a threat to us – nor are we grieving for the loss of sons and lovers. Rather we feel moral indignation. The fear of the doomed prisoners and the sorrow of the townsfolk contribute, along with the atrocity of the execution, to the viewer's righteous anger. Thus, that anger, in part, is caused by the emotions of the depicted persons. But our emotions are not the same – not identical.

Nevertheless, there is a certain degree of similitude between what the characters can be imagined to feel and what the viewer is likely to feel: namely, they are of a similar or converging valence. That is, if the emotions can be mapped as falling between the poles of euphoria and dysphoria, the emotions of the depicted characters, on the one hand, and the viewers, on the other hand, that are engendered by the Goya painting all fall on the dysphoric side of the mapping.

Thus, though the empathy-as-identification approach is false, it can be amended by something like it by replacing the notion of the sharing of type-identical emotions with that of vectorially converging emotions. Empathy on this new account, then, is a matter of the viewer and the subject possessing similar or (somewhat) like emotions – in the sense of vectorially converging emotions – where the viewer's emotion is caused, at least in part, by the subject or subjects having the emotions they have.

In the Goya painting, both the relevant characters and the viewers are in distress. Their emotions are all plotted on the dysphoric tending portion of the emotion chart. But they are different types of dysphoria, while, albeit, trending in the same direction. Call this notion of empathy *empathy-as-vectorially-converging-emotions*. Moreover, this characterization seems to be the most useful conception of empathy when it comes to the art of painting, since it would appear to cover the largest number of cases unproblematically.

Thus, in Fra Angelico's *Annunciation* (1450), the Virgin Mary is happy because she is being told that she will conceive Jesus Christ. We are pleased as well. We are pleased because Mary is pleased, but our euphoria is not exactly hers, since our emotion has a different object/target. We are not with child, let alone divine child. Consequently, that is neither the target nor the object of our happiness. Rather our joy converges on hers on the bright side of the chart of euphoric/dyphoric emotions.

Moreover, this, it seems to me, is the usual case, since the depicted characters will typically have a given object and/or target of their emotional state, whereas viewers will have as the distinctive object/target of their emotional state the character or characters who are focused upon a different, albeit related, set of circumstances.

Emotional contagion

A phenomenon not mentioned thus far but which might be thought relevant to a discussion of the relation of empathy to painting is what has been called *emotional contagion* (Hatfield et al., 1994). This is a phrase with which I am not altogether happy, since it often applies to states that I think are not always categorized properly as emotions, such as certain reflex responses. However, I will use the label "emotional contagion" since it has become the standard way of referring to the phenomenon.

A familiar, everyday manifestation of emotional contagion occurs when a friend is beset by the giggles, perhaps at an inappropriate moment, and his/her mirth disposes you toward levity as well. Each of you attempts to suppress the chuckling, but just seeing your friend struggling to avoid a smile makes it all the more likely that you both will burst out laughing. It is as if your friend's amusement has infected you. You have caught his/her whimsy.

Television producers began to exploit this phenomenon as early as the 1950s. Realizing how the response to comedies in movie theaters was enhanced by the fact that the laughter was magnified by being seen by audiences of many members who stoked each other's amusement, TV producers added laugh tracks to their programs so that lonely home viewers would be inspired – infected, so to say – by the off-screen, canned laughter.

Or, for another example: often the sight of another weeping makes us cry, or, at least, accentuates our tendency to do so, as when we attend the funerals of distant relatives or mere acquaintances. We cry because his loved ones cry. Humans are mimetic creatures. Among other things, we imitate the emotional states of our conspecifics. Moreover, this often does not occur consciously. With conspicuous regularity, we seem to automatically take on the emotions of others. They may grip us unbidden and sometimes even unwanted, like a contagious illness.

As already suggested in the preceding paragraph, key to this sort of emotional contagion has to do with the human proclivity to imitate. When walking down the corridor with a colleague, we often fall into step with his/her pace. When he/she stands tall, we mirror his/her posture. When conversing with friends, as they lean in, so do we. In addition, we tend to ape the cadence of the voice and even to adopt the facial expressions of our dialogical partners. When they smile, we do. When they frown, we do likewise. In short, we tend to mirror the bodily behaviors of the people with whom we interact. Furthermore, we do this automatically, by reflex.

We may label this kind of behavior the *mirror reflex*, which may be (and I stress *may be*) based in the mirror neuron circuitry in the brain. Moreover, our mirror reflexes are connected to affective states inasmuch as our bodily configurations, especially our facial displays (Ekman, 1983, 2003), stimulate our autonomic nervous system with feedback, thereby giving us an inward glimmering of that which our conspecifics are feeling. This information about what others are feeling, needless to say, may supply us with clues about what they intend and how they are likely to act.

The phenomenon of emotional contagion seems likely to contribute to our empathetic response to paintings. This is perhaps most obvious with respect to the genre of portraiture, where we are invited to contemplate the visage of the sitter not only to assess its likeness to its subject, where there is a living subject, but also in order to intuit something of his/her inner state. In many portraits, emphasis is virtually exclusively on the face of the subject. We study it intently for some sign of what the sitter is feeling. As with our friends and neighbors in daily life, our facial muscles may contort subliminally in imitation of the subject of the painting.

In Anthony van Dyck's *Self-Portrait* (c.1615–17), we catch a sense of the youthful van Dyck's wariness as he glances off to the left side of the painting. As we inspect the portrait, we are apt to move our own eyes leftward, if only slightly, and faintly feel an accompanying tincture or even pale shudder of an unnamed, if merely fleeting, anxiety.

Likewise, viewing Hans Holbein's *Sir Thomas More* (1527), we can ape the downward pressure of his visage, starting with his forehead, feeling something of the intense seriousness of this man, his almost muscular powers of concentration.

Although the face undoubtedly is the key element of affective communication in portraiture, it is often supplemented by the posture of the subject. In Joshua Reynolds's *General John Burgoyne* (1766), the calm, steady look on the general's face already suggests his degree of self-satisfaction, but the left hand planted firmly on his hip and his assured grasp of his sword in his right hand confirm the feeling of pride, almost arrogance, that emanates from him, something that we can begin to feel in our own muscles as we are prompted to dispose them comparably.

Here it is important to point out that the phenomenon of mirror reflexing in these cases should not be mistaken for empathy proper, although mirror reflexing may be connected to empathy. Empathy cannot be reduced to mirror reflexes, pure and simple, because the mirror reflexes here are not emotions-in-full inasmuch as they do not provide us with the objects to which these responses are being directed. Consequently, they do not supply us with the kind of action-guiding, affective appraisals of the relevant targets of the states in questions as do emotions-in-full. They convey broad phenomenological insight into what our conspecifics are feeling qualitatively, but they do not tell us what emotional stance to mobilize in response to them. Should we be suspicious of van Dyck's wariness? Is he up to no good? Or should we feel paternally toward a bashful youth? Should we feel contempt or admiration for General Burgoyne? Does the object of Sir Thomas Moore's gaze warrant its intensity?

Mirror reflexes give us part of the information that we may need to marshal an emotional response to a state of affairs, depicted or otherwise. Specifically, they may impart information toward grasping what qualia our conspecifics are feeling. That is an important contribution to our overall emotional reaction to the situation, but it is not the whole story.

Quite clearly, in terms of the portraits we have discussed so far, part of the reason for this is that we do not know the objects of the affective states portrayed in the pictures by van Dyck, Holbein, and Burgoyne. Thus, we cannot be thought of as emotionally empathizing with them solely on the grounds that the images have activated our mirror reflexes.

To respond emotionally to a depicted character, we need more than access to his/her facial expressions and posture. We need to understand their situation. This information typically will be supplied by placing the characters in question in context – showing us what actions they are performing, what upsets they are suffering, how they are flourishing or not, and so on. (Of course, the title of the painting, if it has one, is quite often also very helpful in this regard, especially if it refers to a well-known historical, religious, or mythological event.)

Consider Poussin's *The Rape of the Sabine Women* (1648). Look at the first woman on the left side of the painting. Imagine abstracting her head and her left arm as a detail. From that one could ascertain, perhaps by mirror reflexing, that she was exhibiting distress. She is not happy. But to realize that that distress is compounded by the immense loss she is feeling because of the murder of her husband and her boy children and the terror she feels at the prospect of being violated brutally requires, so to speak, the whole picture.

Her face and her gestures give us a sense of the generic kind of affect she is suffering; it functions as a sort of range finder, alerting us to the general locale of her upset. The depiction of her situation specifies more precisely the particular emotion within that general range that grips her, which, in turn, helps calibrate the vectorially converging sadness or empathy that we feel toward her.

What is being described here should not be confused with what Dominic McIver Lopes calls "scene expression" (Lopes, 2011). For scene expression, on Lopes's account, refers to the overall expressive impression produced by a scene rather than to an emotion expressed by any of the characters in a scene. A painting of a battle may express a feeling of confusion, without any of the depicted warriors expressing being confused. In the cases I am discussing, the scene clarifies the state of the depicted figures in emotionally relevant ways, thereby making them at least available for empathy. *Contra* what Lopes suggests, I do not think that we empathize with scenes. Rather we empathize, in my sense, with characters in situations whose mental states are disclosed largely by being contextualized in scenes, although sometimes with help, via mirror reflexes, from emotional contagion.

Perspective taking

So far I have restricted the discussion of empathy in painting to the viewer's emotional responses to the figures depicted in the painting with regard to their bodily dispositions and the context in which they are situated. But recently the question has arisen as to whether we may feel empathy in regard to the painting as such, and, if so, what we could possibly mean by this (Robinson, forthcoming).

When we look at a painting such as Edvard Munch's *The Scream* or *Der Schrei der Natur* (I am referring to the 1893 versions), one is immediately struck by its affective unity. One's eye is immediately drawn to the anguished figure in the foreground, his/her/its hand gripping the sides of his/her/its head, which is more like a naked skull, as if in pain or terror or both. But, in addition, the depicted environment appears to reinforce those feelings. The orange sky seems to flow like a fiery, tumultuous river of what to our contemporary eyes looks like pollution, while the landscape to the right of the central figure is in a wavy turmoil, unstable, as if suffering a seizure itself. The painting projects a coherent mood, one of anxiety, of being situated in a precarious place where every element broadcasts a sense of existential vulnerability, which the alternative title of the painting suggests is nothing less than the human condition. Suppose we contemplate taking on the pervasive mood of the *The Scream*. Is that a matter of empathy?

Or, for a less dreary and depressing example, consider Henri Matisse's *The Dance* (the 1909 version). Although we see one of the dancers smiling, the overall affect that we take from the picture comes from the design of the painting. The mood is one of the joy of life, almost the opposite of the feeling conveyed by *The Scream*. But like *The Scream*, this feeling emerges from the composition of the painting as a whole. The dancers seem to be moving swiftly in a manner that connotes high spirits; they compose a circle, a veritable ring, affording a reassuring sense of a community engaged in ritual celebration. Moreover, all the colors are uplifting, the verdant grass below, the embracing blue sky, and, of course, the pinkish bodies of the dancers, projecting health and vivacity, especially when contrasted to the veritable death's head of the figure in *The Scream*. If we imagine feeling the joy of living embodied in *The Dance*, is that empathy?

Jenefer Robinson has argued that there is a case for maintaining this (Robinson, forthcoming). Taking note of the way in which certain pictures present a unified attitude or point of view toward their subject and that empathy involves perspective taking, she regards what I have been calling the coherent mood of the sort of paintings under discussion as an invitation to the viewer to take on the mood or attitude or point of view uniformly articulated by the pictorial composition as a whole – the *angst* of *The Scream* or the *joie de vivre* of *The Dance*, for example. But what grounds this mood? Objects like paintings don't have moods or attitudes or points of view. So where do they allegedly come from?

Robinson hypothesizes that they involve the perspective of the artist (perhaps understood as an implied author) on the subject of the painting and that the painting represents an invitation to the viewer to share that perspective. Following Richard Wollheim, Robinson maintains that "depicted scenes can express the emotions of their creator in a much richer way as depicting how the world might look when construed by a certain sort of person under the influence of a certain sort of emotional attitude" – that is, the artist as he/she is portrayed in the painting in virtue of his/her choices not only of subject but as through his/her manner of presenting said subject. And spectators, in turn, are invited to view the subject in a comparable manner.

Undoubtedly the talk of "how the world might look," here and elsewhere in Robinson's essay, it seems to me, is ill-advised insofar as it suggests that someone might literally see the world as Munch portrays it. But I doubt that many normally sighted subjects, not under the influence of some controlled substance, literally see the world as Munch represents it. Rather than talking about what the world looks like, perhaps it would be more helpful to say that such paintings project what the world feels like or, alternatively, indicate what the world feels like to someone, such as the artist, who experiences the world or some part of it under a particular emotional perspective and who, in turn, invites us to do likewise. Where viewers accept this invitation, then, they are empathizing with the artist (or the implied artist) insofar as they are engaged in perspective sharing with another.

Undoubtedly, there may be cases like this where Robinson's account of painting as involving empathy through perspective taking is precisely what the artist intends. However, there is a question as to whether we are compelled to think that this is always the explanation of pictures that present coherent moods or attitudes toward their subjects.

Homo sapiens responds to certain visual arrays in predictable ways, whether or not their provenance is human. Yellow is associated with happiness; brown is associated with sadness (Green, 2008). Open spaces may stimulate serenity; closed spaces, claustrophobia. And so on. Painters may exploit these responses in order to construct the moods presented in their pictures toward the depicted subjects. They need not have undergone the attitude or mood embodied in the painting nor even imagine having done so, vividly or otherwise. It may be simply a matter of manipulating certain cues; pushing the viewer's "buttons," in a manner of speaking.

That is, there is no need for the artist to possess the attitude, point of view, or mood that organizes a given painting. So even if viewers take up a vectorially converging mood toward the subject of the picture or recognize, perhaps through some emotive process, that the painting is an indication of how the world feels under the influence of a certain mood, it does not seem to entail that that is the mood of the artist whose perspective we are necessarily being invited to share. Something needs to be added to the account to show that perspective taking occurs across the board or to indicate the way in which to identify the cases where it is claimed to obtain. Thus it would seem that, at this point in the discussion, the most fruitful approach to the phenomenon of empathy with respect to painting – that is, the most widely applicable approach – is to regard said empathy as a matter of vectorially converging affects between the subject of the painting and its viewers.

References

Carroll, Noël (2012) "Some Affective Relations between Audiences and Characters in Popular Fictions," in N. Carroll, *Art in Three Dimensions* (Oxford: Oxford University Press), pp. 329–54.

Currie, Gregory (2011) "Empathy for Objects," in *Empathy: Philosophical and Psychological Perspectives*, edited by Amy Coplan & Peter Goldie (Oxford: Oxford University Press), pp. 82–98.

Ekman, Paul (1983) *Emotions in the Human Face* (Cambridge: Cambridge University Press).

Ekman, Paul (1985) *Emotions Revealed: Recognizing Faces and Feelings to Improve Communication and Emotional Life* (New York: Times Books).

Green, Mitchell (2008) "Empathy, Expression and What Artworks Have to Teach," in *Art and Ethical Criticism*, edited by Garry Hagberg (Oxford: Blackwell Publishing), pp. 95–122.

Hatfield, E., J. T. Cacipoppo, & R. L. Rapson (1994) *Emotional Contagion* (Cambridge: Cambridge University Press).

Lopes, Dominic McIver (2011) "An Empathic Eye," in *Empathy: Philosophical and Psychological Perspectives*, edited by Amy Coplan & Peter Goldie (Oxford: Oxford University Press), pp. 118–33.

McFee, Graham (2011) "Empathy: Interpersonal versus Artistic," in *Empathy: Philosophical and Psychological Perspectives*, edited by Amy Coplan & Peter Goldie (Oxford: Oxford University Press), pp. 185–210.

Robinson, Jenefer (Forthcoming) "The Missing Person Found: Expressing Emotions in Pictures," lecture, British Society for Aesthetics, London, September 11, 2014, revised version to be published in *British Journal of Aesthetics*.

Wispé, L. (1987) "History of the Concept of Empathy," in *Empathy and its Development*, edited by N. Eisenberg & J. Strayer (Cambridge: Cambridge University Press), pp. 17–37.

26

EMPATHY IN MUSIC

Jenefer Robinson

Introduction

The roots of the concept of empathy lie in Romanticism, in Herder and Novalis and other "pantheistically inclined romantic thinkers" who thought that nature "is properly understood only if it is seen as an outward symbol of some inner spiritual reality" (Stueber 2006, 7). As Herder wrote, a human being is uniquely able to "feel into everything" ["*einfühlen*" = literally to feel in], an epistemic method meant to distinguish what we would call the humanities from the feeling-less methods of the natural sciences (Stueber 2006, 6). Understanding history, art, or literature is partly a matter of understanding other minds, including the mind of the historian, artist, or writer. By the late nineteenth century, however, "Einfühlung," later translated into English as "empathy," was being treated by such writers as Theodor Lipps, Vernon Lee (pen name of Violet Paget), and Herbert Langfield primarily as a mode of appreciating aesthetic properties of artworks. Gregory Currie (2011) agrees with Lipps and Langfield in thinking that in appreciating visual artworks, one can be aided by the activation of sub-personal motor mimicry, which he treats along with some kinds of empathy as a "simulation" process. Thus, in appreciating the smoothness of a sculpture, it may be that the same motor circuits are activated in the brain as when one actually runs one's hands over it.

Today most theorists treat empathy primarily as a way of understanding other minds, by "feeling our way into" the emotions and other mental states of another person. One way to "feel another person's emotions" is via a low-level process of internal or external mimicry of another person's emotional expressions, including facial and vocal expressions, as well as gestures and postures expressive of emotion. Alvin Goldman (2006) calls this mimicry low-level *simulation* of the other person's emotionally expressive behavior. Theorists of embodied cognition, such as Joel Krueger, describe it as a "bodily-affective resonance and empathic understanding" (2013, 180). The basic idea is captured by the "action-perception model" of low-level empathy or "emotional contagion" advanced by Stephanie Preston and Frans de Waal. By contrast, high-level affective empathy – what Goldman calls "high-level simulational mindreading" – requires higher cognitive activity, such as being able to take the perspective of another person.

In this chapter I will distinguish between these two kinds of empathic process, broadly speaking – low-level perception-action processes, involving mimicry of expressive behavior, and high-level affective empathy, involving "higher" cognitive processes – as they apply to the experience of music. Low-level interactions *through* music can be found in the interactions between parents and their new born babies. Something similar occurs when listeners to music feel *with* the emotional properties of music via so-called "emotional contagion." But there are also certain kinds of music that invite high-level affective empathy *for* the performer of a song, or the "character" enacted by the performer, *for* the composer, and even *for* a "persona" in "pure" instrumental music.

If we consider "empathic processes" very broadly, to include the sub-personal simulation of motor and emotional expressions, then, even though such processes are better described as "emotional contagion" than as affective empathy proper, it is nevertheless true that they can help us to appreciate various emotionally expressive properties in music, as Lipps and Langfield suggested. And in the case of "higher" affective empathy or enactive imagination, we may feel genuine empathic emotions on behalf of an operatic character, a performer, and maybe even a composer, which not only unite us in fellow-feeling for the person with whom we are empathizing, but can also alert us to emotionally expressive properties in the music in a particularly direct and vivid way. Thus the two original meanings of "empathy" turn out to be closely related: low-level motor and emotional mimicry and high-level affective empathy are *both* ways of understanding other minds *and* modes of aesthetic appreciation.

Low-level "contagion" and high-level affective empathy in ordinary life: a brief introduction

Stephanie Preston and Frans de Waal (2002) have developed a "perception-action" model of empathy that relies on automatic, relatively low-level processes of motor and emotional mimicry. Their model of empathy "is grounded in the theoretical idea, adopted by many fields over time, that perception and action share a common code of representation in the brain" (9). For Preston and de Waal, "perception-action is a superordinate class, which includes two basic level categories, motor behavior and emotional behavior" (4).

With respect to motor behavior, "perception of a behavior in another automatically activates one's own representations for the behavior, and output from this shared representation automatically proceeds to motor areas of the brain where responses are prepared and executed" (9–10). This thesis has received empirical support from the discovery of "mirror neurons," which activate both when an action is being performed and when that same action is seen being performed (see Chapter 5 in this volume, "Empathy and mirror neurons").

With respect to emotional behavior, neuroscientists Jean Decety and Julie Grèzes have summarized a wealth of empirical evidence that people "catch the emotions of others as a result of afferent feedback generated by elementary motor mimicry of others' expressive behavior, which produces a simultaneous matching emotional experience" (2006, 8). For instance, "viewing facial expressions triggers expressions on one's own face, even in the absence of conscious recognition of the stimulus," and "observing fearful body expressions not only produces increased activity in brain areas associated with emotional processes but also in areas linked with representation of action and movement" (8). In short, emotional contagion occurs when one feels the same emotion as another person because one has been "infected" by that person's expression of the emotion.

Most theorists of empathy today accept Martin Hoffman's view that an empathic emotion is "an emotion that is more appropriate to the state or situation of someone other than the person who experiences it" (Hoffman 2000). It is an emotion that not only *matches* the emotion of another person, but which is experienced *for* or *on behalf of* that person (Maibom 2014, 5). All by themselves, the low-level processes of emotional contagion described by Preston and de

Waal are not primarily experienced on behalf of another person. Indeed, typically we are not even aware of being infected by someone else's emotion via sub-personal motor or emotional mimicry.

High-level affective empathy involves high-level cognitive abilities. Heidi Maibom identifies three "routes to empathy," one of which is "the perceptual route," i.e., "witnessing the person in the situation" (Maibom 2014, 10). The idea here seems to be that low-level emotional contagion can transmogrify into high-level empathy if one becomes aware that one's feelings are caused by the observed feelings of another. However, as I just remarked, even when consciously experienced, such feelings need not be empathic in the sense that they are felt *for* or on behalf of the other person: it may just be my own personal emotions that are affected. A second route is inferential: "believing that the person is in a certain situation or is experiencing a certain emotion." This kind of "empathy" is often termed "cognitive empathy"; it is an "understanding of others" (Maibom 2014, 2) that need involve no emotion at all, and I will exclude it from my discussion here. Finally, the most characteristic high-level route to affective empathy is through the imagination or perspective-taking: one "takes the perspective" of the other person in the sense that "we imagine what it is like for her or what we would feel were we in her situation" (Maibom 2014, 12). In brief, we engage imaginatively with the other person's point of view.

This phenomenon is what Goldman calls "high-level simulation" or "enactive imagination": we "quarantine" our own beliefs, desires, and emotions, we imagine being in the other person's shoes, and then we 'see' what we would think, feel, want, or intend to do, and ascribe those psychological states to the person we are trying to understand" (Maibom 2014, 12). One of the many problems with Goldman's account is that "imagining being in the other person's shoes" is notoriously difficult and perhaps impossible, and – worse – there are no reliable criteria for success in the endeavor. Other theorists have introduced further distinctions. Amy Coplan, for example, distinguishes between "self-oriented" and "other-oriented" varieties of empathy. I will ignore the niceties of these disputes and focus simply on the idea of *taking the perspective* of another person, while acknowledging that there are different views of what this process is and that any such process is likely to be imperfect.

Empathizing *through* music: emotional interactions between babies and care-givers

Preston and de Waal argue that their perception-action model "subserves the ability of infants to perceive and learn from the expressions of the caregiver. The actions and expressions of the mother are mapped onto existing representations of the infant and generate actions and expressions in response. This facilitates not only the infant's ability to understand the behavior of the mother, but also facilitates coordinated activity in the dyad, necessary for the development of emotion regulation" (2002, 8). One of the striking ways in which parents interact with their babies is through music.

All over the world mothers talk baby-talk to their babies, and when they sing to their babies they do so in a special infant-directed way. In turn, infants much prefer baby-talk and infant-directed singing to adult talk and song. Babies appear "hypnotized" by their mothers' singing and in turn mothers (or other care-givers) "nicely mirror infants' perceptual abilities by singing more slowly, at higher pitch, with exaggerated rhythm, and in a more loving or emotionally engaging manner than when singing alone." Infant-directed speech and song share many of the same acoustic features: both are "characterized by higher pitch, greater pauses between phrases, slower tempo, and simpler structures relative to their [infant-absent] counterparts" (O'Neill et al. 2001, 410). Although fathers do not usually sing at a higher pitch than normal to their infants, as mothers almost always do, both mothers and fathers use a distinctive "baby-style" when they sing to their babies that is "highly engaging" (409) to babies. In both cases melodic contours are "perceptually and acoustically, the salient units" of communication (Papoušek 1992, 245). Parents' melodic contours are not consciously produced and are found pan-culturally in both mothers and fathers. Moreover, "responsiveness to such infant-directed singing appears inborn. Two-day-old hearing infants, born from congenitally deaf parents (who sign and do not sing or speak), prefer infant-directed singing to adult-directed singing" (245).

What Preston and de Waal say about mother-baby interactions in general applies with even greater force to musical interactions: "Infants and their caregivers … use their emotional expressions to reinforce positive affect, transform negative affect and provide breaks when arousal becomes too high" (2002, 8). According to Colwyn Trevarthen, human babies are born with a repertoire of facial expressions, including "pleasure, displeasure, fear, surprise, confusion and interest" (Trevarthen 1979, 323), that are similar to adult expressions of these emotions. They are also born with a repertoire of expressive vocalizations, including sounds of comfort (such as cooing) and discomfort, and cries of pleasure and displeasure, which have distinct frequencies and distinct peak amplitudes (Papoušek 1992, 236–7). Successful interactions are not a matter of the parent demanding some kind of response from the baby, regardless of what the baby seems to want to do. Attentive parents wait and watch as much as vocalize. Trevarthen reports that mothers react to their babies "as agents who are *subordinate* to acts of babies" (1979, 338).

Joel Krueger emphasizes the rhythmic quality of these interactions. Baby and care-giver together establish a "mutual temporal orientation to features of the rhythmic dialogue being shared" (Krueger 2013, 182). The infant orients to the music, and engages in a "musically informed 'mutual tuning-in relationship' with the care-giver" (183). Sucking, swallowing, initiation of eye contact, and an increasingly engaged and attentive bodily posture are just a few of the signs that the baby is actively responding to the sung melody. Such interactions initiate and cement bonding between care-giver and baby, and provide the basis for affective empathy and social bonding in later life. Care-givers and their babies seem to learn to understand and share each other's feelings, as well as to be emotionally responsive to each other more generally.

These musical interactions between care-giver and baby are not confined to mirroring responses, but they instantiate the perception-action model insofar as they are an important pre-linguistic means of mutual understanding through the *perception* of the other's emotional expressions and an appropriate *reaction* to it, which on both sides seems to be to some degree automatically generated. More broadly, these early interactions "set the stage for the subsequent role of music in group bonding" (Trehub 2003, 13), as in the flash mob phenomenon (Higgins 2012), and may anticipate later "interactional synchrony," the "dance between persons" that occurs when we interact with each other socially, adapting our gaze and co-ordinating head movements, hand gestures, and so on (Bunt and Pavlicevic 2001, 194).

Empathizing *with* music: the role of emotional contagion

What emotions music *expresses* belong to the music, whereas what emotions are *aroused* by music belong to the listener. If emotional contagion in ordinary life consists in feeling the same emotions as another person as a result of being "infected" by that person's emotional expressions, then it seems that something very similar can happen when we listen to music (Davies 2013): the music *expresses* sadness or joy and when I listen to it sadness or joy are thereby *aroused* in me. Recall that Preston and de Waal think that both motor and emotional behavior are "contagious" according to their perception-action model. It turns out that music can be a source of both kinds of contagion.

It is widely agreed that music (or most western music at least) essentially involves motion. Tones move upward and downward; they do not merely follow one another like the beeps on a microwave oven, but have rhythm; melodies move energetically or lazily, breezily or heavily. Roger Scruton says that "if we take away the metaphors of movement, of space, of chords as objects, of melodies as advancing and retreating, as moving up and down – if we take those metaphors away, nothing of music remains, but only sound" (1983, 97). Scruton thinks that such talk is necessarily metaphorical. However, the perception-action model and the data on mirroring processes in the human brain suggest that we do not need recourse to metaphors to explain why we hear music as moving: music seems to dispose us to move by virtue of the fact that the motor system is activated when we listen to it. In one experiment discussed by Joel Krueger, a piece of music with an ambiguous rhythm was played to adult listeners who were asked to bounce either on every second beat or every third beat. It turned out that these adults had to "personally bounce their own bodies, and not watch a video of another doing it, in order for their experience of the ambiguous rhythm to covary relative to their particular bounce training." In other words, to learn a rhythm requires actual movement to the rhythm, not just watching someone else move to the rhythm. The motor system needs to be actively involved when we are engaged in "sensitive music listening" (Krueger 2013, 187).

There is a great deal of evidence that music directly affects the motor system. Nakamura et al. have shown correlations between music listening and activity in the motor system in the brain, including the premotor cortex (Nussbaum 2007, 68). Similarly, Chen et al. have found that "listening to musical rhythms recruits motor regions of the brain"; establishing a "groove" also requires activation of the motor system (reported in London 2016, 102). "Listening to piano pieces appears to activate (pre)motor activity in pianists" (Koelsch & Siebel 2005, 582). In other words pianists internally enact the movements they would be making if they were playing the pieces themselves. Moreover, "music perception can interfere with action planning in musicians," suggesting that the motor system is busy helping to process the music and cannot spare resources for planning other actions (582).

Bharucha et al. suggest that the most basic kind of experience of motion induced by music is a "sense of self-motion through space," which "emphatically is not metaphorical but rather physiologically induced," and is probably mediated by the vestibulum, "a proprioceptive organ that detects changes in the spatial state of the organism's body" (Bharucha et al. 2006, 158). There is also good evidence for "rhythmic entrainment" to music, i.e., the powerful, external rhythm of the music interacts with an internal body rhythm of the listener such as the heart rate, such that the latter rhythm adjusts toward and eventually "locks in" to a common periodicity (Levitin 2006, 59; Juslin et al. 2010, 621). However, it seems likely that there are different types of motion experience when we listen to music that may be mediated by different brain systems (Bharucha et al. 2006, 162), for example, distinguish self-motion through space from "the sense of a piece of music as sounding like a moving object" (159) or the more abstract sense of movement in melody, harmony, and tonality which "has the properties of a mathematical space, but … also maps onto a psychological space" (162).

Listeners frequently mimic the movements they hear in music. Much music is written in order to co-ordinate the movements of a group of people. Think of funeral marches, wedding marches, work songs, and all the many varieties of dancing. However, even when movement is inhibited, as when we are sitting quietly in the concert hall, it seems that we often mimic internally the movement of the music we hear. It seems highly plausible, therefore, that the primary means of detecting movement in music is being actually moved ourselves, whether overtly or internally: those who cannot *feel* a rhythm have a hard time *hearing* it.

Scruton says that just as we "transfer an experience of movement to music (which does not move)," so we "transfer an experience of passion to music (which has no passions)" (1983, 109). He assumes that describing music in emotional terms is metaphorical. Again, however, it's not obvious that describing music as melancholy or cheerful or simply as expressive is metaphorical at all. Just as we hear music as moving in various ways because of activity in the motor system caused by the music, so it's likely that we hear music as melancholy or cheerful partly because of the way that the music makes us *feel*. As the perception-action model suggests, "attended perception" of music "automatically activates" the [listener's] representations of emotional expressions in the music, and furthermore, "activation of these representations primes or generates the associated autonomic and somatic responses, unless inhibited" (Preston & de Waal 2002, 4). In other words, listeners hear musical gestures as expressive of emotions and come to enact those same expressions by a process of motor mimicry. Some would deny that internal mimicry is necessary for grasping emotional expression in music (Kivy 1990, Zangwill 2012), and it may well be that experienced listeners can detect emotional qualities in music without being themselves emotionally affected. But for a great many listeners, the way to identify what the music expresses is to feel it, and much of our enjoyment of music involves this kind of emotional involvement with the music.

How do we get from motor mimicry while listening to music to the experience of emotion? We have already seen how musical gestures can activate motor systems in the brain so that listeners mimic – externally or internally – how the music moves. When the movements mimicked are characteristic of a certain emotional state, then the listener can come to have the corresponding emotional feelings. This is what I have called the Jazzercise effect (Robinson 2005, 391–5). William James long ago predicted that adopting the facial expression, posture, gaze, autonomic responses, and/or actions characteristic of a particular type of emotion can induce that same emotion. In his recent book *Feelings: The Perception of Self*, James Laird has amassed a great deal of evidence that James was right: although some people are apparently more responsive to situational cues than to their own behavioral or personal cues, for many people, mimicking the behaviors characteristic of some emotional state induces feelings of that state. Thus, Henry Purcell's *Music on the Death of Queen Mary* (1695) invites the pall-bearers in the funeral procession to move with a solemn, leaden, trudging movement characteristic of profound sorrow, which in turn can induce profound sorrow in those who move in this way. By contrast, the bourrées, gigues, and gavottes in J. S. Bach's orchestral suites invite the listener to dance to or internally mimic the joyful movements in the music.

Moreover, just as music can mirror the way that human beings express their emotions in the way they move and gesture, so too, according to Patrik Juslin and his collaborators, music can mirror the tones of voice and phrasing characteristic of the vocal expression of specific emotions, and by internal mimicry listeners can come to acquire the corresponding emotional feelings. They claim that expressive music and expressive speech use "different channels" (speech and music) but the "same code," i.e., there are marked similarities between speech and music concerning both "the accuracy with which discrete emotions [are] communicated to listeners" and the emotion-specific pattern of acoustic cues (Juslin & Laukka 2003, 770). Juslin is mainly focused on the "prosodic" features of music and language, i.e., their rhythmic and intonational features, which are characteristic of specific emotions. Moreover, according to Juslin's "super-expressive voices" theory (Juslin & Laukka 2003, 803), "what makes a specific music performance on, say, the violin, so moving, is the fact that it sounds a lot like the human voice, whereas at the same time it goes far *beyond* what the human voice [can] do in terms of tempo, pitch range, and timbre" (Juslin & Timmers 2010, 477).

For example, according to Juslin and Timmers, who rely on a number of different studies, the characteristic acoustic cues for sadness in both speech and music include "slow mean tempo, legato articulation, small articulation variability, low sound level, dull timbre, large timing variations, soft duration contrasts, slow tone attacks, flat microintonation, slow vibrato, and final ritardando" (Juslin & Timmers 2010, 463). These are features characteristic of expressions of sadness in both speech and music, and when we hear speech or music with these features, we may mimic them internally and thereby become "infected" by sadness. In short, the perception-action model gives an account of how we can come to experience emotional feelings by mimicking – either externally or internally – emotional expressions either in the human voice or in human movements and gestures. As we listen to music, we mimic its emotional expressions, especially its movement – including its rhythms, phrasing, and intonational patterns – and thereby come to adopt the emotions expressed.

Two important consequences follow from the application of the "perception-action model" to music. First, Preston and de Waal describe emotional contagion as a process whereby we mimic the facial and vocal expressions of another *person* and thereby take on their emotions. But the process whereby we come to feel certain emotional feelings by mimicking vocal expressions and motor activity in *music* is not quite the same. Music is human-*like* and it may sound and move like a human being but it is *not* a human being. In a broad sense, perhaps it is not implausible to say that listeners are "infected" by the music they hear, but I suspect the mechanism cannot be quite the same as in the human-to-human case. Most importantly, empathic emotions are felt *for* or *on behalf of* another person, but in listening to sad or happy music there is no person on whose behalf we feel sadness or happiness. Our feelings belong to ourselves alone.

The second consequence is that just as Currie (2011) argues that "simulations of motor activity at a sub-personal level" can help us appreciate visual art, so simulations of motor activity at a sub-personal level can help us appreciate music. Or perhaps we appreciate musical movement simply by becoming "attuned" to the way the music moves, as the proponents of embodied cognition might think. Either way, even though we do not literally empathize with music, activation of the motor system seems essential to the proper understanding of music. Some formalists, such as Peter Kivy and Nick Zangwill (Kivy 1990, Zangwill 2012), claim that we need only *detect* movements and emotional expressions in music without actually moving or feeling anything ourselves. I would say that the empirical evidence shows that whether we are aware of it or not, our motor systems are typically activated when we listen with understanding to a piece of music. Indeed, anecdotally it is often hard not to dance when we hear dance music. Scruton may well be right when he argues that dancing appropriately to music is a mode of understanding and appreciating it (1997, 357).

If this is correct, then it seems that the two threads in the early history of the concept of empathy are indeed closely related. We come to appreciate certain aesthetic qualities in music, such as qualities of movement – energetic, sprightly, or leaden – by means of external or internal motor mimicry of musical movement. And we can come to appreciate *emotional* qualities in music (which are themselves of course a subset of its aesthetic qualities) in a similar way, by coming to mimic internally or externally vocal and behavioral expressions of emotions in music, a process which has much in common with emotional contagion. Such low-level processes do not count as affective empathy proper but they do enable listeners to experience some of the emotions that music expresses and thereby invite aesthetic appreciation of the corresponding expressive qualities.

Empathy *for* music: high-level affective empathy for musical protagonists

As we have seen, high-level "affective empathy" requires some kind of "higher" cognitive activity. In particular, what I have been calling "affective empathy proper" involves "taking the perspective" of the other person in the sense that "we imagine what it is like for her or what we would feel were we in her situation" (Maibom 2014, 12).

In the musical case, I may be "infected" by a sad tune, and come to realize that my sadness has been induced by the sadness in the music, but, again, the sadness is not felt *for* or *on behalf of* anyone else, so it is somewhat misleading to classify it as genuine empathic sadness. On the other hand, according to Scruton, when "Einfühlung" has as its object an *expressive gesture* rather than a person, and we "enter into" such gestures, we can "transform our observation of another's expression into the imaginative knowledge of 'what it is like'" (1983, 111), where "what it is like" can be captured only by direct *acquaintance* with this specific musical gesture rather than by any verbal *description* of it. Interpreted in this way, "emotional contagion" by music has more in common with empathy than I have allowed. If we imaginatively "adopt" the emotion expressed by a *musical* gesture, and thereby come to enter imaginatively into the specific state of mind that the music expresses, we might, in so doing, come to grasp "what it is like" to feel that emotion and thereby to expand the range of our emotional experiences (Scruton 1997, 362–3). On Scruton's account, we may not be empathizing with anyone in particular, but we are at least empathizing with an imagined person's emotionally expressive gestures. Here we approach closer to "high-level" simulation or affective empathy.

A more natural way of interpreting empathic reactions to songs, however, especially *lyric* songs in which the singer seems to be expressing her own feelings in words and music, is that listeners are not simply adopting emotions expressed by musical gestures but are genuinely empathizing with the "character" or protagonist enacted by the singer, much as we might empathize with a character in a novel or film. When we listen to vocal music, such as Adele's "Someone Like You," we can pay attention to both words and music and thereby come to "imagine what it is like for her or what we would feel were we in her situation" (Maibom 2014, 12). At the same time, we are probably engaging in sub-personal simulations of the melodic movement, as well as internally simulating the rhythmic and intonational patterns of the vocal line, which is expressive of grief, longing, and nostalgia. In short, the song encourages the listener to experience "high-level" empathic grief, longing, and nostalgia on behalf of the character enacted by Adele, reinforced by low-level mimicry processes. Our repertoire of emotional experiences is expanded by genuine affective empathy *for* the feelings of another person (see also Scherer and Zentner 2001, 369–71).

Now it is widely believed that it is problematic to talk of feeling genuine emotions on behalf of fictional creatures. In Robinson (2005) I tried to dissolve this problem by pointing out that our emotion systems respond automatically to certain types of situations – dangers, losses, offenses, and other "core relational themes" – so that whether the object of empathic sorrow and pity is real or fictional, our responses can be equally empathic in both cases. In the musical case, however, there is an important source of reinforcement for any empathic emotions I might feel: if my motor system is responding to the movement in the music, then the sub-personal motor simulation processes Currie emphasizes will reinforce the empathic emotion I am experiencing. Similarly, mimicking the intonational, rhythmic, and melodic contours characteristic of a specific emotion ("emotional contagion" by music) reinforces and is reinforced by "high-level" affective empathy. Indeed I would suggest that one reason why empathy can be so powerfully induced by highly expressive music is because the two systems for inducing emotions in listeners – low-level and high-level – are working together.

The idea that music can arouse emotions only via the mimicry of behavioral characteristics of emotions that have a uniquely identifying set of behaviors associated with them limits the emotions in music with which listeners can empathize (Davies 2006). The same is true of the Jazzercise effect. Juslin and his group at Uppsala University in Sweden mainly study emotions that have distinctive behavioral characteristics, which can be mimicked and thus "infect" other people. Examples include the *basic* emotions of sadness, happiness, and anger. However, many of the emotions that Romantic composers thought of as paradigms of emotions expressible by music, such as love, longing, despair, nostalgia, and tenderness, have no specific behavioral characteristics which listeners can mimic. Nevertheless, Romantic song-writers, such as Franz Schubert and Johannes Brahms, were able to compose songs that express subtle and cognitively complex emotions, such as love and nostalgia (Robinson 2005).

Interestingly, the research group at the University of Geneva, led by Klaus Scherer, has reported – using self-reports by very large numbers of music listeners at music festivals – that the emotions most commonly aroused by music are mostly quite different from the basic emotions and include many "Romantic emotions" such as wonder, tenderness, nostalgia, and feelings of power and transcendence (Zentner et al. 2008). Since, as far as is currently known, no specific behaviors characterize these emotions, presumably we cannot "catch" them from the music by a process of emotional contagion. However, if Scruton is right, then when we listen to music that expresses nostalgia or longing, such as "Someone Like You" or Schubert's "Gute Nacht," the first song in his song cycle *Winterreise*, we are invited to imagine *what it is like* for the protagonist, and we can thereby come to feel the very emotion that he or she is expressing in the song. Broadly speaking, both these songs express a general emotion type: sadness and noasstalgia for a lost love. But the *specific* sadness and nostalgia that each expresses is very different and peculiar to each song. Indeed, the emotions expressed are *ineffable*, in the sense that they are knowable by acquaintance but incapable of being captured adequately by verbal description.

Moreover, when we respond empathically to Schubert's "Gute Nacht" or Adele's "Someone Like You," not only do we feel genuine empathic distress on behalf of the protagonist of the song, the abandoned lover, but also the feelings we experience *enable us to appreciate aesthetically* what is being expressed emotionally not only by the words or even the vocal line, but by the song as a whole. Interestingly, then, it seems that, like low-level contagion, high-level affective empathy can play an important role in the detection of aesthetic properties in music – especially emotionally expressive properties – and that once again the two main roots of empathy are importantly connected.

Empathizing *for* performers, composers, and "personae" in instrumental music

So far I have spoken as if songs express the emotions of the characters who enact them, but sometimes, especially in the case of popular musicians such Adele, it is easy to interpret a song as an expression of emotion in the singer herself, so that when we listen, we may find ourselves empathizing with the singer. In live performance this is probably more likely, because we are not only hearing the emotions expressed but also seeing them in the singer's facial expressions and gestures. Indeed there is evidence that even when listening to instrumental music, we obtain additional cues about the music from *seeing* the performer's facial expressions and expressive gestures (Vines et al. 2006, 2011). In one experiment, for example, subjects watched two clarinetists play the same piece, one using expressive musical gestures, the other playing relatively inexpressively ("just the notes"). The results showed that visual cues are important to how we hear *phrasing* and *tension*, where "tension" was interpreted – perhaps quixotically – as "a proxy for the experience of emotion in a musical piece" (Vines et al. 2006, 83).

Like many philosophers of music, I have talked as if it is *the music itself* that expresses emotions (with which we may or may not empathize), but of course the very same piece can be performed in very different ways to express different emotions or shades of emotion (or lack of emotion), so that what we are responding to is not just a "work of music" but a specific performance by a specific performer. Contrast, for example, the yearning, sorrowful, tender intonation in Eric Clapton's acoustic version of "Layla" with the aggressive, impatient, but more exuberant intonation in the electric version.

In a song the *words* typically tell us about the situation in which the protagonist finds him or herself and it is the words and music together which enable us to understand *what it is like* to be in that situation. However, some theorists have argued that at least in some instrumental music it makes sense to posit a "persona," the "owner" of the emotional states expressed, with whom attentive listeners can empathize (Levinson 1996, 2006; Robinson 2005). In such cases it seems that we imagine ourselves to be in the persona's situation, and feel the very same emotions that he or she seems to be experiencing. This way of listening is most appropriate in my view for some of the great Romantic symphonies of Beethoven and his successors, where there are sometimes good reasons for supposing that it is the composer who is intentionally expressing his own emotions in the music. For example, Aaron Ridley has plausibly suggested that it is "very difficult to conceive of an experience of Mahler's Ninth Symphony which does not involve hearing it as, inter alia, the expression of the evolving psychological state of a highly distinctive persona – as a kind of soul journey" (Ridley 1995, 183–4), and Karl and Robinson have argued that the emotional states expressed in Shostakovich's Tenth Symphony likely belong to the composer himself (1995). But we do not need to hear such pieces as expressions of the composer's emotions. More important is the fact that at least some pieces of Romantic instrumental music should be heard not merely as "purely formal" structures but as "musical plots" (Newcomb 1984) or "expressive genres" (Hatten 1994), in listening to which listeners are invited to "enact" the music's "action plan" in imagination (Nussbaum 2007) and thereby to empathize with the emotions expressed by a persona in the music – the "owner" of the emotions expressed – which gradually unfold over the course of a musical piece (Karl & Robinson 2015).

Empathy in music and empathy in life

Empathy as a personality trait is measured by such instruments as the Interpersonal Reactivity Index (IRI), which taps into the ability to take the perspective of another person, the "tendency to experience feelings of sympathy and compassion for unfortunate others," the tendency to feel "distress and discomfort" at extreme distress in other people, and the tendency to fantasize, i.e., "imaginatively transpose oneself into fictional situations" (IRI; see Davis 1980). An experiment by Clemens Wöllner (2012) found that high-empathy individuals were more accurate in their (multimodal) perceptions of string quartet performers' "expressive intentions" when they played a highly expressive passage. It is noteworthy, however, that Wöllner does not mention empathy for specific individual emotions, but only the general property of "expressiveness" and its relative intensity.

More relevant to empathy is the fact that, according to Vuoskoski & Eerola (2012), people rated as highly empathic according to IRI are more susceptible to experiencing sadness induced in them by listening to unfamiliar sad instrumental music. The fact that the music is unfamiliar is designed to rule out the possibility that sad music induces sadness only because the music reminded listeners of some event in their past lives. That the sadness induced by the unfamiliar music was genuine sadness was confirmed by the fact that the subjects exhibited cognitive biases previously found to be effects of sadness, such as "changes in [sadness]-related memory and judgment" (Vuoskoski and Eerola 2012, 204). For further details about the cognitive biases induced by sadness see Bower (1981), Davidson (1994), and Niedenthal (2001). So not only can high-empathy individuals more easily *recognize* expressiveness in instrumental music, as Wöllner claims; they can also more readily actually *experience* the emotion expressed when they listen to expressive music.

One would expect, however, that vocal music, expressive of personal emotion, might more readily induce empathy in listeners than instrumental music. Andrei Miu and Felicia Baltes (2012) have studied listeners' propensity to empathize with the performer of a song, or, as I would say, with the "character" that the performer is enacting. (They do not distinguish between the two.) In one experiment they showed videos of two opera excerpts, both sung by Cecilia Bartoli: a Vivaldi aria, "Gelido in ogni vena," describing a mother's pain at being about to lose her sons, and "Rataplan," by Maria Malibran, an aria which describes the happy march of a boy drummer in a victory parade. Both pieces were unfamiliar to the experimental subjects. Subjects were divided into "high-empathy" and "low-empathy" conditions. The "high-empathy" participants were given instructions to "imagine as vividly as possible how the performer feels about what is described in the music and try to feel those emotions themselves" (2012, 3). The "low-empathy" participants were instructed "to take an objective perspective toward what is described in the music, and try not to get caught up in how the performer might feel" (3). The participants had their physiological activity recorded and they filled out a questionnaire, using the emotions identified by the Geneva research team as most likely to be experienced in response to music, in which they were asked to rate the emotions they felt as they listened. They were also asked which of the following contributed most to the emotions that they felt as they listened: the music, the lyrics (which were translated into the subjects' language), or the performer's facial expressions.

The results were interesting. A large majority of participants attributed their emotions to the *music* (89% for the Vivaldi, 76.5% for the Malibran). With respect to *manipulated empathy* – i.e., empathy influenced by the experimenters' instructions – the high-empathy condition induced nostalgia to the Vivaldi and feelings of "power" to "Rataplan." The high-empathy manipulation also decreased skin conductance responses to the Vivaldi and increased respiration rate in "Rataplan." Miu and Baltes comment that "the deliberate efforts made by listeners to empathize with the performer and imagine her feelings related to the music she performed, facilitated music-induced emotions and physiological activity," and that the emotions increased by empathy were "closely related to the emotional content of the music" (3), i.e., what the music *expresses* (nostalgia for the Vivaldi and a sense of power for "Rataplan"). On the other hand, the characters also express other emotions such as grief (Vivaldi) and pride ("Rataplan") that the subjects do not seem to have experienced, so even the high-empathy group did not feel exactly "what it was like" to be those operatic characters.

From the point of view of this chapter, the most significant finding was that "voluntarily empathizing with a music performer can modulate negative and positive music-induced emotions, as well as their underlying physiological activity" (5). Other experiments have shown that it is easier to empathize in this way with performers performing music that one likes and/or that one knows (and of course familiarity breeds liking, as we know from the mere exposure effect) (Schubert 2013). This is true of empathy in general, not just empathy for music and characters in music. It is interesting, I think, that empathy seems to help us not only to understand people in daily life by feeling the emotions of another, but also apparently to feel more intensely the emotions expressed in music. Once again, empathy as a mode of understanding other people turns out to increase aesthetic appreciation as well.

Conclusion

I have tried to demonstrate in this chapter that both low-level emotional contagion and high-level affective empathy can function to aid in the understanding of the protagonist in vocal music or the performer, composer, or, more generally, the "persona" in some pieces of pure instrumental music. And this understanding in turn aids in the aesthetic appreciation of the music, especially the emotions that it expresses. Moreover, it seems that there is a direct relation between empathy in life and in music: those induced to take the perspective of an operatic character or the protagonist of a song are more likely to have relevant emotional experiences as they listen to the music.

Bibliography

Bharucha, J., et al. 2006: "Varieties of Musical Experience," *Cognition* 100, 131–72.

Bower, Gordon 1981: "Mood and Memory," *American Psychologist* 36, 129–48.

Bunt, Leslie, & Mercedes Pavlicevic 2001: "Music and Emotion: Perspectives from Music Therapy," in Patrik Juslin & John Sloboda eds., *Music and Emotion: Theory and Research*, New York: Oxford University Press, 181–201.

Chen, J. L., et al. 2008: "Listening to Musical Rhythm Recruits Motor Regions of the Brain," *Cerebral Cortex* 18, 2844–54.

Currie, Gregory 2011: "Empathy for Objects," in Amy Coplan & Peter Goldie eds., *Empathy: Philosophical and Psychological Perspectives*, New York: Oxford University Press, 82–95.

Davidson, Richard J. 1994: "On Emotion, Mood, and Related Affective Constructs," in Paul Ekman & Richard Davidson eds., *The Nature of Emotion*, New York: Oxford University Press, 51–5.

Davies, Stephen 2006: "Artistic Expression and the Hard case of Pure Music," in Matthew Kieran ed., *Contemporary Debates in Aesthetics and the Philosophy of Art*, Oxford: Blackwell, 179–91.

Davies, Stephen 2013: "Music-to-Listener Emotional Contagion," in Tom Cochrane et al. eds., *The Emotional Power of Music*, New York: Oxford University Press, 169–76.

Davis, M. H. 1980: "A Multidimensional Approach to Individual Differences in Empathy," *JSAS Catalog of Selected Documents in Psychology*, vol. 10, 85.

Decety, Jean, & Julie Grèzes 2006: "The Power of Simulation: Imagining One's Own and Others' Behavior," *Brain Research* 1079, 4–14.

Goldman, Alvin 2006: *Simulating Minds: The Philosophy, Psychology, and Neuroscience of Mindreading*, New York: Oxford University Press.

Hatten, Robert 1994: *Musical Meaning in Beethoven*, Indianapolis, IN: University of Indiana Press.

Higgins, Kathleen 2012: *The Music between Us: Is Music a Universal Language?* Chicago, IL: University of Chicago Press.

Hoffman, Martin 2000: *Empathy and Moral Development: Implications for Caring and Justice*, Cambridge: Cambridge University Press.

Juslin, Patrik, & Petri Laukka 2003: "Communication of Emotions in Vocal Expression and Music Performance: Different Channels, Same Code?" *Psychological Bulletin* 770–814.

Juslin, Patrik, et al. 2010; "How Does Music Evoke Emotions?" in Patrik Juslin & John Sloboda eds., *Handbook of Music and Emotion: Theory, Research, Applications*, New York: Oxford University Press, 605–42.

Juslin, Patrik, & Renee Timmers 2010: "Expression and Communication of Emotion in Music Performance," in Patrik Juslin & John Sloboda eds., *Handbook of Music and Emotion: Theory, Research, Applications*, New York: Oxford University Press, 453–89.

Karl, Gregory, & Jenefer Robinson 1995: "Shostakovich's Tenth Symphony and the Musial Expression of Cognitively Complex Emotions," *Journal of Aesthetics and Art Criticism* 53, 401–15.

Karl, Gregory, & Jenefer Robinson 2015: "Yet Again 'Between Absolute and Programme Music,'" *British Journal of Aesthetics* 55, 19–37.

Kivy, Peter 1990: *Music Alone: Philosophical Reflections on the Purely Musical Experience*, Ithaca, NY: Cornell University Press.

Koelsch, Stefan, & Walter Siebel 2005: "Towards a Neural Basis of Music Perception," *Trends in Cognitive Science* 9, 578–84.

Krueger, Joel 2013: "Empathy, Enaction, and Shared Musical Experience: Evidence from Infant Cognition," in Tom Cochrane et al. eds., *The Emotional Power of Music*, New York: Oxford University Press, 177–96.

Laird, James 2007: *Feelings: The Perception of Self*, New York: Oxford University Press.

Levinson, Jerrold 1996: "Musical Expressiveness," in *The Pleasures of Aesthetics*, Ithaca, NY: Cornell University Press, 90–125.

Levinson, Jerrold 2006: "Musical Expressiveness as Hearability-as Expression," in Matthew Kieran ed., *Contemporary Debates in Aesthetics and the Philosophy of Art*, Oxford: Blackwell, 192–204.

Levitin, Daniel 2006: *This Is Your Brain on Music*, New York: Dutton.

London, Justin 2016: "Review of Tiger Roholt's *Groove*," *Journal of Aesthetics and Art Criticism* 74, 101–4.

Maibom, Heidi 2014: "Introduction: (Almost) Everything You Ever Wanted to Know about Empathy," in Heidi Maibom ed., *Empathy and Morality*, New York: Oxford University Press, 1–40.

Miu, Andrei C., & Felicia Rodica Baltes 2012: "Empathy Manipulation Impacts Music-Induced Emotions: A Psychophysiological Study on Opera," *Plos One* 7, 1–6.

Newcomb, Anthony 1983: "Once More 'Between Absolute and Program Music,'" *19th-Century Music* 7, 233–50.

Niedenthal, Paula, et al. 2001: "When Did Her Smile Drop? Facial Mimicry and Influences of Emotional State on the Detection of Change in Emotional Expression," *Cognition and Emotion* 15, 853–64.

Nussbaum, Charles 2007: *The Musical Representation*, Cambridge, MA: MIT Press.

O'Neill, Colleen, et al. 2001: "Infants' Responsiveness to Fathers' Singing," *Music Perception* 18, 409–25.

Papoušek, M. 1992: "Early Ontogeny of Vocal Communication in Parent-Infant Interactions," in Papoušek et al., *Non-Verbal Vocal Communication*, Cambridge: Cambridge University Press, 230–61.

Preston, Stephanie, & Frans de Waal 2002: "Empathy: Its Ultimate and Proximate Bases," *Behavioral and Brain Sciences* 25, 1–72.

Ridley, Aaron 1995: *Music, Value and the Passions*, Ithaca, NY: Cornell University Press.

Robinson, Jenefer 2005: *Deeper than Reason*, especially chapter 9: "A New Romantic Theory of Musical Expression," New York: Oxford University Press.

Scherer, Klaus, & Marcel Zentner 2001: "Emotional Effects of Music: Production Rules," in Patrik Juslin & John Sloboda eds., *Music and Emotion: Theory and Research*, New York: Oxford University Press, 361–92.

Schubert, Emery 2013: "Emotion Felt by the Listener and Expressed by the Music: A Literature Review and Theoretical Perspectives," *Frontiers in Psychology* 4, 1–12.

Scruton, Roger 1983: *The Aesthetic Understanding*, London: Methuen.

Scruton, Roger 1997: *The Aesthetics of Music*, Oxford: Oxford University Press.

Stueber, Karsten 2006: *Rediscovering Empathy: Agency, Folk Psychology, and the Human Sciences*, Cambridge, MA: MIT Press.

Trehub, Sandra 2003: "Musical Predispositions in Infancy: An Update," in R. J. Zatorre & Isabelle Peretz eds., *The Cognitive Neuroscience of Music*, Oxford: Oxford University Press, 3–20.

Trevarthen, Colwyn 1979: "Communication and Cooperation in Early Infancy: A Description of Primary Intersubjectivity," in Margaret Bullowa ed., *Before Speech: The Beginning of Interpersonal Communication*," Cambridge: Cambridge University Press, 321–47.

Vines, Bradley et al. 2006: "Cross-Modal Interactions in the Perception of Musical Performance," *Cognition* 101, 80–113.

Vines, Bradley et al. 2011: "Music to My Eyes: Cross-Modal Interactions in the Perception of Emotions in Musical Performance," *Cognition* 118, 157–70.

Vuoskoski, Jonna, & Tuomas Eerola 2012: "Can Sad Music Really Make You Sad? Indirect Measures of Affective States Induced by Music and Autobiographical Memories," *Psychology of Aesthetics, Creativity, and the Arts* 6, 204–13.

Wöllner, Clemens 2012: "Is Empathy Related to the Perception of Emotional Expression in Music? A Multimodal Time-Series Analysis," *Psychology of Aesthetic Creativity and the Arts* 6, 214–23.

Zangwill, Nick 2012: "Music and Emotion: A Survey of Some Central Problems," *JTLA* (Journal of the Faculty of Letters, The University of Tokyo, Aesthetics) 37, 1–5.

Zentner, Marcel, et al: 2008: "Emotions Evoked by the Sound of Music: Characterization, Classification, and Measurement," *Emotion* 8, 494–521.

27

EMPATHY IN LITERATURE

Eileen John

Literature is a form of art, using the medium of language. The experience of its medium is essential to the understanding and appreciation of a given literary work. This basic conception of literature allows for both fictional and non-fictional literary works; the literary kinds associated with fiction – the novel, short story, drama, and much poetry – raise issues of particular interest in relation to empathy, so fiction will be the focus here. Literary works do not lend themselves easily to generalization, but one thing they do fairly universally is use the resources of language to offer and portray possibilities of experience. Literary works typically explore what can be undergone, done, sensed, felt, and thought by conscious beings. These possibilities can be grasped as belonging to an author, a narrating agent, and to explicitly depicted persons or fictional characters. A literary work can thus produce a complex layering or interrelation of experiential perspectives (see Feagin 1996 on readers' mental "shifts and slides": 59–82; Robinson 2005: 175–88; Goldie 2012: 30). Readers can give uptake to, and link and compare, diverse perspectives in the course of a single work. In the very broad sense of offering experiential shifts issuing from perspectives other than one's own, literature seems to be rather pervasively in the empathy business.

Literature might not seem to be too distinctive in this regard, since art in general can be viewed as a domain of perspective-shifting experience. Though not attempting to make a uniqueness claim, I would still offer literature, both the writing and the reading of it, as a rather extreme manifestation of a human urge to know how lives feel, how minds work, and what a full awareness of interacting agents with distinct subjectivities would amount to (Zunshine 2006). This urge can be pursued in literature through the finely conceptualizing, specifying, ordering, relating, and expressive powers of language. Erich Auerbach says of Homer,

> With the utmost fullness, with an orderliness which even passion does not disturb, Homer's personages vent their inmost hearts in speech; what they do not say to others, they speak in their own minds [...] no speech is so filled with anger or scorn that the particles which express logical and grammatical connections are lacking or out of place.
>
> *(Auerbach 1953: 6)*

Dorrit Cohn notes the perhaps paradoxical reality-effect of fiction that gives us an intimacy with others' inner lives that we do not have with real others: "the special life-likeness of narrative fiction – as compared to dramatic and cinematic fictions – depends on what writers and readers know least in life: how another mind thinks, another body feels" (Cohn 1978: 5–6). These remarks about what seems to be the impossibly perspicuous and accessible rendering of experience in literature raise some issues I will return to. For now I hope they suggest the interest of thinking about empathy in relation to literature.

Reading requires being open at least to the experiential shift involved in letting a stretch of language generated by another occupy one's consciousness. The "occupation" can be intimate, the words closely guiding what is present in a reader's thinking. Some things we read do not aim to trigger processes of connected thought (grocery lists, credit card bills), but literary works engaged with the possibilities of experience are likely to support uptake of processes of perception, thought, and feeling. While this uptake can be said to be empathetic in a very broad sense – the reader's perspective shifts to follow a process of thought that is not of her own making – this would not suffice for empathy as that term is most commonly used.

The narrower conception of empathy that I will focus on is that in empathizing one responds to another conscious being and experiences the response as governed by and to some degree replicating how that other experiences his or her (or its) situation. In empathizing, my sense of another's situation and of his or her concerns in that situation sets the terms for my experiential perspective. Empathy is sometimes described as "feeling with" another, feeling what she feels on the basis of getting inside what she experiences as salient and significant. For various reasons, I will de-emphasize the "success" requirement, namely, the idea that empathetic experience successfully replicates the experience of the "target" (Gibson 2016: 243–4). In empathetic encounters with people, maybe we commonly replicate what the other feels to some extent, but what is more basic is that the empathizer understands the experience in this way, as an activity or state in which another's perspective is at work within one's own experience. We take ourselves to be responding as the other has to her own situation – we feel moved in a way that we experience as making sense from that other's perspective. Eva Dadlez, speaking of empathy with fictional characters, says "the construal is made on behalf of the character" (Dadlez 1997: 183). We sometimes may get evidence suggesting the construal did or did not match the other's experience, but proving the success is elusive (Matravers 2011: 27; McFee 2011). Especially in the literary case, what matters is that we take ourselves to be achieving empathetic alignment and understanding. We find our thoughts and feelings being guided by another's situation and concerns (alignment), and we take this to be informative about their experience (understanding). In the literary context, we often frame the empathetic experience differently than the target would or could frame it, and that framing will interfere with the possibility of purely successful matching. In any case, empathy has the meaning within the empathizer's experience of manifesting the other's perspective and experience.

If empathy requires taking oneself to respond as another has to her lived situation, a reader of fiction would rarely be in a position to empathize with an author. Fictional works will usually not serve to inform and guide readers as to what authors have undergone. Of course the language that an author selects somehow manifests the author's experiential perspective. But the trace of authorial experience that shows up on the page is likely to be too indirect and obscure for a reader to follow, and there is not a convention of fiction-reading that readers should try to follow such traces back toward empathy with an author. Readers are very unlikely to think that they have informative access to an author's experience, despite their close contact with what an author has done in writing the work. This highlights another basic assumption about empathy, namely, that the empathizer is aware of the empathetic experience as such. If I empathize with Donald, the connection with Donald is transparent to me. But the fiction reader's focus is usually the work itself and its representational content, rather than authorial experience. In the case of a memoir, in contrast, focus on the author's experiential perspective can be encouraged and could prompt empathy with the author.

Empathy for fictional characters

Discussions of literature and empathy typically focus on the possibility, mechanisms, and value of empathizing with fictional characters. I will consider these issues in turn, but will start by sketching a few examples. These can be offered as examples only in a suggestive spirit, since empathy is specific to individual reading experiences. The fine variations in response to fiction also do not make it easy to interpret responses as empathetic. I hope these relatively brief and simple passages nonetheless provide a more concrete sense of what can be talked about under this heading.

Toward the middle of Vladimir Nabokov's *Lolita*, there is a scene in which Humbert Humbert leaves Dolores playing tennis with another girl for a few minutes. He returns with cold drinks, "and then a sudden void within my chest made me stop as I saw that the tennis court was deserted" (Nabokov 1991: 163). During Humbert's obsessively isolating travels with the child Dolores, there are numerous incidents like this, in which she appears to have a chance of escaping. At some level, I expect that every reader wants Dolores to escape. However, I also expect that readers have many empathetic experiences aligned with Humbert. A reader, not in any sense "on board" with his project of control and sexual exploitation of Dolores, still seems likely to register the deserted tennis court with a hint of Humbert's alarm and sense of emptiness. *Lolita* sets up a kind of worst-case scenario for achieving this kind of alignment – with a linguistically over-the-top paedophile as its first-person narrator – and still does it.

Another first-person narrator, in Julio Cortázar's story "Axolotl," recounts a detail he observes in the salamander-like axolotls he visits at the aquarium:

> Once in a while a foot would barely move, I saw the diminutive toes poise mildly on the moss. It's that we don't enjoy moving a lot, and the tank is so cramped – we barely move in any direction and we're hitting one of the others with our tail or our head – difficulties arise, fights, tiredness. The time feels like it's less if we stay quietly.
>
> *(Cortázar 1967: 5)*

That first observational sentence is able, I think, to offer a brief empathetic moment in a reader's experience with a generally very puzzling narrator. The careful description of the movement, zeroing in on the small foot and its even smaller toes (and following much description of static axolotls), lets the reader feel the narrator's deepening absorption and even excitement at this sign of life and perhaps intention. The empathetic moment is broken abruptly by the next sentence, which leaps past the narrator's eventual transformation into an axolotl, and proceeds matter-of-factly as if answering a casual question about why axolotls do what they do. The last sentence might shift a reader back toward something more like empathy, now with the narrator-as-axolotl, as it notes the unelaborated but somehow crushing impact of time.

Gish Jen's story "Duncan in China" centers on Chinese-American Duncan who has come to China to teach English in the early 1980s. He has a shaming, uncomfortable meeting with a cousin and the cousin's young son. They scrabble out a marginal living, Duncan finds them coarse and repellent, and they throw Duncan's unthinking good fortune into relief. Afterward, Duncan talks to his Chinese boss:

"I'm going to adopt that child," announced Duncan, though in fact he had not decided what to do. In fact, he wasn't even sure a single man could legally adopt a child […]. Still, it was what he wished to do. Or, more accurately: He wished to be the sort of person who would adopt a child like Bing Bing. […] But was he that person? And if he was, why did he feel as though he needed to lie down and sleep for a long, long time?

(Jen 1999: 87)

A reader might take up various perspectives on Duncan's progress from bold statement of noble intention to yearning for the oblivion of sleep, perhaps seeing through him as an ethical poseur, and also sympathizing with him in his ethically uncomfortable situation. But I think some empathetic "downward momentum" can also lead a reader through this passage, if one feels the steady deflation of his ethical confidence and the desire to hide from his own weakness.

Let me sum up what leads me to offer these cases as examples. As a reader I experienced my responses to them as manifesting, and making evaluative and affective sense from, the position of a given character. That Dolores is not there, that an axolotl moved its toes, or that Duncan's ethical ambition dissipates, and that these circumstances should feel alarming, absorbing, or deflating, are packages of attention, assessment, and affect that seem best described by saying the reader takes up and is moved by the cognitive-perceptual state and concerns of a character. In these cases other perspectives are likely to operate in a reader's experience as well, but I think something important about the reading experience would be missing if that alignment with the character's perspective, and the felt grip of it that I experienced, were discounted. An alternate description of what the reader does – namely, "in-his-shoes" imagining, imagining what I would think and feel if I were in the character's position – seems inaccurate certainly with respect to Humbert and the narrator on the way to becoming an axolotl. I simply would not be moved as they are moved, and what I do feel as a reader makes sense to me as hanging on these characters' tendencies and concerns. Perhaps the Duncan case is more susceptible to an "in-his-shoes" response, as most adult readers could imagine themselves along an ethically deflating path like Duncan's; my inclination is to add such a perspective into the mix – I both take up Duncan's perspective and feel how his situation would pull me in a similar direction.

These examples also illustrate some of the interesting possibilities of empathy in relation to fiction. The positions of Duncan and Humbert are, respectively, ethically unattractive and despicable; we can empathize with them without liking or wanting to be like them, and without endorsing the desires that move them (Currie 1997, 2004, 2010; Dadlez 1997: 190). With the narrator who turns into an axolotl, liking or disliking him is not really the question; the story is not aimed, it seems, at establishing a psychologically comfortable connection between reader and character. Yet even with that narrator, I think the story supports moments of empathy and presses the further question of empathy with the axolotls. A literary work can make the potential, the limits, and strangeness of empathy into themes.

Stepping back from the examples, there are two systematic skeptical questions to be considered. The possibility of empathizing with fictional characters could be challenged as part of the long-standing philosophical debate about the status of attitudes and emotions directed at the merely fictional. There is no person or conscious being to empathize with in the case of a fictional character, so doesn't that immediately squash the possibility of empathy? I will set aside this baldly metaphysical worry. The fact that a fictional character does not exist as a living being does not, as it turns out, prevent readers from experiencing the shifts of perspective that are the juicy core of empathy. Readers have cognitively and affectively cogent bases for identifying their responses as empathetic, in relation to what a given character is represented as undergoing.

James Harold points out that we can argue effectively and make sense of being wrong about empathetic feelings for characters (Harold 2000: 347–8). However the larger debates about fiction are resolved, we need to acknowledge responses to works of fiction that have the important experiential hallmarks and sense of directedness of empathy. Note that the lack of an actually existing target can be considered a reason for downplaying or dismissing the criterion of "successful" matching of feeling as relevant to empathy and fiction (Feagin 1996: 96; Neill 2006: 256; Knight 2006: 274).

A different kind of possibility objection rests on a claim about what fictional characters are, as opposed to what they are not. On this objection, fictional characters are all too obviously not enough like real people to be empathized with. We engage with them as elements of narrative wholes for which demands of genre, thematic unity, and plot structure permeate our interpretive and appreciative engagement (Feagin 1996: 95–100; Knight 2006: 277–9). The psychological and broadly life-sensitive responses appropriate in relation to a person are not what are called for – or, more weakly, they can inform but not govern response – with respect to characters. Keeping the "external perspective" on characters in view, treating them as the constructs of storytelling that they actually are, makes "empathy with a character" seem a misleading label for response to the textual, conventional, and artistic elements offered by fiction. Deborah Knight argues that we need "a more formalist and narratological account" of understanding and appreciation of fiction, in which psychological notions of empathetic response to characters would be strongly subordinated (Knight 2006: 279). Susan Feagin, meanwhile, acknowledges that the "elicitors" of a reader's responses typically differ significantly from what the text presents as eliciting a character's experience, but argues that readers' responses can nonetheless be empathetic if they meet some distinctive conditions: a reader's responses can be structurally similar to processes a character is said to undergo, and readers can, through reflection, integrate the person-centered and literary significance of their responses. I can reasonably attribute emotion to a character when that attribution "makes interpretive sense of the fictional work" (Feagin 1996: 98).

On the one hand, the point about the literary context in which we respond to fictional characters seems obvious and important. What we do with fictional characters is influenced by powers of language, narration, convention, and artistic control that have no obvious parallels in psychologically engaging encounters with people. We are not responding to people, and what is at stake in our responses is different – my empathy for a character is not part of an encounter in which I deal well or badly with another person. My empathy seems to be part of a process in which I hope to do a particular kind of justice to the work. (And we should not assume that empathy with characters is inevitably a way of doing justice – if I unstintingly empathize with Humbert, I will not do justice to *Lolita*.)

On the other hand, empathy for characters seems clearly to mobilize resources for responding to people. The perspectival input offered by a character has, to some extent, the content, organization, and force – the coherence and momentum – of a person's perspective. I do not see a particularly tidy way of explaining how we integrate the literary-fiction-sensitive and the person-sensitive aspects of empathy for characters. Presumably it occurs in some way distinctively with each work. To return to the "Axolotl" example above, the fact that I empathize with Cortázar's character on his way to becoming an axolotl clearly emerges from my awareness of the project of the story: to document such a transformation as if it is a somehow possible outcome of devoted attention to captive axolotls. Without that wonderful fictional trajectory in mind (as announced in the first paragraph of the story, "Now I am an axolotl"), a sentence telling me that someone saw a movement of salamander toes would be very unlikely to trigger an empathetic response. As a reader I am looking for the initiation of the transformation, primed to find what could count as a significant entry into the life of the axolotl. That sentence has, I would say, both "person-shaped" and "story-shaped" force. Gregory Currie, discussing an Anne Brontë novel, stresses that the empathy it triggers is "modified by such other reactions as ironic distance" and "awareness of the author's manipulation of our responses," and more generally that "reflection on the empathic structure of the work" contributes to understanding the author's intentions and the work's structure (Currie 2004: 186–7). A reader's awareness of narrative role and the interpretive significance of empathy is part of why the "successful matching" condition seems implausible in relation to empathy with characters. The empathetic experience is guided by a "person-perspective *plus*," as it were. A work will lead readers to enhance the person-shaped perspective with story-shaped significance and awareness.

Explaining empathetic response to fiction

What are the mechanisms by which literary works prompt empathy with characters? Recalling the Auerbach and Cohn remarks mentioned earlier, it might seem that we have a simple answer at hand. Literary works can put into words what these imagined people perceive, think, feel, and do, thus granting us access to their experiences and enabling us to give uptake to their perspectives. Note that the Nabokov and Cortázar passages report on a physical scene or object that is the focus of the narrator's perceptual attention, and this seems immediately to enable at least a partial alignment of experience in the reader (Coplan 2004: 141–2). The passage from Jen's story gives us direct speech on the part of the character, and then a series of assertions and questions that, if not strictly the words that ran through Duncan's head (they refer to him, for instance, in the third person), appear to record perspicuously what he was thinking. A work of literature can also focus steadily on the thoughts and experiences of a single character, say Dostoyevsky's Underground Man or the protagonist whose husband has left her in Anita Brookner's *A Misalliance*. However, these possibilities for articulation and focus are not especially explanatory, given that they can be in place in a work and yet not prompt empathy. We are introduced to Brookner's character Blanche Vernon with some sharp attention to her state of mind, including first-person reflection: "I am innocent, she felt like proclaiming on particularly inclement days, and I always was. My husband left me for a young woman with a degree in computer sciences and in whom I can discern not the slightest spark of imagination" (Brookner 1986: 5). This novel does, I would say, build up the possibility of some empathetic connection with this character, but not simply because of its careful attention to her circumstances and feelings; it is too amusing, and the narration and the character somehow hold engagement with her at bay. The resources of fiction for focus and psychological report are relevant to why it has potential for establishing empathy with characters, but they are not explanatorily sufficient.

One might also hold that the "impossibly good" resources of literary fiction for presenting experience in fact work against empathizing (Carroll 2001: 312). Alex Neill, contrasting literary and cinematic fictional characters, argues that the detailed information offered about the thoughts and feelings of literary characters can impede empathy: "the motive for empathizing [...] is the desire to understand how things are with them" and "we do not *need* to empathize with them in order to understand them" (Neill 2006: 255). Although it seems right that empathizing, considered as a standing human capacity, serves a need to understand others, it is not so clear that instances of empathy are motivated by the desire to understand another. Do I want to improve my understanding of the characters I empathize with? Sometimes yes, but sometimes I just find myself empathizing with a character such as Humbert, without experiencing myself as curious or as problematically ignorant. I can empathize with characters I take myself to understand well, and ones for whom there really is not much to know (e.g., the doomed side character in a murder mystery, the pig hoping a straw house will fend off the wolf). Needing or not needing to understand another does not seem to distinguish the positions of those likely or not likely to empathize. But Neill's point suggests a related issue, which is whether empathy can be "handed to us on a plate" or whether it requires some kind of independent activity or processing that crosses a gap between self and other. The crucial thing that can be missing in a reader, even when filled with articulate, psychologically revealing detail about a character, is what might be called activation of concern (Giovannelli 2009: 85). That the character finds something to be relevant to her prospects has to be at work in my experience, and whether that happens is not determined by having rich or impoverished understanding of the character. Though I think a work can prepare for and aim to prompt empathy, it is a process that the reader has to complete in some way, and that is not fully under the control of the work.

It need not be under the reader's control either; it is just that it is in the reader that activation of concern occurs. Virginia Woolf's *Mrs. Dalloway* leads up to a society party given by the title character, and she worries that it is not gelling as a party: "Oh dear, it was going to be a failure; a complete failure, Clarissa felt it in her bones as dear old Lord Lexham stood there apologising for his wife" (Woolf 1925: 254). I empathize with Clarissa Dalloway at this point, but for me it is a good question how this concern is activated. The party is filled with self-important, politically conservative types, it is a celebration of upper-class mores and privilege, and Clarissa herself is fairly hard to warm to. The structure of the novel seems to matter, in the way the party brings narrative threads together, and the novel's own questioning of the meaning and value of the party is somehow important. As Knight and Feagin might put it, my empathy is entwined with the character's role and meaning *in the novel*, not just with the woman hosting the party.

Although this line of thought does not lead to a confident account of the "mechanisms" behind empathy with characters, an approach that seems helpful is Currie's appeal to the embedding of empathetic experience in "a project with a certain kind of narrative shape" (Currie 2004: 182; Goldie 2002: 195–9). Currie describes this as a "narrative of inquiry" about the one empathized with (Currie 2004: 185); as just suggested, I would not link empathy too tightly to inquiring about the other. However, it sounds plausible that a work, when prompting empathy, provides the means for tracking the character as a sort of protagonist in at least a mini-narrative. For concern to be activated, it seems that seeing where the other has come from and is trying to go, grasping the path the other hopes to be on, would be the relevant basis. That such tracking is available to the reader is again not sufficient for explaining empathy, and might rather prompt a more detached response, as I had to Brookner's Blanche Vernon, but it is a good candidate for a minimally necessary "mechanism."

So far I have focused on the reader's empathy in terms of what it means for the reader: it shows up in her experiential economy as a matter of being moved by the cognitive-perceptual state and concerns of a character. A great deal of discussion focuses on what exactly the reader could be doing, in order to end up in a state that she takes to have that function. It is difficult to survey this territory because the trickiness of theories of engagement with fiction mix and match with diverse accounts of empathy. Generally some kind of imaginative entertainment of fictional content is assumed, but what is that imaginative activity? Is it a matter of simulating, letting one's own system "run" on the basis of what the work offers, or of assimilating complex information in building up an understanding of a fictional world? Then the nature, frequency, and importance of empathy within the imaginative activity is disputed. You may think that imagining is essential to reading fiction but not to empathy (Walton 1990, 2015), that the reader's imaginative activity centrally involves simulation, as does empathy (Feagin 1996; Currie 1997, 2004, 2010), that empathy for characters need not involve simulation (Kieran 2003), or that empathy is not that common or important in relation to fictional characters, especially because readers and characters are typically in very different informational and evaluative positions (Carroll 1998, 2001, 2011; Goldie 2012: 31–2; Lamarque 2009). The persistent question is to describe what a reader does such that "self-other differentiation" is maintained – the empathizer is aware that another's perspective is at work (Coplan 2004), while allowing for that perspective indeed to be at work. How can I be me, thinking and feeling as I do, while thinking and feeling on behalf of a character (Goldie 2011)?

As my brief examples above were intended to show, experiences with fiction that merit that description seem relatively ordinary. Alternative, perhaps less puzzling accounts – that I am experiencing what I would think and feel in the other's position, or that I am just reacting to the character as an observer – do not seem descriptively adequate. Introspection on these experiences is helpful, I think, with respect to identifying their meaning for the empathizer, but not very helpful with respect to identifying underlying psychological processes. It seems possible that different readers reach empathetic experience by different routes, some using input about a character to simulate the character's experience, and others using it to form and be moved by a gestalt laden with character-based import (Robinson 2005: 128). I do not want to offer an account that is more precise and confident than seems warranted. A broader point that seems relevant is that reading fiction is an activity we seek out partly in order to change our agency and "centeredness" with respect to thought and feeling. There is a relaxation of control, some kind of openness to letting other patterns of attention, conceptualization, and evaluation occupy the experiential foreground. However we ultimately locate "the self" in the psychological processes at work, it seems that empathetic response to characters is one important form of experience enabled by this openness.

The value of empathy in literature

Finally, what is the value of empathy in relation to literature? As a number of theorists point out, empathy is just one amongst a range of responses that need to be acknowledged and understood (Smith 1995; Feagin 1996), and the value of empathetic response may hang on that fact in some way. The sequence, contrast, and comparison of responses may be important to their collective value.

One view emphasizes that empathy and other emotionally charged responses are important to the appreciation of literary works. Jenefer Robinson argues that "emotional responses give us important information about a novel, information that is not available to someone who does not respond emotionally" (Robinson 2005: 133). In Feagin's terms, appreciating a work of literary fiction is a matter of experiencing its value and that includes "being affectively or emotionally moved" – an appreciator reads "with feeling" (Feagin 1996: 1). Empathy, to the extent that it contributes to an informative and full experience of a work, particularly by helping us to understand characters, thus has value within literary practice. One might say that this makes empathy instrumental in appreciation, helping us to "get the value out of" the work (Feagin 1996: 1), without itself having literary value. However, even if empathetic power and experience are instrumental to appreciation, I think Robinson and Feagin are persuasive in showing that reading with feeling – at least for some works of literature – is not contingently instrumental to appreciation. Responding to the affective potential of some works is *the* way to appreciate them, and it is then not obvious why the experiences so central to appreciation would not themselves be part of what we value about the work.

Peter Lamarque suggests that emotional responses, including empathy, "tend to be too reader-relative or culture-specific" to "play a central role in literary criticism" (Lamarque 2009: 247). Since I have said that a work cannot ensure empathetic response, and that this depends on the activation of concern in a given reader, it sounds sensible not to tie the value of a work to its actual effectiveness in prompting empathy. Nonetheless, it seems that we do count empathetic aspirations and achievements as interesting and important with respect to some works (as I do with "Axolotl" and indeed with *Lolita*). Perhaps we have a flexible critical practice that lets empathy and failure of empathy matter when we can tell how those effects figure into the aims and power of a given work. If we think more loosely about the pleasures of reading, not worrying about literary value, it seems that many readers would count empathetic response as part of the pleasure. It is a response that can bind us to a story, making a character vividly present. That a reader finds a work *interesting* can be the result of having formed empathetic connections to its characters.

Views about the value of empathy in response to literature often point beyond the practice of reading and literary appreciation. Feagin thinks of literary fiction in part as "equipment for exercising our minds," helping us to develop "affective flexibility," expanding our ability to imagine possibilities adequately (Feagin 1996: 248). Murray Smith develops a related view in casting narrative art as a kind of "extended mind" technology that allows us to expand and refine empathetic response (Smith 2011). Lisa Zunshine, although more concerned with fiction as exercising our ability to attribute mental states to others (not necessarily depending on empathetic connection), presses the general claim that we take pleasure in fiction because we experience it as pervasively testing and making us aware of our "mind-reading wellbeing" (Zunshine 2006: 21).

Along with finding value in empathetic response as an extension and flexing of imaginative, affective, and mind-reading capacities, one can value the content and specific processes of empathy afforded by fiction. Currie suggests that empathetic experience with fiction can work against complacent entrenchment in one's own outlook: "Few of us have an outlook that is undistorted, wholly reliable, and maximally designed to achieve our own flourishing," and in empathizing we can "try on for size" another outlook (Currie 1997: 73). The relation between emotions and normative judgment is often interestingly at work in empathy, as we may experience emotional alignment with a character caught up in values we do not accept or fully understand, and that awkward position may be illuminating, perhaps enabling critical assessment of the character or of our own value commitments (Dadlez 1997: 187–94). Keith Oatley sees the power of artistic fiction as deriving importantly from the fact that it does not merely engage habitual schemas for emotional response: the empathetic response to a literary character can show we are capable of feeling things "we might not normally admit to ourselves, which we might think belong only to others" (Oatley 2011: 117). Oatley's point suggests that while we know that "the other is the source" of the empathy – we are aware of self-other differentiation (Oatley 2011: 113) – this does not mean that the empathetic experience is safely cordoned off in its significance for the empathizer. We can have reason to probe the basis for our empathy and to consider what we might know about ourselves on that basis.

The specific empathizing projects that a literary work supports may not be focused on celebrating or strengthening empathy, but may exploit those projects for some further purpose. Tzachi Zamir's discussion of Shakespeare's *Richard III* makes the empathetic response to an evil character one part of an engagement with moral skepticism and its psychological bases, and with the limited reach of philosophical argument. The play involves "dimensions of response that counter empathy and conflict with it" (Zamir 2007: 86). Or, as with "Axolotl," a work may be about empathy itself, exploring it as an interesting and potentially problematic form of connectedness. Terry Eagleton, reading Keats's "Ode to a Nightingale" – in which the figure hearing the nightingale feels "too happy in thine happiness," until "Now more than ever seems it rich to die" – takes the poem to address "an empathy so intense that it prefigures the seductive indifference of death" (Eagleton 2009: 71). Joshua Landy, meanwhile, urges us to resist valorizing fictional empathy as if it is inevitably desirable as a servant of real-world empathy, and as if "there is simply no such thing as too much *Mitgefühl*" (Landy 2010: 223). Citing *Lolita* as exemplary for showing that the ideal reader can be "one who continually *stands back* from her empathy" (Landy 2010: 224), Landy further presents Flaubert's *Madame Bovary* as asking readers to cancel out competing empathies and "as a result, to feel, with the hard-bitten, hard-won resignation of the ancient skeptics, the perfect calm of absolutely nothing" (Landy 2010: 229). Empathetic response to fiction can itself be the target of critical scrutiny.

Conclusion

Let me conclude with a few basic thoughts. The literary experience of empathy draws on psychological, imaginative, and interpretive capacities we use in relating to people. It is a manifestation of what we do in "attuning to others" (Oatley 2011: 113) and finding them to be real, interesting, and ethically weighty. Empathy can help fictional characters "come to life" and grip us as readers. But the literary context is also quite different, since it eliminates (most of) the practical engagement and decision-making that empathy ordinarily helps us with. This difference is likely to explain, in part, why empathy can roam as freely and surprisingly as it does in the realm of fiction. With a literary work we respond to an artistic construction, and empathy with a character will be framed within that experience. As many of those cited above note, the literary work can also lead to critical reflection on the empathetic response, in a way that is hard to do (and perhaps inappropriate) in responding to a person.

Literature is an art form offering complex experiential shifts and, very broadly construed, possibilities for empathy. I have supported the more narrowly focused view that some responses to fictional characters are empathetic, where this is not just a matter of imagining oneself in another's shoes. This empathy exemplifies a relaxation of the self's control of perspective, an openness to "activation" by another's concerns, that it seems we seek out in fiction. This activation might involve simulation or other mechanisms that allow a character's perspective to guide a reader's response. My focus has been on the empathetic meaning of the response, where this reflects the person-shaped perspective of the character and the literary context. Echoing a point made by John Gibson, it seems unhelpful to require successful matching of characters' feelings. As Gibson suggests, focusing on the process, "the imaginative project of attempting to grasp" another's perspective (Gibson 2015: 244), is more fruitful for understanding the significance of literary empathy. The empathizing reader is in the process of building a not merely self-oriented sense of the meaningful environment. This experiential openness can benefit the reader as an appreciator of fiction, as well as exercising capacities relevant to attunement to real others.

References

Auerbach, E. (1953) *Mimesis*, Princeton: Princeton University Press.
Brookner, A. (1986) *A Misalliance*, London: Grafton Books.
Carroll, N. (1998) *A Philosophy of Mass Art*, Oxford: Clarendon Press.
——— (2001) "Simulation, Emotions, and Morality," in *Beyond Aesthetics*, Cambridge: Cambridge University Press, 306–16.
——— (2011) "On Some Affective Relations between Audiences and the Characters in Popular Fictions," in A. Coplan and P. Goldie (eds.) *Empathy: Philosophical and Psychological Perspectives*, Oxford: Oxford University Press, 162–84.
Cohn, D. (1978) *Transparent Minds*, Princeton: Princeton University Press.

Coplan, A. (2004) "Empathic Engagement with Narrative Fictions," *Journal of Aesthetics and Art Criticism* 62:2, 141–52.

Cortázar, J. (1967) "Axolotl," in *Blow-up and Other Stories*, P. Blackburn (trans.), New York: Pantheon Books, 3–9.

Currie, G. (1997) "The Paradox of Caring," in M. Hjort and S. Laver (eds.) *Emotion and the Arts*, New York: Oxford University Press, 63–77.

——— (2004) "Anne Brontë and the Uses of Imagination," in *Arts and Minds*, Oxford: Clarendon Press, 173–88.

——— (2010) "Narration, Imitation, and Point of View," in G. L. Hagberg and W. Jost (eds.) *A Companion to the Philosophy of Literature*, Chichester: Wiley-Blackwell, 331–49.

Dadlez, E. (1997) *What's Hecuba to Him?*, University Park: Pennsylvania State University Press.

Eagleton, T. (2009) *Trouble with Strangers*, Chichester: Wiley-Blackwell.

Feagin, S. (1996) *Reading with Feeling*, Ithaca: Cornell University Press.

Gibson, J. (2016) "Empathy," in N. Carroll and J. Gibson (eds.) *Routledge Companion to Philosophy of Literature*, London: Taylor & Francis, 234–46.

Giovannelli, A. (2009) "In Sympathy with Narrative Characters," *Journal of Aesthetics and Art Criticism* 67:1, 83–95.

Goldie, P. (1999) "How We Think of Others' Emotions," *Mind and Language* 14: 394–423.

——— (2002) *The Emotions: A Philosophical Exploration*, Oxford: Oxford University Press.

——— (2011) "Anti-Empathy," in A. Coplan and P. Goldie (eds.) *Empathy: Philosophical and Psychological Perspectives*, Oxford: Oxford University Press, 302–17.

——— (2012) *The Mess Inside: Narrative, Emotion and the Mind*, Oxford: Oxford University Press.

Harold, J. (2000) "Empathy with Fictions," *British Journal of Aesthetics* 40:3, 340–55.

Jen, G. (1999) "Duncan in China," in *Who's Irish?*, New York: Vintage Books, 49–91.

Kieran, M. (2003) "In Search of a Narrative," in M. Kieran and D. M. Lopes (eds.) *Imagination, Philosophy, and the Arts*, London: Routledge, 69–87.

Knight, D. (2006) "In Fictional Shoes: Mental Simulation and Fiction," in N. Carroll and J. Choi (eds.) *Philosophy of Film and Motion Pictures*, Malden: Blackwell, 271–80.

Lamarque, P. (2009) *The Philosophy of Literature*, Malden: Blackwell.

Landy, J. (2010) "Passion, Counter-Passion, Catharsis: Flaubert (and Beckett) on Feeling Nothing," in G. L. Hagberg and W. Jost (eds.) *A Companion to the Philosophy of Literature*, Chichester: Wiley-Blackwell, 218–38.

Matravers, D. (2011) "Empathy as a Route to Knowledge," in A. Coplan and P. Goldie (eds.) *Empathy: Philosophical and Psychological Perspectives*, Oxford: Oxford University Press, 19–30.

McFee, G. (2011) "Empathy: Interpersonal vs Artistic?," in A. Coplan and P. Goldie (eds.) *Empathy: Philosophical and Psychological Perspectives*, Oxford: Oxford University Press, 185–208.

Nabokov, V. (1991) *The Annotated Lolita*, A. Appel (ed.), London: Penguin Books.

Neill, A. (2006) "Empathy and (Film) Fiction," in N. Carroll and J. Choi (eds.) *Philosophy of Film and Motion Pictures*, Malden: Blackwell, 247–59.

Oatley, K. (2011) *Such Stuff as Dreams: The Psychology of Fiction*, Chichester: John Wiley & Sons.

Robinson, J. (2005) *Deeper than Reason*, Oxford: Oxford University Press.

Smith, M. (1995) *Engaging Characters: Fiction, Emotion, and the Cinema*, Oxford: Oxford University Press.

——— (2011) "Empathy, Expansionism, and the Extended Mind," in A. Coplan and P. Goldie (eds.) *Empathy: Philosophical and Psychological Perspectives*, Oxford: Oxford University Press, 99–117.

Walton, K. (1990) *Mimesis as Make-Believe*, Cambridge, MA: Harvard University Press.

——— (2015) *In Other Shoes*, New York: Oxford University Press.

Woolf, V. (1925) *Mrs. Dalloway*, New York: Harcourt, Brace & World.

Zamir, T. (2007) *Double Vision*, Princeton: Princeton University Press.

Zunshine, L. (2006) *Why We Read Fiction*, Columbus: Ohio State University Press.

28

EMPATHY IN FILM

Jane Stadler

The concept of empathy has special significance for the study of cinema as a narrative art form because, from its inception, empathy has been seen as an integral aspect of how people engage with art and come to understand the inner life and emotions of others. Deriving from the German word "Einfühlung," the term "empathy" dates back to the aesthetic criticism of art historian Robert Vischer in 1873. It was later taken up by psychologist Theodor Lipps (1903) and others in the hermeneutic and phenomenological traditions to refer to "feeling into" an aesthetic object, a natural vista, or another person's subjective experience in order to develop an experiential understanding of other minds and works of art (see Chapter 7, "Empathy in the aesthetic tradition"). The epistemological function of empathy is an enduring focal point for research about empathy's role in understanding both art and human experience.

In contemporary film criticism there is little consensus regarding how to differentiate empathy from related terms including sympathy, the vicarious experience and embodied and imaginative simulation that cinematic narratives facilitate, the involuntary sharing of affective states via emotional contagion, the ethical deliberation often involved in perspective taking, or moral emotions such as compassion. This chapter begins with an understanding of cinematic empathy as an emotional process that occurs when audience members perceive, imagine, or hear about a film character's affective and mental state and, in so doing, vicariously experience a shared or congruent state. Philosopher Dan Zahavi's account of the phenomenology of empathy provides a particularly useful starting point for thinking about empathy in film: "empathy is the experience of the embodied mind of the other"; it takes different forms and it involves "a special kind of experiential understanding" that can be understood as "knowledge by acquaintance" (Zahavi 2014: 151). This working definition encompasses important aspects of emotive responses to cinema, including cognitive processes such as imagination as well as perceptual processes and feelings or affective states that may be shared with screen characters. The aesthetic style and content of narrative films can also cue empathy in ways that are not anchored to identification with characters, as discussed in relation to developments in phenomenological film theory later in this chapter.

In film studies, interest in empathy has arisen in relation to spectatorship, emotion, and embodied responses, primarily in the sub-fields of cinematic ethics, cognitive narratology, and phenomenological analysis (see Choi & Frey 2014; Sinnerbrink 2016; Stadler 2008). Writing in the 1920s, Béla Balázs was one of the first to suggest that cinematic close-ups of the human face render the subject's "feelings, emotions, moods, intentions and thoughts" not only visible but also *palpable* (1952: 61). Balázs's work is notable for his emphasis on the "psychological subtleties of moving emotions" revealed in the close-up and its effect on film spectators through the magnification of facial expressions and gestures on screen to subtly convey the human being's embodied subjectivity (1952: 63, 67). This work introduced ideas about the empathic qualities of close-ups, including acoustic close-ups, in ways that prefigured cognitivist studies of facial feedback, contemporary embodiment theory, and phenomenological analysis by some eighty years.

Balázs was ahead of his time in his analysis of acoustic close-ups as an emotive technique available only to cinema, not to stage performances. He observes that "[s]ubtle associations and interrelations of thoughts and emotions can be conveyed by means of very low, soft sound effects. Such emotional or intellectual linkages can play a very decisive dramaturgical part" (Balázs 1952 210–11). Regarding the significance of the cinematic soundscape in empathy, contemporary sound designer Mark Ward emphasizes the non-conscious aspects of affective processes and acoustic aesthetics: "cinema recruits our body's innate capacity for 'feeling into' another's affective state, offering an embodied and noncognitive route to empathy, even if that other is fictional … cinematic sound design is an embodied process of experiential knowing" (2015: 185–6).

Balázs has been particularly influential in his exploration of how imaginative engagement with the materiality of the face and its aesthetic representation provides insight into human subjectivity, suggesting that screen performance and other aspects of film style such as cinematography and sound illuminate the inner life of a character and break down the opposition between self and other. Contemporary researchers have developed related ways of explaining how screen aesthetics may facilitate empathy by fostering emotional perception and social intuition. For example, cognitive film theorist Carl Plantinga analyses "scenes of empathy," which he characterizes as narrative sequences in which the audience sees a film character's face in an expressive close-up so that "the interior emotional experience of a favoured character becomes the locus of attention" (1999: 239). Plantinga notes that in such scenes the character's perceptual experience is often privileged through a shot-reverse-shot sequence that alternates between images of what the character is looking at and close-up reaction shots. Although Balázs does not use the term empathy, he focuses on the same features of cinema that Plantinga later highlights and he distinguishes film from other arts in its capacity to reveal and elicit the affective or embodied dimensions of emotion. Balázs describes a moving example of what Plantinga would call a "scene of empathy" from *Lenin in October* (dir. Mikhail Romm and Dmitriy Vasilev, 1937) wherein Lenin (Boris Shchukin) learns of the assassination of a close friend and his face silently registers love, overlaid by pain, and then hardening into anger. In apprehending the passage of emotions across Lenin's face, the audience comes to the empathic understanding "that hardness was only the reverse side of tenderness, that the revolutionary could hate so fiercely only because he could love so tenderly" (Balázs 1952: 209). This focus on aesthetic strategies used to occasion empathy has become central to debates about narrative empathy and its various manifestations in film, literature, and drama.

Narrative empathy

According to literary theorist Suzanne Keen, narrative empathy involves a vicarious, spontaneous sharing of feeling and perspective-taking that can be evoked by seeing, hearing about, reading about, or imaginatively simulating another person's story and situation (2007: 4). Narrative empathy can be involved in the creative act of narrative production, in narrative's formal and aesthetic strategies, and in mental simulation and narrative reception, but Keen cautions that it should not simply be conflated with character identification. She states, "empathy involves responses not only to sentient beings, but also to inanimate objects and landscape features. It separates aspects of motor mimicry, emotional contagion, and fusion of feelings from the older term sympathy, 'feeling for' or compassion" (Keen 2013: 5). Keen's research critically evaluates claims that fiction, and particularly literary narratives, "may elicit the expression of dispositional empathy, or it may cultivate the sympathetic imagination through the exercise of innate role-taking abilities" (2007: 3).

In relation to cinema, narrative empathy is thought to have a social and ethical function: moral philosophers and moral psychologists understand empathy to involve other-oriented processes such as position taking, which fosters intersubjectivity and may inform altruistic behavior. Significantly, film provides access to both cognitive-imaginative and affective-experiential forms of empathy because audiences are able to share in the sights and sounds of the story world and to mirror characters' emotional expressions, whereas literature primarily facilitates cognitive empathy. Film can also provide powerful cues for perspective shifting, such as subjective sound and imagery and non-diegetic music and voice-over narration that function in similar ways to first-person perspective or deep internal focalization in literature in order to provide access to the inner world of a character. Building on influential work by philosophers such as Martha Nussbaum (1992, 2001) and Stanley Cavell (1996) about the ways that literary and cinematic narratives can exercise and cultivate the moral imagination and associated empathic sensibilities, Robert Sinnerbrink notes that "Schiller's romantic ideal of art serving as a means of educating the senses towards moral maturity through the free of play of the imagination thus finds in cinematic empathy a new lease of life" (2016: 92).

Developments in cognitive film theory

Within the field of cognitive film theory, the term empathy has been used to refer "to a variety of phenomena, ranging from the conscious, imaginative effort to 'perspective take' or put oneself in another's shoes, to affective mimicry and emotional contagion, whereby we 'catch' the emotions of others through a process of low-level, non-conscious, involuntary mimicry" (Smith 2014: 37). Cognitive film theory provides a cogent account of empathy's affective and cognitive elements; however, the definition and use of these terms is contested. Adriano D'Aloia maintains that the cognitivist emphasis typically lies with psychological processes such as perspective taking, "mentalizing," imaginative simulation, and the ascription of intentions and subjective states to others, during which "the viewer adopts the characters' perspectives and deliberately reproduces their mental states" (2015: 188). Murray Smith, one of the key scholars to write about empathy and film from a cognitivist perspective, argues that "empathy is a kind of imagining; in particular it is a type of personal or central imagining" (2011: 100). Smith characterizes the imaginative simulation involved in empathy as the mental simulation of experience and it is this personal, experiential quality that goes beyond the ascription of mental states and distinguishes it from the closely related term "perspective taking." Smith writes: "in imagining how some other specified agent sees the world, and in imagining how they think and feel, I empathize with them. Let us call this type of imagining other-focused personal imagining. Such imagining allows us not merely to recognize or understand, but to grasp directly … the emotional frames of mind of others" (2011: 101). In this view, emotional contagion and affective mimicry can facilitate imaginative simulation; however, some cognitivists reject the personal quality of empathy, neglect the affective dimensions of experience, or even exclude affective mimicry from their accounts of empathy altogether. For example, Amy Coplan argues that emotional contagion, understood as "an automatic and involuntary affective process that can occur when we observe others experiencing emotions," cannot properly be considered to be empathic because it is self-directed and non-volitional (2006: 26). This cognitivist focus on the other-directed, deliberative components of empathy figures in arguments about empathy's role in ethical evaluation.

Ed Tan takes a strong cognitivist position when he maintains that "empathy does not always result in an emotion" and that empathy is "a cognitive state resulting from efforts to understand another person" (2013: 339, 340). Tan's interest is in the extent to which empathy is a process of "mind reading" and in the role screen aesthetics play in cuing intentional empathy while watching films. Tan's thoughtful and systematic work at times neglects the full significance of shared affect and emotion and suggests a limited understanding of the complexity of empathic character engagement, as is the case when he writes: "Not only is it easy or fun to put yourself in the shoes of a protagonist, but also it often seems as if we cannot help but lose ourselves in a character" (2013: 337–8). Fellow cognitivist Plantinga offers a more nuanced account, arguing that film audiences often feel a mixture of sympathy and empathy but rarely mirror a character's emotions identically; rather than empathic mimicry of a character's feelings, he focuses on how film elicits affective congruence, which may be experienced as "vicarious emotion, role taking, and the ability to understand the situation of others" (2009: 101; see also Gaut 2010).

Cognitivist approaches to empathy implicitly point to the significance of "vicarious experience" in understanding how empathy functions in narrative film. Yet, as Pierre Jacob points out, "while empathetic experiences are vicarious experiences, not all vicarious experiences are empathetic. Contagious responses to others' affective states are not empathetic responses, but they are also vicarious experiences" (2015: 5). In other words, not all vicarious experiences necessarily function to help us understand another person's mind or subjective state; sometimes, as with vicarious disgust responses, such experiences are indicative of self-directed concern because they convey an embodied apprehension of substances or actions that we ought to avoid to preserve our own wellbeing (Jacob 2015: 19). For example, a scene in Darren Aronofsky's *Requiem for a Dream* (2000) shows Tyrone (Marlon Wayans) grimace and turn away when he watches his friend Harry (Jared Leto) inject heroin into a suppurating, badly infected vein in his arm. Christine Guo and I conducted a pilot study of emotional responses to the infected vein scene in *Requiem for a Dream* and the curb-stomp scene in *American History X*, using a reverse camera to record audience reactions. The results showed pronounced affective mimicry of the characters' facial expressions, which is a key indicator of somatic empathy. Tyrone's grimace as he flinches indicates that on one level he vicariously experiences his friend's pain, but the overriding emotion expressed on his face when Harry shoots up is disgust. This is not indicative of an empathic reaction to physical or emotional pain. Tyrone's affective reaction may encode a value judgment about self-destructive addictive behavior and his recoil response suggests the self-protective quality of disgust. The film audience mirrors Tyrone's revolted facial expression and his recoil response. Cognitivists like Tan and Coplan would be unlikely to refer to the affective congruence and motor mimicry that takes place between the audience and Tyrone as empathy because the audience experiences this feeling of disgust as their own emotion: this "fellow feeling" is based on responding to the same stimuli as Tyrone and reacting with their own aversive recoil response to the extreme close-up of Harry's putrefying flesh rather than "feeling into" Tyrone's subjective experience. Contrary to Tan and Coplan's position, this visceral capacity to facilitate vicarious experience via shared responses to perceptual and affective stimuli can arguably be understood as a distinctive feature of the cinematic medium that augments film's capacity to elicit somatic empathy.

The concepts of emotional contagion, vicarious experience, and the possibility of "losing oneself" in another person lead back to early theories of empathy. Lipps contends that to experience *Einfühlung* is to feel one's way into another subject and in the process to feel a sense of interconnection or "fusion" so that the demarcation between self and other is eroded (see Chapter 7, "Empathy in the aesthetic tradition"). This ill-defined notion of empathic fusion has been interpreted in many different ways and remains a contentious point in contemporary debates about empathy's meaning and its relationship to film spectatorship, ethics, and intersubjectivity. Lipps's idea of empathic merging or "fusion" has led to concerns that empathy may either result in a loss of self or a projection of oneself into another when a film spectator "feels with" or "feels into" a screen character. For instance, D'Aloia claims there are cases where a "fusion of subjectivities occurs" during films when the spectator identifies strongly with the protagonist and experiences emotional mirroring: "the total assimilation of subjectivities stems from viewers losing self-awareness and fusing their egos with that of the character" (2015: 189). Needless to say, "total assimilation of subjectivities" only occurs in science fiction and would not, in any event, be an instance of empathy. This kind of overstatement is also found in studies of film spectatorship that describe embodied simulation in terms of a "fusion of selves" (Raz & Hendler 2014: 97).

Contrary to those who speak of "assimilation" or "fusion" during vicarious empathic experiences, Smith contends that "we do not lose ourselves in the other, but imagine possessing certain predicates of the other" (1995: 97). He goes on to argue that cinema (and narrative more generally) can function as "cognitive prostheses" that extend the capacity of the mind to grasp the plight of other people by imaginatively and affectively incorporating aspects of their experience to form an empathic connection (Smith 2011: 108–9). Smith writes that in film:

> [o]ur ability to empathise is extended across a wide range of types of person, and sustained and intensified by virtue of the artificial, 'designed' environment of fictional experience ... The possibility of understanding 'from the inside' – that is, empathically imagining – human agents in social situations more or less radically different from our own emerges. We may come not only to see, but to feel, how an agent in a given situation comes to feel.
>
> *(2011: 111)*

In Smith's work we once again find support for the argument that film has an important place in the narrative arts because the aesthetic and technical audiovisual strategies by which it "designs" or represents experience can also reproduce a protagonist's perceptual experience, thereby stimulating both the imaginative and the affective components of empathy. Smith contends that affective empathic processes provide a necessary foundation for imaginative simulation via "direct experiential knowledge" of another person's subjective state (2011: 102). He argues persuasively that affective processes have the capacity to extend one's ability to directly "grasp" the emotional states of others and to become "other-focussed" as we engage in the process of personal imagining or central imagining required for fully fledged empathy (2011: 101).

Developments in phenomenological film theory

Parallel with cognitive film theory, another model of spectatorship has been developed by scholars who ground the aesthetic experience of film in a phenomenological account of embodiment, emotion, and perception, with particular reference to the philosophy of Maurice Merleau-Ponty (1964). Phenomenology is a philosophical method of describing and reflecting on the experience of phenomena as they present themselves to consciousness (see Chapter 3, "Phenomenology, empathy and mindreading"). Film presents an ideal opportunity to study empathy at one remove from subjective experience because, as leading phenomenological film theorist Vivian Sobchack has argued, cinema involves "the perception of expression and the expression of *perception*. Indeed, it is this mutual capacity for and possession of experience through common structures of embodied existence, through similar modes of being in the world, that provide the *intersubjective* basis of objective cinematic communication" (1992: 5). In her account of cinema's perceptual and expressive capacities, I take Sobchack to mean that, on one hand, the audience perceives film's expression of narrative content when it is projected, streamed, or played on a screen. On the other hand, film simultaneously "expresses" not just the sounds and images that its recording technologies "perceive" but also the optical and acoustic point-of-view shots and internal subjective imagery or flashbacks that express what screen characters perceive within the story world. Cinematic empathy or fellow feeling may be facilitated by the experience of shared audiovisual sensations during this reciprocal process of perception and expression. This phenomenological interest in how perception, sensation, and affect give film spectators access to how a character feels is related to the "direct perception" approach that models empathic experience on perceptual experience (see Jacob 2015: 4).

Recent phenomenological research has further examined how film invites sensorial responses from audience members. For example, Christiane Voss has argued for a concept of cinema that includes the spectator's body and "emphasizes the relevance of intertwined sensations, and the interpretation of these sensations, for the aesthetic experience of the medium" (2011: 139). This interest in how the mind simulates bodily sensations in the process of interpretation has its origins in early empathy research. In 1909, when Edward Titchener used the term empathy in his *Lectures on the Experimental Psychology of the Thought Processes*, he built on Lipps's concept of *Einfühlung* in a manner that emphasized what neuroscientists now term "embodied simulation" and what phenomenologists have recently come to refer to as "kinaesthetic empathy" or "somatic empathy." Titchener wrote: "Not only do I see gravity and modesty and pride and courtesy and stateliness, but *I feel or act them in the mind's muscle.* That is, I suppose, a simple case of empathy" (emphasis added, 1909: 21 quoted in Coplan & Goldie 2011: xiii).

Julian Hanich's account of cinematic emotion (2010) explains that somatic empathy comes in three forms: *sensation, motor,* and *affective* mimicry. Although Hanich explicitly takes a phenomenological approach, he does not discount cognitive film theory. In fact, his explanation of somatic empathy draws on Smith's cognitivist terminology when he writes:

> In sensation mimicry I involuntarily and without reflection replicate a similar sensation as the character onscreen: a slimy parasite entering his ear, a hot needle being pierced in her eye … In motor mimicry, we mimic the muscular actions of someone we are observing – think of someone running or throwing a baseball. If we follow the action closely or have a strong interest in its outcome we might tense up, imitating the muscular control of the runner or player. Motor mimicry is therefore a weak or partial simulation of someone else's physical motion.
>
> *(Hanich 2010: 182)*

Affective mimicry, Hanich goes on to state, is "the phenomenon whereby we – pre-cognitively – mimic an emotion or affect expressed by someone else," typically when a close-up provides the audience with access to the character's emotional state and prompts a mirroring of their expression (2010: 183). Other film scholars have referred to this process as sensory-motor empathy, which occurs "when the viewer reproduces the observed movement such as assuming a facial expression similar to that of the character" (D'Aloia 2015: 189).

Phenomenologist Jennifer Barker's account of "kinaesthetic empathy" or muscular empathy goes beyond empathizing or identifying with film characters to claim that audiences may also experience a sense of "fellow feeling" in response to the film itself and aesthetic techniques such as travelling shots that mirror human experiences of time, space, travel, and motion (see Barker 2009: 73). This understanding of empathy privileges the embodied engagement with aesthetic objects put forward by Lipps and Vischer. Contemporary neuroscientific theories of empathy and film suggest that these ideas might be extended and used to advance knowledge of the way the bodies of audience members respond corporeally to films that replicate the kinetic experience of movement, gesture, and expression. In particular, as I discuss below, Vittorio Gallese's research into mirror neurons and "embodied simulation" provides some evidence that the neural mirroring associated with empathy can be cued by camera movement and sound as well as by screen performance.

Developments in neurocinematic approaches to empathy

An emerging field of study that is variously referred to as "neurocinematics" (Hasson et al. 2008), "neurofilmology" (D'Aloia & Eugeni 2014), "psychocinematics" (Shimamura 2013), or "neurophenomenology" (D'Aloia 2015) is complementary to existing cognitivist and phenomenological understandings of cinematic empathy (see also Coëgnarts & Kravanja 2015). This interdisciplinary research indicates that somatic engagement or the embodied simulation of gesture, motion, sensation, and emotion may be more central to cinematic empathy and, by extension, to understandings of ethics and subjectivity than has previously been recognized. Neuroscientific research studying the processing of emotions can provide evidence to support or critique theories and assumptions about cinema spectatorship and empathy by using neuro-imaging techniques and other neurophysiological measures to examine aspects of empathy and film that are unavailable to systematic reflection or textual analysis (Smith 2014: 41). The mirror neuron system is activated to produce a mental simulation of expression, sensation, and movement when experiencing emotions and intentional behavior and when observing or imagining someone else's actions and affective states (see Chapter 5, "Empathy and mirror neurons"). This capacity for internal mirroring seems crucial to human social interaction. As Smith explains, "sensory and affective mimicry enable a rapid, almost seamless, grasp of the basic affective states of the individuals and groups with whom we interact, while motor mimicry enhances not only our ability to recognise with ease and facility the intentions of others (as these are embodied in basic actions), but also our ability to pick up new motor skills" (2014: 37). Increasingly, in empirical neuroscience research, the capacity for internal mirroring is thought to be central to empathy and to empathic responses to cinema (see Chapter 4, "The neuroscience of empathy").

However, as with other theories of empathy including cognitive and phenomenological approaches, social neuroscientists differentiate between affective and cognitive empathy circuits, which involve interconnected processes that take place in different regions of the brain: "The evidence suggests that two empathy related processes, which can be generally referred to as 'embodied simulation' and 'theory of mind,' are driven by distinct neurophysiological systems" (Raz & Hendler 2014: 92; see also Pisters 2014). Embodied simulation, as proposed by Vittorio Gallese and Michel Guerra in "Embodying movies: embodied simulation and film studies" (2012), is an involuntary mirroring of emotional feeling states that relies on motor mimicry and emotional contagion. As D'Aloia points out, "Embodied simulation does not entail inference of mental states or an imaginative substitution. Rather, it is pre-logical and pre-reflexive, rooted at the sensory-motor and neurophysiological level" (2015: 190–1). The aspects of empathy related to motor mimicry or embodied simulation come close to the notion of *Einfühlung* that Vischer and Lipps initially proposed wherein a person imitates a felt, bodily state that they attribute to the subject with whom they empathize (see Zahavi 2014: 113; Raz & Hendler 2014: 93). Theory of mind, by contrast, refers to cognitive processes of attributing and understanding others' mental states.

In relation to the study of cinematic empathy, different aesthetic strategies are thought to be associated with these empathic processes: imaginative simulation is facilitated by *recounting* whereas embodied simulation is facilitated by *enactment* (Raz & Hendler 2014: 104). Specifically, Gal Raz and Talma Hendler have conducted empirical experiments that demonstrate that cognitive cues that prompt inferences about a character's motives and intentions such as extended takes, dialogue, or eye-line matches revealing gaze direction can elicit a cognitive perspective-taking process (2014: 104). By contrast, affective mimicry involving the simulation or resonance of bodily states is facilitated by audiovisual cues foregrounding the character's bodily sounds, facial expressions, and gestures, often with shots that privilege the character's aural and visual perspective (Raz & Hendler 2014: 104). Hand-held cinematography has been shown to elicit stronger mirroring responses and an augmented sense of empathic involvement with characters because it more closely resembles human movement than static camera, zooms, or dolly-mounted tracking shots (Guerra 2015: 153).

A vivid example of the aesthetic strategies used to elicit imaginative and affective modes of empathy occurs in *American History X* (Tony Kaye, 1998), when Danny (Edward Furlong) witnesses his older brother Derek (Edward Norton) brutally assault an African-American man. The scene begins with voice-over narration as Danny recounts the events: "I imagined what would have happened if I hadn't gone to his room and told him …" This cognitive cue invites the audience into Danny's memory, his imagination, and his conscience. A flashback shows Danny tell Derek that someone is trying to steal his car and a shot-reverse-shot sequence establishes motives and intentional cues as Derek furiously loads his gun, ready to retaliate. The audience is primarily cued to adopt Danny's perspective as he looks on in horror. While watching Danny anticipating how his aggressive brother will deal with the car thieves, the audience is invited to imaginatively simulate how fearful and tense Danny must be feeling, his apprehension perhaps already tinged with guilt for having sparked Derek's wrath by alerting him to the theft. A more visceral mode of empathy is triggered when Derek enacts violence, dragging the man who had broken into his car to the roadside and stomping his head against the curb. The unstable hand-held camera provides shaken, intrusive close-ups that convey a palpable sense of apprehension, and the sickening sound of teeth grating on concrete as flesh and bone give way beneath Derek's boot anchors the viewer's senses to the terror and pain of the wounded man. Finally, when a slow-motion close-up reaction shot reveals Danny's horror as he runs to intervene, the audience physically mirrors his wide-eyed expression of shock. The use of aesthetic cues in this disturbing narrative sequence orchestrates the seamless interweaving of affective mimicry and cognitive perspective taking as cinematic empathy facilitates intersubjective understanding of the experiences of the characters present in the scene.

Cinematic empathy, intersubjectivity, and intercorporeality

Recent interdisciplinary research combining neuroscience and film studies indicates that empathy functions as "a key element of human social intelligence" (Gallese 2014: 7). Gallese, who played a pivotal role in the discovery of mirror neurons, proposes that the function of mirror neurons underpins the way we understand other people's goal-directed action. In other words, figuring out how the brain works when observing characters' behavior in films may help us to understand how people come to empathize with other people's goals, actions, emotions, bodily experiences, and psychological states (Gallese 2014: 3). This suggests that affective mirroring and imaginative construal of another person's subjective perspective are not discrete processes; rather, intersubjective understanding of other people includes a kind of *intercorporeality* as well as attributing attitudes, beliefs, and desires to others (Gallese 2014: 4). In conjunction with neurocinematic research, work on embodied spectatorship and the corporeal foundations of empathy in phenomenological film studies by scholars such as Sobchack, Barker, and Hanich, and work by cognitivists such as Plantinga, Tan, and Smith, suggests that watching films may facilitate the development of embodied simulation and imaginative simulation in ways that augment empathic engagement.

The cognitive, phenomenological, and neurological studies of cinematic empathy detailed above demonstrate that film has an important role to play in developing and testing models of empathic engagement and intersubjective understanding. The research overwhelmingly indicates that equal attention must be given to imaginative perspective taking (the kind of mind reading that narrative fiction fosters so adeptly) and to how empathic understanding involves sharing embodied, experiential feelings (the kind of intercorporeality that film can elicit via direct perceptual cues). The mirroring mechanisms that underpin embodied understanding constitute an important source of our knowledge of others and our capacity for empathic insight, just as the mental processes of imagining one's way into another person's subjective state can facilitate understanding of their motives, intentions, desires, and feelings. Rather than reinforcing a value-laden dichotomy denigrating "lower-level" non-volitional, embodied forms of empathy and privileging "higher-order" cognitive-deliberative responses, the study of cinematic narratives, aesthetics, and spectatorship can help illuminate the networked interplay between these processes. Film studies can identify the aesthetic and technical cues, bodily movements and expressions, narrative scenarios, and storytelling strategies that stimulate or inhibit embodied resonance and the moral imagination. In this way the study of cinematic empathy may come to have far-reaching implications for fields as diverse as persuasive communication, intercultural understanding, psychology, and neuroscience.

References

Balázs, B. (1952) *Theory of the Film: Character and Growth of a New Art*, London: Dennis Dobson.

Barker, J. (2009) *The Tactile Eye: Touch and the Cinematic Experience*, Berkeley: University of California Press.

Cavell, S. (1996) *Contesting Tears: The Hollywood Melodrama of the Unknown Woman*, Chicago: University of Chicago Press.

Choi, J., & M. Frey (2014) *Cine-Ethics: Ethical Dimensions of Film Theory, Practice, and Spectatorship*, London: Routledge.

Coëgnarts, M., & P. Kravanja (eds.) (2015) *Embodied Cognition and Cinema*, Leuven: Leuven University Press.

Coplan, A. (2006) "Catching Characters' Emotions: Emotional Contagion Responses to Narrative Fiction Film," *Film Studies* 8.1: 26–38.

Coplan, A., & P. Goldie (2011) "Introduction," in A. Coplan & P. Goldie (eds.) *Empathy: Philosophical and Psychological Perspectives*, Oxford: Oxford University Press, ix–xlvii.

D'Aloia, A. (2015) "The Character's Body and the Viewer: Cinematic Empathy and Embodied Simulation in the Film Experience," in M. Coëgnarts & P. Kravanja (eds.) *Embodied Cognition and Cinema*, Leuven: Leuven University Press, 187–99.

D'Aloia, A., & R. Eugeni (2014) "Neurofilmology: An Introduction," *Cinema&Cie* 14.22/23: 9–26.

Gallese, V. (2014) "Bodily Selves in Relation: Embodied Simulation as Second-Person Perspective on Intersubjectivity," *Philosophical Transactions of the Royal Society B.* 369 (20130177): 1–10.

Gallese, V., & M. Guerra (2012) "Embodying Movies: Embodied Simulation and Film Studies," *Cinema: Journal of Philosophy and the Moving Image* 3: 183–210.

Gaut, B. (2010) "Empathy and Identification in Cinema," *Midwest Studies in Philosophy* 34.1: 136–57.

Guerra, M. (2015) "Modes of Action at the Movies, or Re-thinking Film Style from the Embodied Perspective," in M. Coëgnarts & P. Kravanja (eds.) *Embodied Cognition and Cinema*, Leuven: Leuven University Press, 139–54.

Hanich, J. (2010) *Cinematic Emotion in Horror Films and Thrillers: The Aesthetic Paradox of Pleasurable Fear*, New York: Routledge.

Hasson, U., O. Landesman, B. Knappmeyer, I. Vallines, N. Rubin, & D. J. Heeger (2008) "Neurocinematics: The Neuroscience of Film," *Projections: Journal of Movie and Mind* 2.1: 1–26.

Jacob, P. (2015) "Empathy and the Disunity of Vicarious Experience," *International Journal of Philosophy and Psychology (Rivista Internazionale di Filosofia e Psicologia)* 6.1: 4–23.

Keen, S. (2007) *Empathy and the Novel*, Oxford: Oxford University Press.

Keen, S. (2013) "Narrative Empathy," in *The Living Handbook of Narratology* (www.lhn.uni-hamburg.de).

Lipps, T. (1903) "Empathy, Inward Imitation, and Sense Feelings," in E. F. Carritt (ed.) *Philosophies of Beauty: From Socrates to Robert Bridges Being the Sources of Aesthetic Theory*, Oxford: Clarendon Press [1931], 252–6.

Merleau-Ponty, M. (1964) *The Primacy of Perception*, Evanston, IL: Northwestern University Press.

Nussbaum, M. (1992) *Love's Knowledge: Essays on Philosophy and Literature*, Oxford: Oxford University Press.

Nussbaum, M. (2001) *Upheavals of Thought: The Intelligence of the Emotions*, New York: Cambridge University Press.

Pisters, P. (2014) "Dexter's Plastic Brain: Mentalizing and Mirroring in Cinematic Empathy," *Cinéma & Cie* 14.22/23: 53–63.

Plantinga, C. (1999) "The Scene of Empathy and the Human Face on Film," in G. M. Smith & C. Plantinga (eds.) *Passionate Views: Film, Cognition, and Emotion*, Baltimore: Johns Hopkins University Press, 239–56.

Plantinga, C. (2009) *Moving Viewers: American Film and the Spectator's Experience*, Berkeley: University of California Press.

Raz, G., & T. Hendler (2014) "Forking Cinematic Paths to the Self: Neurocinematically Informed Model of Empathy in Motion Pictures," *Projections: A Journal of Movies and Mind* 8.2: 89–114.

Shimamura, A. (ed.) (2013) *Psychocinematics: Exploring Cognition at the Movies*, New York: Oxford University Press.

Sinnerbrink, R. (2016) *Cinematic Ethics: Exploring Ethical Experience through Film*, Abingdon/New York: Routledge.

Smith, M. (1995) *Engaging Characters: Fiction, Emotion, and the Cinema*, Oxford: Clarendon Press.

Smith, M. (2011) "Empathy, Expansionism and the Extended Mind," in A. Coplan & P. Goldie (eds.) *Empathy: Philosophical and Psychological Perspectives*, Oxford: Oxford University Press, 99–117.

Smith, M. (2014) "The Pit of Naturalism: Neuroscience and the Naturalized Aesthetics of Film," in T. Nannicelli & P. Taberham (eds.) *Cognitive Media Theory*, New York: Routledge, 27–45.

Sobchack, V. (1992) *Address of the Eye: A Phenomenology of Film Experience*, Princeton: Princeton University Press.

Stadler, J. (2008) *Pulling Focus: Intersubjective Experience, Narrative Film, and Ethics*, London: Continuum.

Tan, E. (2013) "The Empathic Animal Meets the Inquisitive Animal in the Cinema: Notes on a Psychocinematics of Mind Reading," in A. Shimamura (ed.) *Psychocinematics: Exploring Cognition at the Movies*, New York: Oxford University Press, 337–67.

Titchener, E. (1909) *Lectures on the Experimental Psychology of the Thought Processes*, New York: Macmillan.

Vischer, R. (1873) "On the Optical Sense of Form: A Contribution to Aesthetics," in H. Mallgrave & E. Ikonomou (eds. and trans.) *Empathy, Form and Space: Problems in German Aesthetics, 1873–1893*, Santa Monica, CA: Getty Center for the History of Art and the Humanities, 89–124.

Voss, C. (2011) "Film Experience and the Formation of Illusion: The Spectator as 'Surrogate Body' for the Cinema," *Cinema Journal* 50.4: 138–50.

Ward, M. (2015) "Art in Noise: An Embodied Simulation Account of Cinematic Sound Design," in M. Coëgnarts & P. Kravanja (eds.), *Embodied Cognition and Cinema*, Leuven: Leuven University Press, 155–86.

Zahavi, D. (2014) *Self and Other: Exploring Subjectivity, Empathy and Shame*, Oxford: Oxford University Press.

29

IMAGINATIVE RESISTANCE AND EMPATHY

Kathleen Stock

1. Introduction

There are some sentences which, if found in the context of a novel or short story, would be experienced as jarring by most readers. For instance:

[GK1] *In killing her baby, Giselda did the right thing: after all, it was a girl.*

(Walton 1994: 37)

Given a standard background ethical sensibility, many readers report an impression of 'resistance' when trying to imagine that [GK1] is true (leaving aside for the present what this impression exactly consists in). Other examples also discussed by philosophers include: *The village elders did their duty before God by forcing the widow on to the funeral pyre (ibid.)* and (in the context of reading Shakespeare's *Macbeth*) *The murder of Duncan was unfortunate only for having interfered with Macbeth's sleep that night* (Moran 1994: 95). Readers' reactions to such sentences don't look typical of responses to ordinary sentences in fictions (compare: *Giselda stood at the bus stop, tears streaming, holding the knife tightly*). With most sentences in fiction, it seems easy to imagine that they are true, even if their content is wildly at odds with what one would expect or even believe to be possible. Consider, for instance, how easy it is when reading Harry Potter books to imaginatively engage with fantastical events concerning flying wizards, disappearing ghosts, and transmogrifying beings.

Following Weatherson (2004), it has become common to distinguish between two explanatory challenges raised by sentences like [GK1]. The first is to explain the impression of resistance. Let's call this 'the phenomenological challenge'. The second is to explain the alleged fact that it doesn't even count as *fictionally true* that *in killing her baby, Giselda did the right thing* (etc.). I'll ignore this, for it seems clear that its central premise is controversial (indeed, I deny it: Stock, forthcoming), and that whether or not we should grant it at all will depend on what theory of fictional content should be endorsed. This is is an issue we cannot settle here.

In what follows I'll describe two common approaches to the phenomenological challenge, and a problem with both of them. I'll then introduce and defend my own preferred type of explanation. Each theory discussed will cite something like a failure of empathy as the typical cause of imaginative resistance; yet each will invoke a slightly different notion of empathy, as we'll see.

2. A 'counterfactual' explanation (COUNT)

Here, in broad outline, is what I'll call a 'counterfactual explanation' (COUNT), applied to [GK1]:

A) In making [GK1] fictionally true, the author is asking the reader to imagine that [GK1] is true.
B) To imagine that [GK1] is true, the reader must generally believe that any real person in a relevantly similar situation to Giselda would be doing the right thing.
C) The reader can't believe that any real person in a relevantly similar situation to Giselda would be doing the right thing. Hence:
D) The reader can't imagine that [GK1] is true.

A) depends on a reasonable assumption: that fictions invite imaginings on the part of readers, and that a reader's imaginative content in response to a fiction F should optimally mirror what is fictionally true in F. This is accepted by most (an exception is Matravers 2014).

The crucial premise of COUNT is B). It assumes that the moral judgements a reader makes 'in imagination' *must* mirror those she would make 'in reality' towards people in relevantly similar situations. If empathy is understood in a relatively loose sense as perspective-taking, and moral perspectives are understood as generalised moral judgements towards people in a certain sort of situation, then COUNT invokes a failure of empathy, in this loose sense. For it says that resistance to [GK1] occurs because the reader cannot adopt or endorse the moral perspective embodied in the narrative.

Instances of COUNT are numerous. For instance, Walton writes, speaking for readers generally: 'I judge characters by the moral standards I myself use in real life' (1994: 37). Walton's explanation for this is that moral principles supervene in exactly the same way on non-evaluative facts, whether described in a fiction or described in reality (1994: 45). For Yablo too, whether or not a thinker can imagine that the judgement *right* applies to a fictional situation is determined by whether she *would judge that situation right*, were she to encounter it as described (2008). Weatherson, meanwhile, presupposes that, relative to individual conceptual schemes, some facts are taken to hold 'in virtue of other facts'. *Rightness*, where it obtains, is a 'higher level fact' that holds *in virtue of* 'lower level facts (e.g. about who did what to whom, and for what reason)'. The reader can't imagine that [GK1] is true because, in actuality, were it the case that a mother killed her daughter because she was a girl, the reader *wouldn't* class it as right, given the mere presence of the lower-level fact that she was a girl, and the absence of any further lower-level facts to justify the action (Weatherson 2004: 24; see also Levin 2011). Driver adds that the connections between moral concepts and lower-level facts are psychologically necessary and so non-negotiable even in fictional situations (2008: 304). Though she possesses different background arguments, Mathani also argues that we resist sentences such as [GK1] partly because we import all and only the moral principles we hold true generally into any given fictional world (2012: 426–7).

A few words are necessary about C). What counts as a 'relevantly similar situation'? There are a couple of options. 'Relevantly similar situation' might mean: as Giselda's situation *is described by [GK1], without any additional detail added*. On this interpretation, all the morally salient facts about Giselda's situation are already mentioned by [GK1]. Effectively, [GK1] is understood here, not as a fragment of some wider story, but as a complete mini-fiction in its own right, to which – as, arguably, with all fictions – it would be conventionally inappropriate for a reader to add details of her own in any substantive unauthorised way (Weatherson 2004: 20).

A second option is to treat [GK1] as a fragment of some wider story whose content is unknown to the reader. Then it looks as if 'relevantly similar situation' means 'relevantly similar to whatever situation Giselda is in, according to the complete story'. In that case, there's a possible world in which the currently resisting reader might have been able to imagine [GK1] as true without resistance after all. For instance, she might have discovered that, according to the complete story, Giselda lives in a state where daughters are sold into a slavery worse than death (Stock 2005: 617). In that possible world, one assumes, the reader might also have believed that anyone in that context would have been doing the right thing in killing their baby. Reverting to the actual world where the resisting reader isn't presented with any such context but only the fragment [GK1], then the explanation of her resistance here is, as before, that she can't, under the present relatively context-free circumstances, believe that any real person in Giselda's situation would have done the right thing. Hence, given premise B), she can't imagine it either.

3. Explanations from lack of intelligibility (INTEL)

COUNT explains resistance in terms of an inability to empathise, understood in a particular sense: namely, the ability to *endorse* a particular moral perspective (that is, the moral perspective requested by the narrative). According to a different approach, which I'll now describe, resistance is to be explained in terms of an inability to empathise, where empathy is understood in a different, weaker sense: an ability to *understand* a particular moral perspective.

I'll call this approach the 'explanation from lack of intelligibility' (INTEL). INTEL rejects premise B) of COUNT– that is, rejects the claim that to imagine that [GK1] is true, one needs to believe that any real person in a relevantly similar situation to Giselda would be doing the right thing. Instead, it proposes a different condition, with consequent adaptations to C) and D) as well:

B)★ To imagine that [GK1] is true, one needs to find the judgement that *any real person in a relevantly similar situation to Giselda would be doing the right thing* intelligible.
C)★ The reader can't find the judgement that *any real person in a relevantly similar situation to Giselda would be doing the right thing* intelligible. Hence:
D)★ The reader can't imagine that [GK1] is true.

Understanding a judgement as intelligible isn't the same as believing it or endorsing it. For instance, a pacifist might find the judgement that it is permissible to wage war under a particular circumstance intelligible without believing it true. Intelligibility looks like it involves (roughly) understanding what conception of the action another person might have, such that it might appear from that other person's perspective as warranting the moral judgement in question. One must be able to see why an action might *look* right (for instance) to someone else, even if ultimately one doesn't believe it is or would *be* right. G. E. M. Anscombe talks in a similar vein of a 'desirability characterization': understanding what would be desirable about a particular action, other things being equal, even if one does not desire that thing oneself (Anscombe 2000 70–2).

According to INTEL, resistance occurs because [GK1] doesn't provide a suitable context, such that the reader can understand the moral judgement contained in [GK1] as intelligible. As with COUNT, this might be either because [GK1] is being understood as a complete mini-fiction in itself, which does not itself provide enough information to make the judgement it contains intelligible; or because [GK1] is understood as a fragment of a wider fiction which might perhaps have provided a context such that the judgement in [GK1] became intelligible, but whose details are unknown. Either way, it would be conventionally inappropriate for the reader to add improvised detail of her own, such that [GK1] and its associated generalised judgement then became intelligible.

A version of INTEL seems to be presented by Stueber (2011). Generally, Stueber says, where we engage in 'perspective-matching' successfully – that is, simulating another's reasons for acting and thinking as they do – we 'quarantine' much of our own mental set, including our moral judgements, from the process (which is effectively to reiterate the point just made, that finding another's judgement upon an action intelligible isn't the same thing as endorsing that judgement). But in cases where we fail to understand another's perspective or to find it intelligible, we cannot quarantine our own moral judgements. This is what happens with cases of resistance, Stueber argues: we don't have enough context to find intelligible and so match the perspective of the utterer of [GK1], who thinks what Giselda did was right; which means we can't quarantine our own negative moral judgement about Giselda's action. (See also Moran 1994: 91 for an explanation of resistance which has elements in common with INTEL.)

Prima facie, INTEL looks a more psychologically plausible position than COUNT. For COUNT apparently leaves little room for imaginatively entertaining a different moral perspective to one's own without believing it. Either you positively believe action *x* would be right in circumstances *C*, or you can't imagine that *x* could be right in circumstances *C*. Yet surely there's an interim state where you don't yet believe that *x* would be right in circumstances *C*, but you can entertain the possibility that it might; you can see how it might look as if *x* would be right, though you don't yet want to commit yourself. Moral argument apparently depends on this, as does imaginative continuity with one's past self who might have differed in moral perspective from one's present self (Moran 1994: 101–2).

4. An objection

There's a problem with both COUNT and INTEL, however. As has often been noted, an author's choice of genre sometimes seems to influence whether imaginative resistance is present or not, in a way apparently at odds with B) and B)★ (see e.g. Gendler 2000: 75; Liao et al. 2014). Say that, for instance, [GK1] was altered in a way clearly indicative of humorous intent on the part of the author: for instance (insert a famous sports club of your choice; preferably one you don't also support):

> [GK2] *In killing her daughter, Giselda did the right thing; after all, she was an Arsenal fan.*

I take it that many readers wouldn't find the last sentence problematic in the way that they might have found [GK1] problematic. This is, of course, not to say that they believe that any real person in the situation as described in [GK2] would be doing the right thing; nor even that they would find such a judgement intelligible. It is only that imaginative resistance does not seem to arise for readers, phenomenologically speaking.

I suppose someone might reply that, in response to this, that the reader of [GK2], doesn't *really* imagine that it's true. She merely sees the humorous intent of the author in writing the sentence, and is amused. But on what grounds might one insist that no imagining occurs?

One can't appeal to the fact that no mental image could adequately convey this scenario; for first, arguably no mental image could convey the 'rightness' of *any* situation, as 'rightness' isn't a thing that is imageable. In any case, there are many fictional sentences more generally that cannot be adequately captured in mental images but yet which obviously can be propositionally imagined (*pace* Kind 2001). Consider the many sentences in nineteenth-century novels about the intentional objects of the characters' complex mental lives, for instance. There's no reason to deny that we don't imagine such sentences are true, even though very often we can't picture anything much relevantly corresponding to them.

Instead, I suppose that our objector might say that no fictional situation she can (propositionally) think of, when fully fleshed out in its particular details, could count as verifying the thought that [GK2] expresses: as entailing that [GK2] would be true. (Something like this is imposed as a condition on *idealised* imagining by Chalmers 2002.) Yet we don't standardly require of imagining in relation to fiction that it be accompanied by any such ability. Fictions regularly contain sentences which ask us to imagine things we cannot fully understand in this way. Consider the following opening line of a fiction:

> Katagiri found a giant frog waiting for him in his apartment. It was powerfully built, standing over six feet tall on its hind legs. A skinny little man no more than five foot three, Katagiri was overwhelmed by the frog's imposing bulk. 'Call me "Frog,"' said the frog in a clear, strong voice.
>
> *(Murukami 2002: 1)*

The reader of such sentences, occurring as they do at the beginning of a story, need have no clear idea what circumstances would have to occur, in detail, to make the sentences true; but it seems that she does not need one in order to do what we normally unproblematically would take to count as imagining their truth. Nor need she be assuming that later parts of the fiction may provide some explanatory context, in order to imagine. Some fictions never explain themselves.

In short, well-functioning or idealised imagining may (for all that has been said) include the capacity to work out details of the imagined scenario in a coherent way, but it would be too demanding to make this a necessary condition of imagining *at all*. When we add to this the fact that, I assume, the reader experiences no phenomenological resistance to [GK2] (or at least, nothing like the degree of felt resistance to [GK1]) I see no reason to deny that what is happening with respect to [GK2] is propositional imagining, akin to that which (we happily accept) happens with respect to other fictional sentences.

A further related objection to COUNT and INTEL is that sometimes fictions in certain genres can describe, in detail, situations towards which, had they occurred in reality, the reader would have had a strong moral response, and yet which she makes no corresponding moral judgement 'in imagination' (a point also noted by Gendler 2000: 75). Take, for instance, erotic fiction and the description of otherwise morally questionable statements and acts:

> 'I'm a sadist, Ana. I like to whip little brown-haired girls like you because you all look like the crack whore – my birth mother ...' He runs a hand through his hair and almost smiles but instead sighs ruefully. 'I'm talking about the heavy shit, Anastasia. You should see what I can do with a cane or a cat.'
>
> *(James 2012: 61)*

Or consider the horror genre:

> The man in red spoke. His voice was water running uphill, birds falling into the sky, sand eroding into rock. *Where is Rafe Baburn?* he asked. The children glanced at one another. One of the girls offered a nervous smile. Later, Kosar would swear that the man never even gave them time to reply ... He grabbed the smiling girl by her long hair, pulled his hand from within the red robes and sliced her throat. His knife seemed

to lengthen into a sword, as if gorging on the fresh blood smearing its blade, and he swung it through the air. Three other children clutched at fatal wounds, shrieking as they disappeared from Kosar's view behind the parapet.

(Lebbon 2006: 6)

In such cases, I suggest, readers familiar with the genres in question won't automatically make the moral judgements they would make were these situations believed to be real and being reported. In the realm of erotic fiction or pornography, clearly people can find arousing fictional situations, where they would find analogous 'real' situations morally repellant and so, presumably, a turn-off in real life. And a reader can read the horror story just sampled, perhaps with moderate excitement but no deep feelings of revulsion, even as it describes the murder of children. These facts also stand in need of explanation.

In the next section, I'll introduce what I think is a better response to the phenomenological challenge of imaginative resistance: one which can explain how, as just observed, whether resistance arises or not seems to vary across fictional genres, even given sentences of similar content and structure.

5. The explanation from an invitation to believe (INVITE)

On a third view, which I'll here call INVITE, many cases of imaginative resistance are to be explained in terms of the following features. (INVITE is elaborated upon in Stock, forthcoming. For a different kind of explanation of imaginative resistance, also citing pragmatics, see Nanay 2010.)

Some imagining, generally speaking, is aimed at the goal of arriving at counterfactuals: beliefs about what would be the case, if such-and-such else were the case. Call this kind of imagining 'counterfactual imagining'. Counterfactual imagining can be done for the purposes of planning, or for working out what one would feel or think or want or do in a given case. Counterfactual imagining is aimed, ultimately, at the acquisition of beliefs: what else would be the case if such-and-such happened? What would I feel? (etc.). As such, counterfactual imagining is subject to epistemic constraints. If counterfactual imagining is my goal, for some cognitive purpose, then I can't just imagine what I like. It is constrained at least partly by relevant existing beliefs already possessed by me. If, for instance, I try to imagine what would happen if Labour won the next general election, I bring to bear my existing beliefs about what tends to happen when there is a change of government, generally.

The fact that counterfactual imagining is aimed at the acquisition of beliefs about what would happen gives rise to a constraint upon it. Namely, to be able to counterfactually imagine that situation S has moral aspect M, I must not already believe that actual instances of S (generally described) are not-M or even have significant doubts that actual instances of S are not-M. So, if for instance I already believe that infanticide on the sole grounds of gender is wrong/have serious doubts that it is, I won't be able to *counterfactually imagine* that infanticide simply on the grounds of gender is right. That is, I won't be able to engage the kind of imagining I normally use to work out what would be the case, with respect to that proposition in particular.

Not all imagining is counterfactual imagining, however. Not all imagining is aimed at beliefs about what would be the case. For instance, fantasising for pleasure is not like this. Often, realisations about what would actually be the case inhibit rather than enable fantasy! Equally, morbid and irrational catastrophising about what just might happen, given a situation S, isn't aimed at gaining beliefs about what *would* be the case, given S. Aimless daydreaming isn't either, precisely because it is aimless. In each of these cases, one is not working out what would happen, or what one would think were other things to happen. This means that they are not constrained by existing beliefs in the same way. It doesn't matter whether or not I believe that winning the lottery actually leads to happiness; even if I don't, I can still fantasise about winning the lottery making me happy.

Authors write fictions with a range of intentions, and the competent reader is able to discern them via a grasp of pragmatic context. Some fictions are intended to invite readers, via discernible pragmatic markers, to engage in counterfactual imagining about the fictional situations they describe. For instance, an author might convey that she intends readers to counterfactually imagine a certain situation, with a view to *working out* what moral judgements they would themselves reach in those situations, were they in them. But some fictions go further: their authors don't just imply that a certain fictional situation is to be counterfactually imagined, leaving it open how the reader exactly imagines it, in terms of its moral aspect; they imply that the reader should counterfactually imagine it a particular way, *including* that it possesses some moral aspect. These are the cases in which resistance arises, according to INVITE.

Resistance arises, on this explanation, where the reader detects, via pragmatic context, that she is supposed to counterfactually imagine a given described situation S as possessing a given moral aspect M; but where she cannot imagine it that way. She cannot imagine it that way either because she already believes that actual instances of S are not-M, or because she at least has significant doubts that they are. As emphasised, the goal of counterfactual imagining is to work out what one would believe, given a certain situation; and so is constrained by one's existing relevant beliefs about what would be the case.

One motive an author might have for intending readers to counterfactually imagine a particular fictional situation S as having moral aspect M is get readers to arrive at a *new* counterfactual belief: that S, if actualised, would indeed be M. Morally didactic fictions such as *Uncle Tom's Cabin* and *To Kill a Mockingbird* explicitly have the aim of inculcating certain moral judgements in this way. But there are other possible motives. In a different sort of case, an author might intend a reader to counterfactually imagine S as M, partly because, she assumes, the reader *already* takes it as uncontroversial that actual instances of S are M, intending her to consciously access this belief. Take the following extract from Conan Doyle's Sherlock Holmes story 'The Adventure of the Three Gables', narrated by Watson, which conveys a racist contempt for a fellow character (where I take it that this is a kind of moral judgement, broadly construed):

> The door had flown open and a huge negro had burst into the room ... His broad face and flattened nose were thrust forward, as his sullen dark eyes, with a smouldering gleam of malice in them, turned from one of us to the other. 'Which of you gen'l'men is Masser Holmes?' he asked ... He swung a huge knotted lump of a fist under my friend's nose. Holmes examined it closely with an air of great interest ... 'I've wanted to meet you for some time,' said Holmes. 'I won't ask you to sit down, for I don't like the smell of you, but aren't you Steve Dixie, the bruiser?' 'That's my name, Masser Holmes, and you'll get put through it for sure if you give me any lip.'

> 'It is certainly the last thing you need,' said Holmes, staring at our visitor's hideous mouth.

> *(Conan Doyle 2006 87)*

Here it looks clear from the pragmatic context that Conan Doyle himself endorses, with respect to actual black people generally, the racist beliefs and attitudes fictionally exhibited by Holmes and Watson to Steve Dixie, and that he cosily expects his readers to already share them. In this case, he seems to intend readers only to consciously access their (to our mind) racist beliefs, and not particularly to acquire new ones.

Putting INVITE a bit more formally, it explains resistance to [GK1] as follows:

A) In making [GK1] fictionally true, the author makes it clear, via discernible pragmatic markers, that she intends the reader to *counterfactually imagine* that [GK1] is true.
B) To counterfactually imagine that [GK1] is true, the reader must not already believe that infanticide simply on the grounds of gender is wrong, or even just seriously doubt that it is right.
C) The reader already believes that infanticide simply on the grounds of gender is wrong or, at least, seriously doubts that it is right.
D) The reader can't counterfactually imagine that [GK1] is true.

The way [GK1] is phrased pragmatically indicates, via its use of 'after all', that the author intends it to be fictionally true, in this story, that there is a justificatory link between Giselda's act of infanticide and the gender of her child, and moreover that the reader is to *counterfactually imagine* this link as holding, not merely imagine it. Of course, [GK1] was originally invented by Walton, a philosopher, for the purposes of an article, which complicates the story about authorial intention. However, the point still applies to the fictional version of [GK1] we are implicitly encouraged by Walton to consider: the imaginary case where [GK1] appears in a story by some other author: presumably, not a philosopher using it for a thought experiment.

How does INVITE differ from COUNT and INTEL? They make general claims about epistemic constraints operating on imagining with ethical content. But this looks suspect: why should imagining generally require such constraints? It is well understood why there should be epistemic constraints, relating to standards of intelligibility, justification, and evidence, on what we can appropriately believe, given that the cost of false belief can be high; but it looks odd to pose parallel constraints on imagining (which is effectively what is being suggested). According to INVITE, epistemic constraints understandably affect counterfactual imagining – imagining in the goal of working out what would be the case – but not imagining generally. There are other goals of imagining – to give oneself pleasure for instance, via fantasising – which do not share such constraints.

According to INVITE, then, the reader *could in other circumstances* imagine that sentences with the content of [GK1] and those in the Conan Doyle extract are true. She could easily imaginatively engage with them if she didn't take herself to be intended to counterfactually imagine them, but rather to imagine them in order to achieve some non-cognitive goal (admittedly, it is hard in these cases to see what that might be). Authors unconcerned with exploring counterfactuals can happily 'authoritatively' tell or imply to readers that certain outlandish values operate in their fictional worlds; and readers can accept this, because there's little cognitive cost to their doing so. In contrast, where a fiction makes clear that it has ambitions to change or reinforce minds about moral matters in the actual world, resistance may well be experienced, depending on the outlandishness of the perspective being displayed. So INVITE also has a more sophisticated account of fiction than COUNT does: it acknowledges that fiction as a medium can be used for different goals. Sometimes the goal is to get the reader to think about the relation between the fictional world and the actual one; but not always.

What's the relation here to empathy? Like the other explanations cited earlier, INVITE also cites empathy, but only in a particular and limited sense. Once again, if moral perspectives are understood as generalised moral judgements towards people in a certain sort of situation, then INVITE, like COUNT and INTEL, cites a failure of empathy – a rejection of a given moral perspective towards actual world facts – as causally relevant to resistance. However, unlike COUNT and INTEL, it also cites a specific understanding on the part of the reader that she is being invited by the author to engage in a particular kind of imagining incompatible with that sort of failure of empathy. Where she does not take herself to be so invited, on this view, resistance doesn't occur. Generally speaking, whether or not one empathises with the perspective that says that infanticide on the grounds of gender is wrong is irrelevant to whether one can imagine that [GK1] is true; it is relevant only to the possibility of *counterfactual* imagining that it is true.

If INVITE is right, then we have a nice explanation of the interaction between resistance and some fictional genres, as noted in the previous section, which COUNT and INTEL apparently lack as they stand. That is: an author's intentional use of a certain fictional genre and its associated conventions of interpretation can make it pragmatically clear to a reader that, *even though* a moral judgement-inclusive sentence appears in the fiction, she is not supposed to *counterfactually imagine* whatever situation is being described, but only to imagine it. Some uses of comic, erotic, and horror genres can be like this. In those cases, it is often as if both authors and readers have signed up to a convention which says that what happens in the fiction does not have any or much relevance to what should be taken to be the case in actuality. This isn't to say that this convention cannot be overridden in many cases by other deliberately employed cues of interpretation, of course. Many comedies have deadly serious things to say about the real world. As usual, everything will depend on a complete specification of the context. However, very often, the purposes of such genres are not to explore what would be the case in reality, but rather to give the reader some fun or thrill.

Relatedly, we can see why, in the case of stories or myths written a long time ago or set in a culture very different to the current reader's own, resistance may be reduced (see Liao et al. 2014): because the reader is simply unable to pragmatically interpret whether she is supposed to counterfactually imagine or not, with respect to them. (Of course, in the case of myths, the notion of a single originating author is itself often inapplicable in any case.)

Another virtue of INVITE is that, in broad outline, it can be extended to non-moral cases. Weatherson cites a range of (once again contrived, deliberately invented-for-the-purpose) examples of non-moral resistance, including the sentences 'Although shape-shifting aliens didn't exist, and until that moment Sam had no evidence that they did, this was a rational belief. False, but rational' (Weatherson 2004: 3) and Yablo's story of a 'five-fingered leaf' which was also an 'oval' (2008: 485). According to INVITE, these sentences evoke resistance on the assumption that the reader takes herself to be invited to counterfactually imagine their truth, but yet she possesses beliefs or doubts incompatible with doing so (about whether unevidenced beliefs are rational, or five-fingered things are oval).

Actually, it seems to me that if these rather unusual examples had actually turned up in real fictions – for instance, in the work of Terry Pratchett or Donald Barthelme, or some other author deemed likely to write fantastical scenarios fully aware of their fantastical nature – the reader wouldn't have experienced resistance to them at all, because it would have been clear that counterfactual imagining wasn't an appropriate response to them. It is only because these are contrived cases, of which the reader is supposed to imagine that she came across them in some context other than a philosophy article, but doesn't know what context that is exactly, that resistance gets a grip at all, if indeed it does for her. Even so, non-moral cases are still likely to arise wherever there's some matter of genuine controversy about which people are likely to differ, including authors and their readers. For instance, imagine the following sentence found in a fiction:

> The ice sheets were melting, but it wasn't because the world was getting warmer. There was no such thing as global warming.

Presumably, if the reader of this passage assumed she was thereby being asked to counterfactually imagine it, and she wasn't a climate change sceptic, she would to some extent resist. If on the other hand, she did not assume this, but took the utterance merely to be asking her to imagine it for some other goal (pleasure or humour, say), she wouldn't. Neither COUNT nor INTEL can easily explain this. Once more, we see that to fail to pay attention to nuances of pragmatics in fictional works is to miss out on a plausible explanation of resistance across various contexts.

Finally, INVITE can also explain how the mere inclusion of a fictional narrator is sometimes, but isn't always, enough to automatically deflect resistance to a description of a fictional situation S as having a particular moral aspect M (Gendler 2000: 64). The inclusion of a fictional narrator deflects resistance where it is clear from pragmatic context that the author does not intend or expect the reader to counterfactually imagine that S is M, but only to imagine that the fictional narrator believes that S is M. It is insufficient to deter resistance, when it is clear, as in the Conan Doyle case, that the author shares the fictional narrator's perspective on actual events, and still expects the reader to counterfactually imagine it that way.

6. Comparison with Gendler's view

Before closing, it is worth briefly comparing the view I've argued for with that expressed in an influential paper of Tamar Gendler (2000), since there are similarities between the two, but also important differences. Gendler distinguishes between 'nondistorting fictions' and 'distorting' fictions. In the former, the author has 'imported' a large number of truths from the actual world (about physical laws, psychological generalisations, and historical facts, for instance). Equally, in these fictions it is appropriate for the reader to 'export' large numbers of fictional truths from the story to the world (which, in other words, means to believe them). In contrast, there are 'distorting' fictions, which represent worlds obviously very unlike our actual one, where the author has 'imported' fewer real-world facts, and where the reader is not free to 'export' to the same extent. Imaginative resistance occurs, Gendler tells us, only with respect to 'nondistorting' fiction. It occurs when a) the reader encounters a deviant moral evaluation in such a fiction, and assumes she is supposed to 'export it' as a truth to the actual world (i.e. believe it); but where b) she 'does not wish to add' it to her 'conceptual repertoire' (2000: 77); that is, she doesn't want to (or presumably better, cannot) believe it.

There are a few differences here with the view I prefer. One very minor difference is that she apparently assumes that in cases of resistance the author (or at least, the fiction – it isn't clear to what extent Gendler is an intentionalist) must be inviting the reader to acquire a new belief, which she doesn't want to adopt. On INVITE, there is space for an alternative motive: the author invites the reader to counterfactually imagine a scenario in order to consciously access a belief which, she assumes, they already have (as in the Conan Doyle case).

A more important disagreement is as follows. Say that an author is writing a novel, and 'imports' a specific real-world fact F as a fictional truth in her story (i.e. she uses the real world as material). This fact on its own doesn't make it appropriate for the reader to believe (or 'export') F simply on the basis of reading the story. It is only if the author pragmatically indicates to the reader, via context, that certain passages, or implications of certain passages, are to believed that this becomes appropriate. At times Gendler goes further, seeming to argue that once real-world material is incorporated in a work, the reader standardly gets licence to believe *any* of the fictional truths in that work (though 'with numerous exceptions', 2000: 76), but clearly this is false.

As it stands, however, the biggest problem with Gendler's view is that she doesn't convincingly explain why rejecting the belief that *infanticide on the grounds of gender is right* might constrain one's ability to imagine that [GK1] is true, as she thinks it generally does. Towards the end of her paper she argues that imagining generally requires a kind of 'participation' that mere supposing something true does not: that in imagining something we take our thought to be partly about the actual world and not 'merely restricted to the hypothetical' as supposing is (2000: 80). (It seems to follow that that in cases where, via the use of genre, statements structurally similar to [GK1] are not resisted, e.g. 'In killing her daughter, Giselda did the right thing: after all it was an Arsenal fan', supposing, not imagining, is taking place.) This is an implausible constraint to place on imagining generally: as we have seen, imagining can be directed towards non-cognitive goals such as fantasising for pleasure, and in such cases there is no need to think of imagining as implying any commitments towards actual world facts. Better to distinguish, amongst cases of imagining, between the kind of imagining directed at finding out what would be the case, counterfactually, and those other kinds of imagining that are not.

7. Summary

In this chapter, I've compared three possible explanations of imaginative resistance, as follows.

Let [RW1] be the proposition that *any real person in a relevantly similar situation to Giselda would be doing the right thing*. According to the first explanation, COUNT, roughly, a reader resists a sentence such as [GK1] because she cannot believe that [RW1] is true, and she needs to believe [RW1] in order to imagine that [GK1] is true. According to the second, INTEL, again roughly, a reader resists [GK1] because she cannot find [RW1] intelligible, and she needs to find [RW1] intelligible in order to imagine that [GK1] is true. According to third, my preferred option INVITE, a reader resists [GK1] because, given an assumed pragmatic context, she takes herself to be intended to counterfactually imagine that [GK1] is true, which requires that she does not already believe that [RW1] is false, or doubt that it is true; yet she does one of the latter. Seeing things this way, I've argued, helps us understand those cases where, apparently, moral judgements are either withheld or deviantly applied in genres such as comedy, erotica, and horror fiction, and yet typically we do not resist them. In those genres, I've suggested, the reader knows she isn't supposed to counterfactually imagine anything as a result of reading; in which case she is free to happily imagine whatever she is asked to, without problem.

References

Anscombe, G. E. M. (2000) *Intention*. 2nd edn. Harvard University Press.
Chalmers, David (2002) 'Does conceivability entail possibility?', in T. Gendler & J. Hawthorne (eds) *Conceivability and Possibility*. Oxford University Press, pp. 145–200.
Conan Doyle, Arthur (2006) *The Casebook of Sherlock Holmes*. Headline Review.
Currie, Gregory (2002) 'Desire in imagination', in T. Gendler & J. Hawthorne (eds) *Conceivability and Possibility*. Oxford University Press, pp. 201–21.
Driver, Julia (2008) 'Imaginative resistance and ontological necessity', *Social Philosophy and Policy* 25(1): 301–13.

Gendler, Tamar (2000) 'The puzzle of imaginative resistance', *Journal of Philosophy* 97(2): 55–81.

Gendler, Tamar (2006) 'Imaginative resistance revisited', in Shaun Nichols (ed.) *The Architecture of the Imagination*. Oxford University Press, pp. 149–73.

James, E. L. (2012) *Fifty Shades Darker*. Arrow Books.

Kind, Amy (2001) 'Putting the image back into the imagination', *Philosophy and Phenomenological Research* 62(1): 85–109.

Kind, Amy (2013) 'The heterogeneity of the imagination', *Erkenntnis* 78: 141–59.

Lebbon, Tim (2006). *Dusk*. Bantam Spectra.

Leslie, Alan (1994) 'Pretending and believing: issues in the theory of ToMM', *Cognition* 50: 211–38.

Levin, Janet (2011) 'Imaginability, possibility, and the puzzle of imaginative resistance', *Canadian Journal of Philosophy* 41(3): 391–421.

Liao, Shen-yi, Strohminger, Nina, & Sekhar Sripada, Chandra (2014) 'Empirically investigating imaginative resistance', *British Journal of Aesthetics* 54(3): 339–55.

Mahtani, Anna (2012) 'Imaginative resistance without conflict', *Philosophical Studies* 158: 415–29.

Matravers, Derek (2014) *Fiction and Narrative*. Oxford University Press.

Moran, Richard (1994) 'The expression of feeling in imagination', *Philosophical Review* 103(1): 75–106.

Murukami, Haruki (2002) 'Super-Frog saves Tokyo', *GQ* magazine, June. www.gq.com/entertainment/books/200206/haruki-murakami-super-frog-saves-tokyo-full-story. Accessed 24 March 2015.

Nanay, Bence (2010) 'Imaginative resistance and conversational implicature', *Philosophical Quarterly* 60(240): 586–600.

Stueber, Karsten (2011) 'Imagination, empathy and moral deliberation: the case of imaginative resistance', *Southern Journal of Philosophy* 49: 156–80.

Stock, Kathleen (2005) 'Resisting imaginative resistance', *Philosophical Quarterly* 55(221): 607–24.

Stock, Kathleen (Forthcoming) *Only Imagine: Fiction, Interpretation and Imagination*. Oxford University Press.

Walton, Kendall (1994) 'Morals in fiction and fictional morality/I', *Aristotelian Society* Supp. Vol. 68: 27–50.

Weatherson, Brian (2004). 'Morality, fiction and possibility', *Philosophers' Imprint* 4(3): 1–27.

Yablo, Stephen (2008) 'Coulda, woulda, shoulda', reprinted in S. Yablo, *Thoughts: Papers on Mind, Meaning and Modality*. Oxford University Press, pp. 103–49.

PART VI

Empathy and individual differences

30

EMPATHY ACROSS CULTURES

Douglas Hollan

The focused and explicit study of empathy across cultures has a relatively short history, despite the fact that anthropologists have long used participant observation and face-to-face communication as key tools in generating knowledge and understanding of other people. While many anthropologists have seemed to presume, at least implicitly, the importance of empathic-like sensibilities in social life and in fieldwork, only a relative handful have explicitly evoked empathy or related concepts in discussing and analyzing their fieldwork engagements, and even fewer have made empathy or empathic-like sensibilities among other people a central focus of their research. This lack of explicit attention to empathy is likely related to the fact that while many anthropologists have presumed that empathic-like capacities are implicated in the ability to feel and imagine one's way into the lives and experiences of other people, many have also been very aware of how fallible these capacities can be, especially with regard to describing other people fairly and accurately.

Clifford Geertz (1984) perfectly captured many anthropologists' ambivalent stance towards empathy in his widely cited essay "'From the Native's Point of View': On the Nature of Anthropological Understanding," in which he strongly criticized the notion that understanding another's point of view involves any kind of special psychological, experiential, perceptual, or transcultural sense. Rather, he argued, "Understanding the form and pressure of, to use the dangerous word one more time, natives' inner lives, is more like grasping a proverb, catching an illusion, seeing a joke – or, as I have suggested, reading a poem – than it is like achieving communion" (Geertz 1984, 135).

Geertz's warnings about the fallibilities of naive empathy and the dangers of ethnocentrism and the unwitting and unrecognized projection of one's own feelings and experiences onto others was a message that resonated deeply in the anthropological community. It brought to the surface and made explicit the ambivalence about empathy that many anthropologists had always intuited, and it helped create a conceptual climate in which anthropologists would be less likely to investigate empathy very actively or explicitly – since empathy was now thought to possibly impede rather than promote understanding – much less extol its value to the ethnographic enterprise.

But the relatively recent "rediscovery" of empathy across a variety of disciplines that the philosopher Karsten Stueber (2006) has observed – fueled at least in part by new neurobiological research into the workings of mirror neurons, processes of facial recognition and emotional contagion, and embodied forms of imitation and attunement – has now caught on in anthropology as well. In the remainder of this chapter, I discuss some of the findings of this new anthropology of empathy. The works I discuss here are ethnographic in nature, an approach that is critical to the study of empathy more broadly because rather than presume the centrality of empathy in human life based on theoretical or conceptual grounds alone, ethnographic studies seek to examine how empathic processes manifest themselves and unfold in the course of everyday, naturally occurring behavior, and how these processes are related to, if not contingent upon, other forms of social knowing, awareness, and communication. The focus of these studies is on more "complex" (Hollan 2012), "reenactive" (Stueber 2006), "higher-level" (Goldman 2006) forms of empathy, those that entail the awareness and knowledge any person must have to understand *why* a person is in a certain emotional or intentional state (Halpern 2001). Such higher-level forms of empathy are certainly emergent from a host of neurobiological processes that underpin basic forms of emotional reactivity and attunement, but they are conscious to people and can be reflected upon and talked about. Ethnographic studies enable us to examine when and why and under what conditions empathy becomes central to human life and when and why it does not, and they help us to determine which aspects of empathic processes people share everywhere – biologically based or not – and which may be more culturally shaped and influenced. I separate out and highlight here a few issues about empathic processes that are emerging from recent ethnographic research, but I must underscore that all of the aspects I discuss are closely interrelated and entail one another. Indeed the ethnographic approach demonstrates the extent to which empathic processes are always deeply embedded in their social, cultural, and political contexts, being influenced by those contexts, but also influencing them.

What *is* empathy in a cross-cultural context?

Although the early philosophers David Hume and Adam Smith both emphasized the importance of social sentiments such as sympathy, compassion, and fellow feeling in human life, the contemporary concept of "empathy" is of relatively recent origin, being coined by Theodor Lipps only a little more than one hundred years ago to describe and capture the experience of feeling one's way into an aesthetic object. This notion of "feeling into" remains at the core of many contemporary, formal definitions of empathy, which usually emphasize – though not without contestation (Coplan & Goldie 2011, Engelen & Rottger-Rossler 2012, Zahavi & Overgaard 2012, Maibom 2014) – that empathy is an experiential way of approximating what another person is thinking, feeling, and/or doing from a quasi first-person point of view, and that this process involves emotional, cognitive, and imaginative aspects. Formal definitions also usually note that while empathy implies an emotional resonance of some kind between the empathizer and the target of empathy, it also requires that the empathizer maintain a clear distinction between his or her own thoughts and feelings and those of the target – which is ostensibly what distinguishes empathy from sympathy, compassion, pity, or some other form of emotional contagion.

As Throop and I have noted elsewhere (Hollan 2012, Hollan 2014, Hollan & Throop 2008, Throop & Hollan 2008, Hollan & Throop 2011b), while recent ethnographic research suggests that many people around the world share concepts or terminology that may overlap with this notion of empathy, far fewer have ones that are identical to it. One common area of overlap is in the notion that empathic-like awareness involves both emotional and cognitive/imaginative aspects. But one would actually tend to expect this kind of overlap, given how few people attempt to identify or maintain the sharp distinction between "thinking" and "feeling" that is often so central to folk and scientific psychologies within the Euro-North American context (Lutz 1988, Wikan 1992).

It is also clear, however, that the vocabulary and conceptualization of empathic-like processes varies considerably through space and time. There seem to be many places in the world, for example in the Pacific region (see Hollan & Throop 2011a), where empathic-like sentiments shade much more closely, both semantically and behaviorally, to what English speakers would refer to as love, compassion, sympathy, concern, pity, or some hyphenated combination of these terms. In the eastern Indonesian society of Toraja, terms suggesting empathic-like awareness but translating more literally into English as "love-compassion-pity" often imply a strong sense of identification or merger with the subject of attention, such that one feels compelled to reach out and help, as if one had no other choice (Hollan 2011, Hollan & Wellenkamp 1994, 1996).

One could argue that this urge to help and the blurring of self and other it entails indicates sympathy or compassion or another sentiment distinct from empathy as defined in the research community. However, the fact that the Toraja and many other people do not have words or concepts that translate very precisely as empathy and that they conflate phenomenological states that English speakers take to be distinct and discriminate among those that English speakers take to be whole and integrated, raises the more general issue of whether "empathy" per se is ever to be found in a relatively pure, isolated state. Or, whether it is in fact an awareness that must be carved out of other closely related social sentiments, with boundaries that remain semantically and behaviorally fuzzy and open to a variety of cultural and symbolic mediations (cf. Zahavi 2012). If the latter – and the available ethnographic evidence clearly points in that direction – it would suggest that there are no complex empathic processes apart from the social, cultural, linguistic, and political contexts in which they are embedded. It would also suggest that our research definitions of empathy must remain open and flexible enough to capture the varieties of empathic processes and expressions we find around the world, rather than arbitrarily exclude forms that may fall outside these relatively arbitrary (and perhaps ethnocentric) definitions. It is for this reason that I regularly refer to "empathy-like" phenomena below, to indicate that that phenomena under discussion may be similar to the kinds of empathy discussed in the research literature, but may not be identical with them.

Marked and unmarked forms of altruistic empathy

In most places in the world, altruistic forms of empathy-like awareness – which can be contrasted with forms that are used to harm (discussed below) – are either encouraged or discouraged depending on the context. And indeed, it is well to remember that much of social life everywhere goes on without intimate knowledge of others' motives and intentions, through habit, routine, common expectation, and widely shared rules of social engagement and etiquette (Wallace 1961). Altruistic forms of empathy are often actively discouraged in contexts where tolerance of fellow feeling or understanding of others would interfere with other highly valued goals such as in the training of soldiers or warriors or in efforts to maintain social and economic hierarchies or ethnic or religious differences of various kinds.

"Unmarked" forms of altruistic empathy are those that occur in everyday contexts and do not draw much attention to themselves: they usually do not involve special or elaborate forms of discernment, relying more on the kind of knowledge of others that one gains by sharing common forms of life with them (Wikan 2012). In Toraja, Indonesia, for example, people readily comprehend the shame and embarrassment others experience when they find themselves unable to contribute animals or money to a funeral feast (Hollan & Wellenkamp 1994, 1996, Hollan 2011). This is "insider" knowledge of others' lives that is not obscured or compromised by ignorance or politics. In many places, such as Yap in Micronesia (Throop 2008), this insider knowledge of others is honed and facilitated through the third-person discourse of gossip, which enables people to share information about others' lives and to compare their own perceptions and understandings of others with those of other bystanders and observers.

Many everyday, unmarked forms of altruistic empathy involve efforts to anticipate the needs of others, as when Bosmun in northeast Papua New Guinea (von Poser 2011) offer food to those whom they presume to be hungry or in need of nurturance. For Bosmun, the giving and withholding of food is inextricably linked to the negotiation and communication of social and emotional meanings and becomes the consummate expression of empathy-like feelings or their withholding. Similar exchanges or withholdings of food, service, and labor to express empathic-like concerns for and evaluations of others are used throughout the Pacific region (Feinberg 2011, Mageo 2011, Throop 2011) and in many other places in the world. Indeed, many everyday, unmarked forms of empathy have this pragmatic orientation: they are expressed more as a doing and a performing than as a passive experiencing, and the focus is on their social consequences and effects. For many people around the world in many contexts, the proof of one's empathic response to another is in one's action or inaction with regards to the other's needs and concerns, not in one's mere understanding of another, no matter how accurate that understanding might be.

Another common form of unmarked empathy is when people try to avoid causing unnecessary harm to others, as when Toraja pretend not to have seen behavior that others might find embarrassing or shameful (Hollan 2008). The aversion of the potentially shaming gaze or interaction is indeed one of the most important forms of empathic communication we find anywhere. In all societies, one must learn when to look away and pretend not to have seen or heard at certain moments.

In contrast to everyday, unmarked forms of empathy, "marked" forms are those that are culturally and symbolically elaborated and highlighted in some way. They often involve the cultivation of special forms of expert knowledge or discernment, such as dream interpretation, spirit possession, or arcane diagnosis, that may require long periods of learning or apprenticeship to master. Throop and I (Hollan & Throop 2008) have hypothesized that marked forms of empathy, such as those we find in patient-healer relationships and in healing and religious rituals of various kinds, often seem to arise at just those knots in the social fabric where more direct, explicit ways of knowing about and understanding others are blocked or limited by politics, anxiety, fear, or ignorance. Kirmayer (2008), for example, has noted the necessity of expert forms of empathy in the contemporary psychiatric or mental health clinic, where puzzling illness and the often radically different social, cultural, and educational backgrounds of physicians and patients challenge mutual understanding. He argues that part of the empathic process that is required in such difficult circumstances is a political and ethical stance that enables a physician to acknowledge the limits of her own understanding of patients while at the same time remaining convinced of patients' basic humanness and intelligibility.

Toraja, Indonesia is one of the places in the world where many people believe that certain types of dreams are prophetic (Hollan & Wellenkamp 1994, 1996). Such dreams often involve a visit from an ancestor figure, who through veiled statements or gestures communicates to the dreamer how the future will unfold. When dreamers get the sense that an ancestor may be upset by or critical of their behavior or is bringing news of impending misfortune, they may seek out a person known for his or her dream interpretive skills who can advise them as to how to assuage the ancestor and avoid the coming misfortune. This advisor is someone whose empathic-like awareness is directed not only towards the anxious and frightened dreamer, but also towards the visiting ancestor figure whose intentions and warnings must be deciphered if the dreamer is to be given relief. The inherent ambiguity of dream imagery encourages similar types of empathic elaboration and expertise in many places in the world where dreams are taken seriously and assumed to be meaningful (Mageo 2003, Lohmann 2003, Laughlin 2011).

The causes of many illness experiences are also inherently ambiguous, especially in places where it is thought that illness may be caused by the gods, spirits, ancestors, or even possibly by other humans, through witchcraft or magic. Among some groups of highland Maya in Chiapas, Mexico (Groark 2008), shamans and curers use not only confession but also pulse taking to diagnose and discern the pervasive ill will and antipathy of everyday village life that is thought to be a major cause of illness there. This form of indirect empathic detection and diagnosis allows curers to penetrate the cloaks of silence and self-concealment that patients and others use to protect themselves from the ill will and hostility they presume surrounds them and to shed light on aspects of social life that are otherwise hidden by people's pervasive fear and mistrust of one another.

> Curers gain direct access to the internal states of their patients through the taking of the pulse (*pikel*). Illness is said to "become known" or "to manifest in the arm" *(-vinaj ta k'ob)* through the quality of the pulse. A male curer explained to me, "the blood tells everything. If you strike your wife, it says so." … The sensory modalities involved in this form of knowing privilege "hearing or listening" (*-a'i*) to the blood by "touching" or pulsing (*-pik*), a process that leads to discernment or clear vision of the underlying social causes of the illness. Indeed, the name for curer (*j'ilol*) means "one who sees" reflecting this gift of clear diagnostic discernment.
>
> *(Groark 2008, 442)*

This is a particularly clear example of a situation in which politics, anxiety, fear, and ignorance limit the ability of people to understand each other and themselves and so lead them to develop specialized forms of empathic knowing and discernment that attempt to transcend such social blindness. It also illustrates well Throop's observation (2012) that when certain sensory modalities of empathic discernment become blocked or are culturally discouraged, other modalities – in this case the sense of touch – often become cultivated and elaborated in their place.

Specific cultural and historical settings may and usually do at times indirectly structure altruistically oriented empathy, whether marked or unmarked, by encouraging interpersonal engagements of a complementary type. For example, in places like Toraja, where people are encouraged or allowed to express their needs and concerns very directly and explicitly at times, a self-revealing stance on the part of one person might be complemented by an other-attending one on the part of another, who then becomes attentive to what the revealer is expressing. In Yap, where the cultural inducements are in the direction of hiding one's subjective experience from others, a self-concealing stance might be complemented by an other-respecting one, in which one empathically feigns ignorance of or indifference to the other's thoughts and feelings. And in places like Bosmun, where people often attempt to fulfill others' needs before they are openly revealed or expressed, especially with regard to food, a self-projecting stance, in which one communicates information about one's subjective states in very subtle, often nonverbal ways, might be complemented and met by an other-anticipating one, in which one attempts to read and interpret the other's subtle projections of needs and concerns. Such culturally preferred orientations to self-other encounters can be combined and shuffled in highly dynamic and complex ways in the course of actual interactions (Hollan & Throop 2011b, 18), and yet they shape and set limits on the sensory modalities and forms of expression through which more complex forms of altruistic empathy are enacted.

Douglas Hollan

Hurtful forms of empathy

Many researchers influenced by evolutionary models of behavior have suggested that empathy is an essentially altruistic impulse or response leading to prosocial and moral behavior unless or until it is suppressed or inhibited in some way (de Waal 2009, Haidt 2012, Harris 2007, Hoffman 2011, Slote 2007). Yet much ethnographic evidence to date suggests that in the context of everyday social practice, first-person-like knowledge of others is rarely, if ever, considered an unambiguously good thing, despite the many positive connotations empathy has in the Euro-North American context. Although empathic-like knowledge of others may be used to help others or to interact with them more effectively, it may also be used to hurt or embarrass them. Because of this, people all over the world seem just as concerned with concealing their first-person experience from others as in revealing it in some way (see, for example, Hollan & Wellenkamp 1994, Rosen 1995, Rumsey & Robbins 2008, Groark 2008, Throop 2008, 2010). Everywhere we find complex concepts of personhood that convey what is appropriate to know about people and what is not, that suggest how porous or impermeable the boundaries of the self should be ideally, and that hint at the damage done when psychic integrity (however defined) is violated. Empathic awareness certainly has the potential to breach these norms of personhood, whether people intend to use it in that way or not.

Some of this widespread wariness of empathic-like knowledge stems from the anticipation of its pragmatic deployment and implementation discussed above: there is an awareness and concern that people tend to "do" something with the empathic-like knowledge they acquire. Even in situations when people can anticipate that empathizers intend to help rather than to harm, they may fear that the first-person-like knowledge that others have obtained about them is inaccurate or that it will be leaked to third parties who could use it to harm or embarrass. This wariness of empathic-like knowledge takes particularly stark form in parts of the Pacific region where some groups make a strong claim that it is difficult, if not impossible, to really know another person's heart or mind (Rumsey & Robbins 2008). While some anthropologists have argued that this belief in the "opacity of other minds" means that people actually avoid thinking or speculating about other people's thoughts, feelings, and intentions (Robbins 2008), most have suggested that the opacity doctrine is not so much an epistemological claim that one cannot know the mind of another as a moral and political one about what is proper to say or publicly acknowledge about another's unexpressed feelings or intentions (Duranti 2008, Keane 2008, Rumsey 2008). It is a claim that another's thoughts and feelings should not be speculated about publicly, and that people have the right to be the first person of their own thoughts and that others have a similar right to be the first person of theirs (Keane 2008, 478). Such claims reflect both a high degree of respect for the autonomy and integrity of another's personhood, but also an awareness of people's vulnerability to the empathic-like knowledge others may have of them.

Beliefs or claims about the difficulty or impossibility of knowing other people's minds express a generalized wariness and concern about the accuracy of empathic-like knowledge and its potentially compromising or harmful uses. But people around the world also recognize that empathy can be used in much more directly and consciously harmful ways, either because they have been the victims of such knowledge or because they have used such knowledge in harmful ways themselves. The degree of harm that empathy can cause ranges on a continuum depending partly on whether the harm is intended or not. At one end are cases in which people accidentally or inadvertently leak empathic-like knowledge that ends up embarrassing or hurting someone, as when empathically oriented gossip escapes and gets back to the person or persons gossiped about. Then there are cases in which people deliberately use empathic-like

346

knowledge against someone, but for ostensibly innocent reasons, as when someone uses such insider information to tease or joke with another or to promote some other prosocial value.

Among the Inuit of the Canadian Arctic, intimate knowledge of others is sometimes used to shame or humiliate people into conventional, morally acceptable behavior. Children in particular can become the focus of such surveillance. Briggs reports (1998, 2008) that Inuit adults may use their empathic-like awareness of the motives underlying children's misbehavior to draw attention to that misbehavior and to create fear, doubt, and shame about it in children's minds, often in a way that disguises the surveillance with humor or playfulness. For example, a child who becomes overly friendly and unguarded with a stranger or non-kin person might be "jokingly" told that the stranger intends to take the child home with him when he leaves. The targets of such emotionally ambiguous interactions, whether adult or child, are often left to wonder, "Are these people commenting on my behavior playing with me or hurting me? Am I 'in trouble' with them or not?" Briggs argues that it is just these kinds of emotionally ambiguous interactions, aroused by empathic-like surveillance, that make core cultural values so salient and motivating to people, because they generate an awareness among actors that "something is at stake" in the interaction. We see here how fuzzy and ambiguous the line between empathy in the service of "help" and harm can sometimes be.

At the other end of the harm continuum are cases when people knowingly and intentionally use empathic-like knowledge to harm people either socially and psychologically or physically. In Toraja, public reputations are most at stake at communal feasts, when seating, food, and drink are all visibly distributed according to one's status and prestige. Although hosts and meat dividers usually try not to offend people during these distributions, they sometimes have reason to assert one person's status over another, and they know just how to do this in the most visible, humiliating way – for example, by giving a high-status person a small and inferior piece of meat when they actually deserve a large and preferred one, or by not displaying a prize sacrificial animal prominently enough, thereby depriving the donor of his or her proper recognition.

Among the Maya that Groark studied, people believe that the witches among them can and do use intimate knowledge of others to cause illness or death. To counteract such presumed ill will and antipathy, many people enact a type of "positive politeness" that is intended to block others' intimate knowledge of themselves and to mask or hide their own thoughts and feelings about others, for fear of inadvertently giving offense. While certain curers, as mentioned above, are periodically allowed the kinds of social access and diagnostic tools, such as pulse taking, necessary to encourage communication and reconciliation among people, the mobilization of such marked and altruistically oriented empathic resources often occurs only in the aftermath of miscommunication and harm already done.

Bubandt and Willerslev argue that these forms of "tactical" empathy – "instances when the empathic incorporation of an alien perspective contains, and in fact is motivated by, seduction, deception, manipulation, and violent intent" (Bubandt & Willerslev 2015, 6) – are generally under-reported and under-studied because of the assumption among many researchers that empathy is inherently virtuous. One of their prime examples of the ubiquity of more malevolent forms of empathy is hunting, in which humans use empathic-like perspective taking to imagine how animals behave in order to stalk and kill them more effectively. In particular, they discuss the elaborate ways in which Yukaghir hunters in Siberia mimic the appearance and behavior of moose in order to get close enough to them to shoot and kill them. They underscore that "Once one starts to look for it, one finds tactical empathy in many forms of human practice," including among poker players, police profilers, military strategists, con artists, Internet scammers, method actors, and everyday romantic Casanovas, all of whom "attempt to assume the perspective and affective stance of an avowed opponent, victim, portrayed figure, or desired subject, and base their future actions on some form of mimicry that allows them to win the game, gain a strategic advantage, capture, fool, portray, or seduce someone else" (Bubandt & Willerslev 2015, 8).

They examine at length the use of tactical empathy in a case of political violence from North Maluku, Indonesia (previously reported in Bubandt 2009) in which individuals from the Muslim community had forged a letter from the head of a Christian church. The purpose of this fake letter, in which the church leader ostensibly encourages his fellow Christians to attack Muslims in order to facilitate a Christian takeover of North Maluku, is to scare the Muslims among whom it is distributed into a united front against the Christian community, by leading them to believe that a Christian offensive is imminent. Bubandt and Willerslev argue that the forged letter was convincing to Muslims only because it was able to capture in an authentically empathic way the kinds of concerns, fears, worries, and ambitions the Christian community might reasonably have had. As I have suggested elsewhere (Hollan 2012), it is certainly arguable that the forged letter was effective not because it demonstrated empathy for Christians – it can be read, instead, as a slanderous caricature of them – but rather for the other Muslims in the community, among whom were those who might have been feeling as alienated, disempowered, and resentful of Christians as the letter writers obviously were. The letter taps into this reservoir of resentment and anxiety, suggesting that Christians on North Maluku really were as deceitful and manipulative as some Muslims might have feared. But in any case, Bubandt and Willerslev illustrate well just how dangerous empathic-like knowledge can be, whether in places and times of social and political unrest or otherwise. Their point that tactical empathy is just as "social" and foundational to human life as is altruistic empathy is one that is well taken.

The politics and morality of empathy

Ethnographic evidence demonstrates just how much empathic forms of awareness can vary from context to context. Everyday forms of altruistic empathy can be culturally encouraged and elaborated into highly visible, marked forms, but they may also be left relatively undeveloped and unmarked or even culturally discouraged or suppressed. It is also clear that many people around the world are wary of empathic forms of knowledge, fearing their possible inaccuracies and fallibilities even when they are obviously meant to help, and knowing how readily they can be deployed for deceptive or hostile purposes. Such evidence challenges the assumption that empathic processes are inherently prosocial or altruistic and instead underscore the extent to which they are embedded within and shaped by politics and morality. Although altruistic forms of empathy create bonds with certain people, they create boundaries with others, and are therefore implicated in the creation and maintenance of power relations, social structures, and identities (Hollan & Throop 2011a). They are generally directed only toward those deemed worthy of empathy, and often flow along lines of kinship or other socially and politically valued relationships. Even within these flows, people often differentiate between those who can "afford" to give empathy and those who receive it, the givers assuming, either implicitly or explicitly, a higher status, prestige, and moral authority (Hermann 2011). Among Yapese, a person's ability to take up a compassionate stance toward another is necessarily an indication and enactment of an elevated position in the social hierarchy (Throop 2011, 2010). Altruistic forms of empathy thus channel and are channeled by social, political, and economic inequalities of various kinds.

The moral ambiguity of empathic awareness becomes clearer in cases where it is used to deceive or harm rather than to help. Some such cases are readily condemned nearly everywhere, as when a person uses empathic-like knowledge to steal from others or to commit unjustified homicide or sexual assault. But other cases of using empathy to deceive or cause harm are more ambiguous and sometimes even justified (or rationalized) morally and politically. Among the Toraja that Jane Wellenkamp and I knew well (Hollan & Wellenkamp 1994, 1996), many people were concerned that others would take advantage of the rules of reciprocity to ask for help when they did not actually need it, those asking for help knowing that people have a hard time refusing requests of almost any kind. And yet, many of these same people often admired those (including themselves) who used their empathic-like, tactical "cleverness" against others to achieve desired goals or to justify morally ambiguous actions. Whether this use of empathic-like awareness was considered deceit or cleverness depended very much on whom it advantaged or disadvantaged: if it advantaged oneself or those with whom one was closely affiliated, it was generally considered to be justifiable and "clever"; if it disadvantaged oneself or those with whom one was closely affiliated, it was generally considered unjustifiable and deceitful.

Ambivalence toward empathy used for deceit or harm may become heightened as the level of harm caused increases, but not necessarily, and very harmful uses of tactical empathy can become morally and politically justified, especially if people can claim that the harm perpetrated is done in the service of some higher value or goal. We see this moral and political justification most graphically in the "terror" violence going on all over the world today. Those seeking to terrorize often attempt to justify their use of empathic-like knowledge to kill others when they are most surprised and defenseless by claiming to be victims of violence or injustice themselves or in the service of a moral authority higher than local or international law, while those seeking to defend against such attacks justify their use of empathically informed torture and preemptive arrest by arguing that it is necessary for counterintelligence and self-defense. The irony here is that empathic resonance with the needs and concerns of those with whom one is closely affiliated may then lead one to use empathic-like knowledge in harmful ways to undermine those whom one perceives as threatening in some way.

Such variability in the way empathic-like awareness is evaluated and deployed supports Battaly's (2011) contention that the foundational intersubjective processes underlying empathic modes of understanding and behavior, sometimes referred to as "basic" empathy (Steuber 2006), are not virtuous in and of themselves; they do not automatically or necessarily lead to non-harmful, altruistic forms of behavior. Rather, they are probably best conceived of as involuntary "capacities," or when they are self-consciously practiced and honed, as voluntary "skills," that can be cultivated and developed (or not) in various ways. They can become powerfully motivating of altruism and concern for others, of course, but only if people self-consciously cultivate them as virtuous-like behaviors and make it socially, politically, and economically feasible for them to be enacted in virtuous-like ways. But such reactive capacities can also be culturally downplayed and marginalized relative to other modes of interaction, and as we have seen, they can also be cultivated and used to harm people rather than to help. Ethnographic studies illuminate the complexity of these socially, culturally, and politically embedded processes and demonstrate the Jamesian (1985[1902]) wisdom of documenting all the varied forms and contexts of a behavioral phenomenon before too quickly building a more general theory about it or its place in human life. Given this, ethnography must be considered a primary tool in the investigation of human empathy, not a secondary or optional one.

Conclusion

Ethnographic evidence available to date suggests that we still have much to learn about how very basic intersubjective processes become developed into more complex, higher-level forms of human empathy. Most basically, it demonstrates that many places around the world do not have words or phrases that translate very precisely as "empathy" in English, but rather, tend to have words or phrases that stretch the semantic and behavioral boundaries of first-person perspective taking more toward what English speakers refer to as compassion, love, or pity – capturing the fact that many people tend to focus more on the social and pragmatic consequences of empathic-like knowledge, rather than on its experiential or perceptual qualities per se.

Ethnography also makes clear that first-person-like perspective taking on other people's behavior is rarely considered to be an unambiguously good thing, because people are acutely aware that such awareness is error prone and that it can be used to harm others as well as to help them. This wariness of and ambivalence toward empathy can be seen in the lengths to which people sometimes go to protect themselves from empathic-like knowledge, up to and including the assertion that it is impossible to know another person's mind or heart.

Although empathy is a foundational intersubjective capacity that enables and affords many different types of human sociality, it is also a capacity that, in turn, is shaped by and responsive to the cultural, moral, and political contexts in which it is always embedded. Empathic-like awareness can become culturally "marked" and developed into highly elaborate forms of expert knowledge and discernment that may takes years to teach and master, or it may be left relatively unmarked and unremarked upon in everyday behavior, relying more on the kind of knowledge of others that one gains by sharing common forms of life with them. When empathy does become highly elaborated, it can often be related to the fact that more direct ways of knowing about others have also become blocked or limited by politics, anxiety, fear, or ignorance.

Empathy can and is evaluated more positively or negatively depending on whether it is used to help or harm and on whether that help or harm advantages or disadvantages the people with whom one is most closely aligned and affiliated. Empathy can certainly build bridges between people, but it may also create boundaries between them, and it necessarily implies a hierarchy between those who can "afford" to empathize and those who are the recipients of empathy. Ethnographic studies bring attention to the variability in which empathic processes and their social consequences are experienced, expressed, and evaluated. In doing so, they implicitly challenge any conception of empathic processes that overemphasizes their innateness, their uniformity, or their moral or political clarity.

References

Battaly, Heather D. 2011. Is Empathy a Virtue? In Amy Coplan & Peter Goldie, eds., *Empathy: Philosophical and Psychological Perspectives*, pp. 277–301. Oxford: Oxford University Press.

Briggs, Jean. 1998. *Inuit Morality Play*. New Haven, CT: Yale University Press.

Briggs, Jean. 2008. Daughter and Pawn: One Ethnographer's Routes to Understanding Children. *Ethos* 36(4): 449–56.

Bubandt, Nils. 2009. From the Enemy's Point of View: Violence, Empathy, and the Ethnography of Fakes. *Cultural Anthropology* 24(3): 553–88.

Bubandt, Nils & Rane Willerslev. 2015. The Dark Side of Empathy: Mimesis, Deception, and the Magic of Alterity. *Comparative Studies in Society and History* 57(1): 5–34.

Coplan, Amy & Peter Goldie. 2011. Introduction. In Amy Coplan & Peter Goldie, eds., *Empathy: Philosophical and Psychological Perspectives*, pp. ix–xlvii. Oxford: Oxford University Press.

De Waal, Franz. 2009. *The Age of Empathy: Nature's Lessons for a Kinder Society*. New York: Harmony Books.

Duranti, Alessandro. 2008. Further Reflections on Reading Other Minds. *Anthropological Quarterly* 81(2): 483–94.

Engelen, Eva-Maria & Birgitt Rottger-Rossler. 2012. Current Disciplinary and Interdisciplinary Debates on Empathy. *Emotion Review* 4(1): 3–8.

Feinberg, Richard. 2011. Do Anutans Empathize? Morality, Compassion, and Opacity of Other Minds. In Douglas W. Hollan & C. Jason Throop, eds., *The Anthropology of Empathy: Experiencing the Lives of Others in Pacific Societies*, pp. 151–68. New York: Berghahn Books.

Geertz, Clifford. 1984. "From the Native's Point of View": On the Nature of Anthropological Understanding. In Richard A. Sweder & Robert A. LeVine, eds., *Culture Theory: Essays on Mind, Self, and Emotion*, pp. 123–36. Cambridge: Cambridge University Press.

Goldman, Alvin I. 2006. *Simulating Minds: The Philosophy, Psychology, and Neuroscience of Mindreading*. New York: Oxford University Press.

Groark, Kevin. 2008. Social Opacity and the Dynamics of Empathic In-Sight among the Tzotzil Maya of Chiapas, Mexico. *Ethos* 36(4): 427–48.

Haidt, Jonathan. 2012. *The Righteous Mind: Why Good People are Divided by Politics and Religion*. New York: Pantheon Books.

Halpern, Jodi. 2001. *From Detached Concern to Empathy: Humanizing Medical Practice*. New York: Oxford University Press.

Harris, James. 2007. The Evolutionary Neurobiology, Emergence and Facilitation of Empathy. In Tom Farrow & Peter Woodruff, eds., *Empathy in Mental Illness*, pp. 168–86. Cambridge: Cambridge University Press.

Hermann, Elfriede. 2011. Empathy, Ethnicity, and the Self among the Banabans in Fiji. In Douglas W. Hollan & C. Jason Throop, eds., *The Anthropology of Empathy: Experiencing the Lives of Others in Pacific Societies*, pp. 25–42. New York: Berghahn Books.

Hoffman, Martin L. 2011. Empathy, Justice, and the Law. In Amy Coplan & Peter Goldie, eds., *Empathy: Philosophical and Psychological Perspectives*, pp. 230–54. Oxford: Oxford University Press.

Hollan, Douglas. 2008. Being There: On the Imaginative Aspects of Understanding Others and Being Understood. *Ethos* 36(4): 475–89.

Hollan, Douglas. 2011. Vicissitudes of "Empathy" in a Rural Toraja Village. In Douglas W. Hollan & C. Jason Throop, eds., *The Anthropology of Empathy: Experiencing the Lives of Others in Pacific Societies*, pp. 195–214. New York: Berghahn Books.

Hollan, Douglas. 2012. Emerging Issues in the Cross-Cultural Study of Empathy. *Emotion Review* 4: 70–8.

Hollan, Douglas. 2014. Empathy and Morality in Ethnographic Perspective. In Heidi L. Maibom, ed., *Empathy and Morality*, pp. 230–50. New York: Oxford University Press.

Hollan, Douglas W. & C. Jason Throop. 2008. Whatever Happened to Empathy? Introduction. *Ethos* 36(4): 385–401.

Hollan, Douglas W. & C. Jason Throop, eds. 2011a. *The Anthropology of Empathy: Experiencing the Lives of Others in Pacific Societies*. New York: Berghahn Books.

Hollan, Douglas W. & C. Jason Throop. 2011b. The Anthropology of Empathy: Introduction. In Douglas W. Hollan & C. Jason Throop, eds., *The Anthropology of Empathy: Experiencing the Lives of Others in Pacific Societies*, pp. 1–21. New York: Berghahn Books.

Hollan, Douglas W. & Jane C. Wellenkamp. 1994. *Contentment and Suffering: Culture and Experience in Toraja*. New York: Columbia University Press.

Hollan, Douglas W. & Jane C. Wellenkamp. 1996. *The Thread of Life: Toraja Reflections on the Life Cycle*. Honolulu: University of Hawaii Press.

James, William. 1985[1902]. *The Varieties of Religious Experience*. New York: Penguin Books.

Keane, Webb. 2008. Others, Other Minds, and Others' Theories of Other Minds. *Anthropological Quarterly* 81(2): 473–82.

Kirmayer, Laurence J. 2008. Empathy and Alterity in Cultural Psychiatry. *Ethos* 36(4): 457–74.

Laughlin, Charles D. 2011. *Communing with the Gods: Consciousness, Culture and the Dreaming Brain*. Brisbane: Daily Grail Publishing.

Lohmann, Roger Ivar, ed. 2003. *Dream Travelers of the Western Pacific: Sleep Experiences and Culture in the Western Pacific*. New York: Palgrave Macmillan.

Lutz, Catherine A. 1988. *Unnatural Emotions: Everyday Sentiments on a Micronesian Atol and their Challenge to Western Theory*. Chicago: University of Chicago Press.

Mageo, Jeannette Marie, ed. 2003. *Dreaming and the Self: New Perspectives on Subjectivity, Identity, and Emotion*. Albany: State University of New York Press.

Mageo, Jeannette. 2011. Empathy and "As-If" Attachment in Samoa. In Douglas W. Hollan & C. Jason Throop, eds., *The Anthropology of Empathy: Experiencing the Lives of Others in Pacific Societies*, pp. 69–94. New York: Berghahn Books.

Maibom, Heidi L. 2014. Introduction: (Almost) Everything You Ever Wanted to Know about Empathy. In Heidi L. Maibom, ed., *Empathy and Morality*, pp. 1–40. New York: Oxford University Press.

Robbins, Joel. 2008. On Not Knowing Other Minds: Confession, Intention, and Linguistic Exchange in a Papau New Guinea Community. *Anthropological Quarterly* 81(2): 421–30.

351

Rosen, Lawrence. 1995. *Other Intentions: Cultural Contexts and the Attributions of Inner States*. Sante Fe: School of American Research.

Rumsey, Alan. 2008. Confession, Anger, and Cross-Cultural Articulation in Papua New Guinea. *Anthropological Quarterly* 81(2): 455–72.

Rumsey, Alan & Joel Robbins, eds. 2008. Anthropology and the Opacity of Other Minds. Special Issue of *Anthropological Quarterly* 81(2).

Slote, Michael. 2007. *The Ethics of Care and Empathy*. New York: Routledge.

Stueber, Karsten. 2006. *Rediscovering Empathy: Agency, Folk Psychology, and the Human Sciences*. Cambridge, MA: MIT Press.

Throop, C. Jason. 2008. On the Problem of Empathy: The Case of Yap, Federated States of Micronesia. *Ethos* 36(4): 402–26.

Throop, C. Jason. 2010. *Suffering and Sentiment: Exploring the Vicissitudes of Experience and Pain in Yap*. Berkeley: University of California Press.

Throop, C. Jason. 2011. Suffering, Empathy, and Ethical Modalities of Being in Yap (Waqab), Federated States of Micronesia. In Douglas W. Hollan & C. Jason Throop, eds., *The Anthropology of Empathy: Experiencing the Lives of Others in Pacific Societies*, pp. 119–50. New York: Berghahn Books.

Throop, C. Jason. 2012. On the Varieties of Empathic Experience: Tactility, Mental Opacity, and Pain in Yap. *Medical Anthropology Quarterly* 26(3): 408–30.

Throop, C. Jason & Douglas W. Hollan, eds. 2008. Whatever Happened to Empathy? Special Issue of *Ethos* 36(4).

von Poser, Anita. 2011. Bosmun Foodways: Emotional Reasoning in a Papau New Guinea Lifeworld. In Douglas W. Hollan & C. Jason Throop, eds., *The Anthropology of Empathy: Experiencing the Lives of Others in Pacific Societies*, pp. 169–94. New York: Berghahn Books.

Wallace, Anthony F. C. 1961. *Culture and Personality*. New York: Random House.

Wikan, Unni. 1992. *Managing Turbulent Hearts: A Balinese Formula for Living*. Chicago: University of Chicago Press.

Wikan, Unni. 2012. *Resonance: Beyond the Words*. Chicago: University of Chicago Press.

Zahavi, Dan. 2012. Basic Empathy and Complex Empathy. *Emotion Review* 4(1): 81–2.

Zahavi, Dan & Soren Overgaard. 2012. Empathy without Isomorphism: A Phenomenological Account. In Jean Decety, ed., *Empathy: From Bench to Bedside*, pp. 3–20. Cambridge, MA: MIT Press.

31

EMPATHIC ACCURACY

Vivian P. Ta and William Ickes

Can we really know what other people are thinking or feeling? Consider the following scenario.

> Your friend, Richard, is distraught because his dog has just died. Because you are a good friend, you try to console Richard and offer your support. You say, "I know how you feel. You'll be mourning the loss of your dog for a little while, but this sadness will go away soon." Instead of feeling appreciative of your support, Richard becomes angry at your assumption and says, "You don't know how I feel! My dog and I had a special bond. Nobody knows how I feel!"

This scenario reveals some interesting complexities. First, Richard is asserting that you could not possibly know how he feels. After all, you are not Richard and you do not have direct access to his thoughts and feelings. His experiences as an individual are unique to him, and therefore the bond that he shared with his dog is fully comprehensible only by him. The philosophical idea of solipsism, which maintains that what is experienced by the individual self is all that can be known for certain to exist, is consistent with Richard's point of view. How can you know how Richard feels if you are not Richard himself? Second, and quite ironically, Richard, by asserting that you do not know how he feels, is implying that *he* knows how *you* feel. But in terms of the previous argument, how can this be if no one can know how another person feels, simply because they are not that person?

This apparent "contradiction of empathy" is one that philosophers have been debating for decades. In the interest of space, we will not discuss either side of this debate but will instead return to our original question: Can people know – at least partially if not completely – what other people are thinking or feeling? The empirical answer to this question, as provided by psychological research, is yes. People do have real – though quite limited – insight into the specific content of other people's thoughts and feelings. Psychologists call the process by which they achieve this insight *empathic inference*, whereas the level of insight they actually achieve is called *empathic accuracy*.

In this chapter, written from the perspective of the research psychologist, we first define the term *empathic accuracy* and briefly discuss the history of this term. We then review some of the factors that have been shown to influence perceivers' empathic accuracy, such as age-related

353

maturational changes and various motivational influences. We also consider how the target person's "readability" can influence the perceiver's empathic accuracy, and how perceivers can improve their empathic accuracy. Finally, we consider the conditions in which empathic accuracy hurts versus helps the partners in close relationships.

What is empathic accuracy?

As noted above, empathic inference is the process by which we attempt to infer the specific content of other people's thoughts and feelings (Ickes, 2009). Empathic accuracy is the extent to which these everyday mind reading attempts are successful (Ickes, 1997, 2003). The historical precedent of the term "empathic accuracy" is Carl Rogers's term "accurate empathy," which he used to describe the ideal clinician's ability to accurately infer the moment-to-moment changes in the content of a client's successive thoughts and feelings (Rogers, 1957).

Empathic accuracy, as operationally defined, is a global measure of how accurately a perceiver is able to infer the specific content of all of the target person's thoughts and feelings. The accuracy of the perceiver's empathic inferences is based on trained raters' judgments of how similar each of the inferred thoughts and feelings were to the actual thoughts and feelings that the target person reported (for procedural details, see Ickes, 2001). The global (overall) measure of empathic accuracy is scaled as a percentage measure, with 0 indicating no accuracy and 100 indicating perfect accuracy. (More precisely, 0 indicates that the perceiver was awarded no "accuracy points" for any of his or her empathic inferences, whereas 100 indicates that the perceiver was awarded all of the available "accuracy points" by the trained raters.)

How is empathic accuracy measured?

During the past twenty-five years of research on empathic accuracy, the construct has been measured and studied using two primary research paradigms: the *unstructured dyadic interaction paradigm* and the *standard stimulus paradigm* (Ickes, 2001; Schmid Mast & Ickes, 2007).

The unstructured dyadic interaction paradigm. In the unstructured dyadic interaction paradigm, two individuals (who may or may not already be acquainted) are escorted to a laboratory "waiting room" by an experimenter who asks them to take a seat on a couch. Consistent with a cover story, the experimenter then leaves them alone together on the pretext of having to retrieve something that is needed for the experiment. At this point, the unstructured dyadic interaction occurs: during the next six minutes, the two participants are unobtrusively video and audio recorded. At the end of this time, the experimenter returns and reveals to the participants that their interaction has been digitally recorded.

If both participants then give their written consent to have the video and audio recordings used as data sources, they proceed to the next phase of the study. In this phase, they are seated in separate cubicles, where they each view a copy of the recording that was made while they were interacting. Their task while watching the recording is to stop it whenever they remember having had a thought or a feeling at a particular point during the interaction. Using a supply of *thought/feeling recording forms*, they write down the specific times when their thoughts or feelings occurred, along with the content of each reported thought or feeling.

When both participants have completed this task, the thought/feeling inference phase of the procedure begins. The participants are asked to infer the specific content of each of their partner's thoughts and feelings, using a supply of *thought/feeling inference forms*. In this phase of the procedure, the experimenter (or an assistant) pauses the recording for each participant at the specific points at which the interaction partner reported having had each of his or her actual thoughts and feelings, and the two perceivers (again working independently) write down each of their thought/feeling inferences.

Later, the empathic accuracy of each perceiver is judged by a group of five to eight raters. The raters assign "accuracy points" to each inference according to how similar it is in content to the thought or feeling that was actually reported by the interaction partner. For example, a reported thought of "This guy is nice" and an inferred thought of "This guy is a jerk" would be rated with a 0, as they have essentially different content. In contrast, ratings of 1 or 2 denote "similar, but not the same, content" and "essentially the same content," respectively. By aggregating and transforming these "accuracy points" into a percent-correct measure, an overall empathic accuracy score is then calculated for each participant. Higher scores indicate higher levels of empathic accuracy on a percentage scale that has a potential range of 0 (none of the possible accuracy points) to 100 (all of the possible accuracy points). With as many as six to eight raters, the interrater reliability of this empathic accuracy measure typically averages about .90; with fewer raters, this value will decline.

The unstructured dyadic interaction paradigm can be used to study asymmetries in empathic accuracy within relationships (Clements, Holtzworth-Munroe, Schweinle, & Ickes, 2007) as well as differences in empathic accuracy across relationships that vary in their degree of intimacy/acquaintanceship (Stinson & Ickes, 1992; Thomas & Fletcher, 2003). On the other hand, the major disadvantage of the paradigm is that each perceiver infers the thoughts and feelings of a unique partner, making the inference task different for each perceiver and confounding the perceiver's empathic ability with the partner's "readability." For a statistical solution to these problems (one that involves additional measurement and is a bit too complicated to describe here), see Simpson, Oriña, & Ickes (2003) and Flury, Ickes, & Schweinle (2008).

The standard stimulus paradigm. The standard stimulus paradigm was originally developed to assess empathic accuracy in a clinically relevant research setting (Marangoni, Garcia, Ickes, & Teng, 1995). The paradigm employs a standard stimulus video, usually composed of excerpts from a set of previously videotaped interactions, although they can be taken from any tapes for which the target person's thoughts and feelings are known. This compilation videotape is used as a standard stimulus tape in subsequent studies, in which participants are asked to make thought and feeling inferences at those points on the tape where the target person(s) reported having had a thought or feeling. The inferred thoughts and feelings are compared to the actual reported thoughts and feelings (as described in the previous section), and participants are assigned an overall empathic accuracy score.

The major advantage of the standard stimulus paradigm is the fact that the task is the same for all perceivers. This feature allows empathic accuracy scores to be compared across perceivers and correlated with relevant perceiver characteristics. It also avoids the problem of confounding target expressivity with perceiver perceptivity. Researchers can therefore meaningfully assess individual differences in empathic ability and then use these data to explore issues such as cross-target consistency (Marangoni et al., 1995) and the correlates of empathic ability (Gleason, Jensen-Campbell, & Ickes, 2009).

How accurate are people, on average?

Strangers infer each other's thoughts and feelings with an average accuracy score of about 20%; close friends make these inferences with an average accuracy score of about 30%; and married couples achieve average accuracy scores that usually range no higher than 35% (Graham, 1994; Stinson & Ickes, 1992; Verhofstadt, Buysse, & Ickes, 2007; Verhofstadt et al., 2008). All of these groups perform significantly better than chance, but there is obviously a lot of room for improvement between 35% accuracy and the theoretical maximum of 100% accuracy. So, the answer to the question we started with is that people do have real – though quite limited – insight into the specific content of other people's thoughts and feelings.

Why are empathic accuracy scores limited to the lower portion of their potential range? One possibility is that "evolutionary pressures operated over countless generations to eventually optimize the effective range of empathic accuracy in humans so that it was high enough to enable us to deal effectively with others but was not so high that we put our genetic futures at grave risk by weighting everyone else's interests as heavily as our own" (Ickes, 2011, p. 201).

Are some people more empathically accurate than others?

Researchers have attempted to relate a number of individual-difference variables to empathic accuracy. So far, however, only two of these variables – age-related maturational change and location on the autism spectrum – have consistently been linked to empathic accuracy. Two other individual-difference variables – intelligence and gender – have not, evidencing only weak and inconsistent relationships at best.

Age-related maturational change

Who would be more empathically accurate: an infant or a ten-year-old? The ten-year-old, obviously. Age-related maturational change is a powerful predictor of empathic accuracy. As normally developing children mature, they learn that other people can have different thoughts and feelings from their own and that these differences derive from what these other people are in a position to know or to perceive (Gopnik & Wellman, 1994). So, at least from infancy through middle to late childhood, age is a strong predictor of empathic accuracy.

But who would be more empathically accurate in *this* case: an eighteen-year-old or a twenty-eight-year-old? We suspect that most people would say that the twenty-eight-year-old would be more empathically accurate, and at first glance that might make sense. After all, the twenty-eight-year-old has had ten more years than the eighteen-year-old to develop his or her interpersonal skills, which might include the specific skills that underlie empathic accuracy. This seems like a reasonable supposition; however, the available research evidence isn't so clear. The preliminary data suggest that empathic accuracy appears to level off following an initial peak during adolescence, with little or no further change evident in adulthood (Perner & Wimmer, 1985). Many researchers now believe that the dramatic increase in empathic accuracy from infancy to middle to late childhood may be attributable to the development of more general skills that collectively facilitate empathic accuracy, rather than to the development of specific mind-reading[1] skills.

Autism

As Hodges, Lewis, & Ickes (2014) have noted, people's location on the Autism Spectrum has also been associated with their empathic accuracy:

> People with severe autism often have severe language deficits and other behavioral disturbances that make testing their empathic accuracy essentially impossible. However, within samples who are high enough functioning to be tested using the Ickes paradigm, people diagnosed with ASD show worse empathic accuracy (Demurie, De Corel, and Roeyers, 2011; Ponnet, Buysse, Roeyers, and De Clercq, 2008). The lack of

predictable structure in a social interaction appears to be an important moderator of this effect (Ponnet et al., 2008). High functioning autistics may be able to understand the "gist" of what the other person is thinking or feeling by learning to apply the relevant social schemas or scripts (see Grandin, Barron, and Zysk, 2005; Hirschfeld, Bartmess, White, and Frith, 2007; White, Hill, Winston, and Frith, 2006).

Intelligence and academic performance

In contrast to the results for autism, which reveal a fairly consistent link to empathic accuracy, the results for measures of intelligence and academic performance have been mixed. Although some studies have shown that university students' grade point average (GPA) predicted their empathic accuracy scores (Ickes et al., 1990, Ponnet, Buysse, Roeyers, & De Clercq, 2008), other studies have failed to replicate this finding (Ponnet, Roeyers, Buysse, De Clercq, & Van der Heyden, 2004, Ickes et al., 2000, Neel & Hodges, 2008).

Gender

Is there an overall gender difference in empathic accuracy that favors female perceivers? Some writers have proposed that because their traditional gender role requires women to be more nurturing and socially sensitive than men, women should also be more empathically accurate than men. This prediction of a female advantage is sometimes confirmed, but it seems to apply only when women are reminded that they are *supposed* to be more socially sensitive than men are (Hodges, Laurent, & Lewis, 2011; Hodges et al., 2010). For example, when they were explicitly asked to rate how accurately they inferred each of the target person's thoughts and feelings immediately following each empathic inference, women achieve a higher degree of empathic accuracy than men (Graham & Ickes, 1997; Ickes, Gesn, & Graham, 2000). Women also inferred a target person's thoughts and feelings more accurately than men when they were first asked how much empathic concern they felt for that person (Klein & Hodges, 2001). Because empathy is an essential part of the socially prescribed female gender role, these cues appear to have selectively enhanced empathic accuracy for women, but not men, by increasing the women's *motivation* to be accurate (Helgeson, 1994; Spence & Helmreich, 1978).

Can people train to improve their empathic accuracy?

If the right kind of training can improve skills such as playing the piano or playing a sport, can it also improve empathic accuracy? A study by Marangoni et al. (1995) suggests that it can. The participants in this study were instructed to infer the thoughts and feelings of clients who appeared in videotaped therapy sessions. Half of the participants (feedback condition) saw the client's actual thought or feeling appear on the video screen immediately after they had written down their thought/feeling inference, whereas the other half of the participants (no-feedback condition) did not. The participants who received feedback were significantly more accurate in their subsequent empathic inferences than those who did not. Impressively, this gain in empathic accuracy was evident after only forty-two feedback trials.

If we are capable of improving our empathic accuracy through training, which of the target person's behaviors should we attend to the most in order to maximize our empathic accuracy: the target's verbal behavior, nonverbal behavior, or both? The available research (Gesn & Ickes, 1999; Hall & Schmid Mast, 2008; Zaki, Bolger, & Ochsner, 2008) provides a clear answer: "In the overwhelming majority of everyday interactions [...] our empathic accuracy appears to rely most upon *what the other person says* (the words themselves), next most upon *how he or she says it* (the paralinguistic cues), and least upon *the accompanying visible nonverbal cues that the other person displays*" (Ickes, 2016).

Are some target persons more "readable" than others?

So far, we have focused on characteristics such as maturation and normal (i.e., non-autistic) development that enable the perceiver to become more empathically accurate. However, we must not forget that empathic accuracy also depends to a large extent on how transparent, or "readable," a target person's thoughts and feelings are in relation to those of other target persons (Ickes et al., 2000). What makes one person more "readable" than others? Not surprisingly, target persons are more "readable" when their thoughts and feelings match what they are currently talking about (Lewis, Hodges, Laurent, Srivastava, & Biancarosa, 2012). This transparency helps to minimize perceivers' confusion when they attempt to infer the target person's thoughts and feelings, and thus to increase their empathic accuracy. In most cases, we can assume that what people say reflects what they are currently thinking or feeling, unless they are either (1) distracted and thinking about something else or (2) using the topic they are talking about to mask or misrepresent their actual thoughts and feelings.

Motivational influences on empathic accuracy

Human behavior is determined by both personal characteristics and features of the situation the person is in (Ross & Nisbett, 1991). We have already discussed a number of personal characteristics that influence empathic accuracy, but what situational factors motivate people to be more empathically accurate?

In a study of opposite-sex (male-female) strangers, Ickes et al. (1990) found that the perceivers were more empathically accurate when their interaction partner was physically attractive, as assessed by a group of trained raters. This finding suggests that having a strong interest in one's partner can motivate greater attention to the partner, which leads in turn to greater empathic accuracy. Evidence from the same study supports this interpretation: the perceivers' empathic accuracy was also positively correlated with (1) the percentage of partner-focused (i.e., target-focused) thoughts and feelings the perceiver had reported, and (2) the percentage of partner-focused attributions the perceiver had reported (e.g., "She's nice," "He seems really nervous"). It appears that an opposite-sex partner's physical attractiveness motivates the perceiver to be both more attentive to the partner and more empathically accurate.

Societal expectations can also affect our empathic accuracy. For example, Thomas & Maio (2008) found that when female perceivers were provided with feedback that challenged their empathic skill, they subsequently displayed more empathic accuracy than male perceivers did. Being empathic and having the ability to understand others is a fundamental part of the female gender role – a societal expectation that conflicted with the specific information that these women were given. This conflict apparently motivated them to work harder to achieve a higher level of empathic accuracy and thereby conform more closely to their gender-role stereotype.

Interestingly, there is evidence that an outside incentive in the form of money can be used to motivate men to achieve higher levels of empathic accuracy. Klein & Hodges (2001) found that men who were paid according to how accurate they were achieved greater empathic accuracy than men who were not paid for their accuracy on the same task. This and the previously mentioned motivational findings suggest that "everyday mind reading" is an effortful process that people engage in for reasons that are largely pragmatic and goal-directed, whether the goal is to get close to an attractive person of the opposite sex, to assert a particular social identity, or to earn more money.

Empathic accuracy in close relationships

Relationship type influences empathic accuracy

Relationships, whether they are with a romantic partner, a family member, a friend, or a co-worker, are vital to our social, mental, and physical well-being (Cohen et al., 2003; Hawkley & Cacioppo, 2007; Hawkley, Thisted, Masi, & Cacioppo, 2010). Not all relationships are created equal, however. For example, we are typically more intimate with a romantic partner than with a co-worker, and we typically exhibit more formal behavior with people we have just met than with our siblings. In other words, our behavior varies from one type of relationship to the next. Does this mean that our average level of empathic accuracy varies in different types of relationships, too?

The answer is yes. Although the relevant research findings are somewhat mixed, the evidence suggests that strangers are less empathically accurate than are close friends (Stinson & Ickes, 1992; Graham, 1994), and that dating partners are more empathically accurate than both friends and strangers (Thomas & Fletcher, 2003). Although the length of time that people have known each other is important, what is *even more* important are the events that take place within the relationship which generate the information from which empathically accurate inferences are derived (Marangoni et al., 1995). In other words, how intimately and how well the perceiver gets to know the target person in whatever time period is being considered accounts for the difference in empathic accuracy between friends and strangers.

Motivated empathic inaccuracy

With regard to romantic relationships, researchers have repeatedly acknowledged that mis-understanding based on miscommunication is one of the most common and damaging problems that couples experience (McCabe, 2006). One might therefore assume that higher levels of empathic accuracy should be associated with greater relationship satisfaction and stability. After all, communication problems would not exist in the first place if people were consistently able to accurately read each other's minds (perhaps talking would even cease to exist if this were the case!). Although some studies have indeed confirmed that empathic accuracy is positively related to relationship satisfaction and stability, other studies have demonstrated an important exception: when the partner's thoughts and feelings have the potential to threaten and destabilize the relationship, greater empathic accuracy is negatively related to satisfaction and stability.

According to the *empathic accuracy model* (Ickes & Simpson, 1997, 2001), relationship partners are motivated to understand each other's thoughts and feelings in order to develop and maintain a close relationship. However, if the partner's thoughts and feelings contain information that has the potential to be hurtful and to threaten the relationship, perceivers are often motivated to *avoid* making accurate inferences that are likely to have such damaging consequences – a phenomenon that Ickes & Simpson (1997, 2001) have labeled *motivated inaccuracy*. In a study by Simpson, Ickes, & Blackstone (1995), dating couples who used motivated inaccuracy to cope with a situation that was highly threatening to their relationship were more likely to still be dating four months later than couples who did not. So is ignorance bliss, after all?

When does empathic accuracy help, versus hurt, relationships?

When is empathic accuracy likely to help, versus hurt, close relationships? Based on available theory and research, empathic accuracy appears to help close relationships when (1) perceivers use it to anticipate and avoid or, failing that, to recognize and resolve problems with their partner (Simpson, Ickes, & Oriña, 2001); (2) perceivers use it to provide the specific type and amount of support that their partner needs (Verhofstadt, Ickes, & Buysse, 2010; Verhofstadt, Davis, & Ickes, 2011); and (3) perceivers use it to coordinate their own goals with their partner's goals (Berscheid, 1985). (For other examples, see Bissonnette, Rusbult, & Kilpatrick, 1997; Goffman, 1974; Ickes, 2003, chapter 8; Noller, 1980, 1981; Sillars, 1998; Stinson & Ickes, 1992; Thomas & Fletcher, 2003; Thomas, Fletcher, & Lange, 1997.)

On the other hand, the available theory and research suggest that empathic accuracy can hurt close relationships (1) when the partners use it to provoke each other and "push each other's buttons" (Ickes, 2003, chapter 11); (2) when it reveals the differences between the partner's viewpoints are much greater than previously recognized, to such an extent that further clarification or discussion will only underscore the tension in the relationship (Aldous, 1977; Kursh, 1971; Sillars, 1985); and (3) when it reveals that certain "benign misconceptions" that the partners previously held about each other are false and can no longer be sustained (Levinger & Breedlove, 1966; Sillars, 1985). (For other examples, see Aldous, 1977; Rausch, Barry, Hertel, & Swain, 1974; Watzlawick, Weakland, & Fisch, 1974.) In these circumstances, partners may be better off if they decide "I'm not going to go there," and avoid making accurate inferences that are likely to result in more harm than benefit.

Conclusion

In summary, there is no need to take an absolutist position regarding the problem of "reading" other people's minds. Although it is true that we cannot have direct access to other people's minds and achieve a perfect knowledge of what they are thinking and feeling, we can – and do – achieve a limited knowledge that is often "good enough" to sustain successful relationships with them. In addition, we can often sense when it is better to stay out of our partners' minds and avoid knowing thoughts and feelings that are likely to cause us pain. The empirical study of empathic accuracy has, over the past thirty years, made it possible to move beyond philosophical speculation and debate and obtain fascinating insights into the complex role that "everyday mind reading" (Ickes, 2003) plays in people's daily lives.

Note

1 Although many psychologists refer to the process of inferring other people's thoughts and feelings as "empathic inference," it is also referred to as "mindreading" or "theory of mind."

References

Aldous, J. (1977). Family interaction patterns. *Annual Review of Sociology*, 3, 105–35.
Berscheid, E. (1985). Compatibility, interdependence, and emotion. In W. Ickes (ed.), *Compatible and incompatible relationships* (pp. 143–61). New York: Springer-Verlag.
Bissonnette, V., Rusbult, C., & Kilpatrick, S. D. (1997). Empathic accuracy and marital conflict resolution. In W. Ickes (ed.), *Empathic accuracy* (pp. 251–81). New York: Guilford Press.
Clements, K., Holtzworth-Munroe, A., Schweinle, W., & Ickes, W. (2007). Empathic accuracy of intimate partners in violent versus nonviolent relationships. *Personal Relationships*, 14, 369–88.

Cohen, S., Doyle, W. J., Turner, R., Alper, C. M., & Skoner, D. P. (2003). Sociability and susceptibility to the common cold. *Psychological Science*, 14(5), 389–95.

Demurie, E., DeCorel, M., & Roeyers, H. (2011). Empathic accuracy in adolescents with autism spectrum disorders and adolescents with attention-deficit/hyperactivity disorder. *Research in Autism Spectrum Disorders*, 5, 126–34.

Flury, J., Ickes, W., & Schweinle, W. (2008). The borderline empathy effect: Do high BPD individuals have greater empathic ability? Or are they just more difficult to "read"? *Journal of Research in Personality*, 42, 312–32.

Gesn, P., & Ickes, W. (1999). The development of meaning contexts for empathic accuracy: Channel and sequence effects. *Journal of Personality and Social Psychology*, 77, 746–61.

Goffman, E. (1974). *Frame analysis: An essay on the organization of experience*. New York: Harper and Row.

Gopnik, A., & Wellman, H. M. (1994). The "theory" theory. In L. A. Hirschfield & S. A. Gelman (eds.), *Mapping the mind: Domain specificity in cognition and culture* (pp. 257–293). Cambridge: Cambridge University Press.

Graham, T. (1994). *Gender, relationship, and target differences in empathic accuracy*. Unpublished master's thesis, University of Texas at Arlington.

Graham, T., & Ickes, W. (1997). When women's intuition isn't greater than men's. In W. Ickes (ed.), *Empathic accuracy* (pp. 117–43). New York: Guilford.

Grandin, T., Barron, S., & Zysk, V. (eds.). (2005). *Unwritten rules of social relationships: Decoding social mysteries through the unique perspectives of autism*. Arlington, TX: Future Horizons.

Hall, J., & Schmidt Mast, M. (2008). Are women always more interpersonally sensitive than men? Impact of content domain and motivation. *Personality and Social Psychology Bulletin*, 34, 144–55.

Hawkley, L. C., & Cacioppo, J. T. (2007). Aging and loneliness: Downhill quickly? *Current Directions in Psychological Science*, 16, 187–91.

Hawkley, L. C., Thisted, R. A., Masi, C. M., & Cacioppo, J. T. (2010). Loneliness predicts increased blood pressure: Five-year cross-lagged analyses in middle-aged and older adults. *Psychology and Aging*, 25, 132–41.

Helgeson, V. (1994). Relation of agency and communion to wellbeing: Evidence and potential explanations. *Psychological Bulletin*, 116, 412–28.

Hirschfeld, L., Bartmess, E., White, S., & Frith, U. (2007). Can autistic children predict behavior by social stereotypes? *Current Biology*, 17(12), 451–2.

Hodges, S. D., Kiel, K. J., Kramer, A. D. I., Veach, D., & Villanueva, B. R. (2010). Giving birth to empathy: The effects of similar experience on empathic accuracy, empathic concern, and perceived empathy. *Personality and Social Psychology Bulletin*, 36, 398–409.

Hodges, S. D., Laurent, S. M., & Lewis, K. L. (2011). Specially motivated, feminine, or just female: Do women have an empathic accuracy advantage? In J. L. Smith, W. Ickes, J. Hall, & S. D. Hodges (eds.), *Managing interpersonal sensitivity: Knowing when – and when not – to understand others* (pp. 59–73). New York: Nova Science Publishers.

Hodges, S. D., Lewis, K. L., & Ickes, W. (2014). The matter of other minds: Empathic accuracy and the factors that influence it. In P. Shaver, M. Mikulincer (eds.), J. A. Simpson, & J. Dovidio (assoc. eds.), *APA handbook of personality and social psychology*, Vol. 2: *Interpersonal relations and group processes* (pp. 319–48). Washington, DC: American Psychological Association.

Ickes, W. (ed.) (1997). *Empathic accuracy*. New York: Guilford Press.

Ickes, W. (2001). Measuring empathic accuracy. In J. A. Hall & F. J. Bernieri (eds.), *Interpersonal sensitivity: Theory and measurement* (pp. 219–41). Mahwah, NJ: Erlbaum.

Ickes, W. (2003). *Everyday mind reading: Understanding what other people think and feel*. Amherst, NY: Prometheus Books.

Ickes, W. (2009). Empathic accuracy: Its links to clinical, cognitive, developmental, social, and physiological psychology. In J. Decety & W. Ickes (eds.), *The social neuroscience of empathy* (pp. 57–70). Cambridge, MA: MIT Press.

Ickes, W. (2011). Everyday mind reading is driven by motives and goals. *Psychological Inquiry*, 22, 200–6.

Ickes, W. (2016). Judging thoughts and feelings. In J. A. Hall, M. Schmid Mast, & T. V. West (eds.), *The social psychology of perceiving others accurately*. New York: Cambridge University Press.

Ickes, W., Buysse, A., Pham, H., Rivers, K., Erickson, J., Hancock, M., Kelleher, J., & Gesn, P. (2000). On the difficulty of distinguishing "good" and "poor" perceivers: A social relations analysis of empathic accuracy data. *Personal Relationships*, 7, 219–34.

Ickes, W., Gesn, P., & Graham, T. (2000). Gender differences in empathic accuracy: Differential ability of differential motivation? *Personal Relationships*, 7, 95–109.

Ickes, W., & Simpson, J. (1997). Managing empathic accuracy in close relationships. In W. Ickes (ed.), *Empathic accuracy* (pp. 218–50). New York: Guilford Press.

Ickes, W., & Simpson, J. (2001). Motivational aspects of empathic accuracy. In G. J. O. Fletcher & M. S. Clark (eds.), *Blackwell handbook in social psychology: Interpersonal processes* (pp. 229–49). Oxford: Blackwell.

Ickes, W., Stinson, L., Bissonnette, V., & Garcia, S. (1990). Naturalistic social cognition: Empathic accuracy in mixed-sex dyads. *Journal of Personality and Social Psychology*, 59, 730–42.

Klein, K., & Hodges, S. (2001). Gender differences, motivation, and empathic accuracy: When it pays to understand. *Personality and Social Psychology Bulletin*, 27, 720–30.

Kursh, C. O. (1971). The benefits of poor communication. *Psychoanalytic Review*, 58, 189–208.

Levinger, G., & Breedlove, J. (1966). Interpersonal attraction and agreement. *Journal of Personality and Social Psychology*, 3, 367–72.

Lewis, K., Hodges, S., Laurent, S., Srivastava, S., & Biancarosa, G. (2012). Reading between the minds: The use of stereotypes in empathic accuracy. *Psychological Science*, 23, 1040–6.

Marangoni, C., Garcia, S., Ickes, W., & Teng, G. (1995). Empathic accuracy in a clinically relevant setting. *Journal of Personality and Social Psychology*, 68, 854–69.

McCabe, M. (2006). Satisfaction in marriage and committed heterosexual relationships: Past, present, and future. *Annual Review of Sex Research*, 17, 39–58.

Neel, R., & Hodges, S. (2008). [Empathic accuracy and verbal intelligence]. Unpublished raw data.

Noller, P. (1980). Misunderstandings in marital communication: A study of couples' nonverbal communication. *Journal of Personality and Social Psychology*, 39, 1135–48.

Noller, P. (1981). Gender and marital adjustment level differences in decoding messages from spouses and strangers. *Journal of Personality and Social Psychology*, 41, 272–8.

Perner, J., & Wimmer, H. (1985). "John thinks that Mary thinks that …": Attribution of second-order beliefs by 5- to 10-year-old children. *Journal of Experimental Child Psychology*, 39, 437–71.

Ponnet, K., Buysse, A., Roeyers, H., & De Clercq, A. (2008). Mind reading in young adults with ASD: Does structure matter? *Journal of Autism and Developmental Disorders*, 38, 905–18.

Ponnet, K., Roeyers, H., Buysse, A., De Clercq, A., & Van Der Heyden, E. (2004). Advanced mind reading in adults with Asperger syndrome. *Autism*, 8, 249–66.

Rausch, H. L., Barry, W. A., Hertel, R. K., & Swain, M. A. (1974). *Communication conflict and marriage*. San Francisco: Jossey-Bass.

Rogers, C. R. (1957). The necessary and sufficient conditions of therapeutic personality change. *Journal of Consulting Psychology*, 21, 95–103.

Ross, L., & Nisbett, R. (1991). *The person and the situation: Perspectives of social psychology*. New York: McGraw-Hill.

Schmid Mast, M. S., & Ickes, W. (2007). Empathic accuracy: Measurement and potential clinical applications. In T. F. D. Farrow & P. W. R. Woodruff (eds.), *Empathy in mental illness* (pp. 408–27). Cambridge: Cambridge University Press.

Sillars, A. (1985). Interpersonal perception in relationships. In W. Ickes (ed.), *Compatible and incompatible relationships* (pp. 277–305). New York: Springer-Verlag.

Sillars, A. L. (1998). (Mis)understanding. In B. H. Spitzberg & W. R. Cupach (eds.), *The dark side of close relationships* (pp. 73–102). Mahwah, NJ: Erlbaum.

Simpson, J., Ickes, W., & Blackstone, T. (1995). When the head protects the heart: Empathic accuracy in dating relationships. *Journal of Personality and Social Psychology*, 69, 629–41.

Simpson, J. A., Ickes, W., & Oriña, M. M. (2001). Empathic accuracy and pre-emptive relationship maintenance. In J. Harvey & A. Werzel (eds.), *Close romantic relationships: Maintenance and enhancement* (pp. 27–46). Mahwah, NJ: Lawrence Erlbaum Associates.

Simpson, J. A., Oriña, M. M., & Ickes, W. (2003). When accuracy hurts, and when it helps: A test of the empathic accuracy model in marital interactions. *Journal of Personality and Social Psychology*, 85, 881–93.

Spence, J., & Helmreich, R. (1978). *Masculinity and femininity: Their psychological dimensions, correlates, and antecedents*. Austin, TX: University of Texas Press.

Stinson, L., & Ickes, W. (1992). Empathic accuracy in the interactions of male friends versus male strangers. *Journal of Personality and Social Psychology*, 62, 787–97.

Thomas, G., & Fletcher, G. (2003). Mind reading accuracy in intimate relationships: Assessing the roles of the relationship, the target, and the judge. *Journal of Personality and Social Psychology*, 85, 1079–94.

Thomas, G., Fletcher, G. J. O., & Lange, C. (1997). On-line empathic accuracy in marital interaction. *Journal of Personality and Social Psychology*, 72, 839–50.

Thomas, G., & Maio, G. R. (2008). Man, I feel like a woman: When and how gender-role motivation helps mind reading. *Journal of Personality and Social Psychology*, 95, 1165–79.

Verhofstadt, L. L., Buysse, A., & Ickes, W. (2007). Social support in couples: An examination of gender differences using self-report and observational methods. *Sex Roles*, 57, 267–82.

Verhofstadt, L. L., Buysse A., Ickes, W., Davis, M., & Devoldre, I. (2008). Support provision in marriage: The role of emotional similarity and empathic accuracy. *Emotion*, 8, 792–802.

Verhofstadt, L., Davis, M., & Ickes, W. (2011). Motivation, empathic accuracy, and spousal support. It's complicated! In J. L. Smith, W. Ickes, J. A. Hall, & S. D. Hodges (eds.), *Managing interpersonal sensitivity: Knowing when and when not to understand others* (pp. 169–92). Hauppauge, NY: Nova Science Publishers.

Verhofstadt, L. L., Ickes, W., & Buysse, A. (2010). Empathic accuracy and support provision in marriage. In K. Sullivan & J. Davila (eds.), *Support processes in intimate relationships* (pp. 71–88). New York: Oxford University Press.

Watzlawick, P., Weakland, J., & Fisch, R. (1974). *Principles of problem formation and problem resolution*. New York: Norton.

White, S., Hill, E., Winston, J., & Frith, U. (2006). An islet of social ability in Asperger syndrome: Judging social attributes from faces. *Brain and Cognition*, 61(1), 69–77.

Zaki, J., Bolger, N., & Ochsner, K. (2008). It takes two: The interpersonal nature of empathic accuracy. *Psychological Science*, 19, 399–404.

32

EMPATHY AND PSYCHOPATHOLOGY

Jeanette Kennett

Introduction

What can we learn about empathy and in particular about its role in morality by studying conditions in which it is significantly impaired? Over the past decade or so philosophers have focused extensively on psychopathy and to a lesser extent on autism in trying to tease out these questions and shed light on the longstanding meta-ethical debates between rationalists and sentimentalists about the basis of moral motivation and judgement. In tandem with this, some positive accounts of morality in both philosophy and psychology have given empathy a central role (e.g. Hoffman 2000, Slote 2010).

There are a variety of ways in which empathy might play an important or essential role in morality. It might be developmentally essential to moral agency. It might be epistemically important. It might be critical for moral regard, moral motivation and the acquisition of virtue.

But what kind of empathy is critical to morality in these ways? What are those philosophers who argue that it is fundamental to morality including in their conception of empathy?

In this chapter I begin by briefly outlining some of the ways in which moral philosophers and others have understood empathy and the claims they have made for its moral importance. I then consider the cases of autism and psychopathy. I suggest against critics that though the underlying causes differ, these two populations are each impaired at the kind of identifying empathy that has been argued to be fundamental to the development of moral concern and to the recognition of the moral status of other persons. Other factors come into play in explaining the moral differences between the two populations and this is made clearer by an examination of alexithymia – a condition that affects the capacity to experience, identify and share emotions.

Empathy and morality

What empathy requires is the ability *to know what the other person thinks or feels despite the fact that it is different from one's own mental state* at the time. In empathy *one shares emotional reactions* to the other person's different state of mind. Empathy presupposes, amongst other things, a recognition of different mental states. It also presupposes that one goes beyond the recognition of difference to *adopt the other person's frame of mind* with *all the consequences of emotional reactions*.

(Frith 1989: 144–5, my emphases)

As Frith describes it, empathy is a complex capacity involving both mindreading and emotion sharing. Mindreading is important for empathy – but in empathy one goes beyond knowledge of the other's mental states to adopt or somehow identify with the other person's perspective and so comes to feel vicariously what the other feels for their situation. It is this kind of empathy, as affective identification and attunement, that I will primarily target here. It is not clear whether Frith's account requires a further congruent but distinct emotional *response* to the mental states and emotions of others. It is the sympathetic responses that arise from affective identification with the other that sentimentalist philosophers tend to focus on in their accounts of moral judgement, motivation and concern.

For Hume, feeling with and for others lies at the basis of moral concern and moral motivation.

> Were I present at any of the more terrible operations of surgery, it is certain, that even before it begun, the preparation of the instruments, the laying of the bandages in order, the heating of the irons, with all the signs of anxiety and concern in the patient and assistants, would have a great effect upon my mind, and excite the strongest sentiments of pity and terror […] we have *no such extensive concern for society but from sympathy*.
>
> *(Treatise 576)*

Hume argues that the transmission of feelings via emotional contagion is based on our similarity to one another. He says "we never remark any passion or principle in others, of which, in some degree or other, we may not find a parallel in ourselves" (*Treatise* 318). In the example given, the vicarious and seemingly unwilled sharing of the patient's terror stimulates pity for their ordeal and a related desire to alleviate their suffering. Basic *empathy* is thus seen as the foundation of our *sympathetic* concern for others' welfare. Hume's claims about the connection between similarity, emotion transmission and care appear to have garnered substantial empirical support via a series of experiments conducted by Daniel Batson to test the Empathy Altruism Hypothesis – *empathic concern produces altruistic motivation*. These experiments show an increase in helping when empathy is primed – usually by providing the subject with a similar target (age, gender, race, background etc.) or by giving instructions to focus on how the target feels. They cannot, however, decisively establish the larger claim that empathy is necessary for altruistic motivation or is the basis of *all* morally motivated action. Empathy is clearly not sufficient for moral motivation even on Hume's account since it may be outcompeted by other motives. Moreover, Hume agrees that morality requires us to take up a more general or universal point of view and it is at least questionable whether empathy itself provides the mechanism that could move us to adopt this universal point of view and extend our concern to all.

A rather different account of the connection may be built from P. F. Strawson's participant reactive attitudes account of social and moral interaction. It is a brute fact that we human beings as social and emotional creatures care about others' attitudes towards us and demand goodwill from each other in our everyday dealings. When those expectations are disappointed we respond with anger and resentment. When they are satisfied we often feel gratitude and affection. Because we just do care about what others think of us we are disposed to be sensitive to their wishes and demands in our ongoing reciprocal interactions. We are also disposed to feel vicarious reactive attitudes on behalf of others and to press their case when the demand for goodwill is violated. Morality is essentially interpersonal and regulates our behaviour by way of these affective mechanisms within the participant stance to create the shared standards and expectations that are the foundation of moral community.

Strawson does not talk about empathy but empathy theorists such as David Shoemaker take themselves to be developing a Strawsonian picture of morality. Shoemaker argues that what he calls *identifying empathy* is crucial to participation in the moral community and to moral *competence*. Identifying empathy in its affective mode involves "the capacity and disposition to *feel* what things are like for that person, to be in sync emotionally with that person's own emotional ups and downs … [to be] vulnerable to them" (Shoemaker 2009: 443).

He argues that emotional forms of empathy – a term that he takes to cover "some kind of experience 'from the inside' of the psychological goings-on of creatures very similar to, yet distinct from, ourselves" (Shoemaker 2015: 157) – provide more than an epistemic aid to moral forms of regard; rather they may be constitutive of moral regard in its pure form. One way to interpret this claim about empathy and moral regard is as follows. Moral regard involves a recognition or apprehension of the other as a source of non-derivative reasons for action – their concerns become concerns for us. We apprehend others in this way via our affective engagement with them. Without the capacity to be affectively in sync with the other we will be insensitive to second-person reasons – we will not have pure moral regard. And without this sensitivity to second-person reasons we could not be held to moral demands.

Shoemaker argues that the comparison between individuals with Mild Mental Retardation (MMR) and psychopaths supports his view. It is the intact affective capacities of the individual with MMR that enable them to "develop moral understanding and motivation" and to participate in the moral community, whereas the psychopath's "emotional deafness is the source of her inability to register the moral appeals of her fellows" with the result that she is incapable of "genuine moral understanding and motivation" (Shoemaker 2009: 444).

I agree that second-person reasons are plausibly the currency of the participant stance and that responsiveness to them is important to smooth social interaction, cooperation and the development of moral concerns. What it is not yet clear is whether emotional forms of empathy provide the only mechanism by which we take others' reasons on board and see them as providing non-derivative reasons for action.

Empathy, psychopathology and moral agency

(i) Psychopathy

The close connection between empathy and morality suggested in sentimentalist accounts appears to gain support by looking at cases where it is notably absent. Lack of empathy is a defining feature of psychopathy (e.g. Blair et al. 2005, Cleckley 1955, Robert Hare 1991) and is usually taken to be the core feature of the disorder that unifies key diagnostic criteria on the widely used Psychopathy Checklist (Revised), for example the Factor One list of personality traits that includes: pathological lying, cunning/manipulative, lack of remorse or guilt, shallow affect (genuine emotion is short-lived and egocentric), callousness, lack of empathy and failure to accept responsibility for own actions (Hare 1991).

There is indeed a strong case to be made that psychopaths' pervasive and fundamental deficits in emotion recognition, emotion experience and emotion responsiveness are causally connected with their amoralism, even if these deficits are not all best described in terms of empathy. Blair (1995) argues that when a normal child sees a victim's distress she associates her own fear and distress with that of the victim and is aversively conditioned to the harmful action. This requires intact systems to detect intention, systems involved in empathetic identification and systems which allow conditioning to aversive stimuli using the fear response. Psychopaths, however, are deficient in the neurocognitive mechanisms required. They show abnormally low physiological response to distress cues from others.

Nichols argues along similar lines that the normal affective response to others' distress infuses social norms against harming others with the special status that we take to be definitive of moral norms. Since psychopaths have a deficiency in their affective response to harm in others "this plausibly explains why they fail to take harm norms seriously" (Nichols 2002: 300). On both these accounts psychopaths lack the internal mechanisms that inhibit harming and promote helping, and failure of basic empathy is the explanation. At least with respect to the negative emotions of fear and sadness they do not experience emotional contagion, vicarious sharing of emotions or, notably, a sympathetic response to the emotions they might attribute to others. (Some psychopaths, however, have a sufficiently good understanding of the negative emotions of others to take pleasure in the distress that they cause.)

These affective deficits are then plausibly at the heart of the psychopath's amoralism. This explains why they cannot meet the conditions for moral competence suggested by Shoemaker – their inability to be in sync with others is the source of their insensitivity to (an important class of) second-person reasons. For psychopaths, to use Carl Elliot's words, other people are "less 'real'. The psychopath seems ... unable to see things through the eyes of others and thus unable to see why the interests of others matter" (Elliot 1992: 210).

Nevertheless, lack of empathy – feeling what the other feels from their perspective – may not be the primary deficit in psychopathy. Heidi Maibom in "Without Fellow Feeling" (2014) suggests that a documented deficit in personal distress may instead play the key role in the moral deficits of psychopaths. Since psychopaths fail to experience personal distress when imagining *themselves* in unpleasant or frightening situations, their perspective taking produces neither personal nor empathic distress. Bird et al. (2014) also note that "a deficit in e.g. the experience of distress emotions would lead to a diminished ability to recognize distress cues in others and therefore a lack of empathy for distress". They argue along similar lines to Blair and Nichols that "[i]f the infant experiences distress less often than is typical, there will be reduced opportunity for the infant to learn which cues reliably signal distress in another". Some degree of personal distress seems critical to feeling distress for others and it is this, Maibom suggests, rather than fellow feeling or sympathy, that most likely plays a key role in inhibiting aggression. Maibom's suggestion seems supported by a variety of studies that indicate that psychopaths are insensitive to punishment and lack the ability to become aversively conditioned (see Blair, Mitchell & Blair 2005: 48–52 for an overview). This might explain the risk-taking and irresponsibility characteristic of psychopathy but the inability to be moved by punishment is not a failure of empathy. A deficit in personal distress might be the more fundamental failure which manifests both as lack of empathy for the suffering of others and insensitivity to punishment.

The suggestion that psychopaths might lack what is sometimes called intrapersonal empathy (Maibom does not use this term) is also seen in Shoemaker (2015). He suggests that the psychopath's flattened affective landscape results in a lack of care for themselves. Nothing matters to them and this explains their often striking imprudence and their insusceptibility to the threat of punishment. This is a promising line of enquiry but I do not think it can be the full explanation.

Other disorders involving impairments of empathy and amorality may not be similarly marked by incapacity to feel or imagine personal distress. Some accounts of narcissism do mention personal distress. Histrionic disorder involves high levels of personal distress but the egocentric focus of the histrionic leaves little space for empathizing with others. Moreover, as Adshead points out in "The Words but not the Music" (2014), many of those detained in secure facilities combine elements of psychopathy with emotional dysregulation and personal distress.

Adshead suggests that the key to understanding moral incapacity in psychopathy might rather be their fragmented and impoverished sense of self as displayed in their high levels of narrative incoherence, especially on moral questions. Adshead argues that coherent narratives are high in self-reflection. By contrast, a number of studies of psychopaths indicate that they violate maxims of relevance, contradict known facts about their lives without noticing it, and make huge unwarranted inferences. They cannot make their stories add up.

The inability to make one's story add up is a striking feature of Cleckley's descriptions of his patients. Consider for example the case of Roberta, described by Cleckley. Cleckley describes her as friendly and helpful and apparently open in her demeanour, but she is also utterly unreliable and engages in frequent theft, truancy and deceptive behaviour about which she seems untroubled. Of her lying, her father had this to say:

> I wouldn't exactly say she's like a hypocrite … When she's caught and confronted with her lies and other misbehaviour she doesn't seem to appreciate the inconsistency of her position. Her conscience seems still untouched.
>
> *(cited in Cleckley 1955: 72)*

Or take the case of Pete, another of Cleckley's patients, a seemingly amiable young man from a good home who has casually engaged in a variety of morally dubious and criminal activities, including theft, forgery, blackmarket dealing and cheating in his exams. From Pete's endlessly changing accounts of the reasons for his behaviour and his frequent contradictory claims and shallow inconsistent goals, Cleckley concludes:

> It seemed … a case of there being nowhere within him any valid contrast between *believing* and *not believing* or even between a thing of this sort being *so* or *not so* …

> He did not seem to feel any need to revise his attitude as the ordinary man does on finding himself in error. The fact that he had been, as admitted by himself, on the wrong track seemed in no way to stimulate him toward getting on another track … It was not hard to get the feeling that he had never been on any track at all, that he had not really been committed to his first proposition and so had nothing to withdraw.
>
> *(1955: 118–20)*

I have argued elsewhere that psychopaths are insensitive to the discomfort of cognitive dissonance and that this puzzling feature of psychopathy seems likely to be a cause as well as a consequence of their empathy deficits (Kennett 2015). Psychopaths' lack of internal coherence and tolerance or unawareness of personal inconsistency interact with and can partially explain both the shallowness of their emotions and their failure to develop a rich sense of self. Central moral emotions such as guilt, shame and regret arguably require a clear persisting sense of self against which one's actions can be judged consistent or inconsistent. There is now a growing body of empirical evidence on how identity motivates action (for an overview, see Hardy & Carlo 2005). The evidence is that people are motivated to act in an identity-congruent way (Vignoles et al. 2008). According to Blasi, as one's sense of self develops and matures there is a greater desire for self-consistency; fidelity with one's core self is seen as a necessity, and self-inconsistency elicits intense negative affect (reported in Hardy & Carlo 2005). The psychopaths described above do not appear to possess a core sense of self and so cannot experience this form of motivation. I suggest (Kennett 2015) that this more complex story provides a rival explanation to lack of empathy alone for many of the items on the psychopathy checklist that contribute to their amoralism, including: need for stimulation/proneness to boredom; poor behavioural controls; lack of realistic long-term goals; impulsivity and irresponsibility; shallow affect; lack of remorse or guilt; and pathological lying (Hare 1991).

While psychopaths undoubtedly have deficits in affective forms of empathy that are related to their moral deficits, precisely how we should understand this requires further investigation. Their deficits manifest in an insensitivity to second-person reasons within the participant stance but the absence of moral concern in psychopaths is also revealed in their lack of core principles – a lack that is not necessarily shared by other populations with empathy impairments.

(ii) Autistic spectrum disorder

According to DSM-5, the American Psychiatric Association's Diagnostic and Statistical Manual of Mental Disorders, an essential feature of this disorder (Criterion A) is "persistent impairment in reciprocal communication and social interaction" (American Psychiatric Association 2013: 53). This includes:

1. Deficits in social-emotional reciprocity, ranging for example from … failure of normal back and forth conversation; to reduced sharing of interests, emotions, or affect; to failure to initiate or respond to social interaction.
2. Deficits in nonverbal communicative behaviours used for social interaction …
3. Deficits in developing, maintaining and understanding relationships, ranging for example, from difficulties adjusting behaviour to suit various social contexts; to difficulties in sharing imaginative play or in making friends; to absence of interest in peers. (American Psychiatric Association 2013: 50)

Autism is on a spectrum and discussions of the impact of autism on moral agency in philosophy have largely been confined to relatively high-functioning autistic people without co-occurring intellectual disability and without the kind of language impairments that would prevent them testifying to their moral concerns (Kennett 2002). Nevertheless, such individuals report significant difficulties in social understanding and interaction. It seems apparent that the kind of identifying empathy that Shoemaker thinks is at the core of morality – the capacity and disposition to *feel* what things are like for the other person, to be in sync emotionally with that person's own emotional ups and downs – may be significantly impaired in autistic people. That degree of synchronicity plausibly requires just those capacities for reciprocal social interaction and adjustment that the person with autism lacks.

Yet many autistic people are morally conscientious and report a range of sincere moral concerns (Kennett 2002). They do recognise other people's concerns as reason giving, though due to their deficiencies in social understanding and interpretation they may have difficulty discerning what those concerns are. This suggests that factors other than empathy may be critical to moral agency and moral motivation.

The claim that autistic people are impaired in empathy has been challenged however. Blair (1996) argues that basic affective empathy in autistic children is unimpaired and it is this that explains their normal performance on a range of moral tasks – at least those that do not require mindreading abilities. Autistic children and adults are claimed to be meaningfully responsive to distress in others when this is made salient to them. It has been suggested (e.g. Bollard 2014) that the distinction between cognitive empathy and affective empathy explains the moral difference between people with autism and psychopathy. Autistic people lack cognitive empathy – they cannot read other people's intentions – but not affective empathy. In psychopaths the deficiency is reversed. The mistake has been to think that there is a common lack of empathy between the two groups and so we must look elsewhere to explain the moral differences between psychopaths and autistic people. I agree that the two populations differ in cognitive empathy but, as we shall see below, it is not so clear that differences in affective empathy can do all the work of explaining their moral differences.

First I doubt that the preserved basic emotion recognition and response claimed for autistic people gets us all the way to the identifying empathy or the degree of affective attunement that Shoemaker suggests is crucial for moral regard, responsiveness to second-person reasons and inclusion in the moral community. A reliance on basic empathy would seem to gloss over the other social deficits that are essential criteria for the diagnosis of autism and which must substantially restrict the individual's capacity to engage in the participant stance with others, and come to regulate their behaviour via affective mechanisms. Attention to others plus some degree of mindreading or cognitive empathy is surely required, as is what Bird et al. (2014) call input from the Situation Understanding System, which they describe as a domain-general appraisal system that provides an estimate of the emotional state of another based upon the situation they are in. Bird et al. say that absent, or incorrect, empathic responses may result from atypical social scripts due to reduced attention to, or opportunity for, social interaction in autism and may also result from Theory of Mind deficits. Even where basic affective empathy is preserved in autism it certainly does not get elaborated in the ordinary ways, and so if empathy is crucial for moral concern we should expect significant deficits in moral concern in autistic people.

However, it may be that the discussion of empathy deficits in autism misses the target. Autistic people do not all share the same empathy-relevant deficits. It is estimated that around 50 per cent of people with autism are severely alexithymic, with the majority showing at least some degree of alexithymia. Alexithymic individuals experience difficulties in experiencing, identifying, expressing and describing emotions. Bird et al. (2014) suggest that co-occurring alexithymia explains a number of the affective impairments seen in autism but that alexithymia is neither necessary nor sufficient for a diagnosis of autism. For example, a study which examined empathic anterior insula response to the pain of another showed that the amount of empathic brain activity was predicted by the degree of alexithymia in both those with autism and those without autism. Autism did not have any independent predictive value (Bird et al. 2010).

If empathy theorists are right about the basis of moral concern – if Hume is right that we have no such concern for others except via the operations of empathy – which includes emotional contagion, emotion sharing via simulation and resultant affectively attuned responses to the situation of the other – then we should expect a marked reduction of moral concern among those with alexithymia. Indeed, since Bird et al. suggest that empathy impairments in alexithymia "arise from a more global (in comparison with psychopathy) impairment in the ability to represent one's own emotion, resulting in an inability to learn associations between cues to affective states in others, and affective states in the self", this condition should be even more morally devastating than psychopathy.

Conversely, if there are morally conscientious alexithymic individuals, with or without autism, then their moral concern must have some basis other than that achieved via affective forms of empathy, and this would further undermine the case that empathy deficits are sufficient to explain the moral deficits of the psychopath.

Alexithymia, moral judgement and moral concern

There is some evidence that alexithymia affects moral judgement. Brewer et al. (2015) cite evidence that increased alexithymia is associated with more utilitarian decision making and increased perceived permissibility of accidentally harming others. This appears to be consistent with studies showing an increase in utilitarian judgements in people with psychopathic traits and might suggest that alexithymia underlies psychopathic moral indifference. However, studies of alexithymia and psychopathy have been inconclusive and according to Adshead (2014) there is not an obvious relation between them.

Work by Brewer et al. (2015) also suggests that there are no easy conclusions to be drawn about the impact of emotion blindness on moral judgement. In a study where individuals with and without Autistic Spectrum Disorder (matched for alexithymia) judged the moral acceptability of emotion-evoking statements, and identified the emotion evoked, alexithymia in non-autistic individuals predicted atypical moral judgement, but it did *not* predict it for those individuals with ASD. Brewer et al. explain the results in line with dual processing accounts which posit that both rational and emotional processes contribute to moral judgement. They say that "while typical individuals judged the moral acceptability of emotion-evoking statements based on the emotion likely to be evoked, and alexithymia, characterized by reduced emotion identification, negatively impacted on this process, those with ASD did not rely on emotion judgments when judging moral acceptability" (Brewer et al. 2015).

Of course judgements of moral acceptability (especially in laboratory settings) are not necessarily reliable indicators of moral concern and commitment or of morally motivated action in line with the judgement. They may just be evidence of acquaintance with the content of this subset of social norms. Is there evidence of deeper moral commitment and understanding in individuals with alexithymia?

In the remainder of this section I will draw upon interviews and writings from alexithymic individuals with and without a diagnosis of autism. I suggest that these are evidence that at least some such individuals display clear moral concerns and a conscientious approach to their dealings with others. Importantly, despite affective flatness and a greatly lessened interest in and need for social interaction, these individuals are nothing like amoral psychopaths. The difference between these alexithymic individuals and psychopaths appears to rest in their conscientiousness and, relatedly, a clear sense of self. (I am not suggesting that all alexithymic individuals have a clear sense of self but some seem to.) The moral profile of these individuals is undoubtedly different to that of neurotypicals, and the expression of their concerns can sound strange to our ears. But on any charitable interpretation they do have moral concerns, they do have moral principles, and this surely puts pressure on the very strong constitutive claims made for empathy by some moral theorists.

Let's recap. Alexithymia is a condition where individuals do not experience or cannot describe, express or identify their emotions. Such individuals may experience many of the physical sensations associated with emotion, for example, tightness in the chest or heart racing, but may have trouble assigning meaning to these sensations and individuating emotions. Alexithymic individuals have manifest difficulties in relating to others and managing social relationships and are often seen by those around them as lacking empathy. But they are also often anxious to get it right and behave appropriately. To the extent that they succeed, they do not succeed by the processes of affective attunement.

Take Fiona. As a child she would watch cartoons to learn social scripts:

> "I used to have pick characters to adopt for certain uses, like if someone insulted me I'd pick a character that seemed good at being angry … or a character good at being caring when someone was upset.

"Most of all, I always identified with aliens or robots with self-awareness. I never really knew why, but now I guess it's because I know I can't connect on an emotional level and try as much as I can I have to accept I'll never really understand, I'll always being watching from the outside."

(Reynolds 2015)

Fiona's concerns may be social rather than moral but other individuals do express moralised concerns about their relationships with others.

Caleb … has visited a cognitive behavioural therapist to help with his social understanding, and through conscious effort he is now better able to analyse the physical feelings and to equate it with emotions that other people may feel. Although it remains a somewhat academic exercise, the process helps him to try to grasp his wife's feelings and to see why she acts the way she does.

"The trade-off is that my relationship with my wife is a conscious choice," he says – he is not acting on a whim but a very deliberate decision to care for her. That has been particularly helpful in the last eight months.

(Robson 2015)

The notion of deliberate choice recurs in these first-personal accounts. One woman says: "When I am happy it is a logical decision to be happy, when I am sad it is a logical decision to be sad" (Reynolds 2015). Jim Sinclair, an able autistic man, says:

But wait. Because I don't *need* other people in my life, I'm free, as non-autistic people can never be free, to *want* other people in my life. Because I don't need relationships with *anyone*, I'm free to choose a relationship with a *someone* – not because I need a relationship, but because I like that person.

(Sinclair 1992)

Sinclair's account of his difficulties in understanding and labelling his own emotions, recognising them in others and sharing in the emotions of others is suggestive of alexithymia. It is clear that his emotional profile is very distinct from neurotypicals and that he does not enjoy the affective attunement with others that undoubtedly facilitates sympathetic concern, co-regulation of conduct (McGeer 2015) and moral community. On Shoemaker's account it must be doubtful that he has practical moral competence; on Hume's account is hard to see how he could achieve a concern for the welfare of others. Indeed, he does often struggle to understand what it is that he should do and does not appear to achieve this understanding by empathic processes. But Sinclair strongly rejects the claim that he lacks concern for others. He points out that not knowing how to respond to other people does not mean being uncaring.

Sometimes I notice the cues but I don't know what they mean. I have to develop a separate translation code for every person I meet – does it indicate an uncooperative attitude if someone doesn't understand information conveyed in a foreign language? Even if I can tell what the cues mean, I may not know what to do about them.

(Sinclair 1992)

Sinclair also cautions against a reliance on a shared system for interpretation and understanding and warns that failures of understanding go both ways:

> … you're assuming a shared system, a shared understanding of signals and meaning, that the child in fact does not share … it takes more work to communicate with someone whose native language isn't yours … You're going to have to back up to levels more basic than you've probably thought about before, to translate and make sure that your translations are understood … Approach respectfully, without preconceptions and with openness to learning new things, and you'll find a world you never imagined.
>
> *(Sinclair 1993)*

Sinclair thinks that both autistic and non-autistic people should strive in these ways. The problem is symmetrical and resolving it requires moral commitment and cognitive effort. It is clear in his writings that he has a sense of the dignity of persons, and respect for persons is for him a core value.

In "Autism, Empathy and Moral Agency" (Kennett 2002) I argued that Sinclair's moral concern was not based in empathy. Bollard (2014) and others have disagreed, citing Blair's work that basic affective empathy is preserved in autism and suggesting that this is what is doing the work in driving moral concern and its elaboration into more cognitive forms of sympathy. But basic empathy is not preserved in those 50 per cent of autistic individuals who are alexithymic and there is little to suggest that basic affective attunement with others is doing the work in Sinclair's case.

The case of Caleb, who is not autistic, drives this point home:

> Caleb may not have been transported to ecstasy by his wedding or the birth of his child, but he has spent most of his life looking within, striving to feel and understand the sensations of himself and the people around him. The result is that he is … thoughtful, and self-aware … someone who seems to know himself, and his limitations, inside out.

> Ultimately, he wants to emphasise that emotional blindness does not make one unkind, or selfish. "It may be hard to believe, but it is possible for someone to be cut off completely from the emotions and imagination that are such a big part of what makes us humans," he says. "*And that a person can be cut off from emotions without being heartless, or a psychopath.*"
>
> *(Robson 2015, my emphasis)*

It is notable that Jim Sinclair and Caleb are highly reflective, self-aware and conscientious. They have a strong sense of self and a moral identity that anchors them across time. It is also apparent that they see respect for others as fundamental to the moral enterprise. These are features lacking in psychopathy. It looks as though empathy is not necessary and not sufficient to deliver them. Elsewhere (Kennett 2008, 2015) I have suggested that the judgement that *other persons matter* and the consequent taking of their interests as reason giving may arise instead from reverence for reason or a sense of awe. Here I just note that these cases should serve as a corrective for some of the more extravagant claims made in both psychology and philosophy about the connection between empathy and morality. There has been an unfortunate tendency to elide the notions of empathy and moral feeling more generally. But not all moral feelings are the result of experiences of emotional contagion, emotion sharing or vicarious emotion. Even sympathy, which is a calibrated moral response to our recognition of another's situation, can be arrived at by other routes. Perhaps as Kant claims in *The Doctrine of Virtue*, sympathy too can be a choice based on moral principles (Kant 1797/1991).

Conclusion: the limits of empathy

While there is no question that empathy is important for participation in moral communities, regulation of behaviour, the sharing of norms and acquisition of morally relevant information that may be very hard to obtain in other ways, an examination of psychopathologies in which empathy is impaired indicates that there are other pathways to moral concern and moral understanding and other processes that are important to moral judgement and moral agency. These other pathways and processes are not just compensatory mechanisms; they operate and are important in the ordinary case.

Hume is correct that the mechanisms of empathy rely on similarity. As this relatively brief survey of psychopathology should illustrate, they do not work or they work far less efficiently in its absence. Psychopaths, many autistic individuals and those with alexithymia thus fail to master and internalise important aspects of the interpretive norms and practices of the communities in which they are situated and so they are disadvantaged in ways that matter for morality. But these disadvantages also arise for we neurotypicals in our interactions with culturally and neurologically diverse populations. The failure of empathy in such cases is symmetrical. As many others have pointed out (e.g. Bloom 2014, Prinz 2011, Singer 2014), empathy tends to be limited, partial and subject to implicit bias.

For example, one study found "no vicarious mapping of the pain of individuals culturally marked as outgroup members on the basis of their skin color ... Importantly, group-specific lack of empathic reactivity was higher in the onlookers who exhibited stronger implicit racial bias" (Avenanti et al. 2010). Havi Carel points out that "[p]eople lack empathy for the diseased. The pain, disability and fear are exacerbated by the apathy and disgust with which you are sometimes confronted when you are ill" (Carel 2008: 41).

Note that these morally objectionable failures of empathy are not the result of the kind of empathy deficits seen in psychopathology. They are the result of apparently inbuilt features of the normal operation of empathy that need to be countered by the adoption of more impartial forms of reasoning if we are to extend our *moral* concern to those beyond the immediate reach of our empathic concern. Why ought we to do so and what could motivate us to do so? Empathy does not provide the answer to these questions. A closer examination of the psychopathologies in which empathy is impaired can help us to map the other factors at play.

References

Adshead, G. (2014) The Words but not the Music: Empathy, Language Deficits and Psychopathy. In Thomas Schramme (ed.) *Psychopathy and Moral Incapacity*. Cambridge, MA: The MIT Press.

American Psychiatric Association (2013) *Diagnostic and Statistical Manual of Mental Disorders*. Fifth Edition. Arlington, VA, American Psychiatric Association.

Avenanti, Alessio et al. (2010) Racial Bias Reduces Empathic Sensorimotor Resonance with Other-Race Pain. *Current Biology* 20(11), 1018–22.

Batson, C. Daniel, Bruce D. Duncan, Paula Ackerman, Terese Buckley, & Kimberly Birch (1981) Is Empathic Emotion a Source of Altruistic Motivation? *Journal of Personality and Social Psychology* 40(2), 290–302.

Batson, C. Daniel (2011) The Empathy-Altruism Hypothesis. In Batson, *Altruism in Humans*. Oxford: Oxford University Press.

Bird, G. & Viding, E. (2014) The Self to Other Model of Empathy: Providing a New Framework for Understanding Empathy Impairments in Psychopathy, Autism, and Alexithymia. *Neuroscience and Biobehavioral Reviews*, 47, 520–32.

Bird, G., Silani, G., Brindley, R., White, S., Frith, U. & Singer, T. (2010) Empathic Brain Responses in Insula Are Modulated by Levels of Alexithymia but not Autism. *Brain* 133, 1515–25.

Blair, J., Mitchell, D. & Blair, K. (2005) *The Psychopath: Emotion and the Brain*. Oxford: Wiley-Blackwell.

Blair, R. J. R. (1995) A Cognitive Developmental Approach to Morality: Investigating the Psychopath. *Cognition* 57, 1–29.

Blair, R. J. R. (1996) Brief Report: Morality in the Autistic Child. *Journal of Autism and Developmental Disorders* 26(5), 571–9.

Blair, R. J. R. (2008) Fine Cuts of Empathy and the Amygdala: Dissociable Deficits in Psychopathy and Autism. *The Quarterly Journal of Experimental Psychology* 61, 157–70.

Blasi, A. (2004) Moral Functioning: Moral Understanding and Personality. In D. K. Lapsley & D. Narvaez (eds.) *Moral Development, Self, and Identity*. Mahwah, NJ: Erlbaum: pp. 189–212.

Bloom, Paul (2014) Forum: Against Empathy: Opening the Debate. *Boston Review* 10 September. https://bostonreview.net/forum/paul-bloom-against-empathy.

Bollard, M. (2014) Psychopathy, Autism and Questions of Moral Agency. In Alexandra Perry & Chris Herrera (eds) *Ethics and Neurodiversity*. Cambridge: Scholars Publishing: pp. 238–59.

Brewer, R., Marsh, A., Catmur, C., Cardinale, E. M., Stoycos, S., Cook, R. & Bird, G. (2015) The Impact of Autism Spectrum Disorder and Alexithymia on Judgments of Moral Acceptability. *Journal of Abnormal Psychology* 124(3), 589–95.

Carel, Havi (2008) *Illness: The Cry of the Flesh*. Stocksfield: Acumen.

Cleckley, H. (1955) *The Mask of Sanity: An Attempt to Clarify Some Issues about the So-Called Psychopathic Personality*. 3rd ed. St Louis: C.V. Mosby.

Elliott, Carl (1992) Diagnosing Blame: Responsibility and the Psychopath. *The Journal of Medicine and Philosophy* 17, 200–14.

Frith, Uta (1989) *Autism: Explaining the Enigma*. Oxford: Basil Blackwell.

Gordon, Robert M. (1995) Sympathy, Simulation and the Impartial Spectator. *Ethics* 105, 727–42.

Hardy, S. A. & Carlo, G. (2005) Identity as a Source of Moral Motivation. *Human Development* 48, 232–56.

Hare, Robert D. (1991) *The Hare Psychopathy Checklist-Revised*. New York: Multi Health Systems.

Hoffman, Martin L. (2000) *Empathy and Moral Development: Implications for Caring and Justice*. Cambridge: Cambridge University Press.

Hume, D. (1978) *A Treatise of Human Nature*, ed. L. A. Selby-Bigge, 2nd ed., revised by P. H. Nidditch. Oxford: Clarendon Press.

Kant, Immanuel (1797/1991) *The Metaphysics of Morals*. Trans. Mary Gregor Cambridge: Cambridge University Press.

Kennett, J. (2002) Autism, Empathy and Moral Agency. *The Philosophical Quarterly* 52(208), 340–57.

Kennett, J. (2008) Reasons, Reverence and Value. In Walter Sinnott-Armstrong (ed.) *Moral Psychology, Volume 3: The Neuroscience of Morality: Emotion, Disease, and Development*. Cambridge, MA: MIT Press.

Kennett, J. (2015) What's Required for Motivation by Principle? In Gunnar Björnsson et al. (eds.) *Motivational Internalism*. New York: Oxford University Press.

Maibom, H. L. (2014) Without Fellow Feeling. In Thomas Schramme (ed.) *Psychopathy and Moral Incapacity*. Cambridge, MA: The MIT Press: pp. 91–110.

McGeer, V. (2015) Mind-Making Practices: The Social Infrastructure of Self-Knowing, Agency and Responsibility. *Philosophical Explorations* 18(2), 259–81.

Nichols, S. (2002) How Psychopaths Threaten Moral Rationalism: Is It Irrational to Be Amoral? *Monist* 85, 285–304.

Prinz, J. (2011) Against Empathy. *The Southern Journal of Philosophy* 49, 214–33. doi: 10.1111/j.2041-6962.2011.00069.x.

Reynolds, Emma (2015) What It's Like to Be Emotionally Blind. www.news.com.au/lifestyle/health/mind/what-its-like-to-be-emotionally-blind/news-story/1cfa69056be707467f275c613396cb62. Accessed 25.3.16.

Robson, D. (2015) What Is It Like to never Have Felt an Emotion? www.bbc.com/future/story/20150818-what-is-it-like-to-have-never-felt-an-emotion. Accessed 25.3.16.

Shoemaker, D. (2009) Responsibility and Disability. *Metaphilosophy* 40, 438–61. doi: 10.1111/ j.1467-9973.2009.01589.x.

Shoemaker, D. (2015) *Responsibility from the Margins.* Oxford: Oxford University Press.

Sinclair, Jim (1992) Bridging the Gaps: An Inside-Out View of Autism (or, Do you know what I don't know?). In E. Schopler, & G. B. Mesibov (eds) *High Functioning Individuals with Autism.* New York: Plenum Press.

Sinclair, Jim (1993) Don't Mourn for Us. *Our Voice.* Newsletter of the Autism Network International.

Singer, P. (2014) Forum: Against Empathy. *Boston Review* 26 August. http://bostonreview.net/forum/ against-empathy/peter-singer-response-against-empathy-peter-singer.

Slote, Michael (2010) *Moral Sentimentalism.* New York: Oxford University Press.

Strawson, P. (1974) Freedom and Resentment. In *Freedom and Resentment and Other Essays.* London: Methuen.

Vignoles, Vivian L., et al. (2008) Identity Motives Underlying Desired and Feared Possible Future Selves. *Journal of Personality* 76(5): 1165–200.

33

GENDER AND EMPATHY

Robyn Bluhm

Are there gender differences in empathy? It may seem a straightforward question, but, of course, the answer depends on how the concept of empathy is understood and measured. Moreover, the operative concept of empathy itself, and the way that data relevant to gender differences in empathy are explained, both depend on researchers' broader background assumptions about the existence and the causes of behavior differences between women and men. In this chapter, I identify three distinct approaches to investigating gender differences in empathy. My aim is both to provide an overview of research on gender differences and to situate this research in the broader social and scientific context within which it is conducted.

Affective empathy and gender socialization

Prior to the late 1970s, there was relatively little research on gender differences in empathy and research that did look for possible differences did so either as a methodological requirement in studies for which gender was only of incidental interest, or as part of a broader survey of gender differences in a variety of cognitive characteristics and abilities. In this section, I will characterize discussions of gender differences in empathy during this time and identify the point at which gender differences in empathy started to become an explicit focus of research.

Early research on gender differences in empathy tended to be conducted by developmental psychologists and, to a lesser extent, by researchers who were interested in the broader question of gender differences in personality, who tended instead to talk of "tender-mindedness" (Feingold, 1994). Within these fields, however, gender differences did not tend to be the primary focus of research. Rather, as Block (1976) suggests, "[m]ost studies in developmental psychology include both sexes routinely and test for sex differences, not because theoretically such differences are expected, but rather with the hope that the *absence* of difference will provide justification for merging the samples of males and females, thus simplifying the analysis and the reporting of results" (p. 288). She further notes that in at least some developmental psychology journals, investigators were expected to report the results of tests for gender differences. Similarly, Feingold says that "gender differences in personality traits were first examined by psychometricians to determine whether separate norms were needed for males and females" (1994, p. 429). In both of these areas of research, then, interest in possible gender differences was more of a technical or a methodological interest than a substantive research question.

In 1974, Maccoby and Jacklin examined research that looked at gender differences in a wide variety of psychological functions including various aspects of perception, learning, verbal and quantitative abilities, personality, and social behavior. They found no differences between women and men (or girls and boys) in the majority of the papers they reviewed, including in their review of studies that examined gender and empathy. They conclude that the only gender differences for which significant evidence existed in psychology were girls' superior verbal abilities, boys' superior performance on both quantitative and visuospatial tasks, and boys' greater levels of aggression.

Shortly after the publication of Maccoby and Jacklin's book, Block (1976) published a review that responded to what she perceived as some shortcomings of their analysis. She pointed out that many of the studies they reviewed had relatively small sample sizes and also used a factorial design (which necessitated the testing of multiple hypotheses, including both main effects and interactions). As a result of these characteristics, the studies may not have had the statistical power to detect sex differences that actually do exist (i.e., they may report false negative results) (Block, 1976, p. 287). Moreover, in cases where a comparison between the sexes did not reach statistical significance (at the p< .05 level), Maccoby and Jacklin simply reported that there was no gender difference, but did not consider the possible effects of the lack of power when discussing their findings. Block also noted that Maccoby and Jacklin included in their review all of the studies they found, regardless of their quality, rather than critically assessing and screening the data that would inform their analysis. Finally, she suggests that children are overrepresented in the studies that Maccoby and Jacklin examine – 75 percent of the studies, across all domains, are based on research participants who are twelve years of age or younger; this limited the overall conclusions that could be drawn about gender differences. (This proportion is also true of the studies on empathy.) Despite these criticisms, in her own review of the literature, Block comes to agree with their conclusion that there are no gender differences established in empathy.

Unlike both of the previous reviews, Hoffman's 1977 paper focused solely on gender differences in empathy. Also unlike the previous reviews, Hoffman concludes that gender differences in empathy do exist. It is worth looking at his arguments in detail, as he makes explicit a number of assumptions about empathy and its measurement, as well as about the likely sources of gender differences, that are rather different from those that inform later research.

Like Block, Hoffman is responding to what he perceives as shortcomings of Maccoby and Jacklin's research. He begins by distinguishing between two different aspects of empathy, which correspond to cognitive and affective empathy, though he does not use this terminology. On the one hand, he says, empathy may refer to "the cognitive awareness of another person's feelings ... affective perspective taking ... or more simply recognition of affect" (Hoffman, 1977, p. 712), while on the other, it involves "a vicarious affective response to another person's feelings." According to Hoffman, the "latter corresponds more closely to what is commonly thought of as empathy," as well as to the kinds of characteristics that figured in widely believed gender stereotypes. Hoffman then argues that Maccoby and Jacklin lump together studies that are best viewed as focusing on different skills, and that only some of them are actually measuring empathy. Maccoby and Jacklin review thirty studies in total; Hoffman subdivides them as follows: six studies measure vicarious affect (affective empathy), seven assess perspective taking (cognitive empathy), and the remainder use measures that reflect "various dimensions of social competence but do not fit either definition of empathy" (p. 713). Moreover, dividing the studies this way complicates Maccoby and Jacklin's conclusion that there are no gender differences in empathy. In the first group of studies, assessing vicarious affect, female participants scored higher on measures of empathy (more on this below), while in the second group there were no differences observed in five studies and females scored higher in two. In studies in the third group, males and females were equally likely to score higher.

Given these perceived problems with the previous analysis, Hoffman reconsiders the evidence, focusing primarily on studies that measure affective empathy. He suggests that the ideal measure would both demonstrate that "(a) affect has been aroused in the observer and (b) the quality and direction of the affect correspond to those experienced by the person being observed" (p. 713). He also acknowledges, however, that there is no such measure. In particular, physiological measurements appear promising, but they do not establish the second criterion, since physiological responses could indicate pleasures in someone else's pain, or merely being startled by the person's behavior, or fear (etc.) for oneself rather than for the person being observed. He therefore excludes studies that use physiological measures from his analysis.

Instead, the majority of studies he includes use an experimental protocol designed by Feshbach and Roe (1968), in which study participants, usually children, are shown a series of slides that depict a child of their own sex in an emotion-inducing situation and are then asked how *they* feel, rather than how the child depicted feels. (Interestingly, this task uses ratings of how the depicted child feels as a comprehension check, rather than as a distinct test of cognitive empathy; I will return to this point below.) Other studies have the experimenters rate children's facial and bodily reactions when they view emotional scenes. Finally, studies in babies use "the closest approximation to an index of empathy in infants" (p. 714), testing whether they cry in response to hearing another infant cry. Hoffman acknowledges that this is not truly an empathetic response, but says that it must be considered "a possible early precursor" (p. 714).

Taken together, Hoffman includes in his analysis eight studies that examine affective empathy in infants and children; these studies include fifteen samples in total. Of the samples, five examine gender differences in reflexive crying in newborns. None of these reached statistical significance, though one sample of twenty infants approached significance (Sagi & Hoffman, 1976). Five samples looked at children's verbal reports of their own affective state after viewing emotion-inducing slides; one of these showed a statistically significant difference, favoring girls (Feshbach & Roe, 1968), while another approached statistical significance (Feshbach & Roe, 1969). The last five samples examined children's facial expressions while they viewed affective films or slides; one of these reached statistical significance (Buck, 1975). One additional study included in Hoffman's review examined gender differences in empathy in adults (Craig & Lowery, 1969). Participants were asked to rate their own level of distress upon seeing a confederate receive a shock. This study did show statistically significant differences between the groups, with women reporting higher levels of distress than men.

Despite these unpromising results, Hoffman summarizes his findings thus: "in every case, regardless of the age of the subjects or the measures used, the females obtained higher scores than did the males." He therefore concludes that "although the magnitude of the difference may not have been great, the findings overall clearly provide a stronger case for the proposition that females are more empathetic through the life cycle than that no sex difference exists" (p. 714). (Although this conclusion may, justifiably, strike contemporary readers as unfounded, Hoffman's conclusions are based on standard methods for conducting literature reviews at the time; the article was published before meta-analysis became the standard for literature reviews.)

Two other features of Hoffman's analysis are of interest, especially, as we shall see, in comparison with later discussions of gender differences in empathy. First, while Hoffman explicitly focuses on what is now generally called affective empathy, he also looks at studies that investigate gender differences in cognitive empathy, as assessed by the ability to recognize affect in others. Here, he looks at twelve studies, comprising sixteen samples, with participants ranging from toddlers to college students. (These included the results of the "comprehension check" in the task developed by Feshbach and Roe.) Only one study (n = 576) reached statistical significance (Borke, 1973), with girls found more likely to select faces that have emotional expressions corresponding to the emotion that a story character is feeling. Of the other studies, the results are a mix of no gender differences, girls scoring higher than boys, and boys scoring higher than girls. Hoffman therefore concludes: "When encountering someone in an emotional situation, both sexes are equally adept at assessing how that person feels, but in females the awareness of the other's feeling is more apt to be accompanied by a vicarious affective response" (p. 716). Using the now-standard distinction, Hoffman's assessment is that there are no gender differences in cognitive empathy, but girls exhibit more affective empathy.

The second thing to note about Hoffman's analysis is that his discussion is couched almost entirely in terms of gender roles and socialization, despite the fact that he focuses on research on young children and newborns. He begins by noting that "[f]emales have traditionally been socialized to acquire expressive traits such as empathy, compassion, and giving and receiving affect," in contrast to males, who are "initially socialized expressively," but then as they get older are encouraged to develop "instrumental traits, such as mastery and problem solving" (p. 712). Only toward the end of the paper does he consider that there may be an innate (biological) component to the observed gender differences in empathy. In particular, the tendency of female infants to be more likely than male infants to cry in response to another infant's cry "is not true empathy, but it does suggest the possibility of a constitutional precursor that together with differences in socialization may account for later sex differences in empathy" (p. 720).

Yet at around the same time that Hoffman's review of the literature on gender differences in empathy was published, the literature itself began to change. These changes are reflected in a 1983 review of the literature on gender differences in empathy by Eisenberg and Lennon. The authors themselves focus on one important change, which is that a wider variety of methods had come to be used to test for gender differences in empathy. In addition, tests were being conducted across a broader range of ages; recall that Hoffman's review included only one study that used adult participants. They also note that researchers tended to use different measures in different age groups (Eisenberg & Lennon, 1983, pp. 102–3), which is not surprising given that different experimental paradigms are likely to be appropriate at different ages. Moreover, although Eisenberg and Lennon do not address this point, whereas older studies were most likely to test for gender differences in the course of testing a different hypothesis, newer studies were more likely to focus explicitly on gender differences. Beginning in the late 1970s, the papers included in Eisenberg and Lennon's review began to include references to "sex differences" or "gender differences" in their titles, indicating that this was a major focus of the study.

Eisenberg and Lennon identified seven distinct approaches to measuring affective empathy. These were: (1) reflexive crying in infants; (2) self-reported emotional responses to emotion-inducing stories or pictures, where the emotion might match that of the individual in the story (this paradigm was used in children); (3) observers' ratings of subjects' facial, gestural, or vocal reactions to emotion-inducing stimuli (children); (4) observers' reports of empathy, using either teacher or peer raters; (5) physiological measures, including heart rate and skin conductance (mainly college students and other adults); (6) self-reported emotional responsiveness, using pencil-and-paper scales, to "simulated distress" scenarios; and (7) self-report scales asking about trait empathy. This last category of study usually used a scale developed by Mehrabian & Epstein (1972) to measure affective empathy. As noted above, reflexive crying was used to assess (proto-) empathy in infants. The second through fourth approaches were used mainly to assess empathy in children, while the sixth and seventh were used mainly in college students and other adults.

After surveying the literature, Eisenberg and Lennon's primary conclusion is that "the results of research concerning sex differences in empathy are highly related to the method of assessing empathy" (p. 199). Specifically, while most of the seven sub-areas of research included in the study reported small or no gender differences in empathy, both research using self-report scales to assess trait empathy and studies using assessments by peers or teachers were nearly unanimous in reporting large sex differences, with females scoring much higher than males. Only one of the studies that used self-report questionnaires did not find a statistically significant difference between women and men in self-reported empathy. Of the others, "[e]specially for adults, the sex differences were frequently so large that they were significant at the $p< .000000001$ level" (p. 116).

Eisenberg and Lennon conclude that the best explanation for the observed pattern of results across studies is that the self-report measures "may be influenced by demand characteristics" (p. 125). That is, both women and men are likely to recognize what is being measured, as well as the stereotypical gender associations with empathy. "Consequently, it is not surprising that a sex difference in empathy is found primarily when subjects are asked to rate themselves on traits that are clearly masculine or feminine" (p. 125). Similarly, in those studies that asked peers or teachers to rate children's levels of empathy, gender stereotypes may be in part responsible for the large gender differences observed.

In this section, I have surveyed research on gender differences in empathy up to the mid-1980s. The major characteristics of this research were: (1) a tendency to focus on affective, rather than cognitive empathy; (2) a tendency to discuss observed differences in social terms (e.g., with reference to socialization or to the influence of gender stereotypes), rather than offering biological explanations. Yet there was also (3) an increasing interest in investigating gender differences in empathy as a primary goal of research, rather than as a mere methodological requirement. This interest was reflected in a growing body of research on gender differences in many areas of biology and psychology. In the next section, I will show that, through the influential work of Simon Baron-Cohen, this broader interest in gender differences has also come to shape research that looks specifically at gender differences in empathy.

Baron-Cohen: from affective to cognitive empathy

An alternative approach to recognizing potential gender differences in empathy began to emerge in the late 1990s, in the work of Simon Baron-Cohen.[1] According to Baron-Cohen women's brains are "specialized" for empathy, while men's are specialized for "systematizing." This theory grew out of Baron-Cohen's work on autism, which he characterizes in terms of the development of an "extreme male brain": whether female or male, people with autism lack the ability to empathize with others and to understand their mental states, while they often show great interest in and facility with systems, including facts and statistics, mathematics, etc.

Several aspects of Baron-Cohen's theory show an interesting contrast with the work in developmental psychology that was discussed above. First, whereas Hoffman and Eisenberg and Lennon were concerned almost entirely with affective empathy, Baron-Cohen uses measures that assess both cognitive and affective empathy and, in fact, describes empathy in primarily cognitive terms. Second, his explanation for gender differences in empathy appeals to biology, particularly to two areas of research that gained prominence during the 1970s: sociobiological/ evolutionary explanations of gender roles and characteristics and (2) the role of exposure to sex hormones during fetal development in shaping the brains of girls/women versus those of boys/men. Perhaps because of his reliance on these biological ideas, Baron-Cohen also tends to view gender differences in empathy as "natural" rather than as the result of differences in the socialization of boys and girls.

Baron-Cohen first presented his "extreme male brain" theory of autism in a 1997 paper co-written with Jessica Hammer. In this paper, they begin by presenting a survey of research that shows that women outperform men on a variety of cognitive tasks, and vice versa for other tasks. The research they survey reflects the conclusions drawn by Maccoby and Jacklin in their review; women tended to perform better than men on linguistic tasks, while men did better than women on tasks that tapped visuospatial abilities. Unlike Maccoby and Jacklin, though, Baron-Cohen and Hammer drew on research in developmental biology and in evolutionary biology to link these performance differences to innate differences in brain function. Their theory is then presented as a unifying explanation for the gender differences they describe: genetic and hormonal factors cause women's and men's brains to develop along different trajectories, resulting in distinct "male" and "female" brain types. With this background in place, they then "operationally define the male brain type as an individual whose spatial (SP) skills are in advance of his or her social (SOC) skills" (Baron-Cohen & Hammer, 1997, p. 6) and the female brain type as the opposite. They are also careful to note that both women and men, as individuals, might have either a male or a female brain type (a claim that sits oddly with their appeal to innate biology), and that the designations are based on evidence that shows *average* differences between the sexes, as well as on differences in biology. In a footnote, they explain that they chose to use the gendered terminology to reflect that fact that the female brain type also comes with additional, especially linguistic, skills in addition to its social skills, while the male brain type comes with other characteristics in addition to visuospatial cognition. They also say that "calling them Brain Types 1 and 2 was another option open to us, but this simply ignores that if you are biologically male or female, you have an increased likelihood of having one brain type over the other" (p. 6). Finally, they suggest a third possible brain type, in which spatial and social skills are roughly equally developed in an individual; they call this the "cognitively balanced" brain type.

Having identified these gender differences, Baron-Cohen and Hammer then propose that individuals with autism or Asperger's syndrome have an extreme form of the male brain, reflecting both the symptoms of these disorders (impairment in social skills and, in many cases, a preoccupation with what Baron-Cohen later comes to call "systematizing" pursuits) and the fact that autism is more prevalent in boys and men than in girls and women. They then present the results of a series of experiments designed to tap either spatial or social skills. Of primary importance for this chapter are the tasks designed to tap the strengths of the "female" brain type. The Faux Pas test examines children's abilities to recognize social missteps. It involves presenting children with brief descriptions of social situations in which one character commits a faux pas and then asking the child which of the three characters "said something they shouldn't have said" (p. 14). In the Reading the Mind in the Eyes test, participants were asked to select from among two words (later changed to four words) the one that describes the emotion depicted by a person in a picture. As the name of the test suggests, the picture shows only the eye region of the person. For both of these tasks, Baron-Cohen and his colleagues found the boys/men performed more poorly than girls/women, and people with autism, whether male or female, did not perform as well as individuals who were not autistic.

By 2003, when Baron-Cohen published a book that presented his theory to a broader public audience, his characterization of female and male brains had undergone a subtle, but important, shift. Whereas an individual with a "male-type" brain was previously described as having spatial skills significantly more developed than his social skills, the book describes the "male brain" as "hardwired for systematizing" (Baron-Cohen, 2003, p. 1). And while Baron-Cohen and Hammer describe an individual with a "female-type" brain as having better social than systematizing skills, the 2003 book describes the "female brain" as "hardwired for empathizing" (p. 1). Moreover, discussion of the linguistic and other skills that purportedly also distinguished between the brain types in Baron-Cohen and Hammer's paper have now disappeared from the discussion and the "male brain" and "female brain" are now associated with a single characteristic each, though in the case of empathy, as I shall show below, this characteristic covers a great deal of behavior. In addition, empathizing and systematizing are now seen as being in competition with each other during brain development (Goldenfeld et al., 2005). Although Baron-Cohen continues to acknowledge that some people have "balanced" brains, empathizing and systematizing have become polar opposites.

These shifts in Baron-Cohen's theory are, I suggest, the result of using the deficits and strengths associated with autism to characterize gender differences. If autism reflects the "extreme male brain" and people with autism lack empathy, then *having* empathy becomes a characteristic of the non-male brain. While Baron-Cohen and Hammer did discuss sex differences on social tasks in their original paper, most of the literature they reviewed was concerned with cognitive traits; it found that on average women performed better on linguistic, and worse on visuospatial tasks. By 2003, the emphasis is almost completely on social skills, reflecting the influence of research on the social deficits associated with autism.

Moreover, because of the influence of autism on Baron-Cohen's theory of gender differences, the concept of empathy that is being used in his research is very different from the concept that was used in the developmental psychology literature discussed above. Recall that both the review paper by Hoffman and the one by Eisenberg and Lennon focus explicitly on tasks that measure *affective* empathy, and that the task developed by Feshbach and Roe uses the cognitive ability to correctly identify others' mental states as a control task designed to ensure that their study participants understood the instructions. By contrast, both the Faux Pas test and the Reading the Mind in the Eyes test tap *cognitive* empathy: they are concerned with whether one recognizes emotional signals, rather than whether one feels them.

Baron-Cohen does recognize a difference between cognitive and affective empathy, but does not tend to consider them separately. The empathy scale he has developed, the Empathy Quotient (EQ), mixes together questions relevant to cognitive with those more relevant to affective empathy, and does not include a subscale that measures them separately. This is somewhat surprising, given that in the paper in which they first introduce the scale, Baron-Cohen & Wheelwright (2004) report that they interviewed fifty patients with autism in order to better understand their results on the EQ. Their participants reported that "even though they have difficulty judging/explaining/anticipating or interpreting another's behavior, it is not the case that they want to hurt another person. When it is pointed out to them that their behavior was hurtful ... they typically feel bad about the hurt they caused" (p. 169). Thus it seems that when people with autism actually *do* recognize others' feelings, they do respond emotionally to them, and in fact several studies (Rogers et al., 2007; Smith, 2009; Jones et al., 2010) have suggested that people with autism have relatively normal affective empathy, and impairments only in cognitive empathy. Despite this, Baron-Cohen and Wheelwright say that not only are the affective and cognitive aspects both "essential to defining empathy," but also that "in most cases, the cognitive and the affective cannot be easily separated" (2004, p. 163).

In addition to including both cognitive and affective empathy in his research on gender differences, Baron-Cohen also expands the range of abilities involved in both affective and cognitive empathy well beyond the traditional understanding of these abilities (Stueber, 2013). Affective empathy, in his view, does not require feeling the *same* emotion as another but includes "respond[ing] intuitively to a change in another's mood with concern, appreciation, understanding, comforting, or whatever the appropriate emotion might be" (Baron-Cohen, 2003,

p. 22). It thus incorporates what other theorists would characterize as a sympathetic, rather than an empathetic, response. Similarly, cognitive empathy has expanded to include the recognition of others' beliefs, in addition to their emotions: "A natural empathizer not only notices others' feelings but also continually thinks about what the other person might be feeling, thinking, or intending" (p. 22). Finally, empathizing, on Baron-Cohen's account, comes both *naturally* ["Empathy is about spontaneously and naturally tuning into the other person's thoughts and feelings, whatever these might be" (p. 21)] and *automatically* ["you are not empathizing if you are doing all of the above in order to appear appropriate, or as an intellectual exercise. You are doing it because you can't help doing it" (p. 24)], and it *influences social behavior* ["[e]mpathizing leads you to pick up the phone and tell someone you are thinking about them and their current situation, even when your own life demands are equally pressing" (p. 22)]. Thus although Baron-Cohen now speaks of empathy, rather than of social skills more generally, as characterizing women's strengths, the concept of empathy has expanded so that the two concepts are virtually synonymous.

Baron-Cohen's research program over the past two decades has been influential, but has also been controversial. Above, I mentioned findings that challenge his claims about the scope of the empathy deficits associated with autism. His claims about gender differences have also been criticized, both with regard to the empirical evidence he has gathered and to the biological framework underlying his theory. Evidence that women have superior cognitive empathy skills is mixed (for review, see Maibom, 2012) and, as with affective empathy, when gender differences *are* observed, it is possible that they are due to women's attempts to conform to gender-appropriate behavior. For example, Klein & Hodges (2001) showed that men's scores on an empathy task equaled women's when a monetary reward for good performance was offered. Baron-Cohen, by contrast, tends to attribute women's superior empathizing to innate biological factors; however, this explanation has been criticized (e.g., Rogers, 2003; Grossi & Fine, 2012; Jordan-Young, 2010). In summary, as with the earlier research on gender differences in affective empathy, support for Baron-Cohen's theory is both equivocal and open to various interpretations.

Neuroscience and gender differences in empathy

Most recently, a third era of research on empathy and gender differences has begun to emerge; this research examines the neurophysiology of empathy. There is not yet enough research published to allow the guiding methods and concepts to be identified definitively; however, in this last section I will discuss the ways that some of the themes that emerged in the two earlier eras are being addressed. Although research on the neuroscience of empathy acknowledges Baron-Cohen's work (and he has in fact conducted some research in this area), the major influences on these studies are, first, neuroscience research on gender differences in emotion processing and, second, neuroscientific work on mirror neurons. The latter influence on neuroimaging research lies mainly in the specific brain regions that are taken to be important in empathy; the former, as I will show below, has shaped discussions of the relationship between affective and cognitive empathy and, more generally, of the (gendered) relationship between emotion and cognition.

A number of themes that arose in earlier work on gender and empathy can be seen in two neuroimaging studies have used similar emotion tasks to assess gender differences in cognitive and affective empathy (Schulte-Rüther et al., 2008; Derntl et al., 2010). Both behavioral and neuroimaging data were collected in these experiments. With regard to behavior, in both studies, men and women viewed pictures of emotional faces and were equally adept at identifying the emotions displayed, suggesting that there were no observed differences in cognitive empathy.

With regard to affective empathy, things are a bit more complicated. Only one study (Schulte-Rüther et al.) asked participants to report their affective reaction to the emotion exhibited by another (affective empathy); they found that women reported greater affective empathy. The other presented participants with hypothetical scenarios and asked them to identify which of two faces expressed the emotion that they would feel if *they* were in that scenario; the authors describe this as assessing "affective responsiveness" rather than affective empathy, and report that they did not find gender differences. Both studies also used pencil-and-paper scales to measure participants' self-reported trait empathy. Schulte-Rüther et al. found that women scored higher on the affective empathy scale developed by Mehrabian and Epstein. Derntl et al. found no difference on this scale, but women in their sample scored higher on another measure of affective empathy, the empathic concern subscale of the Interpersonal Reactivity Index (Davis, 1983).

Both studies, however, reported gender differences in neural activity in all of the experimental conditions. Of particular interest is the way that they interpret these differences. Recall that Hoffman (1997) expressed skepticism about research that used physiological measurements of empathy on the grounds that it is not possible to determine the meaning of any observed responses. In the case of neuroscience research, these interpretations are being made on the basis both of previous neuroimaging research that aimed to localize different cognitive functions and of broader background assumptions about the possible causes of gender differences. For example, in these studies, Schulte-Rüther et al. found that men, but not women, showed activity in an area (the left temporoparietal junction) that is associated with knowledge of cognitive states, when asked to report on their own emotions. They therefore suggest that men may have "a more cognitively driven access to *one's own* feelings in response to the emotions of others" (emphasis added, Schulte-Rüther et al., 2008, p. 400). Similarly, in discussing an analysis that combined the imaging results for three empathy-related tasks, two measuring cognitive empathy and one measuring affective responsiveness,[2] Derntl et al. say that their findings "strongly support the assumption that females recruit more emotion-related regions, whereas males engage a different neural network, rather associated with cognitive evaluation, mentalizing, and behavioral anticipation" (2010, p. 79). This tendency to interpret women's neural activation patterns in terms of greater emotional responses and men's in terms of cognition (even when emotions are being measured) is characteristic of the neuroimaging literature on gender differences in emotion processing (Bluhm, 2013). This interpretation is consistent with gender stereotypes that view women as, in general, more emotional than men.

Yet Derntl et al. do not simply attribute their results to women's greater emotionality. Rather, citing Eisenberg and Lennon, they note that "women assume that it is expected to be more empathetic as a female and thus are more likely to describe themselves according to this gender stereotype" (p. 79). They continue: "these gender stereotypes might even extend to neurobiological responses, prompting stronger activation of emotion-related areas when subjects, in particular females, assume that it is expected to act according to a certain stereotype" (p. 79). Contrary to the common assumption that "biological" means immutable, and is to be contrasted with "social," their analysis recognizes that *any* kind of influence on gender differences must be reflected in brain activity.

Despite this nuanced discussion, the idea that empathy differences can be traced back to evolutionary and developmental causes, which figures prominently in Baron-Cohen's theory, is still influential. A recent review of research relevant to gender and empathy surveys research on empathy "precursors" in nonhuman animals (as well as in infants and young children) and concludes that "selective pressures shaped females' anatomy, physiology, and neurobiology to facilitate sensitivity to infants' internal states and resultant nurturing behavior" (Christov-Moore et al., 2014, p. 610; original in italics). With this as the framework within which differences in empathy between adult women and men are interpreted, any observed differences seem like the inevitable end point of distinct developmental trajectories, rather than as complex behaviors influenced by social expectations and internalized beliefs about (gender) appropriate behavior.

Again, research on the neuroscience of gender differences in empathy is still quite new and it's not possible to predict the specific background assumptions and experimental paradigms that will come to characterize this area of research. Already, however, traces of the questions and assumptions that characterized earlier research can be observed. As noted above, this emerging research also shows the influence of other areas of neuroscience, which will likely interact with the longer-standing trends in empathy research to shape further investigations.

More generally, over time new experimental methods and theoretical approaches have been incorporated into research on gender differences in empathy. With the exception of studies that rely on participants' self-reports, or on others' reports of their behavior, no consistent gender differences in empathy have been observed. This pattern raises the possibility that gender differences in empathy are in the eye of the beholder, and that the beholder is more influenced by gender stereotypes than by empathetic feelings or behaviors themselves. We can draw several conclusions from the existing literature on gender and empathy. First, the continued interest in investigating possible differences speaks to the influence of widely held social beliefs about gender and empathy. Second, in the absence of clear and unequivocal findings of difference, much continues to depend on the way that the data are incorporated into researchers' other theoretical commitments and on how empathy itself is understood and measured. Finally, given that research on gender differences is often contentious, it is important to consider the broader conceptual frameworks within which experiments aiming to identify gender differences in empathy are conducted.

Notes

1 The gap between Eisenberg and Lennon's review and Baron-Cohen's introduction of his theory reflects the fluctuating popularity of research on gender differences. Eagly et al. report that the number of papers published on gender and gender differences in the psychology literature reached a peak in the late 1970s and again in the late 1990s (2012, pp. 5 and 14).
2 The decision to combine the data this way echoes Baron-Cohen's collapsing of the distinction between affective and cognitive empathy.

References

Baron-Cohen, S. 2003. *The Essential Difference: Males, Females, and the Truth about Autism.* New York: Basic Books.

Baron-Cohen, S., Hammer, J. 1997. Is autism an extreme form of the "male" brain? *Advances in Infancy Research* 11: 193–217.

Baron-Cohen, S., Wheelwright, S. 2004. The empathy quotient: An investigation of adults with Asperger syndrome or high functioning autism. *Journal of Autism and Developmental Disorders* 34(2): 162–75.

Block, J. H. 1976. Issues, problems, and pitfalls in assessing sex differences: A critical review of The Psychology of Sex Differences. *Merill-Palmer Quarterly of Behavior and Development* 24(4): 283–308.

Bluhm, R. 2013. Self-fulfilling prophecies: The influence of gender stereotypes on functional neuroimaging research on emotion. *Hypatia* 23(4): 870–86.

Borke, H. 1973. The development of empathy in Chinese and American children between three and six years of age: A cross-culture study. *Developmental Psychology* 9: 102–8.

Buck, R. 1975. Nonverbal communication of affect in children. *Journal of Personality and Social Psychology* 31: 644–53.

Christov-Moore, L., Simpson, E. A., Coudé, G., Grigaityte, K., Iacoboni, M., Ferrari, P. F. 2014. Empathy: Gender effects in brain and behavior. *Neuroscience and Biobehavioral Reviews* 46: 604–27.

Craig, K. D., Lowery, H. J. 1969. Heart-rate components of conditioned vicarious autonomic responses. *Journal of Personality and Social Psychology* 11(4): 381–7.

Davis, M. H. 1983. Measuring individual differences in empathy: Evidence for a multidimensional approach. *Journal of Personality and Social Psychology* 44(1): 113–26.

Derntl, B., Finkelmeyer, A., Eickhoff, S., Kellermann, T., Falkenberg, D. I., Schneider, F., Habel, U. 2010. Multidimensional assessment of empathic abilities: Neural correlates and gender differences. *Psychoneuroendocrinology* 35(1): 67–82.

Eagly, A. H., Eaton, A., Rose, S. M., Riger, S., McHugh, M. C. 2012. Feminism and psychology: Analysis of a half-century of research on women and gender. *American Psychologist* 67(3): 211–30.

Eisenberg, N., Lennon, R. 1983. Sex differences in empathy and related capacities. *Psychological Bulletin* 94(1): 100–31.

Feingold, A. 1994. Gender differences in personality: A meta-analysis. *Psychological Bulletin* 116(3): 429–56.

Feshbach, N. D., Roe, K. 1968. Empathy in six- and seven-year-olds. *Child Development* 39(1): 133–45.

Feshbach, N. D., Roe, K. 1969. The relationship between empathy and aggression in two age groups. *Developmental Psychology* 1(2): 102–7.

Goldenfeld, N., Baron-Cohen, S., Wheelwright, S. 2005. Empathizing and systematizing in males, females, and autism. *Clinical Neuropsychiatry* 2(6): 338–45.

Grossi, G., Fine, C. 2012. The role of fetal testosterone in the development of "the essential difference" between the sexes: Some essential issues. In *Neurofeminism: Issues at the Intersection of Feminism and Cognitive Science*, ed. Robyn Bluhm, Heidi Maibom, & Anne Jaap Jacobson. Basingstoke, UK: Palgrave Macmillan, pp. 73–104.

Hoffman, M. L. 1997. Sex differences in empathy and related behaviors. *Psychological Bulletin* 84(4): 712–22.

Jones, A. P., Happé, F. G. E., Gilbert, F., Burnett, S., Viding, E. 2010. Feeling, caring, knowing: Different types of empathy deficit in boys with psychopathic tendencies and autism spectrum disorder. *Journal of Child Psychology and Psychiatry* 51(11): 1188–97.

Jordan-Young, R. M. 2010. *Brain Storm: The Flaws in the Science of Sex Differences*. Cambridge, MA: Harvard University Press.

Klein, K. J. K., Hodges, S. D. 2001. Gender differences, motivation, and empathic accuracy: When it pays to understand. *Personality and Social Psychology Bulletin* 27(6): 720–30.

Maccoby, E. E., Jacklin, C. N. 1974. *The Psychology of Sex Differences*, Volume 1. Stanford, CA: Stanford University Press.

Maibom, H. 2012. In a different voice? In *Neurofeminism: Issues at the Intersection of Feminism and Cognitive Science*, ed. Robyn Bluhm, Heidi Maibom, & Anne Jaap Jacobson. Basingstoke, UK: Palgrave Macmillan, pp. 56–72.

Mehrabian, A., Epstein, N. 1972 A measure of emotional empathy. *Journal of Personality* 49(4): 525–43.

Rogers, L., 2003. Extreme problems with essential differences. *Cerebrum* Dana Foundation. www.dana.org/Cerebrum/2003/Extreme_Problems_with_Essential_Differences/.

Rogers, K., Dziobek, I., Hassenstab, J., Wolf, O. T., Convit, A. 2007. Who cares? Revisiting empathy in Asperger syndrome. *Journal of Autism and Developmental Disorders* 37(4): 709–15.

Sagi, A., Hoffman, M. L. 1976. Empathic distress in the newborn. *Developmental Psychology* 12(2): 175–6.

Schulte-Rüther, M., Markowitsch, H. J., Shah, N. J., Fink, G. R., Piefke, M. 2008. Gender differences in brain networks supporting empathy. *Neuroimage* 42(1): 393–403.

Smith, A., 2009. The empathy imbalance hypothesis of autism: A theoretical approach to cognitive and emotional empathy in autistic development. *The Psychological Record* 59: 489–510.

Stueber, K. 2013. "Measuring empathy." –Supplement to "Empathy." *Stanford Encyclopedia of Philosophy.* http://plato.stanford.edu/entries/empathy/measuring.html.

INDEX